Usage and Style

Language
20 Writing to the World
21 Language That Builds Common Ground
22 Language Variety
23 Word Choice and Spelling
24 Glossary of Usage

52 STUDENT RESEARCH ESSAY, MLA STYLE

List of Works Cited

pages 243–284

pages 455–512

Sentence Style
25 Coordination, Subordination, and Emphasis
26 Consistency and Completeness
27 Parallelism
28 Shifts
29 Conciseness
30 Sentence Variety

pages 285–314

APA, *Chicago*, and CSE Documentation
53 APA Style
   STUDENT ESSAY, APA STYLE
54 *Chicago* Style
   STUDENT ESSAY, *CHICAGO* STYLE
55 CSE Style
   STUDENT PROPOSAL, CSE STYLE

pages 513–590

Sentence Grammar
31 Basic Grammar
32 Verbs
33 Subject-Verb Agreement
34 Pronouns
35 Adjectives and Adverbs
36 Modifier Placement
37 Comma Splices and Fused Sentences
38 Sentence Fragments

pages 315–396

For Multilingual Writers
56 Writing in U.S. Academic Genres
57 Clauses and Sentences
58 Nouns and Noun Phrases
59 Verbs and Verb Phrases
60 Prepositions and Prepositional Phrases

pages 591–620

Punctuation and Mechanics
39 Commas
40 Semicolons
41 End Punctuation
42 Apostrophes
43 Quotation Marks
44 Other Punctuation
45 Capital Letters
46 Abbreviations and Numbers
47 Italics
48 Hyphens

pages 397–454

Writing in the Disciplines
61 Academic Work in Any Discipline
62 Writing for the Humanities
   STUDENT CLOSE READING
63 Writing for the Social Sciences
   STUDENT REPORT
64 Writing for the Natural and Applied Sciences
   STUDENT LAB REPORT
65 Writing for Business
   STUDENT DOCUMENTS

pages 621–664

MW00718493

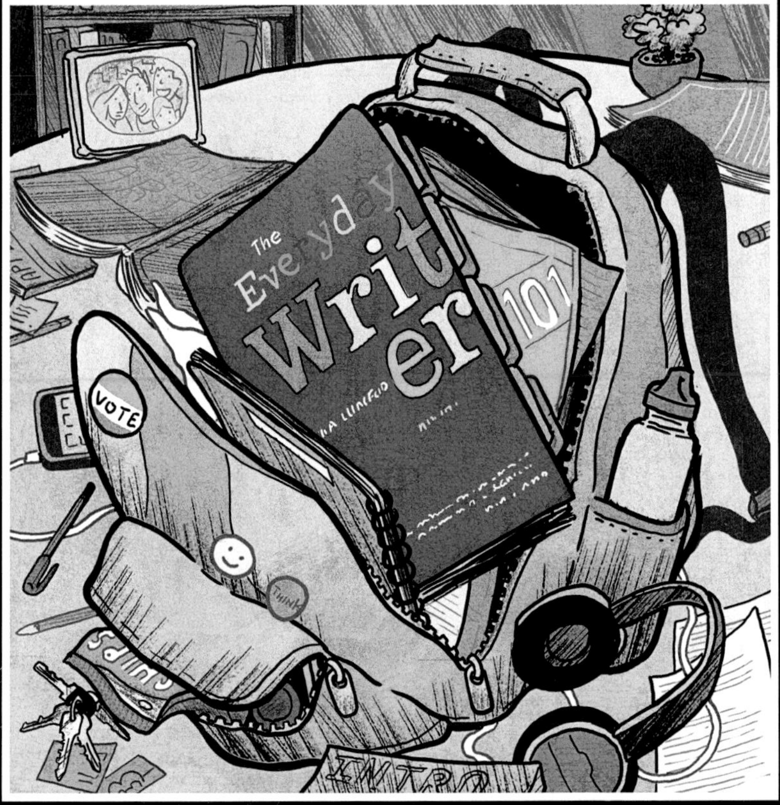

You've Got Access!

The Everyday Writer + LearningCurve

Your access code is on the back of this tab.

Who says grammar practice can't be fun?

LearningCurve, game-like online quizzing, adapts to what you already know and helps you practice what you need to learn.

Note: If the code below does not work, it might be expired. You can purchase access to LearningCurve at **bedfordstmartins.com/everydaywriter/LC**.

For access to LearningCurve:

1. Go to bedfordstmartins.com/everydaywriter/LC
2. Enter your student access code exactly as it appears below, including any dashes, and follow the instructions.

For technical support:

- 1-800-936-6899
- bfwpub.com/techsupport

Students

If you are using *CompClass for The Everyday Writer*, don't use the code below because your LearningCurve activities are already inside of CompClass. To register for CompClass, go to **yourcompclass.com**

STUDENT ACCESS CODE

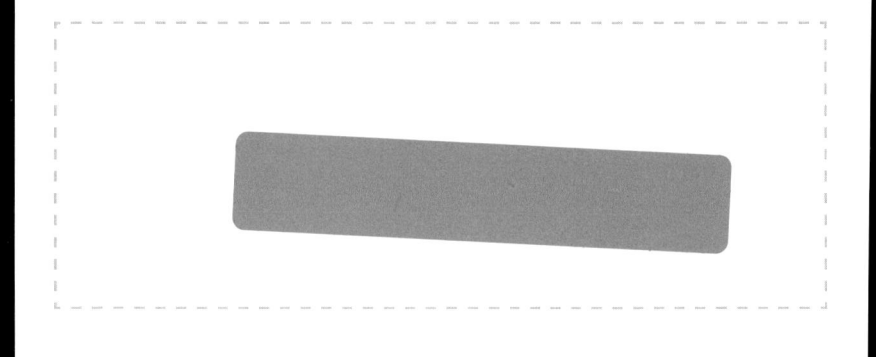

Bedford/St. Martin's e-Book to Go

The Everyday Writer with Exercises, Seventh Edition

for Florida International University

To unlock your custom e-Book to Go:

1. **Get an Adobe ID.** Go to **bedfordstmartins.com/AID**, click **"Don't have an Adobe ID?"** under the yellow sign-in button, and create your Adobe ID.

2. **Download the software.** Choose one of the following:

   Using your computer? Go to bedfordstmartins .com/ADE to download Adobe Digital Editions.

   Using your iPad/iPhone/iOS system or Android? Go to bedfordstmartins.com/BF to download Bluefire to iTunes or search for "Bluefire Reader" from your Application Store directly on your device.

   Using your Nook? Go to bedfordstmartins.com /ADE to download Adobe Digital Editions. Connect your computer via USB and transfer the file.

3. **Download your e-Book to Go.** Go to **www .redeemebooks.com**. Type in your e-Book to Go redemption code exactly as it appears below (including any dashes) and click **Next**. Follow the on-screen instructions that appear until your book has downloaded.

YOUR E-BOOK TO GO REDEMPTION CODE

P9ZEM6-9PUP5V

Technical Support

Visit **macmillanhighered.com/techsupport**.

System Requirements/Supported Devices

Adobe Digital Editions requires the latest version of **Adobe Flash Player** and is compatible with Windows: Intel® Pentium® 4 processor or later, **Windows**® XP SP 3 or Windows® 7 (32 or 64 bit running in 32-bit mode), 512MB of RAM (1GB recommended), 40MB of available hard-disk space; **Mac OS**: Intel Core™ Duo or faster processor, Mac OS X v10.6 or later, 512MB of RAM (1GB recommended), 5MB of available hard-disk space; and Apple Retina Display: Intel Core™ Duo or faster processor, Mac OS X v10.6 or later, compatible with Apple Retina Display, 512MB of RAM (1GB recommended), 75MB of available hard-disk space. If using a **Nook**, connect your Nook directly to your PC via a USB cable and drag your e-Book to Go onto Nook from Adobe Digital Editions.

Bluefire Reader is compatible with your **iOS systems**: iPhone 3GS, iPhone 4, iPhone 4S, iPhone 5, iPod touch (3rd generation), iPod touch (4th generation), iPod touch (5th generation), and iPad. Requires iOS 4.3 or later. This app is optimized for iPhone 5. For **Android**: compatible with Android 2.2, 2.3, 3.1 or later.

The e-Book to Go is not compatible with Kindle.

For maximum readability, we strongly encourage use of a large-screen device, such as your computer or iPad.

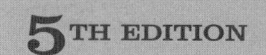

The Everyday Writer

FLORIDA INTERNATIONAL UNIVERSITY EDITION

Andrea A. Lunsford
STANFORD UNIVERSITY

A section for multilingual writers with

Paul Kei Matsuda
ARIZONA STATE UNIVERSITY

Christine M. Tardy
DEPAUL UNIVERSITY

Bedford/St. Martin's
BOSTON ◆ NEW YORK

Manufactured in the United States of America.

8   7   6   5   4   3
f   e   d   c   b   a

For information, write: Bedford/St. Martin's, 75 Arlington Street, Boston, MA 02116   (617-399-4000)

ISBN 978-1-4576-7322-1 (Florida International University custom edition)

The Writing Program at Florida International University

The Writing Program at Florida International University

A Note to FIU Students   *FIU-3*

FIU **Resources for Your Writing**   *FIU-6*

   a *The Everyday Writer* companion Web site   *FIU-6*

   b The Center for Excellence in Writing at Florida
          International University   *FIU-7*

   c Writing in the disciplines   *FIU-10*

   d Using Turnitin.com   *FIU-12*

   e Academic misconduct agreement   *FIU-13*

A Note to FIU Students

From the Writing Program Directors

You might be using this handbook in your first-year writing classes, in your upper-level Gordon Rule courses, or in courses for your major. In any case, we hope that you will find this a valuable resource as you work to enhance your writing skills and to communicate your ideas clearly, convincingly, and gracefully.

A group of writing instructors and students in the English Department chose this handbook as a required text after surveying a number of similar books. Our intention was to provide students with a helpful resource in the areas of grammar, research, and writing style. We also hoped to save you money as you can carry this one handbook with you throughout your writing courses here at FIU.

We encourage you to refer often to *The Everyday Writer* handbook. You might begin with Chapter 1, which covers twenty of the most common errors that student writers make. If you concentrate on avoiding these errors in your writing, you are off to a good start in producing grammatically correct work. The chapters on usage and style (Chapters 20–43) will help you further refine your language skills. If English is not your first language, you should find Chapters 56–60 particularly useful.

Of course, writing is about more than producing grammatically correct sentences. Effective writing must also have solid, thoughtful content; clear and convincing structure; and sensitivity to the overall rhetorical context. In addition, especially in academic settings, high-quality writing should exhibit sound research and attention to documentation conventions. Your handbook offers advice in these areas as well as providing, for example, strategies to help you analyze your audience, discover effective topics, and organize your work. For related help, see Chapters 1–19. Chapters 49–55 provide guidelines for using the most common documentation styles, including MLA and APA. Additionally, Chapters 61–65 provide advice for tackling writing assignments in classes outside of the writing program.

In the next several pages, you will find:

- an explanation of *The Everyday Writer* companion Web site,
- details on the tutoring services offered at the Center for Excellence in Writing,
- comments from FIU professors about writing in their disciplines,
- instructions for using Turnitin.com, and

- a form that your instructor may ask you to sign indicating your awareness of FIU's academic honesty policies.

Best wishes for success in your writing courses here at FIU. If you'd like to provide us with feedback on your handbook, you can email us directly or ask your writing instructor to forward us your comments.

Kimberly Harrison, PhD

Director of Writing Programs

Cindy Chinelly
Robert Saba
Mike Creeden

Associate Directors

From the Teaching Assistants in the Writing Program

Whether or not you realize it now, this custom edition of *The Everyday Writer with Exercises* will become one of your most valuable tools in both your undergraduate and graduate careers. As instructors, as writing tutors, and most importantly as students, we use this tool on an almost daily basis. Although we teach writing, we still need to rely on a writing reference. Whether writing syllabi, assignment sheets, or class papers, we often refer to this handbook before considering any piece of writing completed. Its useful tabs act as a quick reference when we need to look things up at a moment's notice. Frequently, we use it for reviewing citation rules and for ensuring that there are no errors within our own writing. For example, this handbook was a constant companion as we constructed the literature reviews and bibliographies for our own theses and dissertation proposals. Even as graduate students, we haven't memorized every citation rule. While our professors do not expect us to *be* walking handbooks, they do expect us to *use* our handbooks to cite our sources correctly.

As instructors of ENC 1101 and ENC 1102, we see how *The Everyday Writer with Exercises* helps our students to recognize and address their sentence-level errors. Before you submit any paper, we encourage you to look specifically at Chapter 1, and review the rules for avoiding the "top twenty" most common errors made by student writers. When grading student writing, we are quick to notice these errors, but we also realize that, with initiative and diligence, our students can avoid them and present their work without errors that may distract their readers.

When offering feedback on student writing, we often provide students with references to pages in this handbook where they can find guidelines to address particular errors. The section titled "For Multilingual Writers" offers some great advice; we often use this section to assist students during office hours, and we reference it in written feedback we provide on student papers. We also find that the sections on research are especially helpful to our students during the initial stages of brainstorming and research.

Even advanced writers—and advanced students—need a good handbook to help them with their writing. We encourage you to use every tool available to you as you develop your writing skills and strategies throughout your studies here at FIU.

The Teaching Assistants in the Writing Program at FIU

FIU   Resources for Your Writing

FIUa   *The Everyday Writer* companion Web site

Your handbook gives you quick access to practical information about writing and editing. As an FIU student, you also have free access to this handbook's companion Web site. The Web site offers a variety of supplemental resources to help you with your writing. To browse the site's open resources, visit your Student Center on the Web at **bedfordstmartins.com/everydaywriter**.

Among the many resources available are the following:

- Samples of effective student writing across the disciplines
- Quizzes and interactive tutorials on finding and documenting research, designing documents, and editing for common errors
- Exercises for multilingual writers

Taking online quizzes and tutorials is a convenient way to enhance your learning and measure your knowledge. Use the Web site to expand on your understanding of the information in your handbook. Also, ask your instructor for suggestions about resources that will help you with specific assignments.

FIUb   The Center for Excellence in Writing at Florida International University

Visit the Center for Excellence in Writing (CEW) to write in a friendly, supportive environment. Whether you are composing an essay for freshman composition or writing your dissertation, you can work one on one with our trained peer writing consultants. For more information, please visit our Web site or stop by one of our locations:

Modesto A. Maidique Campus
11200 Southwest 8th Street
Miami, FL 33199
Green Library 125
(305) 348-6634

Biscayne Bay Campus
3000 Northeast 151st Street
North Miami, FL 33181
Glenn Hubert Library, First Floor
(305) 919-4036

Engineering Center
10555 West Flagler Street
Miami, FL 33174
Library Services, EC 2780
(305) 348-6634

Find us online at writingcenter.fiu.edu.

Center for Excellence in Writing   @FIUWriting

Online tutoring

For those of you off-campus or with a busy schedule, the Center for Excellence in Writing offers personalized online tutoring sessions to help you improve your writing! All you need is a microphone. You meet remotely and spend one-on-one time with a peer consultant to discuss your paper, just as you would face to face. Online tutoring is available Monday through Friday, 9:00 a.m. to 10:00 p.m. Additionally, the Center for Excellence in Writing now offers online tutoring on weekends (Saturday and Sunday). Please review the Center's scheduler at **fiu.mywconline.net** for online tutor availability during weekend hours.

What we do

We offer individual consultations about any writing you do throughout your years at FIU. Whether you are brainstorming, drafting, revising or polishing, our writing consultants can assist you with projects such as:

- Papers, reports, and projects for any course in any department
- Honors theses, master's theses, dissertations
- Proposals
- Résumés and applications for fellowships and employment
- Personal statements
- Group projects
- PowerPoint presentations and other non-print projects

What we don't do

- We do not grade papers. Only your instructor can determine how well your writing satisfies the requirements of an assignment.
- We do not edit or proofread papers. We provide direction to help you to develop and improve your writing skills.
- We do not recommend bringing in long papers that are due the same day as the session. Longer and more complex assignments take more time to read and review so you should come to the Center early in your writing process.

Want to improve your writing? Make an appointment with one of our consultants!

WHAT DO <u>STUDENTS</u> HAVE TO SAY ABOUT THE WRITING CENTER?

▶ Very informative. Opened my eyes to new style and organizational choices. Very, very helpful. Best constructive criticism I've ever received.

▶ My session was extremely effective. I arrived to the session unsure of the structure, thesis, or the argument I would present in my paper. I left the session with a plan of action and feeling very confident about my paper.

▶ The consultants make you think and come up with solutions to the errors in the essays. They do not just do it for you.

▶ Encouraged me to brainstorm and reflect on new ideas on my own.

▶ The session was entirely effective. I thought that this was my final draft but I realized that there was still some organizing and correcting to do!

▶ I am always recommending students [come] to the writing center, and I will continue to do so as I believe that this program is extremely useful and valuable.

WHAT DO <u>CONSULTANTS</u> HAVE TO SAY ABOUT THE WRITING CENTER?

▶ Students now have a vital resource that enables them to become better writers and empowers them to become critical thinkers.

– FITZGERALD SMITH

▶ Coming to the Center for Excellence in Writing means finding a place to meet both a good reader of your work and a fellow writer. It's a place where your writing process is understood and respected. Because the Center is peer structured, we all essentially have the same goal at heart: to become better thinkers, better readers and ultimately, better writers.

– MARINA PRUNA

▶ The Center for Excellence in Writing is an awesome resource for all students because it is dedicated to the advancement of the individual writer, no matter what the skill level.

– RON BROWN

FIUc   Writing in the disciplines

Here, see what FIU instructors have to say about writing in their fields and expectations for student writing:

Writing in history

Historians seek to understand the past. Historical writing presents a thesis that explains or analyzes an event within an historical context. It uses evidence that demonstrates that the thesis presented is reasonable and consistent with what is known. Evidence might be a document, a speech, a social structure, a law, a myth, a photograph, or a city directory. The possibilities are varied. Sometimes the evidence to be used for your interpretation is provided by the professor. Your task is to develop a thesis that can be defended. Sometimes the best way to develop a thesis is to phrase it to yourself as a question. Your paper, then, answers the question.

– DR. JOYCE PETERSON,
Department of History, Associate Dean

Writing in literature

Integrating writing with reading distinguishes literary analysis from casual reading for enjoyment or information. Through writing, readers engage in larger conversations about the meaning of texts, the experience of aesthetic pleasure, and the cultural and historical roles of language in human life. Students of literature read in order to respond to a text in writing and they write in order to become more analytical and thorough readers. Instructors in literary studies promote this seamless integration of reading, interpretation, and writing, whether students' work is an analytical argument or a creative composition. When I evaluate writing, I not only want to see that students can identify rhetorical and symbolic devices like irony or metaphor, but also that they can use these devices to make their own thinking more complex and flexible. I do not want my students to be only competent writers—clear, precise, and grammatically correct. I hope my students will use reading and writing to become insightful thinkers about how the media of writing and language structures what counts as information, knowledge, and communication.

– DR. YVETTE PIGGUSH,
Department of English, Assistant Professor

Writing in the social sciences

For social science papers, the quality of the research is as important as the quality of the writing. The depth, breadth, and relevance of the sources, therefore, determine how good the paper can be, regardless of how grammatically well written it is. In student papers, the source citations should be complete. Students should avoid the temptation to rely only on their own opinions, but instead base their work on what they have learned from their sources, analyzing and synthesizing the research. Students don't have "feelings" about the subject from their research, they come to conclusions based on the cited material. Except in unusual cases, such as in reporting on important speeches or documents, direct quotations from the research material should not be used. Long quotations should not be a way to avoid stating the information from the source in your own words.

– Dr. Peter Craumer,
Department of International Relations, Associate Professor

Writing in philosophy

Writing in philosophy typically aims to argue for or against a clearly stated thesis. The point is to explain and critically respond to some of the reasoning found in the philosophical readings. In most cases, essays should display a classic structure: (1) an introduction that focuses the topic and states the thesis; (2) an exposition of the thesis-focused topic with accounts of some of the views and reasoning in relevant readings; (3) the main argument for the thesis including responses to anticipated objections; (4) a conclusion that returns to the thesis but with a greater degree of specificity, achieved through the earlier exposition and critical arguments.

Students' essays should provide clarity about assumptions and display a structure of inference from premises to conclusion. The most common lapse is a failure to come down to specifics, both in exposition and in critical argument. A helpful example can often serve as a pivot uniting exposition and critical discussion. The exposition should set up the critical discussion so that the transition to supporting or opposing reasoning flows naturally out of the expository account.

– Drs. Ken Henely and Ken Rogerson,
Department of Philosophy, Professors

FIUd Using Turnitin.com

Creating a new Turnitin.com account (For new users)

1. Go to **turnitin.com**.
2. Click "Create Account."
3. Enter your email address and password, and select that you are a student.
4. Fill in your "Class ID" and the "Class enrollment password." (Both are provided by your instructor.)
5. Enter your user information as directed, and choose a password.

Adding a class (For returning users)

1. Go to **turnitin.com**.
2. Log in using your email address and password.
3. A list of your current classes appears. Click "Enroll in a Class."
4. Fill in the "Class/Section ID" and the "Enrollment Password." (Both will be provided by your instructor.)

Submitting papers to Turnitin.com

1. Log in.
2. Click on the name of your class.
3. Find the assignment for which you want to submit a paper and click "Submit."
4. Enter a submission title for the assignment you want to submit.
5. Click "Browse" to find the assignment on your computer.
6. Click "Submit." A screen appears, displaying the paper you selected.
7. If this is the paper you want to submit, click "Yes, submit." If not, click "No, go back." (If needed, repeat steps 5 and 6.)

FIUe   Academic misconduct agreement

Be sure to read FIU's policies on academic misconduct in your *Student Handbook* before filling out the contract below. See also pages 224–34 in your copy of *The Everyday Writer with Exercises*.

I have read and understood all portions of FIU's Code of Academic Integrity, which includes its definition of plagiarism:

NAME (PRINTED)

_____

STUDENT ID#

_____

SIGNATURE

_____

TODAY'S DATE (MM/DD/YY)

_____

COURSE AND SELECTION NUMBER

_____

INSTRUCTOR

_____.

The
Everyday
Writer

with Exercises

5TH EDITION

The Everyday Writer

with Exercises

Andrea A. Lunsford

STANFORD UNIVERSITY

A section for multilingual writers with

Paul Kei Matsuda
ARIZONA STATE UNIVERSITY

Christine M. Tardy
DEPAUL UNIVERSITY

Bedford / St. Martin's
BOSTON ◆ NEW YORK

For Bedford/St. Martin's

Executive Editor: Carolyn Lengel
Senior Production Editor: Harold Chester
Assistant Production Manager: Joe Ford
Marketing Manager: Scott Berzon
Editorial Assistant: Nicholas McCarthy
Copy Editor: Wendy Polhemus-Annibell
Indexer: Melanie Belkin
Photo Researcher: Connie Gardner
Permissions Manager: Kalina K. Ingham
Art Director: Lucy Krikorian
Text Design: Anne Carter; Claire Seng-Niemoeller
Illustrator: GB Tran
Cover Design: Donna Dennison
Composition: Graphic World
Printing and Binding: Quad Graphics

President, Bedford/St. Martin's: Denise B. Wydra
Presidents, Macmillan Higher Education: Joan E. Feinberg
    and Tom Scotty
Editor in Chief: Karen S. Henry
Director of Development: Erica T. Appel
Director of Marketing: Karen R. Soeltz
Production Director: Susan W. Brown
Associate Production Director: Elise S. Kaiser
Managing Editor: Shuli Traub

Library of Congress Control Number: 2012939679

7   6   5   4   3
f   e   d   c   b

For information, write: Bedford/St. Martin's, 75 Arlington Street, Boston, MA
02116   (617-399-4000)

ISBN 978-1-4576-1267-1 (Student edition)
ISBN 978-1-4576-4055-1 (Instructor's edition)

Acknowledgments

How to Use This Book

T*he Everyday Writer* provides a "short and sweet" writing reference you can use easily on your own—at work, in class, even on the run. Small enough to tuck into a backpack or briefcase, this text has been designed to help you find information quickly, efficiently, and easily. I hope that this book will prove to be an everyday reference—and that the following tips will lead you to any information you need.

You'll find many more free resources—videos, tutorials, and research help—and access to e-books and other premium content on the book's companion Web site at **bedfordstmartins.com/everydaywriter**.

The Quick Access Menu on the inside front cover offers a brief overview of the book's contents, divided into twelve color-coded sections that correspond to the book's tabs. If you're looking for a particular chapter or a general topic, this is the simplest place to start. (You can also use the Contents on the inside back cover, which gives chapter titles and most major headings.)

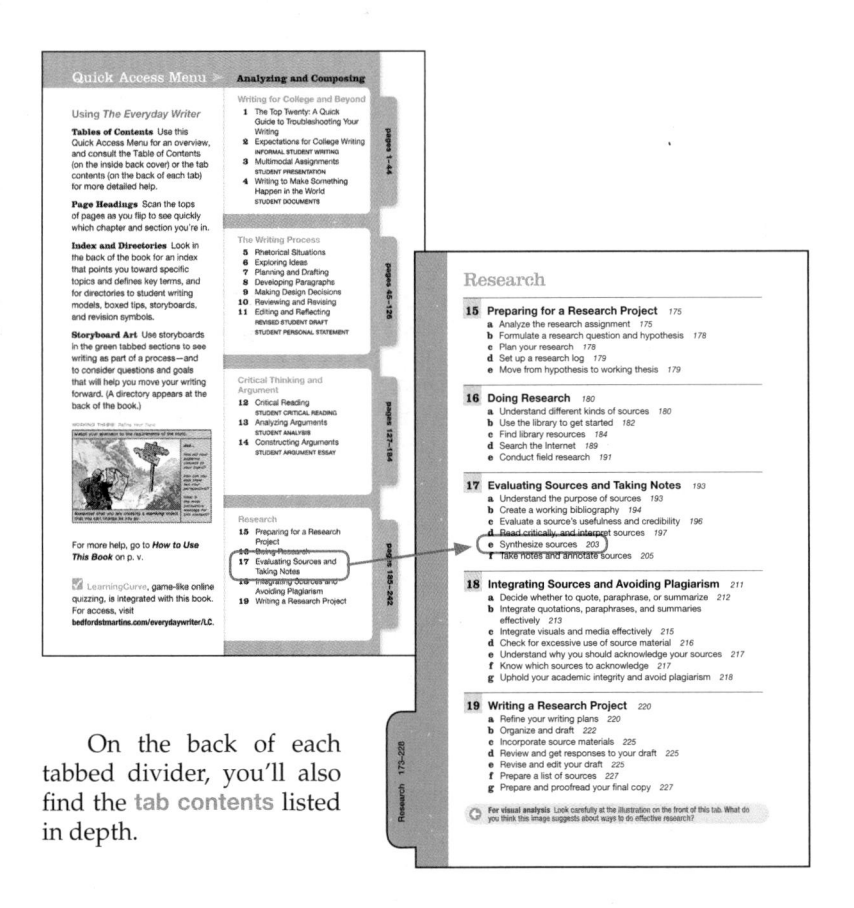

On the back of each tabbed divider, you'll also find the tab contents listed in depth.

The tab contents gives a page number for the beginning of each section, but you can also flip through using the page headers to find the content you're looking for.

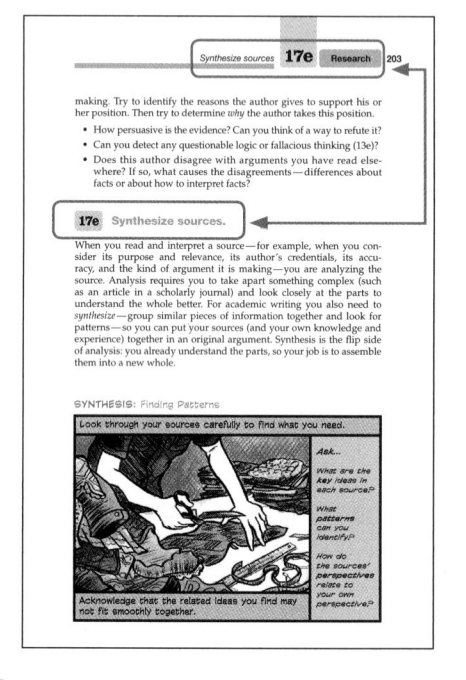

More ways into the book

Directories At the end of the book, you'll find several directories to help you locate special categories of content quickly, including a Directory of Storyboard Art to help you think in new ways about the writing process, a Directory of Student Writing in the book (with more on the Web site), directories of Chapters of Advice and Boxed Tips for multilingual writers, and directories to the "Considering Disabilities" and "Talking the Talk" boxes.

User-Friendly Index The index lists everything covered in the book. You can look up a topic either by its formal name (*ellipses*, for example) or, if you're not sure what the formal name is, by a familiar word you use to describe it (such as *dots*). Important concepts are defined in the index, too, so if you're just looking for a definition, you can find it immediately.

Guide to the Top Twenty Chapter 1 provides guidelines for recognizing, understanding, and editing the most commonly identified issues in student writing today. This section includes brief explanations, hand-edited examples, and cross-references to other places in the book where you'll find more detail on each topic.

Clear Guides to Research and Documentation   Easy-to-follow source maps walk you step-by-step through the processes of selecting, evaluating, using, and citing sources. Documentation models appear in two tabbed sections—gold for MLA style and white for APA, *Chicago*, and CSE styles—with the different documentation styles color-coded in these sections. Most models are also color-coded.

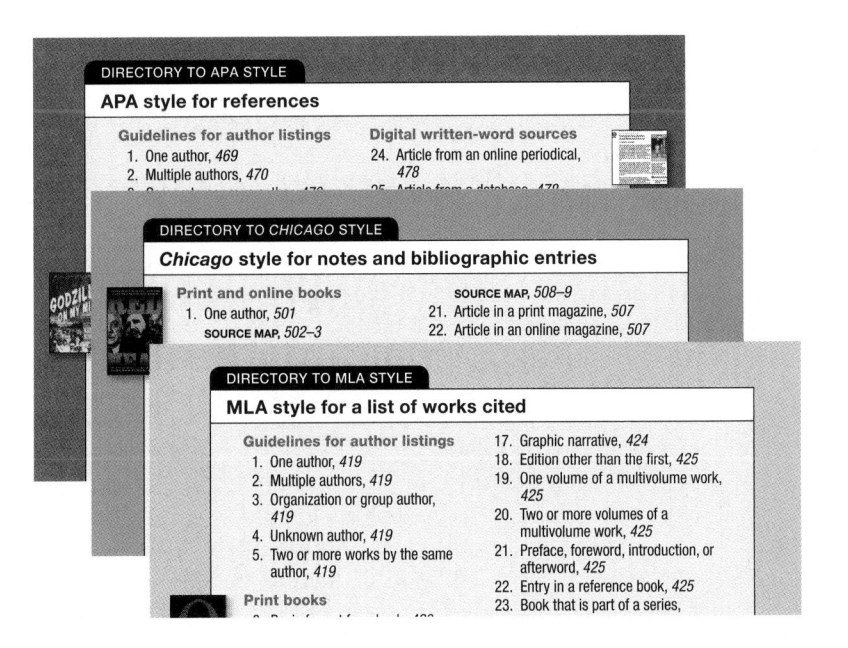

Revision Symbols   If your instructor uses revision symbols to mark your drafts, you can consult the list of symbols at the back of the book and its cross-references to places in the book where you'll find more help.

Glossary of Usage   Chapter 24 gives quick advice on commonly confused and misused words.

Hand-Edited Examples   Many examples are hand-edited in blue, allowing you to see the text and its revision at a glance. Pointers and boldface type make examples easy to spot on the page.

▶ **When him and Zelda were first married, they lived in New York.**
       he

▶ **The boss invited she and her family to dinner.**
                her

Color-Coded Examples Many examples that point out sentence construction or grammar issues use color-coding to focus your attention.

Helping verbs (also called auxiliary verbs) combine with other verbs (often called main verbs) to create verb phrases. Helping verbs include the various forms of *be, do, have* (which can also function as main verbs) and the words *can, could, may, might, must, shall, should, will,* and *would.*

▶ You do need some sleep tonight!
▶ I could have danced all night.
▶ She would prefer to learn Italian rather than Spanish.

See Chapters 32 and 33 for a complete discussion of verbs.

Boxed Tips throughout the Book Look for color-coded boxes to get focused help:

- Green "At a Glance" boxes at the beginning of most chapters (and elsewhere in the book) help you check your drafts with a critical eye and revise or edit.
- Red "Talking the Talk" and "Talking about Style" boxes help you make sense of how writing works in the academic world and help you make stylistic choices for various kinds of writing—in communities, jobs, and disciplines.
- Blue "For Multilingual Writers" boxes offer advice for students whose home language is not exclusively English.
- Gold "Considering Disabilities" boxes help you make your work accessible to readers with disabilities. If you're a writer with a disability, these boxes also point out resources and strategies you may want to use.

Storyboard Art Comic-style art throughout the green-tabbed sections helps you look at the writing process with fresh eyes—and reflect on how your process works. The storyboards are designed so you can think them through on your own. A complete list of storyboards appears in the directory at the back of the book. Exercises to focus your thinking on the storyboards can be found in *The Everyday Writer with Exercises* and on the Web site at **bedfordstmartins .com/everydaywriter**.

RHETORICAL SITUATIONS: Choose Your Topic

Browse around for a topic you care about.

Ask...

What *interesting* topic will meet the requirements for your assignment and context?

What do you know about the topic? What else do you need to find out?

What *message* do you want to convey?

Make sure your topic is manageable and suits your purpose....

Cross-References to the Web Site *The Everyday Writer* Web site expands the book's coverage. The cross-references in the book point you toward practical online resources—tutorials, interactive exercises, model student writing, research and documentation help, and more.

bedfordstmartins.com/everydaywriter
Student Writing

A tutorial on using *The Everyday Writer*, Fifth Edition

For this book to serve you well, you need to get to know it — to know what's inside and how to find it. The following tutorial is designed to help you familiarize yourself with *The Everyday Writer*; the answers appear on the pages following the tutorial.

Getting Started with *The Everyday Writer*

1. Where will you find advice on revising a rough draft of an essay?
2. Where will you find quick information on identifying and fixing sentence fragments?
3. Where will you find guidelines on documenting electronic sources, such as information found on a Web site?
4. Where will you find advice for multilingual writers?

Planning and Drafting

5. Where in *The Everyday Writer* can you find general guidelines on planning and drafting an essay?
6. Where can you find information about how to make and support a claim?
7. Your instructor wants you to give an oral presentation based on a print essay you've written. Where would you find information about planning the presentation?

Doing Research

8. You have a topic but don't know where to begin your research. How can *The Everyday Writer* help you narrow down your options?
9. You've found Web sites related to your topic, but you aren't sure how reliable they are. Where can you find help in evaluating them?
10. Your instructor asks you to become a more critical reader of the sources you have found for your writing project. What section of the handbook will help you understand what to do?
11. You have misplaced the page number of a quotation from an article you want to use in your final project. Can you omit it? Where can you find the answer in *The Everyday Writer*?
12. Your instructor has asked you to use MLA style. How do you document information obtained from a DVD source?

Editing

13. As you edit a final draft, you stop at the following sentence: *Winning may be the name of the game but it isn't a name I care for very much.* Should you put a comma before *but*? How and where do you find this answer?

14. You speak several languages, and you still confuse the English prepositions *in* and *on*. Where can you find help?

15. Your instructor has written *ref* next to this sentence: *Transmitting video signals by satellite is a way of overcoming the problem of scarce airwaves and limiting how they are used.* Where do you look in your handbook for help responding to your instructor's comment?

16. You have spell-checked your document. Do you still need to proofread it? What information does *The Everyday Writer* provide?

Meeting Your Instructor's Expectations

17. You have gotten a draft of your essay back from your instructor with the comment *underdeveloped*. How can your handbook help you find out what you need to do to revise?

18. You want to let your instructor know that you will need to miss class the following day. What advice can *The Everyday Writer* give you about sending a message to someone you don't know very well?

19. You turned in a revised draft, but your instructor says you have only corrected minor errors. Where can you find information on doing thorough revisions?

20. You have been asked to look at a classmate's draft and make suggestions. How can you find out more about reviewing the work of your peers?

Writing in Any Discipline

21. You have a paper due in political science. You've never before written a political science paper, so you're not sure how to proceed. Do political science papers follow any set format? Where can you look for help?

22. You need to write a lab report for your chemistry class. Is there a model in *The Everyday Writer*?

23. For a literature course, you're writing an essay interpreting a poem by Emily Dickinson. Where can you find help?

24. You need to submit a reflective essay to complete the portfolio for your writing class. Where in *The Everyday Writer* can you find information about what to include and how to present the work?

Answers to the tutorial

1. Chapter 10.
2. Chapter 38, on sentence fragments.
3. The gold tab covers documenting sources, including electronic sources, in MLA style; the white tab covers documenting sources in APA, *Chicago*, and CSE styles.

4. The first blue tab includes five chapters (Chapters 56–60) that cover language issues of special interest to students who speak languages in addition to English. At the back of the book you will find a directory to all the materials for multilingual writers.

5. Chapters 6–7 offer guidelines on exploring, planning, and drafting.

6. Looking up *claim* in the index leads you to Chapter 13, on analyzing arguments, and to Chapter 14, on constructing an effective argument.

7. Looking in the directory of student writing points you toward the excerpts from a student presentation in 3c.

8. Chapter 16, "Doing Research," includes section 16b, "Use the library to get started."

9. Skimming the table of contents leads you to Chapter 17, on evaluating sources, and in particular to 17c, on evaluating usefulness and credibility, and to 17d, on reading sources critically.

10. Looking in the index under *reading* or *critical reading* — or checking the table of contents — should lead you to Chapter 12, "Critical Reading," which outlines steps in a critical reading process with examples for various kinds of texts.

11. Consulting the index under *sources* takes you to Chapter 18, "Integrating Sources and Avoiding Plagiarism," where you will find that you must include all of the necessary elements of a citation. "The Top Twenty" in Chapter 1 points out that incomplete documentation is one of the three most common problems in student writing today.

12. The table of contents leads you to the gold tab, which provides a full discussion of MLA documentation conventions. The directory to MLA style, in Chapter 51, points you to the model for citing a DVD.

13. You could turn directly to Chapter 39, on using commas, and look for examples of how to use commas in similar sentences. Looking at "The Top Twenty" in Chapter 1 will show you that omitting a comma in a compound sentence is one of the most common errors students make.

14. The table of contents tells you that Chapter 60 covers prepositions; 60a includes a set of strategies for using prepositions idiomatically, including several examples of sentences using *in* and *on*.

15. A list of revision symbols appears at the back of *The Everyday Writer*. Consulting this list tells you that *ref* refers to "unclear pronoun reference" and that this subject is discussed in 34g.

16. Looking up *proofreading* in the index will take you to an entry on spell checkers and proofreading. The information in section 23e points out that spell checkers miss many kinds of mistakes — there is no substitute for careful proofreading!

17. Looking up *instructor comments* in the index or skimming the table of contents will lead you to section 10c, which includes a chart on learning from instructor comments.

18. The table of contents shows you that section 2e, "Use media to communicate effectively," offers guidelines for sending formal messages, such as an email to an instructor.

19. In the index, you'll find an entry for *reviewing drafts* that directs you to a "Talking the Talk" box in Chapter 10. A directory to all the book's "Talking the Talk" boxes, which answer frequently asked questions about academic work, appears at the back of the book.

20. Looking under *peer review* in the index, or scanning the table of contents, will lead you to section 10b, a detailed look at how to act as a peer reviewer — and how to react when your work is under review.

21. Chapters 61–65 cover academic and professional writing in general, and Chapter 63 covers social science subjects.

22. Consulting the student directory at the back of the book will lead you to a chemistry lab report in Chapter 64, on writing for the natural and applied sciences.

23. Chapter 62, on writing for the humanities, provides guidelines for close readings of literature and a student paper comparing two poems by E. E. Cummings. (On the book's Web site, at **bedfordstmartins.com /everydaywriter**, you can also find a glossary of literary terms.)

24. Looking up *portfolios* in the index or skimming the table of contents will take you to Chapter 11, which includes material on planning a portfolio.

Today, we are in the midst of a literacy revolution the likes of which we haven't seen in at least two thousand years—or perhaps ever. One hallmark of this revolution is that students today are no longer just consumers of information; rather, they are active producers of knowledge. More than ever before, students today are *writers*—every day, every night, all the time; writing is all around them, like the air they breathe, so much so that they don't even notice. From contributing entries to Wikipedia to blogging, texting, tweeting, and posting to YouTube and Facebook, student writers are participating widely in what philosopher Kenneth Burke calls "the conversation of humankind." As access to new writing spaces grows, so too do the potential audiences: many writers, for example, are in daily contact with people around the world, and their work goes out to millions. In such a time, writers need to think more carefully than ever about how to craft effective messages and how best to represent themselves to others.

These ever-expanding opportunities for writers, as well as the challenges that inevitably come with them, have inspired this edition of *The Everyday Writer*—from the focus on thinking carefully about audience and purposes for writing and on attending to the "look" of writing; to an emphasis on moving smoothly between informal, social-media writing and academic writing; to a focus on writing to make something happen in the world; to an emphasis on the ways writing works across disciplines; to the questions that new genres and forms of writing raise about citing and documenting sources and about understanding and avoiding plagiarism. What remains constant is the focus on the "everydayness" of writing and on down-to-earth, practical advice for how to write well in a multitude of situations as well as across a range of genres and media.

What also remains constant is the focus on rhetorical concerns. In a time of such challenging possibilities, taking a rhetorical perspective is particularly important. Why? Because a rhetorical perspective rejects either/or, right/wrong, black/white approaches to writing in favor of asking what choices will be most appropriate, effective, and ethical in a given writing situation. A rhetorical perspective also means paying careful attention to the purposes we want to achieve and the audiences we want to address. Writers today need to maintain such a rhetorical perspective every single day, and *The Everyday Writer*, Fifth Edition, provides them with the tools for doing so.

What's different about this edition?

The Literacy Revolution Has Arrived Students today are writing more than ever to communicate with friends and reach a wider public. The literacy revolution has brought with it opportunities for student writers

to make their voices heard by audiences never before accessible to them; to create texts that include images, sound, and video as well as words; and to present these texts across a range of genres, from brochures and posters to blogs and Web-based reports. My research shows that students often make well-informed decisions in their everyday writing—so *The Everyday Writer* includes new features to help students understand the skills they already have as social writers and use those skills in their academic writing.

A Focus on Bridging Social and Academic Writing *The Everyday Writer* shows students how to use the rhetorical strategies that they employ in their extracurricular writing—including an intuitive understanding of audience and purpose—to create more effective academic writing. Examples throughout show student writers using social media effectively, and advice in several chapters helps students consider the differences between social and academic writing.

An Awareness That Today's Academic Writing Goes Beyond Print Rhetorical advice in *The Everyday Writer* never assumes that students are producing only traditional print products. In addition to new coverage that specifically addresses the rhetorical considerations of tasks such as planning an online text and turning a print text into a presentation, advice throughout the book aims to help students create rhetorically effective texts for any situation.

More Student Writing in More Genres Many students define good writing as active and participatory; they tell me that their most important writing aims to "make something happen in the world." Sample student writing in *The Everyday Writer* reflects the writing students are doing today, both in and out of class—from tweets and event promotions to reports and literary analyses. A new chapter on public writing, Chapter 4, "Writing to Make Something Happen

in the World," helps students understand how to reach their communities with various kinds of texts.

New Attention to Critical Reading — and an Awareness That Students Today Must Respond to Many Kinds of Texts A completely updated chapter on critical reading highlights the wide range of texts that students want, and are asked, to read (or view or listen to) today. Examples in the chapter analyze speeches, blog posts, and photos as well as literary works.

A Focus on the "Why" as Well as the "How" of Documenting Sources New coverage of the basics of various documentation styles helps students understand why academic work calls for more specific citation than popular writing, how to tell the difference between a work from a database and a work online, why medium matters, and more. And additional visual help (including color-coding) with documentation models makes it easy to see what information writers should include in citations.

New Illustrations by *Vietnamerica* Artist GB Tran Because of my own interest in graphic texts and in the ways words and images make meaning together, I'm thrilled that GB Tran, author of *Vietnamerica*, contributed illustrations to this book. In addition to the beautiful part opener  and chapter opener images and other illustrations he created, he and I worked together on six multipanel series on crucial aspects of the writing process (on analyzing rhetorical situations, crafting a working thesis, reading critically, revising and editing, managing peer review, and synthesizing sources). Exercises that ask students to closely examine these panel illustrations appear in *The Everyday Writer with Exercises* and on the Web site at **bedfordstmartins.com /everydaywriter**.

What hasn't changed?

Attention to Good Writing, Not Just to Surface Correctness *The Everyday Writer* helps students understand that effective texts in every genre and medium follow conventions that always depend on their audience, situation, and discipline.

Help for the Most Common Writing Problems   A nationwide study that I conducted with Karen Lunsford—revisiting the original 1986 research that Bob Connors and I did on student writing—shows the problems U.S. college students are most likely to have in their writing today. This book's first chapter presents a quick guide to troubleshooting the Top Twenty—with examples, explanations, and information on where to turn in the book for more detailed information.

Up-to-Date Advice on Research and Documentation   As best practices for research continue to evolve, so does *The Everyday Writer*. In this edition, you'll find integrated coverage of library and online research to help students find authoritative and credible information in any medium, plus advice on integrating sources, avoiding plagiarism, using social bookmarking tools for research, and citing sources in MLA, APA, *Chicago*, and CSE documentation styles. Visual source maps in all four documentation sections show students how to evaluate, use, and document print and online sources.

Comprehensive Coverage of Critical Thinking and Argument   Because first-year writing assignments increasingly call for argument, *The Everyday Writer* provides all the information student writers need to respond effectively to their writing assignments, including practical advice on critical reading and analysis of all kinds of texts, instruction on composing arguments, and two complete student essays.

Essential Help for Writing in the Disciplines   Along with strategies for understanding discipline-specific assignments, vocabulary, style, and use of evidence, this edition offers more student writing samples than ever before, including tweets and Facebook posts, an analysis of a graphic novel in both print-essay and multimodal-presentation form, research projects (in MLA, APA, *Chicago*, and CSE styles), business documents, sample writing from introductory courses in other disciplines, and writing for the public.

Unique Coverage of Language and Style   Unique chapters on language help students think about language in context and about the consequences that language choices have on writers and readers. Boxed tips throughout the book help students communicate effectively across cultures—and use varieties of language both wisely and well.

An Inviting Design   *The Everyday Writer* makes information easy to find and appealing to read.

A User-Friendly, All-in-One Index Entries include both everyday words (such as *that* or *which*) and grammatical terms (such as *pronoun*, which is defined in the index), so students can find what they're looking for quickly and easily.

Available in many formats with a wide array of ancillaries

Print, digital, and integrated media formats

The Everyday Writer, Fifth Edition
- **Comb** binding   ISBN 978-1-4576-0004-3
- **Spiral** binding   ISBN 978-1-4576-1269-5

The Everyday Writer with Exercises, Fifth Edition
Comb-bound book integrated with **LearningCurve adaptive online quizzing** that focuses students on grammar and style topics
ISBN 978-1-4576-1267-1

Visit **bedfordstmartins.com/everydaywriter/LC** for instructor access to LearningCurve.

The Everyday Writer, Fifth Edition, e-books
Assign the *e-Book for The Everyday Writer*, an interactive online e-book with extra tools and content that allow you to easily customize the book for your course and see student progress, or let students choose a downloadable e-book for their computer, tablet, or e-reader.

Customizable online or downloadable e-book formats: **bedfordstmartins .com/everydaywriter/formats**

The Everyday Writer, Fifth Edition, Coursepacks
Free content for your course management system: **bedfordstmartins
.com/coursepacks**

Teaching with Lunsford Handbooks, 2013 Update
ISBN 978-1-4576-1268-8

***From Theory to Practice: A Selection of Essays*,
Third Edition, by Andrea A. Lunsford**
ISBN 978-0-312-56729-3

***Teacher to Teacher*,** Andrea Lunsford's channel
on the award-winning Bedford Bits blog at
bedfordbits.com

Visit **LunsfordHandbooks.com** for these and additional instructor
resources, including downloadable answer keys for *The Everyday Writer
with Exercises* and for the supplemental exercise book available with *The
Everyday Writer.*

Like **Andrea Lunsford on Facebook** to keep up with her research and
travels, and follow **@LunsfordHandbks on Twitter**.

Resources for students

✓ **LearningCurve packaged with *The Everyday Writer***
LearningCurve adaptive online quizzing is available as a package
with *The Everyday Writer* (version without exercises). To order an access
card packaged with the print book, use ISBN 978-1-4576-4370-5 (for
comb-bound) or ISBN 978-1-4576-4369-9 (for spiral-bound). Students
can also purchase access to LearningCurve at **bedfordstmartins.com
/everydaywriter/LC**.

***Student Site for The Everyday Writer*, Fifth Edition**
Go to **bedfordstmartins.com/everydaywriter** for free resources —
tutorials, exercises, documentation help, and more—plus optional
premium content.

***Supplemental Exercises for The Everyday Writer*, Fifth Edition**
ISBN 978-1-4576-2251-9

CompClass for The Everyday Writer
Bedford's online course space includes a dedicated writing and peer
review space, LearningCurve adaptive online quizzing, an interactive
e-book, and more.
ISBN 978-1-4576-2284-7

Acknowledgments

As always, I am most grateful to Carolyn Lengel, my editor for this and
two other handbooks as well: her patience, fortitude, and sheer hard
work, her astute judgment, her wellspring of good ideas, her meticulous attention to detail, and most of all her great wit and sense of humor
are gifts that just keep on giving. I am also thankful to Stephanie Butler
and Adam Whitehurst for their help with planning the overall project
and their advice on handbook media; to Karrin Varucene for her work
on the teaching tab of the Instructor's Edition and for keeping the blog
and Facebook pages on track; to Nick McCarthy for editorial assistance;
to Claire Seng-Niemoeller and Anna Palchik for their brilliant contributions to art and design; to Donna Dennison for cover art; to Wendy
Annibell for her meticulous copyediting; to Sarah Ferguson for her
work on the book's new media components; and to Harold Chester, our
diligent project editor.

Many thanks, also, to the unfailingly generous and supportive
members of the Bedford/St. Martin's team: Joan Feinberg, Denise

Wydra, Erica Appel, Karen Henry, Nancy Perry, Jimmy Fleming, Karen Soeltz, Scott Berzon, Shuli Traub, Nick Carbone, and Joe Ford.

For this edition, I am especially grateful to GB Tran, comics artist and author of *Vietnamerica*, whose simple, elegant, yet "everyday" drawings add immeasurably to the visual appeal of *The Everyday Writer*. I am also indebted to Paul Kei Matsuda and Christine Tardy for their extraordinarily helpful additions to the multilingual writer sections of this book; to Lisa Ede for her ongoing support and advice; and to Lisa Dresdner at Norwalk Community College for her fine work on *Teaching with Lunsford Handbooks*. I have also benefited greatly from the excellent advice of some very special colleagues: Colin Gifford Brooke, Syracuse University; Patrick Clauss, Butler University; Dànielle Nicole DeVoss, Michigan State University; Barbara Fister, Gustavus Adolphus College; Beverly Moss, Ohio State University; Arnold Zwicky, Stanford University; and Marilyn Moller.

I owe special thanks to the group of student writers whose work appears in and enriches this book and its companion Web site: Michelle Abbott, Carina Abernathy, Milena Ateyea, Julie Baird, Jennifer Bernal, Valerie Bredin, Taurean Brown, Tessa Cabello, Ben Canning, Leah Clendening, David Craig, Kelly Darr, Allyson Goldberg, Tara Gupta, Joanna Hays, Dana Hornbeak, Ajani Husbands, Bory Kea, James Kung, Emily Lesk, Nastassia Lopez, Heather Mackintosh-Sims, Merlla McLaughlin, Alicia Michalski, Laura Montgomery, Elva Negrete, Katie Paarlberg, Shannan Palma, Stephanie Parker, Teal Pfeifer, Amrit K. Rao, Heather Ricker, Amanda Rinder, Dawn Rodney, Rudy Rubio, Melissa Schraeder, Bonnie Sillay, Shuqiao Song, Jessica Thrower, Dennis Tyler, and Caroline Warner.

Once again, I have been guided by a group of hardworking and meticulous reviewers, including Teresa Aggen, Pikes Peak Community College; Tom Amorose, Seattle Pacific University; Christopher Baarstad, California State Polytechnic University, Pomona; Michelle Baptiste, University of California, Berkeley; Daisy L. Breneman, James Madison University; Matthew Bryan, University of Central Florida; William Carney, Cameron University; Rebecca Chapman, Vanderbilt University; Karen Culver, University of Miami; Cheryl H. Duffy, Fort Hays State University; Heidi Estrem, Boise State University; Susan Gebhardt-Burns, Norwalk Community College; Angela L. Glover, Simpson College; Melissa A. Goldthwaite, Saint Joseph's University; Andrew Green, University of Miami; Joy A. Hagen, University of California, Santa Cruz; Michelle Hager, San José State University; Chad Hammett, Texas State University, San Marcos; James Harger, Colorado Christian University; Kimberly Harrison, Florida International University; Kristy K. Hodson, California State Polytechnic University; Sarah Klotz, University of California, Davis; Mary R. Lamb, Clayton State University; Tom Lindsley, Iowa State University; Mary M. Mackie, Rogers State University; Anne McCarthy, North

Carolina Central University; Molly McClennen, Marshall University; Holly McSpadden, Missouri Southern State University; Gina Merys, Creighton University; Jennifer Metsker, University of Michigan; Lyle W. Morgan, Pittsburg State University; Beverly Neiderman, Kent State University; Gary Olson, University of Washington; Susan Pagnac, Iowa State University; Shelley Harper Palmer, Rowan-Cabarrus Community College; Jonathan Purkiss, Pulaski Technical College; Carolee Ritter, Southeast Community College; Kathleen J. Ryan, University of Montana; Robert Saba, Florida International University; Charlene Schauffler, Kent State University; Marti Singer, Georgia State University; Rachelle M. Smith, Emporia State University; Mary Tripp, University of Central Florida; Erik Turkman, University of Maryland; Samuel Waddell, York College of Pennsylvania; and Susan Zabowski, University of Miami.

Finally, and always, I continue to learn—from my students, who serve as the major inspiration for just about everything I do; from the very best sisters, nieces, and nephews anyone has ever had; and from my spectacular grand-nieces, Audrey and Lila: this book is for all of you.

Andrea A. Lunsford

The
Everyday
Writer

with Exercises

Writing for College and Beyond

A mind that is stretched by a new experience
can never go back to its old dimensions.

— OLIVER WENDELL HOLMES

Writing for College and Beyond

1 **The Top Twenty: A Quick Guide to Troubleshooting Your Writing** *3*

2 **Expectations for College Writing** *12*
  a Move between social and academic writing *12*
  b Position yourself as an academic writer *14*
  c Read actively *16*
  d Plan research *17*
  e Use media to communicate effectively *18*

3 **Multimodal Assignments** *20*
  a Plan online assignments *20*
  b Join class discussions *24*
  c Prepare for presentations *25*
    STUDENT POWERPOINT PRESENTATION *31*

4 **Writing to Make Something Happen in the World** *36*
  a Decide what should happen *37*
  b Connect with your audience *38*
  c SAMPLE WRITING THAT MAKES SOMETHING HAPPEN IN THE WORLD *39*

For visual analysis Look carefully at the illustration on the front of this tab. What do you think this image suggests about writing for college and beyond?

The Top Twenty: A Quick Guide to Troubleshooting Your Writing

1

Surface errors — grammar, punctuation, word choice, and other small-scale matters — don't always disturb readers. Whether your instructor marks an error in any particular assignment will depend on personal judgments about how serious and distracting it is and about what you should be focusing on in the draft. In addition, not all surface errors are consistently viewed as errors: some of the patterns identified in the research for this book are considered errors by some instructors but as stylistic options by others. Such differing opinions don't mean that there is no such thing as correctness in writing — only that *correctness always depends on some context*, on whether the choices a writer makes seem appropriate to readers.

Research for this book reveals a number of changes that have occurred in student writing over the past twenty-plus years. First, writing assignments in first-year composition classes now focus less on personal narrative and much more on research essays and argument. As a result, students are now writing longer essays than they did twenty years ago and working much more often with sources, both print and digital. Thus it's no surprise that students today are struggling with the conventions for using and citing sources, a problem that did not show up in most earlier studies of student writing.

What else has changed? For starters, wrong-word errors are *by far the most common* errors among first-year student writers today. Twenty years ago, spelling errors were most common by a factor of more than three to one. The use of spell checkers has reduced the number of spelling errors in student writing — but spell checkers' suggestions may also be responsible for some (or many) of the wrong words students are using.

All writers want to be considered competent and careful. You know that your readers judge you by your control of the conventions you have agreed to use, even if the conventions change from time to time. To help you in producing writing that is conventionally correct, you should become familiar with the twenty most common error patterns among U.S. college students today, listed here in order of frequency. A brief explanation and examples of each error are provided in the following sections, and each error pattern is cross-referenced to other places in this book where you can find more detailed information and additional examples.

bedfordstmartins.com/everydaywriter
Top Twenty

AT A GLANCE

The Top Twenty

1. Wrong word
2. Missing comma after an introductory element
3. Incomplete or missing documentation
4. Vague pronoun reference
5. Spelling (including homonyms)
6. Mechanical error with a quotation
7. Unnecessary comma
8. Unnecessary or missing capitalization
9. Missing word
10. Faulty sentence structure
11. Missing comma with a nonrestrictive element
12. Unnecessary shift in verb tense
13. Missing comma in a compound sentence
14. Unnecessary or missing apostrophe (including *its/it's*)
15. Fused (run-on) sentence
16. Comma splice
17. Lack of pronoun-antecedent agreement
18. Poorly integrated quotation
19. Unnecessary or missing hyphen
20. Sentence fragment

---

1 Wrong word

precedence
▶ Religious texts, for them, take ~~prescience~~ over other kinds of sources.
                                    ^

Prescience means "foresight," and *precedence* means "priority."

▶ The child suffered from a severe ~~allegory~~ *allergy* to peanuts.

   Allegory is a spell checker's replacement for a misspelling of *allergy*.

▶ The panel discussed the ethical implications ~~on~~ *of* the situation.

Wrong-word errors can involve using a word with the wrong shade of meaning, using a word with a completely wrong meaning, or using a wrong preposition or another wrong word in an idiom. Selecting a word from a thesaurus without knowing its meaning, or allowing a spell checker to correct spelling automatically, can lead to wrong-word errors, so use these tools with care. If you have trouble with prepositions and idioms, memorize the standard usage. (See Chapter 23 on word choice and spelling and Chapter 60 on prepositions and idioms.)

2 Missing comma after an introductory element

▶ Determined to get the job done, we worked all weekend.

▶ Although the study was flawed, the results may still be useful.

Readers usually need a small pause—signaled by a comma—between an introductory word, phrase, or clause and the main part of the sentence. Use a comma after every introductory element. When the introductory element is very short, you don't always need a comma, but including it is never wrong. (See 39a.)

3 Incomplete or missing documentation

▶ Satrapi says, "When we're afraid, we lose all sense of analysis and reflection" *(263).*

   This quotation comes from a print source, so a page number is needed.

▶ Some experts agree that James Joyce wrote two of the five best novels of all time *("100 Best Novels").*

   The source of this information should be indentified (this online source has no page numbers).

Cite each source you refer to in the text, following the guidelines of the documentation style you are using. (The preceding examples follow MLA style—see Chapters 49–52; for other styles, see Chapters 53–55.) Omitting documentation can result in charges of plagiarism (see Chapter 18).

4 Vague pronoun reference

POSSIBLE REFERENCE TO MORE THAN ONE WORD

▶ Transmitting radio signals by satellite is a way of overcoming the

the airwaves

problem of scarce airwaves and limiting how they are used.
^

In the original sentence, *they* could refer to the signals or to the airwaves.

REFERENCE IMPLIED BUT NOT STATED *a policy*

▶ The company prohibited smoking, ~~which~~ many employees resented.
^

What does *which* refer to? The editing clarifies what employees resented.

A pronoun should refer clearly to the word or words it replaces (called the *antecedent*) elsewhere in the sentence or in a previous sentence. If more than one word could be the antecedent, or if no specific antecedent is present, edit to make the meaning clear. (See Chapter 34.)

5 Spelling (including homonyms)

Reagan

▶ Ronald ~~Regan~~ won the election in a landslide.
^

Everywhere

▶ ~~Every where~~ we went, we saw crowds of tourists.
^

The most common misspellings today are those that spell checkers cannot identify. The categories that spell checkers are most likely to miss include homonyms, compound words incorrectly spelled as separate words, and proper nouns, particularly names. After you run the spell checker, proofread carefully for errors such as these—and be sure to run the spell checker to catch other kinds of spelling mistakes. (See 23e.)

6 Mechanical error with a quotation

▶ "I grew up the victim of a disconcerting confusion,"/ Rodriguez says (249).
^

The comma should be placed *inside* the quotation marks.

Follow conventions when using quotation marks with commas (39h), colons (44d), and other punctuation (43f). Always use quotation marks in pairs, and follow the guidelines of your documentation style for block quotations (43b). Use quotation marks for titles of short works (43c), but use italics for titles of long works (47a).

7 Unnecessary comma

BEFORE CONJUNCTIONS IN COMPOUND CONSTRUCTIONS THAT ARE NOT COMPOUND SENTENCES

▶ This conclusion applies to the United States/and to the rest of the world.

No comma is needed before *and* because it is joining two phrases that modify the same verb, *applies*.

WITH RESTRICTIVE ELEMENTS

▶ Many parents/of gifted children/do not want them to skip a grade.

No comma is needed to set off the restrictive phrase *of gifted children*, which is necessary to indicate which parents the sentence is talking about.

Do not use commas to set off restrictive elements that are necessary to the meaning of the words they modify. Do not use a comma before a coordinating conjunction (*and, but, for, nor, or, so, yet*) when the conjunction does not join parts of a compound sentence. Do not use a comma before the first or after the last item in a series, between a subject and verb, between a verb and its object or complement, or between a preposition and its object. (See 39j.)

8 Unnecessary or missing capitalization

traditional *medicines* *ephedra*
▶ Some ~~T~~raditional Chinese ~~M~~edicines containing ~~E~~phedra remain legal.

Capitalize proper nouns and proper adjectives, the first words of sentences, and important words in titles, along with certain words indicating directions and family relationships. Do not capitalize most other words. When in doubt, check a dictionary. (See Chapter 45.)

9 Missing word

against
▶ The site foreman discriminated women and promoted men with less experience.

Proofread carefully for omitted words, including prepositions (60a), parts of two-part verbs (60b), and correlative conjunctions (31h). Be particularly careful not to omit words from quotations.

10 Faulty sentence structure

▶ The information which *High* high school athletes are presented with mainly includes information on what credits *they* needed to graduate, and thinking about the college which athletes are trying *colleges to try* to play for, and apply. *how to*

A sentence that starts out with one kind of structure and then changes to another kind can confuse readers. Make sure that each sentence contains a subject and a verb (31b), that subjects and predicates make sense together (26b), and that comparisons have clear meanings (26e). When you join elements (such as subjects or verb phrases) with a coordinating conjunction, make sure that the elements have parallel structures (see Chapter 27).

11 Missing comma with a nonrestrictive element

▶ Marina, who was the president of the club, was first to speak.

The clause *who was the president of the club* does not affect the basic meaning of the sentence: Marina was first to speak.

A nonrestrictive element gives information not essential to the basic meaning of the sentence. Use commas to set off a nonrestrictive element (39c).

12 Unnecessary shift in verb tense

▶ Priya was watching the great blue heron. Then she *slipped* slips and *fell* falls into the swamp.

Verbs that shift from one tense to another with no clear reason can confuse readers (28a).

13 Missing comma in a compound sentence

▶ Meredith waited for Samir, and her sister grew impatient.
            ^

Without the comma, a reader may think at first that Meredith waited for both Samir and her sister.

A compound sentence consists of two or more parts that could each stand alone as a sentence. When the parts are joined by a coordinating conjunction, use a comma before the conjunction to indicate a pause between the two thoughts (39b).

14 Unnecessary or missing apostrophe (including *its/it's*)

                                             child's
▶ Overambitious parents can be very harmful to a ~~childs~~ well-being.
                                                  ^

      its   *It's*
▶ The car is lying on it's side in the ditch. Its a white 2004 Passat.
                         ^   ^

To make a noun possessive, add either an apostrophe and an -*s* (*Ed's book*) or an apostrophe alone (*the boys' gym*). Do not use an apostrophe in the possessive pronouns *ours, yours,* and *hers.* Use *its* to mean *belonging to it;* use *it's* only when you mean *it is* or *it has.* (See Chapter 42.)

15 Fused (run-on) sentence

                            but
▶ Klee's paintings seem simple, they are very sophisticated.
                              ^
   Although she
▶ She doubted the value of meditation, she decided to try it once.
   ^   ^

A fused sentence (also called a *run-on*) joins clauses that could each stand alone as a sentence with no punctuation or words to link them. Fused sentences must either be divided into separate sentences or joined by adding words or punctuation. (See Chapter 37.)

16 Comma splice

                        for
▶ I was strongly attracted to her, she was beautiful and funny.
                                 ^

▶ We hated the meat loaf/ *that* the cafeteria served it every Friday.

A comma splice occurs when only a comma separates clauses that could each stand alone as a sentence. To correct a comma splice, you can insert a semicolon or period, connect the clauses with a word such as *and* or *because*, or restructure the sentence. (See Chapter 37.)

17 Lack of pronoun-antecedent agreement

All students *uniforms.*
▶ Every student must provide their own uniform.

its
▶ Each of the puppies thrived in their new home.

Pronouns must agree with their antecedents in gender (male or female) and in number (singular or plural). Many indefinite pronouns, such as *everyone* and *each*, are always singular. When a singular antecedent can refer to a man or a woman, either rewrite the sentence to make the antecedent plural or to eliminate the pronoun, or use *his or her, he or she*, and so on. When antecedents are joined by *or* or *nor*, the pronoun must agree with the closer antecedent. A collective noun such as *team* can be either singular or plural, depending on whether the members are seen as a group or as individuals. (See 34f.)

18 Poorly integrated quotation

showed how color affects taste:
▶ Schlosser cites a 1970s study that "Once it became apparent that the

steak was actually blue and the fries were green, some people

became ill" (Schlosser 565).

According to Lars Eighner,
▶ "Dumpster diving has serious drawbacks as a way of life" (Eighner 383).

Finding edible food is especially tricky.

Quotations should fit smoothly into the surrounding sentence structure. They should be linked clearly to the writing around them (usually with a signal phrase) rather than dropped abruptly into the writing. (See 18b.)

Taking a Writing Inventory

One way to learn from your mistakes is to take a writing inventory. It can help you think critically and analytically about how to improve your writing skills.

1. Collect two or three pieces of your writing to which either your instructor or other students have responded.

2. Read through these writings, adding your own comments about their strengths and weaknesses. How do your comments compare with those of others?

3. Group all the comments into three categories — *broad content issues* (use of evidence and sources, attention to purpose and audience, and overall impression), *organization and presentation* (overall and paragraph-level organization, sentence structure and style, and for-matting), and *surface errors* (problems with spelling, grammar, punc-tuation, and mechanics).

4. Make an inventory of your own strengths in each category.

5. Study your errors. Mark every instructor and peer comment that sug-gests or calls for an improvement, and put all these comments in a list. Consult the relevant part of this book or speak with your instructor if you don't understand a comment.

6. Make a list of the top problem areas you need to work on. How can you make improvements? Then note at least two strengths that you can build on in your writing. Record your findings in a writing log that you can add to as the class proceeds.

19 Unnecessary or missing hyphen

▶ This paper looks at fictional and real life examples.

A compound adjective modifying a noun that follows it requires a hyphen.

▶ The buyers want to fix up the house and resell it.

A two-word verb should not be hyphenated.

A compound adjective that appears before a noun needs a hyphen. However, be careful not to hypenate two-word verbs or word groups that serve as subject complements. (See Chapter 48.)

20 Sentence fragment

NO SUBJECT

▶ Marie Antoinette spent huge sums of money on herself and her favorites.

Her extravagance
A̧nd helped bring on the French Revolution.

NO COMPLETE VERB

was
▶ The old aluminum boat sitting on its trailer.

BEGINNING WITH A SUBORDINATING WORD

where
▶ We returned to the drugstorȩ, W̶h̶e̶r̶e̶ we waited for our buddies.

A sentence fragment is part of a sentence that is written as if it were a complete sentence. Reading your draft out loud, backwards, sentence by sentence, will help you spot sentence fragments. (See Chapter 38.)

 bedfordstmartins.com/everydaywriter
Taking a Writing Inventory

---

2 Expectations for College Writing

Your college instructors—and your future colleagues and supervisors—will expect you to demonstrate your ability to think critically, to consider ethical issues, to find as well as solve problems, to do effective research, to work productively with people of widely different backgrounds, and to present the knowledge you construct in a variety of ways and in a variety of genres and media. Your success will depend on communicating clearly and on making appropriate choices for the context.

2a Move between social and academic writing.

Social connection today involves so much writing—text messages, tweets, Facebook posts, blogs, YouTube videos, and the like—that you probably do more writing out of class than in class. In fact, Web 2.0

and social networking have opened doors for writers like never before. Writing on social networking sites allows writers to get almost instant feedback, and anticipating responses from an audience often has the effect of making online writers very savvy: they know the importance of analyzing the audience and of using an appropriate style, level of formality, and tone to suit the online occasion.

As you know, writers on Twitter tell followers what's going on in short bursts of no more than 140 characters. Here are two representative tweets from the Twitter feed of Stephanie Parker, a college student whose interests include technology and Korean pop culture.

sparker2

Rain's over, going to Trader Joe's to buy some healthy stuff to fight this cold. . suggestions?

Watching Queen Seon Duk/선덕여왕 on @dramafever, love it so far! http://www.dramafever.com/drama/56/ #nowplaying

In these tweets, Stephanie shows a keen awareness both of her audiences on Twitter and of two very common purposes for this kind of informal writing — to seek information (in the first tweet, about foods to fight off a cold) and to share information (in the second tweet, about her view of a Korean drama, with a link so readers can check it out for themselves).

Facebook and similar sites allow for fast-paced conversation between writers. This status update from Alicia Michalski got a response in the form of a link to a YouTube video (of a man exercising to a song called "You Can Do It"), to which Alicia then replied — all in the space of twelve minutes.

Alicia Michalski Long, long day ahead of me. And the toughest won't even be my classes.

Yesterday at 8:14am · Comment · Like

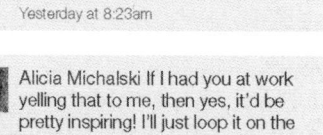

Ryan Sundheimer http://www.youtube.com/watch?v=rCvtldLxu1Y

Tell me that doesn't inspire you!

Yesterday at 8:23am

Alicia Michalski If I had you at work yelling that to me, then yes, it'd be pretty inspiring! I'll just loop it on the speakers there!!

Yesterday at 8:26am

TALKING THE TALK

Conventions

"Aren't conventions just rules with another name?" Not entirely. Conventions — agreed-on language practices of grammar, punctuation, and style — convey a kind of shorthand information from writer to reader. In college writing, you will want to follow the conventions of standard academic English unless you have a good reason to do otherwise. But unlike hard-and-fast rules, conventions are flexible; a convention appropriate for one time or situation may be inappropriate for another. You may even choose to ignore conventions to achieve a particular effect. (You might, for example, write a sentence fragment rather than a full sentence, such as the *Not entirely* near the beginning of this box.) As you become more experienced and confident in your writing, you will develop a sense of which conventions to apply in different writing situations.

Like Stephanie and Alicia, many young writers today are adept at informal social writing across a range of genres and media. You may not think very hard about the audience you'll reach in a tweet or Facebook post, or about your purpose for writing in such spaces, but you are probably more skilled than you give yourself credit for when it comes to making appropriate choices for your informal writing.

Of course, informal writing is not the only writing skill a student needs to master. You'll also need to move back and forth between informal social writing and formal academic writing, and to write across a whole range of genres and media. Look closely at your informal writing: What do you assume about your audience? What is your purpose? How do you achieve a particular tone? In short, why do you write the way you do in these situations? Analyzing the choices you make in a given writing context will help you develop the ability to make good choices in other contexts as well—an ability that will allow you to move between social and academic writing.

2b Position yourself as an academic writer.

If you're like most students, you probably have less familiarity with academic writing contexts than you do with informal contexts. You may not have written anything much longer than five pages of formal academic writing before coming to college, and you may have done only minimal research. The contexts for your college writing will require you to face new challenges; you may be asked, for example, to create a persuasive Web site or to research, write, and deliver a multimedia presentation. You can begin the process of learning by figuring out what your instructors expect from you. Of course, expectations about academic writing vary considerably in different courses and different disciplines (see Chapters 61–65), but becoming familiar with widespread conventions will prepare you well for most academic situations.

Establishing authority

In the United States, most college instructors expect student writers to begin to establish their own authority—to become constructive critics who can analyze and interpret the work of others. But what does establishing authority mean in practice?

- Assume that your opinions count (as long as they are informed rather than tossed out with little thought) and that your audience expects you to present them in a well-reasoned manner.
- Show your familiarity with the ideas and works of others, both from the assigned course reading and from good points your instructor and classmates have made.

Being direct and clear

Your instructors will most often expect you to get to the point quickly and to be direct throughout an essay or other project. Research for this book confirms that readers depend on writers to organize and present their material—using sections, paragraphs, sentences, arguments, details, and source citations—in ways that aid understanding. Good academic writing prepares readers for what is coming next, provides definitions, and includes topic sentences. (See 20c for a description of the organization that instructors often prefer in student essays.) To achieve directness in your writing, try the following strategies:

- State your main point early and clearly.
- Avoid overqualifying your statements. Instead of writing *I think the facts reveal*, come right out and say *The facts reveal*.
- Avoid digressions. If you use an anecdote or example from personal experience, be sure it relates directly to the point you are making.
- Use appropriate evidence, such as examples and concrete details, to support each point.
- Make transitions from point to point obvious and clear. The first sentence of a new paragraph should reach back to the paragraph before and then look forward to what is to come (see Chapter 8).

- Follow logical organizational patterns (see Chapter 8).
- Design and format the project appropriately for the audience and purpose you have in mind (see Chapter 9).
- If your project is lengthy, you may also want to use brief summary statements between sections, but avoid unnecessary repetition.

EXERCISE 2.1

Choose a sample of your own informal writing from a social networking site: a blog, posting, text message, or instant message, for example. Why did you write the post? What did you assume about your readers, and why? Why did you choose the words, images, links, or other parts of the text, and how do these choices contribute to the way the writing comes across to an audience? Does the writing do what you want it to do? Why, or why not?

AT A GLANCE

U.S. Academic Style

- Consider your purpose and audience carefully, making sure that your topic is appropriate to both. (Chapter 5)
- State your claim or thesis explicitly, and support it with examples, statistics, anecdotes, and authorities of various kinds. (Chapter 7)
- Carefully document all of your sources. (Chapters 49–55)
- Make explicit links between ideas. (Chapter 8)
- Consistently use the appropriate level of formality. (Chapter 23)
- Use conventional formats for academic genres. (Chapters 3–4 and 61–64)
- Use conventional grammar, spelling, punctuation, and mechanics. (Chapters 31–48)
- Use an easy-to-read type size and typeface, conventional margins, and double spacing. (Chapter 9)

2c   Read actively.

Your instructors expect you to be an active reader—to offer informed opinions on what readings say. Stating your opinion doesn't require you to be negative or combative, just engaged with the class and the text. The following strategies will help you read actively:

- Note the name of the author and the date and place of publication; these items can give you clues to the writer's purpose and intended audience.

- Understand the overall content of a piece well enough to summarize it (12c).
- Formulate critical questions about the text, and bring these questions up in class.
- Understand each sentence, and make direct connections between sentences and paragraphs. Keep track of repeated themes or images, and figure out how they contribute to the entire piece.
- Note the author's attitude toward and assumptions about the topic. Then you can speculate on how the attitude and assumptions may have affected the author's thinking.
- Note the writer's sources: what evidence does the writer rely on, and why?
- Distinguish between the author's stance and the author's reporting on the stances of others. Watch for key phrases an author uses to signal an opposing argument: *while some have argued that, in the past,* and so on.
- Go beyond content to notice organizational patterns, use of sources, and choice of words.
- Consider annotating your readings, especially if they are very important (12b). Make notes in the margins that record your questions, challenges, or counter-examples to the text.
- If the readings are interactive — that is, if they allow you to post a comment — take advantage of this opportunity to get your voice into the conversation.

2d Plan research.

Much of the work you do in college may turn an informal curiosity into various kinds of more formal research: you might start by wondering how many students on your campus are vegetarians, for example, and end up with a research project for a sociology class that then becomes part of a multimedia presentation for a campus organization. Many of your writing assignments will require extensive formal research with a wide range of sources from various media as well as information drawn from observations, interviews, or surveys.

Research can help you find important information that you didn't know, even if you know a topic very well. And no matter what you discover, college research is an important tool for establishing credibility with your audience members and thus gaining their confidence. Often, what you write will be only as good as the research on which it is based. (For more on research, see Chapters 15–19.)

2e Use media to communicate effectively.

Your instructors will probably expect you to communicate both in and out of class using a variety of media. You may be asked to post to course management systems, lists, blogs, and wikis, and you may respond to the work of others on such sites. In addition, you will probably contact your instructor and classmates using email and text messages. Because electronic communication is so common, it's easy to fall  into the habit of writing very informally. If you forget to adjust style and voice for different occasions and readers, you may undermine your own intentions.

Best practices for formal messages and posts

Email was once seen as highly informal, but you will probably use it today mainly for more formal purposes, particularly to communicate for work and for school. When writing most academic and professional messages, then, or when posting to a public list that may be read by people you don't know well, follow the conventions of standard academic English (2b), and be careful not to offend or irritate your audience—remember that jokes may be read as insults and that ALL CAPS may look like shouting. Finally, proofread to make sure your message is clear and free of errors, and that it is addressed to your intended audience, before you hit SEND.

EMAIL

- Use a subject line that states your purpose clearly.
- Use a formal greeting and closing (*Dear Ms. Aulie* rather than *Hey*).
- Keep messages as concise as possible.
- Conclude your message with your name and email address.
- Ask for permission before forwarding a sensitive message from someone else.
- Consider your email messages permanent and always findable, even if you delete them. Many people have been embarrassed (or worse, prosecuted) because of email trails.
- Make sure that the username on the email account you use for formal messages does not present a poor impression. If your username is *Party2Nite*, consider changing it, or use your school account for academic and professional communication.

DISCUSSION LISTS AND FORUMS

- Avoid unnecessary criticism of others' spelling or language. If a message is unclear, ask politely for a clarification. If you disagree with an assertion, offer what you believe to be the correct information, but don't insult the writer.

- If you think you've been insulted, give the writer the benefit of the doubt. Replying with patience establishes your credibility and helps you appear mature and fair.

- For email discussion lists, decide whether to reply off-list to the sender of a message or to the whole group, and be careful to use REPLY or REPLY ALL accordingly to avoid potential embarrassment.

- Keep in mind that because many discussion forums and email lists are archived, more people than you think may be reading your messages.

Best practices for informal situations

Sometimes audiences expect informality. When you write in certain situations—Twitter posts, for example, and most text messages—you can play with (or ignore) the conventions you would probably follow in formal writing. Most people receiving text messages expect shorthand such as *u* for "you," but be cautious about using such shortcuts with an employer or instructor. You may want to stick to a more formal method of contact if your employer or instructor has not explicitly invited you to send text messages—or texted you first.

Even when you think the situation calls for an informal tone, be attuned to your audience's needs and your purpose for writing. And when writing for any online writing space that allows users to say almost anything about themselves or to comment freely on the postings of others, bear in mind that anonymity sometimes makes online writers feel less inhibited than they would be in a face-to-face discussion. Don't say anything you want to remain private, and even if you disagree with another writer, avoid personal attacks.

 bedfordstmartins.com/everydaywriter
Writing with Digital Media

EXERCISE 2.2: THINKING CRITICALLY

How do you define good college writing? Make a list of the characteristics you come up with. Then make a list of what you think your instructors' expectations are for good college writing, and note how they may differ from yours. (Research suggests that many students today define good writing as "writing that makes something happen in the world." Would that match your definition or that of your instructors?) What might account for the differences — and the similarities — in the definitions and lists? Do you need to alter your ideas about good college writing to meet your instructors' expectations? Why, or why not?

3 Multimodal Assignments

As Clive Thompson noted in *Wired* magazine in 2009, "Before the Internet came along, most Americans never wrote anything, ever, that wasn't a school assignment." Times have indeed changed. More and more Americans are reading and writing for social purposes and for their jobs and communities, not just for school. Your "life writing" is increasingly likely to include blogs, online videos, PowerPoint presentations, and other texts incorporating not just words but images, sound, and video. And college writing classes are increasingly likely to require you to shift gears in similar ways—from writing posts on class forums and creating Web texts to making oral presentations with multimedia support. As one student explains, the multimodal realities of today's academic work require you to become "ambidextrous in the digital age."

3a Plan online assignments.

Writing assignments that your audiences will encounter online may repurpose your print-based work, or they may be entirely new, online-only texts that take advantage of the technology to include material that print texts can't offer, such as sound and video. Whether you are starting with work on a printed page or tackling an online assignment from

---

AT A GLANCE

Guidelines for Creating an Online Text

- Consider purpose, audience, and message. How can your text appeal to the right readers? How will it accomplish its purpose? (Chapter 5)
- Be realistic about the time available for the project, and plan accordingly.
- Think about the various types of online texts you can create, and determine which suits your needs based on what you want or need to do and what your audience expects: text, images, audio, video, or a combination? the latest updates first, or an index page? the ability to collaborate or comment? Make appropriate choices for your project and skills.
- Create an appealing design, or choose a template that follows basic design principles. (Chapter 9)
- Pay attention to user feedback, and make appropriate adjustments.

scratch, you will need to think just as carefully about your online context as you would about any other writing situation.

Rhetorical considerations of online texts

Early on, consider time and technical constraints carefully to make sure that your plan for an online text is manageable. But also remember to think about rhetorical concerns, such as your purpose for creating the text, the needs of your audience, and the main point or message you want to get across.

- Why are you creating this text (5d)? How do you want readers to use it? Considering purpose helps you determine what features your online text will need to incorporate.

- What potential audience (5e) can you identify? Considering audience will help you make good choices about tone, word choice, graphic style and design, level of detail, and many other factors. If your intended audience is limited to people you know (such as a wiki available only to members of your literature class), you may be able to make assumptions about their background, knowledge, and likely responses to your text. If you are covering a particular topic, you may have ideas about the type of audience

you think you'll attract. Plan your text to appeal to the readers you expect— but remember that an online text may reach other, unanticipated audiences.

- What will you talk about? Your topic will also affect the content and design of your project. For example, if you want to write about the latest Hong Kong film releases, you might create a blog; if you want to explore the works of 1940s detective writers, you might produce a Web site. If you prefer to talk about or show information on your topic, you might consider creating an infographic or a video or audio text that you can post to an existing site.

- How do you relate to your subject matter? Your rhetorical stance (5d) determines how your audience will see you. Will you present yourself as an expert, a fan, or a novice seeking input from others? What information will make you seem credible and persuasive to your audience?

Types of online texts

Among the most common types of texts online are Web sites, blogs, wikis, and audio or video texts.

- Web sites and blogs are similar in appearance, and both usually include links to other parts of the site or to other sites. Both are relatively easy to update. Web sites are often organized as a cluster of associations. Readers expect blog content to be refreshed frequently (more often than the contents of a Web page), so blog posts are often time-stamped, and the newest content appears first. Blogs usually invite readers to comment publicly on each post, while Web sites often have a single contact link allowing readers to email the site's creator(s) directly.

- Wikis — collaborative online texts — create communities where all content is peer reviewed and evaluated by other members. They are powerful tools for sharing a lot of information because they draw on the collective knowledge of many contributors.

- Audio and video content can vary as widely as the content found in written-word media — audiobooks, video diaries, pop-culture mashups, radio shows, short documentaries, fiction films, and so on. Writers who create podcasts (which can be downloaded for playback) and streaming media (which can be played without downloading) may produce episodic content united by a common host or theme. Audio and video files can stand alone as online texts on sites such as YouTube, but they can also be embedded on a Web page or blog or included in a presentation to add dimension to still images and written words.

Features of online texts

Choose the features that will enable your audience to get the most from your online text.

- Online readers generally prefer short, manageable chunks of verbal text. If you are writing a long piece, consider breaking it up with headings and visuals. Include enough text to help readers make sense of your content, captions for visuals, sound transcripts (if you include audio files), and so on.

- Links to external sites are one method of documenting sources on-line. You can link to content that helps to prove a point—complex explanations, supporting statistics, bibliographies, referenced Web sites, or additional readings, for example. Links also help readers navigate from one part of a text to another. Each link should have a clear rhetorical purpose and be in an appropriate location. If it's important for users to read the whole paragraph, for instance, you may want to move the link to the end of it.

- Online texts—from blogs and video channels to online newspaper articles—often incorporate interactive features, such as "like" buttons, comments or forums, and a link to contact the writer.

- Online writers who give credit where credit is due have greater authority. If you have not created a verbal text, graphic, or audio or video clip yourself, provide a caption or link identifying the source, and ask permission to use it in a text for an online audience (see Chapter 18).

CONSIDERING DISABILITIES

Accessible Web Texts

Much on the Web remains hard to access and read for persons with disabilities. The Web site for the Americans with Disabilities Act provides guidelines on designing accessible sites, which include offering textual descriptions of any visuals and captions for any sound files. For details, visit www.ada.gov.

Time management

You already know that time management is crucial for your success in any writing situation. How well you can manage decisions will be affected both by your deadline and by how much time you can squeeze out of your other interests and responsibilities to meet that deadline. How much technical expertise do you have, and how much will you need to learn in order to create your text? Allow enough time for that learning to take place. Also consider how much research you will have to do and how long you will need to find, prepare, and seek permission (if needed—see Chapter 16) for any images, sound, or video files you want to use.

Design and organization of online texts

Ultimately, the organization and look of your text depend on what you are trying to achieve. You should make decisions about page length, color, visuals, multimedia, and interactive elements based on rhetorical choices (your audience, purpose, and message) and on practical constraints (the time and tools available). For more on design, see Chapter 9.

Just as you might outline an essay or create a storyboard for a video, you should develop a clear structure for your Web text. Some types of texts are organized in standard ways; others allow you to make choices about how to arrange materials. (For more on organizing a text, see 7d.) Choose a structure that makes sense for your purpose, audience, and message. Arrange your text to allow readers to find what they are looking for as quickly and intuitively as possible. Asking others to try out your site and give you feedback is a good way to learn what works and what doesn't.

3b　Join class discussions.

Make sure your contributions to class discussions—whether live or online—are effective by following these guidelines:

- Be prepared.
- Follow the flow of conversation. Taking notes can help you listen purposefully in a classroom.
- Make sure your comments are relevant. Ask a key question, take the conversation in a new direction, or summarize or analyze what others have said.
- Be specific in your comments: *The passage in the middle of page 42 backs up what you're saying* is more useful than *I agree.*

FOR MULTILINGUAL WRITERS

Speaking Up in Class

Speaking up in class is viewed as inappropriate or even rude in some cultures. In the United States, however, doing so is expected and encouraged. Some instructors even assign credit for such class participation.

3c Prepare for presentations.

More and more students report that formal presentations are becoming part of their work both in and out of class. Good preparation is as necessary for a successful presentation as for any other writing assignment.

Considering your assignment, purpose, and audience for presentations

Begin preparing for a presentation as soon as you get the assignment. Think about how much time you have to prepare; how long the presentation is to be; whether you will use written-out text or note cards; whether visual aids, handouts, or other materials are called for; and what equipment you will need. If you are making a group presentation,

AT A GLANCE

Preparing for Presentations

- How can you ensure that your text meets the expectations of a live audience?
- How does your presentation fulfill your purpose, including the goals of the assignment?
- How do the introduction and conclusion hold the audience's attention?
- Is your organizational structure crystal clear? How do you guide listeners? Are your transitions and signpost language explicit? Do you effectively repeat key words or ideas?
- Have you marked the text you are using for pauses and emphasis?
- Have you prepared all necessary visuals, including presentation slides and other multimedia? Are they large enough to be seen? Would other visuals be helpful?
- Have you practiced your presentation and gotten response to it?

you will need time to divide duties and practice. Make sure that you understand the criteria for evaluation—how will the presentation be graded or assessed?

Consider the purpose of your presentation (5d). Are you to lead a discussion? teach a lesson? give a report? engage a group in an activity? Also consider the audience (5e). If your instructor is a member of the audience, what will he or she expect you to do—and do well? What do audience members know about your topic? What opinions do they already hold about it? What do they need to know to follow your presentation and perhaps accept your point of view?

Student Shuqiao Song got a two-part assignment for her writing class on graphic novels: she had to write an argument essay based on her research on a graphic novel, and then she had to turn that information into a script for a twelve-minute oral presentation with slides. After brainstorming and talking with her instructor, she chose Alison Bechdel's memoir *Fun Home: A Family Tragicomic* as her topic. She realized that although she wanted very much to earn a good grade, she also wanted to convince her classmates that Bechdel's book was complex and important—and she wanted to turn in a truly *impressive* performance in her presentation.

For Shuqiao Song's print essay, see 12e.

Making your introduction and conclusion memorable

Listeners, like readers, tend to remember beginnings and endings most readily, so work extra hard to make these elements memorable. Consider, for example, using a startling statement, opinion, or question; a dramatic anecdote; a powerful quotation; or a vivid image. Shifting language, especially into a variety of language that your audience will identify with, is another effective way to catch their attention (see Chapter 22). Whenever you can link your subject to the experiences and interests of your audience, do so.

Shuqiao Song began her presentation this way:

Welcome, everyone. I'm Shuqiao Song and I'm here today to talk about residents of a dys*FUN*ctional *HOME*. We meet these residents in a graphic memoir called *Fun Home*.

(Here, Shuqiao showed a three-second video clip of author Alison Bechdel saying, "I love words, and I love pictures. But especially, I love them together—in a mystical way that I can't even explain.")

Student Writing

That was Alison Bechdel, author of *Fun Home*. In that clip, she conveniently introduces the topics of my presentation today: Words. Pictures. And the mystical way they work together.

CONSIDERING DISABILITIES

Accessible Presentations

Do all you can to make your presentations accessible.

- Do not rely on color or visuals alone to get across information — some individuals may be unable to pick up such cues.
- If you use video, provide captions to explain any sounds that won't be audible to some audience members.

Note that this presentation opened with a play on words ("dysFUNctional *HOME*") and with a short, vivid video clip that summed up the main topic of the presentation. Also note the use of short sentences and fragments, special effects that act like drumbeats to get and hold the attention of the audience.

Using explicit structure and signpost language

Organize your presentation clearly and carefully, and give an overview of the main points at the outset. (You may want to recall these points toward the end of the talk.) Then, throughout your presentation, call attention to a new point by pausing before it and by using signpost language as an explicit transition: *The second crisis point in the breakup of the Soviet Union occurred shortly after the first* is more explicit than *Another thing went wrong.* (For a list of transitions, see 8e.) Repeated key words and ideas work as signposts, too.

At the end of Shuqiao's introduction, she set forth the structure of her presentation in a very clear, straightforward, and simple way to help her audience follow what came next:

So, let me outline the rest of my presentation. First, I'll

show how text is *insufficient*, but also why it is *necessary* in **Student Writing**

Bechdel's story.

Second, I'll show how images can't be trusted yet why they are still necessary for Bechdel's purpose.

Third and finally, I'll show how the interplay of text and image in *Fun Home* creates a more complex and comprehensive understanding of the story.

Choosing words and sentence structures

Avoid long, complicated sentences, and use straightforward sentence structure (subject-verb-object) as much as possible. Listeners prefer action verbs and concrete nouns to abstractions. You may need to

deal with abstract ideas, but try to provide concrete examples for them (23c).

Shuqiao Song's presentation script included the following example:

Student Writing
> Now, to argue my second point, I'll begin with an image. This is a René Magritte painting. The text means, "This is not a pipe." Is this some surrealist Jedi mind trick? Not really. Now listen to the title of the painting to grasp Magritte's point. The painting is called *The Treason of Images*. Here Magritte is showing us that "this is not a pipe" because it is an *image* of a pipe.

Her short, straightforward sentences and vivid word choice ("Jedi mind trick") help make this passage easy on listeners.

Turning writing into a script for presentation

Even though you will rely on some written material, you will need to adapt it for speech. Depending on the assignment, the audience, and your personal preferences, you may even speak from a full script. If so, double- or triple-space it, and use print that is large enough to read. Try to end each page with the end of a sentence so that you won't have to pause while you turn a page. In addition, you may decide to mark spots where you want to pause and to highlight words you want to emphasize.

Take a look at this paragraph from Shuqiao Song's formal written essay on *Fun Home:*

A PARAGRAPH FROM A WRITTEN ESSAY

Finally, we can see how image and text function together. On the one hand, image and text support each other in that each highlights the subtleties of the other; but on the other hand, the more interesting interaction comes when there is some degree of distance between what is written and what is depicted. In *Fun Home*, there is no one-to-one closure that mentally connects text and image. Rather, Bechdel pushes the boundaries of mental closure between image and text. If the words and pictures match exactly, making the same point, the story would read like a children's book, and that would be too simple for what Bechdel is trying to accomplish. However, text and image can't be so mismatched that meaning completely eludes the readers. Bechdel crafts her story deliberately, leaving just enough mental space for the reader to solve the rest of the puzzle and resolve the cognitive dissonance. The reader's mental closure, which brings coherence to the text and images and draws together loose ends, allows for a more complex and sophisticated understanding of the story.

Student Writing

Now look at how she revised that paragraph into a script for oral presentation:

A PARAGRAPH REVISED FOR A LISTENING AUDIENCE

Finally, image and text can work together. They support each other: each highlights the subtleties of the other. But they are even more interesting when there's a gap — some distance between the story the words tell and the story the pictures tell. In *Fun Home*, text and image are never perfectly correlated. After all, if the words and pictures matched up exactly, the story would read like a kids' book. That would be way too simple for Bechdel's purposes. But we wouldn't want a complete disconnect between words and images either, since we wouldn't be able to make sense of them.

Student Writing

Still, Bechdel certainly pushes the boundaries that would allow us to bring closure between image and text. So what's the take-home point here? That in Bechdel's *Fun Home*, image and text are not just supporting actors of each other. Instead, each offers a *version* of the story. It's for us — the readers. We take these paired versions and weave them into a really rich understanding of the story.

Note that the revised paragraph presents the same information, but this time it is written to be heard, using helpful signpost language, some repetition, simple syntax, and informal varieties of English.

Speaking from notes

If you decide to speak from notes rather than from a full script, here are some tips for doing so effectively:

- In general, use one note card for each point in your presentation.
- Number the cards in case they get scrambled.
- On each card, start with the major point you want to make in large bold text. Include subpoints in a bulleted list below the main point, again printed large enough for you to see easily.
- Include signpost language on each note and use it to guide your listeners.
- Practice your presentation using the notes at least twice.
- Use color or brackets to mark material in your notes that you can skip if you run out of time.

The following note card for Shuqiao Song's introduction reminds her to emphasize her title and her three points. Notice how she has highlighted her signpost language as well as the card's number.

NOTECARD FOR AN ORAL PRESENTATION

[Card 3]
Overview of the rest of the presentation
- First, text is insufficient but necessary
- Second, images can't be trusted but are necessary
- Finally, interplay of text and image creates complex, comprehensive understanding

Using visuals

Visuals are often an integral part of an oral presentation, carrying a lot of the message the speaker wants to convey. So think of your visuals not as add-ons but as a major means of getting your points across. Many speakers use presentation software (such as PowerPoint or Prezi) to help keep themselves on track and to guide the audience. In addition, posters, flip charts, chalkboards, or interactive whiteboards can also help you make strong visual statements.

SLIDES FROM A STUDENT POWERPOINT PRESENTATION

For her presentation, "Words, Images, and the Mystical Way They Work Together in Alison Bechdel's *Fun Home*," Shuqiao Song developed a series of very simple slides aimed at underscoring her points and keeping her audience focused on them. After introducing Bechdel and her book, Shuqiao provided an overview of the presentation as she clicked through the following slides:

So let me tell you, quickly, what I'll be doing in the rest of this presentation:

First, I'll show how text is *insufficient*, but also why it is *necessary* in Bechdel's story.

Second, I'll show how images can't be trusted yet why they are still necessary for Bechdel's purpose.

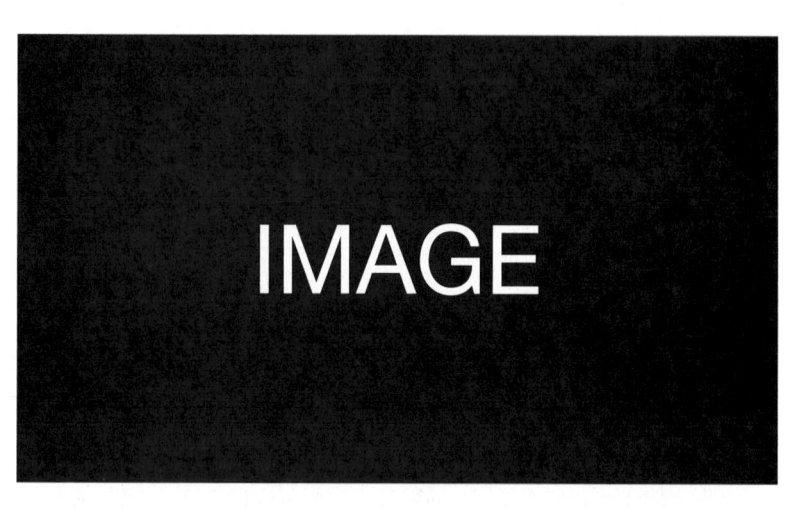

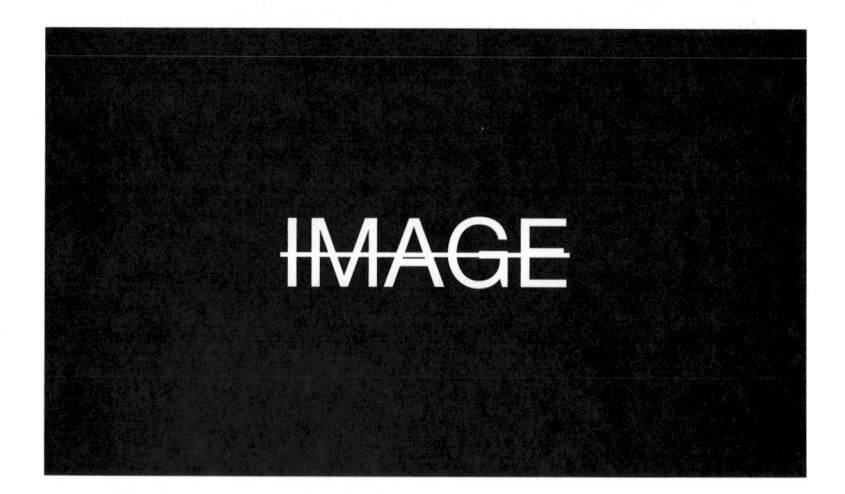

Third and finally, I'll show how the interplay of text and image in *Fun Home* works to create a more complex and comprehensive understanding of this magical story.

Each one of these slides—with simple text and punctuation—serves to emphasize Shuqiao's point and keep the audience's attention on the relationship between word and image.

When you work with visuals for your own presentation, remember that they must be large enough to be easily seen and read. Be sure the information is simple, clear, and easy to understand. And remember *not* to read from your visuals or turn your back on your audience as you refer to them. Most important, make sure your visuals engage and help your listeners rather than distract them from your message. Try out each visual on your classmates, friends, or roommates: if they do not clearly grasp the meaning and purpose of the visual, scrap it and try again.

You may also want to prepare handouts for your audience: pertinent bibliographies, for example, or text too extensive to be presented otherwise. Unless the handouts include material you want your audience to use while you speak, distribute them at the end of the presentation.

TIPS FOR USING PRESENTATION MEDIA

Before you begin designing your presentation, make sure that the equipment you need will be available. As you design presentation slides, keep some simple principles in mind (for more on design, see Chapter 9):

- Audiences can't read and listen to you at the same time, so make the slides support what you are saying as clearly and visually as possible. Just one or two words—or a visual without words—may back up what you are saying more effectively than a list of bullets.

- Never simply read the text of your slides.

- Use your media wisely, and respect your audience's time. If you feel that you need to include more than three or four bullet points (or more than fifty words of text) on a slide, you may be trying to convey information in a slideshow that would make more sense in a report. Rethink your presentation so that what you say and what you show work together to win over your audience.

- Use text on your slides to guide your audience — not as a teleprompter.

- Make sure any text or visual you show is big and clear enough to be visible, and create a clear contrast between text or illustration and background. In general, light backgrounds work better in a darkened room, and dark backgrounds in a lighted one.

- Make sure that sound or video clips are audible and that they relate directly to your topic. If you use sound as background, make sure it does not distract from what you are trying to say.

- Give credit for any visuals or audio that you have not created yourself.

Practicing your presentation

Prepare a draft of your presentation far enough in advance to allow for several run-throughs. Some speakers record their rehearsals and then revise based on the taped performance. Others practice in front of a mirror or in front of colleagues or friends, who can comment on content and style.

Make sure you will be heard clearly. If you are soft-spoken, concentrate on projecting your voice; if your voice tends to rise when you're in the spotlight, practice lowering the pitch. If you speak rapidly, practice slowing down. It's usually best to avoid sarcasm in favor of a tone that conveys interest in your topic and listeners.

Timing your run-throughs will tell you whether you need to cut (or expand) material to make the presentation an appropriate length.

Making your presentation

To calm your nerves and get off to a good start, know your material thoroughly and use the following strategies to good advantage before, during, and after your presentation:

- Visualize your presentation with the aim of feeling comfortable during it.

- Consider doing some deep-breathing exercises before the presentation, and concentrate on relaxing; avoid too much caffeine.
- Be sure you can access everything you need. Assume that microphones are always live, and don't say anything you don't want the audience to hear.
- Pause before you begin, concentrating on your opening lines.
- If possible, stand up. Most speakers make a stronger impression standing rather than sitting.
- Face your audience at all times, and make eye contact as much as possible.
- Allow time for the audience to respond and ask questions.
- Thank your audience at the end of your presentation.

 bedfordstmartins.com/everydaywriter
Student Writing > Multimedia Presentations

EXERCISE 3.1

Attend a lecture or presentation, and analyze its effectiveness. How does the speaker capture and hold your interest? What signpost language and other guides to listening can you detect? How well are visuals integrated into the presentation? How do the speaker's tone of voice, dress, and eye contact affect your understanding and appreciation (or lack of it)? What is most memorable about the presentation, and why? Bring your analysis to class and report your findings.

EXERCISE 3.2: THINKING CRITICALLY

Study the text of an oral or multimedia presentation you've prepared or given. Using the advice in this chapter, see how well your presentation appeals to your audience. Look in particular at how well you catch and hold their attention. How effective is your use of signpost language or other structures that help guide your listeners? How helpful are the visuals (PowerPoint slides, posters) in conveying your message? What would you do to improve this presentation?

 # Writing to Make Something Happen in the World

A large group of college students participating in a research study were asked, "What is good writing?" The researchers expected fairly straightforward answers like "writing that gets its message across," but the students kept coming back to one central idea: good

> **AT A GLANCE**
>
> ## Characteristics of Writing That Makes Something Happen
>
> - Public writing has a very clear *purpose* (to promote a local cause or event; to inform or explain an issue or problem; to persuade others to act; sometimes even to entertain).
> - It is intended for a specific *audience* and addresses those people directly.
> - It uses the *genre* most suited to its purpose and audience (a poster to alert people to an upcoming fund drive, a newsletter to inform members of a group, a brochure to describe the activities of a group, a letter to the editor to argue for a candidate or an issue), and it appears in a *medium* (print, online, or both) where the intended audience will see it.
> - It generally uses straightforward, everyday *language*.

writing "makes something happen in the world." They felt particular pride in the writing they did for family, friends, and community groups—and for many extracurricular activities that were meaningful to them. Furthermore, once these students graduated from college, they continued to create—and to value—these kinds of public writing.

At some point during your college years or soon after, you are highly likely to create writing that is not just something that you turn in for a grade but writing that you do because you want to make a difference. The writing that matters most to many students and citizens, then, is writing that has an effect in the world: writing that gets up off the page or screen, puts on its working boots, and marches out to get something done!

 4a **Decide what should happen.**

When you decide to write to make something happen, you'll generally have some idea of what effect you want that writing to have. Clarify what actions you want your readers to take in response to your writing, and then think about what people you most want to reach—audiences today can be as close as your immediate neighbors or as dispersed as global netizens. Who will be interested in the topic you are writing about? For example, if you are trying to encourage your elementary school to plant a garden, you might try to interest parents, teachers, and PTA members; if you are planning a voter registration drive, you might start with eighteen-year-olds on your campus.

4b Connect with your audience.

Once you have a target audience in mind, you'll need to think carefully about where and how you are likely to find them, how you can get their attention so they will read what you write, and what you can say to get them to achieve your purpose.

If you want to convince your neighbors to pool time, effort, and resources to build a local playground, then you have a head start: you know something about what they value and about what appeals would get their attention and convince them to join in this project. If you want to create a flash mob to publicize ineffective security at chemical plants near your city, on the other hand, you will need to reach as many people as possible, most of whom you will not know.

Genre and media

Even if you know the members of your audience, you still need to think about the genre and medium that will be most likely to reach them. To get neighbors involved in the playground project mentioned above, you might decide that a colorful print flyer delivered door to door and posted at neighborhood gathering places would work best. For a flash mob, however, an easily forwarded message—text, Twitter, or email—will probably work best.

Appropriate language

For all public writing, think carefully about the audience you want to reach—as well as *unintended* audiences your message might reach. Doing so can help you craft writing that will be persuasive without being offensive.

Timing

Making sure your text will appear in a timely manner is crucial to the success of your project. If you want people to plan to attend an event, present your text to them at least two weeks ahead of time. If you are issuing a newsletter or blog, make sure that you create posts or issues often enough to keep people interested (but not so often that readers can't or won't keep up). If you are reporting information based on something that has already happened, make it available as soon as possible so that your audience won't consider your report "old news."

4c   **Sample writing that makes something happen in the world**

On the following pages are some examples of the forms public writing can take.

This poster, created by student Amrit Rao, has a very clear purpose: to attract participants to a walk aimed at raising money in support of AIDS research. In this case, Rao wanted to reach college students in the DC area; students, he felt, would be particularly aware of the need for such research and likely to respond by showing up for the walk. To reach as many students as possible, he decided to distribute the poster in both print and digital forms. He called on friends in the area to help place the poster in key locations on a dozen college campuses, and he emailed PDF versions of the poster to student body presidents on each campus, asking them to help spread the word.

POSTER

Student Global AIDS Walk
——— A Call to Action ———

Fight the AIDS pandemic.
One step at a time.

April 27th 2003   10am   Freedom Plaza   Washington D.C.
The event will occur in 10 major U.S. cities. All proceeds will benefit treatment programs at HIV/AIDS clinics around the world through the Elizabath Glaser Pediatric AIDS Foundation.

REGISTER NOW at www.studentglobalaidswalk.org

FLYER

El Boletin de Trabajadores Temporales

Local 715 SEIU

Volume 1: Issue 3

Servicios educativos para sus hijos:

Necesitan mas ayuda sus niños con la tarea? o Quieren hacer algo despues de la escuela para divertirse? Informece sobre los varios programas que ofrece Stanford para niños que viven en la area cercana. Hay programas para niños de todos años desde la escuela primaria hasta la preparatoria. Ofrecen apoyo academico como ayuca con la tarea y tambien actividades Los programes son durante y despues de la escuela. Para aprender como puede inscribir sus hijos en uno de estos programas, llame a Leticia Rodriguez en la oficina de SEIU Local 715 al (650) 723-3680.

Preocupado por dinero?

Esta endeudado con tarjetas de credito? Quiere saber como obtener su reporte de credito? Nosotros podemos ayudarle a crear un presupuesto mensual, mejorar su puntuacion en su reporte de credito, reducir los intereses que paga en tarjetas de credito, y ahorrar dinero. Para citas gratuitas comuniquese con Araceli Rodriguez o Nancy Villareal a la oficina de SEIU, Local 715 al (650) 723-3680.

OPORTUNIDADES PARA TRABAJOS PERMANENTES

Según el acuerdo en el nuevo contracto de la union, Stanford va a crear 40 posiciones permanentes en los próximos 4 años. Adicionalmente, trabajadores temporales que han trabajado 20 horas por semana por más de cuatro

CUENTO PERSONAL

Student Anna Mumford created and posted copies of this flyer advocating for pay raises for campus workers. Again, her purpose is clear: she wants to raise awareness on her campus of what she views as highly inequitable salaries and working conditions for temporary workers. Her audience in this case is a local one that includes the temporary workers as well as the students, faculty, and administrators on her campus. Mumford did not have an easy way to distribute the information electronically to temporary workers, nor was she certain that all of them had access to computers, so she chose to produce a print flyer that would be easy to distribute across campus. She wrote in Spanish (on an English-speaking campus), the home language of most of the temporary workers, to reach her target audience more effectively.

NEWSLETTER

Asana   Americana

Videos are up!
Joelle on About.com

I spent Memorial Day sequestered in Go Yoga shooting instructional videos for About.com. It was a hot day and my first time on film. (Second time was also this summer in a poet-bike messenger murder mystery set in NY--I play the role of a "senior editor." More about this next month!)

Some of the videos are now live. Take a look. Here's bow pose.

Thank you, Ann Pizer, former student, and current yoga adviser and blogger at About.com, for inviting me to do these videos. Read her blog post about the videos here.

After Labor Day
Back to Normal Teaching Schedule

I was fortunate to go on several retreats this summer. Thanks for your patience as I subbed out my classes. I'm now back to my normal schedule.

Curious about where I went?
I was at the Himalayan Institute, learning the magic of Tantra (it's not what you think!)--studies I'll continue over the next year. I was also in upstate New York at an inspired gathering of women called the Goddess Retreat, run by Kula teacher Alison Sinatra. Super heart-filled--and fun! And finally I attended Omega's Being Yoga conference in Rhinebeck, NY, to interview young PhD and yoga dynamo, Kelly McGonigal, who's developing compassion-based protocols sanctioned by the Dalai Lama.

My Recent Articles & Blog Posts

RECENT ARTICLES & BLOG POSTS:

YogaCityNYC
Interview with my teacher Gary Kraftsow Last Labor Day and again this summer, I interviewed Gary about his life as a student, teacher, and trainer of thousands. He was destined to become a great teacher--the stars foretold it--and has pioneered the field of yoga therapy in the US.

Anatomy Studies for Yoga Teachers: Jason R. Brown took the hard road to learn anatomy, but his new program (ASYT) makes the way much easier for the rest of us.

JOELLE'S YOGA
teaching & writing
NEWSLETTER

TEACHING SCHEDULE
Sunday, 10am open
Monday, 8:15pm basics

at Go Yoga
N6th at Berry, Williamsburg

Privates available by
appointment or for trade

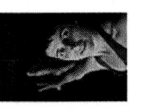

yoganation gmail com

INFO
If you have any questions,
comments, or suggestions
don't hesitate to get in touch.

Namaste!

photos of me by
timknoxphotography.com

As with the writers of the poster and flyer, yoga teacher Joelle Hann has a clear purpose in mind for her e-newsletter: to provide information to her audience—students and others interested in her yoga classes and developments in the yoga community. Emailing the newsletter to her subscribers allows Hann to reach an interested audience quickly and to provide links to more of the content she's discussing, and it also means that she can include photos, illustrations, and color to enhance her document's design impact.

EVENT INVITATION ON SOCIAL NETWORKING SITE

+ Select Guests to Invite

Pure Hell / The Bad Luck Charms / TV Tramps
• Share • Public Event

Time:	Saturday, October 16 · 6:00pm - 9:30pm
Location:	Europa
Created By:	Scenic Nyc, Bryan Swirsky
More Info:	All Ages (16+ with government issued ID, under 16 w/ parent, guardian)
	$8 adv, $10 day of. !!! Early show.

Pure Hell, one of the earliest all-black American punk-rock bands, formed in Philadelphia, Pennsylvania, in 1974, as punk rock was taking off and developing a following in nearby New York City. Discovered by Johnny Thunders during the heyday of the New York Dolls, the band moved to New York. In 1978, they toured Europe and released their only single ("These Boots are Made for Walking" b/w "No Rules"). Live performances by Pure Hell have been compared to the MC5, Sex Pistols, Dead Boys, Germs, and fellow Afropunks the Bad Brains, who identified Pure Hell as an influence. Their album (Noise Addiction), recorded in the late 1970s, was finally released this year. Pure Hell also has an unreleased album (The Black Box) produced in the mid 1990's by former members of L.A. Guns, Nine Inch Nails, and Lemmy Kilmister of Motorhead. Recent performances by Pure Hell in NYC showed that they still have what it takes!

Band promoter Bryan Swirsky used Facebook, where he has many friends who share his interest in punk rock, to reach an audience interested in seeing a reunion show by an all-black punk band that had a cult following in the 1970s. Those invited by Bryan could also invite their own interested friends, allowing news of the event to spread virally.

ONLINE REPORT

Less Trash, More Compost!
A report on a community partnership to reduce trash and promote composting and recycling at a summer camp

Funded in part by the New England Grassroots Environmental Fund

...When campers have something in their hand, they are very likely to ask where is the compost, where is the recycling... and that is exciting...

Counselor, Athol Area YMCA Day Camp

Deb Habib and Kaitlin Doherty
Seeds of Solidarity
November, 2007

Project Background and Goals

"Gross, but fun!" exclaims an eight-year old compost enthusiast, one of over 200 campers, plus counselors and staff at the Athol Area YMCA day camp in Orange, Massachusetts who worked together to successfully divert over one ton of their breakfast and lunch waste from the landfill to compost. And they won't mind telling you that they had fun doing it.

Seeds of Solidarity, a non-profit organization based in Orange, partnered with the summer food service director, the Athol Area YMCA, and a local hauler to implement a composting and recycling initiative, diverting the waste from approximately 3,600 meals at two sites over an eight-week period in the summer of 2007. This pilot project was inspired by success using biodegradable and compostable utensils and plates at the annual North Quabbin Garlic and Arts Festival, also sponsored by Seeds of Solidarity, which results in only two bags of trash for 10,000 people.

Athol and Orange are located in the North Quabbin region, where 20% of the children live below the federal poverty line. Food service director Sherry Fiske runs a state and federally funded summer food service program at 11 sites in Orange and Athol, providing free breakfast and lunch to children and families during the summer months. The YMCA camps based both at the Y site in Athol and Lake Selah in North Orange are among these summer food service sites. While school year lunch programs in the area utilize washable dishes and utensils, the summer food service program is held at temporary sites, resulting in heaping dumpsters of paper, plastic and polystyrene waste.

This report, created by Deb Habib and Kaitlin Doherty of the non-profit group Seeds of Solidarity, provides information about a successful experimental recycling and composting program at a Massachusetts camp. (Only the first page of the twenty-six-page PDF is shown.) Other sections include "Project Description," "Voices of Campers," "Successes and Challenges," "Summary of Key Considerations," and an appendix with additional documents (interviews with campers, letters to campers' parents before the program began, and graphs quantifying the outcomes). The report appears on the organization's Web site, which notes that Seeds of Solidarity "provid[es] people of all ages with the inspiration and practical tools to use renewable energy and grow food in their communities." While the report offers information about an experiment that has already taken place, the document also serves to encourage and inform others who might want to create a similar program.

EXERCISE 4.1: THINKING CRITICALLY

You have probably done quite a bit of writing to make something happen in the world, though you might not have thought of it as official "writing." Yet as this chapter shows, such writing is important to those who do it — and to those affected by it. Think about the groups you belong to — informal or formal, home- or community- or school-based — and choose a piece of writing you have done for the group, whether on your own or with others. Then take a careful look at it: looking at it with a critical eye, is its purpose clear? What audience does it address, and how well does it connect to that audience? Are the genre (newsletter, poster, flyer, brochure, report, etc.) and the medium (print, electronic) appropriate to achieving the purpose and reaching the audience? How might you revise this text to make it even more effective?

The Writing Process

There may be people who like various aspects
of the writing process. For some, it may be the
excitement of facing a blank page. (Hate them!)
For others, it could be a sense of getting a sentence
just right. (Jerks!) There may be those who like
the revision process, who can go over what they've
produced with a cold eye and a keen ear and feel
a satisfaction in making it better. (Liars!)

— RACHEL TOOR

The Writing Process

5 **Rhetorical Situations**   *48*
a Write to connect   *48*
b Make good choices for your rhetorical situation   *48*
c Plan your text's topic and message   *49*
d Consider your purpose and stance as a communicator   *50*
e Analyze your audience   *53*
f Consider other elements of the writing context   *55*
g A sample writing situation   *57*

6 **Exploring Ideas**   *59*
a Try brainstorming   *59*
b Try freewriting or looping   *60*
c Try drawing or creating word pictures   *61*
d Try clustering   *62*
e Ask questions   *63*
f Browse sources   *64*
g Collaborate   *64*

7 **Planning and Drafting**   *66*
a Narrow your topic   *66*
b Craft a working thesis   *67*
c Gather information to support your thesis   *70*
d Organize information   *70*
e Make a plan   *73*
f Create a draft   *76*

8 **Developing Paragraphs**   *78*
a Focus on a main idea   *78*
b Provide details   *80*
c Use effective methods of development   *82*
d Consider paragraph length   *88*
e Make paragraphs flow   *89*
f Work on opening and closing paragraphs   *92*

The Writing Process   45–126

For visual analysis Look carefully at the illustration on the front of this tab. What do you think this image suggests about the writing process?

9 Making Design Decisions *94*

  a Plan a visual structure *94*
  b Choose appropriate formats *96*
  c Use headings appropriately *99*
  d Use visuals effectively *100*

10 Reviewing and Revising *104*

  a Reread *105*
  b Get the most from peer review *106*
  c Consult instructor comments *111*
  d Revise *113*

11 Editing and Reflecting *117*

  a Edit *117*
  b Reflect *122*
     STUDENT REFLECTIVE STATEMENT *124*

5 Rhetorical Situations

What do a documented essay on global warming research, a Facebook message objecting to the latest change to the site's privacy policy, a tweet to other students in your psychology class, a comment on a blog post, a letter to the editor of your local newspaper, and a Web site devoted to sustainability all have in common? To communicate effectively, the writers of these texts must analyze their particular situation and then respond to it in appropriate ways.

Write to connect.

If it is true that "no man [or woman!] is an island," then it is equally true that no piece of writing is an island, isolated and alone. Instead, writing is connected to a web of other writings as a writer extends, responds to, or challenges what others say. This has always been the case, but today it's especially important to remember that all writing exists within a rich and broad context and that all writers listen and respond to what others have said, even as they shape messages about particular topics and for particular purposes that help them connect to their audiences.

5b Make good choices for your rhetorical situation.

A *rhetorical situation* is the full set of circumstances surrounding any communication. When you communicate, whether you're posting on a social networking site, creating a video, or writing an essay for your psychology class, you need to consider and make careful choices about all the elements of your situation.

The rhetorical situation is often depicted as a triangle to present the idea that three important elements are closely connected—your *text*, including your topic and the message you want to convey (5c); your role as the *communicator*, including your purpose and your stance, or attitude toward the text (5d); and your *audience* (5e). If all the pieces making up the larger triangle don't work together, the

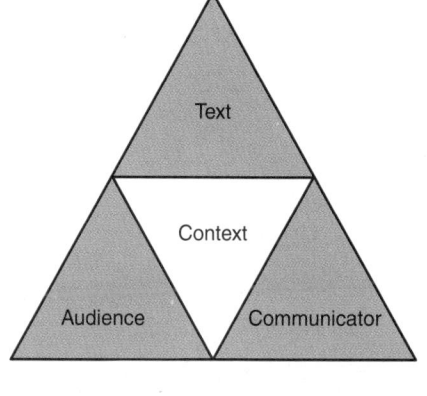

communication will not be effective. But important as these elements are, they are connected to a *context* that shapes all the angles of the triangle. Considering context fully requires you to consider many other questions about the rhetorical situation, such as what kind of text you should create and what conventions you should follow to meet audience expectations for creating and delivering the text (5f).

Informal and formal rhetorical situations

Most people are accustomed to writing in some rhetorical situations without analyzing them closely. When you post something on a friend's social networking page, for example, you probably spend little time pondering what your friend values or finds funny, how to phrase your words, which links or photos would best emphasize your point, or why you're taking the time to post. However, academic and other formal rhetorical situations may seem less familiar than the social writing you share with friends. Until you understand clearly what such situations demand of you, allow extra time to analyze the overall context, the topic and message, the purpose and stance, the audience, and other elements carefully.

5c Plan your text's topic and message.

An instructor or employer may tell you what topic to write about, but sometimes the choice will be yours. When the topic is left open, you may be tempted to put off getting started because you can't decide what to do. Experienced writers say that the best way to choose a topic is literally to let it choose you. Look to the topics that compel, puzzle, confuse, or pose a problem for you: these are likely to engage your interest and hence produce your best writing.

RHETORICAL SITUATIONS: Choose Your Topic

Browse around for a topic you care about.

Make sure your topic is manageable and suits your purpose....

Ask...

What *interesting* topic will meet the requirements for your assignment and context?

What do you know about the topic? What else do you need to find out?

What *message* do you want to convey?

Deciding on a broad topic is an essential step before beginning to write, but you need to go further than that to decide what you want to say about your topic and how you will shape what you want to say into a clear, powerful message.

EXERCISE 5.1

The following assignment was given to an introductory business class: "Discuss in an essay the contributions of the Apple and Microsoft companies to the personal computing industry." What would you need to know about the assignment in order to respond successfully? Using the questions on pp. 51–52, analyze this assignment.

5d Consider your purpose and stance as a communicator.

Whether you choose to communicate for purposes of your own or have that purpose set for you by an instructor or employer, you should consider the purpose for any communication carefully. For the writing you do that is not connected to a class or work assignment, your purpose may be very clear to you: you may want to convince neighbors to support a community garden, get others in your office to help keep the kitchen clean, or tell blog readers what you like or hate about your new phone. Even so, analyzing exactly what you want to accomplish and why can make you a more effective communicator.

RHETORICAL SITUATIONS: Consider Your Purpose and Stance

Always keep your purpose in mind.

Ask...

Why are you writing?

What should the writing accomplish?

Where do you stand on your topic?

Think about how you want your audience to react....

Purposes for academic assignments

An academic assignment may clearly explain why, for whom, and about what you are supposed to write. But sometimes college assignments seem to come out of the blue, with no specific purpose, audience, or topic. Because comprehending the assignment fully and accurately is crucial to your success in responding to it, make every effort to understand what your instructor expects.

- What is the primary purpose of the piece of writing—to explain? to persuade? to entertain? some other purpose?

- What purpose did the person who gave you the assignment want to achieve—to make sure you have understood something? to evaluate your thinking and writing abilities? to test your ability to think outside the box?

- What are your own purposes in this piece of writing—to respond to a question? to learn about a topic? to communicate your ideas? to express feelings? How can you achieve these goals?

- What, exactly, does the assignment ask you to do? Look for such words as *analyze, classify, compare, define, describe, explain, prove,* and *survey.* Remember that these words may differ in meaning from discipline to discipline.

Stances for academic assignments

Thinking about your own position as a communicator and your atti-tude toward your text—your rhetorical stance—is just as important as making sure you communicate effectively.

• Where are you coming from on this topic? What is your overall at-titude toward your topic? How strong are your opinions?

• What social, political, religious, personal, or other influences ac-count for your attitude? Will you need to explain any of these influences?

• What is most interesting to you about the topic? Why do you care?

• What conclusions do you think you'll reach as you complete your text?

• How will you establish your credibility? How will you show you are knowledgeable and trustworthy?

• How will you convey your stance? Should you use words alone, combine words and images, include sound, or something else?

EXERCISE 5.2

Consider a writing project that you are currently working on for a course. What are the purposes of the project in terms of the instructor, the assignment, and you, the writer?

TALKING THE TALK

Assignments

"How do instructors come up with these assignments?" Assignments, like other kinds of writing, reflect particular rhetorical contexts that vary from instructor to instructor. Assignments also change over time. The as-signment for an 1892 college writing contest was to write an essay "on coal." In the twentieth century, many college writing assignments asked students to write about their own experiences; in research conducted for this textbook in the 1980s, the most common writing assignment was a personal narrative. As expectations for college students — and the needs of society — change over time, assignments also change. Competing ef-fectively in today's workforce calls for high-level thinking, for being able to argue convincingly, and for knowing how to do the research neces-sary to support a claim — so it's no surprise that college writing courses today give students assignments that allow them to develop such skills. A recent study of first-year college writing in the United States found that by far the most common assignment today asks students to compose a researched argument. (See Chapters 12–14.)

RHETORICAL SITUATIONS: Imagine Your Audience

> **Think about a target audience for this text.**
>
> **Ask...**
>
> *Who are they? How are they like you? How are they different?*
>
> *How will you reach this audience?*
>
> *What do they already know and care about?*
>
> **Remember to focus on getting your message across.**

5e Analyze your audience.

Every communicator can benefit from thinking carefully about who the audience is, what the audience already knows or thinks, and what the audience needs and expects to find out. One of the characteristics of an effective communicator is the ability to write for a variety of audiences, using language, style, and evidence appropriate to particular readers, listeners, or viewers. Even if your text can theoretically reach people all over the world, focus your analysis on those you most want or need to reach and those who are most likely to take an interest.

Informal and formal audiences

For some informal writing, you know exactly who your audience is, and communicating appropriately may be a simple matter. It's still worth remembering that when you post in a public space, you may not be aware of how large and varied your online audience can be. Can your friend's parents, or her prospective employer, see your posts on her Facebook page? (The answer depends partly on her privacy settings.) Who's reading the blogs you comment on?

Even if you write with intuitive ease in tweets and texts to friends, you may struggle when asked to write for an instructor or for a "general audience." You may wonder, for example, what a general audience might know about your topic, what they value, or what evidence they

> **FOR MULTILINGUAL WRITERS**
> ### Bringing In Other Languages
>
> Even when you write in English, you may want or need to include words, phrases, or whole passages in another language. If so, consider whether your readers will understand that language and whether you need to provide a translation. See 22d for more on bringing in other languages.

will find persuasive. When you are new to academic writing, making assumptions about such questions can be tricky. If you can identify samples of writing that appeal to a similar audience, look for clues about what that audience expects; if still in doubt, check with your instructor or drop by your campus writing center.

Appropriate language for an audience

- Is the language of your text as clear as it needs to be for your audience? If your readers can't understand what you mean, they're not likely to accept your points.

- For academic writing, should you use any specialized varieties of English along with standard academic English? any occupational, professional, regional, or ethnic varieties? any words from a language other than English? any dialogue? (See Chapter 22.) How will these choices help you connect to your audience?

As you think about your audience, consider how you want them to respond to both the words and the images you use. And remember that images can evoke very strong responses in your audience and can affect the tone of your writing (5f), so choose them with special care.

EXERCISE 5.3

Describe one of your courses to three audiences: your best friend, your parents, and a group of high school students attending an open house at your college. Then describe the differences in content, organization, and wording that the differences in audience led you to make.

EXERCISE 5.4: THINKING VISUALLY

Look at the three "Rhetorical Situations" illustrations on pp. 50–53 and analyze the way the visuals are related. Then consider your own writing process for an assignment you are currently working on. What specific decisions have you made about your topic, purpose and stance, and intended audience for the project? Sketch an image that suggests how your topic, stance, and audience will fit together. Will your decisions about this rhetorical situation help you create a unified piece of writing that accomplishes your goals?

CONSIDERING DISABILITIES

Your Whole Audience

Remember that considering your whole audience means thinking about members with varying abilities and special needs. Approximately one in five Americans was living with a disability in the year 2000. All writers need to think carefully about how their words reach out and connect with such very diverse audiences.

5f Consider other elements of the writing context.

After you have chosen a topic, shaped a message, and analyzed your purpose, stance, and audience in relation to your message, you still have other important decisions to make about the text you are developing.

Time and length

- How much time do you have to complete the text? Do you need to schedule research? Do you need to find or create images or media content? Be sure to allow time for revision and editing.

- How long is the finished draft of the writing supposed to be? If you are writing a presentation, what time limits do you face for delivering it? If you are creating a work for the public, how much time can you expect the audience to devote to your work?

Genre, medium, and format

You may be assigned — or able to choose — to work in genres other than straightforward essays or in a medium other than print.

- What genre does your text call for — report? review? argument essay? research project? letter? blog posting? instructions for completing a task? promotional brochure? If you aren't familiar with the conventions of the genre, study examples created by others.

- What format or method of organization is expected for this genre? (See Chapter 7.) Should you conform to traditional formats, or will you gain from going in an unexpected direction?

- In what medium will the text appear — on the Internet? on a password-protected Web site? in a print essay submitted to your instructor? in a spoken presentation? Will your text use images, video, or audio? How will the media you use affect other choices you make?

- What design considerations should you keep in mind? (See Chapter 9.)

Attitude and Point of View in Visuals

Images you choose to include in your work can help establish your credibility, but they always have a point of view and tone of their own. The postcard below, for instance, shows two physical perspectives — a photograph of a highway bridge and a road map showing its location — as well as a time perspective, from 1927, when the bridge was new. Images also reveal attitudes: this one, with the caption "America's Greatest Highway Bridge," sees the construction of the bridge as a triumph of technology, but the image might also convey nostalgia if readers know that the bridge became structurally unsound and had to be demolished in the 1970s. So when you choose an image, think hard about how well it fits in with your topic and purpose. What is the image's perspective and attitude — and do they serve the purpose of your writing?

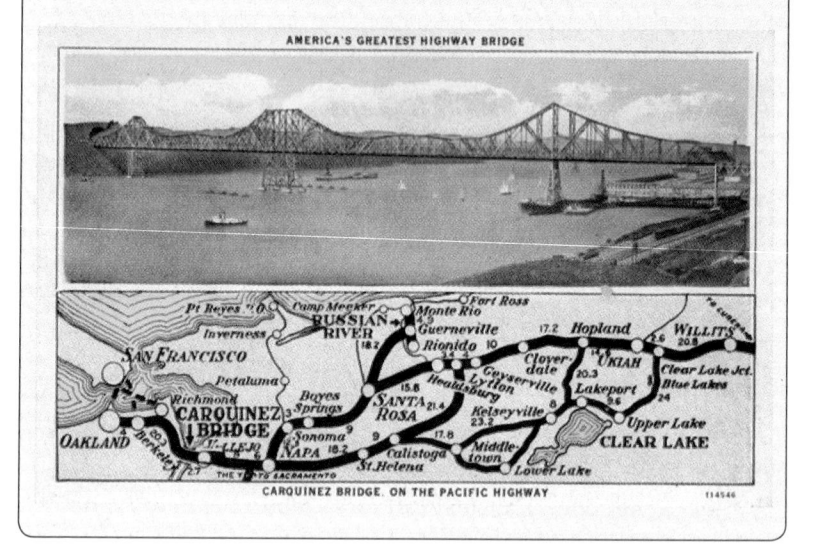

AMERICA'S GREATEST HIGHWAY BRIDGE

CARQUINEZ BRIDGE. ON THE PACIFIC HIGHWAY

Tone and style

- What tone do you want to achieve — humorous? serious? impassioned? ironic? sincere? deeply knowledgeable?

- What words, sentence structures, and images or media will help you achieve this tone?

- Is the tone of the writing appropriate to your audience, purpose, and message? Do the words, images, or sounds you choose have the connotations you intend?

Remember that visual and audio elements can influence the tone of your writing as much as the words you choose. Such elements create associations in viewers' minds: one audience may react more positively than another to an element such as a rap or heavy metal soundtrack, for example—and a presentation with a heavy metal accompaniment will make a far different impression than the same presentation with an easy-listening soundtrack. Writers can influence the way their work is perceived by carefully analyzing their audience and choosing audio and visual elements that set a mood appropriate to the point they want to make.

EXERCISE 5.5

Consider some of the genres that you have encountered as a student, jotting down answers to the following questions and bringing them to class for discussion.

1. What are some genres that you read but don't usually write?
2. What are some genres that you write for teachers?
3. What are some genres that you write to or with other students?
4. What are some genres that you will likely encounter in your major or in your career?
5. How are some of the genres you listed different from those you encountered in high school?

EXERCISE 5.6

Consider a writing assignment you are currently working on. What is its genre? What medium or media does it use? How would you describe the style and tone? Finally, what visuals are you going to include and how well do they work to create the appropriate style and tone?

5g A sample writing situation

Let's take an example of how one writer analyzes a rhetorical situation. Emily Lesk, a student in a first-year English course, gets an assignment that asks her to "explore the ways in which one or more media have affected an aspect of American identity." (More examples of Emily's work appear in the following chapters.) Because Emily is interested in advertising, she plans first to investigate how advertising might help shape American identity. Deciding that such a broad topic is not manageable in the time she has available, however, she shifts her focus to advertising for one company that seems particularly "American," Coca-Cola.

Since Emily's primary audience includes her instructor and her classmates, she needs to find ways to connect with them on an emotional as well as a logical level. She will do so, she decides, first by telling a story about being drawn into buying Coca-Cola products (even though she didn't really like the soft drink) because of the power of the advertising. She thinks that others in her audience may have had similar experiences. Here is a portion of her story and the visual she chose to illustrate it:

Student Writing

Even before setting foot in the Promised Land three years ago, I knew exactly where I could find the Coke T-shirt. The shop in the central block of Jerusalem's Ben Yehuda Street did offer other shirt designs, but the one with the bright white "Drink Coca-Cola Classic" written in Hebrew cursive across the chest was what drew in most of the dollar-carrying tourists. While waiting almost twenty minutes for my shirt (depicted in Fig. 1), I watched nearly everyone ahead of me say "the Coke shirt, *todah rabah* [thank you very much]."

At the time, I never thought it strange that I wanted one, too. Yet, I *had* absorbed sixteen years of Coca-Cola propaganda.

Fig. 1. Hebrew Coca-Cola T-shirt. Personal photograph.

Thinking about how she relates to her audience brings Emily to reflect more deeply on herself as the writer: Why has she chosen this topic? What does it say about her beliefs and values? What is her attitude toward her topic and toward her audience? What does she need to do to establish her credentials to write on this topic and to this audience?

Finally, Emily knows she will need to pay careful attention to the context in which she is writing: the assignment is due in two weeks, so she needs to work fast; the assignment calls for an essay written in academic English, though she plans to include some dialogue and a number of visuals to keep it lively; and since she knows she tends to sound like a know-it-all, she determines to work carefully on her tone and style.

 bedfordstmartins.com/everydaywriter
Student Writing

EXERCISE 5.7: THINKING CRITICALLY

Reading with an Eye for Purpose, Audience, and Context

Advertisements provide good examples of writing that is tailored carefully for specific audiences. Find two ads for the same product in contexts that suggest that the ads aim to appeal to different audiences — for example, men and women. What differences do you see in the messages and photography? What conclusions can you draw about ways of appealing to specific audiences?

Thinking about Your Own Attention to Purpose, Audience, and Context

Analyze a text you have written or are working on right now for an academic course.

- Can you state its purpose(s) clearly and succinctly? If not, what can you do to clarify its purpose(s)?
- What other purposes for this piece of writing can you imagine? How would fulfilling some other purpose change the writing?
- Can you tell from reading the piece who the intended audience is? If so, what in your text clearly relates to that audience? If not, what can you add that will strengthen your appeal to this audience?
- What other audiences can you imagine? How would the writing change if you were to address a different audience? How would it change if you were writing to a largely unknown audience, such as people on the Web?
- What changes would you have to make to create the work in a different genre or medium?
- Does your writing follow the conventions of standard academic English — and if not, should you revise it so that it will? Note your conclusions about purpose and audience in your own writing.

Exploring Ideas 6

The point is so simple that we often forget it: we write best about topics we know well. So among the most important parts of the entire writing process are choosing a topic that will engage your interest, exploring that topic by surveying what you know about it, and determining what you need to find out. You can explore a topic in many ways; the goal is to find strategies that work well for you.

6a Try brainstorming.

One of the best ways to begin exploring a topic is also the most familiar: talk it over with others. Consider beginning with a brainstorming session. Brainstorming means tossing out ideas — often with other people, either in person or online. You can also brainstorm by yourself.

1. Within a time limit of five or ten minutes, list every word or phrase that comes to mind about the topic. Jot down key words and phrases, not sentences. No one has to understand the list but you. Don't worry about whether or not something will be useful—just list as much as you can in this brief span of time.
2. If little occurs to you, try coming up with thoughts about the opposite side of your topic. If you are trying, for instance, to think of reasons to raise tuition and are coming up blank, try concentrating on reasons to lower tuition. Once you start generating ideas in one direction, you'll find that you can usually move back to the other side fairly easily.
3. When the time is up, stop and read over the lists you have made. If anything else comes to mind, add it to your list. Then reread the list, looking for patterns of interesting ideas or one central idea.

6b   Try freewriting or looping.

Freewriting is a method of exploring a topic by writing about it for a period of time *without stopping*.

1. Write for ten minutes or so. Think about your topic, and let your mind wander; write down whatever occurs to you. Don't worry about grammar or spelling. If you get stuck, write anything—just don't stop.
2. When the time is up, look at what you have written. You may discover some important insights and ideas.

If you like, you can continue the process by looping: find the central or most intriguing thought from your freewriting, and summarize it in a single sentence. Freewrite for five more minutes on the summary sentence, and then find and summarize the central thought from the

---

CONSIDERING DISABILITIES

Freespeaking

If you are better at talking out than writing out your ideas, try freespeaking, which is basically the talking version of freewriting. Speak into a tape recorder or into a computer with voice-recognition software, and keep talking about your topic for at least seven to ten minutes. Say whatever comes to your mind — don't stop talking. You can then listen to or read the results of your freespeaking and look for an idea to pursue at greater length.

second "loop." Keep this process going until you discover a clear angle or something about the topic that you can pursue.

6c Try drawing or creating word pictures.

If you're someone who prefers visual thinking, you might either create a drawing about the topic or use figurative language—such as similes and metaphors—to describe what the topic resembles. Working with pictures or verbal imagery can sometimes also help illuminate the topic or uncover some of your unconscious ideas or preconceptions about it.

1. If you like to draw, try sketching your topic. What images do you come up with? What details of the drawing attract you most? What would you most like to expand on? A student planning to write an essay on her college experience began by thinking with pencils and pen in hand. Soon she found that she had drawn a vending machine several times, with different products and different ways of inserting money to extract them (one of her drawings appears  on the right). Her sketches led her to think about what it might mean to see an education as a product. Even abstract doodling can lead you to important insights about the topic and to focus your topic productively.

2. Look for figurative language—metaphors and similes—that your topic resembles. Try jotting down three or four possibilities, beginning with "My subject is _____" or "My subject is like _____." A student working on the subject of genetically modified crops came up with this: "Genetically modified foods are like empty calories: they do more harm than good." This exercise made one thing clear to this student writer: she already had a very strong bias that she would need to watch out for while developing her topic.

Play around a bit with your topic. Ask, for instance, "If my topic were a food (or a song or a movie or a video game), what would it be, and why?" Or write a Facebook status update about your topic, or send

> **FOR MULTILINGUAL WRITERS**
>
> ## Using Your Native Language to Explore Ideas
>
> For generating and exploring ideas — the work of much brainstorming, freewriting, looping, and clustering — you may be most successful at coming up with good ideas quickly and spontaneously if you work in your native language. Later in the process of writing, you can choose the best of these ideas and begin working with them in English.

a tweet about why this topic appeals to you. Such exercises can get you out of the rut of everyday thinking and help you see your topic in a new light.

6d Try clustering.

Clustering is a way of generating ideas using a visual scheme or chart. It is especially helpful for understanding the relationships among the parts of a broad topic and for developing subtopics. You may have a software program for clustering. If not, follow these steps:

1. Write down your topic in the middle of a blank piece of paper or screen and circle it.
2. In a ring around the topic circle, write what you see as the main parts of the topic. Circle each part, and then draw a line from it to the topic.
3. Think of more ideas, examples, facts, or other details relating to each main part. Write each of these near the appropriate part, circle each one, and draw a line from it to the part.
4. Repeat this process with each new circle until you can't think of any more details. Some trails may lead to dead ends, but you will still have many useful connections among ideas.

Here is an example of the clustering Emily Lesk did for her essay about Coca-Cola and American identity:

EMILY LESK'S CLUSTERING

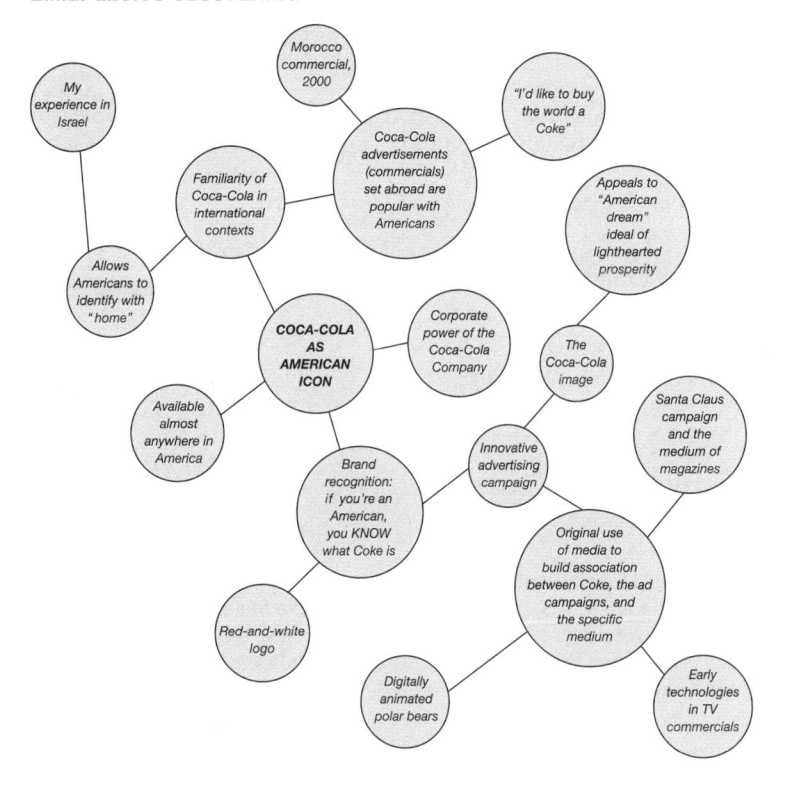

6e Ask questions.

Another basic strategy for exploring a topic and generating ideas is simply to ask and answer questions. Here are two widely used sets of questions to get you started.

Questions to describe a topic

Originally developed by Aristotle, the following questions can help you explore a topic by carefully and systematically describing it:

1. **What is it?** What are its characteristics, dimensions, features, and parts? What does it look like? What do other senses—taste, smell, touch, sound—tell you about it?
2. **What caused it?** What changes occurred to create your topic? How is it changing? How will it change?

3. *What is it like or unlike?* What features make your topic different from others? What comparisons can you make about your topic?
4. *What larger system is your topic a part of?* How does your topic fit into this system?
5. *What do people say about it?* What reactions does your topic arouse? What about the topic causes those reactions?

Questions to explain a topic

The well-known questions *who, what, when, where, why,* and *how,* widely used by news reporters, are especially helpful for explaining a topic.

1. *Who* is doing it?
2. *What* is at issue?
3. *When* does it take place?
4. *Where* is it happening?
5. *Why* does it occur?
6. *How* is it done?

EXERCISE 6.1

Choose a topic that interests you, and explore it by using two of the strategies described in Chapter 6. When you have generated some material, you might try comparing your results with those of other members of the class to see how effective or helpful each strategy was. If you have trouble choosing a topic, use one of the preliminary working theses in Exercise 7.1.

6f Browse sources.

At the library and on the Internet, browse for a topic you want to learn more about. If you have a short list of ideas, do a quick check of reference works to get overviews of topics. You can begin with a general encyclopedia or a specialized reference work that focuses on a specific area, such as psychology (16c). You can also use Wikipedia as a starting point: look at entries that relate to your topic, especially noting the sources they cite. While you should never rely on Wikipedia alone, it is a highly accessible way to begin research.

6g Collaborate.

The texts you write are shaped in part by conversations with others. You might also consider using online tools that facilitate collaborative writing, such as Google Docs or wikis, to gather ideas and generate drafts. Writers often work together to come up with ideas, to respond to

one another's drafts, or even to coauthor something. Here are some strategies for working with
others:

1. Establish a regular meeting time and exchange contact information.
2. Establish ground rules for the group. Be
   sure every member has an equal opportunity—and responsibility—to contribute.
3. With final deadlines in mind, set an agenda
   for each group meeting.
4. Listen carefully to what each person says. If disagreements arise,
   try paraphrasing to see if everyone is hearing the same thing.
5. Use group meetings to work together on particularly difficult
   problems. If an assignment is complex, have each member explain
   one section to all the others. If the group has trouble understanding part of the task, check with whoever made the assignment.
6. Expect disagreement, and remember that the goal is not for
   everyone just to "go along." The challenge is to get a really spir-
   ited debate going and to argue through all possibilities.
7. If you are preparing a group-written document, divide up the
   drafting duties. Set reasonable deadlines for each stage of work.
   Schedule at least two meetings to iron out the final draft by reading it aloud and working for consistency of tone. Have everyone
   proofread the final draft, with one person making the corrections.
8. If the group will be making a presentation, be sure you know
   exactly how much time you will have. Decide how each member
   will contribute to the presentation. Leave time for at least two
   practice sessions.
9. Make a point of assessing the group's effectiveness. What has
   the group accomplished? What has it done best? What has it
   been least successful at? What has each member contributed?
   How could the group function more effectively?

EXERCISE 6.2: THINKING CRITICALLY

Begin by making a list of all the ways in which you collaborate with others. Then
reflect on the kinds of collaboration you find most effective. Finally, take an example
of a recent collaboration you have been part of, and examine how well it worked
by answering the following questions: What did I contribute to the collaboration?
What worked well and did not work well? What could I have done to improve the
collaboration?

7 Planning and Drafting

Some writers just plunge right into their work and develop it as they go along. Others find that they work more effectively by making detailed blueprints before they begin drafting. Your planning and drafting may fall anywhere along this spectrum. As you plan and draft, you narrow your topic, decide on your thesis, organize materials to support that central idea, and sketch out a plan for your writing. As one student said, this is the time in the writing process "when the rubber meets the road."

7a Narrow your topic.

After exploring ideas, you may have found a topic that interests you and that you think would also be interesting to your readers. The topic, however, may be too large to be manageable. If that is the case, narrow your topic using any exploring technique that works for you (see Chapter 6).

Emily Lesk planned to discuss how advertising affects American identity, but she knew that such a topic was far too broad. After thinking about products that are pitched as particularly "American" in their advertising, she posted a Facebook status update asking friends to

WORKING THESIS: Plan Your Approach

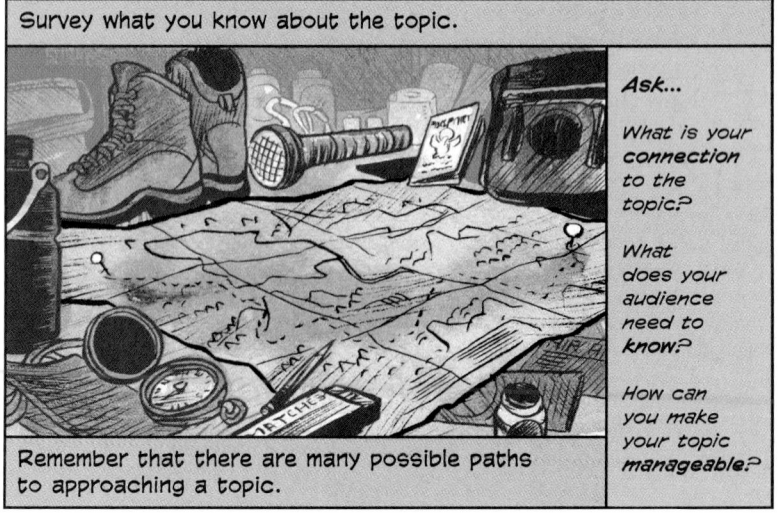

Survey what you know about the topic.

Remember that there are many possible paths to approaching a topic.

Ask...

What is your connection to the topic?

What does your audience need to know?

How can you make your topic manageable?

"name products that seem super-American." She quickly got seventeen responses ranging from Hummers and Winchester rifles to "soft toilet paper," Spam, Wheaties, and apple pie. One friend identified Coca-Cola and Pepsi-Cola, two products that Emily associated with many memorable and well-documented advertising campaigns.

7b Craft a working thesis.

Academic and professional writing in the United States often contains an explicit thesis statement. The thesis functions as a promise to readers, letting them know what the writer will discuss. Your readers may (or may not) expect you to craft the thesis as a single sentence near the beginning of the text. If you want to suggest a thesis implicitly rather than stating one explicitly, if you plan to convey your main argument somewhere other than in your introduction, or if you prefer to make your thesis longer than a single sentence, consider whether the rhetorical situation allows such flexibility. For an academic project, also consult with your instructor about how to meet expectations.

Whether you plan to use an implicit or explicit thesis statement in your text, you should establish a tentative working thesis early in your writing process. The word *working* is important here because your thesis may well change as you write—your final thesis may be very different from the working thesis you begin with. Even so, a working thesis focuses your thinking and research, and helps keep you on track.

WORKING THESIS: Refine Your Topic

Match your approach to the requirements of the topic.

Ask...

How will your audience connect to your topic?

How can you help them see your perspective?

What is the most persuasive message for this context?

Remember that you are creating a **working** thesis that you can change as you go.

A working thesis should have two parts: a topic, which indicates the subject matter the writing is about, and a comment, which makes an important point about the topic.

▶ **In the graphic novel *Fun Home*, illustrations and words combine to make meanings that are more subtle than either words alone or images alone could convey.**

A successful working thesis has three characteristics:

1. It is potentially *interesting* to the intended audience.
2. It is as *specific* as possible.
3. It limits the topic enough to make it *manageable*.

You can evaluate a working thesis by checking it against each of these characteristics, as in the following examples:

▶ **Graphic novels combine words and images.**

INTERESTING? The topic of graphic novels could be interesting, but this draft of a working thesis has no real comment attached to it—instead, it states a bare fact, and the only place to go from here is to more bare facts.

▶ **In graphic novels, words and images convey interesting meanings.**

SPECIFIC? This thesis is not specific. What are "interesting meanings," exactly? How are they conveyed?

WORKING THESIS: Craft Your Message

Draft a working thesis.

Consider this a starting point for organizing and planning your draft....

Ask...

Should your thesis be *implicit* or *explicit* for this context and audience?

Are you conveying your own message—not just facts?

Does your working thesis help you understand where to go next?

▶ **Graphic novels have evolved in recent decades to become an important literary genre.**

MANAGEABLE? This thesis would not be manageable for a short-term project because it would require research on several decades of history and on hundreds of texts from all over the world.

FOR MULTILINGUAL WRITERS

Stating a Thesis Explicitly

In some cultures, stating the main point explicitly may be considered rude or inelegant. In U.S. academic and business practices, however, readers often expect the writer to make key points and positions explicit. Unless your main point is highly controversial or hard for the reader to accept (such as a rejection letter), state your main point early — before presenting the supporting details.

EXERCISE 7.1

Choose one of the following preliminary working theses, and after specifying an audience, evaluate the thesis in terms of its interest, specificity, and manageability. Revise the working thesis as necessary to meet these criteria.

1. The benefits of standardized testing are questionable.

2. Vaccinations are dangerous.

3. Too many American parents try to micromanage their children's college education.

4. Many people are afraid to fly in a plane, although riding in a car is statistically more dangerous.

5. An educated public is the key to a successful democracy.

EXERCISE 7.2

Using the topic you chose in Exercise 6.1, write a preliminary working thesis. Evaluate the thesis in terms of its interest, specificity, and manageability. Revise it as necessary to create a satisfactory working thesis.

EXERCISE 7.3: THINKING VISUALLY

Read and analyze the three "Working Thesis" panels on pp. 66–68. How do the steps shown work as a metaphor for the process of planning and drafting a working thesis as described in 7a–b? How well does this metaphor describe your own process of creating a working thesis? What changes would you make to the metaphor so that it would fit your personal process? Create a brief slide show, video, or written description that clarifies how you moved from your first idea for a piece of writing your're working on to a draft of a working thesis for your project.

7c Gather information to support your thesis.

Once you have a working thesis, consider whether you need to do research for your writing project. Your assignment may require research, or you may decide on your own to find out more about your topic or to locate examples and illustrations that will enhance your writing. You may even need to do research at more than one stage of the writing process as you define, narrow, and perhaps change your topic. Library research, online research, and field research can all help you find the information and visuals you need. (For more on conducting research and working with sources, see Chapters 16 and 17. For more on organizing your support into paragraphs, see Chapter 8.)

7d Organize information.

Remember to consider your audience, purpose, and topic as you think about how you will organize information to make it accessible and persuasive to your audience. At the simplest level, writers most often group information according to four principles—space, time, logic, and association.

Organizing according to space

The organizational principle of space refers to *where* bits of information occur within a setting. If the information you have gathered is descriptive, you may choose to organize it spatially. Using spatial organization allows the reader to "see" your information, to fix it in space.

INFORMATION ORGANIZED SPATIALLY

This photo shows the spatial arrangement described, with the darkened side areas for spectators and the brightly lighted front of the room. The photograph and writing together help readers see the scene vividly.

The scene was being filmed in a windowless building with a corrugated tin roof. We entered through the single side door and sat in folding chairs on a platform along one wall, separated from the rest of the room by beaded red curtains. Behind us was darkness. On the far wall, neon lights glowed dimly, illuminating a few unoccupied barstools on the other side of the room. But the front of the room was ablaze with light. Purple and white floodlights beamed down onto a circular dance floor, creating an almost supernatural glow. The film crew in the center of the room stood silhouetted against the light like an audience waiting for a show to begin.

Organizing according to time

The principle of time refers to *when* bits of information occur, usually chronologically. Chronological organization is the basic method used in cookbooks, lab reports, instruction manuals, and stories. Writers of these products organize information according to when it occurs in some process or sequence of events (narrative).

INFORMATION ORGANIZED CHRONOLOGICALLY

In July of 1877, Eadweard Muybridge photographed a horse in motion with a camera fast enough to capture clearly the split second when the horse's hooves were all off the ground — a moment never before caught on film. Throughout the fall of that year, newspapers were full of the news of Muybridge's achievement. His next goal was to photograph a sequence of

This photo series shows the rapid passage of time, with each image capturing an instant too fast to see with the eye alone. The image and text together give readers a clear idea of Muybridge's achievement.

such rapid images. In the summer of 1878, he set up a series of cameras along a track and snapped successive photos of a horse as it galloped past. Muybridge's technical achievement helped to pave the way for the first motion pictures a decade later.

Organizing according to logic

The principle of logic refers to *how* bits of information are related logically. The most commonly used logical patterns include *illustration, definition, division and classification, comparison and contrast, cause and effect, problem and solution, use of analogies,* and *narration.* The example that follows organizes information logically, according to the principle of division. For other examples of paragraphs organized according to these logical patterns, see Chapter 8.

INFORMATION ORGANIZED LOGICALLY

Burns can be divided into three types based on the severity of tissue damage: (1) Superficial, or first-degree, burns damage only the top layer of skin (epidermis). They are red and painful, but not serious. (2) Partial thickness, or second-degree, burns damage both the epidermis and the layer just below it (dermis). Second-degree burns, which can be very painful, are characterized by blistering, swelling, and redness. (3) Full thickness, or third-degree, burns destroy both the epidermis and the dermis and damage underlying muscle and other tissues. They appear charred and black. The burn area itself is numb, but the surrounding area can be very painful. Third-degree burns can be fatal if the percentage of affected skin is sufficiently large.

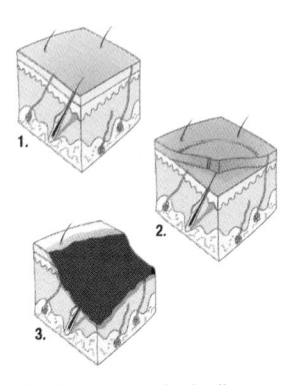

The images are logically arranged to show burns of increasing severity.

Organizing according to association

The principle of association refers to how bits of information are related in terms of visuals, motifs, personal memories, and so on. Many contemporary essays are organized through a series of associations that grow directly out of the writer's memory or experience. Thus, associational organization is often used in personal narrative, where writers can use a chain of associations to render an experience vividly for readers.

INFORMATION ORGANIZED ASSOCIATIONALLY

This image works by association to emphasize the nostalgic charm of homemade ice cream.

Flying from San Francisco to Atlanta, I looked down to see the gentle roll of the Smoky Mountains begin to appear. Almost at once, I was back on my Granny's porch, sitting next to her drinking iced tea and watching all the grownups take turns cranking the ice-cream freezer. Finally the moment came when even the strongest arms could barely turn the churn. Granny lifted the cream can out of the wooden bucket, opened the lid, scooped the gleaming ice cream into a bowl, and topped it with ripe chopped peaches. I still haven't tasted anything better!

In much of your writing, you will want to use two or more principles of organization. In addition, you may want to include not only visuals but sound and other multimedia effects as well.

> **AT A GLANCE**
>
> ## Organizing Visuals
>
> - Use images and visuals to capture your readers' attention and interest in a vivid way, to emphasize a point you make in your text, to present information that is difficult to convey in words, or to communicate with audiences with different language skills.
> - Consider how the image works as an image and in combination with the text, and think about how readers are likely to respond to it.
> - Place each visual as near as possible to the text it illustrates.
> - Introduce each visual clearly: *As the map to the right depicts. . . .*
> - Comment on the significance or effect of the visual: *Figure 1 corroborates the firefighters' statements. . . .*
> - Label each visual appropriately, and cite the source.

EXERCISE 7.4

Using the topic you chose in Exercise 6.1, identify the most effective means of organizing your information. Write a brief paragraph explaining why you chose this particular method (or these methods) of organization.

7e   Make a plan.

At this point, you will find it helpful to create an organizational plan or outline. To do so, simply begin with your thesis; review your exploratory notes, research materials, and visuals; and then list all the examples and other good reasons you have to support the thesis.

A sample organizational plan

One informal way to organize your ideas is to figure out what belongs in your introduction, body paragraphs, and conclusion. Here is how one student, who was writing about solutions to a problem, used this kind of plan:

WORKING THESIS

▶ **Increased motorcycle use demands the reorganization of campus parking lots.**

INTRODUCTION

give background and overview (motorcycle use up dramatically) and use a photograph of overcrowding in a lot

state purpose — to fulfill promise of thesis by offering solutions

BODY

describe the current situation (tell of my research at area parking lots)

describe the problem in detail (report on statistics; cars vs. cycles) and include a graph representing findings

present two possible solutions (enlarge lots or reallocate space)

CONCLUSION

recommend against first solution because of cost and space

recommend second solution, and summarize benefits of it

A formal outline

Even if you have made an informal written plan before drafting, you may also want—or be required—to prepare a formal outline, which can help you see exactly how the parts of your writing will fit together—how your ideas relate, where you need examples, and what the overall structure of your work will be. Most formal outlines follow a conventional format of numbered and lettered headings and subheadings, using roman numerals, capital letters, arabic numerals, and lowercase letters to show the levels of importance of the various ideas and their relationships. Each new level is indented to show its subordination to the preceding level.

Thesis statement
I. First main idea
   A. First subordinate idea
      1. First supporting detail or point
      2. Second supporting detail
      3. Third supporting detail
   B. Second subordinate idea
      1. First supporting detail
      2. Second supporting detail

II. Second main idea
   A. First subordinate idea
      1. First supporting detail
      2. Second supporting detail
   B. Second subordinate idea
      1. First supporting detail
      2. Second supporting detail
         a. First supporting detail
         b. Second supporting detail

Note that each level contains at least two parts, so there is no A without a B, no 1 without a 2. Also keep in mind that headings should be stated in parallel form—either all sentences or all grammatically parallel structures.

A storyboard

The technique of storyboarding—working out a narrative or argument in visual form—can be a good way to come up with an organizational plan, especially if you are developing a Web site or other multimedia project. For such projects you can even find storyboard templates online to help you get started.

For a typical college essay, however, you can create your own storyboard by using note cards or even sticky notes, taking advantage of different colors to keep track of threads of argument, subtopics, and so on. Remember that flexibility is a strong feature of storyboarding: you can move the cards and notes around, trying out different arrangements, until you find an organization that works well for your writing situation. Basic patterns for a storyboard include linear, hierarchical, and spoke-and-hub organization.

LINEAR ORGANIZATION

Use this when you want most readers to move in a particular order through your material. An online report might use the following linear organization:

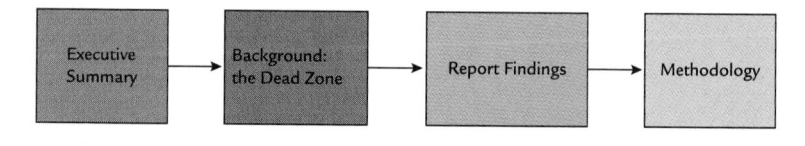

HIERARCHICAL ORGANIZATION

A hierarchy puts the most important material first, with subtopics branching out from the main idea. A multimedia presentation on dog bite prevention might be arranged like this:

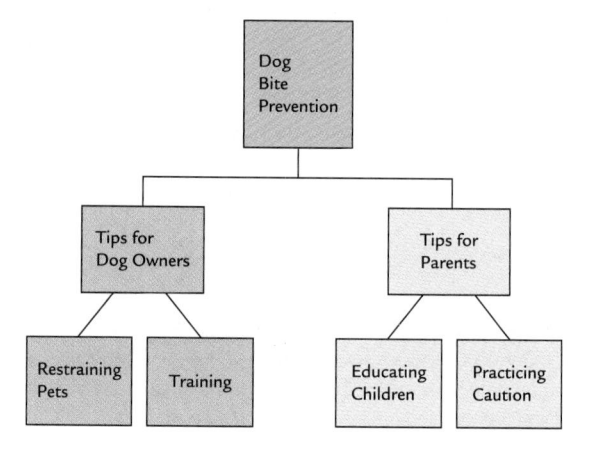

**SPOKE-AND-HUB
ORGANIZATION**

A spoke-and-hub organization allows readers to move from place to place in no particular order. Many portfolio Web sites are arranged as shown at right:

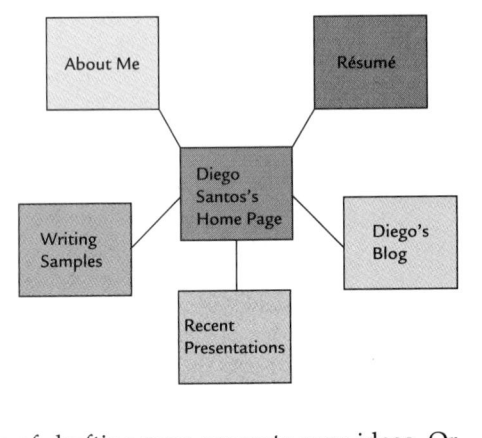

Whatever form your plan takes, you may want or need to change it along the way. Writing has a way of stimulating thought, and the process of drafting may generate new ideas. Or you may find that you need to reexamine some data or information or gather more material.

EXERCISE 7.5

Write out a plan for a piece of writing supporting the working thesis you developed for Exercise 7.2.

7f **Create a draft.**

No matter how good your planning, investigating, and organizing have been, chances are you will need to do more work as you draft. This fact of life leads to the first principle of successful drafting: be flexible. If you see that your plan is not working, don't hesitate to alter it. If some information now seems irrelevant, leave it out—even if you went to great lengths to obtain it. Throughout the drafting process, you may need to refer to points you have already written about. You may learn that you need to do more research, that your whole thesis must be reshaped, or that your topic is still too broad and should be narrowed further. Very often you will continue planning, investigating, and organizing throughout the writing process.

EXERCISE 7.6

Write a draft from the plan you produced for Exercise 7.5.

EXERCISE 7.7: THINKING CRITICALLY

Using the following guidelines, reflect on the process you went through as you prepared for and wrote your draft for Exercise 7.6. Make your answers an entry in your writing log if you are keeping one.

1. How did you arrive at your specific topic?

2. When did you first begin to think about the assignment?

3. What kinds of exploring or planning did you do? What kinds of research did you need to do?

4. How long did it take to complete your draft (including the time spent gathering information)?

5. Where did you write your draft? Briefly describe the setting.

6. How did awareness of your audience help shape your draft?

7. What have you learned from your draft about your own rhetorical stance on your topic?

8. What did you learn about your ideas for this topic by exploring, planning, and talking with others about it?

9. What do you see as the major strengths of your draft? What is your favorite sentence, and why?

10. What do you see as the major weaknesses of your draft? What are you most worried about, and why?

11. What would you like to change about your process of exploring, planning, and drafting?

AT A GLANCE

Drafting

- **Set up a computer folder or file for your essay**. Give the file a clear and relevant name, and save to it often. Number your drafts. If you decide to try a new direction, save the file as a new draft — you can always pick up with a previous one if the new version doesn't work out.

- **Have all your information close at hand and arranged according to your organizational plan**. Stopping to search for a piece of information can break your concentration or distract you.

- **Try to write in stretches of at least thirty minutes**. Writing can provide momentum, and once you get going, the task becomes easier.

- **Don't let small questions bog you down**. Just make a note of them in brackets — or in all caps — or make a tentative decision and move on.

- **Remember that first drafts aren't perfect**. Concentrate on getting all your ideas down, and don't worry about anything else.

- **Stop writing at a place where you know exactly what will come next**. Doing so will help you start easily when you return to the draft.

8 Developing Paragraphs

Paragraphs serve as signposts—pointers that help guide readers through a piece of writing. A look through a popular magazine will show paragraphs working this way: the first paragraph of an article almost always aims to get our attention and to persuade us to read on, and subsequent ones often indicate a new point or a shift in focus or tone.

Put most simply, a paragraph is a group of sentences or a single sentence set off as a unit. All the sentences in a paragraph usually revolve around one main idea.

8a Focus on a main idea.

An effective paragraph often focuses on one main idea. A good way to achieve such paragraph unity is to state the main idea clearly in one sentence and then relate all the other sentences in the paragraph to

---

AT A GLANCE

Editing Paragraphs

- What is the topic sentence of each paragraph? Is it stated or implied? Is the main idea of the paragraph clear? (8a)

- Does the first sentence of each paragraph let readers know what that paragraph is about? Does the last sentence in some way conclude that paragraph's discussion? If not, does it need to?

- Within each paragraph, how does each sentence relate to the main idea? Revise or eliminate any that do not. (8a)

- How completely does each paragraph develop its main idea? What details and images are included? Are they effective? Do any paragraphs need more detail? (8b)

- What other methods of development might make the paragraph more effective? (8c)

- Is each paragraph organized in a way that is easy to follow? Are sentences within each paragraph clearly linked? Do any of the transitions try to create links between ideas that do not really exist? (8e)

- Are the paragraphs clearly linked? Do any links need to be added? Are any of the transitions from one paragraph to another artificial? (8e)

- How does the introductory paragraph catch readers' interest? How does the last paragraph draw the piece to a conclusion? (8f)

FOR MULTILINGUAL WRITERS

Being Explicit

Native readers of English generally expect that paragraphs will have an explicitly stated main idea and that the connections between points in a paragraph will also be stated explicitly. Such step-by-step explicitness may strike you as unnecessary or ineffective, but it follows the traditional paragraph conventions of English.

that idea. The sentence that presents the main idea is called the topic sentence.

Announcing the main idea in a topic sentence

The following paragraph opens with a clear topic sentence, and the rest of the paragraph builds on the idea stated in that sentence:

> *Our friendship was the source of much happiness and many memories.* We grooved on every new recording from Jay-Z. We sweated together in the sweltering summer sun, trying to win the championship for our softball team. I recall the taste of pepperoni pizza as we discussed the highlights of our team's victory. Once we even became attracted to the same person, but luckily we were able to share his friendship.

A topic sentence does not always come at the beginning of a paragraph; it may come at the end. Occasionally a paragraph's main idea is so obvious that it need not be stated explicitly in a topic sentence.

EXERCISE 8.1

Choose an essay you have written, and identify the topic sentence of each paragraph, noting where in the paragraph the topic sentence appears or whether it is implied rather than stated. Experiment with one paragraph, positioning its topic sentence in at least two different places. What difference does the change make? If you have any implied topic sentences, try stating them explicitly. Does the paragraph become easier to read?

Relating each sentence to the main idea

Whether the main idea of a paragraph is stated in a topic sentence or is implied, make sure that all other sentences in the paragraph contribute to the main idea. In the preceding example about friendship, all of the sentences clearly relate to the point that is made in the first sentence. The result is a unified paragraph.

TALKING THE TALK

Paragraph Length

"How long should a paragraph be?" In college writing, paragraphs should address a specific topic or idea and develop that idea with examples and evidence. There is no set rule about how many sentences are required to make a complete paragraph. So write as many sentences as you need — and no more.

8b Provide details.

An effective paragraph develops its main idea by providing enough details — including visual details — to hold the reader's interest. Without such development, a paragraph may seem lifeless and abstract.

A POORLY DEVELOPED PARAGRAPH

No such thing as human nature compels people to behave, think, or react in certain ways. Rather, from our infancy to our death, we are constantly being taught, by the society that surrounds us, the customs, norms, and mores of a distinct culture. Everything in culture is learned, not genetically transmitted.

This paragraph is boring. Although its main idea is clear and its sentences hold together, it fails to gain our interest or hold our attention because it lacks any specific examples or details. Now look at the paragraph revised to include needed specifics.

THE SAME PARAGRAPH, REVISED

A child in Los Angeles decorates a Christmas tree with shiny red ornaments and sparkling tinsel. A few weeks later, a child in Beijing celebrates the Chinese New Year with feasting, firecrackers, and gift money in lucky red envelopes. It is not by instinct that one child knows how to decorate the tree while the other knows how to celebrate the New Year. No such thing as human nature compels people to behave, think, or react in certain ways. Rather, from the time of our infancy to our death, we are constantly being taught, by the society that surrounds us, the customs, norms, and mores of one or more distinct cultures. Everything in culture is learned, not genetically transmitted.

Though both paragraphs present the same point, only the second one comes to life. It does so by bringing in specific details *from* life, including images that show readers what the paragraph describes. We want to read this paragraph because it appeals to our senses (shiny red ornaments, firecrackers) and our curiosity (why are red envelopes considered lucky?).

Details in visual texts

Details are important in both written and visual texts. If you decide to use an image because of a particular detail, make sure your readers will notice what you want them to see. Crop out any unnecessary information, and clarify what's important about the image in your text or with a caption. The first image below shows the original photograph taken to illustrate a blog post about street food. The cropped second image, which appeared on the blog, makes the sandwich the center of the frame.

WEDNESDAY, APRIL 11, 2012

Fresh from the sea!

If the herring at Jan's were any fresher, it would still be swimming!

EXERCISE 8.2

Choose one of the following topic sentences, and spend some time exploring the topic (Chapter 6). Then write a paragraph that includes the topic sentence. Make sure that each of the other sentences relates to it. Assume that the paragraph will be part of a letter you are writing to an acquaintance.

1. I found out quickly that college life was not quite what I had expected.
2. Being part of the "in crowd" used to be essential to me.
3. My work experience has taught me several important lessons.
4. Until recently, I never appreciated my parents fully.
5. One of my high school teachers helped prepare me for life as an adult.

EXERCISE 8.3

Choose an essay you have written recently, and examine the second, third, and fourth paragraphs. Does each have a topic sentence or strongly imply one? Do all the other sentences in the paragraph focus on its main idea? Would you now revise any of these paragraphs — and, if so, how?

8c Use effective methods of development.

As noted in 7d, there are several common methods of development. You can use them to develop paragraphs.

Narrative

A narrative paragraph uses the chronological elements of a story to develop a main idea. The following is one student's narrative paragraph that tells a personal story to support a point about the dangers of racing bicycles with flimsy alloy frames:

> People who have been exposed to the risk of dangerously designed bicycle frames have paid too high a price. I saw this danger myself in last year's Putney Race. An expensive graphite frame failed, and the rider was catapulted onto Vermont pavement at fifty miles per hour. The pack of riders behind him was so dense that other racers crashed into a tangled, sliding heap. The aftermath: four hospitalizations. I got off with some stitches, a bad road rash, and severely pulled tendons. My Italian racing bike was pretzeled, and my racing was over for that summer. Others were not so lucky. An Olympic hopeful, Brian Stone of the Northstar team, woke up in a hospital bed to find that his cycling was over — and not just for that summer. His kneecap had been surgically removed. He couldn't even walk.

Description

A descriptive paragraph uses specific details to create a clear impression. Notice how the following paragraph includes details to describe the appearance of the skyscraper and its effect on those who see it.

The Chrysler Building, completed in 1930, still attracts the eyes of tourists and New Yorkers alike with its shiny steel exterior. The Chrysler cars of the era are incorporated into the design: the eagle-head gargoyles on the upper vertices of the building are shaped like the automobiles' hood ornaments, and winged details imitate Chrysler radiator caps. At night, an elaborate lighting scheme spotlights the sleek, powerful eagles from below—turning them into striking silhouettes—and picks out each of the upper stories' famed triangular windows, arching up into the darkness like the rays of a stylized sun.

Definition

You may often need to write an entire paragraph in order to define a word or concept, as in the following example:

Economics is the study of how people choose among the alternatives available to them. It's the study of little choices ("Should I take the chocolate or the strawberry?") and big choices ("Should we require a reduction in energy consumption in order to protect the environment?"). It's the study of individual choices, choices by firms, and choices by governments. Life presents each of us with a wide range of alternative uses of our time and other resources; economists examine how we choose among those alternatives.

– TIMOTHY TREGARTHEN, Economics

Example

One of the most common ways of developing a paragraph is by illustrating a point with one or more examples.

> The Indians made names for us children in their teasing way. Because our very busy mother kept my hair cut short, like my brothers', they called me Short Furred One, pointing to their hair and making the sign for short, the right hand with fingers pressed close together, held upward, back out, at the height intended. With me this was about two feet tall, the Indians laughing gently at my abashed face. I am told that I was given a pair of small moccasins that first time, to clear up my unhappiness at being picked out from the dusk behind the fire and my two unhappy shortcomings made conspicuous.   – MARI SANDOZ, "The Go-Along Ones"

Division and classification

Division breaks a single item into parts. Classification groups many separate items according to their similarities. A paragraph evaluating one history course might divide the course into several segments—textbooks, lectures, assignments—and examine each one in turn. A paragraph giving an overview of many history courses might classify the courses in a number of ways—by time periods, by geographic areas, by the kinds of assignments demanded, by the number of students enrolled, or by some other principle.

DIVISION

> We all listen to music according to our separate capacities. But, for the sake of analysis, the whole listening process may become clearer if we break it up into its component parts, so to speak. In a certain sense, we all listen to music on three separate planes. For lack of a better terminology, one might name these: (1) the sensuous plane, (2) the expressive plane, (3) the sheerly musical plane. The only advantage to be gained from mechanically splitting up the listening process into these hypothetical planes is the clearer view to be had of the way in which we listen.
> – AARON COPLAND, *What to Listen For in Music*

CLASSIFICATION

> Two types of people are seduced by fad diets. Those who have always been overweight turn to them out of despair; they have tried everything, and yet nothing seems to work. A second group of people to succumb appear perfectly healthy but are baited by slogans such as "look good, feel

good." These slogans prompt self-questioning and insecurity—do I really look good and feel good?—and as a direct result, many healthy people fall prey to fad diets. With both types of people, however, the problems surrounding such diets are numerous and dangerous. In fact, these diets provide neither intelligent nor effective answers to weight control.

Comparison and contrast

When you compare two things, you look at their similarities; when you contrast two things, you focus on their differences. You can structure paragraphs that compare or contrast in two basic ways. One way is to present all the information about one item and then all the information about the other item, as in the following paragraph:

> You could tell the veterans from the rookies by the way they were dressed. The knowledgeable ones had their heads covered by kerchiefs, so that if they were hired, tobacco dust wouldn't get in their hair; they had on clean dresses that by now were faded and shapeless, so that if they were hired they wouldn't get tobacco dust and grime on their best clothes. Those who were trying for the first time had their hair freshly done and wore attractive dresses; they wanted to make a good impression. But the dresses couldn't be seen at the distance that many were standing from the employment office, and they were crumpled in the crush.
>
> – MARY MEBANE, "Summer Job"

Or you can switch back and forth between the two items, focusing on particular characteristics of each in turn.

Malcolm X emphasized the use of violence in his movement and employed the biblical principle of "an eye for an eye and a tooth for a tooth." King, on the other hand, felt that blacks should use nonviolent civil disobedience and employed the theme "turning the other cheek," which Malcolm X rejected as "beggarly" and "feeble." The philosophy of Malcolm X was one of revenge, and often it broke the unity of black Americans. More radical blacks supported him, while more conservative ones supported King. King thought that blacks should transcend their humanity. In contrast, Malcolm X thought they should embrace it and reserve their love for one another, regarding whites as "devils" and the "enemy." The distance between Martin Luther King Jr.'s thinking and Malcolm X's was the distance between growing up in the seminary and growing up on the streets, between the American dream and the American reality.

EXERCISE 8.4

Outline the preceding paragraph on Martin Luther King Jr. and Malcolm X, noting its alternating pattern. Then rewrite the paragraph using block organization: the first part of the paragraph devoted to King, the second to Malcolm X. Finally, write a brief analysis of the two paragraphs, explaining which seems more coherent and easier to follow — and why.

Analogy

Analogies (comparisons that explain an unfamiliar thing in terms of a familiar one) can also help develop paragraphs. In the following paragraph, the writer draws an unlikely analogy — between the human genome and Thanksgiving dinner — to help readers understand what scientists know about the human genome.

> Think of the human genome as the ingredients list for a massive Thanksgiving dinner. Scientists long have had a general understanding of how the feast is cooked. They knew where the ovens were. Now, they also have a list of every ingredient. Yet much remains to be discovered. In most cases, no one knows exactly which ingredients are necessary for making, for example, the pumpkin pie as opposed to the cornbread. Indeed, many, if not most, of the recipes that use the genomic ingredients are missing, and there's little understanding why small variations in the quality of the ingredients can "cook up" diseases in one person but not in another.
> – *USA Today*, "Cracking of Life's Genetic Code Carries Weighty Potential"

Cause and effect

You can often develop paragraphs by explaining the causes of something or the effects that something brings about. The following paragraph discusses how our desire for food that tastes good has affected history:

> The human craving for flavor has been a largely unacknowledged and unexamined force in history. For millennia royal empires have been built, unexplored lands traversed, and great religions and philosophies changed by the spice trade. In 1492 Christopher Columbus set sail to find seasoning. Today the influence of flavor in the world marketplace is no less decisive. The rise and fall of corporate empires — of soft-drink companies, snack-food companies, and fast-food chains — is often determined by how their products taste.
> – Eric Schlosser, *Fast Food Nation*

Process

Paragraphs that explain a process often use the principle of time or chronology to order the stages in the process.

> By the late 20s, most people notice the first signs of aging in their physical appearance. Slight losses of elasticity in facial skin produce the first wrinkles, usually in those areas most involved in their characteristic facial expressions. As the skin continues to lose elasticity and fat deposits build up, the face sags a bit with age. Indeed, some people have drooping eyelids, sagging cheeks, and the hint of a double chin by age 40 (Whitbourne, 1985). Other parts of the body sag a bit as well, so as the years pass, adults need to exercise regularly if they want to maintain their muscle tone and body shape. Another harbinger of aging, the first gray hairs, is usually noticed in the 20s and can be explained by a reduction in the number of pigment-producing cells. Hair may become a bit less plentiful, too, because of hormonal changes and reduced blood supply to the skin.
> – KATHLEEN STASSEN BERGER, *The Developing Person through the Life Span*

Problem and solution

Another way to develop a paragraph is to open with a topic sentence that states a problem or asks a question about a problem and then to offer a solution or answers in the sentences that follow—a technique used in this paragraph from a review of Ted Nordhaus and Michael Shellenberger's book *Break Through: From the Death of Environmentalism to the Politics of Possibility*:

> Unfortunately, at the moment growth means burning more fossil fuel. . . . How can that fact be faced? How to have growth that Americans want, but without limits that they instinctively oppose, and still reduce carbon emissions? [Nordhaus and Shellenberger's] answer is: investments in new technology. Acknowledge that America "is great at imagining, experimenting, and inventing the future," and then start spending. They cite examples ranging from the nuclear weapons program to the invention of the Internet to show what government money can do, and argue that too many clean-energy advocates focus on caps instead.
> – BILL MCKIBBEN, "Can Anyone Stop It?"

Reiteration

Reiteration is a method of development you may recognize from political speeches or some styles of preaching. In this pattern, the writer states the main point of a paragraph and then restates it, hammering home the point and often building in intensity as well. In the following passage from Barack Obama's 2004 speech at the Democratic National Convention, Obama contrasts what he identifies as the ideas of "those who are preparing to divide us" with memorable references to common ground and unity, including repeated references to the United States as he builds to his climactic point:

> Now even as we speak, there are those who are preparing to divide us—the spin masters, the negative ad peddlers who embrace the politics of anything goes. Well, I say to them tonight, there is not a liberal America and a conservative America—there is the United States of America. There is not a black America and a white America and Latino America and an Asian America—there's the United States of America. The pundits like to slice and dice our country into Red States and Blue States: Red States for Republicans, Blue States for Democrats. But I've got news for them, too. We worship an awesome God in the Blue States, and we don't like federal agents poking around in our libraries in the Red States. We coach Little League in the Blue States and yes, we've got some gay friends in the Red States. There are patriots who opposed the war in Iraq and there are patriots who supported the war in Iraq. We are one people, all of us pledging allegiance to the stars and stripes, all of us defending the United States of America.
>
> —BARACK OBAMA

EXERCISE 8.5

Choose two of the following topics or two others that interest you, and brainstorm or freewrite about each one for ten minutes (6a and b). Then use the information you have produced to determine what method(s) of development would be most appropriate for each topic.

1. the pleasure a hobby has given you
2. the different images of two noted athletes
3. how to prepare for a storm
4. why wearing a seat belt should (or should not) be mandatory
5. the best course you've ever taken

EXERCISE 8.6

Take an assignment you have written recently, and study the ways you developed each paragraph. For one of the paragraphs, write a brief evaluation of its development. How would you expand or otherwise improve the development?

8d Consider paragraph length.

Paragraph length is determined by content and purpose. Paragraphs should develop an idea, create any desired effects (such as suspense or humor), and advance the larger piece of writing. Fulfilling these aims will sometimes require short paragraphs, sometimes long ones. For example, if you are writing a persuasive piece, you may put all your evidence into one long paragraph to create the impression of a solid, overwhelmingly convincing argument. In a story about an exciting event, on the other hand, you may use a series of short paragraphs to create suspense, to keep the reader rushing to each new paragraph to find out what happens next.

REASONS TO START A NEW PARAGRAPH

- to turn to a new idea
- to emphasize something (such as an idea or an example)
- to change speakers (in dialogue)
- to get readers to pause
- to take up a subtopic
- to start the conclusion

EXERCISE 8.7

Examine the paragraph breaks in something you have written recently. Explain briefly in writing why you decided on each of the breaks. Would you change any of them now? If so, how and why?

8e Make paragraphs flow.

A paragraph has coherence—or flows—if its details fit together clearly in a way that readers can easily follow. When you arrange information in a particular order (as described in 7d and 8c), you help readers move from one point to another. Regardless of your organization, however, be aware of several other ways to achieve paragraph coherence.

Repeating key words and phrases

Weaving in repeated key words and phrases—or pronouns that point to them—not only links sentences but also alerts readers to the importance of those words or phrases in the larger piece of writing. Notice in the following example how the repetition of the italicized key words and the use of pronouns that refer to those words help hold the paragraph together:

> Over the centuries, *shopping* has changed in function as well as in style. Before the Industrial Revolution, most consumer goods were sold in open-air *markets, customers* who went into an actual *shop* were expected to *buy* something, and *shoppers* were always expected to *bargain* for the best possible *price*. In the nineteenth century, however, the development of the

department *store* changed the relationship between buyers and sellers. Instead of visiting several *market* stalls or small *shops, customers* could now *buy* a variety of merchandise under the same roof; instead of feeling expected to *buy*, they were welcome just to look; and instead of *bargaining* with several merchants, they paid a fixed *price* for each *item*. In addition, *they* could return an *item* to the *store* and exchange *it* for a different one or get their money back. All of these changes helped transform *shopping* from serious requirement to psychological recreation.

EXERCISE 8.8

Look at the essay you drafted for Exercise 7.6, and identify the ways your paragraphs are linked together. Identify each use of repetition, parallel structures, and transitional expressions, and then evaluate how effectively you have joined the paragraphs.

Using parallelism

Parallel structures can help connect the sentences within a paragraph. As readers, we feel pulled along by the force of the parallel structures in the following example:

> William Faulkner's "Barn Burning" tells the story of a young boy trapped in a no-win situation. If he betrays his father, he loses his family. If he betrays justice, he becomes a fugitive. In trying to free himself from his trap, he does both.

Using transitions

Transitions are words such as *so, however,* and *thus* that signal relationships between sentences and paragraphs. Transitions help guide the reader from one idea to another. To understand how important transitions are in directing readers, try reading the following paragraph, from which all transitions have been removed.

A PARAGRAPH WITH NO TRANSITIONS

> In "The Fly," Katherine Mansfield tries to show us the real personality of the boss beneath his exterior. The fly helps her to portray this real self. The boss goes through a range of emotions and feelings. He expresses these feelings to a small but determined fly, whom the reader realizes he unconsciously relates to his son. The author basically splits up the story into three parts, with the boss's emotions and actions changing quite measurably. With old Woodifield, with himself, and with the fly, we see the boss's manipulativeness. Our understanding of him as a hard and cruel man grows.

If we work at it, we can figure out the relationship of these sentences to one another, for this paragraph is essentially unified by one major idea. But the lack of transitions results in an abrupt, choppy rhythm; the paragraph lurches from one detail to the next, dragging the confused reader behind. See how much easier the passage is to read and understand with transitions added.

THE SAME PARAGRAPH WITH TRANSITIONS

In "The Fly," Katherine Mansfield tries to show us the real personality of the boss beneath his exterior. The fly in the story's title helps her to portray this real self. In the course of the story, the boss goes through a range of emotions. At the end, he finally expresses these feelings to a small but determined fly, whom the reader realizes he unconsciously relates to his son. To accomplish her goal, the author basically splits up the story into three parts, with the boss's emotions and actions changing measurably throughout. First with old Woodifield, then with himself, and last with the fly, we see the boss's manipulativeness. With each part, our understanding of him as a hard and cruel man grows.

Commonly used transitions

TO SIGNAL SEQUENCE

again, also, and, and then, besides, finally, first . . . second . . . third, furthermore, last, moreover, next, still, too

TO SIGNAL TIME

after a few days, after a while, afterward, as long as, as soon as, at last, at that time, before, earlier, immediately, in the meantime, in the past, lately, later, meanwhile, now, presently, simultaneously, since, so far, soon, then, thereafter, until, when

TO SIGNAL COMPARISON

again, also, in the same way, likewise, once more, similarly

TO SIGNAL CONTRAST

although, but, despite, even though, however, in contrast, in spite of, instead, nevertheless, nonetheless, on the contrary, on the one hand . . . on the other hand, regardless, still, though, yet

TO SIGNAL EXAMPLES

after all, for example, for instance, indeed, in fact, of course, specifically, such as, the following example, to illustrate

TO SIGNAL CAUSE AND EFFECT

accordingly, as a result, because, consequently, for this purpose, hence, so, then, therefore, thereupon, thus, to this end

TO SIGNAL PLACE

above, adjacent to, below, beyond, closer to, elsewhere, far, farther on, here, near, nearby, opposite to, there, to the left, to the right

TO SIGNAL CONCESSION

although it is true that, granted that, I admit that, it may appear that, naturally, of course

TO SIGNAL SUMMARY, REPETITION, OR CONCLUSION

as a result, as has been noted, as I have said, as mentioned earlier, as we have seen, in any event, in conclusion, in other words, in short, on the whole, therefore, to summarize

8f Work on opening and closing paragraphs.

Opening paragraphs

Even a good piece of writing may remain unread if it has a weak opening paragraph. In addition to announcing your topic, an introductory paragraph must engage readers' interest and focus their attention on what is to follow. One common kind of opening paragraph follows a general-to-specific sequence, in which the writer opens with a general statement and then gets more and more specific, concluding with the thesis. The following paragraph illustrates such an opening:

> The human organism is adapted to function in face-to-face encounters. We know that face-to-face is the most effective way to pitch woo. And face-to-face is obviously the best way to transact an intimate relationship long term. But while we know this, there's much more to face-to-face interaction than meets the naked eye. And it is of grave importance. We risk losing a great deal in any heavy shift of social traffic onto exclusively electronic media. —MARIAM THALOS, "Why I Am Not a Friend"

In this paragraph, the opening sentence introduces a general subject, and the last sentence presents the thesis, which the rest of the essay will develop.

OTHER EFFECTIVE WAYS OF OPENING

- with a quotation: *There is a bumper sticker that reads, "Too bad ignorance isn't painful."* – NIKKI GIOVANNI, "Racism 101"
- with an anecdote: *Social networking pioneer Howard Rheingold begins his digital journalism course each year with a participatory experiment. Shut off your cell phones, he tells his students. Shut your laptop. Now, shut your eyes.* –CATHY DAVIDSON, *Now You See It*
- with a question: *Why are Americans terrified of using nuclear power as a source of energy?*

- with a strong opinion: *Men need a men's movement about as much as women need chest hair.* – JOHN RUSZKIEWICZ, *The Presence of Others*

Concluding paragraphs

A good conclusion wraps up a piece of writing in a satisfying and memorable way. A common and effective strategy for concluding is to restate the central idea (but not word for word), perhaps specifying it in several sentences, and then ending with a much more general statement.

> Lastly, and perhaps greatest of all, there was the ability, at the end, to turn quickly from war to peace once the fighting was over. Out of the way these two men [Generals Grant and Lee] behaved at Appomattox came the possibility of a peace of reconciliation. It was a possibility not wholly realized, in the years to come, but which did, in the end, help the two sections to become one nation again . . . after a war whose bitterness might have seemed to make such a reunion wholly impossible. No part of either man's life became him more than the part he played in this brief meeting in the McLean house at Appomattox. Their behavior there put all succeeding generations of Americans in their debt. Two great Americans, Grant and Lee—very different, yet under everything very much alike. Their encounter at Appomattox was one of the great moments of American history.
> – BRUCE CATTON, "Grant and Lee: A Study in Contrasts"

OTHER EFFECTIVE WAYS OF CONCLUDING

- with a quotation
- with a question
- with a vivid image
- with a call for action
- with a warning

EXERCISE 8.9: THINKING CRITICALLY

Reading with an Eye for Paragraphs

Read something by a writer you admire. Find one or two paragraphs that impress you in some way, and analyze them, using the questions in the At a Glance box on p. 78. Try to decide what makes them effective paragraphs.

Thinking about Your Own Use of Paragraphs

Examine two or three paragraphs you have written, using the guidelines on p. 78, to evaluate the unity, coherence, and development of each one. Identify the topic of each paragraph, the topic sentence (if one is explicitly stated), any patterns of development, and any means used to create coherence. Decide whether or not each paragraph successfully guides your readers, and explain your reasons. Then choose one paragraph, and revise it.

9 Making Design Decisions

Because visual and design elements such as headings, lists, fonts, images, and graphics can help you get and keep a reader's attention, they bring a whole new dimension to writing — what some call *visual rhetoric.*

9a Plan a visual structure.

Effective writers consider the visual structure of any text they create. Their design decisions guide readers by making texts easier on the eyes and easier to understand.

Print and electronic options

One of your first design decisions will be choosing between print delivery and electronic delivery. In general, print documents are easily portable, easy to read without technical assistance, and relatively fast to produce. In addition, the tools for producing print texts are highly developed and stable. Electronic texts, on the other hand, can include sound, animation, and video; updates are easy to make; distribution is fast and efficient; and feedback can be swift. In many writing situations, the assignment will tell you whether to create a print document or an electronic text. Whether you are working to produce a text to be read in print or on a screen (or both), however, you should rely on some basic design principles.

Design principles

Designer Robin Williams, in her *Non-Designer's Design Book*, points out several very simple principles for designing effective texts—contrast, alignment, repetition, and proximity. These principles are illustrated in the examples shown on pp. 95–96.

CONTRAST

Contrast attracts your eye to elements on a page and guides you around it, helping you follow an argument or find information. You may achieve contrast through the use of color, icons, boldface or large type size, headings, and so on. Begin with a focus point—the dominant point, image, or words where you want your reader's eye to go first—and structure the flow of your visual information from this point.

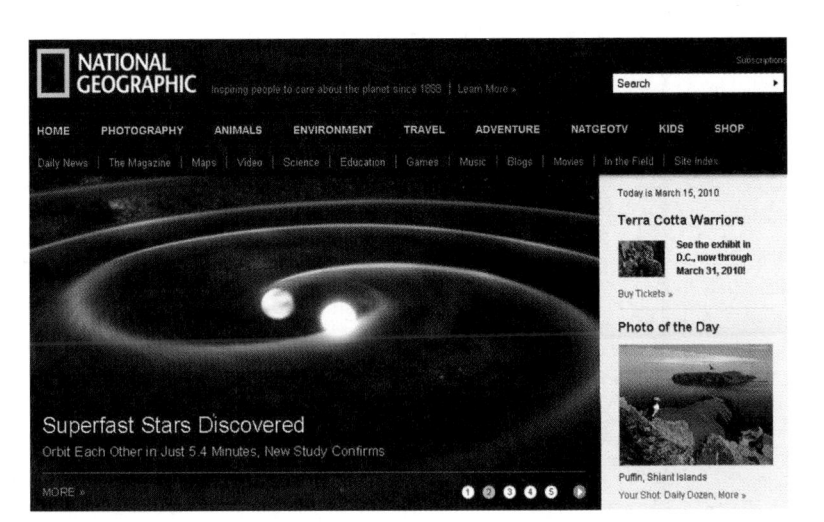

The National Geographic *Web site uses high-contrast yellow and white against a black background.*

ALIGNMENT

Alignment refers to the way visuals and text on a page are lined up, both horizontally and vertically. The overall guideline is not to mix alignments arbitrarily. That is, if you begin with a left alignment, stick with it for the major parts of your page. The result will be a cleaner and more organized look. In this book, for example, headings always align with the left margin.

REPETITION

Readers are guided by the repetition of key words and elements. Use a consistent design throughout your document for such elements as color, typeface, and images.

PROXIMITY

Parts of a text that are closely related should appear together (*proximate* to one another). Your goal is to position related points, text, and visuals near one another and to use clear headings to identify these clusters.

CONSISTENT OVERALL IMPRESSION

Aim for a design that creates the appropriate overall impression or mood for your text. For an academic essay, you will probably make conservative choices that strike a serious scholarly note. In a newsletter for a campus group, you might choose attention-getting images.

This flyer repeats images of generators and buildings to clarify key concepts, and it positions information about safe and unsafe locations for a generator next to illustrations of those locations.

9b   Choose appropriate formats.

With so many options available, you should spend some time thinking about appropriate formatting elements for your text. Although the following guidelines often apply, remember that print documents, Web pages, slide shows, videos, and so on all have their own formatting conventions.

White space

Use white space, or negative space, to emphasize and direct readers to parts of the page. White space determines a page's density—the distance between information bits. You consider white space at the page level (margins), paragraph level (space between paragraphs), and sentence level

---

CONSIDERING DISABILITIES

Color for Contrast

Remember when you are using color that not everyone will see it as you do. Some individuals do not perceive color at all; others perceive color in a variety of ways, especially colors like blue and green, which are close together on the color spectrum. When putting colors next to one another, then, use those on opposite sides of the color spectrum, such as purple and gold, in order to achieve high contrast. Doing so will allow readers to see the contrast, if not the nuances, of color.

(space between sentences). Within the page, you can also use white space around particular content, such as a graphic or list, to make it stand out.

Color

Decisions about color depend to a large extent not only on the kind of equipment you are using—and, for printing, who's paying for the color ink cartridges—but also on the purpose(s) of your document and its intended audience. As you design your documents, keep in mind that some colors can evoke powerful responses, so take care that the colors you use match the message you are sending. Here are some other tips about the effective use of color:

- Use color to draw attention to elements you want to emphasize: headings, bullets, text boxes, or parts of charts or graphs.
- Be consistent in your use of color; use the same color for all sub-heads, for example.
- For most documents, keep the number of colors fairly small; too many colors can create a jumbled or confused look.
- Avoid colors that clash or that are hard on the eyes.

Certain color combinations clash or are hard to read.

Other combinations are easier on the eyes.

- Make sure all color visuals and text are legible in the format where they will be read. What appears readable on the screen—where colors can be sharper—may be less legible in a printed document.

Paper

The quality of the paper affects the overall look and feel of print documents. Although inexpensive paper is fine for your earlier drafts, use 8½" × 11" good-quality white bond paper for your final presentation.

FOR MULTILINGUAL WRITERS

Reading Patterns

In documents written in English and other Western languages, informa-tion tends to flow from left to right and top to bottom — since that is the way English texts are written. In some languages, which may be written from right to left or vertically, documents may be arranged from top right to bottom left. Understanding the reading patterns of the language you are working in will help you design your documents most effectively.

For résumés, you may wish to use parchment or cream-colored bond. For brochures and posters, colored paper may be appropriate as long as your text is still readable. Use the best-quality printer available to you for your final product.

Pagination

Your instructor may ask that you follow a particular pagination format for print texts (for MLA, APA, *Chicago,* and CSE styles, see Chapters 49–55); if not, beginning with the first page of text, place your last name and a number in the upper-right-hand corner of the page.

Type

Computers allow writers to choose among a great variety of type sizes and typefaces, or fonts. For most college writing, the easy-to-read 11- or 12-point type size is best.

This is 12-point Times New Roman
This is 11-point Times New Roman

A serif font, as is used in the main text of this book, is generally easier to read in print than a **sans serif font**. Although unusual fonts might seem attractive at first glance, readers may find such styles distracting and hard to read over long stretches of material.

Remember that typefaces help you create the tone of a document, so consider your audience and purpose when selecting type.

Different fonts convey different feelings.
Different fonts convey different feelings.
DIFFERENT FONTS CONVEY DIFFERENT FEELINGS.
Different fonts convey different feelings.

Most important, be consistent in the size and style of typeface you use, especially for the main part of your text. Unless you are striving for some special effect, shifting sizes and fonts within a document can give an appearance of disorderliness.

Spacing

Final drafts for most of your college writing should be double-spaced, with the first line of paragraphs indented one-half inch. Certain kinds of writing for certain disciplines may call for different spacing. Letters, memorandums, and online texts, for example, are usually single-spaced, with no paragraph indentation. Some long print reports may be printed with one-and-a-half-line spacing to save paper. Other kinds of documents, such as flyers and newsletters, may call for multiple columns. If in doubt, consult your instructor.

In general, leave one space after all punctuation except in the following cases:

- Leave no space before or after a dash (*Please respond—right away—to this message*).
- Leave no space before or after a hyphen (*a red-letter day*).
- Leave no space between punctuation marks (*"on my way,"*).

Computers allow you to decide whether or not you want both side margins justified, or squared off—as they are on this page. Except in posters and other writing where you are trying to achieve a distinctive visual effect, you should always justify the left margin, though you may decide to indent lists and blocks of text that are set off. However, most readers—and many instructors—prefer the right margin to be "ragged," or unjustified.

9c Use headings appropriately.

For brief essays and reports, you may need no headings at all. For longer documents, however, these devices call attention to the organization of the text and thus aid comprehension. Some kinds of reports use set headings (such as *Abstract* and *Summary*), which readers expect and writers therefore must provide; see 53d for an example. When you use headings, you need to decide on type size and style, wording, and placement.

Type size and style

This book, which is a long and complex document, uses various levels of headings. These levels of headings are distinguished by type sizes and fonts as well as by color.

In a college paper, you will usually distinguish levels of headings using only type—for example, all capitals for the first-level headings, capitals and lowercase boldface for the second level, capitals and lowercase italics for the third level, and so on.

FIRST-LEVEL HEADING
Second-Level Heading
Third-Level Heading

Consistent headings

Look for the most succinct and informative way to word headings. In general, state a topic in a single word, usually a noun (*Toxicity*); in a phrase, usually a noun phrase (*Levels of Toxicity*) or a gerund phrase (*Measuring Toxicity*); in a question that will be answered in the text (*How Can Toxicity Be Measured?*); or in an imperative that tells readers what steps to take (*Measure the Toxicity*). Whichever structure you choose, make sure you use it consistently for all headings of the same level.

Positioning

Be sure to position each level of heading consistently throughout the text. And remember not to put a heading at the very bottom of a page, since readers would have to turn to the next page to find the text that the heading is announcing.

9d Use visuals effectively.

Creating a visual design is more likely than ever before to be a part of your process of planning for a completed writing project. Visuals can help make a point more vividly and succinctly than words alone. In some cases, visuals may even be your primary text.

Selecting visuals

Consider carefully what you want visuals to do for your writing before making your selections. What will your audience want or need you to show? Try to choose visuals that will enhance your credibility, allow you to make your point more emphatically, and clarify your overall text. (See the following series of figures for advice on which visuals are best for particular situations.)

Effective visuals can come from many sources—your own drawings or photographs, charts or graphs you create on a computer, or materials created by others. If you are using a visual from another source, be sure to give appropriate credit and to get permission before using any visual that will be posted online or otherwise available to the public.

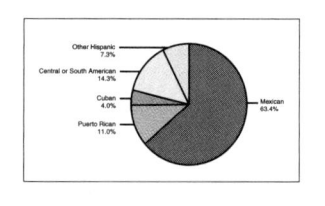

Use *pie charts* to compare parts to the whole.

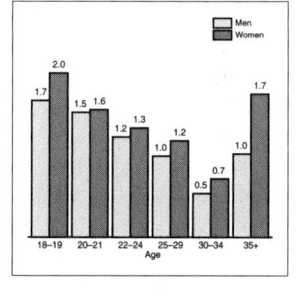

Use *bar graphs* and *line graphs* to compare one element with another, to compare elements over time, or to show correlations and frequency.

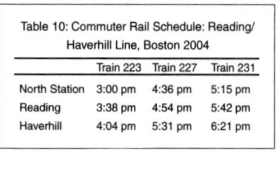

Use *tables* to draw attention to detailed numerical information.

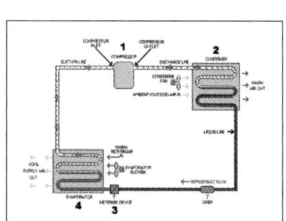

Use *diagrams* to illustrate textual information or to point out details of objects or places described.

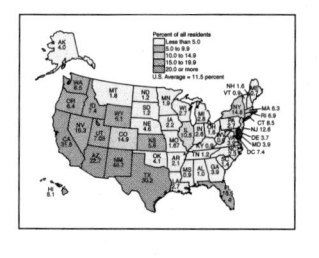

Use *maps* to show geographical locations and to emphasize spatial relationships.

Use *cartoons* to illustrate a point dramatically or comically.

Use *photographs* or *illustrations* to show particular people, places, objects, and situations described in the text or to help readers find or understand types of content.

Identifying visuals in your writing

Position visuals alongside or after the text that refers to them. Number your visuals (number tables separately from other visuals), and give them informative titles. In some instances, you may need to provide captions to give readers additional data as source information.

Figure 1. College Enrollment for Men and Women by Age, 2007 (in millions)

Table 1. Word Choice by Race: *Seesaw* and *Teeter-totter*, Chicago, 1986

Analyzing and altering visuals

Technical tools available to writers and designers today make it relatively easy to manipulate visuals. As you would with any source material, carefully assess any visuals you find for effectiveness, appropriateness, and validity. Here are tips for evaluating visuals:

- Check the context in which the visual appears. Is it part of an official government, school, or library site?
- If the visual is a photograph, are the date, time, place, and setting shown or explained? Is the information about the photo believable?
- If the visual is a chart, graph, or diagram, are the numbers and labels explained? Are the sources of the data given? Will the visual representation help readers make sense of the information, or could it mislead them? (See 18c.)

- Is biographical and contact information for the designer, artist, or photographer given?

At times, you may make certain changes to visuals that you use, such as cropping an image to show the most important detail or digitally brightening a dark image. Here, for example, are separate photos of a mountaintop cabin and a composite that digitally combines the originals into a single panoramic image to convey the setting more accurately. As long as the photograph is identified as a composite, the alteration is ethical.

Combining photos can sometimes be an appropriate choice.

This composite photo conveys the setting more effectively than the individual images.

To ensure that alterations to images are ethical, follow these guidelines:

- Do not attempt to mislead readers. Show things as accurately as possible.
- Tell your audience what changes you have made.
- Include all relevant information about the visual, including the source.

Using Visuals Effectively

- Use visual elements for a specific purpose in your text — to illustrate something, to help prove a point, or to guide readers, for example.
- Tell the audience explicitly what the visual demonstrates, especially if it presents complex information. Do not assume readers will "read" the visual the way you do; your commentary on it is important.
- Number and title all visuals. Number and label tables and figures separately.
- Refer to each visual *before* it appears.
- Follow established conventions for documenting visual sources, and ask permission for use if your work will become available to the public. (18c and e)
- Get responses to your visuals in an early draft. If readers can't follow them or are distracted by them, revise accordingly.
- If you crop, brighten, or otherwise alter visuals to include them in your writing, be sure to do so ethically. (9d)

EXERCISE 9.1

Take an essay or other writing assignment you have done recently, one that makes little use of visuals or the other design elements discussed in this chapter. Reevaluate the effectiveness of your text, and make a note of all the places where visuals and other design elements (color, different type size, and so on) would help you get your ideas across more effectively.

EXERCISE 9.2: THINKING CRITICALLY

Take a look at a piece of writing or a document you have recently completed. Using the advice in this chapter, assess your use of visual structure, consistent use of conventions for guiding readers through your text, and use of headings, color, font size, visuals, and other media. Then write a brief assessment of how well your text is designed and how you could improve it.

10 Reviewing and Revising

The ancient Roman poet Horace advised aspiring writers to get distance from their work by putting it away for *nine years*. Although impractical for most college writers, this advice still holds a nugget of truth: putting the draft away even for a day or two will clear your mind and give you more objectivity about your writing.

10a Reread.

After giving yourself and your draft a rest, review the draft by reread-ing it carefully for meaning; recalling your purpose and audience; re-considering your stance; and evaluating your organization and use of visuals.

Meaning

When you pick up the draft again, don't sweat the small stuff. Instead, concentrate on your message and on whether you have expressed it clearly. Note any places where the meaning seems unclear.

Purpose

If you responded to an assignment, make sure that you have produced what was asked for. If you set out to prove something, have you suc-ceeded? If you intended to propose a solution to a problem, have you set forth a well-supported solution rather than just an analysis of the problem?

Audience

How appropriately do you address your audience members, given their experiences and expectations? Will you catch their interest, and will they be able to follow your discussion?

Stance

Ask yourself one central question: where are you coming from in this draft? Consider whether your stance appropriately matches the stance you started out with, or whether your stance has legitimately evolved.

Organization

One way to check the organization of your draft is to outline it. After numbering the paragraphs, read through each one, jotting down its

---

FOR MULTILINGUAL WRITERS

Asking an Experienced Writer to Review Your Draft

One good way to make sure that your writing is easy to follow is to have someone else read it. You might ask someone who is experienced in the kind of writing you are working on to read over your draft and to point out any words or patterns that are unclear or ineffective.

main idea. Do the main ideas clearly relate to the thesis and to one another? Can you identify any confusing leaps from point to point? Have you left out any important points?

Genre and media

You decided to write in a particular genre, so think again about why you made that choice. Is writing in this genre the best way to achieve your purpose and reach your audience? Does the draft fulfill the requirements of the genre? Would any content in your draft be more effective presented in another medium—for example, as a print handout instead of a Power-Point slide? Should you consider "translating" your work into another medium (see Chapter 3)? Do you need to take any additional steps to make your work as effective as it can be in this medium?

Images and sound

Look closely at the images, audio, and video you have chosen to use. How do they contribute to your draft? Make sure that all visuals and media files are labeled with captions and sources, and remember to refer to visuals and media and to comment on their significance to the rest of your text. Would any information in your draft work better in visual than in verbal form?

EXERCISE 10.1

Take twenty to thirty minutes to look critically at the draft you prepared for Exercise 7.6. Reread it carefully, check to see how well the purpose is accomplished, and consider how appropriate the draft is for the audience. Then write a paragraph about how you would go about revising the draft.

10b   Get the most from peer review.

In addition to your own critical appraisal and that of your instructor (10c), you will probably want to get responses to your draft from friends, classmates, or colleagues. In a writing course, you may be asked to respond to the work of your peers as well as to seek responses from them.

EXERCISE 10.2

To prepare for a peer review, write a description of your purpose, rhetorical stance, and audience for your reviewer(s) to consider. For example, Emily Lesk might write, "I want to figure out why Coca-Cola seems so American and how the company achieves this effect. My audience is primarily college students like me, learning to

---

AT A GLANCE

Guidelines for Peer Response

- *Initial thoughts.* What are the main strengths and weaknesses of the draft? What might confuse readers? What is the most important thing the writer says in the draft? What will readers want to know more about?
- *Assignment.* Does the draft carry out the assignment?
- *Title and introduction.* Do the title and introduction tell what the draft is about and catch readers' interest? How else might the draft begin?
- *Thesis and purpose.* Paraphrase the thesis: *In this paper, the writer will. . . .* Does the draft fulfill that promise?
- *Audience.* How does the draft interest and appeal to its audience?
- *Rhetorical stance.* Where does the writer stand? What words indicate the stance?
- *Supporting points.* List the main points, and review them one by one. How well does each point support the thesis? Do any need more explanation? Do any seem confusing or boring?
- *Visuals and design.* Do visuals, if any, add to the key points? Is the design clear and effective?
- *Organization and flow.* Is the writing easy to follow? How effective are transitions within sentences, between sentences, and between paragraphs?
- *Conclusion.* Does the draft conclude memorably? Is there another way it might end?

FOR MULTILINGUAL WRITERS

Understanding Peer Review

If you are not used to giving or receiving criticisms directly, you may be uneasy with a classmate's challenges to your work. However, constructive criticism is appropriate to peer review. Your peers will also expect you to offer your questions, suggestions, and insights.

analyze their own cultures. I want to sound knowledgeable, and I want this essay to be fun and interesting to read." This type of summary statement can help your reviewers keep your goals in mind as they give you feedback.

Serving as a peer reviewer

One of the main goals of a peer reviewer is to help the writer see his or her draft differently. When you review a draft, you want to *show* the writer what does and doesn't work about particular aspects of the draft.

PEER REVIEW: Work with a Writer

Give your full attention to offering as much help as you can.

Ask...

What does the writer want you to **focus** on for this stage of the draft?

Can you restate the **main points** as you see them?

What **specific** suggestions do you think will **improve** the draft?

Make sure that the writer can move forward when you're finished.

Visually marking the draft can help the writer absorb at a glance the revisions you suggest.

REVIEWING A PRINT DRAFT

When working with a hard copy of a draft, write compliments in the left margin and critiques, questions, and suggestions in the right margin. As long as you explain what your symbols mean, you can also use boxes, circles, single and double underlining, highlighting, or other visual annotations as shorthand for what you have to say about the draft.

REVIEWING A COMPUTER DRAFT

If the draft is an electronic file, the reviewer should save the document in a peer-review folder under an easy-to-recognize name. It's wise to include the writer's name, the assignment, the number of the draft, and the reviewer's initials. For example, the reviewer Ann G. Smith might name the file for the first draft of Javier Jabari's first essay *jabari.essay1.d1.ags.*

The reviewer can then use the word-processing program to add comments, questions, and suggestions to the text. Most such programs have a TRACK CHANGES tool that can show changes to the document in a different color and a COMMENT function that allows you to type a note in the margin. If your word processor doesn't have a COMMENT function, you can comment in footnotes instead.

All-Powerful Coke

I don't drink Coke. Call me picky for disliking the soda's saccharine aftertaste.

Call me cheap for choosing a water fountain over a twleve-ounce aluminum can

that costs a dollar from a vending machine but only pennies to produce. Even call

me unpatriotic for rejecting the potable god that over the last century has come to

represent all the enjoyment and ease to be found in our American way of life. But

don't call me a hypocrite when I admit that I still identify with Coke and the Coca-

Cola culture.

I have a favorite T-shirt that says "Drink Coca-Cola Classic" in Hebrew. It's

Israel's standard tourist fare, like little nested dolls in Russia or painted horses in

Scandinavia, and before setting foot in the Promised Land three years ago I knew

where I could find one. The T-shirt shop in the central block of a Jerusalem shop-

ping center did offer other shirt designs ("Maccabee Beer" was a favorite), but

that Coca-Cola shirt was what drew in most of the dollar-carrying tourists. I waited

almost twenty minutes for mine, and I watched nearly everyone ahead of me say

"the Coke shirt" (and "thanks" in Hebrew).

At the time, I never asked why I wanted the shirt. I do know, though, that the

reason I wear it often, despite a hole in the right sleeve, has to do with its power

as a conversation piece. Few people notice it without asking something like, "Does

that say Coke?" I usually smile and nod. They mumble a compliment and we go our

separate ways. But rarely does anyone want to know what language the world's

most famous logo is written in. And why should they? Perhaps because Coca-Cola

is a cultural icon that shapes American identity.

Comment: I'm not sure your title says enough about what your essay will argue. NL

Comment: The opening sentence is a good attention-getter. Wonder what will come next? NL

Comment: The beginning seems pretty abrupt. BK

Comment: What does this mean?? Will other members of your audience know? BK

Comment: The style of repeating the phrase "call me" is good, but I don't think the first three "call me" statements have much to do with the rest of the paper. NL

Comment: It would be cool to show this. BK

Comment: Not sure you need all these details. Is any of it going to be important later? NL

Comment: one of what? a doll or horse? NL

Comment: Say it in Hebrew? BK

Comment: This transition works really well. I wasn't sure before about where this was going, but the beginning of the paragraph here starts to clue me in. NL

Comment: good detail! Lots of people can relate to a "conversation piece" shirt. NL

Comment: I like the question — but is your next sentence really the answer? NL

Comment: Is this the thesis? Kind of comes out of nowhere. BK

EXERCISE 10.3

Using the questions in the At a Glance box on p. 107 as a guide, analyze the draft you wrote for Exercise 7.6, trying to imagine it through a reviewer's eyes.

EXERCISE 10.4: THINKING VISUALLY

Analyze the "Peer Review: Work with a Writer" panel on p. 108. What does this image suggest about the characteristics of a peer reviewer? How well do those character- istics fit your understanding of what you should do when you review someone else's draft? Using words or images or both, create an analogy that explains your process of commenting on another writer's work.

Reviews of Emily Lesk's draft

On p. 109 are the first three paragraphs of Emily Lesk's draft, as reviewed electronically by two students, Beatrice Kim and Nastassia Lopez. (You'll find earlier appearances of Emily's work in 5g, 6d, and 7a.) Beatrice and Nastassia decided to use highlighting for particular purposes: green for material they found effective, yellow for language that seemed unclear, blue for material that could be expanded, and gray for material that could be deleted.

As this review shows, Nastassia and Bea agree on some of the major problems—and good points—in Emily's draft. The comments on the draft, however, reveal their different responses. You, too, will find that different readers do not always agree on what is effective or ineffective. In addition, you may find that you simply do not agree with their advice.

You can often proceed efficiently by looking first for areas of agreement (*everyone was confused by this sentence—I'd better review it*) or strong disagreement (*one person said my conclusion was "perfect," and someone else said it "didn't conclude"—better look carefully at that paragraph again*).

> ↪ bedfordstmartins.com/everydaywriter
> **Writing Resources > Working Online**

Getting help from peer reviewers

Remember that your reviewers should be acting as coaches, not judges, and that their job is to help you improve your essay as much as

PEER REVIEW: Work with Reviewers

Seek good advice about your draft.

Ask...

What issues do you want reviewers to focus on?

What do they think **works** and **doesn't work** in your draft?

Do you need more information to understand their suggestions?

Think about what reviewers want you to do next.

possible. Listen to and read their comments carefully. If you don't understand a particular suggestion, ask for clarification, examples, and so on. Remember, too, that reviewers are commenting on your writing, not on *you*, so be open and responsive to what they recommend. But you are the final authority on your essay; you will decide which suggestions to follow and which to disregard.

 bedfordstmartins.com/everydaywriter
Student Writing

10c Consult instructor comments.

Instructor comments on any work that you have done can help you identify mistakes, particularly ones that you make repeatedly, and can point you toward larger issues that prevent your writing from being as effective as it could be. Whether or not you will have an opportunity to revise a particular piece of writing, you should look closely at the comments from your instructor.

In responding to student writing, however, instructors sometimes use phrases or comments that are a kind of shorthand—comments that are perfectly clear to the instructor but may be less clear to the students reading them. The instructor comments in the following chart, culled from over a thousand first-year student essays, are among those that you may find most puzzling. Alongside each comment you'll find information intended to allow you to revise as your instructor recommends. If your paper includes a puzzling comment that is not listed here, be sure to ask your instructor what the comment means and how you can fix the problem.

Instructor Comment	Actions to Take in Response
thesis not clear	Make sure that you have a main point, and state it directly. The rest of the paper will need to support the main point, too—this problem cannot be corrected by adding a sentence or two.
trying to do too much covers too much ground	Focus your main point more narrowly (7a) so that you can explain your topic fully in a project of the assigned length. You may need to cut back on some material and then provide evidence and details to expand what remains.

continued

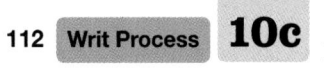

Instructor Comment	Actions to Take in Response
hard to follow *not logical* *incoherent* *jumps around* *parts not connected* *transition*	If overall organization is unclear, try mapping or outlining and rearranging your work. (7d) See if transitions and signals or additional explanation will solve the problem.
too general *vague*	Use concrete language and details, and make sure that you have something specific and interesting to say. (23c) If not, reconsider your topic.
underdeveloped *thin* *sparse*	Add examples and details, and be as specific as possible. (23c) You may need to do more research. (Chapters 15–17)
what about the opposition? *one-sided* *condescending* *overbearing*	Add information on why some people disagree with you, and represent their views fairly and completely before you refute them. Recognize that reasonable people may hold views that differ from yours. (14e)
repetitive *you've already said this*	Revise any parts of your writing that repeat an argument, point, word, or phrase; avoid using the same evidence over and over.
awk *awkward*	Ask a peer or your instructor for suggestions about revising awkward sentences. (Chapters 25–30)
syntax *awkward syntax* *convoluted*	Read the sentence aloud to identify the problem; revise or replace the sentence. (Chapters 25–30)
unclear	Find another way to explain what you mean; add any background information or examples that your audience may need to follow your reasoning.
tone too conversational *not an academic voice* *too informal* *colloquial*	Consider your audience and genre, and revise material that may suggest that you are not serious about the topic, audience, or assignment. (Chapter 23)
pompous *stilted* *stiff*	Make sure you understand the connotations of the words you use. Revise material that adds nothing to your meaning, no matter how impressive it sounds. (23a and b)

continued

Instructor Comment	Actions to Take in Response
set up quotation *integrate quotation*	Read the sentence containing the quotation aloud; revise it if it does not make sense as a sentence. Introduce every quotation with information about the source. Explain each quotation's importance to your work. (Chapter 18)
your words? *source?* *cite*	Mark all quotations clearly. Cite paraphrases and summaries of others' ideas. Give credit for help from others, and remember that you are responsible for your own work. (Chapters 17 and 18)
doc	Check the citations to be sure that you include all of the required information, that you punctuate correctly, and that you omit information not required by the documentation style. (Chapters 49–55)

10d Revise.

Approach comments from peer reviewers or from your instructor in several stages. First, read straight through the comments. Take a few minutes to digest the feedback and get some distance from your work. Then make a revision plan—as elaborate or as simple as you want—that prioritizes the changes needed in your next draft.

REVISION: Read All Comments Carefully

Analyze feedback from your instructor and other readers.

Ask...

What additional questions do you have about the feedback?

Which comments are most important and useful?

Which comments will point you toward the most improved next draft?

Remember: how you respond to suggestions is up to you.

If you have comments from more than one reviewer, you may want to begin by making two lists: (1) areas in which reviewers agree on needed changes, and (2) areas in which they disagree. You will then have to make choices about which advice to heed and which to ignore from both lists. Next, rank the suggestions you've chosen to address.

Focus on comments about your purpose, audience, stance, thesis, and support. Leave any changes to sentences, words, punctuation, and format for later in the process; your revision of bigger-picture issues comes first.

Prepare a file for your revised draft. Use your previous draft as a starting point, renaming it to indicate that it is a revision. (For example, Javier Jabari might rename his file *jabari essay1 d2*, using his name, assignment number, and draft number.)

In the new file, make the changes you identified in your revision plan. Be prepared to revise heavily, if necessary; if comments suggest that your thesis isn't working, for example, you may need to change the topic or the entire direction of your text. Heavy revision is not a sign that there's something wrong with your writing; on the contrary, major revision is a common feature of serious, goal-oriented writing.

Once you are satisfied that your revisions adequately address major concerns, make corrections to sentences, words, and punctuation.

Thesis

Make sure that your thesis states the topic clearly and comments on what is particularly significant about the topic (7b). In addition, ask yourself

REVISION: Plan Your Next Draft

Make big-picture changes.

Ask...

Do you need to rethink your *purpose* or *audience*?

How could you improve your *thesis* or *organization*?

What other *support* do you need?

Keep working until you have a coherent draft.

> **TALKING THE TALK**
>
> ### Revision
>
> "I thought I had revised my assignment, but my instructor said I'd just corrected the typos." It's always a good idea to clarify what *revision* means with a particular instructor. Generally, though, when a writing teacher asks for a revision, minor corrections will not be enough. Plan to review your entire draft, and be prepared to make major changes if necessary. Look for sentence-level errors and typos later, during the editing stage, since these may disappear or change as you revise.

whether the thesis is narrowed and focused enough to be thoroughly proven. If not, take time now to refine or limit your thesis further.

When you revise your thesis, remember also to revise the rest of the draft accordingly.

EXERCISE 10.5

After rereading the draft you wrote for Exercise 7.6, evaluate the revised working thesis you produced for Exercise 7.2. Then evaluate its support in the draft. Identify points that need further support, and list those things you must do to provide that support.

Support

Make sure that each paragraph relates to or supports the thesis and that each paragraph has sufficient detail to support the point it is making. Eliminate unnecessary material, and identify sections that need further details or examples.

Organization

Should any sections or paragraphs be moved to clarify your point or support your thesis more logically? Are there any paragraphs or parts of paragraphs that don't fit with the essay now or that are unnecessary? Look for confusing leaps or omissions, and identify places where transitions would make the writing easier to follow.

Title, introduction, and conclusion

Does the title give information and draw readers in? Does the introduction attract their interest and present the topic in a way that makes them want to keep reading? Does the conclusion leave readers satisfied? Because readers notice beginnings and endings more than other parts of a piece of writing, pay special attention to how you introduce and conclude your work.

Visuals, media, and design

As you check what you've written about your topic, you also need to take a close look at the way your text looks and works. Do your visuals, audio, and video (if any) help you make your points? How can you make this content more effective? Do you use design effectively for your genre and medium? Is your text readable and inviting?

EXERCISE 10.6: THINKING VISUALLY

Analyze the "Peer Review: Work with Reviewers" panel on p. 110. What does this image suggest about your role in dealing with peer reviewers? How well do those characteristics fit your understanding of what you should do when you work with a reviewer of your draft? Using words or images or both, create an analogy that explains your process of accepting comments on your work.

EXERCISE 10.7

Revise the draft you wrote for Exercise 7.6.

EXERCISE 10.8: THINKING VISUALLY

Look at the "Revision" panels on pp. 113–14. How does thinking of your writing as being "under construction" before and during the revision process affect or change your perception of revision? Write a few sentences or sketch an image explaining how close to finished your draft from Exercise 7.6 was before you began to revise.

EXERCISE 10.9: THINKING CRITICALLY

Answer the following questions about your reviewing and revising process.

1. How did you begin reviewing your draft?
2. What kinds of comments on or responses to your draft did you have? How helpful were they, and why?
3. How long did revising take? How many drafts did you produce?
4. What kinds of changes did you tend to make? in organization, paragraphs, sentence structure, wording, adding or deleting information? in the use of visuals?
5. What gave you the most trouble as you were revising?
6. What pleased you most? What is your very favorite sentence or passage in the draft, and why?
7. What would you most like to change about your process of revising, and how do you plan to go about doing so?

Editing and Reflecting **11**

Whether you are writing a wedding invitation, an email to a client, or a history essay, make time to edit and proofread what you write. Editing involves fine-tuning the details of sentence structure, grammar, usage, punctuation, and spelling. Finally, careful proofreading aims at a perfect copy. For important writing, reflecting on how you accomplished the task can prepare you to achieve future writing goals.

11a Edit.

Once you have revised a draft for content and organization, look closely at your sentences and words. Turning a "blah" sentence into a memorable one—or finding exactly the right word to express a thought—can result in writing that is really worth reading. As with life, variety is the spice of sentences. You can add variety to your sentences by looking closely at their length, structure, and opening patterns.

EDITING: Polish Your Draft

Don't forget the details.

Ask...

What does each **sentence** contribute to your purpose?

How can you choose **words** more effectively?

How can you improve your **tone** or **style**?

Follow appropriate conventions for your genre and audience.

Sentence length

Too many short sentences, especially one following another, can sound like a series of blasts on a car horn, whereas a steady stream of long sentences may tire or confuse readers. Most writers aim for some variety in length, breaking up a series of fairly long sentences with a very brief one.

In examining the following paragraph from her essay, Emily Lesk discovered that the sentences were all fairly long. In editing, she decided to shorten the second sentence, thereby offering a shorter sentence between two long ones.

In other words, Coca-Cola has hammered itself into our perceptions — both

conscious and subconscious — of an American cultural identity by equating

As

itself with media that define American culture. ~~When~~ the omnipresent ~~general~~

gave way to

magazine ~~that marked the earlier part of the century fell by the wayside under~~

~~television's power,~~ Coke was there from the beginning. In its 1996 recap of

the previous fifty years in industry history, the publication *Beverage Industry*

cites Coca-Cola as a frontrunner in the very first form of television

advertising: sponsorship of entire programs such as, in the case of Coke, *The*

Bob Dixon Show and *The Adventures of Kit Carson*.

Sentence openings

Opening sentence after sentence in the same way results in a jerky, abrupt, or choppy rhythm. You can vary sentence openings by beginning with a dependent clause, a phrase, an adverb, a conjunctive adverb, or a coordinating conjunction (30b). Another paragraph in Emily Lesk's essay tells the story of how she got her Coke T-shirt in Israel. Before she revised, every sentence in the paragraph opened with the subject, so Emily decided to delete some examples and vary her sentence openings. The final version (which also appears in 5g) is a dramatic and easy-to-read paragraph.

~~I have a favorite T-shirt that says "Drink Coca-Cola Classic" in Hebrew.~~ It's

~~Israel's standard tourist fare, like little nested dolls in Russia or painted horses in~~

Even　　　　　　　　　　*Israel*

~~Scandinavia, and~~ before setting foot in the ~~Promised Land~~ three years ago, I

exactly   *the Coke shirt.*   *'s Ben Yehuda Street*
knew where I could find it. The shop in the central block of a Jerusalem

~~shopping center~~ did offer other shirt designs,("Macabee Beer" ~~was a favorite),~~

but ~~that Coca-Cola shirt~~ was what drew in most of the dollar-carrying tourists.

While waiting   *my shirt,*
~~I waited~~ almost twenty minutes for ~~mine, and~~ I watched nearly everyone

todah rabah [thank you very much]."
ahead of me say "the Coke shirt," ~~(and "thanks" in Hebrew).~~

the one with a bright white "Drink Coca-Cola Classic"
written in Hebrew cursive across the chest

Opening with it and there

As you go over the opening sentences of your draft, look especially at those beginning with *it* or *there*. Sometimes these words can create a special emphasis, as in *It was a dark and stormy night*. But they can also appear too often. Another, more subtle problem with these openings is that they may be used to avoid taking responsibility for a statement. The following sentence can be improved by editing:

The university must
▶ ~~It is necessary~~ to raise student fees.

Tone

Tone refers to the attitude that a writer's language conveys toward the topic and the audience. In examining the tone of your draft, think about the nature of the topic, your own attitude toward it, and that of your intended audience. Does your language create the tone you want to achieve (humorous, serious, impassioned, and so on), and is that tone an appropriate one, given your audience and topic?

Word choice

Word choice—or diction—offers writers an opportunity to put their personal stamp on a piece of writing. Becoming aware of the kinds of words you use should help you get the most mileage out of each word. Check for connotations, or associations, of words and make sure you consider how any use of slang, jargon, or emotional language may affect your audience (see 23a–b).

Spell checkers

While these software tools won't catch every spelling error or identify all problems of style, they can be very useful. Most professional writers use their spell checkers religiously. Remember, however, that spell checkers are limited; they don't recognize most proper names, foreign words, or specialized language, and they do not recognize homonym errors (misspelling *there* as *their*, for example). (See 23e.)

Document design

Before you produce a copy for final proofreading, reconsider one last time the format and the "look" you want your document to have. This is one last opportunity to think carefully about the visual appearance of your final draft. (For more on document design, see Chapter 9. For more on the design conventions of different disciplines, see Chapters 61–65.)

AT A GLANCE

Word Choice

- Are the nouns primarily abstract and general or *concrete* and *specific*? Too many abstract and general nouns can result in boring prose.
- Are there too many nouns in relation to the number of verbs? This sentence is heavy and boring: *The effect of the overuse of nouns in writing is the placement of strain on the verbs.* Instead, say this: *Overusing nouns places a strain on the verbs.*
- How many verbs are forms of *be* — *be, am, is, are, was, were, being, been*? If *be* verbs account for more than about a third of your total verbs, you are probably overusing them.
- Are verbs *active* wherever possible? Passive verbs are harder to read and remember than active ones. Although the passive voice has many uses, your writing will gain strength and energy if you use active verbs.
- Are your words *appropriate*? Check to be sure they are not too fancy — or too casual.

Proofreading the final draft

Take time for one last, careful proofreading, which means reading to correct any typographical errors or other inconsistencies in spelling and punctuation. To proofread most effectively, read through the copy aloud, making sure that you've used punctuation marks correctly and consistently, that all sentences are complete (unless you've used intentional fragments or run-ons for special effects)—and that no words are missing. Then go through the copy again, this time reading backward so that you can focus on each individual word and its spelling.

EXERCISE 11.1

Find a paragraph in your own writing that lacks variety in sentence length, sentence openings, or sentence structure. Then write a revised version.

EXERCISE 11.2: THINKING VISUALLY

Review the "Revision" panels on pp. 113–14 and look at the "Editing" panel on p. 117. What do these images suggest about the relationship between revising and editing? Write a paragraph or draw a sketch explaining how you know when your writing is ready for the editing stage.

EXERCISE 11.3

Using several essays you have written, establish your own editing checklist.

EXERCISE 11.4

Edit and proofread the draft you wrote for Exercise 7.6.

A student's revised draft

Following are the first three paragraphs from Emily Lesk's edited and proofread draft that she submitted to her instructor. Compare these paragraphs with those from her reviewed draft in 10b.

Student Writer

Emily Lesk

Emily Lesk
Professor Arráez
Electric Rhetoric
November 15, 2011

Red, White, and Everywhere

America, I have a confession to make: I don't drink Coke. But don't call me a hypocrite just because I am still the proud owner of a bright red shirt that advertises it. Just call me an American.

Even before setting foot in Israel three years ago, I knew **Student Writing** exactly where I could find the Coke shirt. The shop in the central block of Jerusalem's Ben Yehuda Street did offer other shirt designs, but the one with a bright white "Drink Coca-Cola Classic" written in Hebrew cursive across the chest was what drew in most of the dollar-carrying tourists. While waiting almost twenty minutes for my shirt (depicted in Fig. 1), I watched nearly everyone ahead of me say "the Coke shirt, *todah rabah* [thank you very much]."

Fig. 1. Hebrew Coca-Cola T-shirt.
Personal photograph.

At the time, I never thought it strange that I wanted one, too. After having absorbed sixteen years of Coca-Cola propaganda through everything from NBC's Saturday morning cartoon lineup to the concession stand at Camden Yards (the Baltimore Orioles' ballpark), I associated the shirt with singing along to the "Just for the Taste of It" jingle and with America's favorite pastime, not with a brown fizzy beverage I refused to consume. When I later realized the immensity of Coke's corporate power, I felt somewhat manipulated, but that didn't stop me from wearing the shirt. I still don it often, despite the growing hole in the right sleeve, because of its power as a conversation piece. Few Americans notice it without asking something like "Does that say Coke?" I usually smile and nod. Then they mumble a one-word compliment, and we go our separate ways. But rarely do they want to know what language the internationally recognized logo is written in. And why should they? They are interested in what they can relate to as Americans: a familiar red-and-white logo, not a foreign language. Through nearly a century of brilliant advertising strategies, the Coca-Cola Company has given Americans not only a thirst-quenching beverage but a cultural icon that we have come to claim as our own.

 bedfordstmartins.com/everydaywriter
Student Writing

11b   Reflect.

Research demonstrates a connection between careful reflection and learning: thinking back on what you've learned and assessing it help make that learning stick. As a result, first-year college writing courses are increasingly encouraging students to take time for such reflection. Whether or not your instructor asks you to write a formal reflection, whenever you finish a major piece of writing or a writing course, you should make time to think back over the experience and see what lessons you can learn from it.

Reflecting on your development as a writer

Here are some questions to get you started reflecting productively on your writing:

- What lessons have you learned from writing — from an individual piece of writing or from an entire writing course?
- From what you have learned, what can you apply to the work you will do in other classes?
- What about your writing do you feel most confident about — and why? When did you begin to develop this confidence?
- What about your writing do you find needs additional work, and what plans do you have for improving?
- What confusions did you have while writing, and what did you do to resolve them?
- What major questions do you still have about writing or about an individual piece of writing?
- How has writing helped to clarify your thinking, extend your knowledge, or deepen your understanding?
- Identify a favorite passage of your writing, and then try to articulate what about it pleases you. Can you apply what you learn from this analysis to other writing situations?
- How would you describe your development as a writer?

Portfolios

You may find it useful — or you may be required — to select samples for inclusion in a print or online portfolio of your written work. In preparing a portfolio, use these tips:

- *Consider your purpose and audience.* Do you want to fulfill course requirements for an instructor, show work to a prospective employer, keep a record of what you've done for personal reasons, or something else? Answering these questions will help you decide what to include in the portfolio and whether it should be in print or electronic form.
- *Based on the portfolio's purpose, decide on the number of entries.* You may decide to include a wide range of materials — from essays, problem sets, and photos to Web texts, multimedia presentations, a résumé, or anything else that is relevant — if readers can select only the pieces that interest them. For a portfolio that will be read from beginning to end, however, you should limit yourself to five to seven examples of your writing. You might include an academic essay that argues a claim, a personal essay, a brief report, writing

based on research, significant correspondence, timed writing, or other work that you think shows your strengths as a writer.

- *Consider organization.* What arrangement—in chronological order, by genre, by topic—will make most sense to readers?
- *Think carefully about layout and design.* Will you include a menu, a table of contents, or appendices? How will you use color, font and type size, and other elements of design to enhance your portfolio (see Chapter 9)? Remember to label and date each piece of writing in the portfolio to help readers follow along easily. For print portfolios, number pages in consecutive order.
- *Edit and proofread* each piece in your portfolio and the reflective statement. Ask for responses from peers or an instructor.

Reflective statements

One of the most common writing assignments today is a reflective statement—often in the form of a letter, memo, or home page—that explains and analyzes the work a student has done in a writing course.

To create a reflective statement, think carefully about the impression it should give, and make sure your tone and style set the stage appropriately. Reflect on the strengths and weaknesses of your writing, using specific examples to provide evidence for each point you make. What are the most important things you have learned about writing—and about yourself as a writer—during the course?

If the reflective statement introduces your portfolio, follow your instructor's guidelines carefully. Unless asked to do otherwise, describe the portfolio's contents and explain why you have chosen each piece.

STUDENT REFLECTIVE STATEMENT

Here is a shortened version of the cover letter that James Kung wrote to accompany his first-year writing portfolio.

Student Writer

James Kung

December 6, 2011

Dear Professor Ashdown:

"Writing is difficult and takes a long time." This simple yet powerful statement has been uttered so many times in our class that it has essentially become our motto. During this class, my persuasive writing skills have improved dramatically, thanks to many hours spent writing, revising, polishing, and thinking about my topic. The various drafts, revisions, and other materials in my portfolio show this improvement.

I entered this first-quarter Writing and Rhetoric class with both strengths and weaknesses. I have always written fairly well-organized essays. However, despite this strength, I struggled throughout the term to narrow and define the various aspects of my research-based argument.

Student Writing

The first aspect of my essay that I had trouble narrowing and defining was my major claim, or my thesis statement. In my "Proposal for Research-Based Argument," I proposed to argue about the case of Wen Ho Lee, the Los Alamos scientist accused of copying restricted government documents. I stated, "The Wen Ho Lee incident deals with the persecution of not only one man, but of a whole ethnic group." You commented that the statement was a "sweeping claim" that would be "hard to support."

I spent weeks trying to rework that claim. Finally, as seen in my "Writer's Notebook 10/16/11," I realized that I had chosen the Lee case because of my belief that the political inactivity of Asian Americans contributed to the case against Lee. Therefore, I decided to focus on this issue in my thesis. Later I once again revised my claim, stating that the political inactivity did not cause but rather contributed to racial profiling in the Wen Ho Lee case.

I also had trouble defining my audience. I briefly alluded to the fact that my audience was a "typical American reader." However, I later decided to address my paper to an Asian American audience for two reasons. First, it would establish a greater ethos for myself as a Chinese American. Second, it would enable me to target the people the Wen Ho Lee case most directly affects: Asian Americans. As a result, in my final research-based argument, I was much more sensitive to the needs and concerns of my audience, and my audience trusted me more.

I hope to continue to improve my writing of research-based arguments.

Sincerely,

James Kung

James Kung

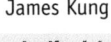

Critical Thinking and Argument

To repeat what others have said requires
education; to challenge it requires brains.

— MARY PETTIBONE POOLE

Critical Thinking and Argument

12 **Critical Reading** *129*
  a Preview the text *129*
  b Read and annotate *131*
  c Summarize the main ideas *135*
  d Analyze the text *136*
  e STUDENT CRITICAL READING OF A TEXT (EXCERPT) *140*

13 **Analyzing Arguments** *143*
  a Think critically about argument *144*
  b Recognize cultural contexts *145*
  c Identify an argument's basic appeals *145*
  d Analyze the elements of argument *148*
  e Think critically about fallacies *151*
  f STUDENT RHETORICAL ANALYSIS *157*

14 **Constructing Arguments** *161*
  a Understand what counts as argument *161*
  b Make a claim and formulate a working thesis *164*
  c Examine your assumptions *164*
  d Shape your appeal to your audience *165*
  e Establish credibility through ethical appeals *165*
  f Use effective logical appeals *167*
  g Use appropriate emotional appeals *172*
  h Consult sources *175*
  i Organize your argument *175*
  j Consider design issues *177*
  k STUDENT ARGUMENT ESSAY *178*

Critical Thinking and
Argument 127–184

For visual analysis Look carefully at the illustration on the front of this tab. What do you think this image suggests about critical thinking and argument?

Critical Reading **12**

Film critic Roger Ebert writes in a notebook as he watches movies, tearing out the pages as he fills them, until he "looks as though he's sitting on top of a cloud of paper," as an *Esquire* profile observed. Reading critically means questioning and commenting thoughtfully on a text—whether an assignment for a psychology class, a graphic novel, a business email, or a YouTube video. Any method you use to keep track of your questions and make yourself concentrate on a text can help you become a better critical reader.

12a Preview the text.

Find out all you can about a text before beginning to look closely at it, considering its context, author, subject, genre, and design.

PREVIEWING THE CONTEXT

- Where have you encountered the work? Are you encountering it in its original context? For example, an essay in a collection of readings may have been previously published in a magazine; a speech you watch on YouTube may have been delivered to a live or televised audience; a painting on a museum wall may have been created for a wealthy patron in a distant country centuries earlier.

- What can you infer from the original or current context of the work about its intended audience and purpose?

LEARNING ABOUT THE AUTHOR OR CREATOR

- What information can you find about the author or creator of the text?

- What purpose, expertise, and possible agenda might you expect this person to have? Where do you think the author or creator is coming from in this text?

CRITICAL READING: Preview

What do you expect to happen in this text?

Ask...

What does the *title* tell you? Who *created* this work?

When, where, and how are you *encountering* the text?

How do *genre, media, and design* affect your expectations?

Prepare to engage the text.

PREVIEWING THE SUBJECT

- What do you know about the subject of the text?
- What opinions do you have about the subject, and on what are your opinions based?
- What would you like to learn about the subject?
- What do you expect the main point to be? Why?

CONSIDERING THE TITLE, MEDIUM, GENRE, AND DESIGN

- What does the title (or caption or other heading) indicate?
- What do you know about the medium (or media) in which the work appears? Is it a text on the Web, a printed advertising brochure, a speech stored in iTunes, an animated cartoon on television, or some combination of media? What role does the medium play in achieving the purpose and connecting to the audience?
- What is the genre of the text — and what can it help illuminate about the intended audience or purpose? Why might the authors or creators have chosen this genre?
- How is the text presented? What do you notice about its formatting, use of color, visuals or illustrations, overall design, general appearance, and other design features?

> **TALKING THE TALK**
>
> ## Critical Thinking
>
> "Are criticizing and thinking critically the same thing?" *Criticize* can sometimes mean "find fault with," and you certainly don't have to be relentlessly negative to think critically. Instead, critical thinking means, first and foremost, asking good questions — and not simply accepting what you see at face value. By asking not only what words and images mean, but also how meaning gets across, critical thinkers consider why a text makes a particular claim, what writers may be leaving out or ignoring, and how to tell whether evidence is accurate and believable. If you're considering questions like these, then you're thinking critically.

Sample preview of an assigned text

A student in a first-year composition class who had been asked to read and analyze Abraham Lincoln's Gettysburg Address made preview notes, a few of which are excerpted here.

> President Lincoln delivered the speech at a ceremony dedicating a national cemetery for Civil War soldiers. Crowds of people gathered in a field near Gettysburg, Pennsylvania, on November 19, 1863, to listen to him and other speakers. In July of that year, a Civil War battle that ended with 7,500 soldiers killed had taken place near where Lincoln spoke.
>
> My textbook has the most famous version of the speech — but nobody knows for sure exactly what Lincoln said 150 years ago. There's obviously no audio recording of him giving the speech! Newspapers at the time reported what listeners heard, but he didn't write the speech out until later.
>
> Lincoln gave this speech in the middle of the war, dedicating a national cemetery, so it must have been a pretty solemn occasion. He probably wanted his audience to think about why the war was worth fighting. He probably also thought that some of the dead soldiers' families might be there listening — as well as people who had seen the battle or its aftermath. Did he think about the possibility that future generations would read and think about this speech? As the leader of the Union, he was probably very interested in showing why the United States needed to stay together.

EXERCISE 12.1

Following the guidelines in 12a, preview a text you have been assigned to read.

12b Read and annotate.

As you read a text for the first time, mark it up (if the medium allows you to do so) or take notes. Consider the text's content, author, intended audience, and genre and design.

CRITICAL READING: Read Carefully

What do you find out by going through the text from start to finish?

Get everything you can from your first reading.

Ask...

How does the text fit with your expectations?

What are the major points in the text? How are they supported?

How well do you understand the content?

READING FOR CONTENT

- What do you find confusing or unclear about the text? Where can you look for explanations or more information? Do you need background information in order to understand fully?
- What key terms and ideas — or key patterns — do you see? What key images stick in your mind?
- What sources or other works does this text cite, refer to, or allude to?
- How does the content fit with what you already know?
- Which points do you agree with? Which do you disagree with? Why?

READING FOR AUTHOR/CREATOR AND AUDIENCE

- Do the authors or creators present themselves as you anticipated in your preview?
- For what audience was this text created? Are you part of its intended audience?
- What underlying assumptions can you identify in the text?
- Are the medium and genre appropriate for the topic, audience, and purpose?

READING FOR DESIGN, COMPOSITION, AND STYLE

- Is the design appropriate for the subject and genre?
- Does the composition serve a purpose — for instance, does the layout help you see what is more and less important in the text?
- Do words, images, sound, and other media work together well?
- How would you describe the style of the text? What contributes to this impression — word choice? references to research or popular culture? formatting? color? something else?

Sample annotation of an assigned text

After previewing the context, author, subject, and other aspects of the following article from the online magazine *Good*, a student assigned to write about the article annotated the text as shown.

Is the Internet Warping Our Brains? **❶**
CORD JEFFERSON, SENIOR EDITOR, *GOOD*

New research from Columbia University psychologist Betsy Sparrow **❷** suggests that Google, your favorite search engine turned email host turned social network, might actually be making you less likely to absorb information. Sparrow's study, "Google Effects on Memory: Cognitive Consequences of Having Information at Our Fingertips," found that people who were confident they could use the internet to access some bit of information in the future were less likely to recall that information themselves. **❸** However, they were more likely to recall how to go about accessing the information if necessary. Sparrow calls it "outsourcing data," letting the internet take care of some stuff so we can save our brains for things that can't be Googled, like parents' birthdays and coworkers' names. **❹**

Is this a bad thing? **❺** Not necessarily, says Sparrow. For instance, for years people in the educational community have known that rote learning — that is, forcing children to memorize facts and dates — is a poor way to educate. **❻** If that's the case, allowing computers to do some of the memorizing for us might be a way to focus more on the more philosophical aspects of learning. **❼**

"Perhaps **❽** those who teach in any context, be they college professors, doctors or business leaders, will become increasingly focused on imparting greater understanding of ideas and ways of thinking, and less focused on memorization," Sparrow told *Time*.

Of course, while you might think that this research suggests people on the internet are using less of their brains than those not online, you'd be wrong. Back in 2008, the neuroscientist Gary Small discovered the difference in brain activity between a person reading a book and a person searching for information on Google. According to Small, the person searching the internet was using a lot more of their mind than the person simply reading a book. **9** Like Sparrow, Small says he's not willing to say if the difference is bad or good, just that our minds react entirely differently when stimulated by the internet as opposed to other forms of media. **10**

[Video: Gary Small discusses "Your Brain on Google" (2:43)] **11**

1 This sounds like a leading question to me — makes me think the author's answer must be "yes."

2 Look for more information on this psychologist and her research.

3 How did the research show this? What were the participants asked to do?

4 Haven't we done this in other ways already — like taking notes so we don't have to remember?

5 Interesting question! Not sure how I would answer.

6 Check out this link to see what the arguments are against "rote learning."

7 This sounds right. But are we really going to become more philosophical if we don't have to remember things? What if we just get more distracted by trivia?

8 Or perhaps not! This seems pretty optimistic.

9 Wow! Seems like it should be a good thing to use more of our brain. But what does it really mean?

10 So the researchers here aren't ready to draw conclusions about what the differences mean for us. (Not that people would stop Googling if it turned out to be a bad thing.)

11 Watch a little of this to see if it might have important information to add.

EXERCISE 12.2

Following is the full text of Abraham Lincoln's Gettysburg Address. Using the guidelines in 12b, read and annotate Lincoln's speech.

Four score and seven years ago our fathers brought forth on this continent a new nation, conceived in Liberty, and dedicated to the proposition that all men are created equal.

Now we are engaged in a great civil war, testing whether that nation, or any nation so conceived and so dedicated, can long endure. We are met on a great battle-field of that war. We have come to dedicate a portion of that field, as a final resting place for those who here gave their lives that that nation might live. It is altogether fitting and proper that we should do this.

But, in a larger sense, we can not dedicate — we can not consecrate — we can not hallow — this ground. The brave men, living and dead, who struggled here, have consecrated it, far above our poor power to add or detract. The world will little note, nor long remember what we say here, but it can never forget what they did here. It is for us the living, rather, to be dedicated here to the unfinished work which they who fought here have thus far so nobly advanced. It is rather for us to be here dedicated to the great task remaining before us — that from these honored dead we take increased devotion to that cause for which they gave the last full measure of devotion — that we here highly resolve that these dead shall not have died in vain — that this nation, under God, shall have a new birth of freedom — and that government of the people, by the people, for the people, shall not perish from the earth. **— ABRAHAM LINCOLN,** *Gettysburg Address*

12c Summarize the main ideas.

When you feel that you have read and thoroughly understood the text, try to summarize the contents in your own words. A summary *briefly* captures the main ideas of a text and omits information that is less important. Try to identify the key points in the text, find the essential evidence supporting those points, and explain the contents concisely and fairly, so that a reader unfamiliar with the original can make sense of it all. Deciding what to leave out can make summarizing a tricky task—but mastering this skill can serve you well in all the reading you do in your academic, professional, and civic life. To test your understanding—and to avoid unintentional plagiarism—it's wise to put the text aside while you write your summary. (For more information on writing a summary, see 17f.)

CRITICAL READING: Summarize

What was that all about?

Make sure you understood the main points of the text.

Ask...

What is the overall **message** of the text?

Can you summarize it in your own words?

Would others get a **fair** and **accurate** impression from your summary?

Sample summary of an assigned text

A student summarized the article "Is the Internet Warping Our Brains?" (12b) as shown below.

> The writer discusses two recent studies, one from 2011 and one from
> 2008, looking at how Internet use affects a person's mind. The 2011 study,
> by psychologist Betsy Sparrow, showed that if a person expects to be able to
> use Google to get information, then he or she is less likely to remember that
> information. Sparrow doesn't see this result as necessarily negative. She hopes
> that the widespread use of Google might lead educators to focus on "imparting
> greater understanding of ideas" rather than on "rote learning," which the writer
> says has been shown to be a bad way to teach students. (A link explains more
> about "rote learning.") The 2008 study, by neuroscientist Gary Small, shows that
> using the Internet actually activates more of a person's brain than reading a
> book. Like Sparrow, Small didn't draw conclusions about whether Internet use is
> therefore better or worse for a person's mind. It's just different.

12d Analyze the text.

When you feel that you understand the meaning of the text, move on to your analysis. You may want to begin the process by asking additional questions about the text.

ANALYZING IDEAS AND EXAMPLES

- What are the main points in this text? Are they implied or explicitly stated?
- Which points do you agree with? Which do you disagree with? Why?
- Does anything in the text surprise you? Why, or why not?
- What kind of examples does the text use? What other kinds of evidence does the text offer to back up the main points? Can you think of other examples or evidence that should have been included?
- Are viewpoints other than those of the author or creator included and treated fairly?
- How trustworthy are the sources the text cites or refers to?
- What assumptions does the text make? Are those assumptions valid? Why, or why not?

CRITICAL READING: Analyze

How does the text get its meaning across?

Assess your overall impression.

Ask...

How does the text accomplish its purposes?

Are the text and its creator credible? Are their assumptions valid?

How effective are the evidence, support, and design?

Visual Texts

"How can an image be a text?" In its traditional sense, a *text* involves words on paper. But we spend at least as much time reading and analyzing images — including moving images — as we spend on printed words. So it makes sense to broaden the definition of "text" to include anything that sends a message. That's why images, ads, videos, films, and the like are often called *visual texts.*

ANALYZING FOR OVERALL IMPRESSION

- Do the authors or creators achieve their purpose? Why, or why not?
- What intrigues, puzzles, or irritates you about the text? Why?
- What else would you like to know?

Sample analysis of a text

Following is a Pulitzer Prize–winning photograph (by Craig F. Walker of the *Denver Post*) and its caption. This image appeared as part of a series documenting the experiences of a Colorado teenager, Ian Fisher, who joined the U.S. Army to fight in Iraq.

During a weekend home from his first assignment at Fort Carson, Colorado, Ian walked through a Denver-area mall with his new girlfriend, Kayla Spitzlberger, on December 15, 2007, and asked whether she wanted to go ring shopping. She was excited, but working out the financing made him nervous. They picked out the engagement ring in about five minutes, but Ian wouldn't officially propose until Christmas Day in front of her family. The couple had met in freshman math class but never really dated until now. She wrote to him during basic training and decided to give Ian a chance. The engagement would end before Valentine's Day.

A student's analysis of this photograph made the following points:

The couple are in the center of the photo—and at the center of our attention. But at this moment of choosing an engagement ring, they do not look "engaged" with each other. Kayla looks excited but uncertain, as if she knows that Ian feels doubts, but she hopes he will change his mind. She is looking right at him, with her body leaning toward him but her head leaning away: she looks very tentative. Ian is looking away from Kayla, and the expression on his face suggests that he's already having second thoughts about the expense of the ring (we see his wallet on the counter by his elbow) and perhaps even about asking Kayla to marry him. The accompanying caption helps us interpret the image, telling us about the couple's brief history together and noting that the engagement will last less than two months after this moment. But the message comes through pretty clearly without words.

Ian and Kayla look as if they're trying on roles in this photograph. She looks ready to take the plunge, and he is resisting. These attitudes conform to stereotypical gender roles for a man and woman considering marriage (or going shopping, for that matter). The woman is expected to want the marriage and the ring; the man knows that he shouldn't show too much enthusiasm about weddings and shopping. It's hard for the reader to tell whether Ian and Kayla really feel that they are making good or careful choices for their situation at this moment or whether they're just doing what they think they're supposed to do under the circumstances.

The reader also can't tell how the presence of the photographer, Craig F. Walker, affected the couple's actions. The photo is part of a series of images documenting Ian Fisher's life after joining the military, so Walker had probably spent a lot of time with Ian before this photo was taken. Did Ian want to give a particular impression of himself on this day? Were he and Kayla trying on "adult" roles in this situation? Were they feeling pressure to produce a memorable moment for the camera? And what was Walker thinking when he accompanied them to the mall and took this photograph? Did he foresee the end of their engagement when he captured this revealing moment? What was his agenda?

EXERCISE 12.3

Write a two- to three-paragraph analysis of a text you have read or seen.

EXERCISE 12.4: THINKING VISUALLY

Look at the four "Critical Reading" panels on pp. 130–37 and think about the last film you watched for fun. What did you know about it before you watched it? What did you feel and learn as you watched? What have you told others about the film, both in terms of summarizing the story and of analyzing what the experience meant to you? Write a paragraph or create a brief slide show describing how you might use the same techniques — previewing, reading, summarizing, and analyzing — the next time you are asked to read a written-word text.

EXERCISE 12.5: THINKING CRITICALLY

Choose a text you have been assigned to read for a class. Read it over carefully, annotating the material, and then write a one- or two-paragraph summary of the contents. Then analyze your summary. Did your annotations help you summarize? Why, or why not? Does your summary interpret the material or aim for an objective stance? What does your summary omit from the original material, and how did you decide what to leave out?

12e Student critical reading of a text (excerpt)

Student Writer

Shuqiao Song

Following are excerpts from a student essay by Shuqiao Song based on her critical reading of Alison Bechdel's graphic memoir *Fun Home: A Family Tragicomic*. Shuqiao's critical reading involved looking closely at the words, at the images, and at how the words and images together create a complex story.

For information on Shuqiao Song's PowerPoint presentation of this essay, see 3c.

bedfordstmartins.com/everydaywriter
Student Writing

Shuqiao Song
Dr. Andrea Lunsford
English 87N
13 March 2012

Residents of a Dys*FUN*ctional *HOME*

In a 2009 online interview, comic artist Alison Bechdel remarked, "I love words, and I love pictures. But especially, I love them together—in a mystical way that I can't even explain" ("Stuck"). Indeed, in her graphic novel memoir, *Fun Home: A Family Tragicomic,* text and image work together in a mystical way: text *and* image. But using both image and text results not in a simple summation but in a strange relationship—as strange as the relationship between Alison Bechdel and her father. These strange pairings have an alluring quality that makes Bechdel's *Fun Home* compelling; for her, both text and image are necessary. As Bechdel tells and shows us, alone, words can fail; alone, images deceive. Yet her life story ties both concepts inextricably to her memories and revelations such that only the interplay of text and image offers the reader the rich complexity, honesty, and possibilities in Bechdel's quest to understand the past. . . .

Song 3

The Bechdels' elaborately restored house is the gilded, but tense, context of young Alison's familial relationships and a metaphor for her father's deceptions. "He used his skillful artifice not to make things, but to make things appear to be what they were not," Bechdel notes alongside an image of her father taking a photo of their family, shown in Fig. 2 (*Fun* 16). The scene represents the nature of her father's artifice; her father is *posing* a photo, an image of their family.

Fig. 2. Alison Bechdel's father posing a family photo (Bechdel, *Fun* 16).

In that same scene, Bechdel also shows her own sleight of hand; she manipulates the scene and reverses her father's role and her own to show young Alison taking the photograph of the family and her father posing in Alison's place (Fig. 3). In the image, young Alison symbolizes Bechdel in the present—looking back through the camera lens to create a

Fig. 3. Alison and her father trade places (Bechdel, *Fun* 17).

Song 4   **Student Writing**

portrait of her family. But unlike her father, she isn't using false images to deceive. Bechdel overcomes the treason of images by confessing herself as an "artificer" to her audience (*Fun* 16). Bechdel doesn't villainize the illusory nature of images; she repurposes their illusory power to reinterpret her memories. . . .

Song 8

Works Cited

Bechdel, Alison. *Fun Home*. Boston: Houghton Mifflin, 2006. Print.

---. "Stuck in Vermont 109: Alison Bechdel." *YouTube*. YouTube, 13 Dec. 2008. Web. 6 Feb. 2009.

Analyzing Arguments **13**

In one important sense, all language has an argumentative edge. When you greet friends, you wish to convince them that you're glad to see them; when advertisers pay for spots that appear alongside your social networking page, they want to persuade you to click and shop. Even apparently objective news reporting has strong argumentative overtones: when a news outlet highlights a particular story, for example, the editors are arguing that this subject is more important than others. Since argument is so pervasive, you need to be able to recognize and use it effectively — and to question your own arguments as well as those put forth by others.

AT A GLANCE

Analyzing an Argument

Here are some questions that can help you judge the effectiveness of an argument:

- What conclusions about the argument can you reach by playing both the believing and the doubting game? (13a)
- What cultural contexts inform the argument, and what do they tell you about where the writer is coming from? (13b)
- What emotional, ethical, and logical appeals is the writer making in support of the argument? (13c)
- How has the writer established credibility to write about the topic? (13c)
- What is the claim (or arguable statement)? Is the claim qualified in any way? (13d)
- What reasons and assumptions support and underlie the claim? (13d)
- What additional evidence backs up the assumption and claim? How current and reliable are the sources? (13d)
- How does the writer use images, graphics, or other visuals to support the argument?
- What fallacies can you identify, and what effect do they have on the argument's persuasiveness? (13e)
- What is the overall impression you get from analyzing the argument? Are you convinced?

13a Think critically about argument.

Critical thinking is a crucial component of argument, for it guides you in recognizing, formulating, and examining arguments. Here are some ways to think critically about argument:

- *Check understanding.* First, make sure you understand what is being argued and why. If you need to find out more about an unfamiliar subject to grasp the argument, do the research.
- *Play the believing — and the doubting — game.* Begin by playing the *believing game:* put yourself in the position of the person creating the argument to see the topic from that person's point of view as much as possible. Once you have given the argument sympathetic attention, play the *doubting game:* look skeptically at each claim, and examine each piece of evidence to see how well (or poorly) it supports the claim. Eventually, this process of believing and doubting will become natural.

- *Ask pertinent questions.* Whether you are thinking about others' ideas or your own, you should question unstated purposes and assumptions, the writer's qualifications, the context, the goal of the argument, and the evidence presented. What objections might be made to the argument?
- *Interpret and assess information.* All information that comes to you has a perspective—a spin. Your job is to identify the perspective and assess it, examining its sources and finding out what you can about its context.
- *Assess your own arguments.* The ultimate goal of all critical thinking is to reach your own conclusions. These, too, you must question and assess.

13b Recognize cultural contexts.

To understand as fully as possible the arguments of others, pay attention to clues to cultural context and to where the writer or creator is coming from. Put yourself in the position of the person creating the argument before looking skeptically at every claim and examining every piece of evidence. Above all, watch out for your own assumptions as you analyze what you read or see. For example, just because you assume that the use of statistics as support for your argument holds more water than, say, precedent drawn from religious belief, you can't assume that all writers agree with you. Take a writer's cultural beliefs into account before you begin to analyze an argument. (See Chapter 20.)

13c Identify an argument's basic appeals.

Aristotle categorized argumentative appeals into three types: emotional appeals that speak to readers' hearts and values (known to the ancient Greeks as *pathos*), ethical appeals that support the writer's character (*ethos*), and logical appeals that use facts and evidence (*logos*).

Emotional appeals

Emotional appeals stir your emotions and remind you of deeply held values. When politicians argue that the country needs more tax relief, they almost always use examples of one or more families they have met, stressing the concrete ways in which a tax cut would improve the quality of their lives. Doing so creates a strong emotional appeal. Some have criticized the use of emotional appeals in argument, claiming that they are a form of manipulation intended to mislead an audience. But emotional appeals are an important part of almost every argument. Critical readers are perfectly capable of "talking back" to such appeals by analyzing them, deciding which are acceptable and which are not.

The accompanying photo shows protesters at an Occupy Wall Street demonstration outside the New York Stock Exchange. The protesters' signs range from a simple logo for the United Auto Workers union to hand-painted cardboard slogans ("This is patriotic") to an American flag. To what emotions are the protesters appealing? Do you find this appeal effective, manipulative, or both? Would you accept this argument?

Ethical appeals

Ethical appeals support the credibility, moral character, and goodwill of the argument's creator. These appeals are especially important for critical readers to recognize and evaluate. We may respect and admire an athlete, for example, but should we invest in the mutual funds the athlete promotes? To identify ethical appeals in arguments, ask yourself these questions: How does the creator of the argument show that he or she has really done the homework on the subject and is knowledgeable and credible about it? What sort of character does he or she build, and how? More important, is that character trustworthy? What does the creator of the argument do to show that he or she has the best interests of an audience in mind? Do those best interests match your own, and, if not, how does that alter the effectiveness of the argument?

Logical appeals

Logical appeals are viewed as especially trustworthy: "The facts don't lie," some say. Of course, facts are not the only type of logical appeals, which also include firsthand evidence drawn from observations, interviews, surveys and questionnaires, experiments, and personal experience; and secondhand evidence drawn from authorities, the testimony of others, statistics, and other print and online sources. Critical readers need to examine logical appeals just as carefully as emotional and ethical ones. What is the source of the logical appeal—and is that source trustworthy? Are all terms defined clearly? Has the logical evidence presented been taken out of context, and, if so, does that change its meaning?

Analyzing appeals in a visual argument

The poster below, from TurnAround, an organization devoted to helping victims of domestic violence, is "intended to strike a chord with abusers as well as their victims." The dramatic combination of words

and image builds on an analogy between a child and a target and makes strong emotional and ethical appeals.

The bull's-eye that draws your attention to the center of the poster is probably the first thing you notice when you look at the image. Then you may observe that the "target" is, in fact, a child's body; it also has arms, legs, and a head with wide, staring eyes. The heading at the upper left, "A child is not a target," reinforces the bull's-eye/child connection.

This poster's stark image and headline appeal to viewers' emotions, offering the uncomfortable reminder that children are often the victims of domestic violence. The design causes viewers to see a target first and only afterward recognize that the target is actually a child—an unsettling experience. But the poster also offers ethical appeals ("Turn-Around can help") to show that the organization is credible and that it supports the worthwhile goal of ending "the cycle of domestic violence" by offering counseling and other support services. Finally, it uses the logical appeal of a statistic, noting that TurnAround has served "more than 10,000 women, children and men each year" and giving specific information about where to get help.

13d   Analyze the elements of argument.

According to philosopher Stephen Toulmin's framework for analyzing arguments, most arguments contain common features: a *claim* or *claims*, *reasons* for the claim, *assumptions* (whether stated or unstated) that underlie the argument, *evidence* (facts, authoritative opinion, examples,

ELEMENTS OF A SAMPLE TOULMIN ARGUMENT

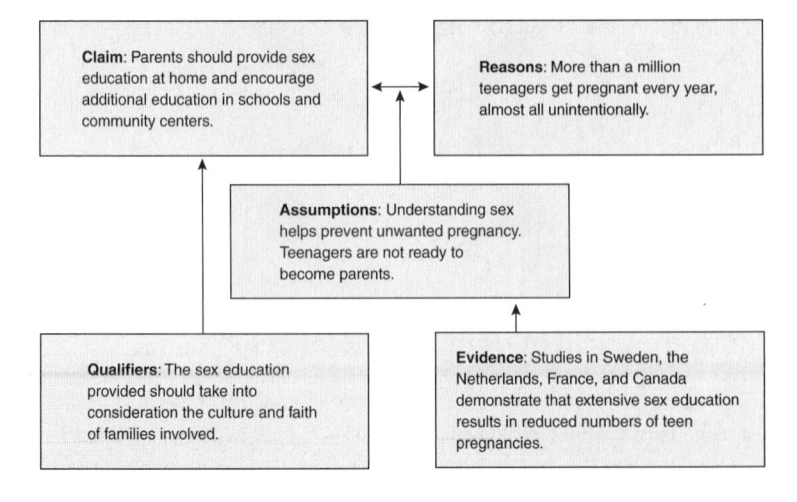

Claim: Parents should provide sex education at home and encourage additional education in schools and community centers.

Reasons: More than a million teenagers get pregnant every year, almost all unintentionally.

Assumptions: Understanding sex helps prevent unwanted pregnancy. Teenagers are not ready to become parents.

Qualifiers: The sex education provided should take into consideration the culture and faith of families involved.

Evidence: Studies in Sweden, the Netherlands, France, and Canada demonstrate that extensive sex education results in reduced numbers of teen pregnancies.

statistics, and so on), and *qualifiers* that limit the claim in some way. In the following discussion, we will examine each of these elements in more detail. The figure on p. 148 shows how these elements might be applied to an argument about sex education.

Claims

Claims (arguable statements) are statements of fact, opinion, or belief that form the backbone of arguments. Claims worthy of arguing are those that are debatable: to say "Ten degrees Fahrenheit is cold" is a claim, but it is probably not debatable—unless you are describing northern Alaska, where ten degrees might seem relatively balmy.

Reasons

A claim is only as good as the reasons explaining why the claim should be accepted. As you analyze claims, look for reasons drawn from facts, from authorities, from personal experience, and from examples. Test each reason by asking how directly it supports the claim, how timely it is, and what counter-reasons you could offer to question it.

Assumptions

Putting a claim and reasons together often results in what Aristotle called an *enthymeme*, an argument that rests on an assumption the writer expects the audience to hold. These assumptions (which Toulmin calls *warrants*) that connect claim and reasons are often the hardest to detect in an argument, partly because they are often unstated, sometimes masking a weak link. As a result, it's especially important to identify the assumptions in arguments you are analyzing. Once the assumption is identified, you can test it against evidence and your own experience before accepting it.

Evidence

As a critical reader, you must evaluate each piece of evidence (what Toulmin calls *backing*) the writer offers. Analyze how the evidence relates to the claim, whether it is appropriate and timely, and whether it comes from a credible source.

Qualifiers

Qualifiers offer a way of limiting or narrowing a claim so that it is as precise as possible. Words or phrases that signal a qualification include *few, often, in these circumstances, rarely, some, typically,* and so on.

Claims having no qualifiers can sometimes lead to overgeneralizations. For example, the statement *Grading damages learning* is less precise than *Grading can damage learning in some circumstances*. Look carefully for qualifiers in the arguments you analyze, since they will affect the strength and reach of the claim.

Analyzing elements of a visual argument

Visual arguments, too, can be analyzed using Toulmin's methods. Look at the accompanying advertising parody: it contains few words, yet it makes a subtle argument. A group of students discussed this advertisement, observing that the image intends to evoke a 1960s-era detergent commercial. They came up with several possible claims that the ad might be making.

POSSIBLE CLAIM   Pharmaceutical companies want to convince consumers that taking drugs to cure depression is no more serious than trying a new detergent.

POSSIBLE CLAIM   Consumers should beware of drug advertisements that make hard-to-prove claims aimed at getting customers to ask for a prescription.

POSSIBLE CLAIM   Buying products will not lead to greater happiness.

All of these claims can be supported by the ad. If you were to choose the first claim, for instance, you might word a reason like this:

This parody of a Prozac ad looks like a detergent commercial from the 1960s, but the product is a chemical that promises to "wash your blues away." With some research into the actual dangers and benefits of antidepressants, you might find evidence that ads for such drugs sometimes minimize their downside and exaggerate their promise. You might also note that the ad's design takes viewers back to a decades-old scene of domestic happiness, suggesting that Prozac could return its users to some mythically perfect time in the past—and you would be well on your way to an analysis of this visual argument.

13e Think critically about fallacies.

Fallacies have traditionally been viewed as serious flaws that damage the effectiveness of an argument. But arguments are ordinarily fairly complex in that they always occur in some specific rhetorical situation and in some particular place and time; thus what looks like a fallacy in one situation may appear quite different in another. The best advice is to learn to identify fallacies but to be cautious in jumping to quick conclusions about them. Rather than thinking of them as errors you can use to discredit an arguer, you might think of them as barriers to common ground and understanding, since they often shut off rather than engender debate.

Verbal fallacies

AD HOMINEM

Ad hominem charges make a personal attack rather than focusing on the issue at hand.

> ▶ **Who cares what that fat loudmouth says about the health care system?**

GUILT BY ASSOCIATION

Guilt by association attacks someone's credibility by linking that person with a person or activity the audience considers bad, suspicious, or untrustworthy.

> ▶ **She does not deserve reelection; her husband had extramarital affairs.**

FALSE AUTHORITY

False authority is often used by advertisers who show famous actors or athletes testifying to the greatness of a product about which they may know very little.

> ▶ **He's today's greatest NASCAR driver—and he banks at National Mutual!**

BANDWAGON APPEAL

Bandwagon appeal suggests that a great movement is underway and the reader will be a fool or a traitor not to join it.

> ▶ **This new phone is everyone's must-have item. Where's yours?**

FLATTERY

Flattery tries to persuade readers by suggesting that they are thoughtful, intelligent, or perceptive enough to agree with the writer.

> You have the taste to recognize the superlative artistry of Bling diamond jewelry.

IN-CROWD APPEAL

In-crowd appeal, a special kind of flattery, invites readers to identify with an admired and select group.

> Want to know a secret that more and more of Middletown's successful young professionals are finding out about? It's Mountainbrook Manor condominiums.

VEILED THREAT

Veiled threats try to frighten readers into agreement by hinting that they will suffer adverse consequences if they don't agree.

> If Public Service Electric Company does not get an immediate 15 percent rate increase, its services to you may be seriously affected.

FALSE ANALOGY

False analogies make comparisons between two situations that are not alike in important respects.

> The volleyball team's sudden descent in the rankings resembled the sinking of the *Titanic*.

BEGGING THE QUESTION

Begging the question is a kind of circular argument that treats a debatable statement as if it had been proved true.

> Television news covered that story well; I learned all I know about it by watching TV.

POST HOC FALLACY

The post hoc fallacy (from the Latin *post hoc, ergo propter hoc,* which means "after this, therefore caused by this") assumes that just because B happened *after* A, it must have been *caused* by A.

> We should not rebuild the town docks because every time we do, a big hurricane comes along and damages them.

NON SEQUITUR

A non sequitur (Latin for "it does not follow") attempts to tie together two or more logically unrelated ideas as if they were related.

> If we can send a spaceship to Mars, then we can discover a cure for cancer.

EITHER-OR FALLACY

The either-or fallacy insists that a complex situation can have only two possible outcomes.

▶ **If we do not build the new highway, businesses downtown will be forced to close.**

HASTY GENERALIZATION

A hasty generalization bases a conclusion on too little evidence or on bad or misunderstood evidence.

▶ **I couldn't understand the lecture today, so I'm sure this course will be impossible.**

OVERSIMPLIFICATION

Oversimplification claims an overly direct relationship between a cause and an effect.

▶ **If we prohibit the sale of alcohol, we will get rid of binge drinking.**

STRAW MAN

A straw-man argument misrepresents the opposition by pretending that opponents agree with something that few reasonable people would support.

▶ **My opponent believes that we should offer therapy to the terrorists. I disagree.**

Visual fallacies

Fallacies can also take the form of misleading images. The sheer power of images can make them especially difficult to analyze—people tend to believe what they see. Nevertheless, photographs and other visuals can be manipulated to present a false impression.

MISLEADING PHOTOGRAPHS

Faked or altered photos have existed since the invention of photography. On the following page, for example, is a photograph of Joseph Stalin, the Soviet Union's leader from 1929 to 1953, with his commissar Nikolai Yezhov. Stalin and the commissar had a political disagreement that resulted in Yezhov's execution in 1940. The second image shows the same photo after Stalin had it doctored to rewrite history.

Today's technology makes such photo alterations easier than ever. But photographs need not be altered to try to fool viewers. Think of all the photos that make a politician look misleadingly bad or good. In these cases, you should closely examine the motives of those responsible for publishing the images.

MISLEADING CHARTS AND GRAPHS

Facts and statistics, too, can be presented in ways that mislead readers. For example, the following bar graph purports to deliver an argument about how differently Democrats, on the one hand, and Republicans and Independents, on the other, felt about an issue:

DATA PRESENTED MISLEADINGLY

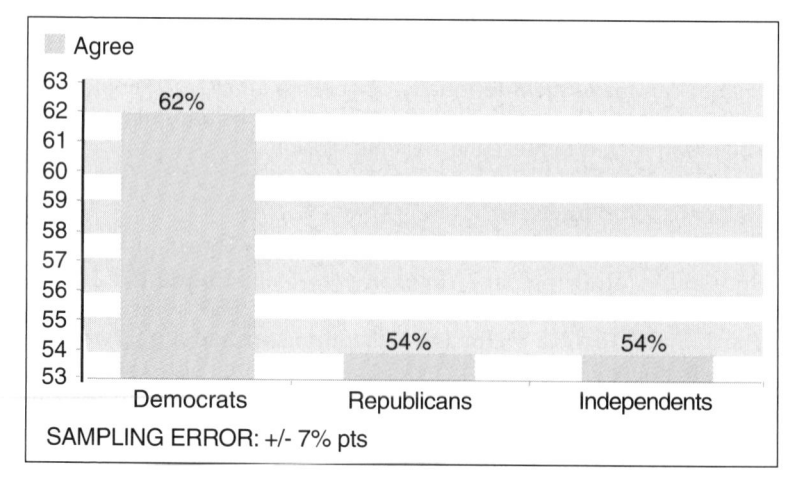

Look closely and you'll see a visual fallacy: the vertical axis starts not at zero but at 53 percent, so the apparently large difference between the groups is misleading. In fact, a majority of all respondents agree about the issue, and only eight percentage points separate Democrats from Republicans and Independents (in a poll with a margin of error of $+/-$ seven percentage points). Here's how the graph would look if the vertical axis began at zero:

DATA PRESENTED MORE ACCURATELY

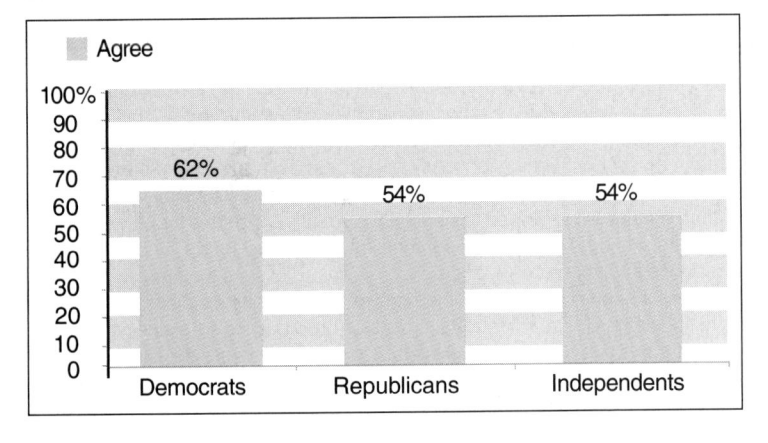

EXERCISE 13.1

Read the following brief essay by Derek Bok, which argues that college administrators should seek to educate and persuade rather than censor students who use speech or symbols that others find deeply offensive. Then carry out an analysis of the argument, beginning with identifying the audience and the author's purpose, and moving to identifying the claim, reason(s), assumption(s), evidence, and qualifiers (if any). As you work, be sure also to identify the emotional, ethical, and logical appeals as well as any fallacies put forward by Bok. You may want to compare your own analysis to the one written by Milena Ateyea in 13f.

> For several years, universities have been struggling with the problem of trying to reconcile the rights of free speech with the desire to avoid racial tension. In recent weeks, such a controversy has sprung up at Harvard. Two students hung Confederate flags in public view, upsetting students who equate the Confederacy with slavery. A third student tried to protest the flags by displaying a swastika.
>
> These incidents have provoked much discussion and disagreement. Some students have urged that Harvard require the removal of symbols that offend many members of the community. Others reply that such symbols are a form of free speech and should be protected.
>
> Different universities have resolved similar conflicts in different ways. Some have enacted codes to protect their communities from forms of speech that are

deemed to be insensitive to the feelings of other groups. Some have refused to impose such restrictions.

It is important to distinguish between the appropriateness of such communications and their status under the First Amendment. The fact that speech is protected by the First Amendment does not necessarily mean that it is right, proper, or civil. I am sure that the vast majority of Harvard students believe that hanging a Confederate flag in public view — or displaying a swastika in response — is insensitive and unwise because any satisfaction it gives to the students who display these symbols is far outweighed by the discomfort it causes to many others.

I share this view and regret that the students involved saw fit to behave in this fashion. Whether or not they merely wished to manifest their pride in the South — or to demonstrate the insensitivity of hanging Confederate flags, by mounting another offensive symbol in return — they must have known that they would upset many fellow students and ignore the decent regard for the feelings of others so essential to building and preserving a strong and harmonious community.

To disapprove of a particular form of communication, however, is not enough to justify prohibiting it. We are faced with a clear example of the conflict between our commitment to free speech and our desire to foster a community founded on mutual respect. Our society has wrestled with this problem for many years. Interpreting the First Amendment, the Supreme Court has clearly struck the balance in favor of free speech.

While communities do have the right to regulate speech in order to uphold aesthetic standards (avoiding defacement of buildings) or to protect the public from disturbing noise, rules of this kind must be applied across the board and cannot be enforced selectively to prohibit certain kinds of messages but not others.

Under the Supreme Court's rulings, as I read them, the display of swastikas or Confederate flags clearly falls within the protection of the free-speech clause of the First Amendment and cannot be forbidden simply because it offends the feelings of many members of the community. These rulings apply to all agencies of government, including public universities.

Although it is unclear to what extent the First Amendment is enforceable against private institutions, I have difficulty understanding why a university such as Harvard should have less free speech than the surrounding society — or than a public university.

One reason why the power of censorship is so dangerous is that it is extremely difficult to decide when a particular communication is offensive enough to warrant prohibition or to weigh the degree of offensiveness against the potential value of the communication. If we begin to forbid flags, it is only a short step to prohibiting offensive speakers.

I suspect that no community will become humane and caring by restricting what its members can say. The worst offenders will simply find other ways to irritate and insult.

In addition, once we start to declare certain things "offensive," with all the excitement and attention that will follow, I fear that much ingenuity will be exerted trying to test the limits, much time will be expended trying to draw tenuous distinctions, and the resulting publicity will eventually attract more attention to the offensive material than would ever have occurred otherwise.

Rather than prohibit such communications, with all the resulting risks, it would be better to ignore them, since students would then have little reason to create such displays and would soon abandon them. If this response is not possible — and one can understand why — the wisest course is to speak with those who perform insensitive acts and try to help them understand the effects of their actions on others.

Appropriate officials and faculty members should take the lead, as the Harvard House Masters have already done in this case. In talking with students, they should seek to educate and persuade, rather than resort to ridicule or intimidation, recognizing that only persuasion is likely to produce a lasting, beneficial effect. Through such effects, I believe that we act in the manner most consistent with our ideals as an educational institution and most calculated to help us create a truly understanding, supportive community.

— DEREK BOK, "Protecting Freedom of Expression at Harvard"

13f Student rhetorical analysis

For a class assignment, Milena Ateyea was asked to analyze the emotional, ethical, and logical appeals in "Protecting Freedom of Expression at Harvard," an essay by Harvard president Derek Bok arguing that colleges should seek to persuade rather than to censor students who use speech or symbols that offend others.

Student Writer

Milena Ateyea

🔘 bedfordstmartins.com/everydaywriter
Student Writing

Provocative title suggests mixed response to Bok

Connects article to her own experience to build credibility (ethical appeal)

Brief overview of Bok's argument

Identifies Bok's central claim

Links Bok's claim to strategies he uses to support it

Direct quotations show appeals to emotion through vivid description

Bok establishes common ground between two positions

Emphasizes Bok's credibility (ethical appeal)

A Curse and a Blessing

In 1991, when Derek Bok's essay "Protecting Freedom of Expression at Harvard" was first published in the *Boston Globe*, I had just come to America to escape the oppressive Communist regime in Bulgaria. Perhaps my background explains why I support Bok's argument that we should not put arbitrary limits on freedom of expression. Bok wrote the essay in response to a public display of Confederate flags and a swastika at Harvard, a situation that created a heated controversy among the students. As Bok notes, universities have struggled to achieve a balance between maintaining students' right of free speech and avoiding racist attacks. When choices must be made, however, Bok argues for preserving freedom of expression.

In order to support his claim and bridge the controversy, Bok uses a variety of rhetorical strategies. The author first immerses the reader in the controversy by vividly describing the incident: two Harvard students had hung Confederate flags in public view, thereby "upsetting students who equate the Confederacy with slavery" (51). Another student, protesting the flags, decided to display an even more offensive symbol—the swastika. These actions provoked heated discussions among students. Some students believed that school officials should remove the offensive symbols, whereas others suggested that the symbols "are a form of free speech and should be protected" (51). Bok establishes common ground between the factions: he regrets the actions of the offenders but does not believe we should prohibit such actions just because we disagree with them.

The author earns the reader's respect because of his knowledge and through his logical presentation of the issue. In partial support of his position, Bok refers to U.S. Supreme Court rulings, which remind us that "the display of swastikas or Confederate flags clearly falls within the protection of the free-speech clause of the First Amendment" (52). The author also emphasizes the danger of the slippery slope of censorship when he warns the reader, "If we begin to forbid flags, it is only a short step to prohibiting offensive speakers" (52). Overall, however, Bok's work lacks the kinds of evidence that statistics, interviews with students, and other representative examples of controversial conduct could provide. Thus, his essay may not be strong enough to persuade all readers to make the leap from this specific situation to his general conclusion.

> Links Bok's credibility to use of logical appeals

> Comments critically on kinds of evidence Bok's argument lacks

Throughout, Bok's personal feelings are implied but not stated directly. As a lawyer who was president of Harvard for twenty years, Bok knows how to present his opinions respectfully without offending the feelings of the students. However, qualifying phrases like "I suspect that" and "Under the Supreme Court's rulings, as I read them" could weaken the effectiveness of his position. Furthermore, Bok's attempt to be fair to all seems to dilute the strength of his proposed solution. He suggests that one should either ignore the insensitive deeds in the hope that students might change their behavior, or talk to the offending students to help them comprehend how their behavior is affecting other students.

> Reiterates Bok's credibility

> Identifies qualifying phrases that may weaken claim

> Analyzes weaknesses of Bok's proposed solution

Nevertheless, although Bok's proposed solution to the controversy does not appear at first reading to be very strong, it may ultimately be effective. There is enough flexibility in his approach to withstand various tests, and Bok's solution is general enough that it can change with the times and adapt to community standards.

> Raises possibility that Bok's imperfect solution may work

In writing this essay, Bok faced a challenging task: to write a short response to a specific situation that represents a very broad and controversial issue. Some people may find that freedom of expression is both a curse and a blessing because of the difficulties it creates. As one who has lived under a regime that permitted very

> Summarizes Bok's task

> Ties conclusion back to title

Returns to own experience, which argues for accepting Bok's solution

limited, censored expression, I am all too aware that I could not have written this response in 1991 in Bulgaria. As a result, I feel, like Derek Bok, that freedom of expression is a blessing, in spite of any temporary problems associated with it.

Work Cited

Bok, Derek. "Protecting Freedom of Expression at Harvard." Rpt. in *Current Issues and Enduring Questions*. Ed. Sylvan Barnet and Hugo Bedau. 6th ed. Boston: Bedford, 2002. 51–52. *Boston Globe* 25 May 1991. Print.

EXERCISE 13.2

Working with one or two classmates, analyze a brief argumentative text — an essay, an advertisement, or an editorial cartoon — by playing the believing and doubting game; identifying emotional, ethical, and logical appeals; and listing claims, reasons, assumptions, evidence, and qualifiers. Then work together to create a collaborative critical response to the text you've chosen.

EXERCISE 13.3: THINKING CRITICALLY

In the following brief review for *Rolling Stone*, music critic James Hunter recaps five CDs that reissue ten Merle Haggard albums from early in the country star's career. What central claim(s) does Hunter make? What emotional, ethical, and logical appeals does he present in support of his claim, and how effective are these appeals?

Outlaw Classics: The Albums That Kept Nashville Real in the Sixties and Seventies

[Review of *Merle Haggard* (Capitol Nashville/EMI)]

By James Hunter

Merle Haggard wasn't the first outsider to rebuke Nashville prissiness in the Sixties — Johnny Cash, who arrived from Sun Records in Memphis, deserves that honor — but Hag was the most down-to-earth soul that the Music City had seen for some time when he loped onto the scene in the mid- to late Sixties. An ex-con from California with Oklahoma roots, he sang eloquently about booze and prison life. His beginnings were in honky-tonk Bakersfield, where he learned first-class musical directness from guys like the great Buck Owens and Wynn Stewart.

For years, Haggard's Sixties and early-Seventies work has been repre-sented chiefly on compilations. This bunch of reissues restores ten of those albums, all with interesting bonus tracks; four of the ten albums have never appeared before on CD. Each showcases Haggard's awesome gifts and inextricable orneriness: There is no Tennessee gothic or flashy Texas ego to this outsider; Haggard was more about subtlety and West Coast calm. A hummable, elastic honky-tonk tune can convey everything he wants to say. His melodies carry a broad range of topics, from cranky love songs ("I'm Gonna Break Every Heart I Can") to prison tunes ("Bring Me Back Home") to perfectly wrought whiskey-and-wine songs, to looks back at his parents' lives. Sometimes, as on the scarily good "I Can't Be Myself," Haggard seems to want to jump out of his own skin; other times, as on "I Threw Away the Rose," he's as centered in his own smooth, crusty tenor as any singer has ever been. In all cases, Haggard sounds like country's coolest customer.

These reissues underscore how Haggard's music far exceeds "Okie from Muskogee," the anti-hippie 1969 smash that made him internationally famous. Cash rocked country up and then went on to become his world's black-clad cul-tural ambassador. George Jones showed how the field needs at least one opera star, and Willie Nelson yoked local songwriting to American poetry. Haggard proved how crucial it was for a country guy to say what was on his mind — and because he was such a sublime recording artist, he was able to make it stick, right from the start.

Constructing Arguments   **14**

You respond to arguments all the time. When you see a stop sign and come to a halt, you've accepted the argument that stopping at such signs is a sensible thing to do. Unfortunately, constructing an ef-fective argument of your own is not as easy as putting up a stop sign. Creating a thorough and convincing argument requires careful reason-ing and attention to your audience and purpose.

14a Understand what counts as argument.

Although winning is an important purpose of argument, it is by no means the only purpose.

TO WIN The most traditional purpose of academic argument, arguing to win, is common in campus debating societies, in political debates, in trials, and often in business. The writer or speaker aims to present a position that will prevail over some other position.

Reviewing Your Argument

- What is the purpose of your argument — to win? to convince others? to explore an issue? (14a)
- Is the point you want to make arguable? (14a)
- Have you formulated a strong working thesis that includes a clear claim and good reasons? (14b)
- Have you considered your audience in shaping your appeals? (14d)
- How have you established your own credibility in the argument? (14e)
- How have you incorporated logical and emotional appeals into your argument? (14f and g)
- If you use sources, how effectively are they integrated into your argument? (14h)
- How is your argument organized? (14i)
- What design elements help you make your argument? (14j)

TO CONVINCE Often, out-and-out defeat of another's position is not only unrealistic but undesirable. Instead, the goal might be to convince another person to change his or her mind. Doing so calls on a writer to provide *compelling reasons* for an audience to accept some or all of the writer's conclusions.

TO EXPLORE AN ISSUE Argument to explore an issue or reach a decision seeks a sharing of information and perspectives in order to make informed choices.

Arguments

"Argument seems so negative — I don't want to attack anybody or contradict what someone else says." Sometimes — in law courts, for example — argument may call for attacking an opponent's credibility, and you may have used the word *argument* to describe a conversation in which the speakers said little more than "I did not!" and "You did, too!" But in college writing, argument usually means something much broader. Instead of attacking or contradicting, you will be expected to explore ideas and to work toward convincing yourself as well as others that these ideas are valuable.

Checking whether a statement can be argued

At school, at home, or on the job, you will often need to convince someone or decide something. To do so, start with an arguable statement, which should meet three criteria:

1. It attempts to convince readers of something, change their minds about something, or urge them to do something—or it explores a topic in order to make a wise decision.
2. It addresses a problem for which no easily acceptable solution exists or asks a question to which no absolute answer exists.
3. It presents a position that readers might realistically have varying perspectives on.

> ARGUABLE STATEMENT Advertising in women's magazines contributes to the poor self-image that afflicts many young women.

This statement seeks to convince, addresses a problem—poor self-image among young women—that has no clear-cut solution, and takes a position many could disagree with.

> UNARGUABLE STATEMENT Women's magazines earn millions of dollars every year from advertising.

This statement does not present a position; it states a fact that can easily be verified and thus offers a poor basis for argument.

EXERCISE 14.1

Using the three characteristics just listed, decide which of the following statements are arguable and which are not.

1. *The Dark Knight* was the best movie of the last decade.
2. The climate of the earth is gradually getting warmer.
3. The United States must further reduce social spending in order to balance the budget.
4. Shakespeare died in 1616.
5. President Roosevelt knew that the Japanese were planning to bomb Pearl Harbor in December 1941.
6. Water boils at 212 degrees Fahrenheit.
7. Van Gogh's paintings are the work of a madman.
8. The incidence of breast cancer has risen in the last ten years.
9. The Federal Emergency Management Agency's response to disasters must be radically improved.
10. A fifty-five-mile-per-hour speed limit lowers accident rates.

bedfordstmartins.com/everydaywriter
Exercise Central > Critical Thinking and Argument

14b Make a claim and formulate a working thesis.

Once you have an arguable statement, you need to develop it into a working thesis (7b). One way to do so is to identify the elements of an argument (13d): the claim or arguable statement; one or more reasons for the claim; and assumptions—sometimes unstated—that underlie the claim and reasons.

To turn a claim into a working thesis for an argument, include at least one good reason to support the arguable statement.

REASON	Pesticides endanger the lives of farmworkers.
WORKING THESIS (CLAIM WITH REASON ATTACHED)	Because they endanger the lives of farmworkers, pesticides should be banned.

EXERCISE 14.2

Using two arguable statements from Exercise 14.1 or two that you create, formulate two working theses, identifying the claim, reason(s), and assumption(s) for each.

14c Examine your assumptions.

Once you have a working thesis, examine your assumptions to help test your reasoning and strengthen your argument. Begin by identifying underlying assumptions that support the working thesis.

WORKING THESIS	Because they endanger the lives of farmworkers, pesticides should be banned.
ASSUMPTION 1	Workers have a right to a safe working environment.
ASSUMPTION 2	Substances that endanger the lives of workers deserve to be banned.

Once you have a working thesis, you may want to use qualifiers to make it more precise and thus less susceptible to criticism. The preceding thesis might be qualified in this way:

▶ Because they *often* endanger the lives of farmworkers, *most* pesticides should be banned.

EXERCISE 14.3

Formulate an arguable statement, and create a working thesis, for two of the following general topics.

1. the Palestinian-Israeli conflict
2. sex education in public schools
3. lowering college tuition
4. reinstatement of a U.S. military draft
5. music downloading

14d Shape your appeal to your audience.

Arguments and the claims they make are effective only if they appeal to the appropriate audience. For example, if you want to argue for increased lighting in parking garages on campus, you might appeal to students by citing examples drawn from their experiences of the safety problems in such dimly lit garages. If you are writing to university administrators, however, you might focus on the negative publicity associated with past attacks in campus garages and evoke the anger that such attacks cause in parents, alumni, and other influential groups.

EXERCISE 14.4

Working with two other members of your class, find two current advertisements you consider particularly eye-catching and persuasive. Then work out what central claim each ad is making, and identify reasons and assumptions in support of the claim. Finally, prepare a brief collaborative report of your findings for the class.

14e Establish credibility through ethical appeals.

To make your argument convincing, you must first gain the respect and trust of your readers, or establish credibility with them. In general, writers can establish credibility by making ethical appeals (13c) in four ways.

Demonstrating knowledge

A writer can establish credibility first by establishing credentials. To decide whether you know enough to argue an issue credibly, consider the following questions:

- Can you provide information about your topic from sources other than your own knowledge?
- How reliable are your sources?
- If sources contradict one another, can you account for or resolve the contradictions?

- Would a personal experience relating to the issue help support your claim?

These questions may well show that you must do more research, check sources, resolve contradictions, refocus your working thesis, or even change your topic.

Establishing common ground

Many arguments between people or groups are doomed to end without resolution because the two sides seem to occupy no starting point of agreement. The following questions can help you find common ground in presenting an argument. (See also Chapter 21.)

- On this issue, how can you discover opinions that differ from your own?
- What are the differing perspectives on the issue?
- What aspects of the issue can all sides agree on?
- How can you express such common ground clearly to all sides? Can you use other languages or varieties of English to establish common ground with those you address? (See Chapter 22.)

Demonstrating fairness

In arguing a position, writers must deal fairly with opposing arguments (also called counterarguments). Audiences are more inclined to listen to writers who seem to consider their opponents' views fairly than to those who ignore or distort such views. The following questions can help you discover ways of establishing yourself as open-minded and evenhanded:

- How can you show that you are taking into account all significant points of view?
- How can you demonstrate that you understand and sympathize with points of view other than your own?
- What can you do to show that you have considered evidence carefully, even when it does not support your position?

Some writers, instead of demonstrating fairness, may make unjustified attacks on an opponent's credibility. Avoid such attacks in your writing.

Visuals that make ethical appeals

In arguments and other kinds of writing, visuals can combine with text to help present a writer or an organization as trustworthy and credible.

Like businesses, many institutions and individuals are using logos and other images to brand themselves as they wish the public to see them. The Sustainable Food Laboratory logo, seen here, suggests that the organization is concerned about both food production and the environment.

Visuals that make ethical appeals add to your credibility and fairness as a writer. Just as you probably consider the impression your Facebook profile photo makes on your audience, you should think about what kind of case you're making for yourself when you choose images and design elements for your argument.

EXERCISE 14.5

List the ways in which the Sustainable Food Laboratory's logo demonstrates knowledge, establishes common ground, and shows fairness. Do you think the visuals are helpful in convincing you of the organization's credibility? Why, or why not?

EXERCISE 14.6

Using a working thesis you drafted for Exercise 14.2 or 14.3, write a paragraph or two describing how you would go about establishing your credibility in arguing that thesis.

14f Use effective logical appeals.

Credibility alone cannot and should not carry the full burden of convincing readers. Indeed, many are inclined to think that the logic of the argument—the reasoning behind it—is as important as its ethos.

Examples, precedents, and narratives

Just as a picture can sometimes be worth a thousand words, so can a well-conceived example be extremely valuable in arguing a point. Examples are used most often to support generalizations or to bring abstractions to life. In making the general statement that popular media send the message that a woman must be thin to be attractive; you might include these examples:

> At the supermarket checkout, a tabloid publishes unflattering photographs of a young singer and comments on her apparent weight gain in shocked captions that ask "What happened?!?" Another praises a star for quickly shedding "ugly pounds" after the recent birth of a child. The cover of *Cosmopolitan* features a glamorously made-up and airbrushed actress in an outfit that reveals her remarkably tiny waist and flat stomach. Every woman in every advertisement in the magazine is thin—and the context makes it clear that we're supposed to think that she is beautiful.

Precedents are examples taken from the past. If, as part of a proposal for increasing lighting in the library garage, you point out that the university has increased lighting in four other garages in the past year, you are arguing on the basis of precedent.

The following questions can help you check any use of example or precedent:

- How representative are the examples?
- Are they sufficient in strength or number to lead to a generalization?
- In what ways do they support your point?
- How closely does a precedent relate to the point you're trying to make? Are the situations really similar?
- How timely is the precedent? (What would have been applicable in 1920 is not necessarily applicable today.)

Because storytelling is universal, *narratives* can be very persuasive in helping readers understand and accept the logic of an argument. Narratives that use video and audio to capture the faces and voices of the people involved are often particularly compelling. In *As We Sow*, a documentary arguing against corporate pork production methods, the farmers shown here tell stories of their struggle to continue raising animals as their families have for generations.

Stories drawn from your own experience can appeal particularly to readers, for they not only help make your point in true-to-life, human terms but also help readers know you better and therefore identify with you more closely.

When you include stories in an argument, ask yourself the following questions:

- Does the narrative support your thesis?
- Will the story's significance to the argument be clear to your readers?
- Is the story one of several good reasons or pieces of evidence—or does it have to carry the main burden of the argument?

In research writing, you must identify your sources for any examples, precedents, or narratives not based on your own knowledge.

Authority and testimony

Another way to support an argument logically is to cite an authority. The use of authority has figured prominently in the controversy over smoking. Since the U.S. surgeon general's 1964 announcement that smoking is hazardous to health, many Americans have quit smoking, largely persuaded by the authority of the scientists offering the evidence.

Ask the following questions to be sure you are using authorities effectively:

- Is the authority *timely*? (The argument that the United States should pursue a policy that was supported by Thomas Jefferson will probably fail since Jefferson's time was so radically different from ours.)
- Is the authority *qualified* to judge the topic at hand? (To cite a movie star in an essay on linguistics may not help your argument.)
- Is the authority likely to be *known and respected* by readers? (To cite an unfamiliar authority without identification will reduce the impact of the evidence.)
- Are the authority's *credentials* clearly stated and verifiable? (Especially with Web-based sources, it is crucial to know whose authority guarantees the reliability of the information.)

Testimony—the evidence that an authority presents in support of a claim—is a feature of much contemporary argument. If testimony is timely, accurate, representative, and provided by a respected authority, then it, like authority itself, can add powerful support.

In research writing (see Chapters 15–19), you should cite your sources for authority and for testimony not based on your own knowledge.

Causes and effects

Showing that one event is the cause or the effect of another can help support an argument. Suppose you are trying to explain, in a petition to change your grade in a course, why you were unable to take the final examination. You would probably trace the causes of your failure to appear—your illness or the theft of your car, perhaps—so that the committee reading the petition would reconsider the effect—your not taking the examination.

Tracing causes often lays the groundwork for an argument, particularly if the effect of the causes is one we would like to change. In an environmental science class, for example, a student may argue that a national law regulating smokestack emissions from utility plants is needed because (1) acid rain on the East Coast originates from emissions at utility plants in the Midwest, (2) acid rain kills trees and other vegetation, (3) utility lobbyists have prevented midwestern states from passing strict laws controlling emissions from such plants, and (4) if such laws are not passed, acid rain will soon destroy most eastern forests. In this case, the fourth point ties all of the previous points together to provide an overall argument from effect: if X, then Y.

Inductive and deductive reasoning

Traditionally, logical arguments are classified as using either inductive or deductive reasoning; in practice, the two almost always work together. Inductive reasoning is the process of making a generalization based on a number of specific instances. If you find you are ill on ten occasions after eating seafood, for example, you will likely draw the inductive generalization that seafood makes you ill. It may not be an absolute certainty that seafood is to blame, but the probability lies in that direction.

Deductive reasoning, on the other hand, reaches a conclusion by assuming a general principle (known as a major premise) and then applying that principle to a specific case (the minor premise). In practice, this general principle is usually derived from induction. The inductive generalization *Seafood makes me ill*, for instance, could serve as the major premise for the deductive argument *Since all seafood makes me ill, the shrimp on this buffet is certain to make me ill.*

Deductive arguments have traditionally been analyzed as syllogisms—reasoning that contains a major premise, a minor premise, and a conclusion.

MAJOR PREMISE	All people die.
MINOR PREMISE	I am a person.
CONCLUSION	I will die.

Syllogisms, however, are too rigid and absolute to serve in arguments about questions that have no absolute answers, and they often lack any appeal to an audience. Aristotle's simpler alternative, the enthymeme, asks the audience to supply the implied major premise. Consider the following example:

> Since violent video games can be addictive and cause psychological harm, players and their parents must carefully evaluate such games and monitor their use.

You can analyze this enthymeme by restating it in the form of two premises and a conclusion.

MAJOR PREMISE	Games that cause harm to players should be evaluated and monitored.
MINOR PREMISE	Violent video games can cause psychological harm to players.
CONCLUSION	These games should be evaluated and monitored.

Note that the major premise is one the writer can count on an audience agreeing with or supplying: safety and common sense demand that potentially harmful games be used with great care. By implicitly asking an audience to supply this premise to an argument, a writer engages the audience's participation.

Toulmin's system (13d) looks for claims, reasons, and assumptions instead of major and minor premises.

CLAIM	Parents should not allow children to play violent video games.
REASON	Exposure to violent video games may make children more indifferent to violence.
ASSUMPTION	Parents do not want their children to be indifferent to violence.

Whether it is expressed as a syllogism, an enthymeme, or a claim, a deductive conclusion is only as strong as the premise or reasons on which it is based.

EXERCISE 14.7

The following sentences contain deductive arguments based on implied major premises. Identify each of the implied premises.

1. The use of marijuana for medical purposes should be legal if it can improve a patient's condition and does not harm anyone.
2. Women soldiers should not serve in combat positions because doing so would expose them to a much higher risk of death.
3. Animals can't talk; therefore they can't feel pain as humans do.

Visuals that make logical appeals

Visuals that make logical appeals can be especially useful in arguments, since they present factual information that can be taken in at a glance. *Mother Jones* used the following simple chart to carry a big message about income distribution in the United States. Consider how long it would take to explain all the information in this chart with words alone.

A VISUAL THAT MAKES A LOGICAL APPEAL

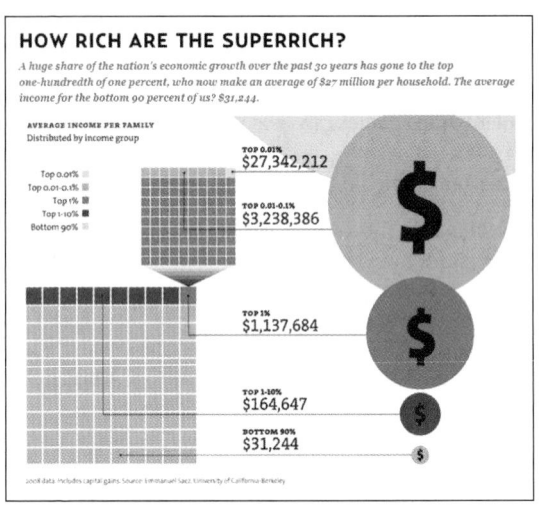

HOW RICH ARE THE SUPERRICH?

A huge share of the nation's economic growth over the past 30 years has gone to the top one-hundredth of one percent, who now make an average of $27 million per household. The average income for the bottom 90 percent of us? $31,244.

EXERCISE 14.8

Using a working thesis you drafted for Exercise 14.2 or 14.3, write a paragraph describing the logical appeals you would use to support the thesis.

14g Use appropriate emotional appeals.

Most successful arguments appeal to our hearts as well as to our minds—as is vividly demonstrated by the campaign to curb the AIDS epidemic in Africa. Facts and figures (logical appeals) convince us that the problem is real and serious. What elicits an outpouring of support, however, is the arresting emotional power of stories and images of people living with the disease. But credible writers take particular care when they use emotional appeals; audiences can easily begin to feel manipulated when an argument tries too hard to appeal to their pity, anger, or fear.

Concrete descriptive details

Like photographs, vivid words can bring a moving immediacy to any argument. A student may amass facts and figures, including diagrams and maps, to illustrate the problem of wheelchair access to the library. But only when the student asks a friend who uses a wheelchair to accompany her to the library does the student writer discover the concrete details necessary to move readers. The student can then write, "Marie inched her heavy wheelchair up the steep entrance ramp, her arms straining, her face pinched with the sheer effort."

Figurative language

Figurative language, or figures of speech, can paint a detailed and vivid picture by making striking comparisons between something you are writing about and something else that helps a reader visualize, identify with, or understand it (23d).

Figures of speech include metaphors, similes, and analogies. Most simply, metaphors compare two things directly: *Richard the Lion-Hearted; old age is the evening of life.* Similes make comparisons using *like* or *as: Richard is as brave as a lion; old age is like the evening of life.* Analogies are extended metaphors or similes that compare an unfamiliar concept or process to a more familiar one.

Visuals can also create vivid comparisons. The panels below come from a cartoon from Tom Tomorrow's comic strip, *This Modern World*, called "If Real Life Were More Like the Internet." Tomorrow, whose work appears regularly online, suggests in these panels that digital content has value, just as physical products and services do—and that those who create such content should be able to earn a living from it.

A VISUAL THAT CREATES A VIVID COMPARISON

Tomorrow adds emotional weight to the comparison by making the cartoon characters who want free content seem selfish and blind to the needs of those who serve them.

A VISUAL THAT MAKES AN EMOTIONAL APPEAL

Visuals that make emotional appeals

Visuals that make emotional appeals can also add substance to your argument. To make sure that such visual appeals will enhance your argument, test them out with several potential readers to see how they interpret the appeal. Consider, for example, the photograph above, which shows a funeral arranged by an American Legion post in Florida to honor four U.S. military veterans who died homeless. Some readers might see this image as an indictment of the government, which allowed soldiers who had fought for their country to end up without a place to live—but others might view it instead (or also) as confirmation that patriots come from every walk of life or that veterans honor their own even when others fail to do so.

EXERCISE 14.9

Make a list of common human emotions that might be attached to each of the following topics, and suggest appropriate ways to appeal to those emotions in a specific audience you choose to address.

1. banning drinking on campus
2. airport security
3. birth control
4. health care reform
5. steroid use among athletes

EXERCISE 14.10

Using a working thesis you formulated for Exercise 14.2 or 14.3, make a list of the emotional appeals most appropriate to your topic and audience. Then spend ten to fifteen minutes brainstorming, looking for descriptive and figurative language as well as images to carry out the appeals.

14h Consult sources.

In constructing an academic argument, it is often essential to use sources. The key to persuading people to accept your argument is providing good reasons; and even if your assignment doesn't specify that you must consult outside sources, they are often the most effective way of finding and establishing these reasons. Sources can help you to do the following:

- provide background information on your topic
- demonstrate your knowledge of the topic to readers
- cite authority and testimony in support of your thesis
- find opinions that differ from your own, which can help you sharpen your thinking, qualify your thesis if necessary, and demonstrate fairness to opposing arguments

For a thorough discussion of finding, gathering, and evaluating sources, see Chapters 15–19.

14i Organize your argument.

Once you have assembled good reasons and evidence in support of an argumentative thesis, you must organize your material to present the argument convincingly. Although there is no universally favored, one-size-fits-all organizational framework, you may find it useful to try one of the following patterns.

The classical system

The system of argument often followed by ancient Greek and Roman orators is now referred to as *classical*. You can adapt the ancient format to written arguments as follows:

1. Introduction
   - Gain readers' attention and interest.
   - Establish your qualifications to write about your topic.
   - Establish common ground with readers.
   - Demonstrate fairness.
   - State or imply your thesis.

2. Background
   - Present any necessary background information, including relevant personal narrative.

3. Lines of argument
   - Present good reasons (including logical and emotional appeals) in support of your thesis.
   - Present reasons in order of importance, with the most important ones generally saved for last.
   - Demonstrate ways your argument may be in readers' best interest.

4. Alternative arguments
   - Examine alternative points of view.
   - Note advantages and disadvantages of alternative views.
   - Explain why one view is better than other(s).

5. Conclusion
   - Summarize the argument if you choose.
   - Elaborate on the implication of your thesis.
   - Make clear what you want readers to think or do.
   - Reinforce your credibility.

The Toulmin system

This simplified form of the Toulmin system (13d and 14f) can help you organize an argumentative essay:

1. Make your claim (arguable statement).

▶ **The federal government should ban smoking.**

2. Qualify your claim if necessary.

▶ **The ban would be limited to public places.**

3. Present good reasons to support your claim.

▶ **Smoking causes serious diseases in smokers.**
▶ **Nonsmokers are endangered by others' smoke.**

4. Explain the assumptions that underlie your claim and your reasons. Provide additional explanations for any controversial assumptions.

ASSUMPTION	The Constitution was established to "promote the general welfare."
ASSUMPTION	Citizens are entitled to protection from harmful actions by others.

ADDITIONAL
EXPLANATION
The United States is based on a political system that is supposed to serve the basic needs of its people, including their health.

5. Provide additional evidence to support your claim (facts, statistics, testimony, and other logical, ethical, or emotional appeals).

STATISTICS Cite the incidence of deaths attributed to secondhand smoke.

FACTS Cite lawsuits won against large tobacco companies, including one that awarded billions of dollars to states in reparation for smoking-related health care costs.

FACTS Cite bans on smoking already imposed on indoor public spaces in many cities.

AUTHORITY Cite the surgeon general.

6. Acknowledge and respond to possible counterarguments.

COUNTER-
ARGUMENT
Smokers have rights, too.

RESPONSE The suggested ban applies only to public places; smokers are free to smoke in private.

7. Finally, state your conclusion in the strongest way possible.

14j Consider design issues.

Most writers today create arguments that are carefully designed to make the best use of space, font style and type size, color, visuals, and technology. Chapter 9 provides extensive information on design issues, and it would be wise to consult that chapter as you design an argument. The following tips will get you thinking about how to produce and design an argument that will add to the ethical, logical, and emotional appeals you are making:

- Spend some time deciding on a distinct visual style for your argument, one that will appeal to your intended readers, set a clear voice or tone for your argument, and guide readers through your text.

- Check out any conventions that may be expected in the kind of argument you are writing. Look for examples of similar arguments, or ask your instructor for information about such conventions (5f).

- Consider the use of white space, titles, and headings and how each page will look. Choose titles, headings, and subheadings that will guide readers from point to point (9c). You may want to set off an especially important part of your argument (such as a list of essential evidence) in a box, carefully labeled.

- Make sure that your visual design is consistent. If you choose a particular color, font, or type style for a particular purpose, such as a second-level heading, make sure that you use the same color, font, or type style for that purpose throughout your paper.
- Be sure to choose readable fonts and font sizes (9b and c).
- Choose colors carefully, and make sure that you use color appropriately for the genre and medium.
- Place images close to the text they illustrate, and label each one clearly. Make sure that audio and video files appear in appropriate places and are identified for users.
- After you have a rough draft of your design, test it out on friends and classmates, asking them to describe how readable it is, how easy it is to follow, and what you need to change to make it more effective. Decide what adjustments you need to make—in format, spacing, alignment, use of color and fonts, and so on.

EXERCISE 14.11

Using the guidelines in this chapter, draft an argument in support of one of the working theses you formulated in Exercise 14.2 or 14.3.

EXERCISE 14.12: THINKING CRITICALLY

Using the checklist on p. 162, analyze an argument you've recently written or the draft you wrote for Exercise 14.11. Decide what you need to do to revise your argument, and write out a brief plan for revision.

14k Student argument essay

Student Writer

Teal Pfeifer

In this essay, Teal Pfeifer argues that images in the media affect how women see themselves, and she offers a solution to a problem. Her essay has been annotated to point out the various parts of her argument as well as her use of good reasons, evidence, and appeals to logic and emotion.

bedfordstmartins.com/everydaywriter
Student Writing

Teal Pfeifer

Professor Rashad

English 102

13 April 2012

Devastating Beauty

Collarbones, hipbones, cheekbones—so many bones. She looks at the camera with sunken eyes, smiling, acting beautiful. Her dress is Versace, or Gucci, or Dior, and it is revealing, revealing every bone and joint in her thin, thin body. She looks fragile and beautiful, as if I could snap her in two. I look at her and feel the soft cushion of flesh that surrounds my own joints, my own shoulders and hips that are broad, my own ribs surrounded by skin and muscle and fat. I am not nearly as fragile or graceful or thin. I look away and wonder what kind of self-discipline it takes to become beautiful like the model in my magazine.

By age seventeen a young woman has seen an average of 250,000 ads featuring a severely underweight woman whose body type is, for the most part, unattainable by any means, including extreme ones such as anorexia, bulimia, and drug use ("The Skinny"). The media promote clothing, cigarettes, fragrances, and even food with images like these. In a culture that has become increasingly visual, the images put out for public consumption feature women that are a smaller size than ever before. In 1950, the White Rock Mineral Water girl was 5′4″ tall and weighed 140 pounds; now she is 5′10″ tall and weighs only 110 pounds, signifying the growing deviation between the weight of models and that of the normal female population (Pipher 184).

This media phenomenon has had a major effect on the female population as a whole, both young and old. Five to ten million women in America today suffer from an eating disorder related

Title uses play on words to pique interest

Opening uses emotional appeals and tries to establish common ground with readers

Presents background information on the problem and cites sources

Introduces problem: ads encourage women's poor body image

to poor self-image, and yet advertisements continue to prey on insecurities fueled by a woman's desire to be thin. Current research shows that "80 percent of American women are dissatisfied with their appearance" and that "45 percent of those are on a diet on any given day" ("Statistics"). Yet even the most stringent dieting will generally fail to create the paper-thin body so valued in the media, and continuing efforts to do so can lead to serious psychological problems such as depression.

While many women express dissatisfaction with their bodies, they are not the only victims of the emaciated images so frequently presented to them. Young girls are equally affected by these images, if not more so. Eighty percent of girls under age ten have already been on a diet and expressed the desire to be thinner and more beautiful (*Slim Hopes*). Thus, from a young age, beauty is equated with a specific size. The message girls get is an insidious one: in order to be your best self, you should wear size 0 or 1. The pressure only grows more intense as girls grow up. According to results from the Kaiser Family Foundation Survey "Reflections of Girls in the Media," 16 percent of ten- to seventeen-year-old girls reported that they had dieted or exercised to look like a TV character. Yet two-thirds of teenage girls acknowledged that these thin characters were not an accurate reflection of "real life" (qtd. in Dittrich, "Children").

It is tragic to see so much of the American population obsessed with weight and reaching an ideal that is, for the most part, ultimately unattainable. Equally troubling is the role magazines play in feeding this obsession. When a researcher asked female students from Stanford University to flip through several magazines containing images of glamorized, super-thin models (see Fig. 1), 68 percent of the women felt significantly worse about themselves after viewing the magazine models (qtd. in Dittrich, "Media"). Another study showed that looking at models on a long-term basis leads to stress, depression, guilt, and

Good reason for thesis: stringent dieting can cause psychological problems

Provides statistical evidence that problem extends across age groups

Uses logical appeals

Good reason for thesis: magazines feed obsession with dieting

Backs up reasons with research and expert opinion

Fig. 1. Young women reading magazines. Personal photograph by author.

lowered self-worth (qtd. in Dittrich, "Media"). As Naomi Wolf points out in *The Beauty Myth*, thinking obsessively about fat and dieting has actually been shown to change thought patterns and brain chemistry.

How do we reject images that are so harmful to the women and young girls who view them? Legislation regarding what can be printed and distributed is not an option because of First Amendment rights. Equally untenable is the idea of appealing to the industries that hire emaciated models. As long as the beauty and clothing industries are making a profit from the physically insecure girls and women who view their ads, nothing will change.

What, however, might happen if women stopped buying the magazines that print such destructive images? A boycott is the most effective way to rid the print medium of emaciated models and eliminate the harmful effects they cause. If women stopped buying magazines that target them with such harmful advertising, magazines would be forced to change the kinds of ads they print. Such a boycott would send a clear message: women and girls reject the victimization that takes place every time they look at

(margin note) Considers and rejects alternative solutions

(margin note) States working thesis: a boycott would effectively solve problem

a skeletally thin model and then feel worse about themselves. Consumers can ultimately control what is put on the market: if we don't buy, funding for such ads will dry up fast.

Good reason: boycotts have been effective

In the past, boycotts have been effective tools for social change. Rosa Parks, often identified as the mother of the modern-day civil rights movement, played a pivotal role in the Montgomery bus boycott in December 1955. When Parks refused to give up her seat to a white bus rider, she was arrested, and this incident inspired the

Presents a precedent/ example as evidence

boycott. For more than a year, the vast majority of African Americans in Montgomery chose to walk instead of ride the buses. Many of them were terrorized or harassed, but the boycott was eventually successful: segregation on buses was declared illegal by the U.S. Supreme Court.

Between 1965 and 1973, Cesar Chavez also used boycotts successfully to change wage policies and working conditions

Presents a second precedent/ example as evidence

for millions of Mexicans and Mexican Americans who were being exploited by growers of grapes and lettuce. In his boycott efforts, Chavez moved on two fronts simultaneously: he asked the workers to withhold their labor, and he asked consumers to refrain from purchasing table grapes (and later, lettuce) in order to show their support for the workers. In this situation, not only did the boycott force an industry to improve existing conditions, but it also made the public aware of pressing labor issues. Thus a bond was formed between the workers and the community their labor was benefiting.

Appeals directly to audience by using "we" in conclusion

As a society, we have much to learn from boycotts of the past, and their lessons can help us confront contemporary social ills. As I have shown, body-image dissatisfaction and eating disorders are rising at an alarming rate among young girls and women in American society. This growing desire for an unrealistically thin body affects our minds and our spirits, especially when we are pummeled dozens of times a day with glamorized images of emaciated and unhealthy women. The resulting anorexia and

Pfeifer 5

bulimia that women suffer from are not only diseases that can be cured; they are also ones that can be prevented—if women will take a solid stand against such supporting advertisements and the magazines that publish them. This is where power lies—in the hands of those who hand over the dollars that support the glorification of unhealthy and unrealistic bodies. It is our choice to exert this power and to reject magazines that promote such images.

Reinforces severity of problem and appeals to emotion

Restates thesis as a call to action

Works Cited

Dittrich, Liz. "About-Face Facts on the Children and the Media."
    About-Face. About-Face, 1996–2010. Web. 10 Mar. 2012.

- - -. "About-Face Facts on the Media." *About-Face*. About-Face,
    1996–2010. Web. 10 Mar. 2012.

Pipher, Mary. *Reviving Ophelia: Saving the Selves of Adolescent Girls*.
    New York: Ballantine, 1994. Print.

"The Skinny on Media and Weight." *Common Sense Media*. Common
    Sense Media Inc., 27 Sept. 2005. Web. 15 Mar. 2012.

Slim Hopes. Dir. Sut Jhally. Prod. Jean Kilbourne. Media Education
    Foundation, 1995. Videocassette.

"Statistics." *National Eating Disorders Association*. National Eating
    Disorders Association, 2005. Web. 14 Mar. 2012.

Wolf, Naomi. *The Beauty Myth*. New York: Harper, 2002. Print.

Young women reading magazines. Personal photograph by author.
    14 Mar. 2012.

Research

Research is formalized curiosity. It is
poking and prying with a purpose.

— ZORA NEALE HURSTON

Research

15 Preparing for a Research Project   *187*

a Analyze the research assignment   *187*
b Formulate a research question and hypothesis   *190*
c Plan your research   *190*
d Set up a research log   *191*
e Move from hypothesis to working thesis   *192*

16 Doing Research   *193*

a Understand different kinds of sources   *193*
b Use the library to get started   *195*
c Find library resources   *196*
d Search the Internet   *202*
e Conduct field research   *203*

17 Evaluating Sources and Taking Notes   *206*

a Understand the purpose of sources   *206*
b Create a working bibliography   *206*
c Evaluate a source's usefulness and credibility   *208*
d Read critically, and interpret sources   *210*
e Synthesize sources   *216*
f Take notes and annotate sources   *218*

18 Integrating Sources and Avoiding Plagiarism   *224*

a Decide whether to quote, paraphrase, or summarize   *225*
b Integrate quotations, paraphrases, and summaries
effectively   *226*
c Integrate visuals and media effectively   *228*
d Check for excessive use of source material   *229*
e Understand why you should acknowledge your sources   *230*
f Know which sources to acknowledge   *231*
g Uphold your academic integrity and avoid plagiarism   *232*

19 Writing a Research Project   *234*

a Refine your writing plans   *234*
b Organize and draft   *236*
c Incorporate source materials   *239*
d Review and get responses to your draft   *239*
e Revise and edit your draft   *239*
f Prepare a list of sources   *241*
g Prepare and proofread your final copy   *241*

For visual analysis Look carefully at the illustration on the front of this tab. What do you think this image suggests about ways to do effective research?

Preparing for a Research Project **15**

Your employer asks you to recommend the best software for a particular project. You want to plan a spring break trip to the beach. Your instructor assigns a term paper about a jazz musician. Each of these situations calls for research, for examining various kinds of sources. Preparing to begin your research means taking a long look at what you already know, the best way to proceed, and the amount of time you have to find out what you need to know. For success in college and beyond, you need to understand how to start the process of academic research.

15a Analyze the research assignment.

In an introductory writing course, you might receive an assignment like this one:

> Choose a subject of interest to you, and use it as the basis for a research essay of approximately two thousand words that makes and substantiates a claim. You should use a minimum of five credible, authoritative sources.

Topic

If your assignment doesn't specify a topic, consider the following questions (see also 5c):

- What subjects do you already know something about? Which of them would you like to explore more fully?
- What subjects do you care about? What might you like to become an expert on?
- What subjects evoke a strong reaction from you, whether positive or negative?

Be sure to get responses about your possible topic from your instructor, classmates, and friends. Ask them whether they would be interested in reading about the topic, whether it seems manageable, and whether they know of any good sources for information on the topic.

Situation

Be sure to consider the rhetorical situation (see Chapter 5) of any research project. Here are detailed questions to think about:

AUDIENCE

- Who will be the audience for your research project (5e)?
- Who will be interested in the information you gather, and why? What will they want to know? What will they already know?
- What do you know about their backgrounds? What assumptions might they hold about the topic?
- What response do you want from them?
- What kinds of evidence will you need to convince them?
- What will your instructor expect?

TALKING THE TALK

Reaching an Audience

"Isn't my audience just my teacher?" To write effectively, you must think of your writing as more than just an assignment you have to complete to get a grade. Recognize that you have something to say — and that in order to get others to pay attention, you have to think about who they are and how to reach them. Of course, your instructor is part of your audience. But who else will be interested in your topic and the unique perspective you bring to it? What does that audience need from you?

PURPOSE

- If you can choose the purpose, what would you like to accomplish (5d)?
- If you have been assigned a specific research project, keep in mind the key words in that assignment. Does the assignment ask that you *describe, survey, analyze, persuade, explain, classify, compare,* or *contrast*? What do such words mean in this field?

YOUR POSITION ON THE TOPIC (STANCE)

- What is your attitude toward your topic? Are you curious about it? critical of it? Do you like it? dislike it? find it confusing?
- What influences have shaped your position (5d)?

SCOPE

- How long is the project supposed to be? Base your research and writing schedule on the scale of the finished project (a short versus a long paper or presentation, a brief oral report or a longer multimedia presentation, a simple versus a complex Web site) and the amount of time you have to complete it.

- How many and what kind(s) of sources should you use (16a)? What kind(s) of visuals—charts, maps, photographs, and so on—will you need? Will you do any field research—interviewing, surveying, or observing (16e)?

Here is a sample schedule for a research project:

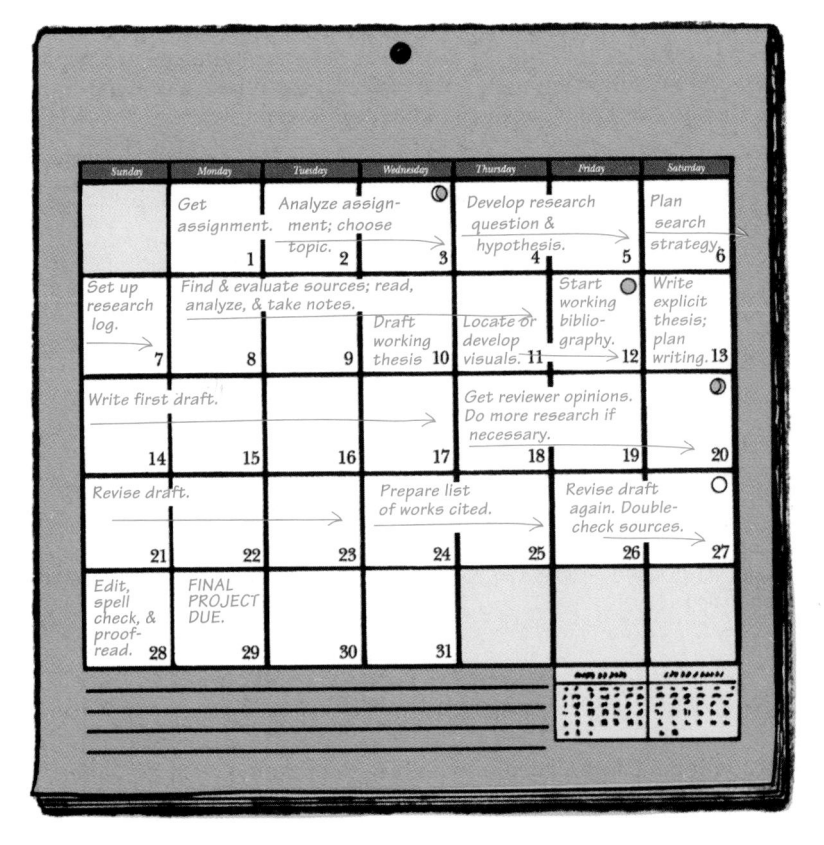

EXERCISE 15.1

Come up with at least two topics you would like to carry out research on. Then write a brief response to some key questions about each topic: How much information do you think is available on this topic? What sources on this topic do you know about or have access to? Who would know about this topic — historians, doctors, filmmakers, psychologists, others?

15b   Formulate a research question and hypothesis.

Once you have analyzed your task, chosen your topic, and narrowed the topic to make it manageable (see 7a), formulate a research question that you can tentatively answer with a hypothesis. The hypothesis, a statement of what you anticipate your research will show, needs to be manageable, interesting, and specific (see 7b). In addition, it must be a debatable proposition that you can prove or disprove with a reasonable amount of research evidence.

David Craig, the student whose research paper appears in Chapter 52, made the following move from general topic to a narrowed topic and then to a research question and hypothesis:

TOPIC	Electronic messaging
NARROWED TOPIC	The language of messaging
ISSUE	The effect of messaging on youth literacy
RESEARCH QUESTION	How has the popularity of messaging affected literacy among today's youth?
HYPOTHESIS	Messaging seems to have a negative influence on the writing skills of young people.

EXERCISE 15.2

Using the tips provided in 15a, write down as much as you can about one of the topics you identified in Exercise 15.1. Then take some time to reread your notes, and jot down the questions you still need to answer as well as the sources you need to find.

15c   Plan your research.

Once you have formulated a hypothesis, determine what you already know about your topic. Tap your memory for sources by listing everything you can remember about *where* you learned about your topic: the Internet, text messages, books, magazines, courses, conversations, television. What you know comes from somewhere, and that somewhere can serve as a starting point for your research. (See Chapter 6 for more strategies for exploring ideas and getting your initial thoughts about a topic down on paper.)

Next, develop a research plan by answering the following questions:

- What kinds of sources (books, journal articles, databases, Web sites, government documents, reference works, and so on) will you need to consult (16a)? How many sources should you consult?

- How current do your sources need to be? For topical issues, especially those related to science, current sources are usually most important. For historical subjects, older sources may offer the best information.

- How can you determine the location and availability of the kinds of sources you need?

One goal of your research plan is to build a strong working bibliography (17b). Carrying out systematic research and keeping careful notes on your sources will make developing your works-cited list or bibliography easier.

15d Set up a research log.

Keeping a research log will make the job of writing and documenting your sources more efficient and accurate. Use your research log to jot down ideas about possible sources and to keep track of materials. When you record an online source in your log, include the URL or other information that will help you find the source again.

Here are a few guidelines for setting up a research log:

1. Create a folder, and label it with a name that will be easy to identify, such as *Research Log for Project on Messaging*.
2. Within this folder, create subfolders that will help you manage your project. These subfolders might include *Notes on Hypothesis and Thesis, Background Information, Visuals, Draft 1, Working Bibliography*, and so on.

You might prefer to begin a blog for your research project. You can use it to record your thoughts on the reading you are doing and, especially, add links from there to Web sites, documents, and articles you have found online.

Whatever form your research log takes, you must clearly distinguish the notes and comments you make from quoted passages you record (see Chapter 17).

15e   Move from hypothesis to working thesis.

As you gather information, search catalogs and databases, and read and evaluate sources, you will probably refine your research question and change your hypothesis significantly. Only after you have explored your hypothesis, tested it, and sharpened it by reading, writing, and talking with others does it become a working thesis.

David Craig, the student whose hypothesis appears in 15b, did quite a bit of research on messaging language, youth literacy, and the possible connection between the two. The more he read, the more he felt that the hypothesis suggested by his discussion with instructors—that messaging had contributed to a decline in youth literacy—did not hold up.

For David Craig's research essay, see Chapter 52.

Thus, he shifted his attention to the positive effects of messaging on communication skills and developed the following working thesis: "Although some educators criticize messaging, it may aid literacy by encouraging young people to use words and to write—even if messaging requires a different kind of writing."

In doing your own research, you may find that your interest shifts, that a whole line of inquiry is unproductive, or that your hypothesis is simply wrong. The process of research pushes you to learn more about your hypothesis and to make it more precise.

EXERCISE 15.3: THINKING CRITICALLY

If you have done research for an essay or research project before, go back and evaluate the work you did as a researcher and as a writer in light of the principles developed in this chapter. What was the purpose of the research? Who was your audience? How did you narrow and focus your topic? What kinds of sources did you use? Did you use a research log? What about your research and your essay pleased you most? What pleased you least? What would you do differently if you were to revise the essay now?

Doing Research **16**

How would you find out where to get the best coffee in town, or how to find sources for a Web project on a 1930s film star? Whether you are researching pizza or Picasso, you need to be familiar with the kinds of sources you are likely to use, the searches you can perform, and the types of research you will do most often: library, Internet, and field research.

16a Understand different kinds of sources.

Sources can include data from interviews and surveys, books and articles in print and online, Web sites, film, video, images, and more. Consider these important differences among sources.

Primary and secondary sources

Primary sources provide firsthand knowledge, while secondary sources report on or analyze the research of others. Primary sources are basic sources of raw information, including your own field research; films, works of art, or other objects you examine; literary works you read; and eyewitness accounts, photographs, news reports, and historical documents (such as letters and speeches). Secondary sources are descriptions or interpretations of primary sources, such as researchers' reports, reviews, biographies, and encyclopedia articles. Often what constitutes a primary or secondary source depends on the purpose of your research. A critic's evaluation of a film, for instance, serves as a secondary source if you are writing about the film but as a primary source if you are studying the critic's writing.

Scholarly and popular sources

While nonacademic sources like magazines can help you get started on a research project, you will usually want to depend more heavily on authorities in a field, whose work generally appears in scholarly journals in print or online. The following list will help you distinguish scholarly and popular sources:

SCHOLARLY	POPULAR

Ecology and Society	

Title often contains the word *Journal*

Journal usually does not appear in title

Source available mainly through libraries and library databases

Source generally available outside of libraries (at newsstands or from a home Internet connection)

Few commercial advertisements

Many advertisements

Authors identified with academic credentials

Authors are usually journalists or reporters hired by the publication, not academics or experts

Summary or abstract appears on first page of article; articles are fairly long

No summary or abstract; articles are fairly short

Articles cite sources and provide bibliographies

Articles may include quotations but do not cite sources or provide bibliographies

Older and more current sources

Most projects can benefit from both older, historical sources and more current ones. Some older sources are classics, essential for understanding later scholarship. Others are simply dated. Whether a source appeared hundreds of years ago or this morning, evaluate it carefully to determine how useful it will be for you.

16b Use the library to get started.

Many beginning researchers are tempted to assume that all the information they could possibly need is readily available on the Internet from a home connection. However, it is a good idea to begin almost any research project with the sources available in your college library.

Reference librarians

The purpose of a college reference library is to help students find information—and the staff of your library, especially reference librarians, will willingly help you figure out how to get started, what resources to choose for your project, and how to research more effectively. When in doubt, ask your librarian! You can make an appointment to talk with a librarian about your research project and get specific recommendations about databases and other helpful places to begin your research. In addition, many libraries have online tours and chat environments where students can ask questions about their research.

Catalogs and databases

Your library's computers hold many resources not accessible to students except through the library's system. In addition to the library's own catalog of books and other holdings, most college libraries also subscribe to a large number of databases—electronic collections of information, such as indexes to journal and magazine articles, texts of news stories and legal cases, lists of sources on particular topics, and compilations of statistics—that students can access for free.

Reference works

Consulting general reference works is another good way to get started on a research project. These works are especially helpful for getting an overview of a topic, identifying subtopics, finding more specialized sources, and identifying useful keywords for electronic searches.

Wikis as Sources

"Why doesn't my instructor want me to use Wikipedia as a source?" Wikis are sites that users can add to and edit as they see fit; as a result, their contents are not always reliable. It's true that Wikipedia, a hugely popular site, has such a large and enthusiastic audience that users are likely to catch mistakes and remove deliberately false information quickly. But you can never be certain that a wiki entry has not been tampered with. Use wikis as sources for preliminary research and then make sure that you double-check any information you find there.

ENCYCLOPEDIAS

Encyclopedias offer general background on a subject and often include bibliographies that can point you to more specialized sources. Remember that encyclopedias will serve as a place to start your research—not as major sources for a research project.

BIOGRAPHICAL RESOURCES

The lives and historical settings of famous people are the topics of biographical dictionaries and indexes.

BIBLIOGRAPHIES

Bibliographies are collections of resources available on a subject—for example, Shakespeare or World War II. Bibliographies may be databases or bound collections, and they may list books alone, both books and articles, or media such as film or video. A bibliography may simply list or describe each resource it includes, or it may include analysis of the resources.

ALMANACS, YEARBOOKS, AND ATLASES

Almanacs and yearbooks contain data on current events and statistical information. Look in an atlas for maps and other geographic data.

16c Find library resources.

The library is one of a researcher's best friends, especially in an age of digital communication. Your college library houses a great number of print materials and gives you access to electronic catalogs, indexes, and databases. Check your library's Web site or ask a librarian for an introduction to the available resources.

Advanced search page from a library catalog that incorporates Boolean operators

Search options

The most important tools your library offers are its online catalog and databases. Searching these tools will always be easier and more efficient if you use carefully chosen words to limit the scope of your research.

SUBJECT WORD SEARCHING

Catalogs and databases usually index their contents not only by author and title but also by subject headings—standardized words and phrases used to classify the subject matter of books and articles. (For books, most U.S. academic libraries use the *Library of Congress Subject Headings*, or LCSH, for this purpose.) When you search the catalog by subject, you need to use the exact subject words.

KEYWORD SEARCHING

Searches using keywords, on the other hand, make use of the computer's ability to look for any term in any field of the electronic record, including not just subject but also author, title, series, and notes. In article databases, a keyword search will look in abstracts and summaries of articles as well. Keyword searching is less restrictive, but it requires you to put some thought into choosing your search terms in order to get the best results.

ADVANCED SEARCHING

Many library catalogs and database search engines offer advanced search options (sometimes on a separate page) to help you combine keywords, search for an exact phrase, or exclude items containing particular keywords. Often they limit your search in other ways as well, such as by date, language, country of origin, or location of the keyword within a site.

Many catalogs and databases offer a search option using the Boolean operators AND, OR, and NOT, and some allow you to use parentheses to refine your search or wildcards to expand it. Note that much Boolean decision making is done for you when you use an advanced search option (as on the advanced search page shown above). Note, too, that search engines vary in the exact terms and symbols they use to refine searches, so check before you search.

- AND *limits your search.* If you enter the terms *messaging* AND *language* AND *literacy,* the search engine will retrieve only those items that contain *all* the terms. Some search engines use a plus sign (+) instead of AND.

- OR *expands your search.* If you enter the terms *messaging* OR *language,* the computer will retrieve every item that contains the term *messaging* and every item that contains the term *language.*

- NOT *limits your search.* If you enter the terms *messaging* NOT *language,* the search engine will retrieve every item that contains *messaging* except those that also contain the term *language.* Some search engines use a minus sign (−) or AND NOT instead of NOT.

- *Parentheses customize your search.* Entering *messaging* AND (*literacy* OR *linguistics*), for example, will locate items that mention either of those terms in connection with messaging.

- *Wildcards expand your search.* Use a wildcard, usually an asterisk (*) or a question mark (?), to find related words that begin with the same letters. Entering *messag** will locate *message, messages,* and *messaging.*

- *Quotation marks narrow your search.* Most search engines interpret words within quotation marks as a phrase that must appear with the words in that exact order.

Books

The library catalog lists all the library's books.

CATALOG INFORMATION

Library catalogs follow a standard pattern of organization, with each holding identified by three kinds of entries: one headed by the *author's name,* one by the *title,* and one or (usually) more by the *subject.* If you can't find a particular source under any of these headings, you can search the catalog by using a combination of subject headings and keywords. Such searches may turn up other useful titles as well.

Catalog entries for books list not only the author, title, subject, and publication information but also a call number that indicates how the book is classified and where it is shelved. Many online catalogs allow you to save the information about the book while you continue searching and then retrieve the call numbers for all of the books you want to find in one list. Once you have the call number for a book, look for a library map or shelving plan to tell you where the book is housed. Take the time to browse through the books near the call number you are looking for. Often you will find other books related to your topic nearby.

Following is a page of results for noted linguist and author David Crystal. Many electronic catalogs indicate whether a book has been checked out and, if so, when it is due to be returned. Sometimes you must click on a link to check the availability of the book.

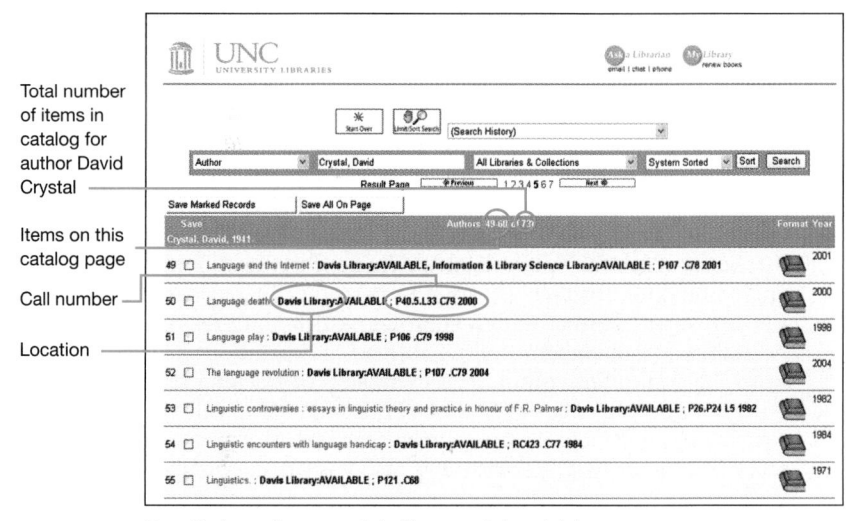

Results for author search in library catalog database

BOOK INDEXES

Indexes can help you quickly locate complete bibliographic information on a book when you know only one piece of it—the author's last name, perhaps, or the title. Indexes can also alert you to other works by a particular author or on a particular subject. If you are looking for an older book, you may find the information you need in a print index rather than in an electronic database.

REVIEW INDEXES

A review index will help you find reviews of books you are interested in so that you can check the relevance of a source or get a thumbnail sketch of its contents before you track it down. For reviews more than ten years old, you will generally need to consult the print version of the index.

Periodical articles

Titles of periodicals held by a library appear in its catalog, but the titles of individual articles do not. To find the contents of periodicals, you will need to use an index source.

PERIODICAL INDEXES

Periodical indexes are databases or print volumes that hold information about articles published in newspapers, magazines, and scholarly journals. Different indexes cover different groups of periodicals. Ask a reference librarian for guidance about the most relevant index for your topic.

General indexes of periodicals list articles from general-interest magazines (such as *Time* or *Newsweek*), newspapers, or a combination of these. General indexes usually provide current sources on a topic, but you may need to look further for in-depth articles.

Many disciplines have *specialized indexes and abstracts* to help researchers find detailed information. To use these resources most efficiently, ask a reference librarian for help.

Some electronic periodical indexes offer the full text of articles and some offer abstracts (short summaries) of the articles. Be sure not to confuse an abstract with a complete article. Full-text databases can be extremely convenient—you can read and print out articles directly from the computer, without the extra step of tracking down the periodical in question. However, don't limit yourself to full-text databases, which may not include the sources that would benefit your research most. Databases that offer abstracts give you an overview of the article's

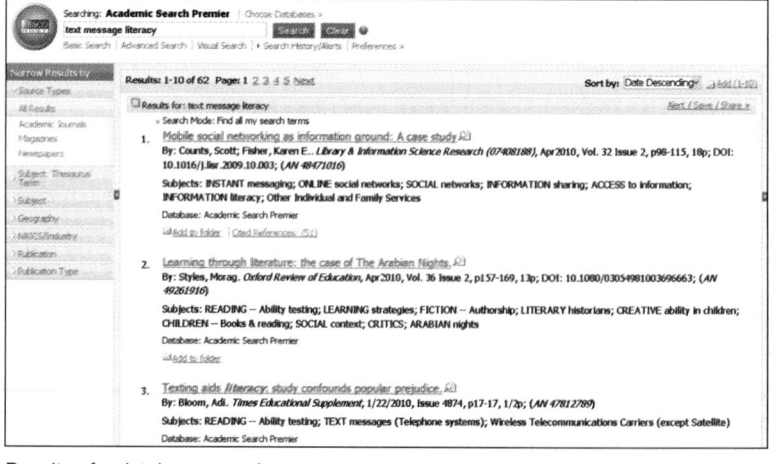

Results of a database search

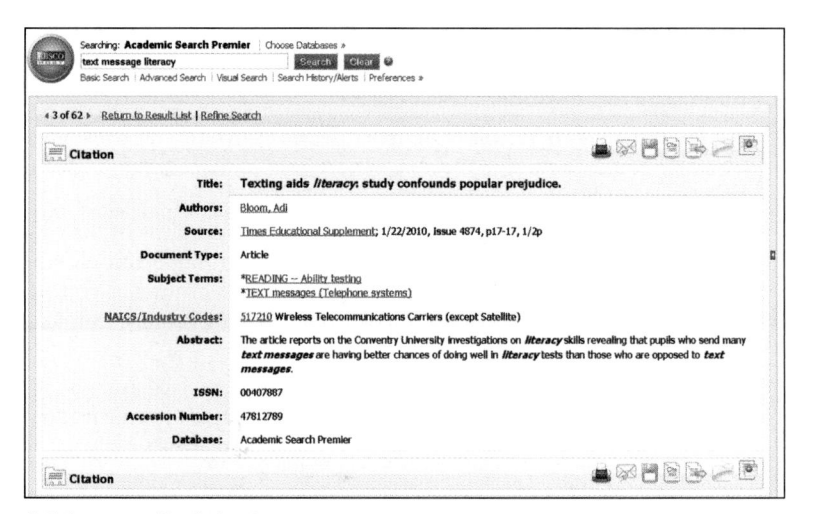

Article page with abstract

contents that can help you decide whether you need to spend time finding and reading the full text.

To locate an indexed article that seems promising for your research project, you can check the library catalog to see whether the periodical is available electronically and, if so, whether your library has access to it. Using the library computer network for access can help you avoid paying to view the text of the article that is available online only for subscribers or for a fee.

If the periodical is not available electronically (some scholarly journals, for example, are not), the library catalog also will tell you whether a print version is available in your library's periodicals room. This room probably has recent issues of hundreds or even thousands of newspapers, magazines, and scholarly journals, and it may also contain bound volumes of past issues and microfilm copies of older newspapers.

Bibliographies

Bibliographies (lists of sources) in books or articles you are using for your research can lead you to other valuable resources. In addition, check with a reference librarian to find out whether your library has more extensive bibliographies devoted to the area of your research.

Other library resources

In addition to books and periodicals, libraries give you access to many other useful materials that might be appropriate for your research.

- *Special collections and archives.* Your library may house archives (collections of valuable papers) and other special materials that are often available to student researchers.
- *Audio, video, multimedia, and art collections.* Many libraries have areas devoted to media and art, where they collect films, videos, paintings, and sound recordings.
- *Government documents.* Many libraries have collections of historical documents produced by local or state government offices. You can also look at the online version of the U.S. Government Printing Office (GPO Access) for electronic versions of government publications from the past decade or so.
- *Interlibrary loans.* To borrow books, videos, copies of journal articles, or audio materials from another library, use an interlibrary loan. Some loans can take time, so be sure to plan ahead.

16d   Search the Internet.

The Internet is many college students' favorite way of accessing information, and it's true that much information—including authoritative sources identical to those your library provides—can be found online, sometimes for free. However, information in library databases comes from identifiable and professionally edited sources; because no one is responsible for regulating information on the Web, you need to take special care to find out which information online is reliable and which is not. (See Chapter 17 for more on evaluating sources.)

Internet searches

Research using a search tool such as Google usually begins with a keyword search. Because the Internet contains vastly more material than the largest library catalog or database, Internet searching requires care in the choice of keywords. For example, if you need information on legal issues regarding the Internet and enter *Internet* and *law* as keywords in a Google search, you will get over three million hits. You may find what you need on the first page of hits, but if not, you will need to choose new keywords that lead to more specific sources.

Bookmarking tools

Today's powerful bookmarking tools can help you browse, sort, and track resources online. Social bookmarking sites allow users to tag information and share it with others. Once you register on a social bookmarking site, you can tag an online resource with any words you choose. Users' tags are visible to all other users. If you find a helpful site, you can check to see how others have tagged it and quickly browse similar tags to find related information. You can sort and group information according to your tags. Fellow users whose tags you like and trust can become part of your network so that you can follow their sites of interest.

Web browsers can also help you bookmark and return to online resources that you have found. However, unlike the bookmarking tools in a Web browser, which are tied to one machine, social bookmarking tools are available from any computer with an Internet connection.

Authoritative sources online

You can find many sources online that are authoritative and reliable. For example, the Internet enables you to enter virtual libraries that allow access to some collections in libraries other than your own. Online collections housed in government sites can also be reliable and useful sources. The Library of Congress, the National Institutes of Health, and the U.S. Census Bureau, for example, have large online collections of articles. For current national news, consult online versions of reputable newspapers such as the *Washington Post* or the *Chicago Tribune*, or electronic sites for news services such as C-SPAN. To limit your searches to scholarly works, try Google Scholar.

Some scholarly journals (such as those from Berkeley Electronic Press) and general-interest magazines (including *Slate* and *Salon*) are published only on the Web, and many other publications, like *Newsweek*, the *New Yorker*, and the *New Republic*, make at least some of their contents available online for free.

16e Conduct field research.

For many research projects, particularly those in the social sciences and business, you will need to collect field data. The "field" may be many things—a classroom, a church, a laboratory, or the corner grocery store. As a field researcher, you will need to discover *where* you can find relevant information, *how* to gather it, and *who* might be your best providers of information.

Interviewing

Some information is best obtained by asking direct questions of other people. If you can talk with an expert—in person, on the telephone, or via the Internet—you might get information you could not obtain

through any other kind of research. In addition to getting an expert
opinion, you might ask for firsthand accounts or suggestions of other
places to look or other people to consult.

AT A GLANCE
Conducting an Interview

1. Determine your purpose, and be sure it relates to your research question and your hypothesis.
2. Set up the interview well in advance. Specify how long it will take, and if you wish to record the session, ask permission to do so.
3. Prepare a written list of factual and open-ended questions. Brainstorming or freewriting can help you come up with questions (6a and b). Leave plenty of space for notes after each question. If the interview proceeds in a direction that seems fruitful, do not feel that you have to ask all of your prepared questions.
4. Record the subject, date, time, and place of the interview.
5. Thank those you interview, either in person or in a letter or email.

Observing

Trained observers report that making a faithful record of an observation requires intense concentration and mental agility. Moreover, an observer is never neutral—he or she always has an angle on what is being observed.

AT A GLANCE
Conducting an Observation

1. Determine the purpose of the observation, and be sure it relates to your research question and hypothesis.
2. Brainstorm about what you are looking for, but don't be rigidly bound to your expectations.
3. Develop an appropriate system for recording data. Consider using a split notebook or page: on one side, record your observations directly; on the other, record your thoughts and interpretations.
4. Record the date, time, and place of the observation.

Conducting surveys

Surveys usually depend on questionnaires. On any questionnaire, the questions should be clear and easy to understand and designed so that you can analyze the answers easily. Questions that ask respondents to say *yes* or *no* or to rank items on a scale are particularly easy to tabulate:

> The parking facilities on our campus are adequate.
>
> **O** Strongly   **O** Somewhat   **O** Unsure   **O** Somewhat   **O** Strongly
>   agree   agree   disagree   disagree

AT A GLANCE

Designing a Survey Questionnaire

1. Write out your purpose, and review your research question and hypothesis to determine the kinds of questions to ask.
2. Figure out how to reach the respondents you need.
3. Draft potential questions, and make sure that each question calls for a short, specific answer.
4. Test the questions on several people, and revise questions that seem unfair, ambiguous, too hard to answer, or too time consuming.
5. For a questionnaire that is to be mailed or emailed, draft a cover letter explaining your purpose.
6. On the final version of the questionnaire, leave adequate space for answers.
7. Proofread the questionnaire carefully.

Analyzing, synthesizing, and interpreting data from field research

To make sense of your data, find a focus for your analysis, since you can't pay attention to everything. Then synthesize the data by looking for recurring words or ideas that fall into patterns. Establish a system for coding your information, labeling each pattern you identify—a plus sign for every positive response, for example. Finally, interpret your data by summing up the meaning of what you have found. What is the significance of your findings? Be careful not to make large generalizations.

EXERCISE 16.1: THINKING CRITICALLY

Begin to analyze the research project you are now working on by examining the ways in which you conducted your research: What use did you make of primary and secondary sources? What library, online, and field research did you carry out? What aspect of the research process was most satisfying? What was most disappointing or irritating? How could you do research more efficiently? Bring your answers to these questions to class.

17 Evaluating Sources and Taking Notes

The difference between a useful source and a poor one depends to a great extent on your topic, purpose, and audience. On almost any topic you can imagine (Why do mosquitoes bite? Who reads fan fiction? What musicians influenced Sonic Youth?), you will need research—looking into sources, gathering data, and thinking critically about these sources—to answer the question. With most topics, in fact, your problem will not be so much finding sources as figuring out *which* sources to consult in the limited time you have available. Learning how to tell which sources are best for you allows you to use your time wisely, and taking effective notes allows you to put the sources to work for you.

17a   Understand the purpose of sources.

Why do writers decide to use one source rather than another? Sources serve different purposes, so part of evaluating sources involves deciding what you need the source to provide for your research projects. You may need background information or context that your audience will need to follow your writing; explanations of concepts unfamiliar to your audience; verbal and visual emphasis for your points; authority or evidence for your claims, which can help you create your own authority; other perspectives on your topic; or counter-examples or counter-evidence that you need to consider.

As you begin to work with your sources, make notes in your research log about why you plan to use a particular source. You should also begin your working bibliography.

17b   Create a working bibliography.

A working bibliography is a list of sources that you may potentially use for your project. As you find and begin to evaluate research sources—articles, books, Web sites, and so on—you should record source information for every source you think you might use. (Relevant information includes everything you need to find the source again and cite it correctly; the information you will need varies based on the type of source, whether you found it in a library or not, and whether you consulted it in print or online.) The emphasis here is on *working* because the list will probably include materials that end up not being useful. For this reason, you don't absolutely need to put all entries into the documentation style you will use (see Chapters 49–55). If you do follow the required documentation style, however, that part of your work will be done when you prepare the final draft.

The following chart will help you keep track of the sorts of information you should try to find:

Type of Source	Information to Collect (if applicable)
Print book	Library call number, author(s) or editor(s), title and subtitle, place of publication, publisher, year of publication, any other information (translator, edition, volume)
Part of a book	Call number, author(s) of part, title of part, author(s) or editor(s) of book, title of book, place of publication, publisher, year of publication, inclusive page numbers for part
Print periodical article	Call number of periodical, author(s) of article, title of article, name of periodical, volume number, issue number, date of issue, inclusive page numbers for article
Electronic source	Author(s), title of document, title of site, editor(s) of site, sponsor of site, publication information for print version of source, name of database or online service, date of electronic publication or last update, date you accessed the source, URL

For other kinds of sources (films, recordings, visuals), you should also list the information required by the documentation style you are using (see Chapters 49–55), and note where you found the information.

Annotated bibliography

You might wish to annotate your working bibliography to include your own description and comments as well as publishing information (whether or not annotations are required) because annotating can help you understand and remember what the source says. If your instructor requires an annotated bibliography, be sure to ask for the specific guidelines you are to follow in creating the bibliography.

Annotations can sometimes be very detailed and may include summaries of the main points in a source and evaluations of the source's usefulness. However, most annotations students do on their own include fairly brief descriptions and comments.

TALKING THE TALK

Research with an Open Mind

"What's wrong with looking for sources that back up what I want to say?" When you start researching a topic, keep an open mind: investigate every important source, even if you think you won't agree with it. If all your sources take the same position you take, you may be doing some pretty selective searching — and you may be missing a big part of the picture. Who knows? You may change your position after learning more about the topic. Even if you don't, ignoring counterarguments and other points of view harms your credibility, suggesting that you haven't done your homework.

ANNOTATED BIBLIOGRAPHY ENTRY

Gere, Anne Ruggles. "Kitchen Tables and Rented Rooms: The Extracurriculum
of Composition." *Literacy: A Critical Sourcebook*. Ed. Ellen Cushman,
Eugene R. Kintgen, Barry M. Kroll, and Mike Rose. Boston: Bedford, 2001.
275–89. Print. This history of writing instruction argues that people teach
writing and learn to write—and always have—more often in informal
places like kitchens than in traditional writing classrooms. Gere presents
numerous examples and comments on their importance to the study of
writing today.

 bedfordstmartins.com/everydaywriter
Student Writing

17c Evaluate a source's usefulness and credibility.

Since you want the information and ideas you glean from sources to be reliable and persuasive, you must evaluate each potential source carefully. The following guidelines can help you assess the usefulness and credibility of sources you are considering:

- *Your purpose.* What will this source add to your research project? Does it help you support a major point, demonstrate that you have thoroughly researched your topic, or help establish your own credibility through its authority?

- *Relevance.* How closely related is the source to the narrowed topic you are pursuing? You may need to read beyond the title and opening paragraph to check for relevance.

- *Level of specialization and audience.* General sources can be helpful as you begin your research, but you may then need the authority or currency of more specialized sources. On the other hand, extremely specialized works may be very hard to understand. Who was the source originally written for — the general public? experts in the field? advocates or opponents? How does this fit with your concept of your own audience?

- *Credentials of the publisher or sponsor.* What can you learn about the publisher or sponsor of the source you are using? For example, is it a newspaper known for integrity, or is it a tabloid? Is it a popular source, or is it sponsored by a professional or governmental organization or academic institution? If you're evaluating a book, is the publisher one you recognize or can find described on its own Web site? No hard and fast rules exist for deciding what kind of source to use. But knowing the sponsor's or publisher's credentials can help you determine whether a source is appropriate for your research project.

- *Credentials of the author.* As you do your research, note names that come up from one source to another, since these references may indicate that the author is influential in the field. An author's credentials may also be presented in the article, book, or Web site, or you can search the Internet for information about the author. In U.S. academic writing, experts and those with significant experience in a field have more authority on the subject than others.

- *Date of publication.* Recent sources are often more useful than older ones, particularly in the sciences or other fields that change rapidly. However, in some fields — such as the humanities — the most authoritative works may be older ones. The publication dates of Internet sites can often be difficult to pin down. And even for sites that include dates of posting, remember that the material posted may have been composed some time earlier.

- *Accuracy of the source.* How accurate and complete is the information in the source? How thorough is the bibliography or list of works cited that accompanies the source? Can you find other sources that corroborate what your source is saying?

- *Stance of the source.* Identify the source's point of view or rhetorical stance, and scrutinize it carefully. Does the source present facts, or does it interpret or evaluate them? If it presents facts, what is included and what is omitted, and why? If it interprets or evaluates information that is not disputed, the source's stance may be obvious, but at other times, you will need to think carefully about the source's goals (17d). What does the author or sponsoring group want? to convince you of an idea? sell you something? call you to action in some way?

- *Cross-references to the source.* Is the source cited in other works? If you see your source cited by others, notice how they cite it and what they say about it to find additional clues to its credibility.

For more on evaluating Web sources and periodical articles, see the Source Maps on pp. 212–215.

17d Read critically, and interpret sources.

For those sources that you want to analyze more closely, reading with a critical eye can make your research process more efficient. Use the following tips to guide your critical reading.

Your research question

As you read, keep your research question in mind, and ask yourself the following questions:

- How does this material address your research question and support your hypothesis?
- What quotations from this source might help support your thesis?
- Does the source include counterarguments to your hypothesis that you will need to answer? If so, what answers can you provide?

The author's stance and tone

Even a seemingly factual report, such as an encyclopedia article, is filled with judgments, often unstated. Read with an eye for the author's overall rhetorical stance, or perspective, as well as for facts or explicit opinions. Also pay attention to the author's tone, the way his or her attitude toward the topic and audience is conveyed. The following questions can help:

- Is the author a strong advocate or opponent of something? a skeptical critic? a specialist in the field?
- Are there any clues to why the author takes this stance?
- How does this stance affect the author's presentation and your reaction to it?
- What facts does the author include? Can you think of any important fact that is omitted?
- What is the author's tone? Is it cautious, angry, flippant, serious, impassioned? What words indicate this tone?

> **AT A GLANCE**
>
> ## Guidelines for Examining Potential Sources
>
> Looking quickly at the various parts of a source can provide useful in-
> formation and help you decide whether to explore that particular source
> more thoroughly. You are already familiar with some of these basic el-
> ements: title and subtitle, title page and copyright page, home page,
> table of contents, index, footnotes, and bibliography. Be sure to check
> other items as well.
>
> - *Abstracts* — concise summaries of articles and books — routinely pre-
>   cede journal articles and are often included in indexes and databases.
> - A *preface* or *foreword* generally discusses the writer's purpose and thesis.
> - *Subheadings* within the text can alert you to how much detail is given on
>   a topic.
> - A *conclusion* or *afterword* may summarize or draw the strands of an
>   argument together.
> - For a digital source, click on some of the *links* to see if they're useful,
>   and see if the overall *design* of the site is easy to navigate.

The author's argument and evidence

Every piece of writing takes a position. Even a scientific report implicitly "argues" that we should accept it and its data as reliable. As
you read, look for the main point or the main argument the author
is making. Try to identify the reasons the author gives to support
his or her position. Then try to determine *why* the author takes this
position.

- How persuasive is the evidence? Can you think of a way to refute it?
- Can you detect any questionable logic or fallacious thinking (13e)?
- Does this author disagree with arguments you have read elsewhere? If so, what causes the disagreements — differences about
  facts or about how to interpret facts?

EXERCISE 17.1

Choose two sources that seem well suited to your topic, and evaluate their usefulness and credibility using the criteria presented in this chapter. If possible, analyze
one print source and one digital source. Bring the results of your analysis to class for
discussion.

SOURCE MAP: Evaluating Web Sources

Is the sponsor credible?

1 Who is the **sponsor or publisher** of the source? See what information you can get from the URL. The domain names for government sites may end in *.gov* or *.mil* and for educational sites in *.edu*. The ending *.org* may — but does not always — indicate a nonprofit organization. If you see a tilde (~) or percent sign (%) followed by a name, or if you see a word such as *users* or *members*, the page's creator may be an individual, not an institution. In addition, check the header and footer, where the sponsor may be identified. The page shown here, from the domain **niemanwatchdog.org**, is from a site sponsored by the nonprofit Nieman Foundation for Journalism at Harvard University.

2 Look for an *About* page or a link to a home page for background information on the sponsor. Is a mission statement included? What are the sponsoring organization's purpose and point of view? Does the mission statement seem balanced? What is the purpose of the site (to inform, to persuade, to advocate for a cause, to advertise, or something else)? Does the information on the site come directly from the sponsor, or is the material reprinted from another source? If it is reprinted, check the original.

Is the author credible?

3 What are the **author's credentials**? Look for information accompanying the material on the page. You can also run a search on the author to find out more. Does the author seem qualified to write about this topic?

Is the information credible and current?

4 When was the information **posted or last updated**? Is it recent enough to be useful?

5 Does the page document sources with **footnotes or links**? If so, do the sources seem credible and current? Does the author include any additional resources for further information? Look for ways to corroborate the information the author provides.

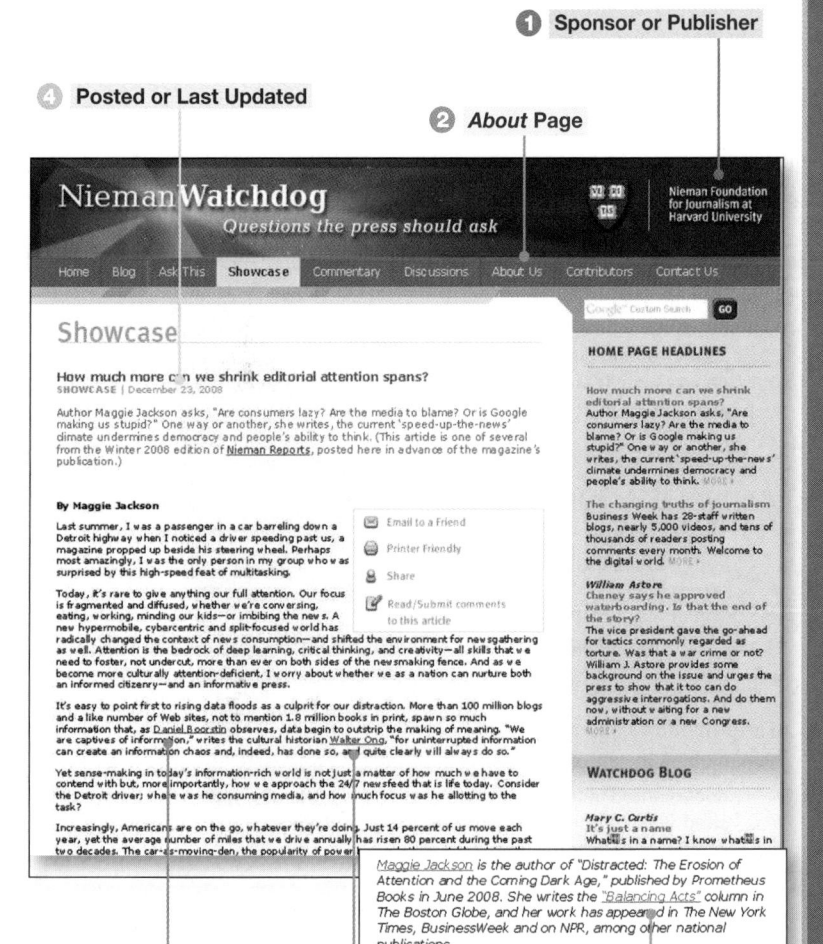

3 Author's Credentials

5 Links

213

SOURCE MAP: Evaluating Articles

Determine the relevance of the source.

1 Look for an **abstract**, which provides a summary of the entire article. Is this source directly related to your research? Does it provide useful information and insights? Will your readers consider it persuasive support for your thesis?

Determine the credibility of the publication.

2 Consider the publication's **title**. Words in the title such as *Journal*, *Review*, and *Quarterly* may indicate that the periodical is a scholarly source. Most research projects rely on authorities in a particular field, whose work usually appears in scholarly journals. For more on distinguishing between scholarly and popular sources, see 16a.

3 Try to determine the **publisher or sponsor**. This journal is published by Johns Hopkins University Press. Academic presses such as this one generally review articles carefully before publishing them and bear the authority of their academic sponsors.

Determine the credibility of the author.

4 Evaluate the **author's credentials**. In this case, they are given in a note, which indicates that the author is a college professor and has written at least two books on related topics.

Determine the currency of the article.

5 Look at the **publication date**, and think about whether your topic and your credibility depend on your use of very current sources.

Determine the accuracy of the article.

6 Look at the **sources cited** by the author of the article. Here, they are documented in footnotes. Ask yourself whether the works the author has cited seem credible and current. Are any of these works cited in other articles you've considered?

In addition, consider the following questions:

- What is the article's stance or point of view? What are the author's goals? What does the author want you to know or believe?
- How does this source fit in with your other sources? Does any of the information it provides contradict or challenge other sources?

HUMAN RIGHTS QUARTERLY

2 Title of Publication

Prisons and Politics in Contemporary Latin America

1 Abstract

Mark Ungar*

America   915

ABSTRACT

Despite democratization throughout Latin America, massive human rights abuses continue in the region's prisons. Conditions have become so bad that most governments have begun to enact improvements, including new criminal codes and facility decongestion. However, once in place, these reforms are undermined by chaotic criminal justice systems, poor policy administration, and rising crime rates leading to greater detention powers for the police. After describing current prison conditions in Latin America and the principal reforms to address them, this article explains how political and administrative limitations hinder the range of agencies and officials responsible for implementing those changes.

an. In Venezuela, the
er 100, but jumped to
tice Ministry agency in
even prisoners, far from
state alone, the number
1997.[11] Inmates form
la Capital (PCC)—with
d prisoners. In the riots
001—which began in
hat amount, and spread
000 inmates—the PCC
cation of PCC leaders.
all sizes and security
—often at unaffordable
country's largest, some
mmed into tiny airless
en of inmates living in
d many of those in the
curity La Paz facility of
al en la Lucha Contra el
to nearly airless cells of
ns lack potable water,
infested with rats and
also bring in weapons
trade in cocaine and
ouse by prison officials,
the National Guard in
often face retribution.
39 prisoners protesting
colony of El

I. INTRODUCTION

4 Author's Credentials

Prison conditions not only constitute some of the worst human rights violations in contemporary Latin American democracies, but also reveal fundamental weaknesses in those democracies. Unlike most other human rights problems, those in the penitentiary system cannot be easily explained with authoritarian legacies or renegade officials. The systemic killing, overcrowding, disease, torture, rape, corruption, and due process abuses all occur under the state's twenty-four hour watch. Since the mid-1990s,

* Mark Ungar is Associate Professor of Political Science at Brooklyn College, City University of New York. Recent publications include the books *Elusive Reform: Democracy and the Rule of Law in Latin America* (Lynne Rienner, 2002) and *Violence and Politics: Globalization's Paradox* (Routledge, 2001) as well as articles and book chapters on democratization, policing, and judicial access. He works with Amnesty International USA and local rights groups in Latin America.

Human Rights Quarterly 25 (2003) 909–934 © 2003 by The Johns Hopkins University Press

5 Publication Date

3 Publisher

10. Inspector General de Cárceles, Informe Annual (Caracas: Ministerio de Justicia 1994).
11. *Overcrowding Main Cause of Riots in Latin American Prisons*, AFP, 30 Dec. 1997.
12. Interviews with inmates, speaking on condition of anonymity in San Pedro prison (19 July 2000); Interviews with inmates, speaking on condition of anonymity in La Paz FELCN Prison (20 July 2000).
13. Typhus, cholera, tuberculosis, and scabies run rampant and the HIV rate may be as high as 25 percent. The warden of Retén de la Planta, where cells built for one inmate house three or four, says the prisons "are collapsing" because of insufficient budgets to train personnel. "Things fall apart and stay that way." Interview, Luis A. Lara Roche, Warden of Retén de la Planta, Caracas, Venezuela, 19 May 1995. At El Dorado prison in Bolívar state, there is one bed for every four inmates, cells are infested with vermin, and inmates lack clean bathing water and eating utensils.
14. *La Crisis Penitenciaria*, El Nacional (Caracas), 2 Sept. 1988, at D2. On file with author.

6 Sources Cited

17e   Synthesize sources.

When you read and interpret a source—for example, when you consider its purpose and relevance, its author's credentials, its accuracy, and the kind of argument it is making—you are analyzing the source. Analysis requires you to take apart something complex (such as an article in a scholarly journal) and look closely at the parts to understand the whole better. For academic writing you also need to *synthesize*—group similar pieces of information together and look for patterns—so you can put your sources (and your own knowledge and experience) together in an original argument. Synthesis is the flip side of analysis: you already understand the parts, so your job is to assemble them into a new whole.

To synthesize sources for a research project, try the following tips:

- *Read the material carefully.* For tips on reading with a critical eye, see Chapter 12.

- *Determine the important ideas in each source.* Take notes on each source (17f). Identify and summarize the key ideas of each piece.

- *Formulate a position.* Review the key ideas of each source and figure out how they fit together. Look for patterns: discussions of causes and effects, specific parts of a larger issue, background informa-

SYNTHESIS: Finding Patterns

Look through your sources carefully to find what you need.

Ask...

What are the key ideas in each source?

What patterns can you identify?

How do the sources' perspectives relate to your own perspective?

Acknowledge that the related ideas you find may not fit smoothly together.

SYNTHESIS: Combining Ideas

Weave your sources into your text.

Make sure your sources support your own voice and message.

Ask...

Why are you using each source?

How do your sources fit with what you want to say?

How can you arrange your ideas and others' ideas for the best effect?

tion, and so on. Be sure to consider the complexity of the issue, and demonstrate that you have considered more than one perspective.

- *Summon evidence to support your position.* You might use paraphrases, summaries, or direct quotations from your sources as evidence (18a), or your personal experience or prior knowledge. Integrate quotations properly (see Chapter 18), and keep your ideas central to the piece of writing.

- *Deal with counterarguments.* You don't have to use every idea or every source available — some will be more useful than others. However, ignoring evidence that opposes your position makes your argument weaker. You should acknowledge the existence of valid opinions that differ from yours, and try to explain why they are incorrect or incomplete.

- *Combine your source materials effectively.* Be careful to avoid simply summarizing or listing your research. Think carefully about how the ideas in your reading support your argument. Try to weave the various sources together rather than discussing your sources one by one.

EXERCISE 17.2: THINKING VISUALLY

Read and analyze the two "Synthesis" panels on pp. 216–17. Then look closely at each source you are using for a research project you are working on now or for one you have done in the past. How do the sources fit into the overall pattern of your writing? How have you brought the sources together and integrated them into your own writing? How have you made sure that your sources don't drown out your own voice? Try your hand at sketching a picture that captures the role the sources play in the argument you're making.

17f   Take notes and annotate sources.

Note-taking methods vary greatly from one researcher to another, so you may decide to use a computer file, a notebook, or index cards. Regardless of the method, however, you should (1) record enough information to help you recall the major points of the source; (2) put the information in the form in which you are most likely to incorporate it into your research essay, whether a summary, a paraphrase, or a quotation; and (3) note all the information you will need to cite the source accurately. The following example shows the major items a note should include:

ELEMENTS OF AN ACCURATE NOTE

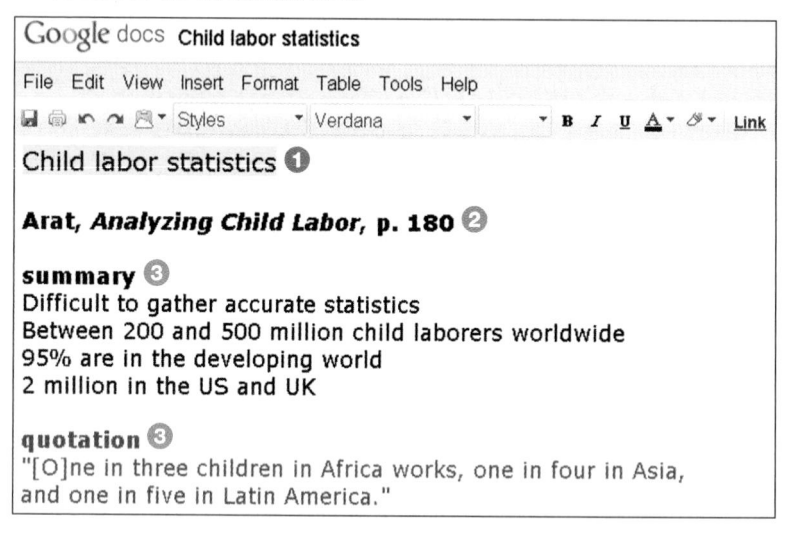

1. *Use a subject heading.* Label each note with a brief but descriptive subject heading so that you can group similar subtopics together.

2. *Identify the source.* List the author's name and a shortened title of the source, and a page number, if available. Your working-bibliography entry (17b) for the source will contain the full bibliographic information, so you don't need to repeat it in each note.

3. *Indicate whether the note is a direct quotation, paraphrase, or summary.* Make sure quotations are copied accurately. Put square brackets around any change you make, and use ellipses if you omit material.

Taking complete notes will help you digest the source information as you read and incorporate the material into your text without inadvertently plagiarizing the source (see Chapter 18). Be sure to reread each note carefully, and recheck it against the source to make sure quotations, statistics, and specific facts are accurate.

Quoting

Some of the notes you take will contain quotations, which give the *exact words* of a source. Here, for example, is a note with a quotation that David Craig planned to use in his research paper:

QUOTATION NOTE

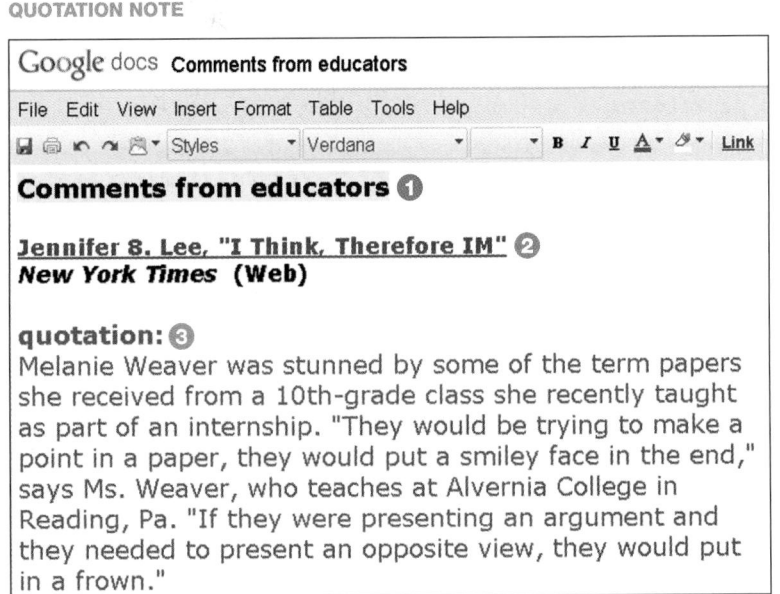

1. Subject heading

2. Author and short title of source (no page number for electronic source)

3. Direct quotation

AT A GLANCE

Guidelines for Taking Notes

- Copy quotations carefully, with punctuation, capitalization, and spelling *exactly* as in the original.

- Enclose the quotation in quotation marks; don't rely on your memory to distinguish your own words from those of the source.

- Use square brackets if you introduce words of your own into a quotation or make changes in it, and use ellipses if you omit material. If you later incorporate the quotation into your essay, copy it faithfully — brackets, ellipses, and all. (44b)

- Record the author's name, the shortened title, and the page number(s) on which the quotation appears. If the note refers to more than one page, use a slash (/) within the quotation to indicate where one page ends and another begins. For sources without page numbers, record the paragraph or other section number(s), if any.

- Make sure you have a corresponding working-bibliography entry with complete source information. (17b)

- Label the note with a subject heading, and identify it as a quotation.

Paraphrasing

A paraphrase accurately states all the relevant information from a passage *in your own words and sentence structures*, without any additional comments or elaborations. A paraphrase is useful when the main points of a passage, their order, and at least some details are important but— unlike passages worth quoting—the particular wording is not. Unlike a summary, a paraphrase always restates *all* the main points of a passage in the same order and often in about the same number of words.

ORIGINAL

Language play, the arguments suggest, will help the development of pronunciation ability through its focus on the properties of sounds and sound contrasts, such as rhyming. Playing with word endings and decoding the syntax of riddles will help the acquisition of grammar. Readiness to play with words and names, to exchange puns and to engage in nonsense talk, promotes links with semantic development. The kinds of dialogue interaction illustrated above are likely to have consequences for the development of conversational skills. And language play, by its nature, also contributes greatly to what in recent years has been called *metalinguistic awareness*, which is turning out to be of critical importance in the development of language skills in general and of literacy skills in particular.

– DAVID CRYSTAL, *Language Play* (180)

UNACCEPTABLE PARAPHRASE: STRAYING FROM THE AUTHOR'S IDEAS

Crystal argues that playing with language — creating rhymes, figuring out how riddles work, making puns, playing with names, using invented words, and so on — helps children figure out a great deal about language, from the basics of pronunciation and grammar to how to carry on a conversation. Increasing their understanding of how language works in turn helps them become more interested in learning new languages and in pursuing education (180).

This paraphrase starts off well enough, but it moves away from paraphrasing the original to inserting the writer's ideas; Crystal says nothing about learning new languages or pursuing education.

UNACCEPTABLE PARAPHRASE: USING THE AUTHOR'S WORDS

Crystal suggests that language play, including rhyme, helps children improve pronunciation ability, that looking at word endings and decoding the syntax of riddles allows them to understand grammar, and that other kinds of dialogue interaction teach conversation. Overall, language play may be of critical importance in the development of language and literacy skills (180).

Because the highlighted phrases are either borrowed from the original without quotation marks or changed only superficially, this paraphrase plagiarizes.

UNACCEPTABLE PARAPHRASE: USING THE AUTHOR'S SENTENCE STRUCTURES

Language play, Crystal suggests, will improve pronunciation by zeroing in on sounds such as rhymes. Having fun with word endings and analyzing riddle structure will help a person acquire grammar. Being prepared to play with language, to use puns and talk nonsense, improves the ability to use semantics. These playful methods of communication are likely to influence a person's ability to talk to others. And language play inherently adds enormously to what has recently been known as *metalinguistic awareness*, a concept of great magnitude in developing speech abilities generally and literacy abilities particularly (180).

Here is a paraphrase of the same passage that expresses the author's ideas accurately and acceptably:

ACCEPTABLE PARAPHRASE: IN THE STUDENT WRITER'S OWN WORDS

Crystal argues that playing with language — creating rhymes, figuring out riddles, making puns, playing with names, using invented words, and so on — helps children figure out a great deal, from the basics of pronunciation and grammar to how to carry on a conversation. This kind of play allows children to understand the overall concept of how language works, a concept that is key to learning to use — and read — language effectively (180).

AT A GLANCE

Guidelines for Paraphrasing

- Include all main points and any important details from the original source, in the same order in which the author presents them.
- State the meaning in your own words and sentence structures. If you want to include especially memorable language from the original, enclose it in quotation marks.
- Save your comments, elaborations, or reactions on another note.
- Record the author's name, the shortened title, and the page number(s) on which the original material appears. For sources without page numbers, record the paragraph, screen, or other section number(s), if any.
- Make sure you have a corresponding working-bibliography entry with complete source information. (17b)
- Label the note with a subject heading, and identify it as a paraphrase.

Summarizing

A summary is a significantly shortened version of a passage or even of a whole chapter or work that captures main ideas *in your own words.* Unlike a paraphrase, a summary uses just enough information to record

SUMMARY NOTE

Google docs **Language development**

File Edit View Insert Format Table Tools Help

Styles   •   Verdana   •   14pt   •   **B**   *I*   U   A▾   ✎▾

Language development ❶

Crystal, *Language Play*, p. 180 ❷

summary: ❸

Crystal argues that various kinds of language play contribute to awareness of how language works, and therefore, to literacy.

❶   Subject heading
❷   Author, title, page reference
❸   Summary of source

the main points you wish to emphasize. To summarize a short passage, read it carefully and, without looking at the text, write a one- or two-sentence summary. On p. 222 is David Craig's note recording a summary of the Crystal passage on p. 220. Notice that it states the author's main points selectively—and without using his words.

For a long passage or an entire chapter, skim the headings and topic sentences, and make notes of each; then write your summary in a paragraph or two. For a whole book, you may want to refer to the preface and introduction as well as chapter titles, headings, and topic sentences—and your summary may take a page or more.

AT A GLANCE

Guidelines for Summarizing

- Include just enough information to recount the main points you want to cite. A summary is usually far shorter than the original.

- Use your own words. If you include any language from the original, enclose it in quotation marks.

- Record the author, shortened title, and page number(s) on which the original material appeared. For sources without page numbers, record the paragraph, screen, or other section number(s), if any.

- Make sure you have a corresponding working-bibliography entry with complete source information. (17b)

- Label the note with a subject heading, and identify it as a summary.

FOR MULTILINGUAL WRITERS

Identifying Sources

While some language communities and cultures expect audiences to recognize the sources of important documents and texts, thereby eliminating the need to cite them directly, conventions for writing in North America call for careful attribution of any quoted, paraphrased, or summarized material. When in doubt, explicitly identify your sources.

Annotating sources

Sometimes you may photocopy or print out a source you intend to use. In such cases, you can annotate the photocopies or printouts with your thoughts and questions and highlight interesting quotations and key terms.

You can copy online sources electronically, paste them into a computer file, and annotate them there. Try not to rely too heavily on copying or printing out whole pieces, however; you still need to read the material very carefully. And resist the temptation to treat copied material as notes, an action that could lead to inadvertent plagiarizing. (In a computer file, using a different color for text pasted from a source will help prevent this problem.)

EXERCISE 17.3

Choose an online source you are sure you will use in your research project. Then download and print out the source, record all essential publication information for it, and annotate it as you read it.

EXERCISE 17.4: THINKING CRITICALLY

Take a careful look at the sources you have gathered for your research project. How many make points that support your own point of view? How many provide counterarguments to your point of view? Which sources are you relying on most — and why? Which sources seem most credible to you — and why? Which sources, if any, are you suspicious of or worried about? Bring the results of this investigation to class for discussion.

18 Integrating Sources and Avoiding Plagiarism

In some ways, there really is nothing new under the sun, in writing and research as well as in life. Whatever writing you do has been influenced by what you have already read and experienced. As you work on your research project, you will be joining a scholarly conversation and responding to the work of others. Thus you will need to know how to use, integrate, and acknowledge the work of others.

Integrating sources into your writing can be quite a challenge. In fact, as a beginning researcher, you might do what Professor Rebecca Howard calls "patchwriting": that is, rather than integrate the sources smoothly and accurately, you patch together words, phrases, and even structures from sources into your own writing, sometimes without citation. The author of this textbook remembers doing just such "patchwriting" for a report in middle school on her hero, Dr. Albert Schweitzer. Luckily, she had a teacher who sat patiently with her, showing her how

> **AT A GLANCE**
>
> ## When to Quote, Paraphrase, or Summarize
>
> **QUOTE**
> - wording that is so memorable or powerful, or expresses a point so perfectly, that you cannot change it without weakening its meaning
> - authors' opinions you wish to emphasize
> - authors' words that show you are considering varying perspectives
> - respected authorities whose opinions support your ideas
> - authors whose opinions challenge or vary greatly from those of others in the field
>
> **PARAPHRASE**
> - passages you do not wish to quote but that use details important to your point
>
> **SUMMARIZE**
> - long passages in which the main point is important to your point but the details are not

to paraphrase and summarize and quote from the sources correctly and effectively. So it takes time and effort—and good instruction—to learn to integrate sources appropriately into your writing rather than patchwriting, which is sometimes considered plagiarism even if you didn't mean to plagiarize.

All writers need to understand current definitions of plagiarism (which have changed over time and differ from culture to culture) as well as the concept of intellectual property—the works protected by copyright and other laws—so they can give credit where credit is due.

18a Decide whether to quote, paraphrase, or summarize.

You tentatively decided to quote, paraphrase, or summarize material when you took notes on your sources (17f). As you choose some of these sources for your research project and decide how to use them, however, you may reevaluate those decisions. The following guidelines can help you decide whether to quote, paraphrase, or summarize.

18b   Integrate quotations, paraphrases, and summaries effectively.

Here are some general guidelines for integrating source materials into your writing.

Incorporating quotations

Quotations from respected authorities can help establish your credibility and show that you are considering various perspectives. However, because your essay is primarily your own work, limit your use of quotations.

BRIEF QUOTATIONS

Short quotations should run in with your text, enclosed by quotation marks (43a).

> In Miss Eckhart, Welty recognizes a character who shares with her "the love of her art and the love of giving it, the desire to give it until there is no more left" (10).

LONG QUOTATIONS

If you are following the style of the Modern Language Association (MLA), set off a prose quotation longer than four lines. If you are following the style of the American Psychological Association (APA), set off a quotation of more than forty words or more than one paragraph. If you are following *Chicago* style, set off a quotation of more than one hundred words or more than one paragraph. Begin such a quotation on a new line. For MLA style, indent every line one inch; for APA style, five to seven spaces; for *Chicago* style, indent the text or use a smaller font (check your instructor's preference). Quotation marks are unnecessary. Introduce long quotations with a signal phrase or a sentence followed by a colon.

The following long quotation follows MLA style:

A good seating arrangement can prevent problems; however, *withitness*, as defined by Woolfolk, works even better:

> Withitness is the ability to communicate to students that you are aware of what is happening in the classroom, that you "don't miss anything." With-it teachers seem to have "eyes in the back of their heads." They avoid becoming too absorbed with a few students, since this allows the rest of the class to wander. (359)

This technique works, however, only if students actually believe that their teacher will know everything that goes on.

INTEGRATING QUOTATIONS SMOOTHLY INTO YOUR TEXT

Carefully integrate quotations into your text so that they flow smoothly and clearly into the surrounding sentences. Use a signal phrase or verb, such as those identified in the following examples and listed below.

> As Eudora Welty notes, "learning stamps you with its moments. Childhood's learning," she continues, "is made up of moments. It isn't steady. It's a pulse" (9).

> In her essay, Haraway strongly opposes those who condemn technology outright, arguing that we must not indulge in a "demonology of technology" (181).

Notice that the examples alert readers to the quotations by using signal phrases that include the author's name. When you cite a quotation in this way, you need put only the page number in parentheses.

SIGNAL VERBS

acknowledges	concludes	emphasizes	replies
advises	concurs	expresses	reports
agrees	confirms	interprets	responds
allows	criticizes	lists	reveals
answers	declares	objects	says
asserts	describes	observes	states
believes	disagrees	offers	suggests
charges	discusses	opposes	thinks
claims	disputes	remarks	writes

BRACKETS AND ELLIPSES

In direct quotations, enclose in brackets any words you change or add, and indicate any deletions with ellipsis points (44f).

> "There is something wrong in the [Three Mile Island] area," one farmer told the Nuclear Regulatory Commission after the plant accident ("Legacy" 33).

> Economist John Kenneth Galbraith has pointed out that "large corporations cannot afford to compete with one another. . . . In a truly competitive market someone loses" (qtd. in Key 17).

Incorporating paraphrases and summaries

Introduce paraphrases and summaries clearly, usually with a signal phrase that includes the author of the source, as the highlighted words in this example indicate.

Professor of linguistics Deborah Tannen says that she offers her book *That's Not What I Meant!* to "women and men everywhere who are trying their best to talk to each other" (19). Tannen goes on to illustrate how communication between women and men breaks down and then to suggest that a full awareness of "genderlects" can improve relationships (297).

EXERCISE 18.1

Take a source-based piece of writing you have done recently or a research project you are working on now, and examine it to see how successfully you have integrated quotations. Have you used accurate signal verbs and introduced the sources of the quotations? Have you used square brackets and ellipses accurately to indicate changes in quotations?

EXERCISE 18.2

Read the brief original passage that follows, and then look closely at the five attempts to quote or paraphrase it. Decide which attempts are acceptable and which plagiarize, prepare notes on what supports your decision in each case, and bring your notes to class for discussion.

The strange thing about plagiarism is that it's almost always pointless. The writers who stand accused, from Laurence Sterne to Samuel Taylor Coleridge to Susan Sontag, tend to be more talented than the writers they lift from.

— MALCOLM JONES, "Have You Read This Story Somewhere?"

1. According to Malcolm Jones, writers accused of plagiarism are always better writers than those they are supposed to have plagiarized.
2. According to Malcolm Jones, writers accused of plagiarism "tend to be more talented than the writers they lift from."
3. Plagiarism is usually pointless, says writer Malcolm Jones.
4. Those who stand accused of plagiarism, such as Senator Joseph Biden, tend to be better writers than those whose work they use.
5. According to Malcolm Jones, "plagiarism is . . . almost always pointless."

18c Integrate visuals and media effectively.

Choose visuals and media wisely, whether you use video, audio, photographs, illustrations, charts and graphs, or other kinds of images. Integrate all visuals and media smoothly into your text.

- *Does each visual or media file make a strong contribution to the written message?* Tangential or purely decorative visuals and media may weaken the power of your writing.

- *Is each visual or media file appropriate and fair to your subject?* An obviously biased perspective may seem unfair or manipulative to your audience.

- *Is each visual or media file appropriate for and fair to your audience?* Visuals and media should appeal to various members of your likely audience.

Whenever you post documents containing visuals or media to the Web, make sure you check for copyright information. While it is considered "fair use" to use such materials in an essay or other project for a college class, once that project is published on the Web, you might infringe on copyright protections if you do not ask the copyright holder for permission to use the visual or media file. U.S. copyright law considers the reproduction of works for purposes of teaching and scholarship to be "fair use" not bound by copyright, but the law is open to multiple intepretations. If you have questions about whether your work might infringe on copyright, ask your instructor for help.

Like quotations, paraphrases, and summaries, visuals and media need to be introduced and commented on in some way.

- Refer to the visual, audio, or video in the text (*As Fig. 3 demonstrates . . .*) and position it as close as possible after the first reference.

- Explain or comment on the relevance of the visual or media file. This can be done after the insertion point.

- Check the documentation system you are using to make sure you label visuals and media appropriately; MLA, for instance, asks that you number and title tables and figures (*Table 1: Average Amount of Rainfall by Region*).

- If you are posting your document or essay on a Web site, make sure you have permission to use any visuals or media files that are covered by copyright.

For more on using visuals, see 9d.

18d Check for excessive use of source material.

Your text needs to synthesize your research in support of your own argument; it should not be a patchwork of quotations, paraphrases, and summaries from other people. You need a rhetorical stance that represents you as the author. If you cite too many sources, your own voice will disappear, a problem the following passage demonstrates:

Saying Something New

"What can I say about my topic that experts haven't already said?" All writers — no matter how experienced — face this problem. As you read more about your topic, you will soon see areas of disagreement among experts, who may not be as expert as they first appear. Notice what your sources say and, especially, what they don't say. Consider how your own interests and experiences give you a unique perspective on the topic. Slowly but surely you will identify a claim that you can make about the topic, one related to what others say but taking a new angle or adding something different to the discussion.

The United States is one of the countries with the most rapid population growth. In fact, rapid population increase has been a "prominent feature of American life since the founding of the republic" (Day 31). In the past, the cause of the high rate of population growth was the combination of large-scale immigration and a high birth rate. As Day notes, "Two facts stand out in the demographic history of the United States: first, the single position as a receiver of immigrants; second, our high rate of growth from natural increase" (31).

Nevertheless, American population density is not as high as in most European countries. Day points out that the Netherlands, with a density of 906 persons per square mile, is more crowded than even the most densely populated American states (33).

18e   Understand why you should acknowledge your sources.

Acknowledging sources says to your reader that you have done your homework, that you have gained expertise on your topic, and that you are credible. Acknowledging sources can also demonstrate fairness—that you have considered several points of view. In addition, recognizing your sources can help provide background for your research by placing it in the context of other thinking. Most of all, you should acknowledge sources to help your readers follow your thoughts, understand how your ideas relate to the thoughts of others, and know where to go to find more information on your topic.

18f Know which sources to acknowledge.

As you carry out research, it is important to understand the distinction between materials that require acknowledgment (in in-text citations, footnotes, or endnotes; and in the works-cited list or bibliography) and those that do not.

Materials that do not require acknowledgment

- *Common knowledge.* If most readers already know a fact, you probably do not need to cite a source for it. You do not need to credit a source for the statement that Barack Obama was elected in 2008, for example.
- *Facts available in a wide variety of sources.* If a number of encyclopedias, almanacs, or textbooks include a certain piece of information, you usually need not cite a specific source for it.

- *Your own findings from field research.* If you conduct observations or surveys, simply announce your findings as your own. Acknowledge people you interview as individuals rather than as part of a survey.

Materials that require acknowledgment

Some of the information you use may need to be credited to a source.

- *Quotations, paraphrases, and summaries.* Whenever you use another person's words, ideas, or opinions, credit the source. Even though the wording of a paraphrase or summary is your own, you should still acknowledge the source.
- *Facts not widely known or claims that are arguable.* If your readers would be unlikely to know a fact, or if an author presents as fact a claim that may or may not be true, cite the source. If you are not sure whether a fact will be familiar to your readers or whether a statement is arguable, cite the source.
- *Visuals from any source.* Credit all visual and statistical material not derived from your own field research, even if you yourself create a graph or table from the data provided in a source.
- *Help provided by others.* If an instructor gave you a good idea or if friends responded to your draft or helped you conduct surveys, give credit.

18g   Uphold your academic integrity and avoid plagiarism.

One of the cornerstones of intellectual work is academic integrity. This principle accounts for our being able to trust those sources we use and to demonstrate that our own work is equally trustworthy. While there are many ways to damage academic integrity, two that are especially important are inaccurate or incomplete acknowledgment of sources in citations—sometimes called unintentional plagiarism—and plagiarism that is deliberately intended to pass off one writer's work as another's.

Whether it is intentional or not, plagiarism can result in serious consequences. At some colleges, students who plagiarize fail the course automatically; at others, they are expelled. Instructors who plagiarize, even inadvertently, have had their degrees revoked and their books withdrawn from publication. And outside academic life, eminent political, business, and scientific leaders have been stripped of candidacies, positions, and awards because of plagiarism.

Inaccurate or incomplete citation of sources

If your paraphrase is too close to the wording or sentence structure of a source (even if you identify the source), if you do not identify the source of a quotation (even if you include the quotation marks), or if you fail to indicate clearly the source of an idea that you obviously did not come up with on your own, you may be accused of plagiarism even if your intent was not to plagiarize. Inaccurate or incomplete acknowledgment

---

FOR MULTILINGUAL WRITERS

Plagiarism as a Cultural Concept

Many cultures do not recognize Western notions of plagiarism, which rest on a belief that language and ideas can be owned by writers. Indeed, in many countries other than the United States, and even within some communities in the United States, using the words and ideas of others without attribution is considered a sign of deep respect as well as an indication of knowledge. In academic writing in the United States, however, you should credit all materials except those that are common knowledge, that are available in a wide variety of sources, or that are your own creations (photographs, drawings, and so on) or your own findings from field research.

> **AT A GLANCE**
>
> ## Avoiding Plagiarism
>
> - Maintain an accurate and thorough working bibliography. (17b)
> - Establish a consistent note-taking system, listing sources and page numbers and clearly identifying all quotations, paraphrases, summaries, statistics, and visuals. (17f)
> - Identify all quotations with quotation marks — both in your notes and in your essay. Be sure your summaries and paraphrases use your own words and sentence structures. (18b)
> - Give a citation or note for each quotation, paraphrase, summary, arguable assertion or opinion, statistic, and visual that is from a source. Prepare an accurate and complete list of sources cited according to the required documentation style. (See Chapters 49–55.)
> - Plan ahead on writing assignments so that you can avoid the temptation to take shortcuts.

of sources often results either from carelessness or from not learning how to borrow material properly in the first place. Still, because the costs of even unintentional plagiarism can be severe, it's important to understand how it can happen and how you can guard against it.

As a writer of academic integrity, you will want to take responsibility for your research and for acknowledging all sources accurately. One easy way to keep track is to keep photocopies or printouts as you do your research; then you can identify needed quotations right on the copy.

Deliberate plagiarism

Deliberate plagiarism—handing in an essay written by a friend or purchased (or simply downloaded) from an essay-writing company; cutting and pasting passages directly from source materials without marking them with quotation marks and acknowledging your sources; failing to credit the source of an idea or concept in your text—is what most people think of when they hear the word *plagiarism*. This form of plagiarism is particularly troubling because it represents dishonesty and deception: those who intentionally plagiarize present the hard thinking and hard work of someone else as their own, and they claim knowledge they really don't have, thus deceiving their readers.

Deliberate plagiarism is also fairly simple to spot: your instructor will be well acquainted with your writing and likely to notice any sudden shifts in the style or quality of your work. In addition, by typing a few words from an essay into a search engine, your instructor can identify "matches" very easily.

 bedfordstmartins.com/everydaywriter
Research Tutorials

EXERCISE 18.3: THINKING CRITICALLY

Look at a recent piece of your writing that incorporates material from sources, and try to determine how completely and accurately you acknowledged them. Did you properly cite every quotation, paraphrase, and summary? every opinion or other idea from a source? every source you used to create visuals? Did you unintentionally plagiarize someone else's words or ideas? Make notes, and bring them to class for discussion.

19 Writing a Research Project

Everyday decisions often call for research and writing. In trying to choose between colleges in different towns, for example, one student made a long list of questions to answer: Which location had the lower cost of living? Which school offered more financial aid? Which program would be more likely to help graduates find a job? After conducting careful research, he was able to write a letter of acceptance to one place and a letter of regret to the other. In much the same way, when you are working on an academic project, there comes a time to draw the strands of your research together and articulate your conclusions in writing.

19a Refine your writing plans.

You should by now have notes containing facts, opinions, paraphrases, summaries, quotations, and other material; you probably have some images or media to include as well. You may also have ideas about how to synthesize these many pieces of information. And you should have some sense of whether your hypothesis has sufficient support. Now is the time to reconsider your purpose, audience, stance, and working thesis.

- What is your central purpose? What other purposes, if any, do you have?
- What is your stance toward your topic? Are you an advocate, a critic, a reporter, an observer?
- What audience(s) are you addressing?
- How much background information or context does your audience need?
- What supporting information will your readers find convincing—examples? quotations from authorities? statistics? graphs, charts, or other visuals? data from your field research?
- Should your tone be that of a colleague, an expert, a student?
- How can you establish common ground with your readers and show them that you have considered points of view other than your own? (See 14e and Chapter 21.)
- What is your working thesis trying to establish? Will your audience accept it?

Developing an explicit thesis

Writing out an explicit thesis statement allows you to articulate your major points and to see how well they carry out your purpose and appeal to your audience. Before you begin a full draft, then, try to develop your working thesis into an explicit statement.

David Craig developed the following explicit thesis statement:

Instant messaging seems to be a positive force in the development of youth literacy because it promotes regular contact with words, the use of a written medium for communication, and the development of an alternative form of literacy.

For David Craig's research essay, see Chapter 52.

FOR MULTILINGUAL WRITERS

Asking Experienced Writers to Review a Thesis

You might find it helpful to ask one or two classmates who have more experience with the particular type of academic writing to look at your explicit thesis. Ask if the thesis is as direct and clear as it can be, and revise accordingly.

Testing your thesis

Although writing out an explicit thesis will often confirm your research, you may find that your hypothesis is invalid, inadequately supported, or insufficiently focused. In such cases, you need to rethink your original research question and perhaps do further research. To test your thesis, consider the following questions:

- How can you state your thesis more precisely or more clearly (7b)? Should the wording be more specific?
- In what ways will your thesis interest your audience? What can you do to increase that interest?
- Will your thesis be manageable, given your limits of time and knowledge? If not, what can you do to make it more manageable?
- What evidence from your research supports each aspect of your thesis? What additional evidence do you need?

EXERCISE 19.1

Take the thesis from your current research project, and test it against the questions provided in 19a. Make revisions if your analysis reveals weaknesses in your thesis.

Considering design

As you move toward producing a draft, take some time to think about how you want your research essay or project to look. What font size will you use? Should you use color? Do you plan to insert text boxes, visuals, or media files? Will you need headings and subheadings? (See Chapter 9.)

19b　Organize and draft.

Experienced writers differ considerably in the ways they go about organizing ideas and information, and you will want to experiment until you find a method that works well for you. (For more on organizational strategies, see 7d.)

Organizing by subject

You may find it useful to have physical notes to arrange—note cards or sticky notes, for example, or printouts of your slides or of notes you have been keeping online that you mark in some way to make the subject categories easy to identify. You can group the pieces around subject headings and reorder the parts until they seem to make sense. Shuqiao Song,

Sticky notes used to organize a presentation

whose critical analysis appears in 12e, organized the plans for her Power-Point presentation (3c) by moving sticky notes around on her window, as shown in her photo above.

Grouping your notes will help you see how well you can support your thesis and help you see if you have missed any essential points. Do you need to omit any ideas or sources? Do you need to find additional evidence for a main or supporting point? Once you have gathered everything together and organized your materials, you can see how the many small pieces of your research fit together. Make sure that your evidence supports your explicit thesis; if not, you may need to revise it or do additional research—or both.

Once you have established initial groups, skim through the notes and look for ways to organize your draft. Figure out what background your audience needs, what points you need to make first, how much detail and support to offer for each point, and so on.

Outlining

You can use outlines in various ways and at various stages. Some writers group their notes, write a draft, and then outline the draft to study its tentative structure. Others develop an informal working outline from their notes and revise it as they go along. Still other writers prefer to plot out their organization early on in a formal outline. (For more on outlines, see 7e.)

Drafting

For most college research projects, drafting should begin *at least* two weeks before the instructor's deadline in case you need to gather more information or do more drafting. Set a deadline for having a complete draft, and structure your work with that date in mind. Gather your notes, outline, and sources, and read through them, getting involved in your topic. Most writers find that some sustained work (two or three hours at a time) pays off at this point. Begin drafting a section that you feel confident about. For example, if you are not sure how you want to introduce the draft but do know how you want to approach a particular point, begin with that, and return to the introduction later. The most important thing is to get started.

WORKING TITLE AND INTRODUCTION

The title and introduction play special roles, for they set the stage for what is to come. Ideally, the title announces the subject of the research essay or project in an intriguing or memorable way. The introduction should draw readers in and provide any background they will need to understand your discussion. Here are some tips for drafting an introduction to a research essay:

- It is often effective to *open with a question*, especially your research question. Next, you might explain what you will do to answer the question. Then *end with your explicit thesis statement*—in essence, the answer.
- Help readers by *forecasting your main points*.
- *Establish your own credibility* by revealing how you have become knowledgeable about the topic.
- A quotation can be a good attention-getter, but you may not want to open with a quotation if doing so will give that source too much emphasis.

CONCLUSION

A good conclusion to a research project helps readers know what they have learned. Its job is not to persuade (the body of the essay or project should already have done that) but to contribute to the overall effectiveness of your argument. Here are some strategies that may help:

- Refer to your thesis, and then expand to a more general conclusion that reminds readers of the significance of your discussion.

- If you have covered several main points, you may want to remind readers of them. Be careful, however, to provide more than a mere summary.
- Try to end with something that will have an impact—a provocative quotation or question, a vivid image, a call for action, or a warning. But guard against sounding preachy.

19c Incorporate source materials.

When you reach the point of drafting your research project, a new task awaits: weaving your source materials into your writing. The challenge is to use your sources yet remain the author—to quote, paraphrase, and summarize other voices while remaining the major voice in your work. (See Chapter 18 for tips on integrating sources.)

19d Review and get responses to your draft.

Once you've completed your draft, reread it slowly. As you do so, answer the following questions, and use them as a starting point for revision:

- What do you now see as its *purpose*? How does this compare with your original purpose? Does the draft do what your assignment requires?
- What *audience* does your essay address?
- What is your *stance* toward the topic?
- What is your *thesis*? Is it clearly stated?
- What *evidence* supports your thesis? Is the evidence sufficient?

Next, ask friends, classmates, and, if possible, your instructor to read and respond to your draft. Asking specific questions of your readers will result in the most helpful advice. (See Chapter 10.)

19e Revise and edit your draft.

When you have considered your reviewers' responses and your own analysis, you can turn to revising and editing. See the box on p. 240 and sections 10d and 11a for more information.

AT A GLANCE

Guidelines for Revising a Research Project

- *Take responses into account.* Look at specific problems that reviewers think you need to solve or strengths you might capitalize on. For example, if they showed great interest in one point but no interest in another, consider expanding the first and deleting the second.

- *Reconsider your original purpose, audience, and stance.* Have you achieved your purpose? If not, consider how you can. How well have you appealed to your readers? Make sure you satisfy any special concerns of your reviewers. If your rhetorical stance toward your topic has changed, does your draft need to change, too?

- *Assess your research.* Think about whether you have investigated the topic thoroughly and consulted materials with more than one point of view. Have you left out any important sources? Are the sources you use reliable and appropriate for your topic? Have you synthesized your research findings and drawn warranted conclusions?

- *Assess your use of visuals and media,* making sure that each one supports your argument, is clearly labeled, and is cited appropriately.

- *Gather additional material.* If you need to strengthen any points, first check your notes to see whether you already have the necessary information. In some instances, you may need to do more research.

- *Decide what changes you need to make.* List everything you must do to perfect your draft. With your deadline in mind, plan your revision.

- *Rewrite your draft.* Many writers prefer to revise first on paper rather than on a computer. However you revise, be sure to save copies of each draft. Begin with the major changes, such as adding content or reorganizing. Then turn to sentence-level problems and word choice. Can you sharpen the work's dominant impression?

- *Reevaluate the title, introduction, and conclusion.* Is your title specific and engaging? Does the introduction capture readers' attention and indicate what the work discusses? Does your conclusion help readers see the significance of your argument?

- *Check your documentation.* Make sure you've included a citation in your text for every quotation, paraphrase, summary, visual, and media file you incorporated, following your documentation style consistently.

- *Edit your draft.* Check grammar, usage, spelling, punctuation, and mechanics. Consider the advice of computer spell checkers (23e) and grammar checkers carefully before accepting it.

19f Prepare a list of sources.

Once you have your final draft and source materials in place, you are ready to prepare a list of sources. Create an entry for each source used in your essay. Then double-check your essay against your list of sources cited; be sure that you have listed every source mentioned in the in-text citations or notes and that you have not listed any sources not cited in your essay. (For guidelines on documentation styles, see Chapters 49–55.)

19g Prepare and proofread your final copy.

To make sure that the final version of your essay puts your best foot forward, proofread it carefully. Work with a hard copy, since reading on-screen often leads to inaccuracies and missed typos. Proofread once for typographical and grammatical errors and once again to make sure you haven't introduced new errors. (To locate examples of student writing in this book and on the Web site, see the Directory of Student Writing at the back of this book.)

EXERCISE 19.2: THINKING CRITICALLY

Reflect on the research project you have completed. How did you go about organizing your information? What would you do to improve this process? What problems did you encounter in drafting? How did you solve these problems? How many quotations did you use, and how did you integrate them into your text? When and why did you use summaries and paraphrases? If you used visuals, how effective were they in supporting your points? What did you learn from revising?

Language

Many people think of language as a set
of rules; break them, and you're wrong.
But that's not how language works.

— ROBERT LANE GREENE

Language

20 **Writing to the World**   *245*
  a Think about what seems "normal"   *245*
  b Clarify meaning   *246*
  c Meet audience expectations   *247*

21 **Language That Builds Common Ground**   *250*
  a Examine assumptions and avoid stereotypes   *251*
  b Examine assumptions about gender   *251*
  c Examine assumptions about race and ethnicity   *253*
  d Consider other kinds of difference   *254*

22 **Language Variety**   *256*
  a Use standard varieties of English appropriately   *256*
  b Use varieties of English to evoke a place or community   *257*
  c Use varieties of English to build credibility with a community   *259*
  d Bring in other languages appropriately   *259*

23 **Word Choice and Spelling**   *260*
  a Choose appropriate formality   *261*
  b Consider denotation and connotation   *265*
  c Use general and specific language effectively   *265*
  d Use figurative language effectively   *267*
  e Make spell checkers work for you   *269*
  f Master spelling rules   *272*

24 **Glossary of Usage**   *274*

For visual analysis Look carefully at the illustration on the front of this tab. What do you think this image suggests about using language effectively?

Writing to the World **20**

People today often communicate instantaneously across vast distances and cultures. Businesspeople complete multinational transactions with a single click, students in Ohio take online classes at MIT or chat with hundreds of Facebook friends, and bloggers in Baghdad find readers in Atlanta.

Who will read what you write? What choices do you need to make in your writing to have the desired effect on your audience? When the whole world can potentially read your work, it's time to step back and think about how to communicate successfully with such a diverse group—how to become a world writer.

20a Think about what seems "normal."

Your judgment on what's "normal" may be based on assumptions you are not even aware of. But remember: behavior that is considered out of place in one context may appear perfectly normal in another. What's considered "normal" in a text message would be anything but in a request for an internship with a law firm. If you want to communicate with people across cultures, try to learn something about the norms in those cultures and be aware of the norms that guide your own behavior.

Like most people, you may tend to see your own way as the "normal" way to do things. How do your own values and assumptions guide your thinking and behavior? Keep in mind that if your ways seem inherently right, then—even without thinking about it—you may assume that other ways are somehow less than right.

- Know that most ways of communicating are influenced by cultural contexts and differ widely from one culture to the next.

- Pay close attention to the ways that people from cultures other than your own communicate, and be flexible.

- Pay attention to and respect the differences among individual people within a given culture. Don't assume that all members of a community behave in the same way or value the same things.
- Remember that your audience may be made up of people from many backgrounds who have very different concepts about what is appropriate or "normal." So don't assume unanimity!

20b Clarify meaning.

When an instructor called for "originality" in his students' essays, what did he mean? A Filipina student thought *originality* meant going to an original source and explaining it; a student from Massachusetts thought *originality* meant coming up with an idea entirely on her own. The professor, however, expected students to read multiple sources and develop a critical point of their own about those sources. In subsequent classes, this professor defined *originality* as he was using it in his classes, and he gave examples of student work he judged original.

This brief example points to the challenges all writers face in trying to communicate across space, across languages, across cultures. While there are no foolproof rules, here are some tips for communicating with people from cultures other than your own:

- Listen carefully. Don't hesitate to ask people to explain or even repeat a point if you're not absolutely sure you understand.
- Take care to be explicit about the meanings of the words you use.

- Invite response — ask whether you're making yourself clear. This kind of back-and-forth is particularly easy (and necessary) in email.
- Remember that sometimes a picture is worth a thousand words. A visual may help make your meaning absolutely clear.

20c Meet audience expectations.

When you do your best to meet an audience's expectations about how a text should work, your writing is more likely to have the desired effect. In practice, figuring out what audiences want, need, or expect can be difficult—especially when you are writing in public spaces online and your audiences can be composed of anyone, anywhere. If you do know something about your readers' expectations, use what you know to present your work effectively. If you know little about your potential audiences, however, carefully examine your assumptions about your readers.

Expectations about your authority as a writer

In the United States, students are often asked to establish authority in their writing—by drawing on certain kinds of personal experience, by reporting on research they or others have conducted, or by taking a position for which they can offer strong evidence and support. But this expectation about writerly authority is by no means universal. Indeed, some cultures view student writers as novices whose job is to reflect what they learn from their teachers. One Japanese student, for example, said he was taught that it's rude to challenge a teacher: "Are you ever so smart that you should challenge the wisdom of the ages?"

As this student's comment reveals, a writer's tone also depends on his or her relationship with listeners and readers. As a world writer, you need to remember that those you're addressing may hold a wide range of attitudes about authority.

- What is your relationship to those you are addressing?
- What knowledge are you expected to have? Is it appropriate for or expected of you to demonstrate that knowledge—and, if so, how?
- What is your goal—to answer a question? to make a point? to agree? something else?
- What tone is appropriate? If in doubt, show respect: politeness is rarely if ever inappropriate.
- What level of control do you have over your writing? In a report, you may have the final say. But if you are writing on a wiki, where you share control with others, sensitivity to communal standards is key.

Expectations about persuasive evidence

How do you decide what evidence will best support your ideas? The answer depends, in large part, on the audience you want to persuade. American academics generally give great weight to factual evidence.

Differing concepts of what counts as evidence can lead to arguments that go nowhere. Consider, for example, how rare it is for a believer in creationism to be persuaded by what the theory of evolution presents as evidence—or for a supporter of evolutionary theory to be convinced by what creationists present as evidence. Think carefully about how you use evidence in writing, and pay attention to what counts as evidence to members of other groups you are trying to persuade.

- Should you rely on facts? concrete examples? firsthand experience? religious or philosophical texts? other sources?
- Should you include the testimony of experts? Which experts are valued most, and why?
- Should you use analogies as support? How much will they count?
- When does evidence from unedited Web sites such as blogs offer credible support, and when should you question or reject it?

Once you determine what counts as evidence in your own thinking and writing, think about where you learned to use and value this kind of evidence. You can ask these same questions about the use of evidence by members of other cultures.

Expectations about organization

As you make choices about how to organize your writing, remember that the patterns you find pleasing are likely to be ones that are deeply embedded in your own culture. For example, the organizational pattern favored by U.S. engineers, highly explicit and leaving little or nothing unsaid or unexplained, is probably familiar to most U.S. students: introduction and thesis, necessary background, overview of the parts to follow, systematic presentation of evidence, consideration of other viewpoints, and conclusion. If a piece of writing follows this pattern, American readers ordinarily find it well organized and coherent.

In the United States, many audiences (especially those in the academic and business worlds) expect a writer to get to the point as directly as possible and to take on the major responsibility of articulating that point efficiently and unambiguously. But not all audiences have such expectations. For instance, a Chinese student with an excellent command of English heard from her U.S. teachers that her writing was "vague," with too much "beating around the bush." As it turned out, her teachers in China had prized this kind of indirectness, expecting audiences to read between the lines.

When writing for audiences who may not share your expectations, then, think about how you can organize material to get your message across effectively. There are no hard and fast rules to help you organize your writing for effectiveness across cultures, but here are a few options to consider:

- Determine when to state your thesis—at the beginning? at the end? somewhere else? not at all?

- Consider whether digressions are a good idea, a requirement, or best avoided with your intended audience.

- Remember that electronic communication may call for certain ways of organizing. In messages or postings, you need to place the most important information first and be as succinct as possible. Or you may need to follow a template, as in submitting a résumé online.

Expectations about style

As with beauty, good style is most definitely in the eye of the beholder—and thus is always affected by language, culture, and rhetorical tradition. In fact, what constitutes effective style varies broadly across cultures and depends on the rhetorical situation—purpose, audience, and so on (see Chapter 5). Even so, there is one important style question to consider when writing across cultures: what level of formality is most appropriate? In most writing to a general audience in the United States, a fairly informal style is often acceptable, even appreciated. Many cultures, however, tend to value a more formal approach. When in doubt, it may be wise to err on the side of formality in writing to people from other cultures, especially to elders or to those in authority.

- Be careful to use proper titles:

  Dr. Atul Gawande   Professor Jaime Mejía

- Avoid slang and informal structures such as fragments.

- Do not use first names of people you do not know in correspondence (even in text messages) unless invited to do so. Note, however, that an invitation to use a first name could come indirectly; if someone signs a message to you with his or her first name, you are implicitly invited to use the first name as a term of address. (See 2e for more on electronic communication.)

- For business correspondence, use complete sentences and words; avoid contractions. Open with the salutation "Dear Mr. / Ms. " or the person's title, if you know it. Write dates with the day before the month, and spell out the name of the month: *7 June 2010.*

Beyond formality, other stylistic preferences vary widely, and context matters. Long, complex sentences and ornate language may be exactly what some audiences are looking for. On Twitter, on the other hand, writers have to limit their message to 140 characters—so using abbreviated words, symbols, and fragments is expected, even desirable.

World writers, then, should take very little about language for granted. To be an effective world writer, aim to recognize and respect stylistic differences as you move from community to community and to meet expectations whenever you can.

EXERCISE 20.1: THINKING CRITICALLY

Choose one or two recent essays or other pieces of writing, and examine them carefully, noting what you assume about what counts as persuasive evidence, good organization, and effective style. How do you represent yourself in relation to your audience? What assumptions do you make about the audience and are such assumptions warranted? What other unstated assumptions about good writing can you identify?

21 Language That Builds Common Ground

The golden rule of language use might be "Speak to others the way you want them to speak to you." The words we select have power: they can praise, delight, inspire — and also hurt, offend, or even destroy. Words that offend prevent others from identifying with you and thus damage your credibility. Few absolute guidelines exist for using

---

AT A GLANCE

Using Language That Builds Common Ground

- Check for stereotypes and other assumptions that might come between you and your readers. Look, for instance, for language implying approval or disapproval and for the ways you use *we*, *you*, and *they*. (21a)

- Avoid potentially sexist language. (21b)

- Make sure your references to race, religion, sexual orientation, and so on are relevant or necessary to your discussion. If they are not, leave them out. (21c and d)

- Check that the terms you use to refer to groups are accurate and acceptable. (21c and d)

words that respect differences and build common ground. Two rules, however, can help: consider carefully the sensitivities and preferences of others, and watch for words that betray your assumptions, even when you have not directly stated them.

21a Examine assumptions and avoid stereotypes.

Unstated assumptions that enter into thinking and writing can destroy common ground by ignoring important differences between others and ourselves. For example, a student in a religion seminar who uses *we* to refer to Christians and *they* to refer to members of other religions had better be sure that everyone in the class identifies as Christian, or some may feel left out of the discussion.

At the same time, don't overgeneralize about or stereotype a group of people. Because stereotypes are often based on half-truths, misunderstandings, and hand-me-down prejudices, they can lead to intolerance, bias, and bigotry.

Sometimes stereotypes and assumptions lead writers to call special attention to a group affiliation when it is not relevant to the point, as in *a woman plumber* or *a white basketball player*. Even positive stereotypes — for example, *Jewish doctors are the best* — or neutral ones — *all college students like pizza* — can hurt, for they inevitably ignore the uniqueness of an individual. Careful writers make sure that their language doesn't stereotype any group or individual.

21b Examine assumptions about gender.

Powerful gender-related words can subtly affect our thinking and our behavior. For instance, at one time many young women were discouraged from pursuing careers in medicine or engineering at least partially because speakers commonly referred to hypothetical doctors or engineers as *he* (and then labeled a woman who worked as a doctor *a woman doctor*, as if to say, "She's an exception; doctors are normally men"). Similarly, a label like *male nurse* may offend by reflecting stereotyped assumptions about proper roles for men. Equally problematic is the traditional use of *man* and *mankind* to refer to people of both sexes and the use of *he* and *him* to refer generally to any human being. Because such usage ignores half of the people on earth, it hardly helps a writer build common ground.

Sexist language, those words and phrases that stereotype or ignore members of either sex or that unnecessarily call attention to gender, can usually be revised fairly easily. There are several alternatives to using masculine pronouns to refer to persons whose gender is unknown to the writer. One option is to recast the sentence using plural forms.

> *Lawyers*   *they*
> ▶ ~~A~~ lawyer must pass the bar exam before he can begin to practice.
>   ^   ^

Another option is to substitute pairs of pronouns such as *he or she*, *him or her*, and so on.

>   *or she*
> ▶ A lawyer must pass the bar exam before he can begin to practice.
>   ^

Yet another way to revise the sentence is to eliminate the pronouns.

>   *beginning*
> ▶ A lawyer must pass the bar exam before ~~he can begin~~ to practice.
>   ^

Beyond the pronoun issue, try to eliminate sexist nouns from your writing.

INSTEAD OF	TRY USING
anchorman, anchorwoman	anchor
businessman	businessperson, business executive
chairman, chairwoman	chair, chairperson
congressman	member of Congress, representative
fireman	firefighter
mailman	mail carrier
male nurse	nurse
man, mankind	humans, human beings, humanity, the human race, humankind
manpower	workers, personnel
mothering	parenting
policeman, policewoman	police officer
salesman	salesperson, sales associate
woman engineer	engineer

EXERCISE 21.1

The following excerpt is taken from the 1948 edition of Dr. Benjamin Spock's *Baby and Child Care*. Read it carefully, noting any language we might now consider sexist. Then try bringing it up-to-date by revising the passage, substituting nonsexist language as necessary.

When you suggest something that doesn't appeal to your baby, he feels he *must* assert himself. His nature tells him to. He just says "no" in words or actions, even about things that he likes to do. The psychologists call it "negativism"; mothers call it "that terrible *no* stage." But stop and think what would happen to him if he never felt like saying "no." He'd become a robot, a mechanical man. You wouldn't be able to resist the temptation to boss him all the time, and he'd stop learning and developing. When he was old enough to go out into the world, to school and later to work, everybody else would take advantage of him, too. He'd never be good for anything.

21c Examine assumptions about race and ethnicity.

In building common ground, writers must watch for any words that ignore differences not only among individual members of a race or ethnic group but also among subgroups. Writers must be aware, for instance, of the many nations to which American Indians belong and of the diverse places from which Americans of Spanish-speaking ancestry have emigrated.

Preferred terms

Identifying preferred terms is sometimes not an easy task, for they can change often and vary widely.

The word *colored*, for example, was once widely used in the United States to refer to Americans of African ancestry. By the 1950s, the preferred term had become *Negro*. This changed in the 1960s, however, as *black* came to be preferred by most, though certainly not all, members of that community. Then, in the late 1980s, some leaders of the American black community urged that *black* be replaced by *African American*.

The word *Oriental*, once used to refer to people of East Asian descent, is now often considered offensive. At the University of California at Berkeley, the Oriental Languages Department is now known as the East Asian Languages Department. One advocate of the change explained that *Oriental* is appropriate for objects—like rugs—but not for people.

Once widely preferred, the term *Native American* is being challenged by those who argue that the most appropriate way to refer to indigenous people is by the specific name of the tribe or pueblo, such as *Chippewa* or *Tesuque*. In Alaska and parts of Canada, many indigenous peoples once referred to as *Eskimos* now prefer *Inuit* or a specific term such as *Tlingit*. It has also become fairly common for tribal groups to refer to themselves as *Indians* or *Indian tribes*.

Among Americans of Spanish-speaking descent, the preferred terms of reference are many: *Chicano/Chicana, Hispanic, Latin American, Latino/Latina, Mexican American, Dominican,* and *Puerto Rican*, to name but a few.

Clearly, then, ethnic terminology changes often enough to challenge even the most careful writers — including writers who belong to the groups they are writing about. The best advice may be to consider your words carefully, to *listen* for the way members of groups refer to themselves (or *ask* about preferences), and to check any term you're unsure of in a current dictionary.

21d Consider other kinds of difference.

Age

Mention age if it is relevant, but be aware that age-related terms (*matronly, well-preserved*, and so on) can carry derogatory connotations. Describing Mr. Fry as *elderly but still active* may sound polite to you, but chances are Mr. Fry would prefer being called *an active seventy-eight-year-old* — or just *a seventy-eight-year-old*, which eliminates the unstated assumption of surprise that he is active at his age.

Class

Take special care to examine your words for assumptions about class. As a writer, you should not assume that all your readers share your background or values — that your classmates all own cars, for instance. And avoid using any words — *redneck, blueblood,* and the like — that might alienate members of an audience.

Geographical area

You should not assume that geography determines personality or lifestyle. New Englanders are not all thrifty and tight-lipped; people in "red states" may hold liberal views; midwesterners are not always polite. Be careful not to make simplistic assumptions.

Check also that you use geographical terms accurately.

AMERICA, AMERICAN Although many people use these words to refer to the United States alone, such usage will not necessarily be acceptable to people from Canada, Mexico, and Central or South America.

BRITISH, ENGLISH Use *British* to refer to the island of Great Britain, which includes England, Scotland, and Wales, or to the United Kingdom of Great Britain and Northern Ireland. In general, do not use *English* for these broader senses.

ARAB This term refers only to people of Arabic-speaking descent. Note that Iran is not an Arab nation; its people speak Farsi, not Arabic. Note

> **CONSIDERING DISABILITIES**
> ## Knowing Your Readers
> Nearly 10 percent of first-year college students — about 155,000 — identify themselves as having one or more disabilities. That's no small number. Effective writers consider their own and their readers' disabilities so that they can find ways to build common ground.

also that *Arab* is not synonymous with *Muslim* or *Moslem* (a believer in Islam). Most (but not all) Arabs are Muslim, but many Muslims (those in Pakistan, for example) are not Arab.

Physical ability or health

When writing about a person with a serious illness or physical disability, ask yourself whether mentioning the disability is relevant to your discussion and whether the words you use carry negative connotations. You might choose, for example, to say someone *uses* a wheelchair rather than to say he or she is *confined to* one. Similarly, you might note a subtle but meaningful difference in calling someone a *person with AIDS* rather than an *AIDS victim*. Mentioning the person first and the disability second, such as referring to a *child with diabetes* rather than a *diabetic child* or a *diabetic*, is always a good idea.

Religion

Assumptions about religious groups are very often inaccurate and unfair. For example, Roman Catholics hold a wide spectrum of views on abortion, Muslim women do not all wear veils, and many Baptists are not fundamentalists. In fact, many people do not believe in or practice a religion at all, so be careful of such assumptions. As in other cases, do not use religious labels without considering their relevance to your point.

Sexual orientation

If you wish to build common ground, do not assume that readers all share one sexual orientation. As with any label, reference to sexual orientation should be governed by context. Someone writing about Representative Barney Frank's legislative record would probably have little if any reason to refer to his sexual orientation. On the other hand, someone writing about diversity in U.S. government might find it important to note that Frank was the first U.S. congressman to voluntarily make his homosexuality public.

 bedfordstmartins.com/everydaywriter
Exercise Central > Language That Builds Common Ground

EXERCISE 21.2: THINKING CRITICALLY

Writer and filmmaker Ruth Ozeki has written widely on issues related to the environment. In this June 2009 posting from her blog, Ozeki appeals to readers to step back and cultivate silence as a necessary prelude to making difficult decisions. Who is the "we" that Ozeki addresses? What views and values do you think she expects her readers to share with her? Note the strategies the writer uses to establish common ground with readers in this paragraph.

> I'm more and more convinced that we need to cultivate mindful silence, and share it with others whenever possible, if we are going to be able to make the careful and difficult choices we will need to make in order to survive in a wired and warming world. This seems to me to be a key piece of activism and eco-pedagogy that we can all learn to cultivate.   — RUTH OZEKI, *Ozekiland*

 # Language Variety

Comedian Dave Chappelle has said, "Every black American is bilingual. We speak street vernacular, and we speak job interview." As Chappelle understands, English comes in many varieties that differ from one another in pronunciation, vocabulary, usage, and grammar. You probably already adjust the variety of language you use depending on how well — and how formally — you know the audience you are addressing. Adding language variety to your writing can improve your communication with your audience if you think carefully about the effect you want to achieve.

22a Use standard varieties of English appropriately.

How do writers decide when to use another language or switch from one variety of English to another? Even writers who are perfectly fluent in several languages must think for a moment before switching linguistic gears.

AT A GLANCE

Language Variety

You can use different varieties of language to good effect for the following purposes:

- to repeat someone's exact words
- to evoke a person, place, or activity
- to establish your credibility and build common ground
- to make a strong point
- to connect with an audience

The key to shifting among varieties of English and among languages is appropriateness: you need to consider when such shifts will help your audience appreciate your message and when shifts may be a mistake. Used appropriately and wisely, *any* variety of English can serve a good purpose.

One variety of English, often referred to as the "standard" or "standard academic," is that taught prescriptively in schools, represented in this and most other textbooks, used in the national media, and written and spoken widely by those wielding social and economic power. As the language used in business and most public institutions, standard English is a variety you will want to be completely familiar with. Standard English, however, is only one of many effective varieties of English and itself varies according to purpose and audience, from the more formal style used in academic writing to the informal style characteristic of casual conversation.

22b Use varieties of English to evoke a place or community.

"Ever'body says words different," said Ivy. "Arkansas folks says 'em different from Oklahomy folks says 'em different. And we seen a lady from Massachusetts, an' she said 'em differentest of all. Couldn' hardly make out what she was sayin'." —JOHN STEINBECK, *The Grapes of Wrath*

Using the language of a local community is an effective way to evoke a character or place. Author and radio host Garrison Keillor, for example, peppers his tales of his native Minnesota with the homespun English spoken there: "I once was a tall dark heartbreaker who, when I slouched into a room, women jumped up and asked if they could get me something, and now they only smile and say, 'My mother is a big fan of yours. You sure are a day-brightener for her. You sure make her chuckle.'"

> **FOR MULTILINGUAL WRITERS**
>
> **Global Varieties of English**
>
> Like other world languages, English is used in many countries, so it has many global varieties. For example, British English differs somewhat from U.S. English in certain vocabulary (*bonnet* for hood of a car), syntax (*to hospital* rather than *to the hospital*), spelling (*centre* rather than *center*), and pronunciation. If you have learned a non-American variety of English, you will want to recognize, and to appreciate, the ways in which it differs from the variety widely used in U.S. academic settings.

Weaving together regionalisms and standard English can also be effective in creating a sense of place. Here, an anthropologist writing about one Carolina community takes care to let the residents speak their minds—and in their own words:

> For Roadville, schooling is something most folks have not gotten enough of, but everybody believes will do something toward helping an individual "get on." In the words of one oldtime resident, "Folks that ain't got no schooling don't get to be nobody nowadays."
>
> —SHIRLEY BRICE HEATH, *Ways with Words*

Varieties of language can also help writers evoke other kinds of communities. In this panel from *One! Hundred! Demons!*, Lynda Barry uses playground language to present a vivid image of remembered childhood games. See how kids' use of slang ("Dag") and colloquialisms ("Whose up is it?") helps readers join in the experience.

22c Use varieties of English to build credibility with a community.

Whether you are American Indian or trace your ancestry to Europe, Asia, Latin America, Africa, or elsewhere, your heritage lives on in the diversity of the English language.

See how one Hawaiian writer uses a local variety of English to paint a picture of young teens hearing a "chicken skin" story from their grandmother.

> "—So, rather dan being rid of da shark, da people were stuck with many little ones, for dere mistake."
> Then Grandma Wong wen' pause, for dramatic effect, I guess, and she wen' add, "Dis is one of dose times. . . . Da time of da sharks."
> Those words ended another of Grandma's chicken skin stories. The stories she told us had been passed on to her by her grandmother, who had heard them from her grandmother. Always skipping a generation.
> —RODNEY MORALES, "When the Shark Bites"

Notice how the narrator of the story uses both standard and nonstandard varieties of English—presenting information necessary to the story line mostly in standard English and using a local, ethnic variety to represent spoken language. One important reason for the shift from standard English is to demonstrate that the writer is a member of the community whose language he is representing and thus to build credibility with others in the community.

Take care, however, in using the language of communities other than your own. When used inappropriately, such language can have an opposite effect, perhaps destroying credibility and alienating your audience.

EXERCISE 22.1

Identify the purpose and audience for one of this chapter's examples of regional, ethnic, or communal varieties of English. Then rewrite the passage to remove all evidence of any variety of English other than the "standard." Compare your revised version with the original and with those produced by some of your classmates. What differences do you notice in tone (is it more formal? more distant? something else?) and in overall impression? Which version seems most appropriate for the intended audience and purpose? Which do you prefer, and why?

22d Bring in other languages appropriately.

You might use a language other than English for the same reasons you might use different varieties of English: to represent the actual words of a speaker, to make a point, to connect with your audience, or to get their attention. See how Gerald Haslam uses Spanish to capture his great-grandmother's words and to make a point about his relationship to her.

> "*Expectoran su sangre!*" exclaimed Great-grandma when I showed her the small horned toad I had removed from my breast pocket. I turned toward my mother, who translated: "They spit blood."
> "*De los ojos,*" Grandma added. "From their eyes," mother explained, herself uncomfortable in the presence of the small beast.
> I grinned, "Awwwwwww."
> But my Great-grandmother did not smile. "*Son muy tóxicos,*" she nodded with finality. Mother moved back an involuntary step, her hands suddenly busy at her breast. "Put that thing down," she ordered.
> "His name's John," I said.
>
> – GERALD HASLAM, *California Childhood*

EXERCISE 22.2: THINKING CRITICALLY

The following description of a meal features English that is characteristic of the Florida backwoods in the 1930s. Using this passage as an example, write a description of a memorable event from your daily life. Try to include some informal dialogue. Then look at the language you used — do you use more than one variety of English? What effect does your use of language have on your description?

> Jody heard nothing; saw nothing but his plate. He had never been so hungry in his life, and after a lean winter and a slow spring . . . his mother had cooked a supper good enough for the preacher. There were poke-greens with bits of white bacon buried in them; sandbuggers made of potato and onion and the cooter he had found crawling yesterday; sour orange biscuits and at his mother's elbow the sweet potato pone. He was torn between his desire for more biscuits and another sandbugger and the knowledge, born of painful experience, that if he ate them, he would suddenly have no room for pone. The choice was plain.
>
> — MARJORIE KINNAN RAWLINGS, *The Yearling*

23 Word Choice and Spelling

Deciding which word is the right word can be a challenge. It's not unusual to find many words that have similar but subtly different meanings, and each makes a different impression on your audience. For instance, the "pasta with marinara sauce" presented in a restaurant may look and taste much like the "macaroni and gravy" served at an Italian family dinner, but the choice of one label rather than the other

---

> **AT A GLANCE**
>
> ## Editing for Appropriate Language and Spelling
>
> - Check to see that your language reflects the appropriate level of formality for your audience, purpose, and topic. (23a)
> - Unless you are writing for a specialized audience that will understand jargon, either define technical terms or replace them with words that are easy to understand. (23a)
> - Consider the connotations of words carefully. If you say someone is *pushy*, be sure you mean to be critical; otherwise, use a word like *assertive*. (23b)
> - Use both general and specific words. If you are writing about the general category *beds*, for example, do you give enough concrete detail (*an antique four-poster bed*)? (23c)
> - Look for clichés, and replace them with fresher language. (23d)
> - Use spell checkers with care. (23e)

tells us not only about the food but also about the people serving it and the people they expect to serve it to.

Ensuring that you choose the correct spelling for the word you want to use is also important. Spell checkers can help you avoid some errors, but they can also make other mistakes more likely, including word choice errors, so use them with care (see 23e).

23a Choose appropriate formality.

Choose a level of formality that matches your audience, purpose, and topic. In an email or letter to a friend or close associate, informal language is often appropriate. For most academic and professional writing, however, more formal language is appropriate because you are addressing people you do not know well. Compare the following responses to a request for information about a job candidate:

EMAIL TO SOMEONE YOU KNOW WELL

Maisha is great — hire her if you can!

LETTER OF RECOMMENDATION TO SOMEONE YOU DO NOT KNOW

I am pleased to recommend Maisha Fisher. She will bring good ideas and extraordinary energy to your organization.

TALKING THE TALK

Texting Abbreviations

"Can I use text-message slang when I contact my teacher?" In a chat or text message, abbreviations such as *u* for *you* may be conventional, but using such shortcuts when communicating with an instructor can be a mistake. At least some of your instructors are likely to view them as disrespectful, unprofessional, or simply sloppy writing. Unless you are working to create a special effect for a special purpose and audience, keep to the conventions of standard English for college writing—and for contacting your instructor.

Slang and colloquial language

Slang, or extremely informal language, is often confined to a relatively small group and usually becomes obsolete rather quickly, though some slang gains wide use (*workaholic, duh*). Colloquial language, such as *a lot, in a bind,* or *snooze,* is less informal, more widely used, and longer lasting than most slang.

Writers who use slang and colloquial language run the risk of not being understood or of not being taken seriously. If you are writing for a general audience about gun-control legislation, for example, and you use the term *gat* to refer to a weapon, some readers may not know what you mean, and others may be irritated by what they see as a frivolous reference to a deadly serious subject.

EXERCISE 23.1

Choose something or someone to describe — a favorite cousin, a stranger on the bus, an automobile, a musical instrument, whatever strikes your fancy. Describe your subject using colloquial language and slang. Then rewrite the description, this time using neither of these. Read the two passages aloud, and note what different effects each version creates.

Jargon

Jargon is the special vocabulary of a trade or profession, enabling members to speak and write concisely to one another. Reserve jargon for an audience that will understand your terms. The example that follows, from a blog about fonts and typefaces, uses jargon appropriately for an interested and knowledgeable audience.

The Modern typeface classification is usually associated with Didones and display faces that often have too much contrast for text use. The Ingeborg family was designed with the intent of producing a Modern face that was readable at any size. Its roots might well be historic, but its approach is very contemporary. The three text weights (Regular, Bold, and Heavy) are functional and discreet while the Display weights (Fat and Block) catch the reader's eye with a dynamic form and a whole lot of ink on the paper. The family includes a boatload of extras like unicase alternates, swash caps, and a lined fill.

−FONTSHOP.COM BLOG

Depending on the needs of the audience, jargon can be irritating and incomprehensible—or extremely helpful. Terms that begin as jargon for specialists (such as *asynchronous* or *vertical integration*) can quickly become part of the mainstream if they provide a useful shorthand for an otherwise lengthy explanation. Before you use technical jargon, remember your readers: if they will not understand the terms, or if you don't know them well enough to judge, then say what you need to say in everyday language.

Pompous language, euphemisms, and doublespeak

Stuffy or pompous language is unnecessarily formal for the purpose, audience, or topic. It often gives writing an insincere or unintentionally humorous tone, making a writer's ideas seem insignificant or even unbelievable.

POMPOUS

Pursuant to the August 9 memorandum regarding the increased unit cost of automotive fuels, it is incumbent upon us to endeavor to make maximal utilization of electronic or telephonic communication in lieu of personal visitation.

REVISED

As noted in the August 9 memo, higher gasoline prices require us to email or telephone whenever possible rather than make personal visits.

As these examples illustrate, some writers use words in an attempt to sound expert, and these puffed-up words can easily backfire.

FOR MULTILINGUAL WRITERS

Avoiding Fancy Language

In writing standard academic English, which is fairly formal, students are often tempted to use many "big words" instead of simple language. Although learning impressive words can be a good way to expand your vocabulary, it is usually best to avoid flowery or fancy language in college writing. Academic writing at U.S. universities tends to value clear, concise prose.

INSTEAD OF	TRY USING	INSTEAD OF	TRY USING
ascertain	find out	optimal	best
commence	begin	parameters	boundaries
finalize	finish, complete	peruse	look at
impact (as verb)	affect	ramp up	increase
methodology	method	utilize	use

Euphemisms are words and phrases that make unpleasant ideas seem less harsh. *Your position is being eliminated* seeks to soften the blow of being fired or laid off. Other euphemisms include *pass on* or *pass away* for *die* and *plus-sized* for *fat*. Although euphemisms can sometimes appeal to an audience by showing that you are considerate of people's feelings, they can also sound insincere or evasive.

Doublespeak is language used to hide or distort the truth. During massive layoffs and cutbacks in the business world, companies speak of firings as *employee repositioning* or *proactive downsizing,* and of unpaid time off as a *furlough*. The public — and particularly those who lose their jobs — recognize these terms for what they are.

EXERCISE 23.2

Revise each of these sentences to use formal language consistently. Example:

> *Although*   *be enthusiastic*   *as soon as*
> I can get all enthused about writing, but I sit down to write, and my
>   *blank.*
> mind goes right to sleep.

1. In Shakespeare's *Othello*, Desdemona just lies down like some kind of wimp and accepts her death as inevitable.

2. The budget office doesn't want to cough up the cash to replace the drafty windows, but cranking up the heat in the building all winter doesn't come cheap.

3. Finding all that bling in King Tut's tomb was one of the biggest archeological scores of the twentieth century.

4. In unfamiliar settings or with people he did not know well, Duncan often came off as kind of snooty, but in reality he was scared to death.

5. My family lived in Trinidad for the first ten years of my life, and we went through a lot of bad stuff there, but when we came to the United States, we thought we finally had it made.

23b Consider denotation and connotation.

Thinking of a stone tossed into a pool and ripples spreading out from it can help you understand the distinction between *denotation*, the dictionary meaning of a word (the stone), and *connotation*, the associations that accompany the word (the ripples). The words *enthusiasm, passion,* and *obsession,* for instance, all carry roughly the same denotation. But the connotations are quite different: an *enthusiasm* is a pleasurable and absorbing interest; a *passion* has a strong emotional component and may affect someone positively or negatively; an *obsession* is an unhealthy attachment that excludes other interests.

Note the differences in connotation among the following three statements:

▶ **Students Against Racism (SAR) erected a temporary barrier on the campus oval. They say it symbolizes "the many barriers to those discriminated against by university policies."**

▶ **Left-wing agitators threw up an eyesore on the oval to stampede the university into giving in to their demands.**

▶ **Supporters of human rights for all students challenged the university's investment in racism by erecting a protest barrier on campus.**

The first statement is the most neutral, merely stating facts; the second, using words with negative connotations (*agitators, eyesore, stampede*), is strongly critical; the third, using a phrase with positive connotations (*supporters of human rights*) and presenting assertions as facts (*the university's investment in racism*), gives a favorable slant to the story.

23c Use general and specific language effectively.

Effective writers balance general words, which name or describe groups or classes, with specific words, which identify individual and particular things. Some general words are abstract; they refer to things we cannot perceive through our five senses. Specific words are often concrete; they name things we can see, hear, touch, taste, or smell. We can seldom draw a clear-cut line between general or abstract words on the one hand and specific or concrete words on the other. Instead, most words fall somewhere in between.

GENERAL	LESS GENERAL	SPECIFIC	MORE SPECIFIC
book	dictionary	abridged dictionary	the fourth edition of *The American Heritage College Dictionary*

EXERCISE 23.3

From the parentheses, choose the word with the denotation that makes most sense in the context of the sentence. Use a dictionary if necessary.

1. She listened (*apprehensively / attentively*) to the lecture and took notes.
2. The telemarketers were told to (*empathize / emphasize*) more expensive items.
3. The interns were (*conscientious / conscious*) workers who listened carefully and learned fast.
4. Franklin advised his readers to be frugal and (*industrial / industrious*).
5. All (*proceedings / proceeds*) from the bake sale went to the athletics program.

EXERCISE 23.4

Study the italicized words in each of the following passages, and decide what each word's connotations contribute to your understanding of the passage. Think of a synonym for each word, and see if you can decide what difference the new word would make on the effect of the passage.

1. If boxing is a sport, it is the most *tragic* of all sports because, more than any human activity, it consumes the very excellence it displays: Its very *drama* is this consumption. — JOYCE CAROL OATES, "On Boxing"

2. Then one evening Miss Glory told me to serve the ladies on the porch. After I set the tray down and turned toward the kitchen, one of the women asked, "What's your name, *girl*?" — MAYA ANGELOU, *I Know Why the Caged Bird Sings*

3. The Kiowas are a summer people; they *abide* the cold and keep to themselves; but when the season *turns* and the land becomes warm and *vital*, they cannot *hold still*. — N. SCOTT MOMADAY, "The Way to Rainy Mountain"

ABSTRACT	LESS ABSTRACT	CONCRETE	MORE CONCRETE
culture	visual art	painting	van Gogh's *Starry Night*

Strong writing usually provides readers with both an overall picture and specific examples or concrete details to fill in that picture. In the following passage, the author might have simply made a general statement — *their breakfast was always liberal and good* — or simply given the details of the breakfast. Instead, he is both general and specific.

> There would be a brisk fire crackling in the hearth, the old smoke-gold of morning and the smell of fog, the crisp cheerful voices of the people and their ruddy competent morning look, and the cheerful smells of breakfast, which was always liberal and good, the best meal that they had: kidneys and ham and eggs and sausages and toast and marmalade and tea.
> — THOMAS WOLFE, *Of Time and the River*

EXERCISE 23.5

Rewrite each of the following sentences to be more specific and concrete.

1. The entryway of the building was dirty.
2. The sounds at dawn are memorable.
3. Our holiday dinner tasted good.
4. The attendant came toward my car.
5. I woke up.

23d Use figurative language effectively.

Figurative language, or figures of speech, can paint pictures in a reader's mind, allowing one to "see" a point readily and clearly. Far from being merely decorative, such language can be crucial to understanding.

Similes, metaphors, and analogies

Similes use *like, as, as if,* or *as though* to make explicit the similarity between two seemingly different things.

> ▶ **You can tell the graphic-novels section in a bookstore from afar, by the young bodies sprawled around it like casualties of a localized disaster.**
> — PETER SCHJELDAHL

> ▶ **The comb felt as if it was raking my skin off.**
> — MALCOLM X, "My First Conk"

Metaphors are implicit comparisons, omitting the *like, as, as if,* or *as though* of similes.

> ▶ **The Internet is the new town square.** — JEB HENSARLING

Mixed metaphors make comparisons that are inconsistent.

> ▶ **The lectures were like brilliant comets streaking through the night sky,**

dazzling   *flashes*
~~showering~~ listeners with ~~a torrential rain~~ of insights.
^   ^

The images of streaking light and heavy precipitation are inconsistent; in the revised sentence, all of the images relate to light.

Analogies compare similar features of two dissimilar things; they explain something unfamiliar by relating it to something familiar.

▶ One way to establish that peace-preserving threat of mutual assured destruction is to commit yourself beforehand, which helps explain why so many retailers promise to match any competitor's advertised price. Consumers view these guarantees as conducive to lower prices. But in fact offering a price-matching guarantee should make it less likely that competitors will slash prices, since they know that any cuts they make will immediately be matched. It's the retail version of the doomsday machine.   — JAMES SUROWIECKI

▶ One Hundred and Twenty-fifth Street was to Harlem what the Mississippi was to the South, a long traveling river always going somewhere, carrying something.   — MAYA ANGELOU, *The Heart of a Woman*

FOR MULTILINGUAL WRITERS
Learning Idioms

Why do you wear a diamond *on* your finger but *in* your ear? See 60a.

Clichés

A cliché is a frequently used expression such as *busy as a bee*. By definition, we use clichés all the time, especially in speech, and many serve usefully as shorthand for familiar ideas or as a way of connecting to an audience. But if you use too many clichés in your writing, readers may conclude that what you are saying is not very new or interesting — or true. To check for clichés, use this rule of thumb: if you can predict exactly what the next word in a phrase will be, the phrase stands a good chance of being a cliché.

 **bedfordstmartins.com/everydaywriter**
Exercise Central > Appropriate Language

EXERCISE 23.6

Return to the description you wrote in Exercise 23.1. Note any words that carry strong connotations, and identify the concrete and abstract language as well as any use of figurative language. Revise any inappropriate language you find.

EXERCISE 23.7: THINKING CRITICALLY

Read the following brief poem. What dominant feeling or impression does the poem produce in you? Identify the specific words and phrases that help create that impression.

What happens to a dream deferred?

Does it dry up
Like a raisin in the sun?
Or fester like a sore —
And then run?
Does it stink like rotten meat?
Or crust and sugar over —
Like a syrupy sweet?

Maybe it just sags
Like a heavy load.

Or does it explode?

— LANGSTON HUGHES, "Harlem (A Dream Deferred)"

23e Make spell checkers work for you.

Research conducted for this textbook shows that spelling errors have changed dramatically in the past twenty years — and the reason is spell checkers. Although these programs have weeded out many once-common misspellings, they are not foolproof. Spell checkers still allow typical kinds of errors that you should look out for.

Common errors with spell checkers

- **Homonyms.** Spell checkers cannot distinguish between words such as *affect* and *effect* that sound alike but are spelled differently.

- **Proper nouns.** A spell checker cannot tell you when you have misspelled a proper name. Proofread names with special care.

- **Compound words written as two words.** Spell checkers will not see a problem if *nowhere* is incorrectly written as *no where*. When in doubt, check a dictionary.

- **Typos.** The spell checker will not flag *heat* even if you meant to type *heart*.

Spell checker use

To make spell checkers work best for you, you need to learn to adapt them to your own needs.

- Always proofread carefully, even after you have used the spell checker. The more important the message or document, the more careful you should be about its accuracy and clarity.

- Use a dictionary to look up any word the spell checker highlights that you are not sure of.

- If your spell checker's dictionary allows you to add new words, enter proper names, non-English words, or specialized language you use regularly and have trouble spelling. Be careful to enter the correct spelling!

- If you know that you mix up certain homonyms, such as *there* and *their*, check for them after running your spell checker.

- Remember that spell checkers are not sensitive to capitalization. If you write "the united states," the spell checker won't question it.

- Do *not* automatically accept the spell checker's suggestions: you may end up with a word you don't really want.

TALKING THE TALK

Spell Checkers and Wrong-Word Errors

"Can I trust spell checkers to correct a word I've spelled wrong?" In a word, no. The spell checker may suggest bizarre substitutes for many proper names and specialized terms (even when you spell them correctly) and for certain typographical errors, thus introducing wrong words into your paper if you accept its suggestions automatically. For example, a student who had typed *fantic* instead of *frantic* found that the spell checker's first choice was to substitute *fanatic* — a replacement that made no sense. Wrong-word errors are the most common surface error in college writing today (see Chapter 1), and spell checkers are partly to blame. So be careful not to take a spell checker's recommendation without paying careful attention to the replacement word.

EXERCISE 23.8

The following paragraph has been checked with a spell checker. Proofread carefully and correct any errors that the spell checker missed.

I see that you have send me a warning about a computer virus that can destroy my hard drive, mangle my soft ware, and generally reek havoc on my computer. How ever, you may not be aware oft he fact that warnings like this one are almost never real. When a message axes you to foreword it to every one in you're address book, you should know immediately that its a hoax. User who send false warnings about viruses to hundreds of there friends are not doing any one a favor; instead, they are simple slowing down traffic on line and creating problems that maybe worst then any technical difficulties cause by the

FOR MULTILINGUAL WRITERS

Recognizing American Spellings

Different varieties of English often use different spelling conventions. If you have learned British or Indian English, for example, you will want to be aware of some of the more common spelling differences in American English. For example, words ending in *–yse* or *–ise* in British/Indian English (*analyse, criticise*) usually end in *–yze* or *–ize* in American English (*analyze, criticize*); words ending in *–our* in British/Indian English (*labour, colour*) usually end in *–or* in American English (*labor, color*); and words ending in *–re* in British/Indian English (*theatre, centre*) usually end in *–er* in American English (*theater, center*).

virus — if the virus even exist. Please insure that warnings contain a grain of true before you past them on. If your worried that my computer might be in danger, set you mind at easy. I will except responsibility if the machine goes hay wire.

Homonyms

A relatively small number of homonyms — just eight groups — cause writers the most frequent trouble.

accept (to take or receive)	to (in the direction of)
except (to leave out)	too (in addition; excessive)
affect (an emotion; to have an influence)	two (number between *one* and *three*)
effect (a result; to cause to happen)	weather (climatic conditions) whether (if)
its (possessive of *it*) it's (contraction of *it is* or *it has*)	who's (contraction of *who is* or *who has*)
their (possessive of *they*) there (in that place) they're (contraction of *they are*)	whose (possessive of *who*) your (possessive of *you*) you're (contraction of *you are*)

If you tend to confuse particular homonyms, try creating a special memory device to help you remember the differences. For example, "*We* all complain about the *weather*" will remind you that *weather* (the climate) starts with *we*.

In addition, pay close attention to homonyms that may be spelled as one word or two, depending on the meaning.

▶ Of course, they did not wear *everyday* clothes *every day*.

▶ Before the six lawyers were *all ready* to negotiate, it was *already* May.

▶ The director *may be* on time. But *maybe* she'll be late.

For additional advice on commonly confused words, see the glossary of usage in Chapter 24.

EXERCISE 23.9

Choose the appropriate word in parentheses to fill each blank.

If _____ (*your/you're*) looking for summer fun, _____ (*accept/except*) the friendly _____ (*advice/advise*) of thousands of happy adventurers: spend three _____ (*weaks/weeks*) kayaking _____ (*thorough/threw/through*) the inside passage _____ (*to/too/two*) Alaska. For ten years, Outings, Inc., has _____ (*lead/led*) groups of novice kayakers _____ (*passed/past*) some of the most breathtaking scenery in North America. The group's goal is simple: to give participants the time of _____ (*their/there/they're*) lives and show them things they don't see _____ (*every day/everyday*). As one of last year's adventurers said, "_____ (*Its/It's*) a trip that is _____ (*already/all ready*) one of my favorite memories. It _____ (*affected/effected*) me powerfully."

23f Master spelling rules.

General spelling rules can help writers enormously, but many rules have exceptions. When in doubt, consult a dictionary.

i *before* e *except after* c

Here is a slightly expanded version of the "*i* before *e*" rule:

I BEFORE *E*	ach*ie*ve, br*ie*f, f*ie*ld, fr*ie*nd
EXCEPT AFTER *C*	c*ei*ling, rec*ei*pt, perc*ei*ve
OR WHEN PRONOUNCED *AY*	*ei*ghth, n*ei*ghbor, r*ei*gn, w*ei*gh
OR IN WEIRD EXCEPTIONS	*ei*ther, for*ei*gn, h*ei*ght, l*ei*sure, n*ei*ther, s*ei*ze

Word endings (suffixes)

FINAL SILENT *E*

Drop the final silent *e* when you add an ending that starts with a vowel.

imagine + -able = imaginable   exercise + -ing = exercising

Generally, keep the final *e* if the ending starts with a consonant. Common exceptions include *argument*, *judgment*, *noticeable*, and *truly*.

force + -ful = forceful   state + -ly = stately

FINAL *Y*

When adding an ending to a word that ends in a consonant plus *y*, change the *y* to an *i* in most cases.

try, tried   busy, busily

Keep the *y* if it is part of a proper name or if the ending begins with *i*.

Kennedy, Kennedyesque   dry, drying

FINAL CONSONANTS

When adding an ending beginning with a vowel to a word that ends with a vowel and a consonant, double the final consonant if the original word is one syllable or if the accent is on the same syllable in both the original and the new word.

stop, stopped   begin, beginner   refer, referral

Otherwise, do not double the final consonant.

bait, baiting   start, started   refer, reference

Plurals

ADDING -S OR -ES

For most nouns, add -*s*. For words ending in *s*, *ch*, *sh*, *x*, or *z*, add -*es*.

pencil, pencils   church, churches   bus, buses

In general, add -*s* to nouns ending in *o* if the *o* is preceded by a vowel. Add -*es* if the *o* is preceded by a consonant.

rodeo, rodeos   patio, patios   potato, potatoes   hero, heroes

For some nouns ending in *f* or *fe*, change *f* to *v*, and add -*s* or -*es*.

calf, calves   life, lives   hoof, hooves

For compound nouns written as separate or hyphenated words, make the most important part plural, whether or not it is the last part of the compound.

lieutenant governors   brothers-in-law

For plurals of numbers and words used as terms, see 42c.

CONSIDERING DISABILITIES

Spelling

Spelling is especially difficult for people who have trouble processing letters and sounds in sequence. Technology can help: "talking pens" can scan words and read them aloud, and voice-recognition programs can transcribe dictated text.

---

bedfordstmartins.com/everydaywriter
Exercise Central > Spelling

24 Glossary of Usage

Conventions of usage might be called the "good manners" of discourse. And just as manners vary from culture to culture and time to time, so do conventions of usage. Matters of usage, like other language choices you must make, depend on what your purpose is and on what is appropriate for a particular audience at a particular time.

a, an   Use *a* with a word that begins with a consonant (*a book*), a consonant sound such as "y" or "w" (*a euphoric moment, a one-sided match*), or a sounded *h* (*a hemisphere*). Use *an* with a word that begins with a vowel (*an umbrella*), a vowel sound (*an X-ray*), or a silent *h* (*an honor*).

accept, except   The verb *accept* means "receive" or "agree to." *Except* is usually a preposition that means "aside from" or "excluding." *All the plaintiffs except Mr. Kim decided to accept the settlement.*

advice, advise   The noun *advice* means "opinion" or "suggestion"; the verb *advise* means "offer advice." *Doctors advise everyone not to smoke, but many people ignore the advice.*

affect, effect   As a verb, *affect* means "influence" or "move the emotions of"; as a noun, it means "emotions" or "feelings." *Effect* is a noun meaning "result"; less commonly, it is a verb meaning "bring about." *The storm affected a large area. Its effects included widespread power failures. The drug effected a major change in the patient's affect.*

aggravate   The formal meaning is "make worse." *Having another mouth to feed aggravated their poverty.* In academic and professional writing, avoid using *aggravate* to mean "irritate" or "annoy."

all ready, already   *All ready* means "fully prepared." *Already* means "previously." *We were all ready for Lucy's party when we learned that she had already left.*

all right, alright   Avoid the spelling *alright*.

all together, altogether   *All together* means "all in a group" or "gathered in one place." *Altogether* means "completely" or "everything considered." *When the board members were all together, their mutual distrust was altogether obvious.*

allude, elude   *Allude* means "refer indirectly." *Elude* means "avoid" or "escape from." *The candidate did not even allude to her opponent. The suspect eluded the police for several days.*

allusion, illusion   An *allusion* is an indirect reference. An *illusion* is a false or misleading appearance. *The speaker's allusion to the Bible created an illusion of piety.*

a lot   Avoid the spelling *alot*.

already   See *all ready, already.*

alright   See *all right, alright.*

altogether   See *all together, altogether.*

among, between   In referring to two things or people, use *between*. In referring to three or more, use *among*. *The relationship between the twins is different from that among the other three children.*

amount, number   Use *amount* with quantities you cannot count; use *number* for quantities you can count. *A small number of volunteers cleared a large amount of brush.*

an   See *a, an.*

and/or   Avoid this term except in business or legal writing. Instead of *fat and/or protein*, write *fat, protein,* or *both.*

any body, anybody, any one, anyone   *Anybody* and *anyone* are pronouns meaning "any person." *Anyone* [or *anybody*] *would enjoy this film. Any body* is an adjective modifying a noun. *Any body of water has its own ecology. Any one* is two adjectives or a pronoun modified by an adjective. *Customers could buy only two sale items at any one time. The winner could choose any one of the prizes.*

anyplace   In academic and professional discourse, use *anywhere* instead.

anyway, anyways   In writing, use *anyway*, not *anyways.*

apt, liable, likely   *Likely to* means "probably will," and *apt to* means "inclines or tends to." In many instances, they are interchangeable. *Liable* often carries a more negative sense and is also a legal term meaning "obligated" or "responsible."

as   Avoid sentences in which it is not clear if *as* means "when" or "because." For example, does *Carl left town as his father was arriving* mean "at the same time as his father was arriving" or "because his father was arriving"?

as, as if, like   In academic and professional writing, use *as* or *as if* instead of *like* to introduce a clause. *The dog howled as if* [not *like*] *it were in pain. She did as* [not *like*] *I suggested.*

assure, ensure, insure   *Assure* means "convince" or "promise"; its direct object is usually a person or persons. *She assured voters she would not raise taxes. Ensure* and *insure* both mean "make certain," but *insure* usually refers specifically to protection against financial loss. *When the city rationed water to ensure that the supply would last, the Browns could no longer afford to insure their car-wash business.*

as to   Do not use *as to* as a substitute for *about*. *Karen was unsure about* [not *as to*] *Bruce's intentions.*

at, where   See *where.*

awhile, a while   Always use *a while* after a preposition such as *for, in,* or *after. We drove awhile and then stopped for a while.*

bad, badly   Use *bad* after a linking verb such as *be, feel,* or *seem*. Use *badly* to modify an action verb, an adjective, or another verb. *The hostess felt bad because the dinner was badly prepared.*

bare, bear   Use *bare* to mean "uncovered" and *bear* to refer to the animal or to mean "carry" or "endure": *The walls were bare. The emptiness was hard to bear.*

because of, due to   Use *due to* when the effect, stated as a noun, appears before the verb *be*. *His illness was due to malnutrition.* (*Illness*, a noun, is the effect.) Use *because of* when the effect is stated as a clause. *He was sick because of malnutrition.* (*He was sick*, a clause, is the effect.)

being as, being that   In academic or professional writing, use *because* or *since* instead of these expressions. *Because* [not *being as*] *Romeo killed Tybalt, he was banished to Padua.*

beside, besides   *Beside* is a preposition meaning "next to." *Besides* can be a preposition meaning "other than" or an adverb meaning "in addition." *No one besides Francesca would sit beside him.*

between   See *among, between.*

brake, break   *Brake* means "to stop" and also refers to a stopping mechanism: *Check the brakes. Break* means "fracture" or an interruption: *The coffee break was too short.*

breath, breathe   *Breath* is a noun; *breathe,* a verb. *"Breathe,"* said the nurse, so *June took a deep breath.*

bring, take   Use *bring* when an object is moved from a farther to a nearer place; use *take* when the opposite is true. *Take the box to the post office; bring back my mail.*

but that, but what   Avoid using these as substitutes for *that* in expressions of doubt. *Hercule Poirot never doubted that* [not *but that*] *he would solve the case.*

but yet   Do not use these words together. *He is strong but* [not *but yet*] *gentle.*

can, may   *Can* refers to ability and *may* to possibility or permission. *Since I can ski the slalom well, I may win the race.*

can't hardly   *Hardly* has a negative meaning; therefore, *can't hardly* is a double negative. This expression is commonly used in some varieties of English but is not used in academic English. *Tim can* [not *can't*] *hardly wait.*

can't help but   This expression is redundant. Use *I can't help going* rather than *I can't help but go.*

censor, censure   *Censor* means "remove that which is considered offensive." *Censure* means "formally reprimand." *The newspaper censored stories that offended advertisers. The legislature censured the official for misconduct.*

compare to, compare with   *Compare to* means "regard as similar." *Jamie compared the loss to a kick in the head. Compare with* means "examine to find differences or similarities." *Compare Tim Burton's films with David Lynch's.*

complement, compliment   *Complement* means "go well with." *Compliment* means "praise." *Guests complimented her on how her earrings complemented her gown.*

comprise, compose   *Comprise* means "contain." *Compose* means "make up." *The class comprises twenty students. Twenty students compose the class.*

conscience, conscious   *Conscience* means "a sense of right and wrong." *Conscious* means "awake" or "aware." *Lisa was conscious of a guilty conscience.*

consensus of opinion   Use *consensus* instead of this redundant phrase. *The family consensus was to sell the old house.*

consequently, subsequently   *Consequently* means "as a result"; *subsequently* means "then." *He quit, and subsequently his wife lost her job; consequently, they had to sell their house.*

continual, continuous *Continual* means "repeated at regular or frequent intervals." *Continuous* means "continuing or connected without a break." *The damage done by continuous erosion was increased by the continual storms.*

could of *Have*, not *of*, should follow *could, would, should*, or *might*. *We could have* [not *of*] *invited them.*

criteria, criterion *Criterion* means "standard of judgment" or "necessary qualification." *Criteria* is the plural form. *Image is the wrong criterion for choosing a president.*

data *Data* is the plural form of the Latin word *datum*, meaning "fact." Although *data* is used informally as either singular or plural, in academic or professional writing, treat *data* as plural. *These data indicate that fewer people are smoking.*

different from, different than *Different from* is generally preferred in academic and professional writing, although both phrases are widely used. *Her lab results were no different from* [not *than*] *his.*

discreet, discrete *Discreet* means "tactful" or "prudent." *Discrete* means "separate" or "distinct." *The leader's discreet efforts kept all the discrete factions unified.*

disinterested, uninterested *Disinterested* means "unbiased." *Uninterested* means "indifferent." *Finding disinterested jurors was difficult. She was uninterested in the verdict.*

distinct, distinctive *Distinct* means "separate" or "well defined." *Distinctive* means "characteristic." *Germany includes many distinct regions, each with a distinctive accent.*

doesn't, don't *Doesn't* is the contraction for *does not*. Use it with *he, she, it*, and singular nouns. *Don't* stands for *do not*; use it with *I, you, we, they*, and plural nouns.

due to See *because of, due to*.

each other, one another Use *each other* in sentences involving two subjects and *one another* in sentences involving more than two.

effect See *affect, effect*.

elicit, illicit The verb *elicit* means "draw out." The adjective *illicit* means "illegal." *The police elicited from the criminal the names of others involved in illicit activities.*

elude See *allude, elude*.

emigrate from, immigrate to *Emigrate from* means "move away from one's country." *Immigrate to* means "move to another country." *We emigrated from Norway in 1999. We immigrated to the United States.*

ensure See *assure, ensure, insure*.

enthused, enthusiastic Use *enthusiastic* rather than *enthused* in academic and professional writing.

equally as good Replace this redundant phrase with *equally good* or *as good*.

every day, everyday *Everyday* is an adjective meaning "ordinary." *Every day* is an adjective and a noun, meaning "each day." *I wore everyday clothes almost every day.*

every one, everyone *Everyone* is a pronoun. *Every one* is an adjective and a pronoun, referring to each member of a group. *Because he began after everyone else, David could not finish every one of the problems.*

except See *accept, except.*

explicit, implicit *Explicit* means "directly or openly expressed." *Implicit* means "indirectly expressed or implied." *The explicit message of the ad urged consumers to buy the product, while the implicit message promised popularity if they did so.*

farther, further *Farther* refers to physical distance. *How much farther is it to Munich? Further* refers to time or degree. *I want to avoid further delays.*

fewer, less Use *fewer* with nouns that can be counted. Use *less* with general amounts that you cannot count. *The world needs fewer bombs and less hostility.*

finalize *Finalize* is a pretentious way of saying "end" or "make final." *We closed* [not *finalized*] *the deal.*

firstly, secondly, etc. *First, second,* etc., are more common in U.S. English.

flaunt, flout *Flaunt* means to "show off." *Flout* means to "mock" or "scorn." *The drug dealers flouted authority by flaunting their wealth.*

former, latter *Former* refers to the first and *latter* to the second of two things previously mentioned. *Kathy and Anna are athletes; the former plays tennis, and the latter runs.*

further See *farther, further.*

good, well *Good* is an adjective and should not be used as a substitute for the adverb *well. Gabriel is a good host who cooks well.*

good and *Good and* is colloquial for "very"; avoid it in academic and professional writing.

hanged, hung *Hanged* refers to executions; *hung* is used for all other meanings.

hardly See *can't hardly.*

herself, himself, myself, yourself Do not use these reflexive pronouns as subjects or as objects unless they are necessary. *Jane and I* [not *myself*] *agree. They invited John and me* [not *myself*].

he/she, his/her Better solutions for avoiding sexist language are to write out *he or she,* to eliminate pronouns entirely, or to make the subject plural. Instead of writing *Everyone should carry his/her driver's license,* try *Drivers should carry their licenses* or *People should carry their driver's licenses.*

himself See *herself, himself, myself, yourself.*

hisself Use *himself* instead in academic or professional writing.

hopefully *Hopefully* is often used informally to mean "it is hoped," but its formal meaning is "with hope." *Sam watched the roulette wheel hopefully* [not *Hopefully, Sam will win*].

hung See *hanged, hung.*

illicit See *elicit, illicit.*

illusion See *allusion, illusion.*

immigrate to See *emigrate from, immigrate to.*

impact Some readers object to the colloquial use of *impact* or *impact on* as a verb meaning "affect." *Population control may reduce [not impact] world hunger.*

implicit See *explicit, implicit.*

imply, infer To *imply* is to suggest indirectly. To *infer* is to guess or conclude on the basis of an indirect suggestion. *The note implied they were planning a small wedding; we inferred we would not be invited.*

inside of, outside of Use *inside* and *outside* instead. *The class regularly met outside [not outside of] the building.*

insure See *assure, ensure, insure.*

interact, interface *Interact* is a vague word meaning "do something that somehow involves another person." *Interface* is computer jargon; when used as a verb, it means "discuss" or "communicate." Avoid both verbs in academic and professional writing.

irregardless, regardless *Irregardless* is a double negative. Use *regardless.*

is when, is where These vague expressions are often incorrectly used in definitions. *Schizophrenia is a psychotic condition in which [not is when or is where] a person withdraws from reality.*

its, it's *Its* is the possessive form of *it. It's* is a contraction for *it is* or *it has. It's important to observe the rat before it eats its meal.*

kind, sort, type These singular nouns should be modified with *this* or *that,* not *these* or *those,* and followed by other singular nouns, not plural nouns. *Wear this kind of dress [not those kind of dresses].*

kind of, sort of Avoid these colloquialisms. *Amy was somewhat [not kind of] tired.*

know, no Use *know* to mean "understand." *No* is the opposite of *yes.*

later, latter *Later* means "after some time." *Latter* refers to the second of two items named. *Juan and Chad won all their early matches, but the latter was injured later in the season.*

latter See *former, latter* and *later, latter.*

lay, lie *Lay* means "place" or "put." Its main forms are *lay, laid, laid.* It generally has a direct object, specifying what has been placed. *She laid her books on the desk. Lie* means "recline" or "be positioned" and does not take a direct object. Its main forms are *lie, lay, lain. She lay awake until two.*

leave, let *Leave* means "go away." *Let* means "allow." *Leave alone* and *let alone* are interchangeable. *Let me leave now, and leave [or let] me alone from now on!*

lend, loan In academic and professional writing, do not use *loan* as a verb; use *lend* instead. *Please lend me your pen so that I may fill out this application for a loan.*

less See *fewer, less.*

let See *leave, let.*

liable See *apt, liable, likely.*

lie See *lay, lie.*

like See *as, as if, like.*

likely See *apt, liable, likely.*

literally *Literally* means "actually" or "exactly as stated." Use it to stress the truth of a statement that might otherwise be understood as figurative. Do not use *literally* as an intensifier in a figurative statement. *Mirna was literally at the edge of her seat* may be accurate, but *Mirna is so hungry that she could literally eat a horse* is not.

loan See *lend, loan.*

loose, lose *Lose* is a verb meaning "misplace." *Loose* is an adjective that means "not securely attached." *Sew on that loose button before you lose it.*

lots, lots of Avoid these informal expressions meaning "much" or "many" in academic or professional discourse.

man, mankind Replace these terms with *people, humans, humankind, men and women,* or similar wording.

may See *can, may.*

may be, maybe *May be* is a verb phrase. *Maybe* is an adverb that means "perhaps." *He may be the head of the organization, but maybe someone else would handle a crisis better.*

media *Media* is the plural form of the noun *medium* and takes a plural verb. *The media are* [not *is*] *obsessed with scandals.*

might of See *could of.*

moral, morale A *moral* is a succinct lesson. *The moral of the story is that generosity is rewarded. Morale* means "spirit" or "mood." *Office morale was low.*

myself See *herself, himself, myself, yourself.*

no See *know, no.*

nor, or Use *either* with *or* and *neither* with *nor.*

number See *amount, number.*

off, of Use *off* without *of. The spaghetti slipped off* [not *off of*] *the plate.*

OK, O.K., okay All are acceptable spellings, but avoid the term in academic and professional discourse.

on account of Use this substitute for *because of* sparingly or not at all.

one another See *each other, one another.*

or See *nor, or.*

outside of See *inside of, outside of.*

owing to the fact that Avoid this and other wordy expressions for *because.*

passed, past Use *passed* to mean "went by" or "received a passing grade": *The marching band passed the reviewing stand.* Use *past* to refer to a time before the present: *Historians study the past.*

per Use the Latin *per* only in standard technical phrases such as *miles per hour.* Otherwise, find English equivalents. *As mentioned in* [not *As per*] *the latest report, the country's average food consumption each day* [not *per day*] *is only 2,000 calories.*

percent, percentage Use *percent* with a specific number; use *percentage* with an adjective such as *large* or *small. Last year, 80 percent of the members were female. A large percentage of the members are women.*

plenty *Plenty* means "enough" or "a great abundance." *They told us America was a land of plenty.* Colloquially, it is used to mean "very," a usage you should avoid in academic and professional writing. *He was very* [not *plenty*] *tired.*

plus *Plus* means "in addition to." *Your salary plus mine will cover our expenses.* In academic writing, do not use *plus* to mean "besides" or "moreover." *That dress does not fit me. Besides* [not *Plus*]*, it is the wrong color.*

precede, proceed *Precede* means "come before"; *proceed* means "go forward." *Despite the storm that preceded the ceremony, the wedding proceeded on schedule.*

pretty Except in informal situations, avoid using *pretty* as a substitute for "rather," "somewhat," or "quite." *Bill was quite* [not *pretty*] *disagreeable.*

principal, principle When used as a noun, *principal* refers to a head official or an amount of money; when used as an adjective, it means "most significant." *Principle* means "fundamental law or belief." *Albert went to the principal and defended himself with the principle of free speech.*

proceed See *precede, proceed.*

quotation, quote *Quote* is a verb, and *quotation* is a noun. *He quoted the president, and the quotation* [not *quote*] *was preserved in history books.*

raise, rise *Raise* means "lift" or "move upward." (Referring to children, it means "bring up.") It takes a direct object; someone raises something. *The guests raised their glasses to toast. Rise* means "go upward." It does not take a direct object; something rises by itself. *She saw the steam rise from the pan.*

rarely ever Use *rarely* by itself, or use *hardly ever. When we were poor, we rarely went to the movies.*

real, really *Real* is an adjective, and *really* is an adverb. Do not substitute *real* for *really.* In academic and professional writing, do not use *real* or *really* to mean "very." *The old man walked very* [not *real* or *really*] *slowly.*

reason is because Use either *the reason is that* or *because* — not both. *The reason the copier stopped is that* [not *is because*] *the paper jammed.*

reason why This expression is redundant. *The reason* [not *reason why*] *this book is short is market demand.*

regardless See *irregardless, regardless.*

respectfully, respectively *Respectfully* means "with respect." *Respectively* means "in the order given." *Karen and David are, respectively, a juggler and an acrobat. The children treated their grandparents respectfully.*

rise See *raise, rise.*

set, sit *Set* usually means "put" or "place" and takes a direct object. *Sit* refers to taking a seat and does not take an object. *Set your cup on the table, and sit down.*

should of See *could of.*

since Be careful not to use *since* ambiguously. In *Since I broke my leg, I've stayed home*, the word *since* might be understood to mean either "because" or "ever since."

sit See *set, sit.*

so In academic and professional writing, avoid using *so* alone to mean "very." Instead, follow *so* with *that* to show how the intensified condition leads to a result. *Aaron was so tired that he fell asleep at the wheel.*

someplace Use *somewhere* instead in academic and professional writing.

some time, sometime, sometimes *Some time* refers to a length of time. *Please leave me some time to dress. Sometime* means "at some indefinite later time." *Sometime I will take you to London. Sometimes* means "occasionally." *Sometimes I eat sushi.*

sort See *kind, sort, type*.

sort of See *kind of, sort of*.

stationary, stationery *Stationary* means "standing still"; *stationery* means "writing paper." *When the bus was stationary, Pat took out stationery and wrote a note.*

subsequently See *consequently, subsequently*.

supposed to, used to Be careful to include the final *-d* in these expressions. *He is supposed to attend.*

sure, surely Avoid using *sure* as an intensifier. Instead, use *certainly*. *I was certainly glad to see you.*

take See *bring, take*.

than, then Use *than* in comparative statements. *The cat was bigger than the dog.* Use *then* when referring to a sequence of events. *I won, and then I cried.*

that, which A clause beginning with *that* singles out the item being described. *The book that is on the table is a good one* specifies the book on the table as opposed to some other book. A clause beginning with *which* may or may not single out the item, although some writers use *which* clauses only to add more information about an item being described. *The book, which is on the table, is a good one* contains a *which* clause between the commas. The clause simply adds extra, nonessential information about the book; it does not specify which book.

theirselves Use *themselves* instead in academic and professional writing.

then See *than, then*.

thorough, threw, through *Thorough* means "complete": *After a thorough inspection, the restaurant reopened. Threw* is the past tense of *throw*, and *through* means "in one side and out the other": *He threw the ball through a window.*

to, too, two *To* generally shows direction. *Too* means "also." *Two* is the number. *We, too, are going to the meeting in two hours.* Avoid using *to* after *where*. *Where are you flying* [not *flying to*]?

two See *to, too, two*.

type See *kind, sort, type*.

uninterested See *disinterested, uninterested*.

unique Some people argue that *unique* means "one and only" and object to usage that suggests it means merely "unusual." In formal writing, avoid constructions such as *quite unique*.

used to See *supposed to, used to*.

very Avoid using *very* to intensify a weak adjective or adverb; instead, replace the adjective or adverb with a stronger, more precise, or more colorful word. Instead of *very nice*, for example, use *kind, warm, sensitive, endearing*, or *friendly*.

way, ways   When referring to distance, use *way*. *Graduation was a long way* [not *ways*] *off.*

well   See *good, well.*

where   Use *where* alone, not with words such as *at* and *to*. *Where are you going* [not *going to*]?

which   See *that, which.*

who, whom   Use *who* if the word is the subject of the clause and *whom* if the word is the object of the clause. *Monica, who smokes incessantly, is my godmother.* (*Who* is the subject of the clause; the verb is *smokes*.) *Monica, whom I saw last winter, lives in Tucson.* (*Whom* is the object of the verb *saw*.)

who's, whose   *Who's* is a contraction for *who is* or *who has*. *Who's on the patio? Whose* is a possessive form. *Whose sculpture is in the garden? Whose is on the patio?*

would of   See *could of.*

yet   See *but yet.*

your, you're   *Your* shows possession. *Bring your sleeping bag along. You're* is the contraction for *you are. You're in the wrong sleeping bag.*

yourself   See *herself, himself, myself, yourself.*

Sentence Style

Look: wear your black some days, and
wear your purple others. There is no
other rule besides pulling it off.

— ZADIE SMITH

Sentence Style

25 Coordination, Subordination, and Emphasis   287
a Use coordination to relate equal ideas   288
b Use subordination to distinguish main ideas   289
c Use closing and opening positions for emphasis   293

26 Consistency and Completeness   295
a Revise faulty sentence structure   295
b Match up subjects and predicates   296
c Use elliptical structures carefully   297
d Check for missing words   298
e Make comparisons complete, consistent, and clear   298

27 Parallelism   299
a Make items in a series parallel   299
b Make paired ideas parallel   300
c Include all necessary words   302

28 Shifts   303
a Revise unnecessary shifts in verb tense   303
b Revise unnecessary shifts in mood   303
c Revise unnecessary shifts in voice   303
d Revise unnecessary shifts in person and number   304
e Revise shifts between direct and indirect discourse   304
f Revise shifts in tone and word choice   305

29 Conciseness   307
a Eliminate unnecessary words   308
b Eliminate redundant words   308
c Eliminate empty words   308
d Replace wordy phrases   309
e Simplify sentence structure   309

30 Sentence Variety   311
a Vary sentence length   311
b Vary sentence openings   312

For visual analysis Look carefully at the illustration on the front of this tab. What do you think this image suggests about using style effectively?

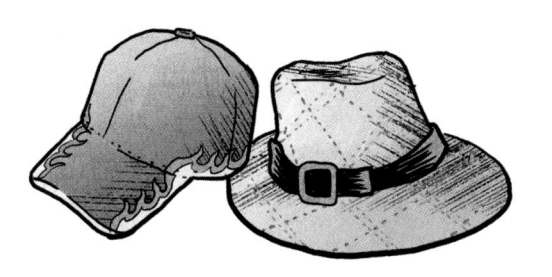

Coordination, Subordination, and Emphasis 25

Coordination and subordination are ways of joining ideas in sentences that show relationships between ideas and emphasize more important ideas. In speech, people tend to use *and* and *so* as all-purpose connectors.

I'm leaving now, and I'll see you later.

The meaning of this sentence may be perfectly clear in speech, which provides clues with voice, facial expressions, and gestures. But in writing, the sentence could have multiple meanings, including these:

Although I'm leaving now, I'll see you later.

I'm leaving now because I'll see you later.

A coordinating conjunction such as *and* gives ideas equal emphasis, and a subordinating conjunction such as *although* or *because* emphasizes one

---

AT A GLANCE

Editing for Coordination, Subordination, and Emphasis

How do your ideas flow from one sentence to another? Do they connect smoothly and clearly? Are the more important ideas given more emphasis than less important ones?

- Look for strings of short sentences that might be combined to join related ideas. (25a)

  ▶ The report was short. It was persuasive. It changed my mind.
  but it /, *it* /;

- If you use *and* excessively, decide whether all the ideas are equally important. If they are not equal, edit to subordinate the less important ones. (25b)

---

continued

- Make sure that the most important ideas appear in independent clauses that can stand alone as complete sentences. (25b)

  Even though the
  ▶ ~~The~~ report was short, ~~even though~~ it changed my mind.

- Identify the word or words you want to receive special emphasis. If those words are buried in the middle of a sentence, edit the sentence to change their position. The end and the beginning are generally the most emphatic. (25c)

- If a sentence includes a series of three or more words, phrases, or clauses, try to arrange the items in the series in climactic order, with the most important item last. (25c)

idea more than another. Choosing appropriate conjunctions also allows a writer to specify how the ideas are related.

25a Use coordination to relate equal ideas.

When used well, coordination relates separate but equal ideas. The element that links the ideas, usually a coordinating conjunction (*and, but, for, nor, or, so, yet*) or a semicolon, makes the precise relationship clear. The following sentences by N. Scott Momaday all use coordination, but the relationship between independent clauses differs in each sentence:

▶ They acquired horses, **and** their ancient nomadic spirit was suddenly free of the ground.

▶ There is perfect freedom in the mountains, **but** it belongs to the eagle and the elk, the badger and the bear.

▶ No longer were they slaves to the simple necessity of survival; they were a lordly and dangerous society of fighters and thieves, hunters and priests of the sun.

 –N. Scott Momaday, *The Way to Rainy Mountain*

Momaday uses coordination in these sentences carefully in order to achieve very specific effects. In the first sentence, for example, the use of *and* gives a sense of adding on: "They acquired horses" *and*, of equal importance, "their ancient nomadic spirit was suddenly free." Momaday might have made other, equally correct choices, but they would have resulted in slightly different sentences. Compare these altered versions with Momaday's sentences. How do the changes affect your understanding?

▶ They acquired horses, **so** their ancient nomadic spirit was suddenly free of the ground.

▶ **There is perfect freedom in the mountains; it belongs to the eagle and the elk, the badger and the bear.**

In your own writing, think about exactly what information you want to convey with coordination. You, too, may have several correct options—so make the choice that works best for your situation and audience.

Coordination can help make explicit the relationship between two ideas.

▶ **Generations have now grown up with** *The Simpsons,*/ **Bart, Lisa, and**

Maggie never get older, but today's college students may have been

watching the show since before they could talk.

Connecting these two sentences with a semicolon strengthens the connection between two closely related ideas.

When you connect ideas within a sentence, make sure the relationship between the ideas is clear.

but

▶ **Watching television is a common way to spend leisure time, and it**

makes viewers apathetic.

What does television's being a common form of leisure have to do with viewers' being apathetic? Changing *and* to *but* better relates the two ideas.

EXERCISE 25.1

Using coordination to signal equal importance or to create special effects, combine and revise the following fourteen short sentences into several longer and more effective ones. Add or delete words as necessary.

The auditorium was filled with people. The sea of faces did not intimidate me. I had decided to appear in a musical with my local community theater group. There was no going back now. I reminded myself of how I had gotten here. It took hard work. I refused to doubt my abilities. Besides, the director and her staff had held auditions. I had read the heroine's part. I had sung a song. They had chosen me for the role. I was untrained. My skills as an actor would now be judged publicly. I felt ready to rise to the challenge.

25b Use subordination to distinguish main ideas.

Subordination allows you to distinguish major points from minor points or to bring in supporting details. If, for instance, you put your main idea in an independent clause—words that could stand alone as a sentence (31m)—you might then put any less significant ideas in dependent clauses, phrases, or even single words. The following sentence highlights the subordinated point:

► **Mrs. Viola Cullinan was a plump woman who lived in a three-bedroom house somewhere behind the post office.**

– MAYA ANGELOU, "My Name Is Margaret"

The dependent clause adds important information about Mrs. Cullinan, but it is subordinate to the independent clause.

Notice that the choice of what to subordinate rests with the writer and depends on the intended meaning. Angelou might have given the same basic information differently.

► **Mrs. Viola Cullinan, a plump woman, lived in a three-bedroom house somewhere behind the post office.**

Subordinating the information about Mrs. Cullinan's size to that about her house would suggest a slightly different meaning, of course. When you write, think carefully about what you want to emphasize and subordinate information accordingly.

Subordination also establishes logical relationships among ideas. These relationships are often specified by relative pronouns—such as *which, who,* and *that*—and by subordinating conjunctions.

COMMON SUBORDINATING CONJUNCTIONS

after	if	though
although	in order that	unless
as	once	until
as if	since	when
because	so that	where
before	than	while
even though		

The following sentence highlights the subordinate clause and underlines the subordinating word:

► **She usually rested her smile until late afternoon <u>when</u> her women friends dropped in and Miss Glory, the cook, served them cold drinks on the closed-in porch.** – MAYA ANGELOU, "My Name Is Margaret"

Using too many coordinate structures can be monotonous and can make it hard for readers to recognize the most important ideas. Subordinating lesser ideas can help highlight the main ideas.

▶ Many people check email in the evening, and so they turn on

Though they

the computer. ~~They~~ may intend to respond only to urgent messages,
^

which

a friend sends a link to a blog post, ~~and they~~ decide to read it
^

Eventually,

for just a short while/, ~~and they~~ get engrossed in Facebook, and they
^

end up spending the whole evening in front of the screen.

Determining what to subordinate

Although our

▶ ~~Our~~ new boss can be difficult, ~~although~~ she has revived and maybe
^

even saved the division.

The editing puts the more important information—that she has saved part
of the company—in an independent clause and subordinates the rest.

TALKING ABOUT STYLE

Subordination

Carefully used subordination can create powerful effects. Some particularly fine examples come from Martin Luther King Jr.

Perhaps it is easy for those who have never felt the stinging darts of segregation to say, "Wait." But *when* you have seen vicious mobs lynch your mothers and fathers at will and drown your sisters and brothers at whim; *when* you have seen hate-filled policemen curse, kick, and even kill your black brothers and sisters; . . . *when* you have to concoct an answer for a five-year-old son who is asking: "Daddy, why do white people treat colored people so mean?"; *when* you take a cross-country drive and find it necessary to sleep night after night in the uncomfortable corners of your automobile because no motel will accept you; . . . *when* your first name becomes "nigger," your middle name becomes "boy" (however old you are) and your last name becomes "John," and your wife and mother are never given the respected title "Mrs."; . . . *when* you are forever fighting a degenerating sense of "nobodiness" — then you will understand why we find it difficult to wait.

– MARTIN LUTHER KING JR., "Letter from Birmingham Jail"

Avoiding excessive subordination

When too many subordinate clauses are strung together, readers may have trouble keeping track of the main idea.

TOO MUCH SUBORDINATION

▶ **Philip II sent the Spanish Armada to conquer England, which was ruled by Elizabeth, who had executed Mary because she was plotting to overthrow Elizabeth, who was a Protestant, whereas Mary and Philip were Roman Catholics.**

REVISED

▶ **Philip II sent the Spanish Armada to conquer England, which was ruled by Elizabeth, a Protestant. She had executed Mary, a Roman Catholic like Philip, because Mary was plotting to overthrow her.**

Putting the facts about Elizabeth executing Mary into an independent clause makes key information easier to recognize.

EXERCISE 25.2

Combine each of the following sets of sentences into one sentence that uses subordination to signal the relationships among ideas. Example:

I was looking through the cupboard.
I noticed the cookies were gone.
This snack is a favorite of my roommate.

While I was looking through the cupboard, I noticed that the cookies, one of my roommate's favorite snacks, were gone.

1. The original *Star Trek* television show ran from 1966 to 1969.
   It was critically acclaimed.
   It had low ratings and was canceled by the network.

2. Athena was the goddess of wisdom.
   Ancient Greeks relied on Athena to protect the city of Athens.
   Athens was named in Athena's honor.

3. Harry Potter is a fictional wizard.
   He turns eleven years old.
   He is taken to Hogwarts School of Witchcraft and Wizardry.

4. Flappers seemed rebellious to their parents' generation.
   They broke with 1920s social conventions.
   They cut their hair short and smoked in public.

5. Skateboarding originated in Venice, California.
   The time was the mid-seventies.
   There was a drought.
   The swimming pools were empty.

→ **bedfordstmartins.com/everydaywriter**
Exercise Central > Coordination and Subordination

25c Use closing and opening positions for emphasis.

When you read a sentence, the part you are most likely to remember is the ending. This part of the sentence should move the writing forward by providing new information, as it does in the following example:

▶ **Employers today expect college graduates to have excellent writing skills.**

A less emphatic but still important position in a sentence is the opening, which often connects the new sentence with what has come before.

▶ **Today's employers want a college-educated workforce that can communicate well. Excellent writing skills are high on the list of qualifications.**

If you place relatively unimportant information in the memorable closing position of a sentence, you may undercut what you want to emphasize or give more emphasis to the closing words than you intend.

Last month, she   *$500,000.*
▶ **She gave $500,000 to the school capital campaign last month.**
    ‸   ‸

Moving *$500,000* to the end of the sentence emphasizes the amount.

Using climactic order to emphasize important ideas

When you arrange ideas in order of increasing importance, power, or drama, your writing builds to a climax. By saving its most dramatic item for last, the following sentence makes its point forcefully and memorably:

▶ **After they've finished with the pantry, the medicine cabinet, and the attic, [neat people] will throw out the red geranium (too many leaves), sell the dog (too many fleas), and send the children off to boarding school (too many scuffmarks on the hardwood floors).**
                            – SUSANNE BRITT, "Neat People vs. Sloppy People"

The original version of the next sentence fails to achieve strong emphasis because its verbs are not sequenced in order of increasing power; the editing provides climactic order.

                        offend our ears,   *and*
▶ **Violent video games assault our eyes, damage our brains, and offend our ears.**
                              ‸   ‸   ‸

TALKING ABOUT STYLE

Anticlimax and Humor

Sometimes it's fun to turn the principle of climactic order upside down, opening with grand or exaggerated language only to end anticlimactically, with everyday words.

> He is a writer for the ages — the ages of four to eight.
>
> — DOROTHY PARKER

Parker builds up high expectations at the beginning of the sentence — only to undercut them unexpectedly by shifting the meaning of *ages.* Having led readers to expect something dramatic, she makes us laugh, or at least smile, with words that are decidedly undramatic.

EXERCISE 25.3

Revise each of the following sentences to highlight what you take to be the main or most important ideas. Example:

Theories about dinosaurs have run the gamut — simple lizards, fully adapted warm-blooded creatures, hybrids of cold-blooded capabilities.

1. The president persuaded the American people, his staff, and Congress.

2. We can expect a decade of record-breaking tropical storms and hurricanes, if meteorologists are correct in their predictions.

3. From the sightseeing boat, we saw a whale dive toward us and then, before crashing its tail on the waves, lift itself out of the water.

4. I did not realize that living in the city would mean eating canned soup every night, selling my car, and losing half my closet space.

5. Jake experienced several side effects from the medication, including dizziness, severe abdominal pain, and dry mouth.

⟳ **bedfordstmartins.com/everydaywriter**
  Exercise Central > Emphasis

EXERCISE 25.4: THINKING CRITICALLY

Analyze two paragraphs from one of your drafts. Do the independent clauses contain the main ideas? How many dependent clauses do you find? Should the ideas in the dependent clauses be subordinate to those in the independent clauses? Revise the paragraphs to use coordination and subordination effectively. What conclusions can you draw about your use of coordination and subordination?

Consistency and Completeness **26**

In conversation, you will hear inconsistent and incomplete structures all the time. For instance, during an interview with journalist Bill
Moyers, Jon Stewart discussed the supposed objectivity of news reporting.

> But news has never been objective. It's always . . . what does every news-
> cast start with? "Our top stories tonight." That's a list. That's a subjec-
> tive . . . some editor made a decision: "Here's our top stories. Number one:
> There's a fire in the Bronx."

Because Stewart is talking casually, some of his sentences begin one
way but then move in another direction. The mixed structures pose no
problem for the viewer—they sound like conversations we hear every
day—but sentences such as these can be confusing in writing.

26a   Revise faulty sentence structure.

One inconsistency that poses problems for writers and readers is a mixed structure, which
results from beginning a sentence with one
grammatical pattern and then switching to another one.

MIXED   The fact that I get up at 5:00 AM, a
wake-up time that explains why
I'm always tired in the evening.

The sentence starts out with a subject (*The fact*) followed by a dependent
clause (*that I get up at 5:00 AM*). The sentence needs a predicate to complete the independent clause, but instead it moves to another phrase
followed by a dependent clause (*a wake-up time that explains why I'm always tired in the evening*), and what results is a fragment.

REVISED   The fact that I get up at 5:00 AM explains why I'm always
tired in the evening.

Deleting *a wake-up time that* changes the rest of the sentence into a predicate.

REVISED   I get up at 5:00 AM, a wake-up time that explains why I'm
always tired in the evening.

Deleting *The fact that* turns the beginning of the sentence into an independent clause.

(For information about subjects and predicates, see 31j and k; for information about independent and dependent clauses, see 31m.)

26b   Match up subjects and predicates.

Another kind of mixed structure, called faulty predication, occurs when a subject and predicate do not fit together grammatically or simply do not make sense together. Many cases of faulty predication result from using forms of *be* when another verb would be stronger.

> *generosity.*
> ► A characteristic that I admire is ~~a person who is generous.~~

A person is not a characteristic.

> *require*
> ► The rules of the corporation ~~expect~~ employees to be on time.

Rules cannot expect anything.

Is when, is where, *and* the reason . . . is because

Constructions using *is when, is where,* and *the reason . . . is because* are used frequently in informal contexts, but they may be inappropriate in academic writing because they describe a noun using an adverb clause (31m).

> *an unfair characterization of*
> ► A stereotype is ~~when someone~~ characterizes a group ~~unfairly.~~

AT A GLANCE

Editing for Consistency and Completeness

- If you find an especially confusing sentence, check to see whether it has a subject and a predicate. If not, revise as necessary. (26a) If you find both a subject and a predicate, and you are still confused, see whether the subject and verb make sense together. (26b)

- Revise any *is when, is where,* and *reason . . . is because* constructions. (26b)

  > *the practice of sending*
  > ► Spamming is ~~where companies send~~ electronic junk mail.

- Check all comparisons for completeness. (26e)

  > *we like*
  > ► We like Lisa better than Margaret.

> *a place*
> A confluence is ~~where~~ two rivers join to form one.
> ^

> ~~The reason~~ I like to play soccer is ~~because~~ it provides aerobic exercise.

EXERCISE 26.1

Revise each of the following sentences in two ways to make its structures consistent in grammar and meaning. Example:

> *Because*
> ~~The fact~~ ~~that~~ our room was cold, we put a heater between our beds.
> ^

> *led us to*
> The fact that our room was cold, we put a heater between our beds.
> ^

1. To enroll in film school being my primary goal, so I am always saving my money and watching for scholarship opportunities.
2. The reason air-pollution standards should not be relaxed is because many people would suffer.
3. By turning off the water when you brush your teeth, saving up to eight gallons of water per day.
4. Irony is when you expect one thing and get something else.
5. The best meal I've ever eaten was sitting by a river eating bread and cheese from a farmers' market.

26c Use elliptical structures carefully.

Sometimes writers omit a word in a compound structure. This type of structure, known as an elliptical structure, is appropriate when the word omitted later in the compound is exactly the same as the word earlier in the compound.

> That bell belonged to the figure of Miss Duling as though it grew directly out of her right arm, as wings grew out of an angel or a tail [grew] out of the devil. — EUDORA WELTY, *One Writer's Beginnings*

If the omitted word does not match a word in the other part of the compound, readers might be confused, so the omission is inappropriate in formal writing.

> *is*
> His skills are weak, and his performance only average.
> ^

The verb *is* does not match the verb in the other part of the compound (*are*), so the writer needs to include it.

26d   Check for missing words.

The best way to catch inadvertent omissions is to proofread carefully.

> ▶ The new Web site makes it easier to look ^*at* and choose from the company's inventory.

26e   Make comparisons complete, consistent, and clear.

When you compare two or more things, the comparison must be complete, logically consistent, and clear.

> ▶ I was embarrassed because my parents were so different ^*from my friends' parents.*

> Different from what? Adding *from my friends' parents* tells readers with what the comparison is being made.

UNCLEAR   Aneil always felt more affection for his brother than his sister.

CLEAR   Aneil always felt more affection for his brother than his sister did.

CLEAR   Aneil always felt more affection for his brother than he did for his sister.

EXERCISE 26.2

Revise each of the following sentences to eliminate any inappropriate elliptical constructions; to make comparisons complete, logically consistent, and clear; and to supply any other omitted words that are necessary for meaning. Example:

> Most of the candidates are bright, and one ^*is* brilliant.

1. Convection ovens cook more quickly and with less power.
2. Argentina and Peru were colonized by Spain, and Brazil by Portugal.
3. She argued that children are even more important for men than women.
4. Do you think the barbecue sauce in Memphis is better than North Carolina?
5. The equipment in our new warehouse is guaranteed to last longer than our current facility.

bedfordstmartins.com/everydaywriter
Exercise Central > Consistency and Completeness

Read over three or four paragraphs from a draft or completed essay you have written recently. Check for mixed sentences and incomplete or missing structures. Revise the paragraphs to correct any problems you find. If you find any, do you recognize any patterns? If so, make a note of them for future reference.

Parallelism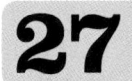

Parallel grammatical structures show up in many familiar phrases: *sink or swim, rise and shine, shape up or ship out.* If you look and listen for these structures, you will see parallelism in everyday use. Bumper stickers often use parallel grammatical structures to make their messages memorable (*Minds are like parachutes; both work best when open*), but the pleasing effects of parallel structures can benefit any kind of writing.

27a Make items in a series parallel.

Parallelism makes a series both graceful and easy to follow.

▶ In the eighteenth century, armed forces could fight **in open fields** and **on the high seas**. Today, they can clash **on the ground anywhere**, **on the sea**, **under the sea**, and **in the air**.

– DONALD SNOW AND EUGENE BROWN, *The Contours of Power*

AT A GLANCE

Editing for Parallelism

- Look for any series of three or more items, and make all of the items parallel in structure. (27a)

- Be sure items in lists and in related headings are parallel. (27a)

- Check for places where two ideas are paired in the same sentence. Often these ideas will appear on either side of *and, but, or, nor, for, so,* or *yet,* or after each part of *both . . . and, either . . . or, neither . . . nor, not only . . . but also, whether . . . or,* or *just as . . . so.* Edit to make the two ideas parallel in structure. (27b)

- Check parallel structures to be sure that you have included all necessary words — prepositions, the *to* of the infinitive, and so on. (27c)

The parallel phrases, as well as the parallel structure of the sentences themselves, highlight the contrast between warfare in the eighteenth century and warfare today.

In the following sentences, note how the revisions make all items in the series parallel:

▶ The quarter horse skipped, pranced, and ~~was~~ *sashayed.* ~~sashaying.~~

▶ The children ran down the hill, skipped over the lawn, and *jumped* into the swimming pool.

▶ The duties of the job include babysitting, housecleaning, and *preparing* ~~preparation of~~ meals.

Items in a list, on a formal outline (p. 74), and in headings in a paper (p. 100) should be parallel.

▶ Kitchen rules: (1) Coffee to be made only by library staff. (2) Coffee service to be closed at 4:00 PM. (3) Doughnuts to be kept in cabinet. (4) *Coffee materials not to be handled by faculty.* ~~No faculty members should handle coffee materials.~~

27b   Make paired ideas parallel.

Parallel structures can help you pair two ideas effectively. The more nearly parallel the two structures are, the stronger the connection between the ideas will be.

▶ History became popular, and historians became alarmed.
– WILL DURANT

▶ I type in one place, but I write all over the house.
– TONI MORRISON

▶ Writers are often more interesting on the page than they are in *the flesh.* ~~person.~~

In these examples, the parallel structures help readers see an important contrast between two ideas or acts.

With coordinating conjunctions

When you link ideas with a coordinating conjunction—*and, but, or, nor, for, so,* or *yet*—try to make the ideas parallel in structure.

▶ Consult a friend in your class or *who is* good at math.

▶ The wise politician promises the possible and ~~should accept~~ *accepts* the inevitable.

In both sentences, the editing links the two ideas by making them parallel.

With correlative conjunctions

Use the same structure after both parts of a correlative conjunction: *either . . . or, both . . . and, neither . . . nor, not . . . but, not only . . . but also, just as . . . so,* and *whether . . . or.*

▶ I wanted not only to go away to school but also *live in* to New England.

Balancing *to go* with *to live* links the two ideas and makes the sentence easier to read.

EXERCISE 27.1

Complete the following sentences, using parallel words or phrases in each case. Example:

The wise politician *promises the possible, faces the unavoidable,* and *accepts the inevitable.*

1. Before buying a used car, you should ____, ____, and ____.
2. Three activities I'd like to try are ____, ____, and ____.
3. Working in a restaurant taught me not only ____ but also ____.
4. We must either ____ or ____.
5. To pass the time in the waiting room, I ____, ____, and ____.

EXERCISE 27.2

Revise the following sentences as necessary to eliminate any errors in parallel structure. Example:

walking
I enjoy skiing, playing the guitar, and ~~I walk~~ on the beach in warm weather.

1. I remember watching it the first time, realizing I'd never seen anything like it, and immediately vowed never to miss an episode of *The Daily Show*.
2. A crowd stood outside the school and were watching as the graduates paraded by.
3. An effective Web site is well designed, provides useful information, and links are given to other relevant sites.

4. It is impossible to watch *The Office* and not seeing a little of yourself in one of the characters.

5. Lila was the winner not only of the pie-eating contest but also won the yodeling competition.

27c　Include all necessary words.

In addition to making parallel elements grammatically similar, be sure to include any words—prepositions, articles, verb forms, and so on—that are necessary for clarity, grammar, or idiom.

> *in*
> ▶ We'll move to a town in the Southwest or ∧Mexico.

To a town in Mexico or to Mexico in general? The editing makes the meaning clear.

 LearningCurve game-like quizzing can take you to the next level.
bedfordstmartins.com/everydaywriter/LC > Parallelism

EXERCISE 27.3: THINKING CRITICALLY

Reading with an Eye for Parallelism

Read the following paragraph about a bareback rider practicing her circus act, and identify all the parallel structures. Consider what effect they create on you as a reader, and try to decide why the author chose to put his ideas in such overtly parallel form. Try imitating the next-to-last sentence, the one beginning *In a week or two*.

> The richness of the scene was in its plainness, its natural condition — of horse, of ring, of girl, even to the girl's bare feet that gripped the bare back of her proud and ridiculous mount. The enchantment grew not out of anything that happened or was performed but out of something that seemed to go round and around and around with the girl, attending her, a steady gleam in the shape of a circle — a ring of ambition, of happiness, of youth. (And the positive pleasures of equilibrium under difficulties.) In a week or two, all would be changed, all (or almost all) lost: the girl would wear makeup, the horse would wear gold, the ring would be painted, the bark would be clean for the feet of the horse, the girl's feet would be clean for the slippers that she'd wear. All, all would be lost.
>
> — E. B. WHITE, "The Ring of Time"

Thinking about Your Own Use of Parallelism

Read carefully several paragraphs from a draft you have recently written, noting any series of words, phrases, or clauses. Using the guidelines in this chapter, determine whether the series are parallel, and if not, revise them for parallelism. Then reread the paragraphs, looking for places where parallel structures would add emphasis or clarity, and revise accordingly. Can you draw any conclusions about your use of parallelism?

Shifts 28

A shift in writing is an abrupt change that results in inconsistency. Sometimes a writer or speaker will shift deliberately, as linguist Geneva Smitherman does in this passage from *Word from the Mother*: "There are days when I optimistically predict that Hip Hop will survive—and thrive. . . . In the larger realm of Hip Hop culture, there is cause for optimism as we witness Hip Hop younguns tryna git they political activist game togetha."

Smitherman's shift from formal academic language to vernacular speech calls out for and holds our attention. Although writers make shifts for good rhetorical reasons, unintentional shifts in verb tenses, pronouns, and tone can be confusing to readers.

28a Revise unnecessary shifts in verb tense.

If the verbs in a passage refer to actions occurring at different times, they may require different tenses. Be careful, however, not to change tenses for no reason.

> A few countries produce almost all of the world's illegal drugs, but
> *affects*
> addiction ~~affected~~ many countries.

> **LearningCurve** game-like quizzing can take you to the next level.
> **bedfordstmartins.com/everydaywriter/LC > Verbs**

28b Revise unnecessary shifts in mood.

Be careful not to shift from one mood to another without good reason. The mood of a verb can be indicative (he *closes* the door), imperative (*close* the door), or subjunctive (if the door *were closed*) (32h).

> Keep your eye on the ball, and ~~you should~~ bend your knees.

28c Revise unnecessary shifts in voice.

Do not shift without reason between the active voice (she *sold* it) and the passive voice (it *was sold*). Sometimes a shift in voice is justified, but often it only confuses readers (32g).

> *me*
> Two youths approached me/ and I~~was~~ asked for my wallet.
>   ^

The original sentence shifts from the active (*youths approached*) to the passive (*I was asked*), so it is unclear who asked for the wallet. Making both verbs active clears up the confusion.

28d   Revise unnecessary shifts in person and number.

Unnecessary shifts in point of view among first person (*I, we*), second person (*you*), and third person (*he, she, it, they*), or between singular and plural subjects can be very confusing to readers.

> *You*
> ~~Someone~~ can do well on this job if you budget your time.
> ^

Is the writer making a general statement or giving advice? Eliminating the shift eliminates this confusion.

28e   Revise shifts between direct and indirect discourse.

When you quote someone's exact words, you are using direct discourse: *She said, "I'm an editor."* When you report what someone says without repeating the exact words, you are using indirect discourse: *She says she is an editor.* Shifting between direct and indirect discourse in the same sentence can cause problems, especially with questions.

AT A GLANCE

Confusing Shifts

- Make sure you have a reason for shifting from one verb tense to another. (28a)
- Revise any shifts in mood — perhaps from an indicative statement to an imperative — that are not necessary. (28b)
- Check for shifts from active (*She asks questions*) to passive voice (*Questions are asked*). Are they intentional? (28c)
- Make sure you have good reasons for any shifts in person or number — from *we* to *you*, for example. (28d)
- Check your writing for consistency in tone and word choice. (28f)

> *he*
> ▶ **Viet asked what could he do to help?**

The editing eliminates an awkward shift by reporting Viet's question indirectly. It could also be edited to quote Viet directly: *Viet asked, "What can I do to help?"*

EXERCISE 28.1

Revise the following sentences to eliminate unnecessary shifts in tense, mood, voice, or person and number and between direct and indirect discourse. Most of the items can be revised in more than one way. Examples:

> When a person goes to college, you face many new situations.
> When a person goes to college, he or she faces many new situations.
> When people go to college, they face many new situations.

1. The greed of the 1980s gave way to the occupational insecurity of the 1990s, which in turn gives way to reinforced family ties in the early 2000s.
2. The building inspector suggested that we apply for a construction permit and that we should check with his office again when the plans are complete.
3. The instructor grabbed her coat, wondered why was the substitute late, and ran out of the room.
4. Suddenly, we heard an explosion of wings off to our right, and you could see a hundred or more ducks lifting off from the water.
5. In my previous job, I sold the most advertising spots and was given a sales excellence award.
6. A cloud of snow powder rose as skis and poles fly in every direction.
7. The flight attendant said, "Please turn off all electronic devices," but that we could use them again after takeoff.
8. The real estate market was softer than it had been for a decade, and a buyer could practically name their price.
9. When in Florence, be sure to see the city's famed cathedral, and many tourists also visit Michelangelo's statue *David*.
10. The freezing weather is threatening crops such as citrus fruits, which were sensitive to cold.

28f Revise shifts in tone and word choice.

Tone, a writer's attitude toward a topic or audience, is related to word choice and to overall formality or informality. Watch out for tone or diction shifts that can confuse readers and leave them wondering what your real attitude is (5f).

FOR MULTILINGUAL WRITERS
Shifting Tenses in Reported Speech

If Al said to Maria, "I will marry you," why did she then correctly tell her mom, "He said that he *would* marry me"? For guidelines on reporting speech, see 59b.

INCONSISTENT TONE

> The question of child care forces a society to make profound decisions about its economic values. Can most families with young children actually live adequately on only one salary? If some conservatives had their way, June Cleaver would still be stuck in the kitchen baking cookies for Wally and the Beaver and waiting for Ward to bring home the bacon, except that, with only one income, the Cleavers would be lucky to afford hot dogs.

In this version, the first two sentences set a serious, formal tone by discussing child care in fairly general, abstract terms. But in the third sentence, the writer shifts suddenly to sarcasm, to references to television characters of an earlier era, and to informal language like *stuck* and *bring home the bacon*. Readers cannot tell whether the writer is presenting a serious analysis or preparing for a humorous satire. The revision makes the tone consistently formal.

REVISED

> The question of child care forces a society to make profound decisions about its economic values. Can most families with young children actually live adequately on only one salary? Some conservatives believe that women with young children should not work outside the home, but many mothers are forced to do so for financial reasons.

 **bedfordstmartins.com/everydaywriter**
Exercise Central > Shifts

EXERCISE 28.2: THINKING CRITICALLY

Reading with an Eye for Shifts

The following paragraph includes several necessary shifts in person and number. Read the paragraph carefully, marking all such shifts. Notice how careful the author must be as he shifts back and forth among pronouns.

> It has been one of the great errors of our time to think that by thinking about thinking, and then talking about it, we could possibly straighten out and tidy up our minds. There is no delusion more damaging than to get the idea in your head that you understand the functioning of your own brain. Once you acquire such a notion, you run the danger of moving in to take charge, guiding your thoughts,

shepherding your mind from place to place, controlling it, making lists of regula-tions. The human mind is not meant to be governed, certainly not by any book of rules yet written; it is supposed to run itself, and we are obliged to follow it along, trying to keep up with it as best we can. It is all very well to be aware of your awareness, even proud of it, but never try to operate it. You are not up to the job. — LEWIS THOMAS, "The Attic of the Brain"

Thinking about Any Shifts in Your Own Writing

Find an article about a well-known person you admire. Then write a paragraph or two about him or her, making a point of using both direct and indirect discourse. Using the information in 28e, check your writing for any inappropriate shifts between direct and indirect discourse, and revise as necessary.

Conciseness  29

If you have a Twitter account, you know a lot about being con-cise — that is, about getting messages across without wasting words (Twitter limits writers to 140 characters). Recently, *New York Times* edi-tor Bill Keller decided to start a discussion by tweeting, "Twitter makes you stupid. Discuss." That little comment drew a large number of responses, including one from his wife that read, "I don't know if Twit-ter makes you stupid, but it's making you late for dinner. Come home."

No matter how you feel about the effects of Twitter on the brain (or stomach!), you can make any writing more effective by using clear structures and choosing words that convey exactly what you mean to say.

AT A GLANCE

Editing for Conciseness

- Look for redundant words. If you are unsure about a word, read the sentence without it; if meaning is not affected, leave the word out. (29a and b)

- Take out empty words — words like *aspect* or *factor*, *definitely* or *very*. (29c)

- Replace wordy phrases with a single word. Instead of *because of the fact that*, try *because*. (29d)

- Reconsider any sentences that begin with *it is* or *there is/are*. Unless they create special emphasis, try recasting the sentences without these words. (29e)

29a Eliminate unnecessary words.

Usually you'll want to make your point in the fewest possible words.

WORDY One thing that her constant and continual use of vulgar expressions or four-letter words indicated to the day-care workers was that she might really have a great deal of trouble in terms of her ability to get along in a successful manner with other six-year-olds in her age group.

Why write that sentence when you could instead write the following?

REVISED Her constant use of four-letter words told the day-care workers she might have trouble getting along with other six-year-olds.

29b Eliminate redundant words.

Sometimes writers say that something is large *in size* or red *in color* or that two ingredients should be *combined together*. Such words are redundant, or unnecessary for meaning, as are the deleted words in the following examples:

Attendance
▶ ~~Compulsory~~ attendance at assemblies is required.
  ^

▶ Many different forms of hazing occur, such as physical abuse and mental abuse.

29c Eliminate empty words.

Empty words are so general or overused that they contribute no real meaning to a sentence.

EMPTY WORDS

angle, area, aspect, case, character, element, factor, field, kind, nature, scope, situation, thing, type

Many modifiers are so common that they have become empty words.

MEANINGLESS MODIFIERS

absolutely, awesome, awfully, central, definitely, fine, great, literally, major, quite, really, very

When you cannot simply delete empty words, think of a more specific way to say what you mean.

▶ *Housing* ~~The housing~~ situation can have a ~~really~~ *strongly influence* ~~significant impact on the~~
~~social~~ aspect of a student's life. *social*

29d Replace wordy phrases.

Wordy phrases can be reduced to a word or two with no loss in meaning.

WORDY	CONCISE
at all times	always
at that point in time	then
at the present time	now/today
due to the fact that	because
for the purpose of	for
in order to	to
in spite of the fact that	although
in the event that	if

29e Simplify sentence structure.

Using the simplest grammatical structures possible can tighten and strengthen your sentences considerably.

▶ Hurricane Katrina, ~~which was certainly~~ one of the most powerful storms
widespread
ever to hit the Gulf Coast, caused damage ~~to a very wide area.~~

Reducing a clause to an appositive, deleting unnecessary words, and replacing five words with one tighten the sentence and make it easier to read.

Using strong verbs

Be verbs (*is, are, was, were, been*) often result in wordiness.

harms
▶ A high-fat, high-cholesterol diet ~~is bad for~~ your heart.

Avoiding there is, there are, *and* it is

Sometimes expletive constructions—*there is, there are,* and *it is*—can introduce a topic effectively; often, however, your writing will be better without them.

> ~~There are~~ ^{Many} ~~many~~ people ~~who~~ fear success because they believe they do not deserve it.

> ^{Presidential} ^{need}
> ~~It is necessary for presidential~~ candidates ~~to~~ perform well on television.

Using active voice

Some writing situations call for the passive voice (32g), but it is always wordier than the active—and often makes for dull or even difficult reading.

> ^{Gower}
> ~~In Gower's research, it was~~ found that pythons often dwell in trees.

EXERCISE 29.1

Look at the following sentences, which use the passive voice. Then rewrite each sentence in the active voice, and decide which version you prefer and why. Example:

> ^I   ^{you}
> ~~You are~~ hereby relieved of your duties. ~~by me.~~

1. Mistakes were made.
2. Musical legends such as Ray Charles, Billie Holiday, and Johnny Cash have all influenced Norah Jones.
3. Numerous reports of loud music from bars and shouting neighbors were taken by the city's new noise complaint hotline.
4. The violin solo was performed by an eight-year-old.
5. In a patient with celiac disease, intestinal damage can be caused by the body's immunological response to gluten.

EXERCISE 29.2

Revise the following paragraph to eliminate unnecessary words, nominalizations, expletives, and inappropriate use of the passive voice.

> As dogs became tamed and domesticated by humans over many thousands of years, the canine species underwent an evolution into hundreds of breeds designed to perform particular, specific tasks, such as pulling sleds and guarding sheep. Over time, there was a decreased need for many breeds. For example, as humans evolved from hunter-gatherers into farmers, it was no

longer at all necessary for them to own hunting dogs. Later, as farming societies became industrialized, there was a disappearance of herd animals, and fewer shepherds watching sheep meant that there were fewer sheepdogs. But by this time humans had grown accustomed to dogs' companionship, and breeding continued. Today, most dogs are kept by their owners simply as companions, but some dogs still do the work they were intentionally bred for, such as following a scent, guarding a home, or leading the blind.

 bedfordstmartins.com/everydaywriter
Exercise Central > Conciseness

EXERCISE 29.3: THINKING CRITICALLY

Reading with an Eye for Conciseness

Bring two pieces of writing to class: one that is not just short, but concise — wasting no words but conveying its meaning clearly — and one that uses too many words to say too little. Bring both pieces to class to compare with those chosen by your classmates.

Thinking about Your Own Writing

Find two or three paragraphs you have written recently, and study them with an eye for empty words. Eliminate meaningless words such as *quite* and *very*. Compare notes with one or two classmates to see what empty words, if any, you tend to use. Finally, make a note of the empty words you use, and try to avoid them in the future.

Sentence Variety 30

R ow upon row of trees identical in size and shape may appeal to our sense of orderliness, but in spite of that appeal, the rows soon become boring. Constant uniformity in anything, in fact, soon gets tiresome. Variety is important in sentence structures because too much uniformity results in dull, listless prose. This chapter examines ways to revise sentences by creating variety in length and in openings.

30a Vary sentence length.

Is there a "just right" length for a particular sentence or idea? The answer depends partly on your purpose, intended audience, and topic. But note that after one or more long sentences with complex ideas or images, the punch of a short sentence can be refreshing.

AT A GLANCE

Editing for Sentence Variety

- Count the words in each of your sentences. If the difference between the longest and shortest sentences is fairly small — say, five words or fewer — try revising your sentences to create greater variety. (30a)
- If many sentences have fewer than ten words, consider whether any of them need more detail or should be combined with other sentences.
- How do your sentences open? If all or most of them open with a subject, try recasting some sentences to begin with a transition, a phrase, or a dependent clause. (30b)

▶ To become a doctor, you spend so much time in the tunnels of preparation—head down, trying not to screw up, just going from one day to the next—that it is a shock to find yourself at the other end, with someone offering you a job. **But the day comes.**   – ATUL GAWANDE, *Better*

EXERCISE 30.1

The following paragraph can be improved by varying sentence length. Read it aloud to get a sense of how it sounds. Then revise it, creating some short, emphatic sentences and combining other sentences to create more effective long sentences. Add words or change punctuation as you need to.

Before planting a tree, a gardener needs to choose a good location and dig a deep enough hole. The location should have the right kind of soil, sufficient drainage, and enough light for the type of tree chosen. The hole should be slightly deeper than the root-ball and about twice as wide. The gardener must unwrap the root-ball, for even burlap, which is biodegradable, may be treated with chemicals that will eventually damage the roots. The roots may have grown into a compact ball if the tree has been in a pot for some time, and they should be separated or cut apart in this case. The gardener should set the root-ball into the hole and then begin to fill the hole with loose dirt. After filling the hole completely, he or she should make sure to water the tree thoroughly. New plantings require extra water and extra care for about three years before they are well rooted.

30b   Vary sentence openings.

If sentence after sentence begins with a subject, a passage may become monotonous or hard to read.

▶ The way football and basketball are played is as interesting as the

          Because football   *each*
players. Football is a game of precision, Each play is diagrammed to

---

TALKING ABOUT STYLE

Technical Writing

For some types of writing, varying sentence structure and length is not always appropriate. Many technical writers, particularly those who write manuals that will be translated into other languages, must follow stringent rules for sentence structure and length. One computer company, for example, requires writers to adhere to a strict subject-verb-object order and limit all sentences to no more than fifteen words. Learn the style conventions of your field as fully as possible, and bring them to bear on your own sentence revisions.

however,
accomplish a certain goal. Basketball, is a game of endurance.

In fact, a
A basketball game looks like a track meet; the team that drops of

exhaustion first, loses. Basketball players are often compared to artists/,

their
The players' moves and slam dunks are their masterpieces.

The editing adds variety by using a subordinating word (*Because*) and a prepositional phrase (*In fact*) and by linking sentences. Varying sentence openings prevents the passage from seeming to jerk or lurch along.

You can add variety to your sentence openings by using transitions, various kinds of phrases, and dependent clauses.

TRANSITIONAL EXPRESSIONS

▶ **In contrast,** our approach will save time and money.

▶ **Nevertheless,** the show must go on.

PHRASES

▶ **Before dawn,** tired commuters drink their first cups of coffee.

▶ **Frustrated by the delays,** the drivers started honking their horns.

▶ **To qualify for flight training,** one must be in good physical condition.

▶ **Our hopes for victory dashed,** we started home.

DEPENDENT CLAUSES

▶ **What they want** is a place to call home.

▶ **Because the hills were dry,** the fire spread rapidly.

🔵 **bedfordstmartins.com/everydaywriter**
Exercise Central > Sentence Variety

EXERCISE 30.2: THINKING CRITICALLY

Reading with an Eye for Sentence Variety

Read something by an author you admire. Analyze two paragraphs for sentence length, opening, and type. Compare the sentence variety in these paragraphs with that in one of your paragraphs. What similarities or differences do you recognize, and what conclusions can you draw about sentence variety?

Thinking about Your Own Sentence Variety

Choose a piece of writing you have recently completed, and analyze two or three pages for sentence variety. Note sentence length, opening, and type (grammatical, functional, and rhetorical). Choose a passage you think can be improved for variety, and make those revisions.

Sentence Grammar

Most of us don't know a gerund from
a gerbil and don't care, but we'd like to
speak and write as though we did.

— PATRICIA T. O'CONNER

Sentence Grammar

31 Basic Grammar 318
  a The basic grammar of sentences 318
  PARTS OF SPEECH
  b Verbs 320
  c Nouns 321
  d Pronouns 321
  e Adjectives 324
  f Adverbs 324
  g Prepositions 325
  h Conjunctions 326
  i Interjections 328
  PARTS OF SENTENCES
  j Subjects 329
  k Predicates 331
  l Phrases 333
  m Clauses 335
  TYPES OF SENTENCES
  n Grammatical classifications 338
  o Functional classifications 339

32 Verbs 340
  a Understand the five forms of verbs 340
  b Use helping (auxiliary) verbs appropriately 342
  c Use appropriate forms of irregular verbs 342
  d Choose between *lie* and *lay*, *sit* and *set*, *rise* and *raise* 346
  e Use verb tenses appropriately 347
  f Sequence verb tenses effectively 350
  g Use active and passive voice effectively 352
  h Use mood effectively 353

33 Subject-Verb Agreement 355
  a Match verb forms with third-person singular subjects 355
  b Check subjects and verbs separated by other words 356
  c Make verbs agree with compound subjects 357
  d Make verbs agree with collective-noun subjects 358
  e Make verbs agree with indefinite-pronoun subjects 359
  f Make verbs agree with antecedents of *who*, *which*, and *that* 360
  g Use appropriate forms of linking verbs 360

For visual analysis Look carefully at the illustration on the front of this tab. What do you think this image suggests how grammar works?

h Make verbs agree with subjects that are plural in form but
singular in meaning *360*

i Make verbs agree with subjects that follow verbs *361*

j Make verbs agree with titles and words used as words *361*

34 Pronouns *363*

a Consider a pronoun's role in the sentence *364*

b Use *who*, *whoever*, *whom*, and *whomever* appropriately *365*

c Consider case in compound structures *368*

d Consider case in elliptical constructions *368*

e Use *we* and *us* appropriately before a noun *368*

f Make pronouns agree with antecedents *369*

g Make pronouns refer to clear antecedents *372*

35 Adjectives and Adverbs *374*

a Use adjectives after linking verbs *374*

b Use adverbs to modify verbs, adjectives, and adverbs *375*

c Choose appropriate comparative and superlative forms *377*

36 Modifier Placement *380*

a Revise misplaced modifiers *381*

b Revise disruptive modifiers *383*

c Revise dangling modifiers *384*

37 Comma Splices and Fused Sentences *385*

a Separate the clauses into two sentences *387*

b Link the clauses with a comma and a coordinating
conjunction *387*

c Link the clauses with a semicolon *387*

d Rewrite the clauses as one independent clause *389*

e Rewrite one independent clause as a dependent clause *389*

f Link the two clauses with a dash *390*

38 Sentence Fragments *392*

a Revise phrase fragments *393*

b Revise compound-predicate fragments *394*

c Revise dependent-clause fragments *394*

31 Basic Grammar

The grammar of our first language comes to us almost automatically, without our thinking much about it or even being aware of it. Listen in, for instance, on a conversation between a six-year-old and her sister.

> AUDREY: My new bike that Daddy got me has a pink basket and a loud horn, and I love it.
>
> LILA: Can I ride it?
>
> AUDREY: Sure, as soon as you get big enough.

This simple conversation features sophisticated grammar used effortlessly. Every language has grammar (basic structures), and native speakers understand and use these structures long before they learn what to call parts of a sentence or the different options for putting the pieces of sentences together effectively. Thinking carefully about the basic structures of English can help you make wise choices for your audience and your rhetorical situation.

31a The basic grammar of sentences

A sentence is a grammatically complete group of words that expresses a thought. In standard English, a grammatically complete sentence must contain a subject, which identifies what the sentence is about, and a predicate, which says or asks something about the subject or tells the subject to do something.

SUBJECT	PREDICATE
I	have a dream.
The rain in Spain	stays mainly in the plain.
Stephen Colbert, who hosts a cable TV show,	pretends to be a conservative.

Some sentences have only a one-word predicate with an implied, or understood, subject (for example, *Stop!*). Most sentences, however, contain additional words that expand the basic subject and predicate. In the preceding example, for instance, the subject might have been simply *Stephen Colbert;* the words *who hosts a cable TV show* tell us more about the subject. Similarly, the predicate of that sentence could grammatically be *pretends;* the words *to be a conservative* expand the predicate by telling us what Colbert pretends.

EXERCISE 31.1

Identify the subject and the predicate in each of the following sentences, underlining the subject once and the predicate twice. Example:

> The roaring lion at the beginning of old MGM films is part of movie history.

1. Scientific experiments on human subjects are now carefully regulated.
2. Her first afternoon as a kindergarten teacher had left her exhausted.
3. The Croatian news media is almost entirely owned by the state.
4. Our office manager, a stern taskmaster with a fondness for Chanel suits, has been terrifying interns since 1992.
5. Reading edited prose shows writers how to communicate.
6. The security officer at the border questioned everyone suspiciously.
7. People in the nineteenth century communicated constantly through letters.
8. Disease killed off a large number of the tomato plants in the northeastern United States last year.
9. What do scientists know about dinosaurs?
10. The hula-hoop craze of the 1960s has made a comeback among adults looking for fun ways to exercise.

TALKING THE TALK

Grammatical Terms

"I never learned any grammar." You may lack *conscious* knowledge of grammar and grammatical terms (and if so, you are not alone — American students today rarely study English grammar). But you probably understand the ideas that grammatical terms such as *auxiliary verb* and *direct object* represent, even if the terms themselves are unfamiliar. Brushing up on the terms commonly used to talk about grammar will make it easier for you and your instructor — as well as other readers and reviewers — to share a common language when you want to discuss the best ways to get your ideas across clearly and with few distractions.

Parts of Speech

All English words belong to one or more of eight grammatical categories called parts of speech: verbs, nouns, pronouns, adjectives, adverbs, prepositions, conjunctions, and interjections. Many English words regularly function as more than one part of speech. Take the word *book,* for example: when you *book a flight,* it is a verb; when you *take a good book to the beach,* it is a noun; and when you *have book knowledge,* it is an adjective.

31b   Verbs

Verbs are among the most important words because they move the meanings of sentences along. Verbs show actions of body or mind (*skip, speculate*), occurrences (*become, happen*), or states of being (*be, seem*). They can also change form to show *time, person, number, voice,* and *mood.*

TIME	we work, we worked
PERSON	I work, she works
NUMBER	one person works, two people work
VOICE	she asks, she is asked
MOOD	we see, if we saw

Helping verbs (also called auxiliary verbs) combine with other verbs (often called main verbs) to create verb phrases. Helping verbs include the various forms of *be, do,* and *have* (which can also function as main verbs) and the words *can, could, may, might, must, shall, should, will,* and *would.*

▶ **You do need some sleep tonight!**

▶ **I could have danced all night.**

▶ **She would prefer to learn Italian rather than Spanish.**

See Chapters 32 and 33 for a complete discussion of verbs.

EXERCISE 31.2

Underline each verb or verb phrase in the following sentences. Example:

Drivers should expect weather-related delays.

1. The story was released to the press late on Friday evening.
2. Most athletes will be arriving well before the games.
3. Housing prices have fallen considerably in the past year.
4. No one spoke in the room where the students were taking the exam.
5. The suspect has been fingerprinted and is waiting for his lawyer.

31c Nouns

A noun names a person (*aviator, child*), place (*lake, library*), thing (*truck, suitcase*), or concept (*happiness, balance*). Proper nouns name specific people, places, things, and concepts: *Bill, Iowa, Supreme Court, Buddhism.* Collective nouns name groups: *team, flock, jury* (33d).

You can change most nouns from singular (one) to plural (more than one) by adding *-s* or *-es: horse, horses; kiss, kisses.* Some nouns, however, have irregular plural forms: *woman, women; alumnus, alumni; mouse, mice; deer, deer.* Noncount nouns—such as *dust, peace,* and *prosperity*—do not have a plural form because they name something that cannot easily be counted (58a).

To show ownership, nouns take the possessive form by adding an apostrophe plus *-s* to a singular noun or just an apostrophe to a plural noun: *the horse's owner, the boys' dilemma* (42a).

FOR MULTILINGUAL WRITERS

Using Count and Noncount Nouns

Do people conduct *research* or *researches*? See 58a for a discussion of count and noncount nouns.

EXERCISE 31.3

Identify the nouns and the articles in each of the following sentences. Underline the nouns once and the articles twice. Example:

The Puritans hoped for a different king, but Charles II regained his father's

throne.

1. After Halloween, the children got sick from eating too much candy.
2. Although June is technically the driest month, severe flooding has occurred in the late spring.
3. Baking is no longer a common activity in most households around the country.
4. A sudden frost turned the ground into a field of ice.
5. The cyclist swerved to avoid an oncoming car that had run a red light.

31d Pronouns

Pronouns often take the place of nouns, other pronouns, or other words functioning as a noun. Pronouns serve as short forms so that you do not have to repeat a word or group of words you have already mentioned.

A word or group of words that a pronoun replaces or refers to is called the antecedent of the pronoun. (See Chapter 34.)

ANTECEDENT   PRONOUN
▶ *Caitlin* **refused the invitation even though** *she* **wanted to go.**

Here are the categories of pronouns:

PERSONAL PRONOUNS

Personal pronouns refer to specific persons or things.

I, me, you, he, she, him, her, it, we, us, they, them

▶ **When Keisha saw the dogs, she called them, and they ran to her.**

POSSESSIVE PRONOUNS

Possessive pronouns are personal pronouns that indicate ownership.

my, mine, your, yours, her, hers, his, its, our, ours, their, theirs

▶ **My roommate lost her keys.**

REFLEXIVE PRONOUNS

Reflexive pronouns refer back to the subject of the sentence and end in *-self* or *-selves*.

myself, yourself, himself, herself, itself, oneself, ourselves, yourselves, themselves

▶ **The seals sunned themselves on the warm rocks.**

INTENSIVE PRONOUNS

Intensive pronouns have the same form as reflexive pronouns. They emphasize a noun or another pronoun.

▶ **He decided to paint the apartment himself.**

INDEFINITE PRONOUNS

Indefinite pronouns do not refer to specific nouns, although they may refer to identifiable persons or things. The following is a partial list:

all, another, anybody, both, each, either, everything, few, many, most, neither, none, no one, nothing, one, some, something

▶ **Everybody screamed, and someone fainted, when the lights went out.**

DEMONSTRATIVE PRONOUNS

Demonstrative pronouns point to specific nouns.

this, that, these, those

▶ **These are Peter's books.**

INTERROGATIVE PRONOUNS

Interrogative pronouns are used to ask questions.

who, which, what

▶ **Who can help set up the chairs for the meeting?**

RELATIVE PRONOUNS

Relative pronouns introduce dependent clauses and relate the information to the rest of the sentence (31m). The interrogative pronoun *who* and the relative pronouns *who* and *whoever* have different forms depending on how they are used in a sentence (34b).

who, which, that, what, whoever, whichever, whatever

▶ **Maya, who hires interns, is the manager whom you should contact.**

RECIPROCAL PRONOUNS

Reciprocal pronouns refer to individual parts of a plural antecedent.

each other, one another

▶ **The business failed because the partners distrusted each other.**

EXERCISE 31.4

Identify the pronouns and any antecedents in each of the following sentences, underlining the pronouns once and any antecedents twice. Example:

As identical twins, they really do understand each other.

1. He told the volunteers to help themselves to the leftovers.
2. There are two kinds of people: those who divide people into two kinds and those who don't.
3. Who is going to buy the jeans and wear them if the designer himself finds them uncomfortable?
4. Before an annual performance review, employees are asked to take a hard look at themselves and their work habits.
5. Forwarding an email warning about a computer virus to everyone in your address book is never a good idea.

31e   Adjectives

Adjectives modify nouns and pronouns, usually by describing, identifying, or limiting those words. Some people refer to the identifying or quantifying adjectives as *determiners* (58c).

▶ The **red** Corvette ran off the road. [describes]
▶ **That** Corvette needs to be repaired. [identifies]
▶ We saw **several** Corvettes race by. [quantifies]

In addition to their basic forms, most descriptive adjectives have other forms that allow you to make comparisons: *small, smaller, smallest; foolish, more foolish, most foolish, less foolish, least foolish* (35c). Many words that function in some sentences as pronouns (31d) can function as identifying adjectives when they are followed by a noun.

▶ **That** is a dangerous intersection. [pronoun]
▶ **That** intersection is dangerous. [identifying adjective]

Adjectives usually precede the words they modify, though they may follow linking verbs: *The car was defective.*

Other kinds of identifying or quantifying adjectives are articles (*a, an, the*) and numbers (*three, sixty-fifth*).

Proper adjectives are adjectives formed from or related to proper nouns (*British, Emersonian*). Proper adjectives are capitalized (45b).

FOR MULTILINGUAL WRITERS

Deciding When Articles Are Necessary

Do you say "I'm working on *a* paper" or "I'm working on *the* paper"? Deciding when to use the articles *a, an,* and *the* can be challenging for multilingual writers since many languages have nothing directly comparable to them. For help using articles, see 58d.

31f   Adverbs

Adverbs modify verbs, adjectives, other adverbs, or entire clauses. They often answer the questions *when? where? why? to what extent?* Many adverbs have an *-ly* ending, though some do not (*always, never, very, well*), and some words that end in *-ly* are not adverbs but adjectives (*scholarly, lovely*). One of the most common adverbs is *not*.

▶ **Jabari recently visited his roommate's family in Maine.** [modifies the verb *visited*]
▶ **It was an unexpectedly exciting trip.** [modifies the adjective *exciting*]
▶ **The visit ended too soon.** [modifies the adverb *soon*]
▶ **Frankly, he would have liked to stay another month.** [modifies the independent clause that makes up the rest of the sentence]

Many adverbs, like many adjectives, take other forms when making comparisons: *forcefully, more forcefully, most forcefully, less forcefully, least forcefully* (35c).

Conjunctive adverbs modify an entire clause and help connect the meaning between that clause and the preceding clause (or sentence). Examples of conjunctive adverbs include *however, furthermore, therefore,* and *likewise* (31h).

EXERCISE 31.5

Identify the adjectives and adverbs in each of the following sentences, underlining the adjectives once and the adverbs twice. Remember that articles and some pronouns are used as adjectives. Example:

Inadvertently, the two agents misquoted their major client.

1. The small, frightened child firmly squeezed my hand and refused to take another step forward.
2. Meanwhile, she learned that the financial records had been completely false.
3. Koalas are generally quiet creatures that make loud grunting noises during mating season.
4. The huge red tomatoes looked lovely, but they tasted disappointingly like cardboard.
5. The youngest dancer in the troupe performed a brilliant solo.

31g Prepositions

Prepositions are important structural words that express relationships—in time, space, or other senses—between nouns or pronouns and other words in a sentence.

▶ **We did not want to leave during the game.**
▶ **The contestants waited nervously for the announcement.**
▶ **Drive across the bridge, and go down the avenue past three stoplights.**

SOME COMMON PREPOSITIONS

about	at	down	near	since
above	before	during	of	through
across	behind	except	off	toward
after	below	for	on	under
against	beneath	from	onto	until
along	beside	in	out	up
among	between	inside	over	upon
around	beyond	into	past	with
as	by	like	regarding	without

SOME COMPOUND PREPOSITIONS

according to	except for	instead of
as well as	in addition to	next to
because of	in front of	out of
by way of	in place of	with regard to
due to	in spite of	

Research for this book shows that many writers today—including native speakers of English—have trouble using prepositions correctly. If you aren't sure which preposition to use, consult a dictionary.

EXERCISE 31.6

Identify and underline the prepositions in the following sentences. Example:

In the dim interior of the hut crouched an old man.

1. The supervisor of the night shift requested that all available personnel work extra hours from October through December.
2. The hatchlings emerged from their shells, crawled across the sand, and swam into the sea.
3. Instead of creating a peaceful new beginning, the tribunal factions are constantly fighting among themselves.
4. After some hard thinking on a weeklong camping trip, I decided I would quit my job and join the Peace Corps for two years.
5. The nuclear power plant about ten miles from the city has the worst safety record of any plant in the country.

31h Conjunctions

Conjunctions connect words or groups of words to each other and tell something about the relationship between these words.

Coordinating conjunctions

Coordinating conjunctions (25a) join equivalent structures—two or more nouns, pronouns, verbs, adjectives, adverbs, prepositions, conjunctions, phrases, or clauses.

▶ A strong **but** warm breeze blew across the desert.

▶ Please print **or** type the information on the application form.

▶ Taiwo worked two shifts today, **so** she is tired tonight.

COORDINATING CONJUNCTIONS

and	for	or	yet
but	nor	so	

Correlative conjunctions

Correlative conjunctions join equal elements, and they come in pairs.

▶ **Both** Bechtel **and** Kaiser submitted bids on the project.

▶ Jeff **not only** sent a card **but also** visited me in the hospital.

CORRELATIVE CONJUNCTIONS

both . . . and	just as . . . so	not only . . . but also
either . . . or	neither . . . nor	whether . . . or

Subordinating conjunctions

Subordinating conjunctions introduce adverb clauses and signal the relationship between an adverb clause and another clause. For instance, in the following sentence, the subordinating conjunction *while* signals that the two events in the sentence happened simultaneously:

▶ Sweat ran down my face **while** I frantically searched for my child.

SOME SUBORDINATING CONJUNCTIONS

after	if	unless
although	in order that	until
as	once	when
as if	since	where
because	so that	whether
before	than	while
even though	though	

Conjunctive adverbs

Conjunctive adverbs signal a logical relationship between parts of a sentence and, when used with a semicolon, can link independent clauses (31m).

▶ The cider tasted bitter; **however,** each of us drank a tall glass of it.

▶ The cider tasted bitter; each of us, **however,** drank a tall glass of it.

SOME CONJUNCTIVE ADVERBS

also	however	moreover	similarly
anyway	incidentally	namely	still
besides	indeed	nevertheless	then
certainly	instead	next	therefore
finally	likewise	now	thus
furthermore	meanwhile	otherwise	undoubtedly

EXERCISE 31.7

Underline the coordinating, correlative, and subordinating conjunctions as well as the conjunctive adverbs in each of the following sentences. Example:

We used sleeping bags, <u>even though</u> the cabin had sheets <u>and</u> blankets.

1. After waiting for an hour and a half, both Jenny and I were disgruntled, so we went home.

2. The facilities were not only uncomfortable but also dangerous.

3. I usually get a bonus each January; however, sales were down this year, so the company did not give us any extra money.

4. Although I had completed a six-week training regimen of running, swimming, and cycling, I did not feel ready, so I withdrew from the competition.

5. Enrique was not qualified for the job because he knew one of the programming languages but not the other; still, the interview encouraged him.

31i   Interjections

Interjections express surprise or emotion: *oh, ouch, ah, hey.* Interjections often stand alone. Even when interjections are part of a sentence, they do not relate grammatically to the rest of the sentence.

▶ **Hey, no one suggested that we would find an easy solution.**

AT A GLANCE

Basic Sentence Patterns

1. subject/verb

      S   V

▶   **Babies drool.**

2. subject/verb/subject complement

      S   V   SC

▶   **Babies smell sweet.**

3. subject/verb/direct object

      S   V   DO

▶   **Babies drink milk.**

4. subject/verb/indirect object/direct object

      S   V   IO   DO

▶   **Babies give grandparents pleasure.**

5. subject/verb/direct object/object complement

      S   V   DO   OC

▶   **Babies keep parents awake.**

Parts of Sentences

Knowing a word's part of speech helps you understand how to use that word. But you also need to look at the part the word plays in a particular sentence. Consider, for instance, the word *description.*

    SUBJECT

▶ **This *description* conveys the ecology of the Everglades.**

    DIRECT OBJECT

▶ **I read a *description* of the ecology of the Everglades.**

> *Description* is a noun in both sentences, yet in the first it serves as the subject of the verb *conveys,* while in the second it serves as the direct object of the verb *read.*

31j Subjects

The subject of a sentence identifies what the sentence is about. The simple subject consists of one or more nouns or pronouns; the complete subject consists of the simple subject with all its modifiers.

> **Baseball is a summer game.**

┌─── COMPLETE SUBJECT ───┐
> **Sailing over the fence, the ball crashed through Mr. Wilson's window.**

┌─── COMPLETE SUBJECT ───┐
> **Those who sit in the bleachers have the most fun.**

A compound subject contains two or more simple subjects joined with a coordinating conjunction (*and, but, or*) or a correlative conjunction (*both . . . and, either . . . or, neither . . . nor*). (See 31h.)

> **Baseball and softball developed from cricket.**
> **Both baseball and softball developed from cricket.**

The subject usually comes before the predicate, or verb, but sometimes writers reverse this order to achieve a special effect.

> **Up to the plate stepped Casey.**

In imperative sentences, which express requests or commands, the subject *you* is usually implied but not stated.

> **(You) Keep your eye on the ball.**

In questions and certain other constructions, the subject usually appears between the auxiliary verb (31b) and the main verb.

> **Did Casey save the game?**

In sentences beginning with *there* or *here* followed by a form of *be*, the subject always follows the verb. *There* and *here* are never the subject.

> **There was no joy in Mudville.**

EXERCISE 31.8

Identify the complete subject and the simple subject in each sentence. Underline the complete subject once and the simple subject twice. Example:

The tall, powerful woman defiantly blocked the doorway.

1. That container of fried rice has spent six weeks in the back of the refrigerator.
2. Did the new tour guide remember to stop in the ancient Greek gallery?
3. There was one student still taking the exam when the bell rang.
4. Japanese animation, with its cutting-edge graphics and futuristic plots, has earned many American admirers.
5. Sniffer dogs trained to detect drugs, blood, and explosives can help solve crimes and save lives.

31k Predicates

In addition to a subject, every sentence has a predicate, which asserts or asks something about the subject or tells the subject to do something. The hinge, or key word, of a predicate is the verb. The simple predicate of a sentence consists of the main verb and any auxiliaries (31b); the complete predicate includes the simple predicate plus any modifiers of the verb and any objects or complements and their modifiers.

> ┌─── COMPLETE PREDICATE ───┐
> ▶ **Both of us are planning to major in history.**

A compound predicate contains two or more verbs that have the same subject, usually joined by a coordinating or a correlative conjunction.

> ┌─────── COMPOUND PREDICATE ───────┐
> ▶ **Omar shut the book, put it back on the shelf, and sighed.**

> ┌─────── COMPOUND PREDICATE ───────┐
> ▶ **The Amish neither drive cars nor use electricity.**

On the basis of how they function in predicates, verbs can be divided into three categories: linking, transitive, and intransitive.

Linking verbs

A linking verb links, or joins, a subject with a subject complement (SC), a word or group of words that identifies or describes the subject.

> ┌─── SC ───┐
> ▶ **Nastassia is a single mother.**

> ┌─ SC ─┐
> ▶ **She is patient.**

If it identifies the subject, the complement is a noun or pronoun (*a single mother*). If it describes the subject, the complement is an adjective (*patient*).

The forms of *be*, when used as main verbs rather than as auxiliary verbs, are linking verbs (like *are* in this sentence). Other verbs—such as *appear, become, feel, grow, look, make, seem, smell,* and *sound*—can also function as linking verbs, depending on the sense of the sentence.

Transitive verbs

A transitive verb expresses action that is directed toward a noun or pronoun, called the direct object (DO) of the verb.

```
       ┌────── DO ──────┐
```
▶ **He peeled all the rutabagas.**

In the preceding example, the subject and verb do not express a complete thought. The direct object completes the thought by saying *what* he peeled.

A direct object may be followed by an object complement, a word (C) or word group that describes or identifies the direct object. Object complements may be adjectives, as in the next example, or nouns, as in the second example.

```
   ┌────────────── DO ──────────────┐┌──── OC ────┐
```
▶ **I find cell-phone conversations in restaurants very annoying.**

```
        ┌──── DO ────┐   ┌──── OC ────┐
```
▶ **Alana considers Keyshawn her best friend.**

A transitive verb may also be followed by an indirect object, which tells to whom or what, or for whom or what, the verb's action is done. You might say the indirect object is the recipient of the direct object.

```
              IO ┌────── DO ──────┐
```
▶ **The sound of the traffic gave me a splitting headache.**

Intransitive verbs

An intransitive verb expresses action that is not directed toward an object. Therefore, an intransitive verb does not have a direct object.

▶ **The Red Sox persevered.**
▶ **Their fans watched anxiously.**

The verb *persevered* has no object (it makes no sense to ask, *persevered what?*), and the verb *watched* has an object that is implied but not expressed.

Some verbs that express action can be only transitive or only intransitive, but most can be used either way, with or without a direct object.

```
                  ┌── DO ──┐
```
▶ **A maid wearing a uniform opened the door.**

The verb *opened* is transitive here.

▶ **The door opened silently.**

The verb *opened* is intransitive here.

EXERCISE 31.9

Underline the predicate in each of the following sentences. Then label each verb as linking (LV), transitive (TV), or intransitive (IV). Finally, label all subject and object complements and all direct and indirect objects. Example:

TV   ⌐ DO ⌐   OC
We considered city life unbearable.

1. He is proud of his heritage.
2. The horrifying news story made me angry.
3. The old house looks deserted.
4. Rock and roll will never die.
5. Chloe's boss offered her a promotion.

311 Phrases

A phrase is a group of words that lacks either a subject or a predicate or both.

Noun phrases

A noun phrase consists of a noun and all its modifiers. In a sentence, a noun phrase can play the role of a subject, object, or complement.

┌──────── SUBJECT ────────┐
► **Delicious, gooey peanut butter is surprisingly healthful.**

⌐ OBJECT ⌐
► **Dieters prefer green salad.**

⌐ COMPLEMENT ⌐
► **A tuna sandwich is a popular lunch.**

Verb phrases

A main verb and its auxiliary verbs make up a verb phrase, which can function only one way in a sentence: as a predicate.

► **I can swim for a long time.**
► **His headaches might have been caused by tension.**

Prepositional phrases

A prepositional phrase includes a preposition, a noun or pronoun (called the object of the preposition), and any modifiers of the object. Prepositional phrases usually serve as adjectives or adverbs.

ADJECTIVE   Our house in Maine is a cabin.

ADVERB   From Cadillac Mountain, you can see the Northern Lights.

Verbal phrases

Verbals are verb forms that do not function as verbs. Instead, they stand in for nouns, adjectives, or adverbs. A verbal phrase is made up of a verbal and any modifiers, objects, or complements. There are three kinds of verbals: participles, gerunds, and infinitives.

PARTICIPIAL PHRASES

A participial phrase always functions as an adjective and can include either a present participle (the *crying* child) or a past participle (the *spoken* word).

▶ A dog **howling at the moon** kept me awake.

▶ **Irritated by the delay,** Louise complained.

GERUND PHRASES

A gerund has the same form as a present participle, ending in *-ing*. But a gerund or a gerund phrase always functions as a noun.

┌ SUBJECT ┐
▶ **Recycling** is not always easy.

┌─────── DIRECT OBJECT ───────┐
▶ He ignored **the loud wailing from the sandbox.**

INFINITIVE PHRASES

An infinitive phrase can function as a noun, adjective, or adverb. The infinitive is the *to* form of a verb: *to be, to write.*

┌── ADJECTIVE ──┐
▶ A vote would be a good way **to end the meeting.**

┌── ADVERB ──┐
▶ **To perfect a draft,** always proofread carefully.

┌───── NOUN ─────┐
▶ My goal is **to be a biology teacher.**

Absolute phrases

An absolute phrase usually includes a noun or pronoun and a participle. It modifies an entire sentence rather than a particular word and is usually set off from the rest of the sentence with commas (39a).

▶ I stood on the deck, **the wind whipping my hair.**

▶ **My fears laid to rest,** I climbed into the plane for my first solo flight.

Appositive phrases

A noun phrase that renames the noun or pronoun immediately preceding it is called an appositive phrase.

▶ **The report, a hefty three-volume work, included sixty recommendations.**

▶ **A single desire, to change the corporation's policies, guided our actions.**

EXERCISE 31.10

Read the following sentences, and identify and label all of the prepositional, verbal, absolute, and appositive phrases. Notice that one kind of phrase may appear within another kind. Example:

```
┌──────────── ABSOLUTE ────────────┐              ┌── PREP ──┐
His voice breaking with emotion, Ed thanked us for the award.
                    └── PREP ──┘
```

1. Chantelle, the motel clerk, hopes to be certified as a river guide.
2. Carpets made by hand are usually the most valuable.
3. My stomach doing flips, I answered the door.
4. Floating on my back, I ignored my practice requirements.
5. Driving across town during rush hour can take thirty minutes or more.

31m Clauses

A clause is a group of words containing a subject and a predicate. There are two kinds of clauses: independent and dependent.

Independent clauses (also known as main clauses) can stand alone as complete sentences: *The window is open.* Pairs of independent clauses may be joined with a comma and a coordinating conjunction (*and*, *but*, *for*, *or*, *nor*, *so*, or *yet*).

▶ **The window is open,** *so* **we'd better be quiet.**

Like independent clauses, dependent clauses (also known as subordinate clauses) contain a subject and a predicate, but they cannot stand alone as complete sentences because they begin with a subordinating word (25b). Dependent clauses function as nouns, adjectives, or adverbs.

▶ **Because the window is open, the room feels cool.**

In this combination, the subordinating conjunction *because* transforms the independent clause *the window is open* into a dependent clause. In doing so, it indicates a causal relationship between the two clauses.

Noun clauses

Noun clauses can function as subjects, direct objects, subject complements, or objects of prepositions. A noun clause is always contained
within another clause. Noun clauses usually begin with a relative pronoun (*that, which, what, who, whom, whose, whatever, whoever, whomever,
whichever*) or with *when, where, whether, why,* or *how.*

▶ **That she had a good job was important to him.**

▶ **He asked where she went to college.**

▶ **The real question was why he wanted to know.**

▶ **He was looking for whatever information was available.**

Notice that in each of these sentences the noun clause is an integral part
of the independent clause that makes up the sentence. For example, in
the second sentence, the independent clause is not just *he asked* but *he
asked where she went to college.*

Adjective clauses

Adjective clauses modify nouns and pronouns in other clauses. Usually
adjective clauses immediately follow the words they modify. Most of
these clauses begin with the relative pronoun *who, whom, whose, that,* or
which. Some begin with *when, where,* or *why.*

▶ **The surgery, which took three hours, was a complete success.**

▶ **It was performed by the surgeon who had developed the procedure.**

▶ **The hospital was the one where I was born.**

Sometimes the relative pronoun introducing an adjective clause may be
omitted.

▶ **That is one book [that] I intend to read.**

Adverb clauses

Adverb clauses modify verbs, adjectives, or other adverbs. They begin
with a subordinating conjunction (31h) and, like adverbs, they usually
tell when, where, why, how, or to what extent.

▶ We hiked **where there were few other hikers.**

▶ My backpack felt heavier **than it ever had.**

▶ I climbed as swiftly **as I could** under the weight of my backpack.

EXERCISE 31.11

Identify the independent and dependent clauses and any subordinating conjunctions and relative pronouns in each of the following sentences. Example:

```
┌───────DEPENDENT CLAUSE───────┐ ┌──────INDEPENDENT CLAUSE──────┐
```
If I were going on a really long hike, I would carry a lightweight stove.

If is a subordinating conjunction.

1. The hockey game was postponed because one of the players collapsed on the bench.
2. She eventually discovered the secret admirer who had been leaving notes in her locker.
3. After he completed three advanced drawing classes, Jason was admitted into the fine arts program, and he immediately rented a small studio space.
4. The test was easier than I had expected.
5. I could tell that it was going to rain, so I tried to get home quickly.

EXERCISE 31.12

Expand each of the following sentences by adding at least one dependent clause to it. Be prepared to explain how your addition improves the sentence. Example:

As the earth continued to shake, the
~~The~~ books tumbled from the shelves.
      ^

1. The economy gradually began to recover.
2. Simone waited nervously by the phone.
3. New school safety rules were instituted this fall.
4. Rob always borrowed money from friends.
5. The crowd grew louder and more disorderly.

Types of Sentences

Like words, sentences can be classified in different ways: grammatically and functionally.

31n Grammatical classifications

Grammatically, sentences may be classified as simple, compound, complex, and compound-complex.

Simple sentences

A simple sentence consists of one independent clause and no dependent clause.

 ┌──────────── INDEPENDENT CLAUSE ──────────┐
▶ **The trailer is surrounded by a wooden deck.**

 ┌──────────── INDEPENDENT CLAUSE ──────────┐
▶ **Both my roommate and I left our keys in the room.**

Compound sentences

A compound sentence consists of two or more independent clauses and no dependent clause. The clauses may be joined by a comma and a coordinating conjunction (*and, but, or, nor, for, so, yet*) or by a semicolon.

 ┌──────── IND CLAUSE ────────┐   ┌──── IND CLAUSE ────┐
▶ **Occasionally, a car goes up the dirt trail, and dust flies everywhere.**

 ┌──────── IND CLAUSE ────────┐ ┌──────── IND CLAUSE ────────┐
▶ **Angelo is obsessed with soccer; he eats, breathes, and lives the game.**

Complex sentences

A complex sentence consists of one independent clause and at least one dependent clause.

 ┌──── IND CLAUSE ────┐ ┌──── DEP CLAUSE ────┐
▶ **Many people believe that anyone can earn a living.**

Compound-complex sentences

A compound-complex sentence consists of two or more independent clauses and at least one dependent clause.

 ┌──── IND CLAUSE ────┐ ┌──── DEP CLAUSE ────┐   ┌──── IND CLAUSE ────┐
▶ **I complimented Luis when he finished the job, and he seemed pleased.**

 ┌──────── IND CLAUSE ────────┐   ┌──── IND CLAUSE ────┐
▶ **Sister Lucy tried her best to help Martin, but he was an undisciplined**

 ┌──────── DEP CLAUSE ────────┐
boy who drove many teachers to despair.

310 Functional classifications

In terms of function, sentences can be classified as declarative (making a statement), interrogative (asking a question), imperative (giving a command), or exclamatory (expressing strong feeling).

DECLARATIVE	He sings with the Grace Church Boys' Choir.
INTERROGATIVE	How long has he sung with them?
IMPERATIVE	Comb his hair before the performance starts.
EXCLAMATORY	What voices those boys have!

EXERCISE 31.13

Classify each of the following sentences as simple, compound, complex, or compound-complex. In addition, note any sentence that may be classified as interrogative, imperative, or exclamatory.

1. The boat rocked and lurched over the rough surf as the passengers groaned in agony.
2. Is this the coldest winter on record, or was last year even worse?
3. After waiting for over an hour, I was examined by the doctor for only three minutes!
4. Keeping in mind the terrain, the weather, and the length of the hike, decide what you need to take.
5. The former prisoner, who was cleared by DNA evidence, has lost six years of his life, and he needs a job right away.

 bedfordstmartins.com/everydaywriter
Exercise Central > Basic Grammar

EXERCISE 31.14: THINKING CRITICALLY

The following sentences come from the openings of well-known works. Identify the independent and dependent clauses in each sentence. Then choose one sentence, and write a sentence of your own imitating its structure, clause for clause and phrase for phrase. Example:

Ten days after the war ended, my sister Laura drove a car off a bridge.
— MARGARET ATWOOD, *The Blind Assassin*

1. We observe today not a victory of party but a celebration of freedom, symbolizing an end as well as a beginning, signifying renewal as well as change.
— JOHN F. KENNEDY, *Inaugural Address*

2. Once in a long while, four times so far for me, my mother brings out the metal tube that holds her medical diploma.
— MAXINE HONG KINGSTON, "Photographs of My Parents"

32 Verbs

Restaurant menus often spotlight verbs in action. One famous place in Boston, for instance, offers to bake, broil, pan-fry, deep-fry, poach, sauté, fricassée, blacken, or scallop any of the fish entrées on its menu. To someone ordering—or cooking—at this restaurant, the important distinctions lie entirely in the verbs.

When used skillfully, verbs can be the heartbeat of prose, moving it along, enlivening it, carrying its action. (See Chapter 33 for advice on subject-verb agreement and Chapter 59 for more about verbs for multilingual writers.)

32a Understand the five forms of verbs.

Except for *be*, all English verbs have five forms.

BASE FORM	PAST TENSE	PAST PARTICIPLE	PRESENT PARTICIPLE	-S FORM
talk	talked	talked	talking	talks
adore	adored	adored	adoring	adores

AT A GLANCE

Editing the Verbs in Your Own Writing

- Check verb endings that cause you trouble. (32a and c)
- Double-check forms of *lie* and *lay*, *sit* and *set*, *rise* and *raise*. See that the words you use are appropriate for your meaning. (32d)
- If you are writing about a literary work, remember to refer to the action in the work in the present tense. (32e)
- If you have problems with verb tenses, use the guidelines on p. 320 to check your verbs.
- Check all uses of the passive voice for appropriateness. (32g)
- Check all verbs used to introduce quotations, paraphrases, and summaries. If you rely on *say*, *write*, and other very general verbs, try substituting more vivid, specific verbs (*claim*, *insist*, and *wonder*, for instance).

BASE FORM	We often go to Legal Sea Foods.
PAST TENSE	Grandpa always ordered bluefish.
PAST PARTICIPLE	Grandma has tried the oyster stew.
PRESENT PARTICIPLE	Juanita is getting the shrimp platter.
-S FORM	The chowder needs salt and pepper.

-s *and* -es *endings*

Except with *be* and *have*, the -s form consists of the base form plus -s or -es. In standard English, this form indicates action in the present for third-person singular subjects. All singular nouns; the personal pronouns *he*, *she*, and *it*; and many other pronouns (such as *this*, *anyone*, *everything*, and *someone*) are third-person singular.

	SINGULAR	PLURAL
FIRST PERSON	I wish	we wish
SECOND PERSON	you wish	you wish
THIRD PERSON	he/she/it wishes	they wish
	Joe wishes	children wish
	someone wishes	many wish

Forms of be

Be has three forms in the present tense and two in the past tense.

BASE FORM	be
PAST PARTICIPLE	been
PRESENT PARTICIPLE	being
PRESENT TENSE	I am, he/she/it is, we/you/they are
PAST TENSE	I/he/she/it was, we/you/they were

TALKING ABOUT STYLE

Everyday Use of *Be*

Spoken varieties of English may follow rules for the use of *be* that differ from the rules in standard English. For instance, you may have heard speakers say sentences like "She ain't here now" (instead of the standard English *She isn't here now*) or "He be at work every Saturday" (instead of the standard English *He is at work every Saturday*). You may sometimes want to quote dialogue featuring such spoken usages of *be* when you write. In most academic and professional writing, however, you will want to follow the conventions of standard English. (For help on using varieties of English appropriately, see Chapter 22.)

32b Use helping (auxiliary) verbs appropriately.

Use helping (auxiliary) verbs with a base form, present participle, or past participle to form verb tenses, questions, and negatives. The most common helping verbs are forms of *be*, *do*, and *have*.

▶ We **have considered** all viewpoints.

▶ The problem **is ranking** them fairly.

▶ **Do** you **know** the answer? No, I **do not know** it.

A special set of helping verbs known as auxiliaries—*can, could, might, may, must, ought to, shall, will, should, would*—indicate future actions, possibility, necessity, obligation, and so on.

▶ You **can see** three states from the top of the mountain.

▶ She **should visit** this spot more often.

FOR MULTILINGUAL WRITERS

Using Modal Auxiliaries

Why do we not say "Alice can to read Latin"? For a discussion of *can* and other modal auxiliaries, see 59b.

32c Use appropriate forms of irregular verbs.

A verb is regular when its past tense and past participle are formed by adding *-ed* or *-d* to the base form.

BASE FORM	PAST TENSE	PAST PARTICIPLE
love	loved	loved
honor	honored	honored
obey	obeyed	obeyed

A verb is irregular when it does not follow the *-ed* or *-d* pattern. If you are not sure whether a verb form is regular or irregular, or what the correct form is, consult the following list or a dictionary. Dictionaries list any irregular forms under the entry for the base form.

Some common irregular verbs

BASE FORM	PAST TENSE	PAST PARTICIPLE
arise	arose	arisen
be	was/were	been

BASE FORM	PAST TENSE	PAST PARTICIPLE
beat	beat	beaten
become	became	become
begin	began	begun
bite	bit	bitten, bit
blow	blew	blown
break	broke	broken
bring	brought	brought
broadcast	broadcast	broadcast
build	built	built
burn	burned, burnt	burned, burnt
burst	burst	burst
buy	bought	bought
catch	caught	caught
choose	chose	chosen
come	came	come
cost	cost	cost
dig	dug	dug
dive	dived, dove	dived
do	did	done
draw	drew	drawn
dream	dreamed, dreamt	dreamed, dreamt
drink	drank	drunk
drive	drove	driven
eat	ate	eaten
fall	fell	fallen
feel	felt	felt
fight	fought	fought
find	found	found
fly	flew	flown
forget	forgot	forgotten, forgot
freeze	froze	frozen
get	got	gotten, got
give	gave	given
go	went	gone
grow	grew	grown

BASE FORM	PAST TENSE	PAST PARTICIPLE
hang (suspend)[1]	hung	hung
have	had	had
hear	heard	heard
hide	hid	hidden
hit	hit	hit
keep	kept	kept
know	knew	known
lay	laid	laid
lead	led	led
leave	left	left
lend	lent	lent
let	let	let
lie (recline)[2]	lay	lain
lose	lost	lost
make	made	made
mean	meant	meant
meet	met	met
prove	proved	proved, proven
put	put	put
read	read	read
ride	rode	ridden
ring	rang	rung
rise	rose	risen
run	ran	run
say	said	said
see	saw	seen
send	sent	sent
set	set	set
shake	shook	shaken
shoot	shot	shot
show	showed	showed, shown
shrink	shrank	shrunk

[1]*Hang* meaning "execute by hanging" is regular: *hang, hanged, hanged.*
[2]*Lie* meaning "tell a falsehood" is regular: *lie, lied, lied.*

BASE FORM	PAST TENSE	PAST PARTICIPLE
sing	sang	sung
sink	sank	sunk
sit	sat	sat
sleep	slept	slept
speak	spoke	spoken
spend	spent	spent
spring	sprang, sprung	sprung
stand	stood	stood
steal	stole	stolen
strike	struck	struck, stricken
swim	swam	swum
swing	swung	swung
take	took	taken
tear	tore	torn
throw	threw	thrown
wake	woke, waked	waked, woken
wear	wore	worn
write	wrote	written

EXERCISE 32.1

Complete each of the following sentences by filling in each blank with the past tense or past participle of the verb listed in parentheses. Example:

They had already _eaten_ (eat) the entrée; later they _ate_ (eat) the dessert.

1. The babysitter _____ (let) the children play with my schoolbooks, and before I _____ (come) home, they had _____ (tear) out several pages.
2. After they had _____ (review) the evidence, the jury _____ (find) the defendant not guilty.
3. Hypnosis _____ (work) only on willing participants.
4. My parents _____ (plant) a tree for me in the town where I was born, but I have never _____ (go) back to see it.
5. Some residents _____ (know) that the levee was leaking long before the storms, but authorities _____ (ignore) the complaints.
6. I _____ (paint) a picture from a photograph my sister had _____ (take) at the beach.
7. When the buzzer sounded, the racers _____ (spring) into the water and _____ (swim) toward the far end of the pool.

8. We had _____ (assume) for some time that surgery was a possibility, and we had _____ (find) an excellent facility.

9. Once the storm had _____ (pass), we could see that the old oak tree had _____ (fall).

10. Some high-level employees _____ (decide) to speak publicly about the cover-up before the company's official story had _____ (be) released to the media.

32d   Choose between *lie* and *lay*, *sit* and *set*, *rise* and *raise*.

These pairs of verbs cause confusion because both verbs in each pair have similar-sounding forms and related meanings. In each pair, one of the verbs is transitive, meaning that it is followed by a direct object (*I laid the cloth on the table*). The other is intransitive, meaning that it does not have an object (*He lay on the floor when his back ached*). The best way to avoid confusing these verbs is to memorize their forms and meanings.

BASE FORM	PAST TENSE	PAST PARTICIPLE	PRESENT PARTICIPLE	-S FORM
lie (recline)	lay	lain	lying	lies
lay (put)	laid	laid	laying	lays
sit (be seated)	sat	sat	sitting	sits
set (put)	set	set	setting	sets
rise (get up)	rose	risen	rising	rises
raise (lift)	raised	raised	raising	raises

> ▶ The doctor asked the patient to ~~lay~~ *lie* on his side.

> ▶ She ~~sat~~ *set* the vase on the table.

> ▶ He ~~raised~~ *rose* up in bed and glared at us.

EXERCISE 32.2

Underline the appropriate verb form in each of the following sentences. Example:

The guests (*raised*/*rose*) their glasses to the happy couple.

1. That cat (*lies*/*lays*) on the sofa all morning.

2. The chef (*lay*/*laid*) his knives carefully on the counter.

3. The two-year-old walked carefully across the room and (*set*/*sat*) the glass vase on the table.

4. Grandpa used to love (*sitting* / *setting*) on the front porch and telling stories of his childhood.

5. Almost immediately, the dough (*sitting* / *setting*) by the warm oven began to (*raise* / *rise*).

32e Use verb tenses appropriately.

Verb tenses show when the action takes place. The three simple tenses are the present tense, the past tense, and the future tense.

PRESENT TENSE	I ask, write
PAST TENSE	I asked, wrote
FUTURE TENSE	I will ask, will write

More complex aspects of time are expressed through progressive, perfect, and perfect progressive forms of the simple tenses.

PRESENT PROGRESSIVE	she is asking, is writing
PAST PROGRESSIVE	she was asking, was writing
FUTURE PROGRESSIVE	she will be asking, will be writing
PRESENT PERFECT	she has asked, has written
PAST PERFECT	she had asked, had written
FUTURE PERFECT	she will have asked, will have written
PRESENT PERFECT PROGRESSIVE	she has been asking, has been writing
PAST PERFECT PROGRESSIVE	she had been asking, had been writing
FUTURE PERFECT PROGRESSIVE	she will have been asking, will have been writing

The simple tenses locate an action only within the three basic time frames of present, past, and future. Progressive forms express continuing actions; perfect forms express actions completed before another action or time in the present, past, or future; perfect progressive forms express actions that continue up to some point in the present, past, or future.

Present tense

SIMPLE PRESENT

Use the simple present to indicate actions occurring now and those occurring habitually.

▶ **I eat breakfast every day at 8:00 AM.**

▶ **Love conquers all.**

Use the simple present when writing about action in literary works.

> *realizes*   *is*
> Ishmael slowly ~~realized~~ all that ~~was~~ at stake in the search for
> the white whale.

General truths or scientific facts should be in the simple present, even when the predicate of the sentence is in the past tense.

> *makes*
> Pasteur demonstrated that his boiling process ~~made~~ milk safe.

When you are quoting, summarizing, or paraphrasing a work, in general use the present tense.

> *writes*
> Keith Walters ~~wrote~~ that the "reputed consequences and promised
> blessings of literacy are legion."

But in an essay using APA (American Psychological Association) style, report your experiments or another researcher's work in the past tense (*wrote, noted*) or the present perfect (*has reported*). (See Chapter 53.)

> *noted*
> Comer (1995) ~~notes~~ that protesters who deprive themselves of food
> (for example, Gandhi) are seen not as dysfunctional but rather as
> "caring, sacrificing, even heroic" (p. 5).

PRESENT PROGRESSIVE

Use the present progressive to indicate actions that are ongoing in the present: *You are driving too fast.*

PRESENT PERFECT

Use the present perfect to indicate actions begun in the past and either completed at some unspecified time in the past or continuing into the present: *Uncontrolled logging has destroyed many forests.*

PRESENT PERFECT PROGRESSIVE

Use the present perfect progressive to indicate an ongoing action begun in the past and continuing into the present: *The two sides have been trying to settle the case out of court.*

Past tense

SIMPLE PAST

Use the simple past to indicate actions that occurred at a specific time and do not extend into the present: *Germany invaded Poland on September 1, 1939.*

PAST PROGRESSIVE

Use the past progressive to indicate continuing actions in the past: *Lenin was living in exile in Zurich when the tsar was overthrown.*

PAST PERFECT

Use the past perfect to indicate actions that were completed by a specific time in the past or before some other past action occurred: *By the fourth century, Christianity had become the state religion.*

PAST PERFECT PROGRESSIVE

Use the past perfect progressive to indicate continuing actions in the past that began before a specific time or before some other past action began: *Carter had been planning a naval career until his father died.*

Future tense

SIMPLE FUTURE

Use the simple future to indicate actions that have yet to begin: *The Vermeer show will come to Washington in September.*

FUTURE PROGRESSIVE

Use the future progressive to indicate continuing actions in the future: *The loans will be coming due over the next two years.*

FUTURE PERFECT

Use the future perfect to indicate actions that will be completed by a specified time in the future: *In ten years, your investment will have doubled.*

FUTURE PERFECT PROGRESSIVE

Use the future perfect progressive to indicate continuing actions that will be completed by some specified time in the future: *In May, I will have been working at IBM for five years.*

EXERCISE 32.3

Fill in the blank in each sentence with an appropriate form of the verb in parentheses. If more than one form is acceptable, be ready to explain your choices. Example:

The supply of a product _rises_ (rise) when the demand is great.

1. History _____ (show) that crime usually decreases as the economy improves.
2. Ever since the first nuclear power plants were built, opponents _____ (fear) disaster.
3. Thousands of Irish peasants _____ (emigrate) to America after the potato famine of the 1840s.
4. The soap opera *General Hospital* _____ (be) on the air since 1963.
5. Olivia _____ (direct) the play next year.
6. While they _____ (eat) in a local café, they witnessed a minor accident.
7. By this time next week, each of your clients _____ (receive) an invitation to the opening.
8. By the time a child born today enters first grade, he or she _____ (watch) thousands of television commercials.
9. In one of the novel's most famous scenes, Huck _____ (express) his willingness to go to hell rather than report Jim as an escaped slave.
10. A cold typically _____ (last) for about a week and a half.

AT A GLANCE

Editing Verb Tenses

If you have trouble with verb tense in standard English, make a point of checking for these common trouble spots as you proofread.

- Problems with verb form: writing *seen* for *saw*, for example, which confuses the past-participle and past-tense forms. (32c)
- Problems with tense: using the simple past (*Uncle Charlie arrived*) when meaning requires the present perfect (*Uncle Charlie has arrived*). (32e)
- Think carefully before using a regional or ethnic variety of English (*she nervous*) in situations calling for standard academic English (*she is nervous*). (See Chapter 22.)

32f　Sequence verb tenses effectively.

Careful and accurate use of tenses is important for clear writing. Even the simplest narrative describes actions that take place at different times; when you use the appropriate tense for each action, readers can follow such time changes easily.

▶ **By the time he lent her the money, she had declared bankruptcy.**

Use an infinitive (*to* plus a base form: *to go*) to indicate actions occurring at the same time as or later than the action of the predicate verb.

▶ **Each couple hopes to win the dance contest.**

The hoping is in the present; the winning is in the future.

Use a present participle (base form plus *-ing*) to indicate actions occurring at the same time as that of the predicate verb.

▶ **Seeking to relieve unemployment, Roosevelt established several public works programs.**

A past participle or a present-perfect participle (*having* plus a past participle) indicates actions occurring before that of the predicate verb.

Flown
▶ **Flying to the front, the troops joined their hard-pressed comrades.**
         ^

The past participle *flown* shows that the flying occurred before the joining.

Having crushed
▶ **Crushing all opposition at home, he launched a war of conquest.**
         ^

He launched the war after he crushed the opposition.

One common error is to use *would* in both clauses of a sentence with an *if* clause. Use *would* only in one clause.

had
▶ **If I would have played harder, I would have won.**
         ^

 LearningCurve game-like quizzing can take you to the next level.
bedfordstmartins.com/everydaywriter/LC > Verbs

EXERCISE 32.4

Edit each sentence to create the appropriate sequence of tenses. Example:

have sent
He needs to send in his application before today.
              ^

1. When she saw *Chicago*, it had made her want to become an actress even more.
2. Leaving England in December, the settlers arrived in Virginia in May.
3. I hoped to make the football team, but injuries prevented me from trying out.
4. Working with great dedication as a summer intern at the magazine, Mohan called his former supervisor in the fall to ask about a permanent position.
5. As we waited for the bus, we would watch the taxis pass by.

TALKING ABOUT STYLE

Technical and Scientific Writing

Much technical and scientific writing uses the passive voice effectively to highlight what is being studied rather than who is doing the studying.

The Earth's plates are created where they separate and are recycled where they collide, in a continuous process of creation and destruction.

— FRANK PRESS AND RAYMOND SIEVER, *Understanding Earth*

32g   Use active and passive voice effectively.

Voice tells whether a subject is acting (*He questions us*) or being acted upon (*He is questioned*). When the subject is acting, the verb is in the active voice; when the subject is being acted upon, the verb is in the passive voice. Most contemporary writers use the active voice as much as possible because it livens up their writing.

PASSIVE   Huge pine trees were uprooted by the storm.

ACTIVE   The storm uprooted huge pine trees.

The passive voice can work to good advantage in some situations. Newspaper reporters often use the passive voice to protect the confidentiality of their sources, as in the familiar expression *it is reported that*. You can also use the passive voice when you want to emphasize the recipient of an action rather than the performer of the action.

DALLAS, Nov. 22 — President John Fitzgerald Kennedy was shot and killed by an assassin today.   — TOM WICKER, *New York Times*

Wicker uses the passive voice with good reason: to focus on Kennedy, not on who killed him.

To shift a sentence from passive to active voice, make the performer of the action the subject of the sentence.

destroyed his acting career.
▶ His acting career was destroyed by his unprofessional behavior on the set.
                                                                        ^

   LearningCurve game-like quizzing can take you to the next level.
bedfordstmartins.com/everydaywriter/LC > Active and Passive Voice

EXERCISE 32.5

Convert each sentence from active to passive voice or from passive to active, and note the differences in emphasis these changes make. Example:

> *The*   *is advised by Machiavelli*
> Machiavelli advises the prince to gain the friendship of the people.
> ^   ^

1. The surfers were informed by the lifeguard of a shark sighting.
2. The cartoonist sketched a picture of Sam with huge ears and a pointy chin.
3. For months, the baby kangaroo is protected, fed, and taught by its mother.
4. The gifts were given out to the children by volunteers dressed as elves.
5. A new advertising company was chosen by the board members.

32h Use mood effectively.

The mood of a verb indicates the attitude of the writer. The indicative mood states facts or opinions and asks questions: *I did the right thing.* The imperative mood gives commands and instructions: *Do the right thing.* The subjunctive mood (used primarily in dependent clauses beginning with *that* or *if*) expresses wishes and conditions that are contrary to fact: *If I were doing the right thing, I'd know it.*

Forming and using the subjunctive

The present subjunctive uses the base form of the verb with all subjects.

▶ **It is important that children be psychologically ready for a new sibling.**

The past subjunctive is the same as the simple past except for the verb *be,* which uses *were* for all subjects.

▶ **He spent money as if he had infinite credit.**
▶ **If the store were better located, it would attract more customers.**

Because the subjunctive creates a rather formal tone, many people today tend to substitute the indicative mood in informal conversation.

▶ **If the store *was* better located, it would attract more customers.**

For academic or professional writing, use the subjunctive in the following contexts:

CLAUSES EXPRESSING A WISH

                                            were
▶ **He wished that his mother was still living nearby.**
                                    ^

THAT CLAUSES EXPRESSING A REQUEST OR DEMAND

be
▶ The job demands that employees are in good physical condition.
                                         ^

IF CLAUSES EXPRESSING A CONDITION THAT DOES NOT EXIST

were
▶ If the federal government was to ban the sale of tobacco, tobacco
                            ^
companies and distributors would suffer a great loss.

EXERCISE 32.6

Revise any of the following sentences that do not use the appropriate subjunctive verb forms required in formal writing. Example:

were
I saw how carefully he moved, as if he was holding an infant.
                                         ^

1. Josh kept spending money as if he was still earning high commissions.
2. She wished that she was able to take her daughter along on the business trip.
3. Protesters demanded that the senator resign from her post.
4. If the vaccine was more readily available, the county health department would recommend that everyone receive the shot.
5. It is critical that the liquid remains at room temperature for seven hours.

FOR MULTILINGUAL WRITERS

Using the Subjunctive

"If you were to practice writing every day, it would eventually seem much easier to you." For a discussion of this and other uses of the subjunctive, see 57f.

bedfordstmartins.com/everydaywriter
Exercise Central > Verbs

EXERCISE 32.7: THINKING CRITICALLY

Reading with an Eye for Verbs

Some years ago a newspaper in San Francisco ran the headline "Giants Crush Cardinals, 3–1," provoking the following friendly advice from John Updike about the art of sports-headline verbs:

The correct verb, San Francisco, is *whip*. Notice the vigor, force, and scorn obtained.... [These examples] may prove helpful: 3–1 — *whip*; 3–2 — *shade*; 2–1 — *edge*. 4–1 gets the coveted verb *vanquish*. Rule: Any three-run margin, *provided the winning total does not exceed ten*, may be described as a vanquishing.

Take the time to study a newspaper with an eye for its verbs. Copy down several examples of strong verbs as well as a few examples of weak or overused verbs. For the weak ones, try to come up with better choices.

Thinking about Your Own Use of Verbs

Writing that relies too heavily on the verbs *be, do,* and *have* almost always bores readers. Look at something you've written recently to see whether you rely too heavily on these verbs, and revise accordingly.

Subject-Verb Agreement 33

Subjects and verbs are at work in almost every statement you make, and you make them agree effortlessly most of the time. Look, for instance, at three sentences taken from a recent broadcast of a baseball game.

> The pitcher powers another blistering curveball over the plate.

> The Yanks move on to Milwaukee tomorrow.

> The duel of the no-hitters continues into the eighth.

Take time to listen to someone reporting an event—a play-by-play announcer, perhaps, or an on-the-scene reporter. Note some of the subject-verb combinations. Do you find any that don't sound right, that might not agree?

33a Match verb forms with third-person singular subjects.

To make a verb in the present tense agree with a third-person singular subject, add *-s* or *-es* to the base form.

▶ **A vegetarian diet lowers the risk of heart disease.**

▶ **What you eat affects your health.**

In the preceding example, the subject is the noun clause *what you eat.* The clause is singular, so the base form of the verb *affect* takes an *-s.*

To make a verb in the present tense agree with any other subject, use the base form of the verb.

▶ **I miss my family.**

▶ **They live in another state.**

AT A GLANCE

Editing for Subject-Verb Agreement

- Identify the subject that goes with each verb. Cover up any words between the subject and the verb to identify agreement problems more easily. (33b)
- Check compound subjects. Those joined by *and* usually take a plural verb. With those subjects joined by *or* or *nor*, however, the verb agrees with the part of the subject closer or closest to the verb. (33c)
- Check collective-noun subjects. These nouns take a singular verb when they refer to a group as a single unit, but they take a plural verb when they refer to the multiple members of a group. (33d)
- Check indefinite-pronoun subjects. Most take a singular verb. *Both*, *few*, *many*, *others*, and *several* take a plural verb, and *all*, *any*, *enough*, *more*, *most*, *none*, and *some* can be either singular or plural. (33e)

Have and *be* do not follow the *-s* or *-es* pattern with third-person singular subjects. *Have* changes to *has*; *be* has irregular forms in both the present and past tenses (32a).

▶ **War is hell.**

▶ **The soldier was brave beyond the call of duty.**

33b Check subjects and verbs separated by other words.

Make sure the verb agrees with the subject and not with another noun that falls in between.

▶ **A vase of flowers makes a room attractive.**

have
▶ **Many books on the best-seller list has little literary value.**

The simple subject is *books*, not *list*.

Be careful when you use phrases beginning with *as well as*, *along with*, *in addition to*, *together with*, and similar prepositions. They do not make a singular subject plural.

was
▶ **A passenger, as well as the driver, were injured in the accident.**

Though this sentence has a grammatically singular subject, it suggests a plural subject. The sentence makes better sense with a compound subject: *The driver and a passenger were injured in the accident.*

EXERCISE 33.1

Underline the appropriate verb form in each of the following sentences. Example:

The benefits of family planning (*is* / *are*) not apparent to many peasants.

1. Soldiers who are injured while fighting for their country (*deserves* / *deserve*) complete medical coverage.

2. The dog, followed by his owner, (*races* / *race*) wildly down the street every afternoon.

3. Just when I think I can go home, another pile of invoices (*appears* / *appear*) on my desk.

4. The pattern of secrecy and lies (*needs* / *need*) to stop in order for counseling to be successful.

5. A substance abuser often (*hides* / *hide*) the truth to cover up his or her addiction.

6. The police chief, in addition to several soldiers and two civilians, (*was* / *were*) injured in the explosion.

7. Garlic's therapeutic value as well as its flavor (*comes* / *come*) from sulfur compounds.

8. The fiber content of cereal (*contributes* / *contribute*) to its nutritional value.

9. The graphics on this computer game often (*causes* / *cause*) my system to crash.

10. Current research on AIDS, in spite of the best efforts of hundreds of scientists, (*leaves* / *leave*) serious questions unanswered.

33c Make verbs agree with compound subjects.

Subjects joined by *and* generally require a plural verb form.

were
▶ A backpack, a canteen, and a rifle was issued to each recruit.

When subjects joined by *and* are considered a single unit or refer to the same person or thing, they take a singular verb form.

▶ George W. Bush's older brother and political ally was the governor of Florida.

remains
▶ Drinking and driving remain a major cause of highway accidents and fatalities.

In this sentence, *drinking and driving* is considered a single activity, and a singular verb is used.

If the word *each* or *every* precedes subjects joined by *and*, the verb form is singular.

▶ **Each boy and girl chooses one gift to take home.**

With subjects joined by *or* or *nor*, the verb agrees with the part closer or closest to the verb.

▶ **Either the witnesses or the defendant *is* lying.**

> If you find this sentence awkward, put the plural noun closer to the verb: *Either the defendant or the witnesses are lying.*

33d Make verbs agree with collective-noun subjects.

Collective nouns—such as *family, team, audience, group, jury, crowd, band, class,* and *committee*—refer to a group. Collective nouns can take either singular or plural verbs, depending on whether they refer to the group as a single unit or to the multiple members of the group. The meaning of a sentence as a whole is your guide to whether a collective noun refers to a unit or to the multiple parts of a unit.

▶ **After deliberating, the jury *reports* its verdict.**

> The jury acts as a single unit.

▶ **The jury still *disagree* on a number of counts.**

> The members of the jury act as multiple individuals.

▶ **The family of ducklings** scatters **when the cat approaches.**

> *Family* here refers to the many ducks; they cannot scatter as one.

Treat fractions that refer to singular nouns as singular and those that refer to plural nouns as plural.

▶ **Two-thirds of the park *has* burned.**

> *Two-thirds* refers to the single portion of the park that burned.

▶ **Two-thirds of the students *were* commuters.**

> *Two-thirds* here refers to the students who commuted as many individuals.

Even though *eyeglasses, scissors, pants,* and other such words refer to single items, they take plural verbs because they are made up of pairs.

▶ Where *are* my reading glasses?

Treat phrases starting with *the number of* as singular and with *a number of* as plural.

SINGULAR   The number of applicants for the internship *was* amazing.

PLURAL   A number of applicants *were* put on the waiting list.

33e Make verbs agree with indefinite-pronoun subjects.

Indefinite pronouns do not refer to specific persons or things. Most take singular verb forms.

SOME COMMON INDEFINITE PRONOUNS

another	each	much	one
any	either	neither	other
anybody	everybody	nobody	somebody
anyone	everyone	no one	someone
anything	everything	nothing	something

▶ Of the two jobs, **neither holds** much appeal.

depicts
▶ Each of the plays depict a hero undone by a tragic flaw.

Both, few, many, others, and *several* are plural.

▶ Though **many apply, few are** chosen.

All, any, enough, more, most, none, and *some* can be singular or plural, depending on the noun they refer to.

▶ All of the cake *was* eaten.

▶ All of the candidates *promise* to improve the schools.

33f   Make verbs agree with antecedents of *who*, *which*, and *that*.

When the relative pronouns *who*, *which*, and *that* are used as a subject, the verb agrees with the antecedent of the pronoun (see 31d and 34f).

▶ Fear is an **ingredient** that **goes** into creating stereotypes.

▶ Guilt and fear are **ingredients** that **go** into creating stereotypes.

Problems often occur with the words *one of the*. In general, *one of the* takes a plural verb, while *the only one of the* takes a singular verb.

> work
▶ Carla is one of the employees who always ~~works~~ overtime.

Some employees always work overtime. Carla is among them. Thus *who* refers to *employees*, and the verb is plural.

> works
▶ Ming is the only one of the employees who always ~~work~~ overtime.

Only one employee always works overtime, and that employee is Ming. Thus *one*, not *employees*, is the antecedent of *who*, and the verb form is singular.

33g   Use appropriate forms of linking verbs.

A linking verb (31k) should agree with its subject, which usually precedes the verb, not with the subject complement, that follows it.

> are
▶ The three key treaties ~~is~~ the topic of my talk.

The subject is *treaties*, not *topic*.

> was
▶ Nero Wolfe's passion ~~were~~ orchids.

The subject is *passion*, not *orchids*.

33h   Make verbs agree with subjects that are plural in form but singular in meaning.

Some words that end in *-s* appear plural but are singular in meaning and thus take singular verb forms.

strikes
▶ **Measles still ~~strike~~ many Americans.**
^

Some nouns of this kind (such as *statistics* and *politics*) may be either singular or plural, depending on context.

SINGULAR   Statistics *is* a course I really dread.

PLURAL   The statistics in that study *are* highly questionable.

33i Make verbs agree with subjects that follow verbs.

In English, verbs usually follow subjects. When this order is reversed, make the verb agree with the subject, not with a noun that precedes it.

stand
▶ **Beside the barn ~~stands~~ silos filled with grain.**
^

The subject is *silos*; it is plural, so the verb must be *stand*.

In sentences beginning with *there is* or *there are* (or *there was* or *were*), *there* serves only as an introductory word; the subject follows the verb.

▶ **There are five basic positions in classical ballet.**

33j Make verbs agree with titles and words used as words.

describes
▶ *One Writer's Beginnings* ~~describe~~ Eudora Welty's childhood.
^

is
▶ *Steroids* ~~are~~ a little word that packs a big punch in the world of sports.
^

EXERCISE 33.2

Revise any of the following sentences as necessary to establish subject-verb agreement. (Some of the sentences do not require any change.) Example:

darts
Into the shadows ~~dart~~ the frightened raccoon.
^

1. Room and board are the most expensive part of my college education.
2. *Three Cups of Tea* tell the story of one man's mission to establish schools in poor, remote areas of Pakistan.

3. Hanging near the *Mona Lisa* is many more Renaissance paintings.

4. Most of the students oppose the shortened dining hall hours.

5. Each of the security workers are considered trained after viewing a twenty-minute videotape.

6. Neither his expensive clothes nor his charm were enough to get him the job.

7. The committee were expected to produce its annual report two weeks early.

8. My grandmother is the only one of my relatives who still goes to church.

9. Sweden was one of the few European countries that was neutral in 1943.

10. Economics involve the study of the distribution of goods and services.

 LearningCurve game-like quizzing can take you to the next level.
bedfordstmartins.com/everydaywriter/LC > Subject-Verb Agreement

EXERCISE 33.3: THINKING CRITICALLY

Reading with an Eye for Subject-Verb Agreement

The following passage, from a 1990 essay questioning a "traditional" view of marriage, includes several instances of complicated subject-verb agreement. Note the rules governing subject-verb agreement in each case.

> Marriage seems to me more conflict-ridden than ever, and the divorce rate — with or without new babies in the house — remains constant. The fabric of men-and-women-as-they-once-were is so thin in places no amount of patching can weave that cloth together again. The longing for connection may be strong, but even stronger is the growing perception that only people who are real to themselves can connect. Two shall be as one is over, no matter how lonely we get.
>
> — VIVIAN GORNICK, "Who Says We Haven't Made a Revolution?"

Thinking about Your Own Use of Subject-Verb Agreement

Visiting relatives is / are treacherous. Either verb makes a grammatically acceptable sentence, yet the verbs result in two very different statements. Write a brief explanation of the two possible meanings. Then write a paragraph or two about visiting relatives. Using the information in this chapter, examine each subject and its verb. Do you maintain subject-verb agreement throughout? Revise to correct any errors you find. If you find any patterns, make a note to yourself of things to look for routinely as you revise your writing.

Pronouns 34

As words that stand in for nouns, pronouns carry a lot of weight in everyday language. These directions show one of the reasons why it's important to use pronouns clearly:

> When you see a dirt road turning left off Winston Lane, follow it for two more miles.

The word *it* could mean either the dirt road or Winston Lane. Pronouns can improve understanding, but only when they're used carefully and accurately.

AT A GLANCE

Editing Pronouns

- Are all pronouns after forms of the verb *be* in the subjective case? *It's me* is common in spoken English, but in formal writing use *It is I.* (34a)

- To check for use of *who* and *whom* (and *whoever* and *whomever*), try substituting *he* or *him*. If *he* is correct, use *who* (or *whoever*); if *him*, use *whom* or *whomever*. (34b)

- In compound structures, make sure any pronouns are in the same case they would be in if used alone (*She and Jake were living in Spain*). (34c)

- When a pronoun follows *than* or *as*, complete the sentence mentally. If the pronoun is the subject of an unstated verb, it should be subjective (*I like her better than he [likes her]*). If it is the object of an unstated verb, make it objective (*I like her better than [I like] him*). (34d)

- If you have used *he, his,* or *him* to refer to *everyone* or another singular indefinite pronoun that includes both males and females, revise the sentence. If you have used *they* to refer to a singular indefinite pronoun, rewrite the sentence. (34f)

- For each pronoun, identify a specific word that it refers to. If you cannot find one specific word, supply one. If the pronoun refers to more than one word, revise the sentence. (34g)

- Check each use of *it, this, that,* and *which* to be sure the pronoun refers to a specific word. (34g)

- Be sure that any use of *you* refers to your specific reader or readers. (34g)

34a Consider a pronoun's role in the sentence.

Most speakers of English know intuitively when to use *I*, *me*, and *my*. Our choices reflect differences in case, the form a pronoun takes to indicate how it acts in a sentence. Pronouns acting as subjects are in the subjective case (*I*); those acting as objects are in the objective case (*me*); those acting as possessives are in the possessive case (*my*).

SUBJECTIVE PRONOUNS	OBJECTIVE PRONOUNS	POSSESSIVE PRONOUNS
I	me	my/mine
we	us	our/ours
you	you	your/yours
he/she/it	him/her/it	his/her/hers/its
they	them	their/theirs
who/whoever	whom/whomever	whose

Subjective case

A pronoun should be in the subjective case (*I*, *we*, *you*, *he/she/it*, *they*, *who*, *whoever*) when it is a subject, a subject complement, or an appositive renaming a subject or subject complement.

SUBJECT

She was passionate about recycling.

SUBJECT COMPLEMENT

The main supporter of the recycling program was she.

APPOSITIVE RENAMING A SUBJECT OR SUBJECT COMPLEMENT

Three colleagues—Peter, John, and she—worked on the program.

Americans routinely use the objective case for subject complements, especially in conversation: *Who's there? It's me*. If the subjective case for a subject complement sounds stilted or awkward (*It's I*), try rewriting the sentence using the pronoun as the subject (*I'm here*).

> *She was the*
> ▶ The first person to see Kishore after the awards was she.

Objective case

Use the objective case (*me*, *us*, *you*, *him/her/it*, *them*) when a pronoun functions as a direct or indirect object, an object of a preposition, an appositive renaming an object, or a subject of an infinitive.

DIRECT OBJECT

The boss surprised her with a big raise.

INDIRECT OBJECT

The owner gave him a reward.

OBJECT OF A PREPOSITION

Several friends went with me.

APPOSITIVE RENAMING AN OBJECT

The students elected two representatives, Joan and me.

SUBJECT OF AN INFINITIVE

The students convinced him to vote for the school bond.

Possessive case

Use the possessive case when a pronoun shows possession or owner-ship. The adjective forms of possessive pronouns (*my, our, your, his/her/its, their, whose*) are used before nouns or gerunds, and noun forms (*mine, ours, yours, his/hers/its, theirs, whose*) take the place of a possessive noun. Possessive pronouns do not include apostrophes (42a).

BEFORE A NOUN

The sound of her voice came right through the walls.

IN PLACE OF A POSSESSIVE NOUN

The responsibility is hers.

Pronouns before a gerund should be in the possessive case.

his
▶ I remember him singing.
       ^

His modifies the gerund *singing.*

34b Use *who, whoever, whom,* and *whomever* appropriately.

A common problem with pronoun case is deciding whether to use *who* or *whom.* Even when traditional grammar requires *whom,* many Americans use *who* instead, especially in speech. Nevertheless, you should understand the difference between *who* and *whom* so that you can make

Correctness or Stuffiness?

"I think *Everyone has their opinion* sounds better than *Everyone has his or her opinion.* And nobody says *whom.* Why should I write that way?" Over time, the conventions governing certain usages — such as *who* versus *whom*, or *their* versus *his* or *her* when it refers to an indefinite pronoun like *everyone* — have become much more relaxed. To many Americans, *Whom did you talk to?* and *No one finished his or her test* — both of which are technically "correct" — sound unpleasantly fussy. However, other people object to less formal constructions such as *Who did you talk to?* and *No one finished their test*; to them, such usages signal a lack of discrimination. Unfortunately, you can't please everyone. Use whatever you are most comfortable with in speaking, but be more careful in formal writing. If you don't know whether your audience will prefer more or less formality, try recasting your sentence.

informed choices in situations such as formal college writing that may call for the use of *whom* (or *whomever*) in the objective case. The most common confusion with *who* and *whom* occurs when they begin a question and when they introduce a dependent clause.

In questions

You can determine whether to use *who* or *whom* at the beginning of a question by answering the question using a personal pronoun. If the answer is *he, she,* or *they,* use *who*; if it is *him, her,* or *them,* use *whom.*

> *Whom*
> ▶ ~~Who~~ did you visit?
>   ^

> I visited *them. Them* is objective; thus *whom* is correct.

> *Who*
> ▶ ~~Whom~~ do you think wrote the story?
>   ^

> I think *she* wrote the story. *She* is subjective; thus *who* is correct.

In dependent clauses

The case of a pronoun in a dependent clause is determined by its purpose in the clause, no matter how that clause functions in the sentence. If the pronoun acts as a subject or subject complement in the clause, use *who* or *whoever*. If the pronoun acts as an object in the clause, use *whom* or *whomever*.

> *who*
> ▶ **Anyone can hypnotize someone whom wants to be hypnotized.**
>   ^

The verb of the clause is *wants*, and its subject is *who*.

> *Whomever*
> ▶ **Whoever the party suspected of disloyalty was executed.**
>   ^

Whomever is the object of *suspected* in the clause *whomever the party suspected of disloyalty*.

If you are not sure, try separating the dependent clause from the rest of the sentence and looking at it in isolation. Then rewrite the clause as a new sentence, and substitute a personal pronoun for *who(ever)* or *whom(ever)*. If you substitute *he*, *she*, or *they*, use *who* or *whoever*; if *him*, *her*, or *them* is correct, use *whom* or *whomever*.

> ▶ **The minister grimaced at (*whoever* / *whomever*) made any noise.**

Isolate the clause *whoever/whomever made any noise*. Substituting a personal pronoun gives you *they made any noise*. *They* acts as the subject; therefore, *The minister grimaced at whoever made any noise.*

> ▶ **The minister smiled at (*whoever* / *whomever*) she greeted.**

Isolate and rearrange the clause to get *she greeted whoever/whomever*. Substituting a personal pronoun gives you *she greeted them*. *Them* acts as an object; therefore, *The minister smiled at whomever she greeted.*

> ▶ **The minister grimaced at *whoever* she thought made the noise.**

Ignore such expressions as *he thinks* and *she says* when you isolate the clause.

EXERCISE 34.1

Insert *who, whoever, whom,* or *whomever* appropriately in the blank in each of the following sentences. Example:

She is someone _who_ will go far.

1. _____ did you say was our most likely suspect?
2. _____ the audience chooses will move up to the next level.
3. The awards banquet will recognize _____ made the honor roll.
4. Professor Quiñones asked _____ we wanted to collaborate with.
5. _____ received the highest score?

34c   Consider case in compound structures.

When a pronoun is part of a compound subject, complement, object, or appositive, put it in the same case you would use if the pronoun were alone.

▶ When ~~him~~ *he* and Zelda were first married, they lived in New York.

▶ The boss invited ~~she~~ *her* and her family to dinner.

▶ This morning saw yet another conflict between my sister and ~~I~~ *me*.

▶ Both panelists—Javonne and ~~me~~ *I*,—were stumped.

To decide whether to use the subjective or objective case in a compound structure, mentally delete the rest of the compound and try the pronoun alone.

▶ Come to the park with Anh and ~~I~~ *me*.

> Mentally deleting *Anh and* results in *Come to the park with I.* Rewrite as *Come to the park with Anh and* <u>me</u>.

34d   Consider case in elliptical constructions.

In elliptical constructions, some words are understood but left out. When an elliptical construction ends in a pronoun, put the pronoun in the case it would be in if the construction were complete.

▶ His sister has always been more athletic than *he* [is].

In some elliptical constructions, the case of the pronoun depends on the meaning intended.

▶ Willie likes Lily more than *she* [likes Lily].

> *She* is the subject of the omitted verb *likes*.

▶ Willie likes Lily more than [he likes] *her*.

> *Her* is the object of the omitted verb *likes*.

34e   Use *we* and *us* appropriately before a noun.

If you are unsure about whether to use *we* or *us* before a noun, recast the sentence without the noun. Use whichever pronoun would be correct if the noun were omitted.

We
▶ **Us fans never give up hope.**
    ^

Without *fans, we* would be the subject.

us
▶ **The Rangers depend on we fans.**
                            ^

Without *fans, us* would be the object of a preposition.

EXERCISE 34.2

Underline the appropriate pronoun from the pair in parentheses in each of the following sentences. Example:

> The possibility of (*their*/*them*) succeeding never occurred to me.

1. Max has had more car accidents than Gabriella, but he still insists he is a better driver than (*she*/*her*).
2. Fixing the dock with Hank and (*they*/*them*) reminded me of our summers at the lake.
3. The coach gave honorable-mention ribbons to the two who didn't win any races — Aiden and (*I*/*me*).
4. There seemed to be no reason for (*them*/*their*) voluntarily studying on a Saturday night.
5. Tomorrow (*we*/*us*) recruits will have our first on-the-job test.

34f Make pronouns agree with antecedents.

The antecedent of a pronoun is the word the pronoun refers to. The antecedent usually appears before the pronoun—earlier in the sentence or in the prior sentence. Pronouns and antecedents are said to agree when they match up in person, number, and gender.

SINGULAR   The choirmaster raised his baton.

PLURAL   The boys picked up their music.

Compound antecedents

Compound antecedents joined by *and* require plural pronouns.

▶ **My parents and I tried to resolve our disagreement.**

When *each* or *every* precedes a compound antecedent, however, it takes a singular pronoun.

Every plant and animal has its own ecological niche.

With a compound antecedent joined by *or* or *nor*, the pronoun agrees with the nearer or nearest antecedent. If the parts of the antecedent are of different genders, however, this kind of sentence can be awkward or ambiguous and may need to be revised.

> AWKWARD   Neither Annie nor Barry got *his* work done.
>
> REVISED   Annie didn't get *her* work done, and neither did Barry.

When a compound antecedent contains both singular and plural parts, the sentence may sound awkward unless the plural part comes last.

▶ Neither the newspaper nor the radio stations would reveal *their* sources.

Collective-noun antecedents

A collective noun that refers to a single unit (*herd, team, audience*) requires a singular pronoun.

▶ The *audience* fixed *its* attention on center stage.

When such an antecedent refers to the multiple parts of a unit, however, it requires a plural pronoun.

▶ The director chose this *cast* for the play because *they* had experience in the roles.

Indefinite-pronoun antecedents

Indefinite pronouns are those that do not refer to specific persons or things. Most indefinite pronouns are always singular; a few are always plural. Some can be singular or plural depending on the context.

▶ **One** of the ballerinas lost **her** balance.

▶ **Many** in the audience jumped to **their** feet.

> SINGULAR   *Some* of the furniture was showing *its* age.
>
> PLURAL   *Some* of the farmers abandoned *their* land.

Sexist pronouns

Indefinite pronouns often serve as antecedents that may be either male or female. Writers used to use a masculine pronoun, known as the

---

AT A GLANCE

Editing Out Sexist Pronouns

Everyone should know <u>his</u> *legal rights.*

Here are three ways to express the same idea without *his*:

1. Revise to make the antecedent a plural noun.
   All citizens should know <u>their</u> *legal rights.*
2. Revise the sentence altogether.
   Everyone should have some knowledge of basic legal rights.
3. Use both masculine and feminine pronouns.
   Everyone should know <u>his</u> *or* <u>her</u> *legal rights.*

This third option, using both masculine and feminine pronouns, can be awkward, especially when repeated several times in a passage.

---

generic *he,* to refer to such indefinite pronouns. However, such wording ignores or even excludes females.

When the antecedent is *anybody, each,* or *everyone,* some people avoid the generic *he* by using a plural pronoun.

▶ *Everyone* **should know** *their* **legal rights.**

You will hear such sentences in conversation and even see them in writing, but many people in academic contexts still consider *anybody, each,* and *everyone* singular, and they think using *their* with singular antecedents is too informal. They prefer one of the solutions in the box.

EXERCISE 34.3

Revise the following sentences as needed to create pronoun-antecedent agreement and to eliminate the generic *he* and any awkward pronoun references. Some can be revised in more than one way. Example:

or her
Every graduate submitted his diploma card.

All graduates   their   cards.
Every graduate submitted his diploma card.

1. While shopping for a new computer for school, I noticed that a laptop costs much less than they used to.
2. Congress usually resists a president's attempt to encroach on what they consider their authority.
3. Marco and Ellen were each given a chance to voice their opinion.
4. An emergency room doctor needs to be swift and decisive; he also needs to be calm and careful.
5. Every dog and cat has their own personality.

34g   Make pronouns refer to clear antecedents.

The antecedent of a pronoun is the word the pronoun substitutes for. If a pronoun is too far from its antecedent, readers will have trouble making the connection between the two.

Ambiguous antecedents

Readers have trouble when a pronoun can refer to more than one antecedent.

▶ The car went over the bridge just before ~~it~~ *the bridge* fell into the water.

> What fell into the water—the car or the bridge? The revision makes the meaning clear.

▶ Kerry told Ellen, *"I* she should be ready soon." *"*

> Reporting Kerry's words directly, in quotation marks, eliminates the ambiguity.

Vague use of it, this, that, *and* which

The words *it, this, that,* and *which* often function as a shortcut for referring to something mentioned earlier. But such shortcuts can cause confusion. Like other pronouns, each must refer to a specific antecedent.

▶ When the senators realized the bill would be defeated, they tried to postpone the vote but failed. ~~It~~ *The entire effort* was a fiasco.

▶ Nancy just found out that she won the lottery, ~~which~~ *and that news* explains her sudden resignation from her job.

Indefinite use of you, it, *and* they

In conversation, we frequently use *you, it,* and *they* in an indefinite sense in such expressions as *you never know; in the paper, it said;* and *they say.* In academic and professional writing, however, use *you* only to mean "you, the reader," and *they* or *it* only to refer to a clear antecedent.

▶ Commercials try to make ~~you~~ *people* buy without thinking.

▶ ~~On the~~ *The* Weather Channel, it reported that an earthquake devastated parts of Pakistan.

Many restaurants in France
▶ ~~In France, they allow dogs~~ in many restaurants.
   ^   ^

Possessive antecedents

A possessive may *suggest* a noun antecedent but does not serve as a clear antecedent.

her   *Alexa*
▶ In Alexa's formal complaint, ~~she~~ showed why the test question was
   ^   ^
wrong.

EXERCISE 34.4

Revise each of the following items to clarify pronoun reference. Most of the items can be revised in more than one way. If a pronoun refers ambiguously to more than one possible antecedent, revise the sentence to reflect each possible meaning. Example:

Miranda found Jane's keys after
After Jane left,/ ~~Miranda found her keys.~~
 ^   ^
Miranda found her own keys after
After Jane left,/ ~~Miranda found her keys.~~
 ^   ^

1. All scholarship applicants must fill out a financial aid form, meet with the dean, and write a letter to the committee members. The deadline is October 24, so they should start the process as soon as possible.
2. Patients on medication may relate better to their therapists, be less vulnerable to what disturbs them, and be more responsive to them.
3. Ms. Dunbar wanted to speak to my mother before she spoke to me.
4. In Texas, you often hear about the influence of big oil corporations.
5. A small band of protestors picketed the new shopping center, which outraged many residents.

EXERCISE 34.5

Revise the following paragraph to establish a clear antecedent for every pronoun that needs one.

In the summer of 2005, the NCAA banned the use of mascots that could be considered offensive to American Indians at any of their championship games. In order to understand this, it is important to consider that movies and television programs for years portrayed them as savage warriors that were feared and misunderstood. That is why some schools have chosen to use Indians as their mascot, a role typically played by wild animals or fictional beasts. You would not tolerate derogatory terms for other ethnic groups being used for school mascots. In the NCAA's new ruling, they ask schools to eliminate mascots that may be hurtful or offensive to America's Indian population.

LearningCurve game-like quizzing can take you to the next level.
bedfordstmartins.com/everydaywriter/LC > Pronouns

EXERCISE 34.6: THINKING CRITICALLY

Turn to a recent piece of your writing (something at least two pages long), and analyze your use of pronouns. Look carefully at the pronoun case you tend to use most; if it is first person, ask whether *I* is used too much. And if you find that you rely heavily on any one case (*you*, for example), decide whether your writing seems monotonous as a result. Take a look as well at whether you tend to use masculine pronouns exclusively to refer to people generally; if so, ask whether you would be more inclusive if you used both masculine and feminine pronouns or if you should revise to use plural pronouns that are not marked as either masculine or feminine (such as *we* or *they*). Finally, check to make sure that your pronouns and their antecedents agree and that the pronouns refer clearly and directly to antecedents.

35 Adjectives and Adverbs

Adjectives and adverbs often bring indispensable differences in meaning to the words they modify. In basketball, for example, there is an important difference between a *flagrant* foul and a *technical* foul, a *layup* and a *reverse layup*, and an *angry* coach and an *abusively angry* coach. In each instance, the modifiers are crucial to accurate communication.

Adjectives modify nouns and pronouns; they answer the questions *which? how many?* and *what kind?* Adverbs modify verbs, adjectives, and other adverbs; they answer the questions *how? when? where?* and *to what extent?* Many adverbs are formed by adding *-ly* to adjectives (*slight, slightly*), but many adverbs are formed in other ways (*outdoors*) or have forms of their own (*very*).

35a Use adjectives after linking verbs.

When adjectives come after linking verbs, they usually serve as a subject complement, to describe the subject: *I am patient*. Note that in specific sentences, some verbs may or may not be linking verbs—*appear, become, feel, grow, look, make, prove, seem, smell, sound,* and *taste,* for instance. When a word following one of these verbs modifies the subject, use an adjective; when it modifies the verb, use an adverb.

ADJECTIVE   Fluffy looked *angry*.

AT A GLANCE

Editing Adjectives and Adverbs

- Scrutinize each adjective and adverb. Consider synonyms for each word to see whether you have chosen the best word possible.

- See if a more specific noun would eliminate the need for an adjective (*mansion* rather than *enormous house*, for instance). Do the same with verbs and adverbs.

- Look for places where you might make your writing more specific or vivid by adding an adjective or adverb.

- Check that adjectives modify only nouns and pronouns and that adverbs modify only verbs, adjectives, and other adverbs. (35b) Check especially for proper use of *good* and *well*, *bad* and *badly*, *real* and *really*. (35b and c)

- Make sure all comparisons are complete. (35c)

- If English is not your first language, check that adjectives are in the right order. (58e)

ADVERB   Fluffy looked *angrily* at the poodle.

Linking verbs suggest a state of being, not an action. In the preceding examples, *looked angry* suggests the state of being angry; *looked angrily* suggests an angry action.

FOR MULTILINGUAL WRITERS

Using Adjectives with Plural Nouns

In Spanish, Russian, and many other languages, adjectives agree in number with the nouns they modify. In English, adjectives do not change number this way: *the kittens are cute* (not *cutes*).

35b Use adverbs to modify verbs, adjectives, and adverbs.

In everyday conversation, you will often hear (and perhaps use) adjectives in place of adverbs. For example, people often say *go quick* instead of *go quickly*. When you write in standard academic English, however, use adverbs to modify verbs, adjectives, and other adverbs.

carefully.
▶ You can feel the song's meter if you listen careful.

really
▶ The audience was real disappointed by the show.

Good, well, bad, *and* badly

The modifiers *good, well, bad,* and *badly* cause problems for many writers because the distinctions between *good* and *well* and between *bad* and *badly* are often not observed in conversation. Problems also arise because *well* can function as either an adjective or an adverb. *Good* and *bad* are always adjectives, and both can be used after a linking verb.

▶ **The weather looks *good* today.**

▶ **He plays the trumpet good and the trombone not bad.**
well *badly.*

Badly is an adverb and can modify a verb, an adjective, or another adverb. After a linking verb, use *bad* instead.

bad
▶ **I feel badly for the Toronto fans.**

The linking verb *feel* requires the adjective *bad.*

As an adjective, *well* means "in good health"; as an adverb, it means "in a good way" or "thoroughly."

ADJECTIVE   After a week of rest, Julio felt *well* again.

ADVERB   She plays *well* enough to make the team.

EXERCISE 35.1

Revise the following sentences to correct adverb and adjective use. Then identify each adjective or adverb you have revised and the word each modifies. Example:

superbly
The attorney delivered a superb conceived summation.

1. Getting tickets at this late date is near impossible.
2. Derek apologized for behaving so immature on the football field.
3. Nora felt badly that the package would arrive one week later than promised.
4. It is real dangerous to hike those mountains in the winter.
5. He spoke confident about winning the race, but we doubted his abilities.
6. Paramedics rushed to help the victim, who was bleeding bad from the head.
7. The car ran good until the last two miles of the trip.
8. Arjun felt terrifically about his discussion with Professor Greene.
9. After we added cinnamon, the stew tasted really well.
10. Scientists measured the crater as accurate as possible.

35c Choose appropriate comparative and superlative forms.

Most adjectives and adverbs have three forms: positive, comparative, and superlative.

POSITIVE	COMPARATIVE	SUPERLATIVE
large	larger	largest
early	earlier	earliest
careful	more careful	most careful
happily	more happily	most happily

▶ Canada is **larger** than the United States.

▶ My son needs to be **more careful** with his money.

▶ They are the **most happily** married couple I know.

Form the comparative and superlative of most one- or two-syllable adjectives by adding *-er* and *-est*. With some two-syllable adjectives, longer adjectives, and most adverbs, use *more* and *most: scientific, more scientific, most scientific; elegantly, more elegantly, most elegantly.* If you are not sure, consult the dictionary entry for the simple form.

Irregular adjectives and adverbs

Some short adjectives and adverbs have irregular comparative and superlative forms.

POSITIVE	COMPARATIVE	SUPERLATIVE
good, well	better	best
bad, badly	worse	worst
little (quantity)	less	least
many, much, some	more	most

Comparatives vs. superlatives

Use the comparative to compare two things; use the superlative to compare three or more.

▶ Rome is a much **older** city than New York.

▶ Damascus is one of the ~~older~~ *oldest* cities in the world.

Double comparatives and superlatives

Double comparatives and superlatives are those that unnecessarily use both the *-er* or *-est* ending and *more* or *most*. Occasionally, these forms can act to build a special emphasis, as in the title of Spike Lee's movie *Mo' Better Blues*. In academic and professional writing, however, do not use *more* or *most* before adjectives or adverbs ending in *-er* or *-est*.

▶ Paris is the ~~most~~ loveliest city in the world.

Incomplete comparisons

In speaking, we sometimes state only part of a comparison because the context makes the meaning clear. For example, you might tell a friend "Your car is better," but the context makes it clear that you mean "Your car is better *than mine*." In writing, take the time to check for incomplete comparisons — and to complete them if they are unclear.

▶ The patients taking the drug appeared healthier. *than those receiving a placebo.*

Absolute concepts

Some readers consider modifiers such as *perfect* and *unique* to be absolute concepts; according to this view, a construction such as *more unique* is illogical because a thing is either unique or it isn't, so modified forms of the concept don't make sense. However, many seemingly absolute words have multiple meanings, all of which are widely accepted as correct. For example, *unique* may mean *one of a kind* or *unequaled*, but it can also simply mean *distinctive* or *unusual*.

If you think your readers will object to a construction such as *more perfect* (which appears in the U.S. Constitution) or *somewhat unique* (which was used by J. D. Salinger), then avoid such uses.

EXERCISE 35.2

Revise each of the following sentences to use modifiers correctly, clearly, and effectively. Many of the sentences can be revised in more than one way. Example:

bill to approve a financial plan for the
He is sponsoring a housing project. ~~financial plan approval bill.~~

1. Alicia speaks both Russian and German, but she speaks Russian best.
2. The summers are more rainier in New York than they are in Seattle.
3. He glanced at the menu and ordered the expensivest wine on the list.
4. Most of the elderly are women because women tend to live longer.
5. Minneapolis is the largest of the Twin Cities.
6. She came up with the most silliest plan for revenge.
7. Our theater company has produced several of the famousest classical Greek plays.
8. The student cafeteria is operated by a college food service system chain.
9. It is safer to jog in daylight.
10. Evan argued that subtitled films are boringer to watch than films dubbed in English.

TALKING ABOUT STYLE

Multiple Negation

Speakers of English sometimes use more than one negative at a time (*I can't hardly see you*). Multiple negatives, in fact, have a long history in English and can be found in the works of Chaucer and Shakespeare. It was only in the eighteenth century, in an effort to make English more uniform, that double negatives came to be seen as incorrect. Emphatic double negatives — and triple, quadruple, and more — are used in many varieties of spoken English (*Don't none of you know nothing at all*).

Even though multiple negatives occur in many varieties of English (and in many other languages), in academic or professional writing you will play it safe if you avoid them — unless you are quoting dialogue or creating a special effect.

bedfordstmartins.com/everydaywriter
Exercise Central > Adjectives and Adverbs

EXERCISE 35.3: THINKING CRITICALLY

Reading with an Eye for Adjectives and Adverbs

Gwendolyn Brooks "describes the 'graceful life' as one where people glide over floors in softly glowing rooms, smile correctly over trays of silver, cinnamon, and cream, and retire in quiet elegance."

— MARY HELEN WASHINGTON, "Taming All That Anger Down"

Identify the adjectives and adverbs in the preceding passage, and comment on what they add to the writing. What would be lost if they were removed?

Thinking about Your Own Use of Adjectives and Adverbs

Take a few minutes to study something you can observe or examine closely. In a paragraph or two, describe your subject for someone who has never seen it. Using the guidelines in this chapter, check your use of adjectives and adverbs, and revise your paragraphs. How would you characterize your use of adjectives and adverbs?

36 Modifier Placement

Modifiers enrich writing by making it more concrete or vivid, often adding important or even essential details. To be effective, modifiers should refer clearly to the words they modify and be positioned close to those words. Consider, for example, a sign seen recently in a hotel:

DO NOT USE THE ELEVATORS IN CASE OF FIRE.

Should we really avoid the elevators altogether for fear of causing a fire? Repositioning the modifier *in case of fire* eliminates such confusion—and makes clear that we are to avoid the elevators only if there is a fire: IN CASE OF FIRE, DO NOT USE THE ELEVATORS. This chapter reviews the conventions of accurate modifier placement.

AT A GLANCE

Editing Misplaced or Dangling Modifiers

1. Identify all the modifiers in each sentence, and draw an arrow from each modifier to the word it modifies.

2. If a modifier is far from the word it modifies, try to move the two closer together. (36a)

3. Does any modifier seem to refer to a word other than the one it is intended to modify? If so, move the modifier so that it refers clearly to only the intended word. (36a)

4. If you cannot find the word to which a modifier refers, revise the sentence: supply such a word, or revise the modifier itself so that it clearly refers to a word already in the sentence. (36c)

36a Revise misplaced modifiers.

Modifiers can cause confusion or ambiguity if they are not close enough to the words they modify or if they seem to modify more than one word in the sentence.

> *on voodoo*
> ► She teaches a seminar this term ~~on voodoo~~ at Skyline College.

The voodoo was not at the college; the seminar is.

> *He*   *billowing from every window.*
> ► ~~Billowing from every window,~~ he saw clouds of smoke.

People cannot billow from windows.

> *After he lost the 1962 gubernatorial race,*
> ► Nixon told reporters that he planned to get out of politics. ~~after he lost the 1962 gubernatorial race.~~

The unedited sentence implies that Nixon planned to lose the race.

EXERCISE 36.1

Revise each of the following sentences by moving any misplaced modifiers so that they clearly modify the words they should. Example:

When they propose sensible plans, politicians
Politicians earn support from the people. ~~when they propose sensible plans.~~

1. The comedian had the audience doubled over with laughter relating her stories in a deadpan voice.

2. News reports can increase a listener's irrational fears that emphasize random crime or rare diseases.

3. Studying legal documents and court records from hundreds of years ago, ordinary people in the Middle Ages teach us about everyday life at that time.

4. Risking their lives in war zones, civilians learn about the conflict from the firsthand accounts of journalists abroad.

5. Melena saw lions in the wild on a safari in Africa last spring.

6. Doctors recommend a new test for cancer, which is painless.

7. Every afternoon I find flyers for free pizza left on my windshield.

8. Screeching strings told the audience that the killer was coming after the opening credits.

9. The coach awarded a medal to the most valuable player made of solid brass.

10. Hanging on by a thread, the five-year-old finally lost her tooth.

Limiting modifiers

Be especially careful with the placement of limiting modifiers such as *almost, even, just, merely,* and *only*. In general, these modifiers should be placed right before or after the words they modify. Putting them in other positions may produce not just ambiguity but a completely different meaning.

AMBIGUOUS	The court *only* hears civil cases on Tuesdays.
CLEAR	The court hears only civil cases on Tuesdays.
CLEAR	The court hears civil cases on Tuesdays only.

In the first sentence, placing *only* before *hears* makes the meaning ambiguous. Does the writer mean that civil cases are the only cases heard on Tuesdays or that those are the only days when civil cases are heard?

> *almost*
> ▶ **The city ~~almost~~ spent $20 million on the new stadium.**
> ^

The original sentence suggests the money was almost spent; moving *almost* makes clear that the amount spent was almost $20 million.

Squinting modifiers

If a modifier can refer to either the word before it or the word after it, it is a squinting modifier. Put the modifier where it clearly relates to only a single word.

SQUINTING	Students who practice writing *often* will benefit.
REVISED	Students who often practice writing will benefit.
REVISED	Students who practice writing will often benefit.

EXERCISE 36.2

Revise each of the following sentences in at least two ways. Move the limiting or squinting modifier so that it unambiguously modifies one word or phrase in the sentence. Example:

> *completely*
> The course we hoped would engross us ~~completely~~ bored us.
> ^

> *completely.*
> The course we hoped would engross us ~~completely~~ bored us./
> ^

1. The division that profited most deserves the prize.
2. The soldier was apparently injured by friendly fire.
3. The collector who owned the painting originally planned to leave it to a museum.

4. Alcoholics who try to quit drinking on their own frequently tend to relapse.

5. Ever since I was a child, I have only liked green peas with ham.

36b Revise disruptive modifiers.

Disruptive modifiers interrupt the connections between parts of a grammatical structure or a sentence, making it hard for readers to follow the progress of the thought.

If they are cooked too long, vegetables will
▶ Vegetables will, if they are cooked too long, lose most of their
nutritional value.

In general, do not place a modifier between the *to* and the verb of an infinitive (*to often complain*). Doing so makes it hard for readers to recognize that the two go together.

surrender
▶ Hitler expected the British to fairly quickly ͜ surrender.

In some sentences, however, a modifier sounds awkward if it does not split the infinitive. In such cases, it may be best to reword the sentence to eliminate the infinitive altogether.

SPLIT   I hope *to* almost *equal* my last year's income.

REVISED   I hope that I will earn almost as much as I did last year.

EXERCISE 36.3

Revise each of the following sentences by moving the disruptive modifier so that the sentence reads smoothly. Example:

During the recent economic depression, many
Many unemployed college graduates during the recent economic depression
attended graduate school.

1. Strong economic times have, statistics tell us, led to increases in the college dropout rate.

2. During finals an otherwise honest student, facing high levels of stress, may consider cheating to achieve a higher grade.

3. The director encouraged us to loudly and enthusiastically applaud after each scene.

4. Michael Jordan earned, at the pinnacle of his career, roughly $40 million a year in endorsements.

5. The stock exchange became, because of the sudden trading, a chaotic circus.

36c Revise dangling modifiers.

Dangling modifiers modify nothing in particular in the rest of a sentence. They often *seem* to modify something that is implied but not actually present in the sentence. Dangling modifiers frequently appear at the beginnings or ends of sentences.

DANGLING   Driving nonstop, Salishan Lodge is located two hours from Portland.

REVISED   Driving nonstop from Portland, you can reach Salishan Lodge in two hours.

To revise a dangling modifier, often you need to add a subject that the modifier clearly refers to. In some cases, however, you have to revise the modifier itself, turning it into a phrase or a clause.

> *our family gave away*
> Reluctantly, the hound ~~was given away~~ to a neighbor.

In the original sentence, was the dog reluctant, or was someone else who is not mentioned reluctant?

> *When he was*
> As a young boy, his grandmother told stories of her years as a country schoolteacher.

His grandmother was never a young boy.

> *My*
> ~~Thumbing through the magazine,~~ my eyes automatically noticed the
> *as I was thumbing through the magazine.*
> perfume ads.

Eyes cannot thumb through a magazine.

EXERCISE 36.4

Revise each of the following sentences to correct the dangling phrase. Example:

a viewer gets
Watching television news, an impression is ~~given~~ of constant disaster.

1. No longer obsessed with being the first to report a story, information is now presented as entertainment.

2. Trying to attract younger viewers, news is blended with comedy on late-night talk shows.

3. Highlighting local events, important international news stories may get overlooked.

4. Chosen for their looks, the journalistic credentials of newscasters may be weak.

5. As an interactive medium, people can find information online that reinforces views they already hold.

bedfordstmartins.com/everydaywriter
Exercise Central > Modifier Placement

EXERCISE 36.5: THINKING CRITICALLY

Reading with an Eye for Modifiers

Look at the limiting modifier italicized in the following passage. Identify which word or words it modifies. Then try moving the modifier to some other spot in the sentence, and consider how the meaning of the sentence changes as a result.

> It was, among other things, the sort of railroad you would occasionally ride *just* for the hell of it, a higher existence into which you would escape unconsciously and without hesitation. — E. B. WHITE, "Progress and Change"

Thinking about Your Own Use of Modifiers

As you examine two pages of a draft, check for clear and effective modifiers. Can you identify any misplaced, disruptive, or dangling modifiers? Using the guidelines in this chapter, revise as need be. Then look for patterns — in the kinds of modifiers you use and in any problems you have placing them. Make a note of what you find.

Comma Splices and Fused Sentences **37**

A comma splice results from placing only a comma between clauses. We often see comma splices in advertising and other slogans, where they can provide a catchy rhythm.

> Dogs have owners, cats have staff.
> – BUMPER STICKER

Another related construction is a fused, or run-on, sentence, which results from joining two independent clauses with no punctuation or connecting word between them. The bumper sticker as a fused sentence would be "Dogs have owners cats have staff."

You will seldom profit from using comma splices or fused sentences in academic or professional writing. In fact, doing so will almost always draw an instructor's criticism.

AT A GLANCE

Editing for Comma Splices and Fused Sentences

Two independent clauses — groups of words that can stand alone as sentences — joined with no punctuation form a fused sentence. Two such clauses joined only by a comma form a comma splice. Here are six methods of editing comma splices and fused sentences. As you edit, look at the sentences around the ones you are revising to determine how a particular method will affect the rhythm of the passage.

1. Separate the clauses into two sentences. (37a)

   ▶ *Education* is an elusive word, *It* it often means different things to different people.

2. Link the clauses with a comma and a coordinating conjunction (*and, but, or, nor, for, so,* or *yet*). (37b)

   ▶ *Education* is an elusive word, *for* it often means different things to different people.

3. Link the clauses with a semicolon. (37c)

   ▶ *Education* is an elusive word, *;* it often means different things to different people.

   If the clauses are linked with only a comma and a conjunctive adverb — a word like *however, then, therefore* — add a semicolon.

   ▶ *Education* is an elusive word, *;* indeed, it often means different things to different people.

4. Recast the two clauses as one independent clause. (37d)

   ▶ *An elusive word, education*
   Education is an elusive word, it often means different things to different people.

5. Recast one independent clause as a dependent clause. (37e)

   ▶ *Education* is an elusive word, *because* it often means different things to different people.

6. In informal writing, link the clauses with a dash. (37f)

   ▶ *Education* is an elusive word, — its meaning varies.

37a Separate the clauses into two sentences.

The simplest way to revise comma splices or fused sentences is to separate them into two sentences.

COMMA
SPLICE

> My mother spends long hours every spring tilling the
>
> *This*
> soil and moving manure/. this part of gardening is
>   ^
>
> nauseating.

FUSED
SENTENCE

> My mother spends long hours every spring tilling the
>
> *This*
> soil and moving manure. this part of gardening is
>   ^
>
> nauseating.

If the two clauses are very short, making them two sentences may sound abrupt and terse, so some other method of revision is probably preferable.

37b Link the clauses with a comma and a coordinating conjunction.

If the two clauses are closely related and equally important, join them with a comma and a coordinating conjunction (*and, but, or, nor, for, so,* or *yet*). (See 25a.)

COMMA
SPLICE

> *and*
> I got up feeling bad, I feel even worse now.
>   ^

FUSED
SENTENCE

> *but*
> I should pay my tuition, I need a new car.
>   ^

37c Link the clauses with a semicolon.

If the ideas in the two clauses are closely related and you want to give them equal emphasis, link them with a semicolon.

COMMA
SPLICE

> This photograph is not at all realistic/; it even uses
>   ^
> dreamlike images to convey its message.

FUSED SENTENCE	The practice of journalism is changing dramatically; advances in technology have sped up news cycles.

Be careful when you link clauses with a conjunctive adverb or a transitional phrase. You must precede such words and phrases with a semicolon (see Chapter 40), with a period, or with a comma combined with a coordinating conjunction (25a).

COMMA SPLICE	Many developing countries have very high birthrates/; therefore, most of their citizens are young.

FUSED SENTENCE	Many developing countries have very high birthrates. *T* therefore, most of their citizens are young.

FUSED SENTENCE	Many developing countries have very high birthrates, *and,* therefore, most of their citizens are young.

SOME CONJUNCTIVE ADVERBS AND TRANSITIONAL PHRASES

also	in contrast	next
anyway	indeed	now
besides	in fact	otherwise
certainly	instead	similarly
finally	likewise	still
furthermore	meanwhile	then
however	moreover	therefore
in addition	namely	thus
incidentally	nevertheless	undoubtedly

FOR MULTILINGUAL WRITERS

Judging Sentence Length

In U.S. academic contexts, readers sometimes find a series of short sentences "choppy" and undesirable. If you want to connect two independent clauses into one sentence, be sure to join them using one of the methods discussed in this chapter so that you avoid creating a comma splice or fused sentence. Another useful tip for writing in American English is to avoid writing several very long sentences in a row. If you find this pattern in your writing, try breaking it up by including a shorter sentence occasionally. (See Chapter 30.)

TALKING ABOUT STYLE

Comma Splices in Context

Spliced and fused sentences appear frequently in literary and journalistic writing, where they can create momentum with a rush of details:

> Bald eagles are common, ospreys abound, we have herons and mergansers and kingfishers, we have logging with Percherons and Belgians, we have park land and nature trails, we have enough oddballs, weirdos, and loons to satisfy anybody.
>
> – ANNE CAMERON

Context is critical. Depending on audience, purpose, and situation, structures commonly considered errors can be appropriate and effective.

37d Rewrite the clauses as one independent clause.

Sometimes you can reduce two spliced or fused independent clauses to a single independent clause.

COMMA SPLICE

Most
A ~~large part~~ of my mail is advertisements/ *and* ~~most of the~~ ~~rest is~~ bills.

37e Rewrite one independent clause as a dependent clause.

When one independent clause is more important than the other, try converting the less important one to a dependent clause (25b).

COMMA SPLICE

which reacted against mass production,
The arts and crafts movement, called for handmade objects/. ~~it reacted against mass production.~~

In the revision, the writer chooses to emphasize the first clause, the one describing what the movement advocated, and to make the second clause, the one describing what it reacted against, into a dependent clause.

FUSED SENTENCE

Although
Zora Neale Hurston is regarded as one of America's major novelists, she died in obscurity.

In the revision, the writer chooses to emphasize the second clause and to make the first one into a dependent clause by adding the subordinating conjunction *although*.

37f Link the two clauses with a dash.

In informal writing, you can use a dash to join the two clauses, especially when the second clause elaborates on the first clause.

COMMA
SPLICE
Exercise trends come and go, this year yoga is hot.

✓ **LearningCurve** game-like quizzing can take you to the next level.
bedfordstmartins.com/everydaywriter/LC > Comma Splices and Fused Sentences

EXERCISE 37.1

Using two of the methods discussed in this chapter, revise each item to correct its comma splice or fused sentence. Use each of the methods at least once. Example:

so
I had misgivings about the marriage, I did not attend the ceremony.

Because
I had misgivings about the marriage, I did not attend the ceremony.

1. Many motorists are unaware of the dangers of texting while driving, lawmakers have taken the matter into their own hands.

2. The tallest human on record was Robert Wadlow he reached an amazing height of eight feet, eleven inches.

3. Some employers provide on-site care for the children of their employees, others reimburse workers for day-care costs.

4. The number of vaccine manufacturers has plummeted the industry has been hit with a flood of lawsuits.

5. Most crustaceans live in the ocean, some also live on land or in freshwater habitats.

6. She inherited some tribal customs from her grandmother, she knows the sewing technique called Seminole patchwork.

7. Don't throw your soda cans in the trash recycle them.

8. My West Indian neighbor has lived in New England for years, nevertheless, she always feels betrayed by winter.

9. The Hope diamond in the Smithsonian Institution is impressive in fact, it looks even larger in person than online.

10. You signed up for the course now you'll have to do the work.

EXERCISE 37.2

Revise the following paragraph, eliminating all comma splices by using a period or a semicolon. Then revise the paragraph again, this time using any of the other methods discussed in this chapter. Comment on the two revisions. What differences in rhythm do you detect? Which version do you prefer, and why?

We may disagree on the causes of global warming, however, we cannot ignore that it is happening. Of course we still experience cold winters, on the other hand, average global temperatures have risen drastically for the last three decades. Polar ice caps are melting, as a result, sea levels are rising. Scientists predict more extreme weather in the coming decades, droughts will probably be more common, in addition, flooding and tropical storm activity may increase. Some experts fear that rising temperatures may cause large amounts of methane gases to be released, this could be disastrous for our atmosphere. Climate change may have human causes, it might be a natural occurrence, nevertheless, we must find ways to save our planet.

 bedfordstmartins.com/everydaywriter
Exercise Central > Comma Splices and Fused Sentences

EXERCISE 37.3: THINKING CRITICALLY

Reading with an Eye for Special Effects

Roger Angell is known as a careful and correct stylist, yet he often deviates from the "correct" to create special effects, as in this passage about pitcher David Cone:

And then he won. Next time out, on August 10th, handed a seven-run lead against the A's, he gave up two runs over six innings, with eight strike-outs. He had tempo, he had poise.   — ROGER ANGELL, "Before the Fall"

Angell uses a comma splice in the last sentence to emphasize parallel ideas; any conjunction, even *and*, would change the causal relationship he wishes to show. Because the splice is unexpected, it attracts just the attention that Angell wants for his statement.

Look through some stories or essays to find comma splices and fused sentences. Copy down one or two and enough of the surrounding text to show context, and comment in writing on the effects they create.

Thinking about Any Comma Splices and Fused Sentences in Your Own Writing

Go through some essays you have written, checking for comma splices and fused sentences. Revise any you find, using the methods discussed in this chapter. Comment on your chosen methods.

38   Sentence Fragments

S entence fragments are often used to make writing sound conversational, as in this Facebook status update:

> Realizing that there are no edible bagels in this part of Oregon. Sigh.

Fragments—groups of words that are punctuated as sentences but are not sentences—are often seen in intentionally informal writing and in public writing, such as advertising, that aims to attract attention or give a phrase special emphasis. But you should think carefully before using fragments in academic or professional writing, where some readers might regard them as errors.

AT A GLANCE

Editing for Sentence Fragments

A group of words must meet three criteria to form a complete sentence. If it does not meet all three, it is a fragment. Revise a fragment by combining it with a nearby sentence or by rewriting it as a complete sentence.

1. A sentence must have a subject. (31j)

2. A sentence must have a verb, not just a verbal. A verbal cannot function as a sentence's verb without an auxiliary verb. (31k and l)

    VERB   The terrier is *barking*.

    VERBAL   The terrier *barking*.

3. Unless it is a question, a sentence must have at least one clause that does not begin with a subordinating word. (31h) Following are some common subordinating words:

although	if	when
as	since	where
because	that	whether
before	though	which
how	unless	who

38a Revise phrase fragments.

Phrases are groups of words that lack a subject, a verb, or both (311). When verbal phrases, prepositional phrases, noun phrases, and appositive phrases are punctuated like sentences, they become fragments. To revise these fragments, attach them to an independent clause, or make them a separate sentence.

▶ NBC is broadcasting the debates. With discussions afterward.
(with)

> *With discussions afterward* is a prepositional phrase, not a sentence. The editing combines the phrase with an independent clause.

▶ The town's growth is controlled by zoning laws. A strict set of
(a)

regulations for builders and corporations.

> *A strict set of regulations for builders and corporations* is an appositive phrase renaming the noun *zoning laws*. The editing attaches the fragment to the sentence containing that noun.

▶ Kamika stayed out of school for three months after Linda was born.

She did so to
To recuperate and to take care of the baby.

> *To recuperate and to take care of the baby* includes verbals, not verbs. The revision—adding a subject (*she*) and a verb (*did*)—turns the fragment into a separate sentence.

Fragments beginning with transitions

If you introduce an example or explanation with one of the following transitions, be certain you write a sentence, not a fragment.

also	for example	like
as a result	for instance	such as
besides	instead	that is

▶ Joan Didion has written on many subjects. Such as the Hoover Dam
(such)

and migraine headaches.

> The second word group is a phrase, not a sentence. The editing combines it with an independent clause.

38b Revise compound-predicate fragments.

A compound predicate consists of two or more verbs, along with their modifiers and objects, that have the same subject. Fragments occur when one part of a compound predicate lacks a subject but is punctuated as a separate sentence. These fragments usually begin with *and*, *but*, or *or*. You can revise them by attaching them to the independent clause that contains the rest of the predicate.

▶ They sold their house. ̷And̷ moved into an apartment.
and

EXERCISE 38.1

Revise each of the following items to eliminate any sentence fragments, either by combining fragments with independent clauses or by rewriting them as separate sentences. Example:

Zoe looked close to tears. Standing with her head bowed./
Zoe looked close to tears.

Zoe looked close to tears. Standing with her head bowed.
She was standing

1. Long stretches of white beaches and shady palm trees. Give tourists the impression of an island paradise.

2. Forgetting to study for an exam. That is what many college students are afraid of.

3. Much of New Orleans is below sea level. Making it susceptible to flooding.

4. Uncle Ron forgot to bring his clarinet to the party. Fortunately for us.

5. Oscar night is an occasion for celebrating the film industry. And criticizing the fashion industry.

6. Diners in Creole restaurants might try shrimp gumbo. Or order turtle soup.

7. In the late 1940s, women began hosting Tupperware parties. Casual gatherings in which the hosts act as salespersons.

8. Attempting to lose ten pounds in less than a week. I ate only cottage cheese and grapefruit.

9. Our parents did not realize that we were hoarding our candy. Under our beds.

10. Thomas Edison was famous for his inventions. For example, the phonograph and the first practical lightbulb.

38c Revise dependent-clause fragments.

Dependent clauses contain both a subject and a verb, but they cannot stand alone as sentences; they depend on an independent clause to complete their meaning. Dependent clauses usually begin with words such as *after, because, before, if, since, though, unless, until, when, where, while, who, which,* and *that.* You can usually combine dependent-clause fragments with a nearby independent clause.

▶ **When I decided to work part-time,/ I gave up a lot of my earning potential.**

If you cannot smoothly attach a clause to a nearby independent clause, try deleting the opening subordinating word and turning the dependent clause into a sentence.

▶ **The majority of injuries in automobile accidents occur in two ways.**

An

~~When an~~ occupant either is hurt by something inside the car or is

thrown from the car.

EXERCISE 38.2

Identify all the sentence fragments in the following items, and explain why each is grammatically incomplete. Then revise each one in at least two ways. Example:

Controlling my temper,/ That has been one of my goals this year.

One of my goals this year has been controlling
~~Controlling my temper. That has been one of my goals this year.~~

1. As soon as the seventy-five-year-old cellist walked onstage. The audience burst into applause.
2. The patient has only one intention. To smoke behind the doctor's back.
3. Some reality shows feature people working in dangerous situations. Such as fishing for Alaskan king crab or logging in swamps.
4. After writing and rewriting for almost three years. She finally felt that her novel was complete.
5. In the wake of the earthquake. Relief workers tried to provide food and shelter to victims.
6. Forster stopped writing novels after *A Passage to India.* Which is one of the greatest novels of the twentieth century.
7. Because only two students signed up. The class was canceled this semester.
8. I started running in April. And ran my first marathon in September.
9. We sat stunned as she delivered her monologue. A ten-minute speech about everything we had done to annoy her.
10. All primates have opposable thumbs. Which sets them apart from other mammals.

LearningCurve game-like quizzing can take you to the next level.
bedfordstmartins.com/everydaywriter/LC > Fragments

EXERCISE 38.3: THINKING CRITICALLY

Reading with an Eye for Fragments

Identify the fragments in the following passage. What effect does the writer achieve by using fragments rather than complete sentences?

> On Sundays, for religion, we went up on the hill. Skipping along the hexagon-shaped tile in Colonial Park. Darting up the steps to Edgecomb Avenue. Stopping in the candy store on St. Nicholas to load up. Leaning forward for leverage to finish the climb up to the church. I was always impressed by this particular house of the Lord.   — KEITH GILYARD, *Voices of the Self*

Thinking about Any Fragments in Your Own Writing

Read through some essays you have written. Using the guidelines in this chapter, see whether you find any sentence fragments. If so, do you recognize any patterns? Do you write fragments when you're attempting to add emphasis? Are they all dependent clauses? phrases? Note any patterns you discover, and make a point of routinely checking your writing for fragments. Finally, revise any fragments to form complete sentences.

Punctuation
and Mechanics

The function of most punctuation . . . is to add
precision and complexity to meaning. It increases
the information potential of strings of words.

— LOUIS MENAND

Punctuation and Mechanics

39 Commas *400*

 a Use commas to set off introductory words, phrases, and clauses *400*
 b Use commas with conjunctions that join clauses in compound sentences *402*
 c Use commas to set off nonrestrictive elements *403*
 d Use commas with items in a series *405*
 e Use commas to set off parenthetical and transitional expressions *406*
 f Use commas to set off contrasting elements, interjections, direct address, and tag questions *407*
 g Use commas with dates, addresses, titles, and numbers *408*
 h Use commas to set off most quotations *409*
 i Use commas to prevent confusion *410*
 j Eliminate unnecessary commas *410*

40 Semicolons *412*

 a Use semicolons to link independent clauses *412*
 b Use semicolons to separate items in a series containing other punctuation *413*
 c Revise misused semicolons *414*

41 End Punctuation *415*

 a Periods *416*
 b Question marks *416*
 c Exclamation points *417*

42 Apostrophes *419*

 a Use apostrophes appropriately to show possession *419*
 b Use apostrophes in contractions *421*
 c Avoid apostrophes in most plural forms *421*

43 Quotation Marks *422*

 a Use quotation marks to identify direct quotations *423*
 b Punctuate block quotations and poetry appropriately *424*
 c Use quotation marks for titles of short works *425*
 d Use quotation marks appropriately for definitions *425*
 e Use quotation marks to identify irony and invented terms *425*

For visual analysis Look carefully at the illustration on the front of this tab. How might it relate to the idea of punctuation and other mechanical features of writing?

f Follow conventions for other punctuation with quotation marks   *426*

g Revise misused quotation marks   *427*

---

44 Other Punctuation   *428*
a Parentheses   *429*
b Brackets   *430*
c Dashes   *431*
d Colons   *432*
e Slashes   *434*
f Ellipses   *434*

---

45 Capital Letters   *437*
a Capitalize the first word of a sentence or line of poetry   *437*
b Capitalize proper nouns and proper adjectives   *438*
c Capitalize titles of works   *439*
d Revise unnecessary capitalization   *440*

---

46 Abbreviations and Numbers   *442*
a Abbreviate some titles before and all titles after proper names   *442*
b Abbreviate years and hours appropriately   *443*
c Abbreviate some business, government, and science terms   *443*
d Use abbreviations in official company names   *444*
e Use Latin abbreviations appropriately   *444*
f Use symbols and unit abbreviations appropriately   *444*
g Use other abbreviations according to convention   *444*
h Spell out numbers expressed in one or two words   *446*
i Spell out numbers that begin sentences   *446*
j Use figures according to convention   *446*

---

47 Italics   *448*
a Italicize titles of long works   *448*
b Italicize words, letters, and numbers used as terms   *449*
c Italicize non-English words and phrases   *449*

---

48 Hyphens   *450*
a Use hyphens with compound words   *451*
b Use hyphens with prefixes and suffixes   *452*
c Avoid unnecessary hyphens   *452*

39 Commas

Commas often play a crucial role in meaning. See how important the comma is in the following directions for making hot cereal:

Add Cream of Wheat slowly, stirring constantly.

That sentence tells the cook to *add the cereal slowly*. If the comma came before the word *slowly,* however, the cook might add all of the cereal at once and *stir slowly*. Using commas correctly can help you communicate more effectively.

39a Use commas to set off introductory words, phrases, and clauses.

► However, health care costs keep rising.

► In the end, only you can decide.

► Wearing new running shoes, Logan prepared for the race.

► To win the contest, Connor needed skill and luck.

► Pencil poised in anticipation, Audrey waited for the drawing contest to begin.

► While her friends watched, Lila practiced her gymnastics routine.

Some writers omit the comma if the introductory element is short and does not seem to require a pause after it.

► *At the racetrack* Henry lost his entire paycheck.

However, you will seldom be wrong if you use a comma after an introductory element.

EXERCISE 39.1

In the following sentences, add any commas that are needed after the introductory element. Example:

To find a good day-care provider, parents usually need both time and money.

1. After the concession speech the senator's supporters drifted out of the room.
2. To our surprise the charity auction raised enough money to build a new technology center.
3. Unaware that the microphone was on the candidate made an offensive comment.
4. Whenever someone rings the doorbell her dog goes berserk.
5. Therefore Sasha must take a summer course to receive her diploma.
6. With the fifth century came the fall of the Roman Empire.
7. A tray of shrimp in one hand and a pile of napkins in the other the waiter avoided me.
8. Toward the rapids floated an empty rubber raft.
9. When they woke up the exhausted campers no longer wanted to hike.
10. Tears in his eyes Keflezighi won the marathon.

AT A GLANCE

Editing for Commas

Research for this book shows that five of the most common errors in college writing involve commas. Check your writing for these errors:

1. Check every sentence that doesn't begin with the subject to see whether it opens with an introductory element (a word, phrase, or clause that describes the subject or tells when, where, how, or why the main action of the sentence occurs). Use a comma to separate the introductory material from the main part of the sentence. (39a)

2. Look at every sentence that contains one of the conjunctions *and*, *but*, *or*, *nor*, *for*, *so*, or *yet*. If the groups of words both before and after the conjunction function as complete sentences, you have a compound sentence. Make sure to use a comma before the conjunction. (39b)

3. Look at each adjective clause beginning with *which*, *who*, *whom*, *whose*, *when*, or *where*, and at each phrase and appositive. (31m) Is the element essential to the meaning of the sentence? If the sentence would be unclear without it, do not set off the element with commas. (39c)

4. Make sure that adjective clauses beginning with *that* are not set off with commas. (39c and j) Do not use commas between subjects and verbs, verbs and objects or complements, or prepositions and objects; to separate parts of compound constructions other than compound sentences; to set off restrictive clauses; or before the first or after the last item in a series. (39j)

5. Do not use a comma alone to separate sentences (see Chapter 37).

39b Use commas with conjunctions that join clauses in compound sentences.

A comma usually precedes a coordinating conjunction (*and, but, or, nor, for, so,* or *yet*) that joins two independent clauses in a compound sentence (31m).

▶ The title sounds impressive‚ but *administrative clerk* is just another word for *photocopier.*

▶ The show started at last‚ and the crowd grew quiet.

With very short clauses, you can sometimes omit the comma.

▶ She saw her chance and she took it.

Always use the comma if there is any chance the sentence will be misread without it.

▶ I opened the junk drawer‚ and the cabinet door jammed.

Use a semicolon rather than a comma when the clauses are long and complex or contain their own commas.

▶ When these early migrations took place, the ice was still confined to the lands in the far north; but eight hundred thousand years ago, when man was already established in the temperate latitudes, the ice moved southward until it covered large parts of Europe and Asia.
　　　　　　　　　　　　　　　 – ROBERT JASTROW, *Until the Sun Dies*

EXERCISE 39.2

Use a comma and a coordinating conjunction (*and, but, for, nor, or, so,* or *yet*) to combine each of the following pairs of sentences into one sentence. Delete or rearrange words if necessary. Example:

I had finished studying for the test‚/ᵴᵒ‚ I went to bed.

1. The chef did not want to serve a heavy dessert. She was planning to have a rich stew for the main course.

2. My mother rarely allowed us to eat sweets. Halloween was a special exception.

3. Scientists have mapped the human genome. They learn more every day about how genes affect an individual's health.

4. Perhaps I will change my name when I get married. Maybe I will keep my maiden name.

5. Penguins cannot fly. They cannot walk the way other birds do.

39c Use commas to set off nonrestrictive elements.

Nonrestrictive elements are word groups that do not limit, or restrict, the meaning of the noun or pronoun they modify. Setting nonrestrictive elements off with commas shows your readers that the information is not essential to the meaning of the sentence. Restrictive elements, on the other hand, *are* essential to meaning and should *not* be set off with commas. The same sentence may mean different things with and without the commas:

▶ **The bus drivers rejecting the management offer remained on strike.**

▶ **The bus drivers, rejecting the management offer, remained on strike.**

The first sentence says that only *some* bus drivers, the ones rejecting the offer, remained on strike. The second says that *all* the drivers did.

Since the decision to include or omit commas affects how readers interpret your sentence, you should think especially carefully about what you mean and use commas (or omit them) accordingly.

RESTRICTIVE   Drivers *who have been convicted of drunken driving* should lose their licenses.

In the preceding sentence, the clause *who have been convicted of drunken driving* is essential because it explains that only drivers who have been convicted of drunken driving should lose their licenses. Therefore, it is *not* set off with commas.

NONRESTRICTIVE   The two drivers involved in the accident, *who have been convicted of drunken driving,* should lose their licenses.

In the second sentence, however, the clause *who have been convicted of drunken driving* is not essential to the meaning because it merely provides more information about what it modifies, *The two drivers involved in the accident.* Therefore, the clause is set off with commas.

To decide whether an element is restrictive or nonrestrictive, read the sentence without the element, and see if the deletion changes the meaning of the rest of the sentence. If the deletion does change the meaning, the element is probably restrictive, and you should not set it off with commas. If it does not change the meaning, the element is probably nonrestrictive and requires commas.

Adjective and adverb clauses

An adjective clause that begins with *that* is always restrictive; do not set it off with commas. An adjective clause beginning with *which* may be either restrictive or nonrestrictive; however, some writers prefer to use *which* only for nonrestrictive clauses, which they set off with commas.

▶ **The claim** *that men like seriously to battle one another to some sort of finish* **is a myth.**   – JOHN MCMURTRY, "Kill 'Em! Crush 'Em! Eat 'Em Raw!"

The *that* clause is necessary to the meaning because it explains which claim is a myth; therefore, the clause is not set off with commas.

▶ **The man/ who rescued Jana's puppy/ won her eternal gratitude.**

The *who* clause is necessary to the meaning because only the man who rescued the puppy won the gratitude; therefore, the clause takes no commas.

▶ **I borrowed books from the rental library of Shakespeare and Company,** *which was the library and bookstore of Sylvia Beach at 12 rue de l'Odeon.*
          – ERNEST HEMINGWAY, *A Moveable Feast*

The clause describing Shakespeare and Company is not necessary to the meaning of the sentence and therefore is set off with a comma.

In general, set off an adverb clause that follows a main clause only if it begins with *although, even though, while,* or another subordinating conjunction expressing contrast.

▶ **He uses semicolons frequently, while she prefers periods and short**

sentences.

The clause *while she prefers periods and short sentences* expresses contrast; therefore, it is set off with a comma.

Do *not* set off any other adverb clause that follows a main clause.

▶ **Remember to check your calculations/ before you submit the form.**

Phrases

Participial phrases may be restrictive or nonrestrictive. Prepositional phrases are usually restrictive, but sometimes they are not essential to the meaning of a sentence and are set off with commas (311).

▶ **Frédéric Chopin, in poor health, still composed prolifically.**

The phrase *in poor health* does not limit the meaning of *Frédéric Chopin* and so is set off with commas.

Appositives

An appositive renames a nearby noun (311). When an appositive is not essential to identify what it renames, it is set off with commas.

NONRESTRICTIVE APPOSITIVES

▶ **Jon Stewart, the comic and news commentator, often pokes fun at political leaders.**

Jon Stewart's name identifies him; the appositive *the comic and news commentator* provides extra information.

RESTRICTIVE APPOSITIVES

▶ **Mozart's opera/ *The Marriage of Figaro*/ was considered revolutionary.**

The appositive is restrictive because Mozart wrote more than one opera.

EXERCISE 39.3

Use commas to set off nonrestrictive clauses, phrases, and appositives in any of the following sentences that contain such elements.

1. What can you buy for the person who has everything?
2. Embalming is a technique that preserves a cadaver.
3. The enormous new house which was the largest in the neighborhood had replaced a much smaller old home.
4. The rescue workers exhausted and discouraged stared ahead without speaking.
5. The new mall has the same stores and restaurants as all the other malls in town.
6. Viruses unlike bacteria can reproduce only by infecting live cells.
7. Napoléon was imprisoned after his defeat at the battle of Waterloo.
8. Hammurabi an ancient Babylonian king created laws that were carved on a stone for public display.
9. Birds' hearts have four chambers whereas reptiles' have three.
10. A female cheetah hisses and swats if another animal gets too close to her young.

39d Use commas with items in a series.

▶ **He has plundered our seas, ravaged our coasts, burnt our towns, and destroyed the lives of our people.** – Declaration of Independence

You may see a series with no comma after the next-to-last item, particularly in newspaper writing. Occasionally, however, omitting the comma can cause confusion.

▶ **All the cafeteria's vegetables—broccoli, green beans, peas, and carrots— were cooked to a gray mush.**

Without the comma after *peas,* you wouldn't know if there were three choices (the third being a *mixture* of peas and carrots) or four.

When the items in a series contain commas of their own or other punctuation, separate them with semicolons rather than commas (40b).

Coordinate adjectives, those that relate equally to the noun they modify, should be separated by commas.

▶ **The long, twisting, muddy road led to a shack in the woods.**

In a sentence like *The cracked bathroom mirror reflected his face,* however, *cracked* and *bathroom* are not coordinate because *bathroom mirror* is the equivalent of a single word, which is modified by *cracked.* Hence, they are *not* separated by commas.

You can usually determine whether adjectives are coordinate by inserting *and* between them. If the sentence makes sense with the *and*, the adjectives are coordinate and should be separated by commas.

▶ **They are sincere *and* talented *and* inquisitive researchers.**

The sentence makes sense with the *and*s, so the adjectives should be separated by commas: *They are sincere, talented, inquisitive researchers.*

▶ **Byron carried an elegant *and* pocket watch.**

The sentence does not make sense with *and,* so the adjectives *elegant* and *pocket* should not be separated by commas: *Byron carried an elegant pocket watch.*

EXERCISE 39.4

Revise any of the following sentences that require commas to set off words, phrases, or clauses in a series.

1. The students donated clothing school supplies and nonperishable food.
2. The hot humid weather did not stop the fans from flocking to the free outdoor concert.
3. The ball sailed over the fence across the yard and through the Wilsons' window.
4. Several art historians inspected the Chinese terra-cotta figures.
5. The young athletes' parents insist on calling every play judging every move and telling everyone within earshot exactly what is wrong with the team.

39e Use commas to set off parenthetical and transitional expressions.

Parenthetical expressions add comments or information. Because they often interrupt the flow of a sentence or digress, they are usually set off with commas.

▶ Some studies have shown that chocolate, of all things, helps to prevent tooth decay.

▶ Roald Dahl's stories, it turns out, were often inspired by his own childhood.

Transitional expressions, conjunctive adverbs (words such as *however* and *furthermore*), and other words and phrases used to connect parts of sentences are usually set off with commas (8e).

▶ Ozone is a by-product of dry cleaning, for example.

▶ Ceiling fans are, moreover, less expensive than air conditioners.

39f Use commas to set off contrasting elements, interjections, direct address, and tag questions.

CONTRASTING ELEMENTS

▶ On official business it was she, not my father, one would usually hear on the phone or in stores.

— RICHARD RODRIGUEZ, "Aria: A Memoir of a Bilingual Childhood"

INTERJECTIONS

▶ My God, who wouldn't want a wife?   — JUDY BRADY, "I Want a Wife"

DIRECT ADDRESS

▶ Remember, sir, that you are under oath.

TAG QUESTIONS

▶ The governor did not veto the unemployment bill, did she?

EXERCISE 39.5

Revise each of the following sentences, using commas to set off parenthetical and transitional expressions, contrasting elements, interjections, words used in direct address, and tag questions.

1. One must consider the society as a whole not just its parts.
2. Drinking caffeinated beverages can in fact be good for your health.
3. You don't expect me to read this speech do you?
4. Coming in ahead of schedule and under budget it appears is the only way to keep this client happy.
5. Believe me Jenna I had no idea things would turn out this way.

39g Use commas with dates, addresses, titles, and numbers.

Dates

Use a comma between the day of the week and the month, between the day of the month and the year, and between the year and the rest of the sentence, if any.

▶ The attacks on the morning of Tuesday, September 11, 2001, took the United States by surprise.

Do not use commas with dates in inverted order or with dates consisting of only the month and the year.

▶ She dated the letter *26 August 2008.*

▶ Thousands of Germans swarmed over the wall in *November 1989.*

Addresses and place-names

Use a comma after each part of an address or place-name, including the state if there is no ZIP code. Do not precede a ZIP code with a comma.

▶ Forward my mail to the Department of English, The Ohio State University, Columbus, Ohio 43210.

▶ Portland, Oregon, is much larger than Portland, Maine.

Titles

Use commas to set off a title such as *MD* or *PhD* from the name preceding it and from the rest of the sentence. The titles *Jr.* and *Sr.,* however, often appear without commas.

▶ Oliver Sacks, MD, has written about the way the mind works.

▶ Martin Luther King Jr. was one of the twentieth century's greatest orators.

Numbers

In numerals of five digits or more, use a comma between each group of three, starting from the right.

▶ The city's population rose to 158,000 in the 2000 census.

The comma is optional within numerals of four digits but never occurs in four-digit dates, street addresses, or page numbers.

► The college had an enrollment of *1,789* [or *1789*] in the fall of 2008.

► My grandparents live at *2428* Loring Place.

► Turn to page *1566.*

EXERCISE 39.6

Revise each of the following sentences, using commas appropriately with dates, addresses, place-names, titles, and numbers.

1. The city of Dublin Ireland has a population of over 500000.
2. I rode a total of almost 1200 miles on my bike in 2009.
3. New Delhi India and Islamabad Pakistan became the capitals of two independent nations at midnight on August 15 1947.
4. MLA headquarters are at 26 Broadway New York New York 10004.
5. I was convinced that the nameplate I. M. Well MD was one of my sister's pranks.

39h Use commas to set off most quotations.

Commas set off a quotation from words used to introduce or identify the source of the quotation. A comma following a quotation goes inside the closing quotation mark. (See 44d for advice about using colons instead of commas to introduce quotations.)

► A German proverb warns, "Go to law for a sheep, and lose your cow."

► "All I know about grammar," said Joan Didion, "is its infinite power."

Do not use a comma after a question mark or exclamation point.

► "What's a thousand dollars?/" asks Groucho Marx in *Cocoanuts.*
   "Mere chicken feed. A poultry matter."

► "Out, damned spot!/" cries Lady Macbeth.

Do not use a comma when you introduce a quotation with *that.*

► The writer of Ecclesiastes concludes that/ "all is vanity."

Do not use a comma before an indirect quotation—one that does not use the speaker's exact words.

► Patrick Henry declared/ that he wanted either liberty or death.

EXERCISE 39.7

Insert a comma in any of the following sentences that require one.

1. "The public be damned!" William Henry Vanderbilt was reported to have said. "I'm working for my stockholders."
2. My mother was fond of telling me "You'd make coffee nervous!"
3. I refuse to believe the old saying that "nice guys finish last."
4. "Learning without thought is labor lost; thought without learning is perilous" Confucius argued.
5. "Do you have any idea who I am?" the well-dressed man asked belligerently.

39i Use commas to prevent confusion.

Sometimes commas are necessary to make sentences easier to read or understand.

▶ The members of the dance troupe strutted in, in matching costumes.

▶ Before, I had planned to major in biology.

39j Eliminate unnecessary commas.

Excessive use of commas can spoil an otherwise fine sentence.

Around restrictive elements

Do not use commas to set off restrictive elements—elements that limit, or define, the meaning of the words they modify or refer to (39c).

▶ I don't let my children watch films/ that are violent.

▶ A law/ reforming campaign financing/ was passed in 2002.

▶ My only defense/ against my allergies/ is to stay indoors.

▶ The actor/ Philip Seymour Hoffman/ might win the award.

Between subjects and verbs, verbs and objects or complements, and prepositions and objects

Do not use a comma between a subject and its verb, a verb and its object or complement, or a preposition and its object. This rule holds true even if the subject, object, or complement is a long phrase or clause.

▶ Watching movies late at night/ is a way for me to relax.

▶ Parents must decide/ how much television their children may watch.

▶ The winner of/ the community-service award stepped forward.

In compound constructions

In compound constructions (other than compound sentences—see 39b), do not use a comma before or after a coordinating conjunction that joins the two parts.

▶ Improved health care/ and more free trade were two of the administration's goals.

The *and* here joins parts of a compound subject, which should not be separated by a comma.

▶ Donald Trump was born rich/ and used his money to make money.

The *and* here joins parts of a compound predicate, which should not be separated by a comma.

Before the first or after the last item in a series

▶ The auction included/ furniture, paintings, and china.

▶ The swimmer took slow, elegant, powerful/ strokes.

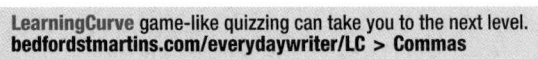

✓ **LearningCurve** game-like quizzing can take you to the next level.
bedfordstmartins.com/everydaywriter/LC > Commas

EXERCISE 39.8: THINKING CRITICALLY

Reading with an Eye for Commas

The following poem uses commas to create rhythm and guide readers. Read the poem aloud, listening especially to the effect of the commas at the end of the first and fifth lines. Then read it again as if those commas were omitted, noting the difference. What is the effect of the poet's decision not to use a comma at the end of the third line?

> Some say the world will end in fire,
> Some say in ice.
> From what I've tasted of desire
> I hold with those who favor fire.
> But if it had to perish twice,
> I think I know enough of hate
> To say that for destruction ice
> Is also great
> And would suffice.

> — ROBERT FROST, "Fire and Ice"

Thinking about Your Own Use of Commas

Choose a paragraph that you have written. Remove all of the commas, and read it aloud. What is the effect of leaving out the commas? Now, punctuate the passage with commas, consulting this chapter. Did you replace all of your original commas? Did you add any new ones? Explain why you added the commas you did.

40 Semicolons

The following public-service announcement, posted in New York City subway cars, reminded commuters what to do with a used newspaper at the end of the ride:

> Please put it in a trash can; that's good news for everyone.

The semicolon in the subway announcement separates two clauses that could have been written as separate sentences. Semicolons, which create a pause stronger than that of a comma but not as strong as the full pause of a period, show close connections between related ideas.

40a Use semicolons to link independent clauses.

Though a comma and a coordinating conjunction often join independent clauses, semicolons provide writers with subtler ways of signaling closely related clauses. The clause following a semicolon often restates an idea expressed in the first clause; it sometimes expands on or presents a contrast to the first.

> ▶ **Immigration acts were passed; newcomers had to prove, besides moral correctness and financial solvency, their ability to read.**
> – MARY GORDON, "More Than Just a Shrine"

AT A GLANCE

Editing for Semicolons

- If you use semicolons, be sure they appear only between independent clauses — groups of words that can stand alone as sentences (40a) — or between items in a series. (40b)
- If you find few or no semicolons in your writing, ask yourself whether you should add some. Would any closely related ideas in two sentences be better expressed in one sentence with a semicolon? (40a)

Gordon uses a semicolon to join the two clauses, giving the sentence an abrupt rhythm that suits the topic: laws that imposed strict requirements.

A semicolon should link independent clauses joined by conjunctive adverbs such as *therefore, however,* and *indeed* or transitional expressions such as *in fact, in addition,* and *for example* (31h).

▶ **The circus comes as close to being the world in microcosm as anything I know; in a way, it puts all the rest of show business in the shade.**
– E. B. WHITE, "The Ring of Time"

If two independent clauses joined by a coordinating conjunction contain commas, you may use a semicolon instead of a comma before the conjunction to make the sentence easier to read.

▶ **Every year, whether the Republican or the Democratic party is in office, more and more power drains away from the individual to feed vast reservoirs in far-off places; and we have less and less say about the shape of events which shape our future.**
– WILLIAM F. BUCKLEY JR., "Why Don't We Complain?"

EXERCISE 40.1

Combine each of the following pairs of sentences into one sentence by using a semicolon. Example:

meet

Take the bus to Henderson Street./; ~~Meet~~ me under the clock.

1. Abalone fishing in California is strictly regulated. A person is allowed to harvest only twenty-four of these large mollusks per year.
2. City life offers many advantages. In many ways, however, life in a small town is much more pleasant.
3. The door contains an inflatable slide to be used in an emergency. In addition, each seat can become a flotation device.
4. Most car accidents occur within twenty-five miles of the home. Therefore, you should wear a seat belt on every trip.
5. Involvement in team sports provides more than just health benefits for young girls. It also increases their self-confidence.

40b Use semicolons to separate items in a series containing other punctuation.

Ordinarily, commas separate items in a series (39d). But when the items themselves contain commas or other marks of punctuation, using semicolons to separate the items will make the sentence clearer and easier to read.

▶ Anthropology encompasses archaeology, the study of ancient civilizations through artifacts; linguistics, the study of the structure and development of language; and cultural anthropology, the study of language, customs, and behavior.

40c Revise misused semicolons.

A comma, not a semicolon, should separate an independent clause from a dependent clause or phrase.

▶ The police found fingerprints; which they used to identify the thief.

▶ The new system would encourage students to register for courses online; thus streamlining registration.

A colon, not a semicolon, should introduce a series or list.

▶ The reunion tour includes the following bands; Urban Waste, Murphy's Law, Rapid Deployment, and Ism.

EXERCISE 40.2

Revise the following passage, eliminating any misused or overused semicolons and, if necessary, replacing them with other punctuation.

Hosting your first dinner party can be very stressful; but careful planning and preparation can make it a success. The guest list must contain the right mix of people; everyone should feel comfortable; good talkers and good listeners are both important; while they don't need to agree on everything, you don't want them to have fistfights, either. Then you need to plan the menu; which should steer clear of problem areas; for vegans; no pork chops; for guests with shellfish allergies, no lobster; for teetotallers; no tequila. In addition; make sure your home is clean and neat, and check that you have enough chairs; dishes; glasses; napkins; and silverware. Leave enough time to socialize with your guests; and save a little energy to clean up when it's over!

 **bedfordstmartins.com/everydaywriter**
Exercise Central > Semicolons

EXERCISE 40.3: THINKING CRITICALLY

Reading with an Eye for Semicolons

Read the following paragraph, which describes a solar eclipse, with attention to the use of semicolons. What different effect would the paragraph have if the author had used periods instead of semicolons? What if she had used commas and coordinating conjunctions? What is the effect of all the semicolons?

You see the wide world swaddled in darkness; you see a vast breadth of hilly land, and an enormous, distant, blackened valley; you see towns' lights, a river's path, and blurred portions of your hat and scarf; you see your husband's face looking like an early black-and-white film; and you see a sprawl of black sky and blue sky together, with unfamiliar stars in it, some barely visible bands of cloud, and over there, a small white ring. The ring is as small as one goose in a flock of migrating geese — if you happen to notice a flock of migrating geese. It is one 360th part of the visible sky. The sun we see is less than half the diameter of a dime held at arms' length. — ANNIE DILLARD, "Solar Eclipse"

Thinking about Your Own Use of Semicolons

Think of something you might take five or ten minutes to observe — a football game, a brewing storm, an argument between friends — and write a paragraph describing your observations point by point and using semicolons to separate each point, as Annie Dillard does in the preceding paragraph. Then, look at the way you used semicolons. Are there places where a period or a comma and a coordinating conjunction would better serve your meaning? Revise appropriately. What can you conclude about effective ways of using semicolons?

End Punctuation 41

Periods, question marks, and exclamation points often appear in advertising to create special effects or draw readers along from line to line.

> You have a choice to make.
> Where can you turn for advice?
> Ask our experts today!

End punctuation tells us how to read each sentence—as a matter-of-fact statement, a query, or an emphatic request. Making appropriate choices with end punctuation allows readers to understand exactly what you mean.

AT A GLANCE

Editing for End Punctuation

- If all or almost all of your sentences end with periods, see if some of them might be phrased more effectively as questions or exclamations. (41a–c)
- Check to be sure you use question marks appropriately. (41b)
- If you use exclamation points, consider whether each is justified. Does the sentence call for extra emphasis? If in doubt, use a period instead. (41c)

41a Periods

Use a period to close sentences that make statements or give mild commands.

▶ **All books are either dreams or swords.** – Amy Lowell

▶ **Don't use a fancy word if a simpler word will do.**
– George Orwell, "Politics and the English Language"

▶ **Please close the door.**

A period also closes indirect questions, which report rather than ask questions.

▶ **I asked how old the child was.**

▶ **We all wonder who will win the election.**

Until recently, periods have been used with most abbreviations in American English (see Chapter 46). However, more and more abbreviations are appearing without periods.

Mr.	MD	BC *or* B.C.
Ms.	PhD	BCE *or* B.C.E.
Mrs.	MBA	AD *or* A.D.
Jr.	RN	AM *or* a.m.
Dr.	Sen.	PM *or* p.m.

Some abbreviations rarely if ever appear with periods. These include the postal abbreviations of state names, such as *FL* and *TN* (though the traditional abbreviations, such as *Fla.* and *Tenn.*, do call for periods), and most groups of initials (*GE, CIA, AIDS, UNICEF*). If you are not sure whether a particular abbreviation should include periods, check a dictionary, or follow the style guidelines (such as those of the Modern Language Association) you are using in a research paper.

41b Question marks

Use question marks to close sentences that ask direct questions.

▶ **How is the human mind like a computer, and how is it different?**
– Kathleen Stassen Berger and Ross A. Thompson,
The Developing Person through Childhood and Adolescence

Question marks do not close *indirect* questions, which report rather than ask questions.

▶ **She asked whether I opposed his nomination.**

Do not use a comma or a period immediately after a question mark that ends a direct quotation.

▶ "Am I my brother's keeper?/" Cain asked.

▶ Cain asked, "Am I my brother's keeper?/"

Questions in a series may have question marks even when they are not separate sentences.

▶ I often confront a difficult choice: should I go to practice? finish my homework? spend time with my friends?

A question mark in parentheses indicates that a writer is unsure of a date, a figure, or a word.

▶ Quintilian died in AD 96 (?).

41c Exclamation points

Use an exclamation point to show surprise or strong emotion.

▶ In those few moments of geologic time will be the story of all that has happened since we became a nation. And what a story it will be!
— JAMES RETTIE, "But a Watch in the Night"

Use exclamation points very sparingly because they can distract your readers or suggest that you are exaggerating.

▶ This university is so large, so varied, that attempting to tell someone everything about it would take three years!.

Do not use a comma or a period immediately after an exclamation point that ends a direct quotation.

▶ On my last visit, I looked out the sliding glass doors and ran breathlessly to Connor in the kitchen: "There's a *huge* black pig in the backyard!"/
— ELLEN ASHDOWN, "Living by the Dead"

EXERCISE 41.1

Revise each of the following sentences, adding appropriate punctuation and deleting any unnecessary punctuation you find. Example:

She asked the travel agent, "What is the air fare to Greece?"/

1. Social scientists face difficult questions: should they use their knowledge to shape society, merely describe human behavior, or try to do both.

2. The court denied a New Jersey woman's petition to continue raising tigers in her backyard!

3. I screamed at Jamie, "You rat. You tricked me."

4. The reporter wondered whether anything more could have been done to save lives?

5. Zane called every store within fifty miles and asked if they had the Wii game he wanted

6. "Have you seen the new George Clooney film?," Mia asked.

bedfordstmartins.com/everydaywriter
Exercise Central > End Punctuation

EXERCISE 41.2: THINKING CRITICALLY

Reading with an Eye for End Punctuation

Consider the use of end punctuation in the following paragraph. Then experiment with the end punctuation. What would be the effect of deleting the exclamation point from the quotation by Cicero or of changing it to a question mark? What would be the effect of changing Cicero's question to a statement?

> To be admired and praised, especially by the young, is an autumnal plea-sure enjoyed by the lucky ones (who are not always the most deserving). "What is more charming," Cicero observes in his famous essay *De Senectute*, "than an old age surrounded by the enthusiasm of youth! . . . Attentions which seem trivial and conventional are marks of honor — the morning call, being sought after, precedence, having people rise for you, being escorted to and from the forum. . . . What pleasures of the body can be compared to the prerogatives of influence?" But there are also pleasures of the body, or the mind, that are enjoyed by a greater number of older persons.
>
> — MALCOLM COWLEY, *The View from 80*

Thinking about Your Own Use of End Punctuation

Look through something you have written recently, noting its end punctuation. Using the guidelines in this chapter, see if your use of end punctuation follows any pat-terns. Try revising the end punctuation in a paragraph or two to emphasize (or de-emphasize) some point. What conclusions can you draw about ways of using end punctuation to draw attention to (or away from) a sentence?

Apostrophes 42

The little apostrophe can make a big difference in meaning. The following sign at a neighborhood swimming pool, for instance, says something different from what the writer probably intended:

> Please deposit your garbage (and your guests) in the trash receptacles before leaving the pool area.

The sign indicates that guests should be put in the trash. Adding a single apostrophe would offer a more neighborly statement: *Please deposit your garbage (and your guests') in the trash receptacles before leaving the pool area* asks that the guests' garbage, not the guests themselves, be thrown away.

42a Use apostrophes appropriately to show possession.

The possessive case denotes ownership or possession of one thing by another.

Singular nouns and indefinite pronouns

Add an apostrophe and *-s* to form the possessive of most singular nouns, including those that end in *-s,* and of indefinite pronouns (31d). Do not use apostrophes with the possessive forms of personal pronouns: *yours, his, hers, its, ours, theirs.*

AT A GLANCE

Editing for Apostrophes

- Check each noun that ends in *-s* and shows possession. Is the apostrophe in the right place, either before or after the *-s*? (42a)
- Check the possessive form of each indefinite pronoun, such as *someone's.* Be sure the apostrophe comes before the *-s.* (42a)
- Check each personal pronoun that ends with *-s* (*yours, his, hers, its, ours, theirs*) to make sure it does not include an apostrophe. (42a)
- Does each *it's* mean *it is* or *it has*? If not, remove the apostrophe. (42b)
- Make sure other contractions use apostrophes correctly. (42b)

▶ The **bus's** fumes overpowered her.

▶ *Star Wars* made George **Lucas's** fortune.

▶ **Anyone's** guess is as good as mine.

Plural nouns

To form the possessive case of plural nouns not ending in -s, add an apostrophe and -s.

▶ The **men's** department sells business attire.

For plural nouns ending in -s, add only the apostrophe.

▶ The three **clowns'** costumes were bright green and orange.

Compound nouns

For compound nouns, make the last word in the group possessive.

▶ The **secretary of state's** speech was televised.

▶ Both her **daughters-in-law's** birthdays fall in July.

▶ My **in-laws'** disapproval dampened our enthusiasm for the new house.

Two or more nouns

To signal individual possession by two or more owners, make each noun possessive.

▶ Great differences exist between **Jerry Bruckheimer's** and **Ridley Scott's** films.

  Bruckheimer and Scott have produced different films.

To signal joint possession, make only the last noun possessive.

▶ **Wallace and Gromit's** creator is Nick Park.

  Wallace and Gromit have the same creator.

EXERCISE 42.1

Complete each of the following sentences by inserting 's or an apostrophe alone to form the possessive case of the italicized words. Example:

  A.J.'s older *brother's* name is Griffin.

1. Grammar is not *everybody* favorite subject.

2. An *ibis* wingspan is about half as long as a *flamingo*.

3. *Charles and Camilla* first visit to the United States as a married couple included a stop at the White House.

4. The long debate over *states* rights culminated in the Civil War.

5. *Kobe Bryant and Tiger Woods* personal crises have threatened to overshadow their athletic careers.

6. She insists that her personal life is *nobody* business.

7. Parents often question *their children* choice of friends.

8. This dog has a *beagle* ears and a *St. Bernard* face.

9. The sidewalk smokers disregarded the *surgeon generals* warnings.

10. *Anna and Tobias* income dropped dramatically after Anna lost her job.

42b Use apostrophes in contractions.

Contractions are two-word combinations formed by leaving out certain letters, which are indicated by an apostrophe.

it is, it has/it's	I would, I had/I'd	will not/won't
was not/wasn't	he would, he had/he'd	let us/let's
I am/I'm	would not/wouldn't	cannot/can't
he is, he has/he's	do not/don't	who is, who
you will/you'll	does not/doesn't	has/who's

Contractions are common in conversation and informal writing. Academic and professional work, however, often calls for greater formality.

Distinguishing it's *and* its

Its is the possessive form of *it*. *It's* is a contraction for *it is* or *it has*.

▶ **This disease is unusual; its symptoms vary from person to person.**

▶ **It's a difficult disease to diagnose.**

42c Avoid apostrophes in most plural forms.

Many style guides now advise against using apostrophes for any plurals.

▶ **The gymnasts need marks of *8s* and *9s* to qualify for the finals.**

Others use an apostrophe and –*s* to form the plural of numbers, letters, and words referred to as terms.

▶ **The five *Shakespeare's* in the essay were spelled five different ways.**

Check your instructor's preference.

EXERCISE 42.2

The following sentences, from which all apostrophes have been deleted, appear in Langston Hughes's "Salvation." Insert apostrophes where appropriate. Example:

"Sister Reed, what is this childs name?"

1. There was a big revival at my Auntie Reeds church.
2. I heard the songs and the minister saying: "Why dont you come?"
3. Finally Westley said to me in a whisper: . . . "Im tired o sitting here. Lets get up and be saved."
4. So I decided that maybe to save further trouble, Id better lie. . . .
5. That night . . . I cried, in bed alone, and couldnt stop.

✔ **LearningCurve** game-like quizzing can take you to the next level.
bedfordstmartins.com/everydaywriter/LC > Apostrophes

EXERCISE 42.3: THINKING CRITICALLY

Write a brief paragraph, beginning "I've always been amused by my neighbor's (or roommate's) _____." Then note every use of an apostrophe. Use the guidelines in this chapter to check that you have used apostrophes correctly.

43 Quotation Marks

A s a way of bringing other people's words into your own, quotations can be a powerful writing tool.

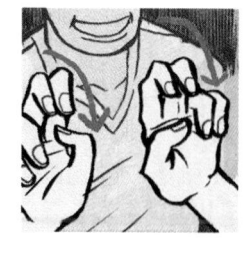

> Mrs. Macken encourages parents to get books for their children, to read to them when they are "li'l," and when they start school to make certain they attend regularly. She holds herself up as an example of "a millhand's daughter who wanted to be a schoolteacher and did it through sheer hard work." — Shirley Brice Heath, *Ways with Words*

The writer lets her subject speak for herself—and lets readers hear Mrs. Macken's voice.

43a Use quotation marks to identify direct quotations.

▶ President Obama asked Congress to "try common sense."

▶ She smiled and said, "Son, this is one incident that I will never forget."

Use quotation marks to enclose the words of each speaker within running dialogue. Mark each shift in speaker with a new paragraph.

> "I want no proof of their affection," said Elinor; "but of their engagement I do."
> "I am perfectly satisfied of both."
> "Yet not a syllable has been said to you on the subject, by either of them." —JANE AUSTEN, *Sense and Sensibility*

AT A GLANCE

Editing for Quotation Marks

- Use quotation marks around direct quotations and titles of short works. (43a and c)
- Do not use quotation marks around set-off quotations of more than four lines of prose or more than three lines of poetry, or around titles of long works. Consult a style guide, such as that of the Modern Language Association (MLA), for guidelines. (43b and c)
- Use quotation marks to signal irony and invented words, but do so sparingly. (43e)
- Check other punctuation used with closing quotation marks. (43f)

  Periods and commas should be *inside* the quotation marks.

  Colons, semicolons, and footnote numbers should be *outside*.

  Question marks, exclamation points, and dashes should be *inside* if they are part of the quoted material, *outside* if they are not.
- Never use quotation marks around indirect quotations. (43g)
- Do not use quotation marks just to add emphasis to words. (43g)

Single quotation marks

Single quotation marks enclose a quotation within a quotation. Open and close the quoted passage with double quotation marks, and change any quotation marks that appear *within* the quotation to single quotation marks.

▶ Baldwin says, "The title 'The Uses of the Blues' does not refer to music; I don't know anything about music."

43b Punctuate block quotations and poetry appropriately.

If the prose passage you wish to quote is more than four typed lines, set the quotation off by starting it on a new line and indenting it one inch from the left margin. This format, known as block quotation, does not require quotation marks.

> In "Suspended," Joy Harjo tells of her first awareness of jazz as a child:
>
> My rite of passage into the world of humanity occurred then, via jazz.
> The music made a startling bridge between the familiar and strange
> lands, an appropriate vehicle, for . . . we were there when jazz was born.
> I recognized it, that humid afternoon in my formative years, as a way to
> speak beyond the confines of ordinary language. I still hear it. (84)

This block quotation, including the ellipsis dots and the page number in parentheses at the end, follows the style of the Modern Language Association (MLA). The American Psychological Association (APA) has different guidelines for setting off block quotations. (See Chapters 49 and 53.)

When quoting poetry, if the quotation is brief (fewer than four lines), include it within your text. Separate the lines of the poem with slashes, each preceded and followed by a space, in order to tell the reader where one line of the poem ends and the next begins.

> In one of his best-known poems, Robert Frost remarks, "Two roads diverged in a yellow wood, and I — / I took the one less traveled by / And that has made all the difference."

To quote more than three lines of poetry, indent the block one inch from the left margin. Do not use quotation marks. Take care to follow the spacing, capitalization, punctuation, and other features of the original poem.

> The duke in Robert Browning's poem "My Last Duchess" is clearly a jealous, vain person, whose arrogance is illustrated through this statement:
>
> She thanked men — good! but thanked
> Somehow — I know not how — as if she ranked
> My gift of a nine-hundred-years-old name
> With anybody's gift. (lines 31–34)

43c Use quotation marks for titles of short works.

Quotation marks are used to enclose the titles of short poems, short stories, articles, essays, songs, sections of books, and episodes of television and radio programs.

▶ **"Dover Beach" moves from calmness to sadness.** [poem]

▶ **Alice Walker's "Everyday Use" is about more than just quilts.** [short story]

▶ **The *Atlantic* published an article entitled "Illiberal Education."** [article]

▶ **In "Photography," Susan Sontag considers the role of photography in our society.** [essay]

▶ **The *Nature* episode "Echo of the Elephants" portrays ivory hunters unfavorably.** [television series episode]

Use italics rather than quotation marks for the titles of television series, magazines, movies, and other long works (see 47a).

43d Use quotation marks appropriately for definitions.

▶ **In social science, the term *sample size* means "the number of individuals being studied in a research project."**
— KATHLEEN STASSEN BERGER AND ROSS A. THOMPSON,
The Developing Person through Childhood and Adolescence

Use italics for words used as a term, like *sample size* above (see 47b).

43e Use quotation marks to identify irony and invented terms.

To show readers that you are using a word or phrase ironically or that you made it up, enclose it in quotation marks.

▶ **The "banquet" consisted of dried-out chicken and canned vegetables.**

The quotation marks suggest that the meal was anything but a banquet.

▶ **Your whole first paragraph or first page may have to be guillotined in any case after your piece is finished: it is a kind of "forebirth."**
— JACQUES BARZUN, "A Writer's Discipline"

The writer made up the term *forebirth*.

EXERCISE 43.1

Revise each of the following sentences, using quotation marks appropriately to signal titles, definitions, irony, or invented terms.

1. Stephen Colbert introduced Americans to the concept he calls truthiness on the first episode of *The Colbert Report*.
2. Margaret Talbot's article A Risky Proposal examines the constitutionality of state laws that ban gay marriage.
3. "The little that is known about gorillas certainly makes you want to know more," writes Alan Moorehead in his essay A Most Forgiving Ape.
4. My father's way of helping usually meant doing the whole project for me.
5. Should America the Beautiful replace The Star-Spangled Banner as the national anthem?
6. In the chapter called The Last to See Them Alive, Truman Capote shows the utterly ordinary life of the Kansas family.
7. The *30 Rock* episode Reunion won an Emmy for outstanding comedy writing.
8. Several popular films, including *Mamma Mia!* and *Muriel's Wedding*, have used Abba hits such as Dancing Queen and Take a Chance on Me.
9. My dictionary defines *isolation* as the quality or state of being alone.
10. In his poem The Shield of Achilles, W. H. Auden depicts the horror of modern warfare.

43f Follow conventions for other punctuation with quotation marks.

Periods and commas go *inside* closing quotation marks.

▶ **"Don't compromise yourself," said Janis Joplin. "You are all you've got."**

When you follow MLA style for documenting a short quotation, place the period *after* the parentheses with source information (see Chapter 50).

▶ **In places, de Beauvoir "sees Marxists as believing in subjectivity" (Whitmarsh 63).**

For more information on using a comma with a quotation, see 39h.

Colons, semicolons, and footnote numbers go *outside* closing quotation marks.

▶ **I felt one emotion after finishing "Eveline": sorrow.**

▶ **Everything is dark, and "a visionary light settles in her eyes"; this vision, this light, is her salvation.**

▶ **Tragedy is defined by Aristotle as "an imitation of an action that is serious and of a certain magnitude."[1]**

Question marks, exclamation points, and dashes go *inside* if they are part of the quoted material, *outside* if they are not.

PART OF THE QUOTATION

▶ The cashier asked, "Would you like to super-size that?"

▶ "Jump!" one of the firefighters shouted.

NOT PART OF THE QUOTATION

▶ What is the theme of "The Birth-Mark"?

▶ "Break a leg"—that phrase is supposed to bring good luck.

43g Revise misused quotation marks.

Do not use quotation marks for indirect quotations—those that do not use someone's exact words.

▶ Mother said that /̶"̶she was sure she would never forget the incident.̶"̶/̶

Do not use quotation marks just to add emphasis to particular words or phrases.

▶ Michael said that his views might not be /̶"̶politically correct̶"̶/̶ but that he wasn't going to change them for anything.

▶ Much time was spent speculating about their /̶"̶relationship.̶"̶/̶

Do not use quotation marks around slang or colloquial language; they create the impression that you are apologizing for using those words. If you have a good reason to use slang or a colloquial term, use it without quotation marks.

▶ After our twenty-mile hike, we were ready to /̶"̶turn in.̶"̶/̶

FOR MULTILINGUAL WRITERS

Quoting in American English

Remember that the way you mark quotations in American English (" ") may not be the same as in other languages. In French, for example, quotations are marked with *guillemets* (« »), while in German, quotations take split-level marks („ "). Writers of British English use single quotation marks first and, when necessary, double quotation marks for quotations within quotations. If you are writing for an American audience, be careful to follow the U.S. conventions governing quotation marks.

EXERCISE 43.2: THINKING CRITICALLY

Reading with an Eye for Quotation Marks

Read the following passage about the painter Georgia O'Keeffe, and pay particular attention to the use of quotation marks. What effect is created by the author's use of quotation marks with *hardness*, *crustiness*, and *crusty*? How do the quotations by O'Keeffe help support the author's description of her?

> "Hardness" has not been in our century a quality much admired in women, nor in the past twenty years has it even been in official favor for men. When hardness surfaces in the very old we tend to transform it into "crustiness" or eccentricity, some tonic pepperiness to be indulged at a distance. On the evidence of her work and what she has said about it, Georgia O'Keeffe is neither "crusty" nor eccentric. She is simply hard, a straight shooter, a woman clean of received wisdom and open to what she sees. This is a woman who could early on dismiss most of her contemporaries as "dreamy," and would later single out one she liked as "a very poor painter." (And then add, apparently by way of softening the judgment: "I guess he wasn't a painter at all. He had no courage and I believe that to create one's own world in any of the arts takes courage.") This is a woman who in 1939 could advise her admirers that they were missing her point, that their appreciation of her famous flowers was merely sentimental. "When I paint a red hill," she observed coolly in the catalogue for an exhibition that year, "you say it is too bad that I don't always paint flowers. A flower touches almost everyone's heart. A red hill doesn't touch everyone's heart."
>
> — JOAN DIDION, "Georgia O'Keeffe"

Thinking about Your Own Use of Quotation Marks

Choose a topic that is of interest on your campus, and interview one of your friends about it. On the basis of your notes from the interview, write two or three paragraphs about your friend's views, using several direct quotations that support the points you are making. Then see how closely you followed the conventions for quotation marks explained in this chapter. Note any usages that caused you problems.

44 Other Punctuation

Parentheses, brackets, dashes, colons, slashes, and ellipses are everywhere. Every URL includes colons and slashes, many sites use brackets or parentheses to identify updates and embedded media, and dashes and ellipses are increasingly common in writing that expresses conversational informality.

> **AT A GLANCE**
>
> ## Editing for Effective Use of Punctuation
>
> - Be sure that any material enclosed in parentheses or set off with dashes requires special treatment — and that the parentheses or dashes don't make the sentence difficult to follow. Use parentheses to de-emphasize material they enclose and dashes to add emphasis. (44a and c)
> - Use brackets to enclose parenthetical elements in material that is already within parentheses and to enclose words or comments inserted into a quotation. (44b)
> - Use colons to introduce explanations, series, lists, and some quotations. Do not put a colon between a verb and its object or complement, between a preposition and its object, or after expressions like *such as*. (44d)
> - Use slashes to mark line divisions in poetry quoted within your own text. (44e)
> - Use ellipses (three equally spaced dots) to indicate omissions from quoted passages. (44f)

You can also use these punctuation marks for more formal purposes: to signal relationships among parts of sentences, to create particular rhythms, and to help readers follow your thoughts.

44a Parentheses

Use parentheses to enclose material that is of minor or secondary importance in a sentence — material that supplements, clarifies, comments on, or illustrates what precedes or follows it.

▶ Inventors and men of genius have almost always been regarded as fools at the beginning **(and very often at the end)** of their careers.
— FYODOR DOSTOYEVSKY

▶ During my research, I found problems with the flat-rate income tax **(a single-rate tax with no deductions)**.

Enclosing textual citations

▶ Freud and his followers have had a most significant impact on the ways abnormal functioning is understood and treated **(Joseph, 1991)**.
— RONALD J. COMER, *Abnormal Psychology*

▶ Zamora notes that Kahlo referred to her first self-portrait, given to a close friend, as "your Botticelli" **(110)**.

The first in-text citation above shows the style of the American Psychological Association (APA); the second, the style of the Modern Language Association (MLA).

Enclosing numbers or letters in a list

▶ Five distinct styles can be distinguished: (1) Old New England,
(2) Deep South, (3) Middle American, (4) Wild West, and (5) Far West
or Californian. — ALISON LURIE, *The Language of Clothes*

With other marks of punctuation

A period may be placed either inside or outside a closing parenthesis, depending on whether the parenthetical text is part of a larger sentence. A comma, if needed, is always placed *outside* a closing parenthesis (and never before an opening one).

▶ Gene Tunney's single defeat in an eleven-year career was to a
flamboyant and dangerous fighter named Harry Greb ("The Human
Windmill"), who seems to have been, judging from boxing literature,
the dirtiest fighter in history. — JOYCE CAROL OATES, "On Boxing"

Choosing among parentheses, commas, and dashes

In general, use commas when the material to be set off is least interruptive (39c, e, and f), parentheses when it is more interruptive, and dashes when it is the most interruptive (44c).

44b Brackets

Use brackets to enclose parenthetical elements in material that is itself within parentheses and to enclose explanatory words or comments that you are inserting into a quotation.

Setting off material within parentheses

▶ Eventually the investigation had to examine the major agencies
(including the previously sacrosanct National Security Agency [NSA])
that were conducting covert operations.

Inserting material within quotations

▶ Massing notes that "on average, it [Fox News] attracts more than
eight million people daily — more than double the number who
watch CNN."

The bracketed words clarify *it* in the original quotation.

In the quotation in the following sentence, the artist Gauguin's name is misspelled. The bracketed word *sic,* which means "so," tells readers that the person being quoted — not the writer who has picked up the quotation — made the mistake.

▶ One admirer wrote, "She was the most striking woman I'd ever seen — a sort of wonderful combination of Mia Farrow and one of Gaugin's [*sic*] Polynesian nymphs."

EXERCISE 44.1

Revise the following sentences, using parentheses and brackets correctly. Example:

She was in fourth grade (or was it third?) when she became blind.

1. The committee was presented with three options to pay for the new park: 1 increase vehicle registration fees, 2 install parking meters downtown, or 3 borrow money from the reserve fund.

2. The FISA statute authorizes government wiretapping only under certain circumstances for instance, the government has to obtain a warrant.

3. The health care expert informed readers that "as we progress through middle age, we experience intimations of our own morality *sic*."

4. Some hospitals train nurses in a pseudoscientific technique called therapeutic touch TT that has been discredited by many rigorous studies.

5. Because I was carrying an umbrella, which, as it turned out, wasn't even necessary, I was required to enter the stadium through the high-security gate.

44c Dashes

Dashes give more emphasis than parentheses to the material they enclose. Many word-processing programs automatically convert two typed hyphens into a solid dash.

▶ The pleasures of reading itself — who doesn't remember? — were like those of Christmas cake, a sweet devouring.
— EUDORA WELTY, "A Sweet Devouring"

Emphasizing explanatory material

▶ Indeed, several of modern India's greatest scholars — such as the Mughal historian Muzaffar Alam of the University of Chicago — are madrasa graduates. — WILLIAM DALRYMPLE

Emphasizing material at the end of a sentence

▶ In the twentieth century it has become almost impossible to moralize about epidemics — except those which are transmitted sexually.
— SUSAN SONTAG, *AIDS and Its Metaphors*

Marking a sudden change in tone

▶ New York is a catastrophe—but a magnificent catastrophe.
– LE CORBUSIER

Introducing a summary or explanation

▶ In walking, the average adult person employs a motor mechanism that weighs about eighty pounds—sixty pounds of muscle and twenty pounds of bone. — EDWIN WAY TEALE

Indicating hesitation in speech

▶ As the officer approached his car, the driver stammered, "What—what have I done?"

EXERCISE 44.2

Punctuate the following sentences with dashes where appropriate. Example:

He is quick, violent, and mean — they don't call him Dirty Harry for nothing — but appealing nonetheless.

1. Most people would say that Labradors are easy dogs to train but they never met our Millie.
2. Even if marijuana is dangerous an assertion disputed by many studies it is certainly no more harmful to human health than alcohol and cigarettes, which remain legal.
3. If too much exposure to negative news stories makes you feel depressed or anxious and why wouldn't it? try going on a media fast.
4. Union Carbide's plant in Bhopal, India, sprang a leak that killed more than 2,000 people and injured an additional 200,000.
5. Refrigerators especially side-by-side models use up more energy than most people realize.

44d Colons

Use a colon to introduce explanations or examples and to separate some elements from one another.

Introducing an explanation, an example, or an appositive

▶ The men may also wear the getup known as Sun Belt Cool: a pale beige suit, open-collared shirt (often in a darker shade than the suit), cream-colored loafers and aviator sunglasses.
– ALISON LURIE, The Language of Clothes

Introducing a series, a list, or a quotation

▶ At the baby's one-month birthday party, Ah Po gave him the Four
Valuable Things: ink, inkslab, paper, and brush.
— MAXINE HONG KINGSTON, *China Men*

▶ The teachers wondered: "Do boys and girls really learn differently?"

The preceding example could have taken a comma instead of a colon
(see 39h). Use a colon rather than a comma to introduce a quotation
when the lead-in is a complete sentence on its own.

▶ The State of the Union address contained one surprising statement:
"America is addicted to oil."

Separating elements

SALUTATIONS IN FORMAL LETTERS

▶ Dear Dr. Chapman:

HOURS, MINUTES, AND SECONDS

▶ 4:59 PM

▶ 2:15:06

RATIOS

▶ a ratio of 5:1

BIBLICAL CHAPTERS AND VERSES

▶ I Corinthians 3:3–5

TITLES AND SUBTITLES

▶ *The Joy of Insight:*
Passions of a Physicist

CITIES AND PUBLISHERS IN
BIBLIOGRAPHIC ENTRIES

▶ Boston: Bedford, 2012

Editing for colons

Do not put a colon between a verb and its object or complement—
unless the object is a quotation.

▶ Some natural fibers are: cotton, wool, silk, and linen.

Do not put a colon between a preposition and its object or after such
expressions as *such as, especially,* and *including.*

▶ In poetry, additional power may come from devices such as: simile,
metaphor, and alliteration.

EXERCISE 44.3

In the following items, insert a colon in any sentence that needs one and delete any
unnecessary colons. Some sentences may be correct as written. Example:

Images: My Life in Film includes revealing material written by Ingmar Bergman.

1. After discussing the case study, the class reached one main conclusion in any
business, the most important asset is the customer.

2. Another example is taken from Psalm 139 16.

3. Roberto tried to make healthier choices, such as: eating organic food, walking to work, and getting plenty of rest.

4. A number of quotable movie lines come from *Casablanca*, including "Round up the usual suspects."

5. Sofi rushed to catch the 5 45 express but had to wait for the 6 19.

44e Slashes

Use a slash to separate alternatives.

▶ **Then there was Daryl, the cabdriver/bartender.**
— JOHN L'HEUREUX, *The Handmaid of Desire*

Use slashes to mark line divisions between two or three lines of poetry quoted within running text. When using a slash to separate lines of poetry, precede and follow it with a space (43b).

▶ **In Sonnet 29, the persona states, "For thy sweet love rememb'red such wealth brings / That then I scorn to change my state with kings."**

Slashes also separate parts of fractions and Internet addresses.

44f Ellipses

Ellipses, or ellipsis points, are three equally spaced dots. Ellipses usually indicate that something has been omitted from a quoted passage, but they can also signal a pause or hesitation in speech in the same way that a dash can.

Indicating omissions

Just as you should carefully use quotation marks around any material that you quote directly from a source, so you should carefully use ellipses to indicate that you have left out part of a quotation that otherwise appears to be a complete sentence.

The ellipses in the following example indicate two omissions — one in the middle of the sentence and one at the end. When you omit the last part of a quoted sentence, add a period after the ellipses, for a total of four dots. Be sure a complete sentence comes before and after the four points. If you are adding your own ellipses to a quotation that already has other ellipses, enclose yours in brackets.

ORIGINAL TEXT

▶ The quasi-official division of the population into three economic classes called high-, middle-, and low-income groups rather misses the point, because as a class indicator the amount of money is not as important as the source. — PAUL FUSSELL, "Notes on Class"

WITH ELLIPSES

▶ As Paul Fussell argues, "The quasi-official division of the population into three economic classes . . . rather misses the point. . . ."

If your shortened quotation ends with a source (such as a page number, a name, or a title), follow these steps:

1. Use three ellipsis points but no period after the quotation.
2. Add the closing quotation mark, closed up to the third ellipsis point.
3. Add the source documentation in parentheses.
4. Use a period to indicate the end of the sentence.

▶ Packer argues, "The Administration is right to reconsider its strategy . . ." (34).

Indicating hesitation

▶ Then the voice, husky and familiar, came to wash over us — "The winnah, and still heavyweight champeen of the world . . . Joe Louis."
— MAYA ANGELOU, *I Know Why the Caged Bird Sings*

EXERCISE 44.4

The following sentences use the punctuation marks presented in this chapter very effectively. Read the sentences carefully; then choose one, and use it as a model for writing a sentence of your own, making sure to use the punctuation marks in the same way in your sentence.

1. The dad was — how can you put this gracefully? — a real blimp, a wide load, and the white polyester stretch-pants only emphasized the cargo.
— GARRISON KEILLOR, "Happy to Be Here"

2. Not only are the distinctions we draw between male nature and female nature largely arbitrary and often pure superstition: they are completely beside the point. — BRIGID BROPHY, "Women"

3. If no one, including you, liked the soup the first time round (and that's why you've got so much left over), there is no point in freezing it for some hopeful future date when, miraculously, it will taste delicious. But bagging leftovers — say, stews — in single portions can be useful for those evenings when you're eating alone. — NIGELLA LAWSON, *How to Eat*

bedfordstmartins.com/everydaywriter
Exercise Central > Other Punctuation

EXERCISE 44.5: THINKING CRITICALLY

Reading with an Eye for Punctuation

In the following passage, Tom Wolfe uses dashes, parentheses, ellipses, and a colon to create rhythm and build momentum in a very long (178-word) sentence. The editorial comment inserted in brackets calls attention to the fact that the "right stuff" was, in the world Wolfe describes here, always male. Look carefully at how Wolfe and the editors use these punctuation marks, and then try writing a description of something that effectively uses as many of them as possible. Your description should be about the same length as Wolfe's passage, but it need not be all one sentence.

> Likewise, "hassling" — mock dogfighting — was strictly forbidden, and so naturally young fighter jocks could hardly wait to go up in, say, a pair of F-100s and start the duel by making a pass at each other at 800 miles an hour, the winner being the pilot who could slip in behind the other one and get locked in on his [never *her* or *his or her*!] tail ("wax his tail"), and it was not uncommon for some eager jock to try too tight an outside turn and have his engine flame out, whereupon, unable to restart it, he has to eject . . . and he shakes his fist at the victor as he floats down by parachute and his million-dollar aircraft goes *kaboom!* on the palmetto grass or the desert floor, and he starts thinking about how he can get together with the other guy back at the base in time for the two of them to get their stories straight before the investigation: "I don't know what happened, sir. I was pulling up after a target run, and it just flamed out on me."
>
> — TOM WOLFE, *The Right Stuff*

Thinking about Your Own Use of Punctuation

Look through a draft you have recently written or are working on, and check your use of parentheses, brackets, dashes, colons, slashes, and ellipses. Do you follow the conventions presented in this chapter? If not, revise accordingly. Check the material in parentheses to see if it could use more emphasis and thus be set off instead with dashes. Then check any material in dashes to see if it could do with less emphasis and thus be punctuated with commas or parentheses.

Capital Letters **45**

C apital letters are a key signal in everyday life. Look around any store to see their importance: you can shop for Levi's or *any* blue jeans, for Coca-Cola or *any* cola, for Kleenex or *any* tissue. As these examples show, one of the most common reasons for capitalizing a word is to indicate that it is part of a name or title—of a brand, person, article, or something else.

45a **Capitalize the first word of a sentence or line of poetry.**

Capitalize the first word of a sentence. If you are quoting a full sentence, capitalize the first word of the quotation.

▶ **Kennedy said, "Let us never negotiate out of fear."**

Capitalization of a sentence following a colon is optional.

▶ **Gould cites the work of Darwin: The [*or* the] theory of natural selection incorporates the principle of evolutionary ties among all animals.**

AT A GLANCE

Editing for Capitalization

- Capitalize the first word of each sentence. If you quote a poem, follow its original capitalization. (45a)
- Check to make sure you have appropriately capitalized proper nouns and proper adjectives. (45b)
- Review where you have used titles of people or of works to be sure you have capitalized them correctly. (45b and c)
- Double-check the capitalization of geographical directions (*north* or *North*?), family relationships (*dad* or *Dad*?), and seasons of the year (*winter*, not *Winter*). (45d)
- In email, check to see that you have not capitalized whole words or phrases. (45d)

Capitalize a sentence within parentheses unless the parenthetical sentence is inserted into another sentence.

▶ **Gould cites the work of Darwin. (Other researchers cite more recent evolutionary theorists.)**

▶ **Gould cites the work of Darwin (see page 150).**

When citing poetry, follow the capitalization of the original poem. Though most poets capitalize the first word of each line in a poem, some poets do not.

▶ **Morning sun heats up the young beech tree**
leaves and almost lights them into fireflies

– JUNE JORDAN, "Aftermath"

45b Capitalize proper nouns and proper adjectives.

Capitalize proper nouns (those naming specific persons, places, and things) and most proper adjectives (those formed from proper nouns). All other nouns are common nouns and are not capitalized unless they begin a sentence or are used as part of a proper noun: *a street* or *the street where you live,* but *Elm Street.* The following list shows proper nouns and adjectives on the left and related common nouns and adjectives on the right.

PEOPLE

| Ang Lee | the film's director |
| Nixonian | political |

NATIONS, NATIONALITIES, ETHNIC GROUPS, AND LANGUAGES

| Brazil, Brazilian | their native country, his citizenship |
| Italian American | an ethnic group |

PLACES

| Pacific Ocean | an ocean |
| Hawaiian Islands | tropical islands |

STRUCTURES AND MONUMENTS

| the Lincoln Memorial | a monument |
| the Eiffel Tower | a landmark |

SHIPS, TRAINS, AIRCRAFT, AND SPACECRAFT

| the *Queen Mary* | a cruise ship |
| the *City of New Orleans* | the 6:00 train |

ORGANIZATIONS, BUSINESSES, AND GOVERNMENT INSTITUTIONS

United Auto Workers	a trade union
Library of Congress	certain federal agencies

ACADEMIC INSTITUTIONS AND COURSES

University of Maryland	a state university
Political Science 102	my political science course

HISTORICAL EVENTS AND ERAS

the Easter Uprising	a rebellion
the Renaissance	the fifteenth century

RELIGIONS AND RELIGIOUS TERMS

God	a deity
the Qur'an	a holy book
Catholicism, Catholic	a religion, their religious affiliation

TRADE NAMES

Nike	running shoes
Cheerios	cereal

Some contemporary companies use capitals called *InterCaps* in the middle of their own or their product's names. Follow the style you see in company advertising or on the product itself—*eBay, FedEx, iTunes.*

Titles of individuals

Capitalize titles used before a proper name. When used alone or following a proper name, most titles are not capitalized. One common exception is the word *president,* which many writers capitalize whenever it refers to the president of the United States.

Chief Justice Roberts	John Roberts, the chief justice
Professor Lisa Ede	my English professor
Dr. Edward A. Davies	Edward A. Davies, our doctor

45c Capitalize titles of works.

Capitalize most words in titles of books, articles, stories, speeches, essays, plays, poems, documents, films, paintings, and musical compositions. Do not capitalize an article (*a, an, the*), a preposition, a

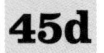
---

conjunction, or the *to* in an infinitive unless it is the first or last word in a title or subtitle.

Walt Whitman: A Life	Declaration of Independence
"As Time Goes By"	*Charlie and the Chocolate Factory*
"Shooting an Elephant"	*Rebel without a Cause*

45d   Revise unnecessary capitalization.

Do not capitalize a compass direction unless the word designates a specific geographic region.

▶ **Voters in the South and much of the West tend to favor socially conservative candidates.**

▶ **John Muir headed West, motivated by the need to explore.**
  west,

Do not capitalize a word indicating a family relationship unless the word is used as part of the name or as a substitute for the name.

▶ **I could always tell when Mother was annoyed with Aunt Rose.**

▶ **When she was a child, my Mother shared a room with my Aunt.**
  mother   *aunt.*

Do not capitalize seasons of the year and parts of the academic or financial year.

spring	fall semester
winter	winter term
autumn	third-quarter earnings

Do not capitalize whole words or phrases for emphasis in online writing, which comes across to readers as SHOUTING. Use italics, boldface, underlining, or (if you can't format text) asterisks to add emphasis.

▶ **Sorry for the abrupt response, but I am *very* busy.**

EXERCISE 45.1

Capitalize words as needed in the following sentences. Example:

> *T. S. Eliot,*   *The Waste Land,*   *Faber   Faber.*
> t.s. eliot, who wrote *the waste land,* was an editor at faber and faber.
> ^   ^   ^

1. the town in the south where i was raised had a statue of a civil war soldier in the center of main street.
2. sarah palin, the former governor, frequently complained that the press had treated her harshly before she accepted a position as an analyst for fox news.
3. the corporation for public broadcasting relies on donations as well as on grants from the national endowment for the arts.
4. during the economic recession, companies such as starbucks had to close some of their stores; others, such as circuit city, went completely out of business.
5. most americans remember where they were when they heard about the 9/11 disaster.
6. accepting an award for his score for the john wayne film *the high and the mighty,* dimitri tiomkin thanked beethoven, brahms, wagner, and strauss.

EXERCISE 45.2

Correct any unnecessary or missing capitalization in the following sentences. Some sentences may be correct as written. Example:

> *southern governors*   *Washington,*
> A group of ~~Southern Governors~~ meets annually in ~~washington,~~ DC.
>   ^   ^

1. The Columbine School Shootings in 1999 prompted a debate about Gun Control Laws in the United States.
2. Every Professor in the department of english has a degree in literature.
3. The Cast included several children, but only two of them had Speaking Roles.
4. Airport checkpoints are the responsibility of the Transportation Security Administration.
5. The price of oil has fluctuated this Winter.

EXERCISE 45.3: THINKING CRITICALLY

The following poem uses unconventional capitalization. Read it over a few times, at least once aloud. What effect does the capitalization have? Why do you think the poet chose to use capitals as she did?

> A little Madness in the Spring
> Is wholesome even for the King,
> But God be with the Clown —
> Who ponders this tremendous scene —
> This whole Experiment of Green —
> As if it were his own!

> — EMILY DICKINSON

46 Abbreviations and Numbers

Any time you look up an address, you see an abundance of abbreviations and numbers, as in the following movie theater listing from a Google map of Berkeley, California:

Oaks Theater   1875 Solano Av   Brk

Abbreviations and numbers allow writers to present detailed information in a small amount of space.

46a Abbreviate some titles before and all titles after proper names.

Ms. Susanna Moller   Henry Louis Gates Jr.

Mr. Aaron Oforlea   Karen Lancry, MD

Dr. Cheryl Gold   Samuel Cohen, PhD

AT A GLANCE

Editing Abbreviations and Numbers

- Use abbreviations and numbers according to the conventions of a specific field (see p. 445): for example, *57%* might be acceptable in a math paper, but *57 percent* may be more appropriate in a sociology essay. (46f)

- If you use an abbreviation readers might not understand, spell out the term the first time you use it, and give the abbreviation in parentheses. (46c)

Other titles—including religious, academic, and government titles—
should be spelled out in academic writing. In other writing, they can
be abbreviated before a full name but should be written out when used
with only a last name.

Rev. Fleming Rutledge   Reverend Rutledge

Prof. Jaime Mejía   Professor Mejía

Gen. Colin Powell   General Powell

Do not use both a title and an academic degree with a person's name.
Use one or the other. Instead of *Dr. Beverly Moss, PhD,* write *Dr. Beverly
Moss* or *Beverly Moss, PhD.* (Note that academic degrees such as *RN* and
PhD often appear without periods; see 41a.)

46b Abbreviate years and hours appropriately.

You can use the following abbreviations with numerals. Notice that
AD precedes the numeral; all other abbreviations follow the numeral.
Today, BCE and CE are generally preferred over BC and AD, and periods
in all four of these abbreviations are optional.

399 BCE ("before the common era") *or* 399 BC ("before Christ")

49 CE ("common era") *or* AD 49 (*anno Domini,* Latin for "year of our
Lord")

11:15 AM (*or* a.m.)

9:00 PM (*or* p.m.)

For these abbreviations, you may use full-size capital letters or small
caps, a typographical option in word-processing programs.

46c Abbreviate some business, government, and science terms.

As long as you can be sure your readers will understand them, use
common abbreviations such as *PBS, NASA, DNA,* and *CIA.* If an abbreviation may be unfamiliar, however, spell out the full term the first time
you use it, and give the abbreviation in parentheses. After that, you can
use the abbreviation by itself.

▶ **The Comprehensive Test Ban (CTB) Treaty was first proposed in the
1950s. For those nations signing it, the CTB would bring to a halt all
nuclear weapons testing.**

46d Use abbreviations in official company names.

Use such abbreviations as *Co., Inc., Corp.,* and *&* if they are part of a company's official name. Do not, however, use these abbreviations in most other contexts.

▶ Sears, Roebuck & Co. was the only large ~~corp.~~ in town.
                                              corporation

▶ Paola has a part-time job at the Warner ~~Brothers~~ store in the mall.
                                            Bros.

46e Use Latin abbreviations appropriately.

In general, avoid these Latin abbreviations except when citing sources:

cf.	compare (*confer*)
e.g.	for example (*exempli gratia*)
et al.	and others (*et alia*)
etc.	and so forth (*et cetera*)
i.e.	that is (*id est*)
N.B.	note well (*nota bene*)
P.S.	postscript (*postscriptum*)

▶ Many firms have policies to help working parents—~~e.g.,~~ flexible hours,
                                                     for example,
parental leave, and day care.

▶ Before the conference began, Haivan unpacked the name tags, programs,
pens, ~~etc.~~
       and so forth.

46f Use symbols and unit abbreviations appropriately.

Symbols such as %, +, $, and = are acceptable in charts and graphs. Dollar signs are acceptable with figures: *$11* (but not with words: *eleven dollars*). Units of measurement can be abbreviated in charts and graphs (*4 in.*) but not in the body of a paper (*four inches*).

46g Use other abbreviations according to convention.

Some abbreviations required in notes and in source citations are not appropriate in the body of a paper.

TALKING ABOUT STYLE

Abbreviations and Numbers in Different Fields

Use of abbreviations and numbers varies in different fields. See a typical example from a biochemistry textbook:

> The energy of a green photon . . . is 57 kilocalories per mole (kcal/mol). An alternative unit of energy is the joule (J), which is equal to 0.239 calorie; 1 kcal/mol is equal to 4.184 kJ/mol.
>
> – LUBERT STRYER, *Biochemistry*

These two sentences demonstrate how useful figures and abbreviations can be; reading the same sentences would be very difficult if the numbers and units of measurement were all written out.

Become familiar with the conventions governing abbreviations and numbers in your field. The following reference books provide guidelines:

MLA Handbook for Writers of Research Papers for literature and the humanities

Publication Manual of the American Psychological Association for the social sciences

Scientific Style and Format: The CSE Manual for Authors, Editors, and Publishers for the natural sciences

The Chicago Manual of Style for the humanities

AIP Style Manual for physics and the applied sciences

CHAPTER AND PAGES	chapter, page, pages (*not* ch., p., pp.)
MONTHS	January, February (*not* Jan., Feb.)
STATES AND NATIONS	California, Mexico (*not* Calif., Mex.) Two exceptions are Washington, D.C., and U.S.

EXERCISE 46.1

Revise each of the following sentences to eliminate any abbreviations that would be inappropriate in most academic writing. Example:

> *United States*
> The population of the U.S. grew considerably in the 1980s.

1. Every Fri., my grandmother would walk a mi. to the P.O. and send a care package to her brother in Tenn.

2. The blue whale can grow to be 180 ft. long and can weigh up to 380,000 lbs.

3. Many a Mich.-based auto co., incl. GM, requested financial aid from the govt.

4. A large corp. like AT&T may help finance an employee's M.B.A.

5. Rosie began by saying, "If you want my two ¢," but she did not wait to see if listeners wanted it or not.

46h Spell out numbers expressed in one or two words.

If you can write out a number in one or two words, do so. Use figures for longer numbers.

▶ Her screams were heard by ~~38~~ *thirty-eight* people, none of whom called the police.

▶ A baseball is held together by ~~two hundred sixteen~~ *216* red stitches.

If one of several numbers *of the same kind* in the same sentence requires a figure, you should use figures for all the numbers in that sentence.

▶ An audio system can range in cost from ~~one hundred dollars~~ *$100* to $2,599.

46i Spell out numbers that begin sentences.

When a sentence begins with a number, either spell out the number or rewrite the sentence.

▶ ~~119~~ *One hundred nineteen* years of CIA labor cost taxpayers sixteen million dollars.

Most readers find it easier to read figures than three-word numbers; thus the best solution may be to rewrite this sentence: *Taxpayers spent sixteen million dollars for 119 years of CIA labor.*

46j Use figures according to convention.

ADDRESSES	23 Main Street; 175 Fifth Avenue
DATES	September 17, 1951; 6 June 1983; 4 BCE; the 1860s
DECIMALS AND FRACTIONS	65.34; 8$^1/_2$
PERCENTAGES	77 percent (*or* 77%)
EXACT AMOUNTS OF MONEY	$7,348; $1.46 trillion; $2.50; thirty-five (*or* 35) cents
SCORES AND STATISTICS	an 8–3 Red Sox victory; a verbal score of 600; an average age of 22; a mean of 53
TIME OF DAY	6:00 AM (*or* a.m.)

Using the Term *Hundred*

The term *hundred* is used idiomatically in English. When it is linked with numbers like two, eight, and so on, the word *hundred* remains singular: *Eight hundred years have passed and still old animosities run deep.* Add the plural -*s* to *hundred* only when no number precedes the term: *Hundreds of priceless books were lost in the fire.*

EXERCISE 46.2

Revise the numbers in the following sentences as necessary for correctness and consistency. Some sentences may be correct as written. Example:

twenty-first

Did the 21st century begin in 2000 or 2001?

1. Al Gore won the popular vote with 50,996,116 votes, but he was still short by 5 electoral votes.
2. 200,000 people may have perished in the 2010 Haitian earthquake.
3. The senator who voted against the measure received 6817 angry emails and only twelve in support of her decision.
4. Walker signed a three-year, $4.5-million contract.
5. In that age group, the risk is estimated to be about one in 2,500.

> **bedfordstmartins.com/everydaywriter**
> **Exercise Central > Abbreviations and Numbers**

EXERCISE 46.3: THINKING CRITICALLY

Reading with an Eye for Abbreviations and Numbers

The paragraph by Roger Angell in Exercise 48.2, at the end of Chapter 48, follows the style of the *New Yorker* magazine, which often spells out numbers in situations where this chapter recommends using figures. Read the paragraph carefully, and then consider whether it would have been easier to read if figures had been used for some of the numbers. If so, which ones? Then consider how the paragraph would have been different if Angell had used *semi-professional* instead of *semi-pro*. What effect does the abbreviated form create?

Thinking about Your Own Use of Abbreviations and Numbers

Look over an essay that you have written, noting all abbreviations and numbers. Check your usage for correctness, consistency, and appropriateness. If you discover a problem with abbreviations or numbers, make a note of it so that you can avoid the error in the future.

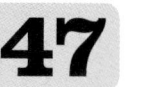

47 Italics

The slanted type known as *italics* is more than just a pretty typeface. Indeed, italics give words special meaning or emphasis. In the sentence "Many people read *People* on the subway every day," the italics (and the capital letter) tell us that *People* is a publication. You may use your computer to produce italic type; if not, underline words that you would otherwise italicize.

AT A GLANCE

Editing for Italics

- Check that all titles of long works are italicized. (47a)
- If you use any words, letters, or numbers as terms, make sure they are in italics. (47b)
- Italicize any non-English words or phrases that are not in an English dictionary. (47c)

47a **italicize titles of long works.**

In general, use italics for titles of long works; use quotation marks for shorter works (43c).

BOOKS	*Fun Home: A Family Tragicomic*
CHOREOGRAPHIC WORKS	Agnes de Mille's *Rodeo*
FILMS AND VIDEOS	*Avatar*
LONG MUSICAL WORKS	*Brandenburg Concertos*
LONG POEMS	*Bhagavad Gita*
MAGAZINES AND JOURNALS	*Ebony,* the *New England Journal of Medicine*
NEWSPAPERS	the *Cleveland Plain Dealer*
PAINTINGS AND SCULPTURE	Georgia O'Keeffe's *Black Iris*
PAMPHLETS	Thomas Paine's *Common Sense*
PLAYS	*Sweeney Todd*
RADIO SERIES	*All Things Considered*
RECORDINGS	*Slade Alive!*
SOFTWARE	*Dreamweaver*
TELEVISION SERIES	*The Wire*
WEB SITES	*Voice of the Shuttle*

47b Italicize words, letters, and numbers used as terms.

▶ On the back of his jersey was the famous *24*.

▶ One characteristic of some New York speech is the absence of postvocalic *r*—for example, pronouncing the word *four* as "fouh."

47c Italicize non-English words and phrases.

Italicize words from other languages unless they have become part of English—like the French "bourgeois" or the Italian "pasta," for example. If a word is in an English dictionary, it does not need italics.

▶ At last one of the phantom sleighs gliding along the street would come to a stop, and with gawky haste Mr. Burness in his fox-furred *shapka* would make for our door.   – VLADIMIR NABOKOV, *Speak, Memory*

EXERCISE 47.1

In each of the following sentences, underline any words that should be italicized, and circle any italicized words that should not be. Example:

The film <u>Good Night, and Good Luck</u> tells the story of a CBS newsman who helped to end the career of Senator Joseph McCarthy.

1. One critic claimed that few people listened to *The Velvet Underground & Nico* when the record was issued but that everyone who did formed a band.

2. Homemade *sushi* can be dangerous, but so can deviled eggs kept too long in a picnic basket.

3. The Web site Poisonous Plants and Animals lists tobacco (Nicotiana tobacum) as one of the most popular poisons in the world.

4. The monster in the Old English epic Beowulf got to tell his own side of the story in John Gardner's novel Grendel.

5. The 2009 film Star Trek imagines the youthful life of James T. Kirk and his early years as a starship captain.

EXERCISE 47.2: THINKING CRITICALLY

Reading with an Eye for Italics

Read the following passage about a graduate English seminar carefully, particularly noting the effects created by the italics. How would it differ without any italic emphasis? What other words or phrases might the author have italicized?

    There were four big tables arranged in a square, with everyone's feet sticking out into the open middle of the square. You could tell who was nervous, and how much, by watching the pairs of feet twist around each other. The Great Man presided awesomely from the high bar of the square. His head was a majestic granite-gray, like a centurion in command; he *looked* famous. His clean shoes twitched only slightly, and only when he was angry.

It turned out he was angry at me a lot of the time. He was angry because he thought me a disrupter, a rioter, a provocateur, and a fool; also crazy. And this was twenty years ago, before these things were *de rigueur* in the universities. Everything was very quiet in those days: there were only the Cold War and Korea and Joe McCarthy and the Old Old Nixon, and the only revolutionaries around were in Henry James's *The Princess Casamassima*.

— CYNTHIA OZICK, "We Are the Crazy Lady"

Thinking about Your Own Use of Italics

Write a paragraph or two describing the most eccentric person you know, italicizing some words for special emphasis. Read your passage aloud to hear the effect of the italics. Now explain each use of italics. If you find yourself unable to give a reason, ask yourself whether the word should be italicized at all.

Then revise the passage to eliminate *all but one* use of italics. Try revising sentences and choosing more precise words to convey emphasis. Decide which version is more effective. Can you reach any conclusions about using italics for emphasis?

48 Hyphens

Hyphens are undoubtedly confusing to many people — hyphen problems are now one of the twenty most common surface errors in student writing. The confusion is understandable. Over time, the conventions for hyphen use in a given word can change (*tomorrow* was once spelled *to-morrow*). New words, even compounds such as *firewall,* generally don't use hyphens, but controversy continues to rage over  whether to hyphenate *email* (or is it *e-mail*?). And some words are hyphenated when they serve one kind of purpose in a sentence and not when they serve another.

AT A GLANCE

Editing for Hyphens

- Double-check compound words to be sure they are properly closed up, separated, or hyphenated. If in doubt, consult a dictionary. (48a)
- Check all terms that have prefixes or suffixes to see whether you need hyphens. (48b)
- Do not hyphenate two-word verbs or word groups that serve as subject complements. (48c)

48a Use hyphens with compound words.

Some compounds are one word (*rowboat, pickup*), some are separate words (*hard drive*), and some require hyphens (*sister-in-law*). You should consult a dictionary to be sure. However, the following conventions can help you decide when to use hyphens with compound words.

Compound adjectives

Hyphenate most compound adjectives that precede a noun but not those that follow a noun.

a *well-liked* boss	My boss is *well liked.*
a *six-foot* plank	The plank is *six feet long.*

In general, the reason for hyphenating compound adjectives is to facilitate reading.

▶ Designers often use potted plants as living-room dividers.

Without the hyphen, *living* may seem to modify *room dividers.*

Never hyphenate an *-ly* adverb and an adjective.

▶ They used a widely⁄distributed mailing list.

Fractions and compound numbers

Use a hyphen to write out fractions and to spell out compound numbers from twenty-one to ninety-nine.

one-seventh	thirty-seven
two and seven-sixteenths	three hundred fifty-four thousand

48b Use hyphens with prefixes and suffixes.

Most words containing prefixes or suffixes are written without hyphens: *antiwar, gorillalike.* Here are some exceptions:

BEFORE CAPITALIZED BASE WORDS	un-American, non-Catholic
WITH FIGURES	pre-1960, post-1945
WITH CERTAIN PREFIXES AND SUFFIXES	all-state, ex-partner, self-possessed, quasi-legislative, mayor-elect, fifty-odd
WITH COMPOUND BASE WORDS	pre-high school, post-cold war
FOR CLARITY OR EASE OF READING	re-cover, anti-inflation, troll-like

Re-cover means "cover again"; the hyphen distinguishes it from *recover,* meaning "get well." In *anti-inflation* and *troll-like,* the hyphens separate confusing clusters of vowels and consonants.

48c Avoid unnecessary hyphens.

Unnecessary hyphens are at least as common a problem as omitted ones. Do not hyphenate the parts of a two-word verb such as *depend on, turn off,* or *tune out* (60b).

▶ Every player must pick-up a medical form before football tryouts.

The words *pick up* act as a verb and should not be hyphenated.

However, be careful to check that two words do indeed function as a verb in the sentence (31b); if they function as an adjective, a hyphen may be needed.

▶ Let's sign up for the early class.

The verb *sign up* should not have a hyphen.

▶ Where is the sign-up sheet?

The compound adjective *sign-up,* which modifies the noun *sheet,* needs a hyphen.

Do not hyphenate a subject complement—a word group that follows a linking verb (such as a form of *be* or *seem*) and describes the subject (31k).

▶ Audrey is almost nine years old.

EXERCISE 48.1

Insert or delete hyphens as necessary in the following sentences. Use your dictionary if you are not sure whether or where to hyphenate a word. Example:

> The governor‸elect joked about the polls.

1. The group seeks volunteers to set-up chairs in the meeting room before the event.

2. Despite concerns about reliability, police line-ups are still frequently used to identify suspects.

3. I was ill-prepared for my first calculus exam, but I managed to pass anyway.

4. Some passengers were bumped from the over-sold flight.

5. Having an ignore the customer attitude may actually make a service-industry job less pleasant.

6. Both pro and antiState Department groups registered complaints.

7. At a yard sale, I found a 1964 pre CBS Fender Stratocaster in mint condition.

8. Applicants who are over fifty-years-old may face age discrimination.

9. Neil Armstrong, a selfproclaimed "nerdy engineer," was the first person to set foot on the moon.

10. Carefully-marketed children's safety products suggest to new parents that the more they spend, the safer their kids will be.

bedfordstmartins.com/everydaywriter
Exercise Central > Hyphens

EXERCISE 48.2: THINKING CRITICALLY

The following paragraph uses many hyphens. Read it carefully, and note how the
hyphens make the paragraph easier to read. Why do you think *semi-pro* is hyphenated? Why is *junior-college* hyphenated in the last sentence?

> All semi-pro leagues, it should be understood, are self-sustaining, and have
> no farm affiliation or other connection with the twenty-six major-league clubs,
> or with the seventeen leagues and hundred and fifty-two teams . . . that make
> up the National Association — the minors, that is. There is no central body of
> semi-pro teams, and semi-pro players are not included among the six hundred
> and fifty major-leaguers, the twenty-five-hundred-odd minor-leaguers, plus all
> the managers, coaches, presidents, commissioners, front-office people, and
> scouts, who, taken together, constitute the great tent called organized ball.
> (A much diminished tent, at that; back in 1949, the minors included fifty-nine
> leagues, about four hundred and forty-eight teams, and perhaps ten thousand
> players.) Also outside the tent, but perhaps within its shade, are five college
> leagues, ranging across the country from Cape Cod to Alaska, where the most
> promising freshman, sophomore, and junior-college ballplayers . . . compete
> against each other. . . .   — ROGER ANGELL, "In the Country"

MLA
Documentation

Careful citation shows your reader that you've
done your homework. . . . It amounts to laying
your intellectual cards on the table.

— JACK LYNCH

MLA Documentation

49 **The Basics of MLA Style** *457*
  a Think about what readers need from your citation *457*
  b Identify the type of source you are using *458*
  c Plan and connect your citations *461*
  d Include notes as needed *462*

50 **MLA Style for In-Text Citations** *463*

51 **MLA Style for a List of Works Cited** *470*

52 **A Student Research Essay, MLA Style** *501*

For visual analysis Look carefully at the illustration on the front of this tab. What do you think this image suggests about the kinds of sources writers might document in MLA style?

The Basics of MLA Style **49**

Different rhetorical situations call for different approaches to citing sources—that is, for different ways of answering the question "Says who?" If you're reading a popular magazine, you probably won't expect the writer to provide careful source citations or a list of references at the end of an article. If you're posting material on a blog, you might follow conventions for citation by simply linking to the material you're talking about. But in other situations, including most academic writing, you will be expected to follow a more rigorous system for citing the information you use. Many courses in English ask writers to follow MLA style, the system developed by the Modern Language Association. For further reference, consult Chapters 50–52 or the *MLA Handbook for Writers of Research Papers,* Seventh Edition (2009).

49a Think about what readers need from your citation.

Why does academic work call for very careful citation practices when writing for the general public may not? The answer to that question is pretty easy: readers of your academic work (your instructor, other students, perhaps even researchers and professionals in your field) expect to get certain information from source citations:

- Source citations demonstrate that while you may not yet be a recognized expert on the topic you've nevertheless done your homework, and you are a part of the conversation surrounding it. You include sources that you find credible and that provide evidence and good reasons to back up your claims, as well as sources that you need to respond to or refute (see 17a). Careful citation shows your readers what you know, where you stand, and what you think is important.

- Source citations show that you understand the need to give credit when you make use of someone else's intellectual property.

Especially in academic writing, when it's better to be safe than sorry, include a citation for any source you think you might need to cite. (See Chapter 18 for details.)

- Source citations give explicit directions to guide readers who want to look for themselves at the works you're using.

The guidelines for MLA style (or APA, *Chicago,* or CSE—if you are asked to use these systems, see Chapters 53–55) help you with this last purpose, giving you instructions on exactly what information to include in your citation and how to format that information.

49b Identify the type of source you are using.

Before you can decide how to cite your source following MLA guidelines, you need to determine what kind of source you're using. This task can be surprisingly difficult. Citing a print book may seem relatively easy (though dizzying complications can arise—such as if the book has an editor or a translator, multiple editions, or chapters written by different people, to name a few possibilities). But citing digital sources may be especially mystifying. How, for instance, can you tell a Web site from a database you access online? What if your digital source reuses material from another source? Who publishes a digital text? Taking a step-by-step approach can help you solve such puzzles.

Print, digital, and other media sources

If your source has printed pages—a book or a newspaper, for instance—and you read the print version, you should look at the Directory to MLA Style on p. 470 for information on citing a print source. If the print source is a regularly issued journal, magazine, or newspaper (look for a date or seasonal information such as "Spring 2012" on the cover or first page), consider it a periodical rather than a book.

Be careful, however. If you access the digital version of a magazine or newspaper article, or if you read a book on an e-reader device such as a Kindle, then you should cite your source not as a print text but as a digital one. A digital version of a source may include updates or corrections that the print version lacks, so MLA guidelines require you to indicate your mode of access and to cite print and digital sources differently. Make sure to provide the correct information!

When you need to cite a source that consists mainly of material other than written words—such as a film, song, or artwork—you will need to provide additional information about how you encountered the material. See the Directory to MLA Style on p. 471 for more information on citing multimedia sources.

Articles from Web and database sources

Many students wonder how to distinguish between a Web source and a source from a database. Both, after all, can be reached from a computer (if you have home access to your school library's online resources, you may be able to reach databases from any wired location). But guidelines for citing articles from the two types of sources are different, and so are considerations for using each type of writing.

DATABASE SOURCES

You need a subscription to look through most databases, so individual researchers almost always gain access to articles in databases through the computer system of a school or community library that pays to subscribe. The easiest way to tell whether a source comes from a database, then, is that its information is *not* available for free to anyone with an Internet connection. Many databases are digital collections of articles that originally appeared in print periodicals. The articles generally have the same written-word content as they did in print form, without changes or updates (some databases omit illustrations that appear in the print versions of articles, but others upload articles as PDFs that show not just words and illustrations but also the original print layout and page numbering). Print periodicals have editors, and some journals are peer-reviewed by experts in a field, ensuring that an authority vouches for the accuracy of the information. Finding information in an article from a database does *not* guarantee its credibility, but such information often has more authority behind it than much of what you find for free on the Web.

David Craig, whose research writing appears in Chapter 52, found the following source in Academic Search Premier, a database he accessed through a library Web site. From this page he was able to click through to the full text of the article. He printed this computer screen in

A SOURCE FROM A DATABASE

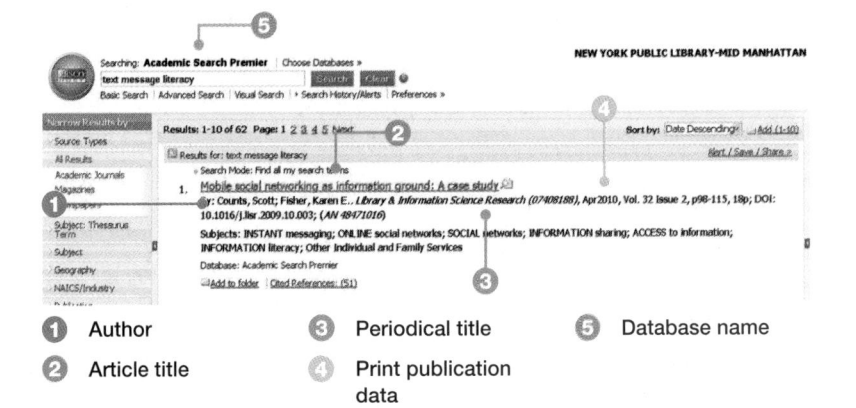

1 Author	**3** Periodical title	**5** Database name
2 Article title	**4** Print publication data	

case he needed to cite the article; the image includes all the information (other than his date of access) that he would need to create a complete MLA citation for an article from a database. Including the original print publication information for the article and the name of the database allows any reader who can access the database to locate the same article.

WEB SOURCES

Almost anyone can create a page on the Web, and information posted there often has not been verified by anyone. Therefore, MLA guidelines ask you to identify the publisher or sponsor for any work from a Web site that you cite in your writing. Information about sponsors and publishers often appears at the bottom of a page, on a home page, or in a separate "About" section on a reputable Web site (see pp. 212–13 in Chapter 17 for details on evaluating Web sources).

If the site doesn't identify a sponsor or publisher, you may still use it (see pp. 490–91), but you should do more digging to find out about the site's creator, and you would be wise to verify information on such a site before including it in your own text. David Craig looked at a Web site called "Text Message 101" while doing his preliminary research; although no author was identified, the information seemed useful. But when he noticed that the site's sponsor was a cell phone provider using the site to sell phone plans, he decided against using the source in his writing project.

Teal Pfeifer, whose paper on how media messages affect body image appears in Chapter 14, downloaded this article by Dr. Sut Jhally, a professor of media studies, from the author's personal Web site.

A WORK FROM A WEB SITE

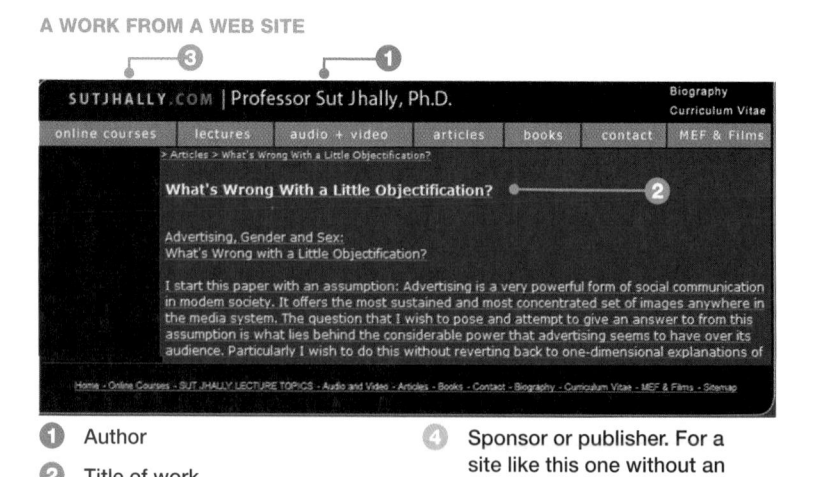

① Author
② Title of work
③ Title of Web site

④ Sponsor or publisher. For a site like this one without an identified publisher, use *N.p.*

⑤ Date of publication. For undated material such as this, use *n.d.*

Web sources for content beyond the written word

Many sources used in academic writing consist mainly of written words, presented either in print or in digital form. But you may also want to include sources in which images and other media are at least as important as written words. Figuring out which model to follow for media sources that appear online can pose additional questions.

While researching her PowerPoint presentation on Alison Bechdel's graphic memoir *Fun Home* (see Chapter 3), Shuqiao Song came across a brief video interview with Bechdel on YouTube that she wanted to play for her audience. However, the YouTube post noted that the interview had originally appeared on a video log called *Stuck in Vermont* and that this interview grew out of, and included passages from, a print interview from a small local print publication. (This kind of complicated backstory is by no means unusual for online media.) Shuqiao had to decide whether the video clip was most like a video, an interview, a work from a Web site, or something else entirely. After consulting with her instructor, she decided to give the full citation for the source as a work from a Web site (see the source map on pp. 490–91), since a YouTube citation seemed likely to make the source most accessible to those who saw her presentation. (For advice on making such decisions when no exact model is available, see the box on p. 494.)

49c Plan and connect your citations.

MLA citations appear in two parts—the brief in-text citation, usually in parentheses in the body of your written text, and the full citation in the list of works cited, to which the in-text citation directs your readers. The most straightforward in-text citations include the author's name and the page number, but many variations on this basic format are discussed in Chapter 50.

In the text of his research essay (see Chapter 52), David Craig includes a paraphrase of material from the print book *Language Play* by linguist David Crystal. As shown here, he cites the book page on which the original information appears in a parenthetical reference that points readers to the entry for "Crystal, David" in his list of works cited. He also cites statistics from a report with four named authors that he found on a Web site sponsored by the nonprofit Pew Internet & American Life Project. The report, like many online texts, does not include page numbers. These examples show just two of the many ways to cite sources using in-text citations and a list of works cited. You'll need to make case-by-case decisions based on the types of sources you include. For more information on in-text citation practices, see Chapter 50; to find models of types of sources for the list of works cited, consult Chapter 51.

to David Crystal, an internationally recognized scholar of linguistics at the University of Wales, as young children develop and learn how words string together to express ideas, they go through many phases of language play. The singsong rhymes and nonsensical chants of preschoolers are vital to their learning language, and a healthy appetite for such wordplay leads to a better command of language later in life (182).

Craig 10

-Year Trend in SAT Scores
h Is Yielding Results: *Reading and Writing Are Causes for Concern*. New York: College Board, 2002. Print.

College Board. "2011 SAT Trends." *Collegeboard.org*. College Board, 14 Sept. 2011. Web. 6 Dec. 2011.

Crystal, David. *Language Play*. Chicago: U of Chicago P, 1998. Print.

The Discouraging Word. "Re: Messaging and Literacy." Message to the author. 13 Nov. 2011. E-mail.

"Is Texting Destroying Kids' Writing Style?" *Curriculum Review* 48.1 (2008): 4-5. *Academic Search Premier*. Web. 7 Dec. 2011.

Leibowitz, Wendy R. "Technology Transforms Writing and the Teaching of Writing." *Chronicle of Higher Education* 26 Nov. 1999: A67-68. Print.

Lenhart, Amanda, Sousan Arafeh, Aaron Smith, and Alexandra Macgill. *Writing, Technology & Teens*. Washington: Pew Internet & Amer. Life Project, 2008. Web. 6 Dec. 2011.

the rise. According to the Pew Internet & American Life Project, 85 percent of those aged 12-17 at least occasionally write text messages, instant messages, or comments on social networking sites (Lenhart, Arafeh, Smith, and Macgill). In 2001, the most

Teenage Life Online: The Rise of *and the Internet's Impact on* *ships*. Washington: Pew Internet . 6 Dec. 2011.

McCarroll, Christina. "Teens Ready to Prove Text-Messaging Skills Can Score SAT Points." *Christian Science Monitor* 11 Mar. 2005. Web. 10 Dec. 2011.

49d   Include notes as needed.

MLA citation style asks you to include explanatory notes for information or comments that don't readily fit into your text but are needed for clarification or further explanation. In addition, MLA permits bibliographic notes for offering information about or evaluation of a source, or to list multiple sources that relate to a single point. Use superscript numbers in the text to refer readers to the notes, which may appear as endnotes (under the heading *Notes* on a separate page immediately before the list of works cited) or as footnotes at the bottom of each page where a superscript number appears.

Although messaging relies on the written word, many messagers disregard standard writing conventions. For example, here is a snippet from an IM conversation between two teenage girls:[1]

1. This transcript of an IM conversation was collected on 20 Nov. 2011. The teenagers' names are concealed to protect their privacy.

MLA Style for In-Text Citations   50

MLA style requires a citation in the text of an essay for every quotation, paraphrase, summary, or other material requiring documentation (see 18f). In-text citations document material from other sources with both signal phrases and parenthetical references. Parenthetical references should include the information your readers need to locate the full reference in the list of works cited at the end of the text. (See Chapter 51.) An in-text citation in MLA style gives the reader two kinds of information: (1) it indicates which source on the works-cited page the writer is referring to, and (2) it explains where in the source the material quoted, paraphrased, or summarized can be found, if the source has page numbers or other numbered sections.

The basic MLA in-text citation includes the author's last name either in a signal phrase introducing the source material (see 18b) or in parentheses at the end of the sentence. For print sources, it also includes the page number in parentheses at the end of the sentence.

DIRECTORY TO MLA STYLE

MLA style for in-text citations

1. Author named in a signal phrase, *464*
2. Author named in a parenthetical reference, *464*
3. Two or three authors, *465*
4. Four or more authors, *465*
5. Organization as author, *465*

➔

MLA style for in-text citations, continued

6. Unknown author, *465*
7. Author of two or more works cited in the same project, *465*
8. Two or more authors with the same last name, *465*
9. Indirect source (author quoting someone else), *466*
10. Multivolume work, *466*
11. Literary work, *466*
12. Work in an anthology or collection, *467*

13. Sacred text, *467*
14. Encyclopedia or dictionary entry, *467*
15. Government source with no author named, *467*
16. Electronic or nonprint source, *467*
17. Entire work, *468*
18. Two or more sources in one parenthetical reference, *468*
19. Visual included in the text, *468*

SAMPLE CITATION USING A SIGNAL PHRASE

In his discussion of Monty Python routines, Crystal notes that the group relished "breaking the normal rules" of language (107).

SAMPLE PARENTHETICAL CITATION

A noted linguist explains that Monty Python humor often relied on "bizarre linguistic interactions" (Crystal 108).

bedfordstmartins.com/everydaywriter
Documenting Sources

Note in the following examples where punctuation is placed in relation to the parentheses.

1. AUTHOR NAMED IN A SIGNAL PHRASE

The MLA recommends using the author's name in a signal phrase to introduce the material and citing the page number(s) in parentheses.

Lee claims that his comic-book creation, Thor, was "the first regularly published superhero to speak in a consistently archaic manner" (199).

2. AUTHOR NAMED IN A PARENTHETICAL REFERENCE

When you do not mention the author in a signal phrase, include the author's last name before the page number(s) in the parentheses. Use no punctuation between the author's name and the page number(s).

The word *Bollywood* is sometimes considered an insult because it implies that Indian movies are merely "a derivative of the American film industry" (Chopra 9).

3. TWO OR THREE AUTHORS

Use all the authors' last names in a signal phrase or in parentheses.

> Gortner, Hebrun, and Nicolson maintain that "opinion leaders" influence other people in an organization because they are respected, not because they hold high positions (175).

4. FOUR OR MORE AUTHORS

Name all the authors in a signal phrase or in parentheses, or use the first author's name and *et al.* ("and others").

> Similarly, as Belenky, Clinchy, Tarule, and Goldberger assert, examining the lives of women expands our understanding of human development (7).

> Similarly, as Belenky et al. assert, examining the lives of women expands our understanding of human development (7).

5. ORGANIZATION AS AUTHOR

Give the group's full name or a shortened form of it in a signal phrase or in parentheses.

> Any study of social welfare involves a close analysis of "the impacts, the benefits, and the costs" of its policies (Social Research Corporation iii).

6. UNKNOWN AUTHOR

Use the full title, if it is brief, in your text — or a shortened version of the title in parentheses.

> One analysis defines *hype* as "an artificially engendered atmosphere of hysteria" ("Today's Marketplace" 51).

7. AUTHOR OF TWO OR MORE WORKS CITED IN THE SAME PROJECT

If your list of works cited has more than one work by the same author, include a shortened version of the title of the work you are citing in a signal phrase or in parentheses to prevent reader confusion.

> Gardner shows readers their own silliness in his description of a "pointless, ridiculous monster, crouched in the shadows, stinking of dead men, murdered children, and martyred cows" (*Grendel* 2).

8. TWO OR MORE AUTHORS WITH THE SAME LAST NAME

Include the author's first *and* last names in a signal phrase or first initial and last name in a parenthetical reference.

> Children will learn to write if they are allowed to choose their own
> subjects, James Britton asserts, citing the Schools Council study of the
> 1960s (37-42).

9. INDIRECT SOURCE (AUTHOR QUOTING SOMEONE ELSE)

Use the abbreviation *qtd. in* to indicate that you are quoting from someone else's report of a source.

> As Arthur Miller says, "When somebody is destroyed everybody finally
> contributes to it, but in Willy's case, the end product would be virtually the
> same" (qtd. in Martin and Meyer 375).

10. MULTIVOLUME WORK

In a parenthetical reference, note the volume number first and then the
page number(s), with a colon and one space between them.

> Modernist writers prized experimentation and gradually even sought to blur
> the line between poetry and prose, according to Forster (3: 150).

If you name only one volume of the work in your list of works cited,
include only the page number in the parentheses.

11. LITERARY WORK

Because literary works are often available in many different editions,
cite the page number(s) from the edition you used followed by a semicolon, and then give other identifying information that will lead readers
to the passage in any edition. Indicate the act and/or scene in a play (37;
sc. 1). For a novel, indicate the part or chapter (*175; ch. 4*).

> In utter despair, Dostoyevsky's character Mitya wonders aloud about the
> "terrible tragedies realism inflicts on people" (376; bk. 8, ch. 2).

For a poem, cite the part (if there is one) and line(s), separated by a
period. If you are citing only line numbers, use the word *line(s)* in the
first reference *(lines 33–34)*.

> Whitman speculates, "All goes onward and outward, nothing collapses, / And
> to die is different from what anyone supposed, and luckier" (6.129-30).

For a verse play, give only the act, scene, and line numbers, separated
by periods.

> The witches greet Banquo as "Lesser than Macbeth, and greater"
> (1.3.65).

12. WORK IN AN ANTHOLOGY OR COLLECTION

For an essay, short story, or other piece of prose reprinted in an anthology, use the name of the author of the work, not the editor of the anthology, but use the page number(s) from the anthology.

> Narratives of captivity play a major role in early writing by women in the
> United States, as demonstrated by Silko (219).

13. SACRED TEXT

To cite a sacred text such as the Qur'an or the Bible, give the title of the edition you used, the book, and the chapter and verse (or their equivalent) separated by a period. In your text, spell out the names of books. In parenthetical references, use abbreviations for books with names of five or more letters (*Gen.* for *Genesis*).

> He ignored the admonition "Pride goes before destruction, and a haughty
> spirit before a fall" (*New Oxford Annotated Bible,* Prov. 16.18).

14. ENCYCLOPEDIA OR DICTIONARY ENTRY

An entry from a reference work—such as an encyclopedia or dictionary—without an author will appear on the works-cited list under the entry's title. Enclose the title in quotation marks and place it in parentheses. Omit the page number for reference works that arrange entries alphabetically.

> The term *prion* was coined by Stanley B. Prusiner from the words
> *proteinaceous* and *infectious* and a suffix meaning *particle* ("Prion").

15. GOVERNMENT SOURCE WITH NO AUTHOR NAMED

Because entries for sources authored by government agencies will appear on your list of works cited under the name of the country (see Chapter 51, item 70), your in-text citation for such a source should include the name of the country as well as the name of the agency responsible for the source.

> To reduce the agricultural runoff into the Chesapeake Bay, the United States
> Environmental Protection Agency has argued that "[h]igh nutrient loading
> crops, such as corn and soybean, should be replaced with alternatives in
> environmentally sensitive areas" (2-26).

16. ELECTRONIC OR NONPRINT SOURCE

Give enough information in a signal phrase or in parentheses for readers to locate the source in your list of works cited. Many works found online or in electronic databases lack stable page numbers; you can omit the page number in such cases. However, if you are citing a work with stable pagination, such as an article in PDF format, include the page number in parentheses.

> As a *Slate* analysis has noted, "Prominent sports psychologists get praised for their successes and don't get grief for their failures" (Engber).

The source, an article on a Web site, does not have stable pagination.

> According to Whitmarsh, the British military had experimented with using balloons for observation as far back as 1879 (328).

The source, an online PDF of a print article, includes stable page numbers.

If the source includes numbered sections, paragraphs, or screens, include the abbreviation (*sec.*), paragraph (*par.*), or screen (*scr.*) number in parentheses.

> Sherman notes that the "immediate, interactive, and on-the-spot" nature of Internet information can make nondigital media seem outdated (sec. 32).

17. ENTIRE WORK

Include the reference in the text, without any page numbers.

> Jon Krakauer's *Into the Wild* both criticizes and admires the solitary impulses of its young hero, which end up killing him.

18. TWO OR MORE SOURCES IN ONE PARENTHETICAL REFERENCE

Separate the information with semicolons.

> Economists recommend that *employment* be redefined to include unpaid domestic labor (Clark 148; Nevins 39).

19. VISUAL INCLUDED IN THE TEXT

When you include an image in your text, number it and include a parenthetical reference in your text (*see Fig. 2*). Number figures (photos, drawings, cartoons, maps, graphs, and charts) and tables separately. Each visual should include a caption with the figure or table number and information about the source—either a complete citation or enough information to direct readers to the works-cited entry. (See 9d.)

> This trend is illustrated in a chart distributed by the College Board as part of its 2011 analysis of aggregate SAT data (see Fig. 1).

Soon after the preceding sentence, readers find the following figure and a caption referring them to the entry on the list of works cited (see Chapter 52 to read the student's entire research paper):

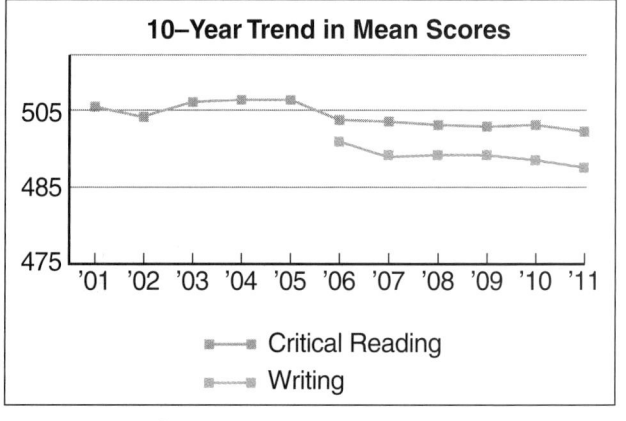

10–Year Trend in Mean Scores

Fig. 1. Ten-year trend in mean SAT reading and writing scores (2001-2011).
Source: College Board, "2011 SAT Trends."

An image that you create might appear with a caption like this (see 14k to see this example used in a student essay):

Fig. 4. Young women reading magazines. Personal photograph by author.

51 MLA Style for a List of Works Cited

A list of works cited is an alphabetical list of the sources you have referred to in your essay. (If your instructor asks you to list everything you have read as background, call the list *Works Consulted*.)

 bedfordstmartins.com/everydaywriter
Documenting Sources

DIRECTORY TO MLA STYLE

MLA style for a list of works cited

Guidelines for author listings
1. One author, *473*
2. Multiple authors, *473*
3. Organization or group author, *473*
4. Unknown author, *473*
5. Two or more works by the same author, *473*

Print books
6. Basic format for a book, *474*
   SOURCE MAP, *476–77*
7. Author and editor both named, *474*
8. Editor, no author named, *474*
9. Anthology, *474*
10. Work in an anthology or chapter in a book with an editor, *475*
11. Two or more items from the same anthology, *475*
12. Translation, *475*
13. Book with both translator and editor, *475*
14. Translation of a section of a book, *475*
15. Translation of a book by an unknown author, *478*
16. Book in a language other than English, *478*

17. Graphic narrative, *478*
18. Edition other than the first, *479*
19. One volume of a multivolume work, *479*
20. Two or more volumes of a multivolume work, *479*
21. Preface, foreword, introduction, or afterword, *479*
22. Entry in a reference book, *479*
23. Book that is part of a series, *479*
24. Republication (modern edition of an older book), *479*
25. Publisher's imprint, *480*
26. Book with a title within the title, *480*
27. Sacred text, *480*

Print periodicals
28. Article in a print journal, *480*
29. Article in a print magazine, *480*
   SOURCE MAP, *482–83*
30. Article in a print newspaper, *481*
31. Article that skips pages, *481*
32. Editorial or letter to the editor, *481*
33. Review, *481*
34. Unsigned article, *484*

MLA style for a list of works cited, continued

Digital written-word sources

35. Work from a database, *485*
    SOURCE MAP, *486–87*
36. Article from the Web site of a journal, *485*
37. Article in a magazine on the Web, *485*
38. Article in a newspaper on the Web, *485*
39. Book on the Web, *488*
40. Poem on the Web, *488*
41. Editorial or letter in a Web periodical, *488*
42. Review in a Web periodical, *488*
43. Entry in a Web reference work, *489*
44. Work from a Web site, *489*
    SOURCE MAP, *490–91*
45. Entire Web site, *489*
46. Academic course Web site, *492*
47. Blog, *492*
48. Post or comment on a blog, *492*
49. Entry in a wiki, *492*
50. Posting to a discussion group or newsgroup, *493*
51. Posting to a social networking site, *493*
52. Email or message on social networking site, *493*
53. Tweet, *493*

Visual, audio, multimedia, and live sources

54. Film or DVD, *494*
55. Online video clip, *494*

56. Television or radio program, *494*
57. Broadcast interview, *495*
58. Unpublished or personal interview, *495*
59. Sound recording, *495*
60. Musical composition, *496*
61. Computer game, *496*
62. Lecture or speech, *496*
63. Live performance, *497*
64. Podcast (streaming), *497*
65. Digital file, *497*
66. Work of art or photograph, *497*
67. Map or chart, *498*
68. Cartoon or comic strip, *498*
69. Advertisement, *499*

Academic, government, and legal sources (including digital versions)

70. Report or pamphlet, *499*
71. Government publication, *499*
72. Published proceedings of a conference, *500*
73. Dissertation, *500*
74. Dissertation abstract, *500*
75. Published interview, *500*
76. Unpublished letter, *500*
77. Manuscript or other unpublished work, *501*
78. Legal source, *501*

Guidelines for author listings

The list of works cited is arranged alphabetically. The in-text citations in your writing point readers toward particular sources on the list (see Chapter 50).

NAME CITED IN SIGNAL PHRASE IN TEXT

 Crystal explains. . . .

NAME IN PARENTHETICAL CITATION IN TEXT

. . . (Crystal 107).

BEGINNING OF ENTRY ON LIST OF WORKS CITED

Crystal, David.

AT A GLANCE

Formatting a List of Works Cited

- Start your list on a separate page after the text of your document and any notes.

- Continue the consecutive numbering of pages.

- Center the heading *Works Cited* (not italicized or in quotation marks) one inch from the top of the page.

- Begin each entry flush with the left margin, but indent subsequent lines one-half inch. Double-space the entire list.

- List sources alphabetically by the first word. Start with the author's name, if available; if not, use the editor's name, if available. If no author or editor is given, start with the title.

- List the author's last name first, followed by a comma and the first name. If a source has multiple authors, subsequent authors' names appear first name first (see model 2).

- Italicize titles of books and long works, but put titles of articles and other short works in quotation marks.

- In general, use a period and a space after each element of the entry; look at the models in this chapter for information on punctuating particular kinds of entries.

- For a book, list the city of publication (add a country abbreviation for non-U.S. cities that may be unfamiliar). Follow it with a colon and a shortened form of the publisher's name — omit *Co.* or *Inc.*, shorten names such as *Simon & Schuster* to *Simon*, and abbreviate *University Press* to *UP*.

- List dates of periodical publication or of access to electronic items in day, month, year order, and abbreviate months except for May, June, and July.

- Give a medium, such as *Print* or *Web*, for each entry.

- List inclusive page numbers for a part of a larger work.

Models 1–5 on p. 473 explain how to arrange author names. The information that follows the name of the author depends on the type of work you are citing—a book (models 6–27); a print periodical (models 28–34); a written text from a digital source, such as an article from a Web site or database (models 35–53); sources from art, film, comics, or other media, including live performances (models 54–69); and academic, government, and legal sources (models 70–78). Consult the model that most closely resembles the kind of source you are using.

1. ONE AUTHOR

Put the last name first, followed by a comma, the first name (and initial, if any), and a period.

> Crystal, David.

2. MULTIPLE AUTHORS

List the first author with the last name first (see model 1). Give the names of any other authors with the first name first. Separate authors' names with commas, and include the word *and* before the last person's name.

> Martineau, Jane, Desmond Shawe-Taylor, and Jonathan Bate.

For four or more authors, either list all the names, or list the first author followed by a comma and *et al.* ("and others").

> Lupton, Ellen, Jennifer Tobias, Alicia Imperiale, Grace Jeffers, and Randi Mates.

> Lupton, Ellen, et al.

3. ORGANIZATION OR GROUP AUTHOR

Give the name of the group, government agency, corporation, or other organization listed as the author.

> Getty Trust.

> United States. Government Accountability Office.

4. UNKNOWN AUTHOR

When the author is not identified, begin the entry with the title, and alphabetize by the first important word. Italicize titles of books and long works, but put titles of articles and other short works in quotation marks.

> "California Sues EPA over Emissions."

> *New Concise World Atlas.*

5. TWO OR MORE WORKS BY THE SAME AUTHOR

Arrange the entries alphabetically by title. Include the author's name in the first entry, but in subsequent entries, use three hyphens followed by a period. (For the basic format for citing a book, see model 6. For the basic format for citing an article from an online newspaper, see model 38.)

Chopra, Anupama. "Bollywood Princess, Hollywood Hopeful." *New York Times*.
New York Times, 10 Feb. 2008. Web. 13 Feb. 2008.

---. *King of Bollywood: Shah Rukh Khan and the Seductive World of Indian Cinema*. New York: Warner, 2007. Print.

Note: Use three hyphens only when the work is by *exactly* the same author(s) as the previous entry.

Print books

6. BASIC FORMAT FOR A BOOK

Begin with the author name(s). (See models 1–5.) Then include the title and subtitle, the city of publication, the publisher, the publication year, and the medium (*Print*). The source map on pp. 476–77 shows where to find this information in a typical book.

Crystal, David. *Language Play*. Chicago: U of Chicago P, 1998. Print.

Note: Place a period and a space after the name, title, and date. Place a colon after the city and a comma after the publisher, and shorten the publisher's name—omit *Co.* or *Inc.*, and abbreviate *University Press* to *UP*.

7. AUTHOR AND EDITOR BOTH NAMED

Bangs, Lester. *Psychotic Reactions and Carburetor Dung*. Ed. Greil Marcus.
New York: Knopf, 1988. Print.

Note: To cite the editor's contribution instead, begin the entry with the editor's name.

Marcus, Greil, ed. *Psychotic Reactions and Carburetor Dung*. By Lester Bangs.
New York: Knopf, 1988. Print.

8. EDITOR, NO AUTHOR NAMED

Wall, Cheryl A., ed. *Changing Our Own Words: Essays on Criticism, Theory, and Writing by Black Women*. New Brunswick: Rutgers UP, 1989. Print.

9. ANTHOLOGY

Cite an entire anthology the same way you would cite a book with an editor and no named author (see model 8).

Walker, Dale L., ed. *Westward: A Fictional History of the American West*.
New York: Forge, 2003. Print.

10. WORK IN AN ANTHOLOGY OR CHAPTER IN A BOOK WITH AN EDITOR

List the author(s) of the selection or chapter; its title, in quotation marks; the title of the book, italicized; *Ed.* and the name(s) of the editor(s); publication information; and the selection's page numbers.

> Komunyakaa, Yusef. "Facing It." *The Seagull Reader.* Ed. Joseph Kelly. New York:
>
> Norton, 2000. 126-27. Print.

Note: Use the following format to provide original publication information for a reprinted selection:

> Byatt, A. S. "The Thing in the Forest." *New Yorker* 3 June 2002: 80-89. Rpt. in
>
> *The O. Henry Prize Stories 2003.* Ed. Laura Furman. New York: Anchor, 2003.
>
> 3-22. Print.

11. TWO OR MORE ITEMS FROM THE SAME ANTHOLOGY

List the anthology as one entry (see model 9). Also list each selection separately with a cross-reference to the anthology.

> Estleman, Loren D. "Big Tim Magoon and the Wild West." Walker 391-404. Print.

> Salzer, Susan K. "Miss Libbie Tells All." Walker 199-212. Print.

12. TRANSLATION

> Bolaño, Roberto. *2666.* Trans. Natasha Wimmer. New York: Farrar, 2008. Print.

13. BOOK WITH BOTH TRANSLATOR AND EDITOR

List the editor's and translator's names after the title, in the order they appear on the title page.

> Kant, Immanuel. *"Toward Perpetual Peace" and Other Writings on Politics, Peace,*
>
> *and History.* Ed. Pauline Kleingeld. Trans. David L. Colclasure. New Haven:
>
> Yale UP, 2006. Print.

14. TRANSLATION OF A SECTION OF A BOOK

If different translators have worked on various parts of the book, identify the translator of the part you are citing.

> García Lorca, Federico. "The Little Mad Boy." Trans. W. S. Merwin. *The Selected*
>
> *Poems of Federico García Lorca.* Ed. Francisco García Lorca and Donald M.
>
> Allen. London: Penguin, 1969. Print.

MLA SOURCE MAP: Books

Take information from the book's title page and copyright page (on the reverse side of the title page), not from the book's cover or a library catalog.

1 **Author.** List the last name first. End with a period. For variations, see models 2–5.

2 **Title.** Italicize the title and any subtitle; capitalize all major words. End with a period.

3 **City of publication.** If more than one city is given, use the first one listed. For foreign cities, add an abbreviation of the country or province (*Cork, Ire.*). Follow it with a colon.

4 **Publisher.** Give a shortened version of the publisher's name (*Oxford UP* for *Oxford University Press*). Follow it with a comma.

5 **Year of publication.** If more than one copyright date is given, use the most recent one. End with a period.

6 **Medium of publication.** End with the medium (*Print*) followed by a period.

A citation for the book on p. 477 would look like this:

Patel, Raj. *The Value of Nothing: How to Reshape Market Society and Redefine Democracy.* New York: Picador, 2009. Print.

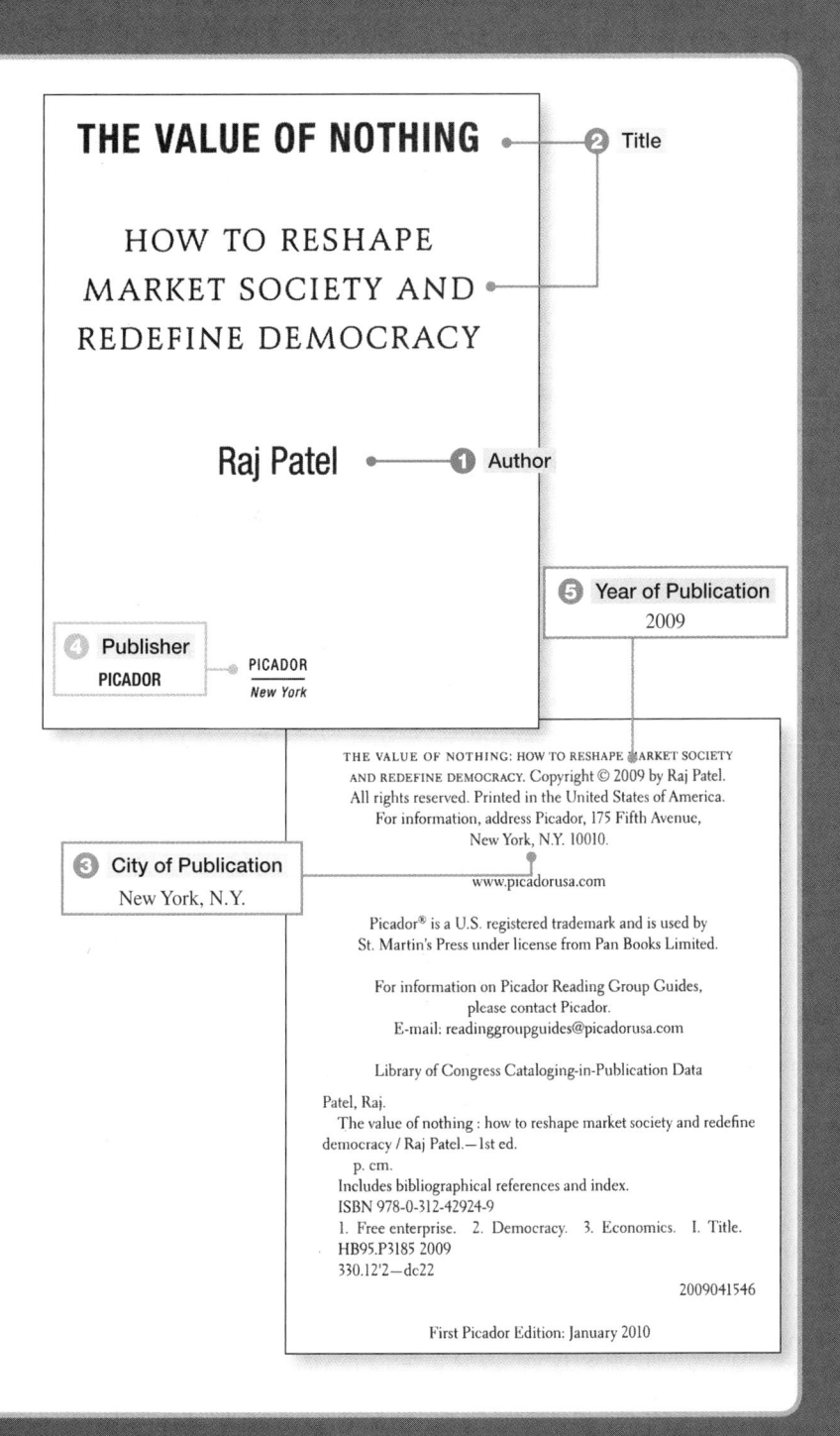

THE VALUE OF NOTHING

2 Title

HOW TO RESHAPE MARKET SOCIETY AND REDEFINE DEMOCRACY

Raj Patel

1 Author

5 Year of Publication
2009

4 Publisher
PICADOR

PICADOR
New York

3 City of Publication
New York, N.Y.

THE VALUE OF NOTHING: HOW TO RESHAPE MARKET SOCIETY AND REDEFINE DEMOCRACY. Copyright © 2009 by Raj Patel. All rights reserved. Printed in the United States of America. For information, address Picador, 175 Fifth Avenue, New York, N.Y. 10010.

www.picadorusa.com

Picador® is a U.S. registered trademark and is used by St. Martin's Press under license from Pan Books Limited.

For information on Picador Reading Group Guides, please contact Picador.
E-mail: readinggroupguides@picadorusa.com

Library of Congress Cataloging-in-Publication Data

Patel, Raj.
  The value of nothing : how to reshape market society and redefine democracy / Raj Patel.—1st ed.
    p. cm.
  Includes bibliographical references and index.
  ISBN 978-0-312-42924-9
  1. Free enterprise. 2. Democracy. 3. Economics. I. Title.
HB95.P3185 2009
330.12'2—dc22

2009041546

First Picador Edition: January 2010

477

Combining Parts of Models

What should you do if your source doesn't match the model exactly? Suppose, for instance, that your source is a translated essay that appears in the fifth edition of an anthology.

- Identify a basic model to follow. If you decide that your source looks most like an essay in an anthology, you would start with a citation that looks like model 10.

- Look for models that show the additional elements in your source. For this example, you would need to add elements of model 14 (for the translation) and model 18 (for an edition other than the first).

- Add new elements from other models to your basic model in the order indicated.

- If you still aren't sure how to arrange the pieces to create a combination model, check the *MLA Handbook* or ask your instructor.

15. TRANSLATION OF A BOOK BY AN UNKNOWN AUTHOR

Grettir's Saga. Trans. Denton Fox and Hermann Palsson. Toronto: U of Toronto P, 1974. Print.

16. BOOK IN A LANGUAGE OTHER THAN ENGLISH

Include a translation of the title in brackets, if necessary.

Benedetti, Mario. *La borra del café [The Coffee Grind]*. Buenos Aires: Sudamericana, 2000. Print.

17. GRAPHIC NARRATIVE

If the words and images are created by the same person, cite a graphic narrative just as you would a book (model 6).

Bechdel, Alison. *Fun Home: A Family Tragicomic*. New York: Houghton, 2006. Print.

If the work is a collaboration, indicate the author or illustrator who is most important to your research before the title of the work. List other contributors after the title, in the order of their appearance on the title page. Label each person's contribution to the work.

Stavans, Ilan, writer. *Latino USA: A Cartoon History*. Illus. Lalo Arcaraz. New York: Basic, 2000. Print.

18. EDITION OTHER THAN THE FIRST

> Walker, John A. *Art in the Age of Mass Media*. 3rd ed. London: Pluto, 2001.
>
> Print.

19. ONE VOLUME OF A MULTIVOLUME WORK

Give the number of the volume cited after the title. Including the total number of volumes after the publication date is optional.

> Ch'oe, Yong-Ho, Peter Lee, and William Theodore De Barry, eds. *Sources of Korean*
>
> *Tradition*. Vol. 2. New York: Columbia UP, 2000. Print. 2 vols.

20. TWO OR MORE VOLUMES OF A MULTIVOLUME WORK

> Ch'oe, Yong-Ho, Peter Lee, and William Theodore De Barry, eds. *Sources of Korean*
>
> *Tradition*. 2 vols. New York: Columbia UP, 2000. Print.

21. PREFACE, FOREWORD, INTRODUCTION, OR AFTERWORD

After the writer's name, describe the contribution. After the title, indicate the book's author (with *By*) or editor (with *Ed.*).

> Atwan, Robert. Foreword. *The Best American Essays 2002*. Ed. Stephen Jay Gould.
>
> Boston: Houghton, 2002. viii-xii. Print.

> Moore, Thurston. Introduction. *Confusion Is Next: The Sonic Youth Story*. By Alec
>
> Foege. New York: St. Martin's, 1994. xi. Print.

22. ENTRY IN A REFERENCE BOOK

For a well-known encyclopedia, note the edition (if identified) and year of publication. If the entries are alphabetized, omit publication information and page number.

> Kettering, Alison McNeil. "Art Nouveau." *World Book Encyclopedia*. 2002 ed.
>
> Print.

23. BOOK THAT IS PART OF A SERIES

Cite the series name (and number, if any) from the title page.

> Nichanian, Marc, and Vartan Matiossian, eds. *Yeghishe Charents: Poet of the*
>
> *Revolution*. Costa Mesa: Mazda, 2003. Print. Armenian Studies Ser. 5.

24. REPUBLICATION (MODERN EDITION OF AN OLDER BOOK)

Indicate the original publication date after the title.

> Austen, Jane. *Sense and Sensibility*. 1813. New York: Dover, 1996. Print.

25. PUBLISHER'S IMPRINT

If the title page gives a publisher's imprint, hyphenate the imprint and the publisher's name.

> Hornby, Nick. *About a Boy*. New York: Riverhead-Penguin Putnam, 1998. Print.

26. BOOK WITH A TITLE WITHIN THE TITLE

Do not italicize a book title within a title. For an article title within a title, italicize as usual and place the article title in quotation marks.

> Mullaney, Julie. *Arundhati Roy's* The God of Small Things: *A Reader's Guide*.
> New York: Continuum, 2002. Print.

> Rhynes, Martha. *"I, Too, Sing America": The Story of Langston Hughes*.
> Greensboro: Morgan, 2002. Print.

27. SACRED TEXT

To cite individual published editions of sacred books, begin the entry with the title.

> *Qur'an: The Final Testament (Authorized English Version) with Arabic Text*. Trans.
> Rashad Khalifa. Fremont: Universal Unity, 2000. Print.

Print periodicals

Begin with the author name(s). (See models 1–5.) Then include the article title, the title of the periodical, the date or volume information, the page numbers, and the medium (*Print*). The source map on pp. 482–83 shows where to find this information in a sample periodical.

28. ARTICLE IN A PRINT JOURNAL

Follow the journal title with the volume number, a period, the issue number (if given), and the year (in parentheses).

> Gigante, Denise. "The Monster in the Rainbow: Keats and the Science of Life."
> *PMLA* 117.3 (2002): 433-48. Print.

29. ARTICLE IN A PRINT MAGAZINE

Provide the date from the magazine cover instead of volume or issue numbers.

> Surowiecki, James. "The Stimulus Strategy." *New Yorker* 25 Feb. 2008: 29. Print.

> Taubin, Amy. "All Talk?" *Film Comment* Nov.-Dec. 2007: 45-47. Print.

AT A GLANCE

Formatting Print Periodical Entries

- Put titles of articles from periodicals in quotation marks. Place the period inside the closing quotation mark.
- Give the title of the periodical as it appears on the magazine's or journal's cover or newspaper's front page; omit any initial *A, An,* or *The.* Italicize the title.
- For journals, include the volume number, a period, the issue number, if given, and the year in parentheses.
- For magazines and newspapers, give the date in this order: day (if given), month, year. Abbreviate months except for May, June, and July.
- List inclusive page numbers if the article appears on consecutive pages. If it skips pages, give only the first page number and a plus sign.
- End with the medium (*Print*).

30. ARTICLE IN A PRINT NEWSPAPER

Include the edition (if listed) and the section number or letter (if listed).

> Longman, Jeré. "Kim Jong-il, Sportsman." *New York Times* 21 Dec. 2011, late ed.: B12. Print.

Note: For locally published newspapers, add the city in brackets after the name if it is not part of the name: *Globe and Mail [Toronto].*

31. ARTICLE THAT SKIPS PAGES

When an article skips pages, give only the first page number and a plus sign.

> Tyrnauer, Matthew. "Empire by Martha." *Vanity Fair* Sept. 2002: 364+. Print.

32. EDITORIAL OR LETTER TO THE EDITOR

Include the writer's name, if given, and the title, if any, followed by a label for the work.

> "California Dreaming." Editorial. *Nation* 25 Feb. 2008: 4. Print.

> Galbraith, James K. "JFK's Plans to Withdraw." Letter. *New York Review of Books* 6 Dec. 2007: 77-78. Print.

33. REVIEW

> Franklin, Nancy. "Teen Spirit." Rev. of *Glee,* by Ryan Murphy, Brad Falchuk, and Ian Brennan. *New Yorker* 10 May 2010: 72-73. Print.

MLA SOURCE MAP: Articles in Print Periodicals

1 **Author.** List the last name first. End with a period. For variations, see models 2–5.

2 **Article title.** Put the title and any subtitle in quotation marks; capitalize all major words. Place a period inside the closing quotation mark.

3 **Periodical title.** Italicize the title; capitalize all major words. Omit any initial *A, An,* or *The.*

4 **Volume and issue / Date of publication.** For journals, give the volume number and issue number (if any), separated by a period; then list the year in parentheses and follow it with a colon.

For magazines, list the day (if given), month, and year.

5 **Page numbers.** List inclusive page numbers. If the article skips pages, put the first page number and a plus sign. End with a period.

6 **Medium.** Give the medium (*Print*). End with a period.

A citation for the magazine article on p. 483 would look like this:

Quart, Alissa. "Lost Media, Found Media: Snapshots from the Future of
  Writing." *Columbia Journalism Review* May/June 2008: 30-34. Print.

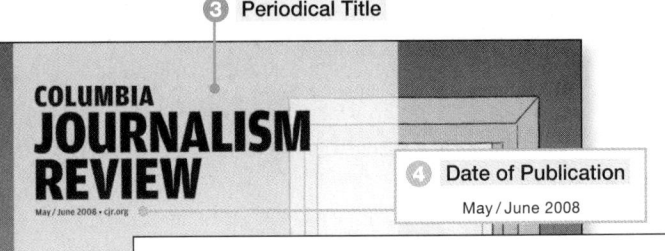

③ Periodical Title

COLUMBIA JOURNALISM REVIEW

May / June 2008 • cjr.org

④ Date of Publication

May / June 2008

The Futur...

Writin...

Nonfiction's disqui...
ALISSA QUART

Kindle isn't it, but...
EZRA KLEIN

UNDER THE SHI...
A reporter recalls...
that got him throu...
CAMERON MCWHIRT...

LOVE THY NEIGH...
The religion beat i...
TIM TOWNSEND

$4.95

② Article Title

become like the people at the ashram after the guru has died.

Right now, journalism is more or less divided into two camps, which I will call Lost Media and Found Media. I went to the Nieman conference partially because I wanted to see how the forces creating this new division are affecting and afflicting the Lost Media world that I love best, not on the institutional level, but for reporters and writers themselves. This world includes people who write for all the newspapers and magazines that are currently struggling with layoffs, speedups, hiring freezes, buyouts, the death or shrinkage of film- and book-review sections, limits on expensive investigative work, the erasure of foreign bureaus, and the general narrowing of institutional ambition. It includes freelance writers competing with hordes of ever-younger competitors willing to write and publish online for free, the fade-out of established journalistic career paths, and, perhaps most crucially, a muddled sense of the meritorious, as blogs level and scramble the value and status of print publications, and of professional writers. The glamour and influence once associated with a magazine elite seem to have faded, becoming a sort of pastiche of winsome articles about yearning and boxers and dinners at Elaine's.

Lost Media, Found Media

Snapshots from the future of writing

BY ALISSA QUART

① Author

ALISSA QUART

If there were an ashram for people who worship contemplative long-form journalism, it would be the Nieman Conference on Narrative Journalism. This March, at the Sheraton Boston Hotel, hundreds of journalists, authors, students, and aspirants came for the weekend event. Seated on metal chairs in large conference rooms, we learned about muscular storytelling (the Q-shaped narrative structure—who knew?). We sipped cups of coffee and ate bagels and heard about reporting history through letters and public documents and how to evoke empathy for our subjects, particularly our most marginal ones. As we listened to reporters discussing great feats—exposing Walter Reed's fetid living quarters for wounded soldiers, for instance—we also renewed our pride in our profession. In short, the conference exemplified the best of the older media models, the ones that have so recently fallen into economic turmoil.

Yet even at the weekend's strongest lectures on interview techniques or the long-form profile, we couldn't ignore the digital elephant in the room. We all knew as writers that the kinds of pieces we were discussing require months of work to be both deep and refined, and that we were all hard-pressed for the time and the money to do that. It was always hard for nonfiction writers, but something seems to have changed. For those of us who believed in the value of the journalism and literary nonfiction of the past, we had

Found Media-ites, meanwhile, are the bloggers, the contributors to Huffington Post-type sites that aggregate blogs, as well as other work that somebody else paid for, and the new nonprofits and pay-per-article schemes that aim to save journalism from 20 percent profit-margin demands. Although these elements are often disparate, together they compose the new media landscape. In economic terms, I mean all the outlets for nonfiction writing that seem to be thriving in the new era or striving to fill niches that Lost Media is giving up in a new order. Stylistically, Found Media tends to feel spontaneous, almost accidental. It's a domain dominated by the young, where writers get points not for following traditions or burnishing them but for amateur and hybrid vigor, for creating their own venues and their own genres. It is about public expression and community—not quite John Dewey's Great Community, which the critic Eric Alterman alluded to in a recent *New Yorker* article on newspapers, but rather a fractured form of Dewey's ideal: call it Great Communities.

To be a Found Media journalist or pundit, one need not be elite, expert, or trained; one must simply produce punchy intellectual property that is in conversation with groups of

Illustration by Tomer Hanuka

⑤ Page Numbers

30

Schwarz, Benjamin. Rev. of *The Second World War: A Short History,* by R. A. C.

   Parker. *Atlantic Monthly* May 2002: 110-11. Print.

34. UNSIGNED ARTICLE

"Performance of the Week." *Time* 6 Oct. 2003: 18. Print.

Digital written-word sources

Digital sources such as Web sites differ from print sources in the ease with which they can be—and frequently are—changed, updated, or even eliminated. In addition, the various electronic media do not organize their works the same way. The most commonly cited electronic sources are documents from Web sites and databases. For help determining which is which, see 49b.

AT A GLANCE

Citing Digital Sources

When citing sources accessed online or from an electronic database, give as many of the following elements as you can find:

1. **Author.** Give the author's name, if available.
2. **Title.** Put titles of articles or short works in quotation marks. Italicize book titles.

For works from databases:	*For works from the Web:*
3. **Title of periodical,** italicized.	3. **Title of the site,** italicized.
4. **Publication information.** After the volume/issue/year or date, include page numbers (or *n. pag.* if no page numbers are listed).	4. **Name of the publisher or sponsor.** This information usually appears at the bottom of the page.
5. **Name of database,** italicized, if you used a subscription service such as Academic Search Premier.	5. **Date of online publication or most recent update.** This information often appears at the bottom of the page. If no date is given, use *n.d.*

6. **Medium of publication.** Use *Web.*
7. **Date of access.** Give the most recent date you accessed the source.

If you think your readers will have difficulty finding the source without a URL, put it after the period following the date of access, inside angle brackets, with a period after the closing bracket.

35. WORK FROM A DATABASE

The basic format for citing a work from a database appears in the source map on pp. 486–87.

For a periodical article that is available in print but that you access in an online database through a library subscription service such as Academic Search Premier, begin with the author's name (if given); the title of the work, in quotation marks; the title of the periodical, italicized; and publication information for the print version of the work (see models 28–34). Include the page numbers from the print version; if no page numbers are available, use *n. pag.* Then give the name of the online database, italicized; the medium (*Web*); and your most recent date of access.

> Collins, Ross F. "Cattle Barons and Ink Slingers: How Cow Country Journalists
>
> Created a Great American Myth." *American Journalism* 24.3 (2007): 7-29.
>
> *Communication and Mass Media Complete.* Web. 7 Feb. 2008.

36. ARTICLE FROM THE WEB SITE OF A JOURNAL

Begin an entry for an online journal article as you would one for a print journal article (see model 28). If an article does not have page numbers, use *n. pag.* End with the medium consulted (*Web*) and the date of access.

> Gallagher, Brian. "Greta Garbo Is Sad: Some Historical Reflections on the
>
> Paradoxes of Stardom in the American Film Industry, 1910-1960."
>
> *Images: A Journal of Film and Popular Culture* 3 (1997): n. pag. Web.
>
> 7 Aug. 2009.

37. ARTICLE IN A MAGAZINE ON THE WEB

See model 29 for print publication information if the article appears in print. After the name of the magazine, give the sponsor of the Web site, the date of publication, the medium (*Web*), and the date of access.

> Shapiro, Walter. "The Quest for Universal Healthcare." *Salon.* Salon Media Group,
>
> 21 Feb. 2008. Web. 2 Mar. 2008.

38. ARTICLE IN A NEWSPAPER ON THE WEB

After the name of the newspaper, give the publisher, publication date, medium (*Web*), and access date.

> Bustillo, Miguel, and Carol J. Williams. "Old Guard in Cuba Keeps Reins." *Los*
>
> *Angeles Times.* Los Angeles Times, 25 Feb. 2008. Web. 26 Feb. 2011.

MLA SOURCE MAP: Articles from Databases

Library subscriptions — such as EBSCOhost and Academic Search Premier — provide access to huge databases of articles.

1 **Author.** List the last name first. End with a period. For variations, see models 2–5.

2 **Article title.** Enclose the title and any subtitle in quotation marks.

3 **Periodical title.** Italicize it. Exclude any initial *A, An,* or *The.*

4 **Print publication information.** List the volume and issue number, if any; the date of publication, including the day (if given), month, and year, in that order; and the inclusive page numbers. If an article has no page numbers, write *n. pag.*

5 **Database name.** Italicize the name of the database.

6 **Medium.** For an online database, use *Web.*

7 **Date of access.** Give the day, month, and year, then a period.

A citation for the article on p. 487 would look like this:

Arnett, Robert P. *"Casino Royale* and Franchise Remix: James Bond as
Superhero." *Film Criticism* 33.3 (2009): 1-16. *Academic Search Premier.*
Web. 16 May 2011.

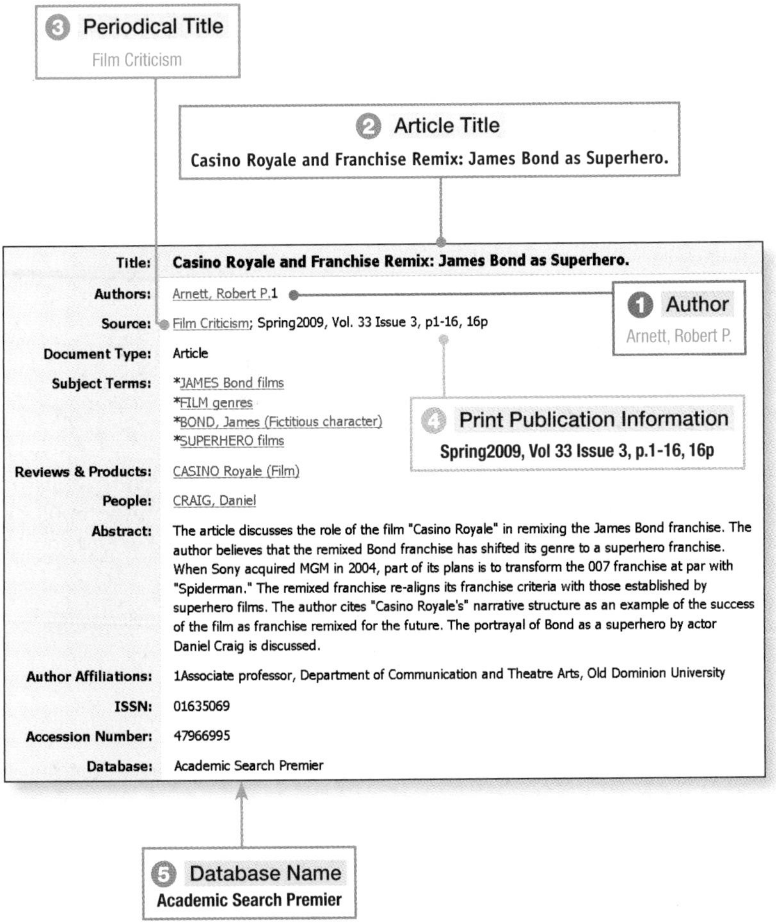

③ Periodical Title

Film Criticism

② Article Title

Casino Royale and Franchise Remix: James Bond as Superhero.

Title:	**Casino Royale and Franchise Remix: James Bond as Superhero.**
Authors:	Arnett, Robert P.1
Source:	Film Criticism; Spring2009, Vol. 33 Issue 3, p1-16, 16p
Document Type:	Article
Subject Terms:	*JAMES Bond films *FILM genres *BOND, James (Fictitious character) *SUPERHERO films
Reviews & Products:	CASINO Royale (Film)
People:	CRAIG, Daniel
Abstract:	The article discusses the role of the film "Casino Royale" in remixing the James Bond franchise. The author believes that the remixed Bond franchise has shifted its genre to a superhero franchise. When Sony acquired MGM in 2004, part of its plans is to transform the 007 franchise at par with "Spiderman." The remixed franchise re-aligns its franchise criteria with those established by superhero films. The author cites "Casino Royale's" narrative structure as an example of the success of the film as franchise remixed for the future. The portrayal of Bond as a superhero by actor Daniel Craig is discussed.
Author Affiliations:	1Associate professor, Department of Communication and Theatre Arts, Old Dominion University
ISSN:	01635069
Accession Number:	47966995
Database:	Academic Search Premier

① Author

Arnett, Robert P.

④ Print Publication Information

Spring2009, Vol 33 Issue 3, p.1-16, 16p

⑤ Database Name

Academic Search Premier

39. BOOK ON THE WEB

Provide information as for a print book (see models 6–27); then give the name of the Web site, the medium, and the date of access.

> Euripides. *The Trojan Women*. Trans. Gilbert Murray. New York: Oxford UP,
>
> 1915. *Internet Sacred Text Archive*. Web. 12 Oct. 2011.

Note: Cite a part of an online book as you would a part of a print book (see models 10 and 21). Give the print publication information (if any); the name of the site; the medium (*Web*); and the date of access.

> Riis, Jacob. "The Genesis of the Gang." *The Battle with the Slum*.
>
> New York: Macmillan, 1902. N. pag. *Bartleby.com: Great Books Online*.
>
> Web. 31 Mar. 2011.

40. POEM ON THE WEB

Include the poet's name, the title of the poem, and the print publication information (if any) as you would for part of an online book (model 39). End with the name of the site, the medium (*Web*), and the date of access.

> Dickinson, Emily. "The Grass." *Poems: Emily Dickinson*. Boston, 1891. *Humanities*
>
> *Text Initiative American Verse Project*. Web. 6 Jan. 2011.

41. EDITORIAL OR LETTER IN A WEB PERIODICAL

Include the word *Editorial* or *Letter* after the author (if given) and title (if any). End with the periodical name, the sponsor of the Web site, the date of posting or most recent update, the medium, and the access date.

> "The Funding Gap." Editorial. *Washington Post*. Washington Post, 5 Nov. 2003.
>
> Web. 19 Oct. 2010.

> Moore, Paula. "Go Vegetarian." Letter. *New York Times*. New York Times, 25 Feb.
>
> 2008. Web. 25 Feb. 2011.

42. REVIEW IN A WEB PERIODICAL

Cite an online review as you would a print review (see model 33). End with the name of the Web site, the sponsor, the date of electronic publication, the medium, and the date of access.

> Seitz, Matt Zoller. "A Modern Horror Film." Rev. of *The Social Network*, dir. David
>
> Fincher. *Salon*. Salon Media Group, 4 Oct. 2010. Web. 24 May 2011.

43. ENTRY IN A WEB REFERENCE WORK

Cite the entry as you would an entry from a print reference work (see model 22). Follow with the name of the Web site, the sponsor, date of publication, medium, and date of access.

"Tour de France." *Encyclopaedia Britannica Online.* Encyclopaedia Britannica,

2006. Web. 21 May 2006.

44. WORK FROM A WEB SITE

For basic information on citing a work from a Web site, see the source map on pp. 490–91. Include all of the following elements that are available: the author; the title of the work in quotation marks; the name of the Web site, italicized; the name of the publisher or sponsor (if none is available, use *N.p.*); the date of publication (if not available, use *n.d.*); the medium (*Web*); and the date of access.

"America: A Center-Left Nation." *Media Matters for America.* Media Matters for

America, 27 May 2009. Web. 31 May 2011.

Stauder, Ellen Keck. "Darkness Audible: Negative Capability and Mark Doty's

'Nocturne in Black and Gold.'" *Romantic Circles Praxis Series.* U of Maryland,

2003. Web. 28 Sept. 2003.

45. ENTIRE WEB SITE

Follow the guidelines for a specific work from the Web, beginning with the name of the author, editor, compiler, director, narrator, or translator, followed by the title of the Web site, italicized; the name of the sponsor or publisher (if none, use *N.p.*); the date of publication or last update; the medium of publication (*Web*); and the date of access.

Bernstein, Charles, Kenneth Goldsmith, Martin Spinelli, and Patrick Durgin, eds.

Electronic Poetry Corner. SUNY Buffalo, 2003. Web. 26 Sept. 2006.

Weather.com. Weather Channel Interactive, 2011. Web. 13 Mar. 2011.

For a personal Web site, include the name of the person who created the site; the title or (if there is no title) a description such as *Home page,* not italicized; the name of the larger site, if different from the personal site's title; the publisher or sponsor of the site (if none, use *N.p.*); the date of the last update; the medium of publication (*Web*); and the date of access.

Ede, Lisa. Home page. *Oregon State.* Oregon State U, 2010. Web. 17 May

2010.

MLA SOURCE MAP: Works from Web Sites

You may need to browse other parts of a site to find some of the following elements, and some sites may omit elements. Uncover as much information as you can.

1 Author. List the last name first. End with a period. If no author is given, begin with the title. For variations, see models 2–5.

2 Title of work. Enclose the title and any subtitle of the work in quotation marks.

3 Title of Web site. Give the title of the entire Web site, italicized.

4 Publisher or sponsor. Look for the sponsor's name at the bottom of the home page. If no information is available, write *N.p.* Follow it with a comma.

5 Date of publication or latest update. Give the most recent date, followed by a period. If no date is available, use *n.d.*

6 Medium. Use *Web* and follow it with a period.

7 Date of access. Give the date you accessed the work. End with a period.

A citation for the work on p. 491 would look like this:

Tønnesson, Øyvind. "Mahatma Gandhi, the Missing Laureate." *Nobelprize.org.*
Nobel Foundation, 1 Dec. 1999. Web. 4 May 2005.

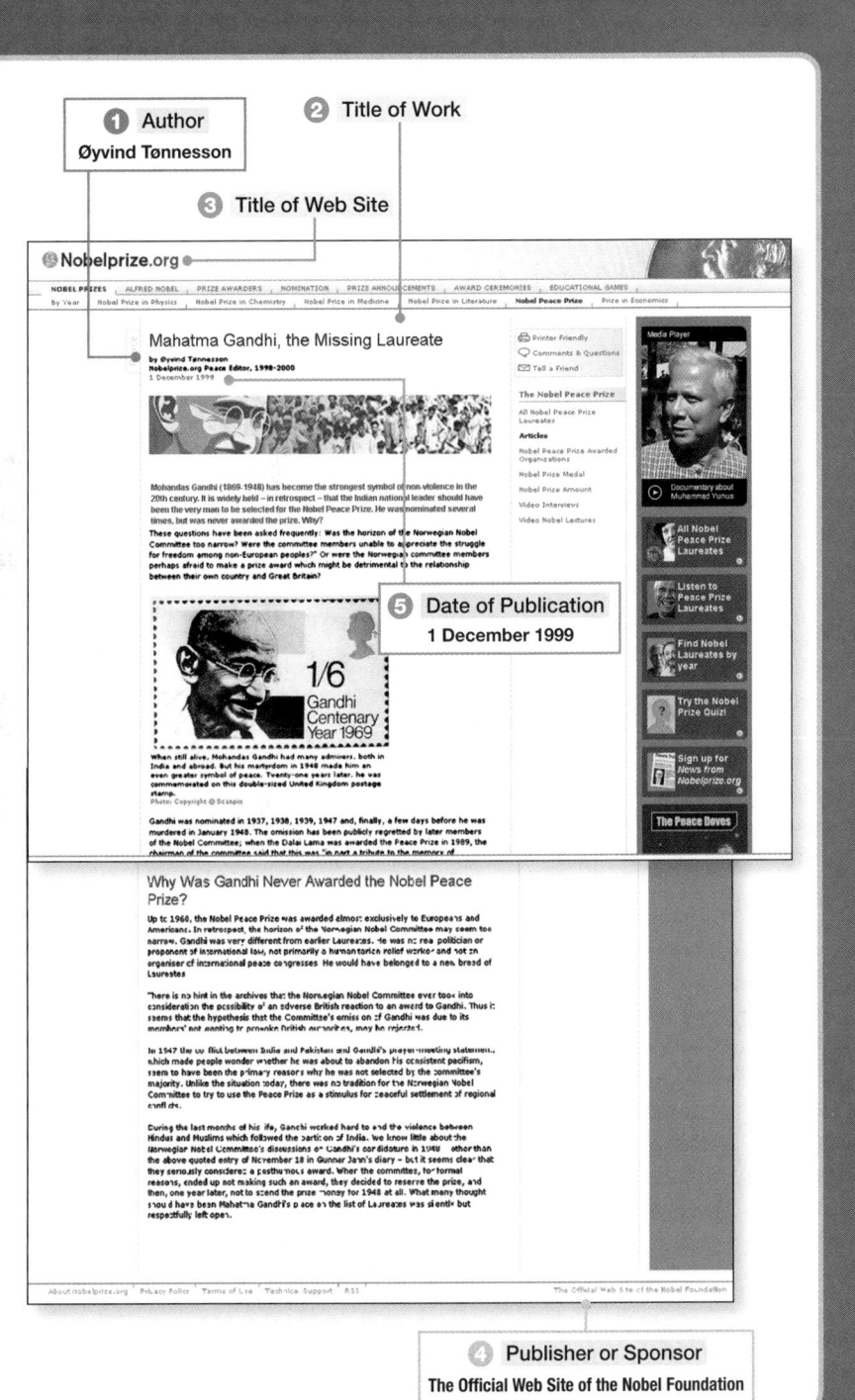

1 Author
Øyvind Tønnesson

2 Title of Work

3 Title of Web Site

5 Date of Publication
1 December 1999

4 Publisher or Sponsor
The Official Web Site of the Nobel Foundation

46. ACADEMIC COURSE WEB SITE

For a course site, include the name of the instructor, the title of the course in quotation marks, the title of the site in italics, the department (if relevant) and institution sponsoring the site, the date (or *n.d.*), the medium (*Web*), and the access date.

Creekmur, Corey K., and Philip Lutgendorf. "Topics in Asian Cinema: Popular

Hindi Cinema." *University of Iowa.* Depts. of English, Cinema, and

Comparative Literature, U of Iowa, 2004. Web. 13 Mar. 2007.

For a department Web site, give the department name, the description *Dept. home page,* the institution (in italics), the site sponsor, the medium (*Web*), and the access information.

English Dept. home page. *Amherst College.* Amherst Coll., n.d. Web. 5 Apr. 2011.

47. BLOG

For an entire blog, give the author's name; the title of the blog, italicized; the sponsor or publisher of the blog (if there is none, use *N.p.*); the date of the most recent update; the medium (*Web*); and the date of access.

Little Green Footballs. Little Green Footballs, 23 Aug. 2011. Web. 23 Aug. 2011.

Note: To cite a blogger who writes under a pseudonym, begin with the pseudonym and then put the writer's real name (if you know it) in square brackets.

Atrios [Duncan Black]. *Eschaton.* N.p., 27 June 2011. Web. 27 June 2011.

48. POST OR COMMENT ON A BLOG

Give the author's name; the title of the post or comment, in quotation marks (if there is no title, use the description *Web log post* or *Web log comment,* not italicized); the title of the blog, italicized; the sponsor of the blog (if there is none, use *N.p.*); the date of the most recent update; the medium (*Web*); and the date of access.

Marcotte, Amanda. "Rights without Perfection." *Pandagon.* N.p., 16 May 2010.

Web. 16 May 2010.

49. ENTRY IN A WIKI

Because wiki content is collectively edited, do not include an author. Treat a wiki as you would a work from a Web site (see model 44). Include the title of the entry; the name of the wiki, italicized; the sponsor or publisher of the wiki (use *N.p.* if there is no sponsor); the date of the latest update; the medium (*Web*); and the date of access. Check with your instructor before using a wiki as a source.

> "Fédération Internationale de Football Association." *Wikipedia.* Wikimedia
>
> Foundation, 27 June 2011. Web. 27 June 2011.

50. POSTING TO A DISCUSSION GROUP OR NEWSGROUP

Begin with the author's name and the title of the posting in quotation marks (or the words *Online posting*). Follow with the name of the Web site, the sponsor or publisher of the site (use *N.p.* if there is no sponsor), the date of publication, the medium (*Web*), and the date of access.

> Daly, Catherine. "Poetry Slams." *Poetics Discussion List.* SUNY Buffalo,
>
> 29 Aug. 2003. Web. 1 Oct. 2005.

51. POSTING TO A SOCIAL NETWORKING SITE

To cite a posting on Facebook or another social networking site, include the writer's name, a description of the posting, the date of the posting, and the medium of delivery. (The MLA does not provide guidelines for citing postings on such sites; this model is based on the MLA's guidelines for citing email.)

> Ferguson, Sarah. Status update. 6 Mar. 2008. Facebook posting.

52. EMAIL OR MESSAGE ON SOCIAL NETWORKING SITE

Include the writer's name; the subject line, in quotation marks (for email); *Message to* (not italicized or in quotation marks) followed by the recipient's name; the date of the message; and the medium of delivery (*E-mail*). (MLA style hyphenates *e-mail.*)

> Harris, Jay. "Thoughts on Impromptu Stage Productions." Message to the
>
> author. 16 July 2006. E-mail.

53. TWEET

Include the writer's real name, if known, with the user name (if different) in parentheses. If you don't know the real name, give just the user name. Include the entire tweet, in quotation marks. End with date and time of message and the medium (*Tweet*).

> BedfordBits. "#4C12 'Think of citations as a guide for the engaged reader.'
>
> Writing center tutor quoted by E. Kleinfeld. See http://citationproject.net/"
>
> 23 Mar. 2012, 4:01 p.m. Tweet.

Visual, audio, multimedia, and live sources

54. FILM OR DVD

If you cite a particular person's work, start with that name. If not, start with the title; then name the director, distributor, and year of release. Other contributors, such as writers or performers, may follow the director. If you cite a DVD instead of a theatrical release, include the original film release date and the label *DVD*. For material found on a Web site, give the name of the site or database, the medium (*Web*), and the access date.

> *Black Swan*. Dir. Darren Aronofsky. Perf. Natalie Portman. Fox Searchlight, 2010.
>
> Film.

> *Spirited Away*. Dir. Hayao Miyazaki. 2001. Walt Disney Video, 2003. DVD.

> Winner, Michael, dir. *Death Wish*. Perf. Charles Bronson. Paramount, 1974.
>
> *Netflix*. Web. 11 Nov. 2011.

55. ONLINE VIDEO CLIP

Cite a short online video as you would a work from a Web site (see model 44).

> Weber, Jan. "As We Sow, Part 1: Where Are the Farmers?" *YouTube*. YouTube, 15
>
> Mar. 2008. Web. 27 Sept. 2010.

56. TELEVISION OR RADIO PROGRAM

In general, begin with the title of the program, italicized. Then list important contributors (narrator, writer, director, actors); the network; the local station and city, if any; the broadcast date; and the medium. To cite

---

AT A GLANCE

Citing Sources without Models in MLA Style

To cite a source for which you cannot find a model, collect as much information as you can find — about the creator, title, sponsor, date of posting or latest update, the date you accessed the site and its location — with the goal of helping your readers find the source for themselves, if possible. Then look at the models in this section to see which one most closely matches the type of source you are using.

In an academic writing project, before citing an electronic source for which you have no model, also be sure to ask your instructor for help.

a particular person's work, begin with that name. To cite a particular episode from a series, begin with the episode title, in quotation marks.

The American Experience: Buffalo Bill. Writ., dir., prod. Rob Rapley. PBS. WNET,

New York, 25 Feb. 2008. Television.

"The Suitcase." *Mad Men.* Writ. Matthew Weiner. Dir. Jennifer Getzinger. AMC,

5 Sept. 2010. Television.

Note: For a streaming version online, give the name of the Web site, italicized. Then give the publisher or sponsor, a comma, and the date posted. End with the medium (*Web*) and the access date.

Limbaugh, Rush. *The Rush Limbaugh Show. RushLimbaugh.com.* Premier Radio

Networks, 29 Feb. 2012. Web. 2 Apr. 2012.

57. BROADCAST INTERVIEW

List the person interviewed and then the title, if any. If the interview has no title, use the label *Interview* and name the interviewer, if relevant. Then identify the source. To cite a broadcast interview, end with information about the program, the date(s) the interview took place, and the medium.

Revkin, Andrew. Interview with Terry Gross. *Fresh Air.* Natl. Public Radio. WNYC,

New York, 14 June 2006. Radio.

Note: If you listened to an archived version online, provide the site's sponsor (if known), the date of the interview, the medium (*Web*), and the access date. For a podcast interview, see model 64.

Revkin, Andrew. Interview with Terry Gross. *Fresh Air. NPR.org.* NPR, 14 June

2006. Web. 12 Jan. 2009.

58. UNPUBLISHED OR PERSONAL INTERVIEW

List the person interviewed; the label *Telephone interview, Personal interview,* or *E-mail interview*; and the date the interview took place.

Freedman, Sasha. Personal interview. 10 Nov. 2011.

59. SOUND RECORDING

List the name of the person or group you wish to emphasize (such as the composer, conductor, or band); the title of the recording or composition; the artist, if appropriate; the manufacturer; and the year of issue. Give the medium (such as *CD, MP3 file,* or *LP*). If you are citing a particular song or selection, include its title, in quotation marks, before the title of the recording.

Bach, Johann Sebastian. *Bach: Violin Concertos.* Perf. Itzhak Perlman and Pinchas
Zukerman. English Chamber Orch. EMI, 2002. CD.

Sonic Youth. "Incinerate." *Rather Ripped.* Geffen, 2006. MP3 file.

Note: If you are citing instrumental music that is identified only by form, number, and key, do not underline, italicize, or enclose it in quotation marks.

Grieg, Edvard. Concerto in A minor, op. 16. Cond. Eugene Ormandy. Philadelphia
Orch. RCA, 1989. LP.

60. MUSICAL COMPOSITION

When you are not citing a specific published version, first give the composer's name, followed by the title.

Mozart, Wolfgang Amadeus. *Don Giovanni,* K527.

Mozart, Wolfgang Amadeus. Symphony no. 41 in C major, K551.

Note: Cite a published score as you would a book. If you include the date the composition was written, do so immediately after the title.

Schoenberg, Arnold. *Chamber Symphony No. 1 for 15 Solo Instruments, Op. 9.*
1906. New York: Dover, 2002. Print.

61. COMPUTER GAME

Include the version after the title, then the city and publisher, date, and medium.

Grand Theft Auto: Tales from Liberty City. PlayStation 3 vers. New York: Rockstar
Games, 2009. DVD-ROM.

Cite an online game as you would a work from a Web site (see model 44).

The Sims 3. PC vers. *TheSims.com.* Electronic Arts, 2011. Web. 30 Nov.
2011.

62. LECTURE OR SPEECH

List the speaker; title, in quotation marks; sponsoring institution or group; place; and date. If the speech is untitled, use a label such as *Lecture.*

Colbert, Stephen. Speech. White House Correspondents' Association Dinner.
YouTube. YouTube, 29 Apr. 2006. Web. 20 May 2011.

Eugenides, Jeffrey. Portland Arts and Lectures. Arlene Schnitzer Concert Hall,

Portland, OR. 30 Sept. 2003. Lecture.

63. LIVE PERFORMANCE

List the title, appropriate names (such as writer or performer), the place, and the date. To cite a particular person's work, begin the entry with that name.

Anything Goes. By Cole Porter. Perf. Klea Blackhurst. Shubert Theater,

New Haven. 7 Oct. 2003. Performance.

64. PODCAST (STREAMING)

Include all of the following that are relevant and available: the speaker, the title of the podcast, the title of the program, the host or performers, the title of the site, the site's sponsor, the date of posting, the medium (*Web*), and the access date. (This model is based on MLA guidelines for a short work from a Web site. For a downloaded podcast, see model 65.)

"Seven Arrested in U.S. Terror Raid." *Morning Report.* Host Krishnan Guru-Murthy.

4 Radio. Channel 4 News, 23 June 2006. Web. 27 June 2010.

65. DIGITAL FILE

A citation for a file that you can download—one that exists independently, not only on a Web site—begins with citation information required for the type of source (a photograph or sound recording, for example). For the medium, indicate the type of file (*MP3 file, JPEG file*).

Officers' Winter Quarters, Army of Potomac, Brandy Station. Mar. 1864. Prints and

Photographs Div., Lib. of Cong. TIFF file.

"Return to the Giant Pool of Money." *This American Life.* Narr. Ira Glass. NPR, 25

Sept. 2009. MP3 file.

66. WORK OF ART OR PHOTOGRAPH

List the artist or photographer; the work's title, italicized; the date of composition (if unknown, use *n.d.*); and the medium of composition (*Oil on canvas, Bronze*). Then cite the name of the museum or other location and the city. To cite a reproduction in a book, add the publication information. To cite artwork found online, omit the medium of composition, and after the location, add the title of the database

---

AT A GLANCE

Citing Visuals That Appear in Your Text

If you choose to include images in your text, you need to cite and caption them correctly (see pp. 468–69).

- For a work that you have created, the works-cited entry should begin with a descriptive phrase from the image's caption ("Bus stop in Los Angeles"), a label ("Photograph by author"), and the date.

- For a visual reproduced from another source, you can include the complete citation information in the caption (see model 19 on p. 468), or you can indicate the source to allow readers to find it on the list of works cited. If you give the complete citation in the caption and do not cite the visual elsewhere in your text, you can omit the visual from your works-cited page.

---

or Web site, italicized; the medium consulted (*Web*); and the date of access.

> Chagall, Marc. *The Poet with the Birds.* 1911. Minneapolis Inst. of Arts. *artsmia.org.* Web. 6 Oct. 2011.

> *General William Palmer in Old Age.* 1810. Oil on canvas. National Army Museum, London. *White Mughals: Love and Betrayal in Eighteenth-Century India.* By William Dalrymple. New York: Penguin, 2002. 270. Print.

> Kahlo, Frida. *Self-Portrait with Cropped Hair.* 1940. Oil on canvas. Museum of Mod. Art, New York.

67. MAP OR CHART

Cite a map or chart as you would a book or a short work within a longer work and include the word *Map* or *Chart* after the title. Add the medium of publication. For an online source, end with the date of access.

> "Australia." Map. *Perry-Castañeda Library Map Collection.* U of Texas, 1999. Web. 4 Nov. 2010.

> *California.* Map. Chicago: Rand, 2002. Print.

68. CARTOON OR COMIC STRIP

List the artist's name; the title (if any) of the cartoon or comic strip, in quotation marks; the label *Cartoon* or *Comic strip*; and the usual publication information for a print periodical (see models 28–31) or a work from a Web site (model 44).

Johnston, Lynn. "For Better or Worse." Comic strip. *FBorFW.com*. Lynn Johnston

Publications, 30 June 2006. Web. 20 July 2006.

Lewis, Eric. "The Unpublished Freud." Cartoon. *New Yorker* 11 Mar. 2002: 80. Print.

69. ADVERTISEMENT

Include the label *Advertisement* after the name of the item or organization being advertised.

Microsoft. Advertisement. *Harper's* Oct. 2003: 2-3. Print.

Microsoft. Advertisement. *New York Times*. New York Times, 11 Nov. 2003. Web.

11 Nov. 2003.

Academic, government, and legal sources (including digital versions)

If an online version is not shown here, use the appropriate model for the source and then end with the medium and date of access.

70. REPORT OR PAMPHLET

Follow the guidelines for a print book (models 6–27) or an online book (model 39).

Allen, Katherine, and Lee Rainie. *Parents Online*. Washington: Pew Internet and

Amer. Life Project, 2002. Print.

Environmental Working Group. *Dead in the Water*. Washington: Environmental

Working Group, 2006. Web. 24 Apr. 2011.

71. GOVERNMENT PUBLICATION

Begin with the author, if identified. Otherwise, start with the name of the government, followed by the agency. For congressional documents, cite the number, session, and house of Congress (*S* for Senate, *H* for House of Representatives); the type (*Report, Resolution, Document*) in abbreviated form; and the number. End with the publication information. The print publisher is often the Government Printing Office (GPO). For online versions, follow the models for a work from a Web site (model 44) or an entire Web site (model 45).

Gregg, Judd. *Report to Accompany the Genetic Information Act of 2003*. US

108th Cong., 1st sess. S. Rept. 108-22. Washington: GPO, 2003. Print.

Kinsella, Kevin, and Victoria Velkoff. *An Aging World: 2001*. US Bureau of the

Census. Washington: GPO, 2001. Print.

> United States. Environmental Protection Agency. Office of Emergency and
> > Remedial Response. *This Is Superfund.* Jan. 2000. *Environmental*
> > *Protection Agency.* Web. 16 Aug. 2002.

72. PUBLISHED PROCEEDINGS OF A CONFERENCE

Cite proceedings as you would a book.

> Cleary, John, and Gary Gurtler, eds. *Proceedings of the Boston Area Colloquium in*
> > *Ancient Philosophy 2002.* Boston: Brill Academic, 2003. Print.

73. DISSERTATION

Enclose the title in quotation marks. Add the label *Diss.,* the school, and
the year the work was accepted.

> Paris, Django. "Our Culture: Difference, Division, and Unity in Multicultural Youth
> > Space." Diss. Stanford U, 2008. Print.

Note: Cite a published dissertation as a book, adding the identification
Diss. and the university after the title.

74. DISSERTATION ABSTRACT

Cite as you would an unpublished dissertation (see model 73). For the
abstract of a dissertation using *Dissertation Abstracts International* (*DAI*),
include the *DAI* volume, year, and page number.

> Huang-Tiller, Gillian C. "The Power of the Meta-Genre: Cultural, Sexual, and
> > Racial Politics of the American Modernist Sonnet." Diss. U of Notre Dame,
> > 2000. *DAI* 61 (2000): 1401. Print.

75. PUBLISHED INTERVIEW

List the person interviewed; the title of the interview (if any) or the
label *Interview* and the interviewer's name, if relevant. Then provide information about the source, following the appropriate model.

> Paretsky, Sara. Interview. *Progressive.* Progressive Magazine, 14 Jan. 2008. Web.
> > 12 Feb. 2011.

> Taylor, Max. "Max Taylor on Winning." *Time* 13 Nov. 2000: 66. Print.

76. UNPUBLISHED LETTER

Cite a published letter as a work in an anthology (see model 10). If the
letter is unpublished, follow this form:

> Anzaldúa, Gloria. Letter to the author. 10 Sept. 2002. MS.

77. MANUSCRIPT OR OTHER UNPUBLISHED WORK

List the author's name; the title (if any) or a description of the material; the form of the material (such as *MS* for manuscript) and any identifying numbers; and the name and location of the library or research institution housing the material, if applicable.

Woolf, Virginia. "The Searchlight." N.d. TS. Ser. III, Box 4, Item 184. Papers of

Virginia Woolf, 1902-1956. Smith Coll., Northampton.

78. LEGAL SOURCE

To cite a court case, give the names of the first plaintiff and defendant, the case number, the name of the court, and the date of the decision. To cite an act, give the name of the act followed by its Public Law (*Pub. L.*) number, the date the act was enacted, and its Statutes at Large (*Stat.*) cataloging number.

Eldred v. Ashcroft. No. 01-618. Supreme Ct. of the US. 15 Jan. 2003. Print.

Museum and Library Services Act of 2003. Pub. L. 108-81. 25 Sept. 2003. Stat.

117.991. Print.

Note: You do not need an entry on the list of works cited when you cite articles of the U.S. Constitution and laws in the U.S. Code.

52 A Student Research Essay, MLA Style

A brief research essay by David Craig appears on the following pages. David followed the MLA guidelines described in the preceding chapters. Note that this essay has been reproduced in a narrow format to allow for annotation.

Student Writer

David Craig

1/2"

Student Writing
MLA

1"

Name,
instructor,
course, date
aligned at left

David Craig

Professor Turkman

English 219

8 December 2011

Title centered

Messaging: The Language of Youth Literacy

Opens with
attention-
getting
statement

The English language is under attack. At least, that is what

many people seem to believe. From concerned parents to local

librarians, everyone seems to have a negative comment on the

state of youth literacy today. They fear that the current generation

of grade school students will graduate with an extremely low level

of literacy, and they point out that although language education

hasn't changed, kids are having more trouble reading and writing

Background on
the problem of
youth literacy

than in the past. When asked about the cause of this situation,

many adults pin the blame on technologies such as texting and

instant messaging, arguing that electronic shortcuts create and

compound undesirable reading and writing habits and discourage

students from learning conventionally correct ways to use language.

But although the arguments against messaging are passionate,

Thesis
statement

evidence suggests that they may not hold up.

The disagreements about messaging shortcuts are profound,

even among academics. John Briggs, an English professor at the

University of California, Riverside, says, "Americans have always

Quotation used
as evidence

been informal, but now the informality of precollege culture is so

ubiquitous that many students have no practice in using language

in any formal setting at all" (qtd. in McCarroll). Such objections

are not new; Sven Birkerts of Mount Holyoke College argued in

1999 that "[students] read more casually. They strip-mine what

they read" online and consequently produce "quickly generated,

casual prose" (qtd. in Leibowitz A67). However, academics are also

among the defenders of texting and instant messaging (IM), with

some suggesting that messaging may be a beneficial force in the

Annotations indicate effective choices or MLA-style formatting.

development of youth literacy because it promotes regular contact with words and the use of a written medium for communication.

Texting and instant messaging allow two individuals who are separated by any distance to engage in real-time, written communication. Although such communication relies on the written word, many messagers disregard standard writing conventions. For example, here is a snippet from an IM conversation between two teenage girls:[1]

> Teen One: sorry im talkinto like 10 ppl at a time
> Teen Two: u izzyful person
> Teen Two: kwel
> Teen One: hey i g2g

As this brief conversation shows, participants must use words to communicate via texting and messaging, but their words do not have to be in standard English.

The issue of youth literacy does demand attention because standardized test scores for language assessments, such as the verbal and writing sections of the College Board's SAT, have declined in recent years. This trend is illustrated in a chart distributed by the College Board as part of its 2011 analysis of aggregate SAT data (see Fig. 1).

The trend lines illustrate a significant pattern that may lead to the conclusion that youth literacy is on the decline. These lines display the ten-year paths (from 2001 to 2011) of reading and writing scores, respectively. Within this period, the average verbal score dropped a few points — and appears to be headed toward a further decline in the future.

Based on the preceding statistics, parents and educators appear to be right about the decline in youth literacy. And this

---

1. This transcript of an IM conversation was collected on 20 Nov. 2011. The teenagers' names are concealed to protect privacy.

Marginal annotations:

Definition and example of messaging

Writer considers argument that youth literacy is in decline

Figure explained in text and cited in parenthetical reference

Discussion of Figure 1

Explanatory note; see 49d.

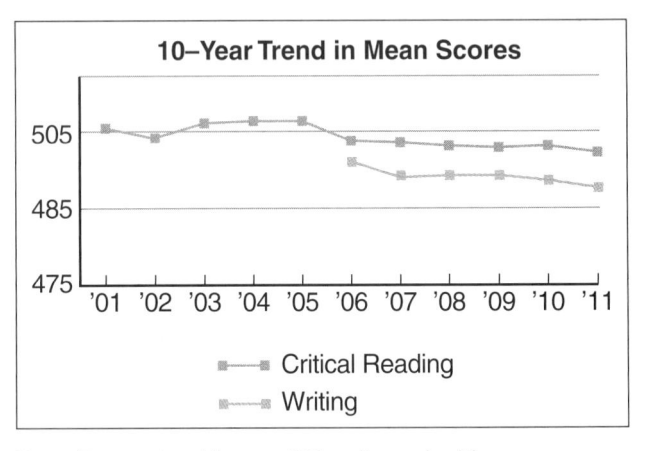

Figure labeled, titled, and credited to source; inserted at appropriate point in text

Fig. 1. Ten-year trend in mean SAT reading and writing scores (2001-2011). Source: College Board, "2011 SAT Trends."

Writer acknowledges part of critics' argument; transition to next point

Statistical evidence cited

trend is occurring while electronic communication is on the rise. According to the Pew Internet & American Life Project, 85 percent of those aged 12-17 at least occasionally write text messages, instant messages, or comments on social networking sites (Lenhart, Arafeh, Smith, and Macgill). In 2001, the most conservative estimate based on Pew numbers showed that American youths spent, at a minimum, nearly three million hours per day on messaging services (Lenhart and Lewis 20). These numbers are now expanding thanks to texting and messaging on popular Web 2.0 sites — such as Facebook. What's more, young messagers seem to be using a new vocabulary.

Writer's field research introduced

In the interest of establishing the existence of a messaging language, I analyzed 11,341 lines of text from IM conversations between youths in my target demographic: U.S. residents aged twelve to seventeen. Young messagers voluntarily sent me chat logs, but they were unaware of the exact nature of my research. Once all of the logs had been gathered, I went through them, recording the number of times messaging language was used in place of conventional words and phrases. Then I generated graphs to display how often these replacements were used.

During the course of my study, I identified four types of messaging language: phonetic replacements, acronyms, abbreviations, and inanities. An example of phonetic replacement is using *ur* for *you are*. Another popular type of messaging language is the acronym; for a majority of the people in my study, the most common acronym was *lol*, a construction that means *laughing out loud*. Abbreviations are also common in messaging, but I discovered that typical IM abbreviations, such as *etc.*, are not new to the English language. Finally, I found a class of words that I call "inanities." These words include completely new words or expressions, combinations of several slang categories, or simply nonsensical variations of other words. My favorite from this category is *lolz*, an inanity that translates directly to *lol* yet includes a terminating *z* for no obvious reason.

In the chat transcripts that I analyzed, the best display of typical messaging lingo came from the conversations between two thirteen-year-old Texan girls, who are avid IM users. Figure 2 is a graph showing how often they used certain phonetic replacements and abbreviations. On the *y*-axis, frequency of replacement is plotted, a calculation that compares the number of times a word or phrase is used in messaging language with the total number of times that it is communicated in any form. On the *x*-axis, specific messaging words and phrases are listed.

My research shows that the Texan girls use the first ten phonetic replacements or abbreviations at least 50 percent of the time in their normal messaging writing. For example, every

Findings of field research presented

Figure introduced and explained

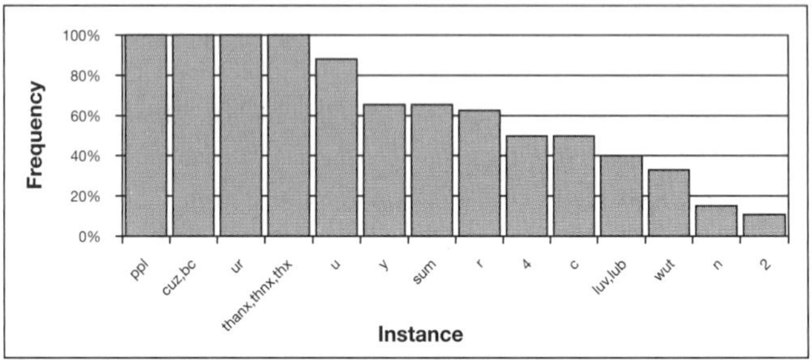

Figure labeled and titled

Fig. 2. Usage of phonetic replacements and abbreviations in messaging.

Discussion of findings presented in Fig. 2

time one of them writes *see*, there is a parallel time when *c* is used in its place. In light of this finding, it appears that the popular messaging culture contains at least some elements of its own language. It also seems that much of this language is new: no formal dictionary yet identifies the most common messaging words and phrases. Only in the heyday of the telegraph or on the rolls of a stenographer would you find a similar situation, but these "languages" were never a popular medium of youth communication. Texting and instant messaging, however, are very popular among young people and continue to generate attention and debate in academic circles.

My research shows that messaging is certainly widespread, and it does seem to have its own particular vocabulary, yet these two factors alone do not mean it has a damaging influence on youth literacy. As noted earlier, however, some people claim that the new technology is a threat to the English language.

Writer returns to opposition argument

Jacquie Ream — a former teacher and author — told a reporter from *Curriculum Review*, "Text messaging is destroying the written word. The students aren't writing letters, they're typing into their cell phones one line at a time. Feelings aren't communicated with

Craig 6

words when you're texting; emotions are sideways smiley faces. Kids are typing shorthand jargon that isn't even a complete thought" (qtd. in "Is Texting Destroying?").

The critics of messaging are numerous. But if we look to the field of linguistics, a central concept — metalinguistics — challenges these criticisms and leads to a more reasonable conclusion — that messaging has no negative impact on a student's development of or proficiency with traditional literacy.

Scholars of metalinguistics offer support for the claim that messaging is not damaging to those who use it. As noted earlier, one of the most prominent components of messaging language is phonetic replacement, in which a word such as *everyone* becomes *every1*. This type of wordplay has a special importance in the development of an advanced literacy, and for good reason. According to David Crystal, an internationally recognized scholar of linguistics at the University of Wales, as young children develop and learn how words string together to express ideas, they go through many phases of language play. The singsong rhymes and nonsensical chants of preschoolers are vital to their learning language, and a healthy appetite for such wordplay leads to a better command of language later in life (182).

As justification for his view of the connection between language play and advanced literacy, Crystal presents an argument for metalinguistic awareness. According to Crystal, *metalinguistics* refers to the ability to "step back" and use words to analyze how language works:

> If we are good at stepping back, at thinking in a more
> abstract way about what we hear and what we say, then
> we are more likely to be good at acquiring those skills
> which depend on just such a stepping back in order
> to be successful — and this means, chiefly, reading

Parenthetical reference uses brief title, author unknown

Transition to support of thesis and refutation of critics

Linguistic authority cited in support of thesis

Block format for a quotation of more than four lines

Ellipses and
brackets
indicate
omissions and
changes in
quotation

and writing. . . . [T]he greater our ability to play with
language, . . . the more advanced will be our command of
language as a whole. (Crystal 181)

If we accept the findings of linguists such as Crystal that
metalinguistic awareness leads to increased literacy, then it seems
reasonable to argue that the phonetic language of messaging can

Writer links
Crystal's views
to thesis

also lead to increased metalinguistic awareness and, therefore,
increases in overall literacy. As messagers develop proficiency
with a variety of phonetic replacements and other types of texting
and messaging words, they should increase their subconscious
knowledge of metalinguistics.

Metalinguistics also involves our ability to write in a variety

Another
refutation of
critics'
assumptions

of distinct styles and tones. Yet in the debate over messaging and
literacy, many critics assume that either messaging or academic
literacy will eventually win out in a person and that the two modes
cannot exist side by side. This assumption is, however, false.
Human beings ordinarily develop a large range of language abilities,
from the formal to the relaxed and from the mainstream to the

Example from
well-known
work of
literature used
as support

subcultural. Mark Twain, for example, had an understanding of local
speech that he employed when writing dialogue for *Huckleberry
Finn*. Yet few people would argue that Twain's knowledge of this
form of English had a negative impact on his ability to write in
standard English.

However, just as Mark Twain used dialects carefully in
dialogue, writers must pay careful attention to the kind of language
they use in any setting. The owner of the language Web site *The
Discouraging Word*, who is an anonymous English literature graduate
student at the University of Chicago, backs up this idea in an
e-mail to me:

Email
correspondence
cited in support
of claim

What is necessary, we feel, is that students learn how to
shift between different styles of writing — that, in other
words, the abbreviations and shortcuts of messaging

should be used online . . . but that they should not be
used in an essay submitted to a teacher. . . . Messaging
might even be considered . . . a different way of reading
and writing, one that requires specific and unique skills
shared by certain communities.

The analytical ability that is necessary for writers to choose
an appropriate tone and style in their writing is, of course,
metalinguistic in nature because it involves the comparison
of two or more language systems. Thus, youths who grasp
multiple languages will have a greater natural understanding of
metalinguistics. More specifically, young people who possess both
messaging and traditional skills stand to be better off than their
peers who have been trained only in traditional or conventional
systems. Far from being hurt by their online pastime, instant
messagers can be aided in standard writing by their experience with
messaging language.

> Writer
> synthesizes
> evidence for
> claim

The fact remains, however, that youth literacy seems to
be declining. What, if not messaging, is the main cause of this
phenomenon? According to the College Board, which collects data
on several questions from its test takers, course work in English
composition and grammar classes decreased by 14 percent between
1992 and 2002 (Carnahan and Coletti 11). The possibility of
messaging causing a decline in literacy seems inadequate when
statistics on English education for US youths provide other evidence
of the possible causes. Simply put, schools in the United States are
not teaching English as much as they used to. Rather than blaming
texting and messaging language alone for the decline in literacy
and test scores, we must also look toward our schools' lack of focus
on the teaching of standard English skills.

> Transition to
> final point
>
> Alternate
> explanation
> for decline in
> literacy

My findings indicate that the use of messaging poses virtually
no threat to the development or maintenance of formal language
skills among American youths aged twelve to seventeen. Diverse

> Transition to
> conclusion

Concluding
paragraph
sums up
argument and
reiterates
thesis

language skills tend to increase a person's metalinguistic awareness
and, thereby, his or her ability to use language effectively to
achieve a desired purpose in a particular situation. The current
decline in youth literacy is not due to the rise of texting and
messaging. Rather, fewer young students seem to be receiving
an adequate education in the use of conventional English.
Unfortunately, it may always be fashionable to blame new tools
for old problems, but in the case of messaging, that blame is not
warranted. Although messaging may expose literacy problems, it
does not create them.

Works Cited

Carnahan, Kristin, and Chiara Coletti. *Ten-Year Trend in SAT Scores Indicates Increased Emphasis on Math Is Yielding Results: Reading and Writing Are Causes for Concern.* New York: College Board, 2002. Print.

College Board. "2011 SAT Trends." *Collegeboard.org.* College Board, 14 Sept. 2011. Web. 6 Dec. 2011.

Crystal, David. *Language Play.* Chicago: U of Chicago P, 1998. Print.

The Discouraging Word. "Re: Messaging and Literacy." Message to the author. 13 Nov. 2011. E-mail.

"Is Texting Destroying Kids' Writing Style?" *Curriculum Review* 48.1 (2008): 4-5. *Academic Search Premier.* Web. 7 Dec. 2011.

Leibowitz, Wendy R. "Technology Transforms Writing and the Teaching of Writing." *Chronicle of Higher Education* 26 Nov. 1999: A67-68. Print.

Lenhart, Amanda, Sousan Arafeh, Aaron Smith, and Alexandra Macgill. *Writing, Technology & Teens.* Washington: Pew Internet & Amer. Life Project, 2008. Web. 6 Dec. 2011.

Lenhart, Amanda, and Oliver Lewis. *Teenage Life Online: The Rise of the Instant-Message Generation and the Internet's Impact on Friendships and Family Relationships.* Washington: Pew Internet & Amer. Life Project, 2001. Web. 6 Dec. 2011.

McCarroll, Christina. "Teens Ready to Prove Text-Messaging Skills Can Score SAT Points." *Christian Science Monitor* 11 Mar. 2005. Web. 10 Dec. 2011.

Heading centered

Report

Graph

Book

Email

Article from database

Print newspaper article

Online report

Subsequent lines of each entry indented

Online newspaper article

APA, *Chicago,* and CSE Documentation

Documentation styles in different disciplines vary according to
what information is valued most highly. Thus in the sciences and
social sciences, where timeliness of publication is crucial, the date
of publication comes up front, right after the author's name.

— ANDREA A. LUNSFORD

APA, *Chicago*, and CSE Documentation

53 APA Style   *515*

a The basics of APA style   *515*
b APA style for in-text citations   *517*
c APA style for a list of references   *521*
d A STUDENT RESEARCH ESSAY, APA STYLE   *541*

54 *Chicago* Style   *551*

a The basics of *Chicago* style   *551*
b *Chicago* style for notes and bibliographic entries   *554*
c AN EXCERPT FROM A STUDENT RESEARCH ESSAY, *CHICAGO* STYLE   *569*

55 CSE Style   *575*

a CSE style for in-text citations   *575*
b CSE style for a list of references   *576*
c AN EXCERPT FROM A STUDENT RESEARCH PROPOSAL, CSE STYLE   *586*

For visual analysis Look carefully at the illustration on the front of this tab. What do you think this image suggests about the kinds of sources writers might document in various disciplines?

APA Style **53**

Chapter 53 discusses the basic formats prescribed by the American Psychological Association (APA), guidelines that are widely used in the social sciences. For further reference, consult the *Publication Manual of the American Psychological Association*, Sixth Edition (2010).

 bedfordstmartins.com/everydaywriter
Documenting Sources

53a The basics of APA style

Why does academic work call for very careful citation practices when writing for the general public may not? The answer is that readers of academic work expect to get certain information from source citations:

- Source citations demonstrate that you've done your homework on your topic and that you are a part of the conversation surrounding it.

- Source citations show that you understand the need to give credit when you make use of someone else's intellectual property. (See Chapter 18 for details.)

- Source citations give explicit directions to guide readers who want to look for themselves at the works you're using.

The guidelines for APA style tell you exactly what information to include in your citation and how to format that information.

TYPES OF SOURCES

Look at the Directory to APA Style on p. 522 for guidelines on citing various types of sources—print books (or parts of print books), print periodicals (journals, magazines, or newspapers), and digital written-word sources (an online magazine or newspaper article, or a book on an e-reader). A digital version of a source may include updates or corrections that the print version of the same work lacks, so it's important to provide the correct information for readers. For sources that consist mainly of material other than written words—such as a film, song, or artwork—consult the "other sources" section of the directory. And if you can't find a model exactly like the source you've selected, see the box on p. 524.

ARTICLES FROM WEB AND DATABASE SOURCES

You need a subscription to look through most databases, so individual researchers almost always gain access to articles in databases through the computer system of a school or community library that pays to subscribe. The easiest way to tell whether a source comes from a database, then, is that its information is *not* generally available for free to anyone with an Internet connection. Many databases are digital collections of articles that originally appeared in edited print periodicals, ensuring that an authority has vouched for the accuracy of the information. Such sources often have more credibility than much of what is available for free on the Web.

Parts of citations

APA citations appear in two parts of your text—a brief in-text citation in the body of your written text and a full citation in the list of references, to which the in-text citation directs readers. The most straightforward in-text citations include the author's name, the publication year, and the page number, but many variations on this basic format are discussed in 53b.

In the text of her research essay (see 53d), Tawnya Redding includes a paraphrase of material from an online journal that she accessed through the publisher's Web site. She cites the authors' names and the year of publication in a parenthetical reference, pointing readers to the entry for "Baker, F., & Bor, W. (2008)" in her references list, shown on the next page.

Content notes

APA style allows you to use content notes, either at the bottom of the page or on a separate page at the end of the text, to expand or supplement your text. Indicate such notes in the text by superscript numerals (^{1}). Double-space all entries. Indent the first line of each note five spaces, but begin subsequent lines at the left margin.

SUPERSCRIPT NUMBER IN TEXT

The age of the children involved in the study was an important factor in the selection of items for the questionnaire.[1]

MOOD MUSIC 9

References

Baker, F., & Bor, W. (2008). Can music preference indicate mental
    health status in young people? *Australasian Psychiatry, 16*(4),
    284–288. Retrieved from http://www3.interscience.wiley.com/
    journal/118565538/home

> types of music can alter the mood of at-risk youth in a negative
> way. This view of the correlation between music and suicide risk
> is supported by a meta-analysis done by Baker and Bor (2008), in
> which the authors assert that most studies reject the notion that
> music is a causal factor and suggest that music preference is more

he association
ioral, and
ogy, 19(2),

y metal music

and adolescent suicidal risk. *Journal of Youth and Adolescence,
    30*(3), 321–332.

Lai, Y. (1999). Effects of music listening on depressed women in

FOOTNOTE

[1]Marjorie Youngston Forman and William Cole of the Child Study Team
provided great assistance in identifying appropriate items for the questionnaire.

53b APA style for in-text citations

DIRECTORY TO APA STYLE

APA style for in-text citations

1. Basic format for a quotation, *518*
2. Basic format for a paraphrase or summary, *518*
3. Two authors, *518*
4. Three to five authors, *519*
5. Six or more authors, *519*
6. Corporate or group author, *519*
7. Unknown author, *519*
8. Two or more authors with the same last name, *519*
9. Two or more works by an author in a single year, *520*
10. Two or more sources in one parenthetical reference, *520*
11. Indirect source, *520*
12. Personal communication, *520*
13. Electronic document, *520*
14. Table or figure reproduced in the text, *521*

An in-text citation in APA style always indicates *which source* on the references page the writer is referring to, and it explains in what year the material was published; for quoted material, the in-text citation also indicates *where* in the source the quotation can be found.

Note that APA style generally calls for using the past tense or present perfect tense for signal verbs: *Baker (2003) showed* or *Baker (2003) has shown.* Use the present tense only to discuss results (*the experiment demonstrates*) or widely accepted information (*researchers agree*).

1. BASIC FORMAT FOR A QUOTATION

Generally, use the author's name in a signal phrase to introduce the cited material, and place the date, in parentheses, immediately after the author's name. The page number, preceded by *p.,* appears in parentheses after the quotation.

> Gitlin (2001) pointed out that "political critics, convinced that the media are
> rigged against them, are often blind to other substantial reasons why their
> causes are unpersuasive" (p. 141).

If the author is not named in a signal phrase, place the author's name, the year, and the page number in parentheses after the quotation: (Gitlin, 2001, p. 141). For a long, set-off quotation (more than forty words), place the page reference in parentheses one space after the final quotation.

For quotations from works without page numbers, you may use paragraph numbers, if the source includes them, preceded by the abbreviation *para.*

> Driver (2007) has noticed "an increasing focus on the role of land" in policy
> debates over the past decade (para. 1).

2. BASIC FORMAT FOR A PARAPHRASE OR SUMMARY

Include the author's last name and the year as in model 1, but omit the page or paragraph number unless the reader will need it to find the material in a long work.

> Gitlin (2001) has argued that critics sometimes overestimate the influence of the
> media on modern life.

3. TWO AUTHORS

Use both names in all citations. Use *and* in a signal phrase, but use an ampersand (*&*) in a parentheses.

> Babcock and Laschever (2003) have suggested that many women do not negotiate
> their salaries and pay raises as vigorously as their male counterparts do.

A recent study has suggested that many women do not negotiate their salaries and pay raises as vigorously as their male counterparts do (Babcock & Laschever, 2003).

4. THREE TO FIVE AUTHORS

List all the authors' names for the first reference.

Safer, Voccola, Hurd, and Goodwin (2003) reached somewhat different conclusions by designing a study that was less dependent on subjective judgment than were previous studies.

In subsequent references, use just the first author's name plus *et al.*

Based on the results, Safer et al. (2003) determined that the apes took significant steps toward self-expression.

5. SIX OR MORE AUTHORS

Use only the first author's name and *et al.* in every citation.

As Soleim et al. (2002) demonstrated, advertising holds the potential for manipulating "free-willed" consumers.

6. CORPORATE OR GROUP AUTHOR

If the name of the organization or corporation is long, spell it out the first time you use it, followed by an abbreviation in brackets. In later references, use the abbreviation only.

FIRST CITATION   (Centers for Disease Control and Prevention [CDC], 2006)

LATER CITATIONS   (CDC, 2006)

7. UNKNOWN AUTHOR

Use the title or its first few words in a signal phrase or in parentheses. A book's title is italicized, as in the following example; an article's title is placed in quotation marks.

The employment profiles for this time period substantiated this trend (*Federal Employment,* 2001).

8. TWO OR MORE AUTHORS WITH THE SAME LAST NAME

If your list of references includes works by different authors with the same last name, include the authors' initials in each citation.

S. Bartolomeo (2000) conducted the groundbreaking study on teenage childbearing.

9. TWO OR MORE WORKS BY AN AUTHOR IN A SINGLE YEAR

Assign lowercase letters (*a, b,* and so on) alphabetically by title, and include the letters after the year.

> Gordon (2004b) examined this trend in more detail.

10. TWO OR MORE SOURCES IN ONE PARENTHETICAL REFERENCE

List sources by different authors in alphabetical order by authors' last names, separated by semicolons: (*Cardone, 1998; Lai, 2002*). List works by the same author in chronological order, separated by commas: (*Lai, 2000, 2002*).

11. INDIRECT SOURCE

Use the phrase *as cited in* to indicate that you are reporting information from a secondary source. Name the original source in a signal phrase, but list the secondary source in your list of references.

> Amartya Sen developed the influential concept that land reform was necessary for
> "promoting opportunity" among the poor (as cited in Driver, 2007, para. 2).

12. PERSONAL COMMUNICATION

Cite any personal letters, email messages, electronic postings, telephone conversations, or interviews as shown. Do not include personal communications in the reference list.

> R. Tobin (personal communication, November 4, 2006) supported his claims
> about music therapy with new evidence.

13. ELECTRONIC DOCUMENT

Cite a Web or electronic document as you would a print source, using the author's name and date.

> Link and Phelan (2005) argued for broader interventions in public health that
> would be accessible to anyone, regardless of individual wealth.

The APA recommends the following for electronic sources without names, dates, or page numbers:

AUTHOR UNKNOWN

Use a shortened form of the title in a signal phrase or in parentheses (see model 7). If an organization is the author, see model 6.

DATE UNKNOWN

Use the abbreviation *n.d.* (for "no date") in place of the year: (*Hopkins, n.d.*).

NO PAGE NUMBERS

Many works found online or in electronic databases lack stable page numbers. (Use the page numbers for an electronic work in a format, such as PDF, that has stable pagination.) If paragraph numbers are included in such a source, use the abbreviation *para.*: (*Giambetti, 2006, para. 7*). If no paragraph numbers are included but the source includes headings, give the heading and identify the paragraph in the section:

> Jacobs and Johnson (2007) have argued that "the South African media is still
>
> highly concentrated and not very diverse in terms of race and class" (South
>
> African Media after Apartheid, para. 3).

14. TABLE OR FIGURE REPRODUCED IN THE TEXT

Number figures (graphs, charts, illustrations, and photographs) and tables separately.

For a table, place the label (*Table 1*) and an informative heading (*Hartman's Key Personality Traits*) above the table; below, provide information about its source.

Table 1

Hartman's Key Personality Traits

Trait category	Color			
	Red	Blue	White	Yellow
Motive	Power	Intimacy	Peace	Fun
Strengths	Loyal to tasks	Loyal to people	Tolerant	Positive
Limitations	Arrogant	Self-righteous	Timid	Uncommitted

Note: Adapted from *The Hartman Personality Profile,* by N. Hayden. Retrieved February 24, 2009, from http://students.cs.byu.edu/~nhayden/Code/index.php

For a figure, place the label (*Figure 3*) and a caption indicating the source below the image. If you do not cite the source of the table or figure elsewhere in your text, you do not need to include the source on your list of references.

53c APA style for a list of references

The alphabetical list of the sources cited in your document is called *References.* If your instructor asks that you list everything you have read—not just the sources you cite—call the list *Bibliography.*

A ll the entries in this section of the book use hanging indent format, in which the first line aligns on the left and the subsequent lines indent one-half inch or five spaces. This is the customary APA format.

DIRECTORY TO APA STYLE

APA style for references

Guidelines for author listings
1. One author, *523*
2. Multiple authors, *524*
3. Corporate or group author, *524*
4. Unknown author, *524*
5. Two or more works by the same author, *524*

Print books
6. Basic format for a book, *525*
   SOURCE MAP, *526–27*
7. Editor, *525*
8. Selection in a book with an editor, *525*
9. Translation, *525*
10. Edition other than the first, *528*
11. Multivolume work, *528*
12. Article in a reference work, *528*
13. Republished book, *528*
14. Introduction, preface, foreword, or afterword, *528*
15. Book with a title within the title, *528*

Print periodicals
16. Article in a journal paginated by volume, *529*
17. Article in a journal paginated by issue, *529*
   SOURCE MAP, *530–31*
18. Article in a magazine, *529*
19. Article in a newspaper, *529*
20. Editorial or letter to the editor, *529*
21. Unsigned article, *529*
22. Review, *529*
23. Published interview, *529*

Digital written-word sources
24. Article from an online periodical, *532*
25. Article from a database, *532*
   SOURCE MAP, *534–35*
26. Abstract for an online article, *532*
27. Document from a Web site, *533*
   SOURCE MAP, *536–37*
28. Chapter or section of a Web document, *538*
29. Email message or real-time communication, *538*
30. Online posting, *538*
31. Blog (Web log) post, *538*
32. Wiki entry, *539*

Other sources (including online versions)
33. Computer software, *539*
34. Government publication, *539*
35. Data set, *539*
36. Dissertation, *539*
37. Technical or research report, *540*
38. Conference proceedings, *540*
39. Paper presented at a meeting or symposium, unpublished, *540*
40. Poster session, *540*
41. Film, video, or DVD, *540*
42. Online audio or video file, *540*
43. Television program, single episode, *540*
44. Television series, *541*
45. Audio podcast (downloaded audio file), *541*
46. Recording, *541*

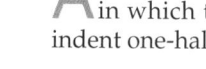

Formatting a List of References

- Start your list on a separate page after the text of your document but before appendices or notes. Continue consecutive page numbers.
- Center the heading *References* one inch from the top of the page.
- Begin each entry flush with the left margin, but indent subsequent lines one-half inch or five spaces. Double-space the entire list.
- List sources alphabetically by authors' (or editors') last names. If no author is given, alphabetize the source by the first word of the title other than *A*, *An*, or *The*. If the list includes two or more works by the same author, list them in chronological order. (For two or more works by the same author published in the same year, see model 5.)
- Italicize titles and subtitles of books and periodicals. Do not italicize titles of articles, and do not enclose them in quotation marks.
- For titles of books and articles, capitalize only the first word of the title and the subtitle and any proper nouns or proper adjectives.
- For titles of periodicals, capitalize all major words.
- Follow the guidelines in 53c for punctuating an entry.

Guidelines for author listings

List authors' last names first, and use only initials for first and middle names. The in-text citations in your text point readers toward particular sources in your list of references (see 53b).

NAME CITED IN SIGNAL PHRASE IN TEXT

Driver (2007) has noted . . .

NAME IN PARENTHETICAL CITATION IN TEXT

. . . (Driver, 2007).

BEGINNING OF ENTRY IN LIST OF REFERENCES

Driver, T. (2007).

Models 1–5 below explain how to arrange author names. The information that follows the name of the author depends on the type of work you are citing—a book (models 6–15), a print periodical (models 16–23), a digital source (models 24–33), or another kind of source (models 34–46).

1. ONE AUTHOR

Give the last name, a comma, the initial(s), and the date in parentheses.

Zimbardo, P. G. (2009).

AT A GLANCE

Combining Parts of Models

What should you do if your source doesn't match the model exactly? Suppose, for instance, that your source is a translation of a republished book with an editor.

- Identify a basic model to follow. If you decide that your source looks most like a republished book, for example, start with a citation that looks like model 13.

- Look for models that show additional elements in your source. For this example, you would need elements of model 9 (for the translation) and model 7 (for the editor).

- Add new elements from other models to your basic model in the order that makes the most sense to you.

- If you still aren't sure how to arrange the pieces to create a combination model, check the *APA Manual* or ask your instructor.

---

2. MULTIPLE AUTHORS

List up to seven authors, last name first, with commas separating authors' names and an ampersand (&) before the last author's name.

Walsh, M. E., & Murphy, J. A. (2003).

Note: For a work with more than seven authors, list the first six, then an ellipsis (. . .), and then the final author's name.

3. CORPORATE OR GROUP AUTHOR

Resources for Rehabilitation. (2003).

4. UNKNOWN AUTHOR

Begin with the work's title. Italicize book titles, but do not italicize article titles or enclose them in quotation marks. Capitalize only the first word of the title and subtitle (if any) and proper nouns and proper adjectives.

Safe youth, safe schools. (2009).

5. TWO OR MORE WORKS BY THE SAME AUTHOR

List two or more works by the same author in chronological order. Repeat the author's name in each entry.

Goodall, J. (1999).

Goodall, J. (2002).

If the works appeared in the same year, list them alphabetically by title, and assign lowercase letters (*a, b,* etc.) after the dates.

> Shermer, M. (2002a). On estimating the lifetime of civilizations. *Scientific American, 287*(2), 33.

> Shermer, M. (2002b). Readers who question evolution. *Scientific American, 287*(1), 37.

Print books

6. BASIC FORMAT FOR A BOOK

Begin with the author name(s). (See models 1–5.) Then include the publication year, title and subtitle, city of publication, country or state abbreviation, and publisher. The source map on pp. 526–27 shows where to find this information in a typical book.

> Levick, S. E. (2003). *Clone being: Exploring the psychological and social dimensions.* Lanham, MD: Rowman & Littlefield.

7. EDITOR

For a book with an editor but no author, list the source under the editor's name.

> Dickens, J. (Ed.). (1995). *Family outing: A guide for parents of gays, lesbians and bisexuals.* London, England: Peter Owen.

To cite a book with an author and an editor, place the editor's name, with a comma and the abbreviation *Ed.,* in parentheses after the title.

> Austin, J. (1995). *The province of jurisprudence determined.* (W. E. Rumble, Ed.). Cambridge, England: Cambridge University Press.

8. SELECTION IN A BOOK WITH AN EDITOR

> Burke, W. W., & Nourmair, D. A. (2001). The role of personality assessment in organization development. In J. Waclawski & A. H. Church (Eds.), *Organization development: A data-driven approach to organizational change* (pp. 55–77). San Francisco, CA: Jossey-Bass.

9. TRANSLATION

> Al-Farabi, A. N. (1998). *On the perfect state* (R. Walzer, Trans.). Chicago, IL: Kazi.

APA SOURCE MAP: Books

Take information from the book's title page and copyright page (on the reverse side of the title page), not from the book's cover or a library catalog.

1. **Author.** List all authors' last names first, and use only initials for first and middle names. For more about citing authors, see models 1–5.

2. **Publication year.** Enclose the year of publication in parentheses.

3. **Title.** Italicize the title and any subtitle. Capitalize only the first word of the title and the subtitle and any proper nouns or proper adjectives.

4. **City and state of publication.** List the city of publication and the country or state abbreviation followed by a colon.

5. **Publisher.** Give the publisher's name, dropping any *Inc.*, *Co.*, or *Publishers*.

A citation for the book on p. 527 would look like this:

Tsutsui, W. (2004). *Godzilla on my mind: Fifty years of the king of monsters.* New York, NY: Palgrave Macmillan.

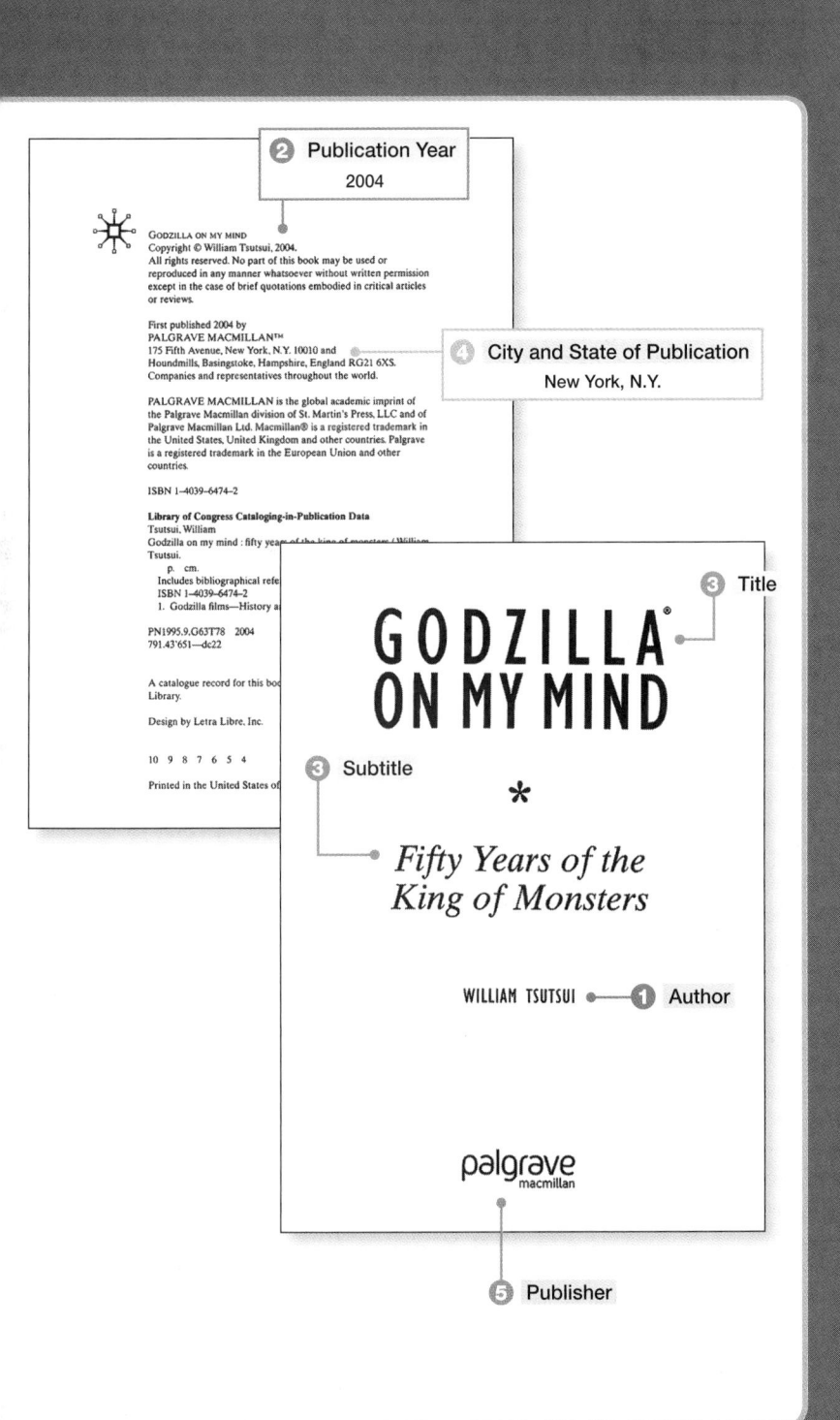

10. **EDITION OTHER THAN THE FIRST**

> Moore, G. S. (2002). *Living with the earth: Concepts in environmental health science* (2nd ed.). New York, NY: Lewis.

11. **MULTIVOLUME WORK**

> Barnes, J. (Ed.). (1995). *Complete works of Aristotle* (Vols. 1–2). Princeton, NJ: Princeton University Press.

Note: If you cite just one volume of a multivolume work, list that volume, not the complete span of volumes, in parentheses after the title.

12. **ARTICLE IN A REFERENCE WORK**

> Dean, C. (1994). Jaws and teeth. In *The Cambridge encyclopedia of human evolution* (pp. 56–59). Cambridge, England: Cambridge University Press.

If no author is listed, begin with the title.

13. **REPUBLISHED BOOK**

> Piaget, J. (1952). *The language and thought of the child*. London, England: Routledge & Kegan Paul. (Original work published 1932)

14. **INTRODUCTION, PREFACE, FOREWORD, OR AFTERWORD**

> Klosterman, C. (2007). Introduction. In P. Shirley, *Can I keep my jersey?: 11 teams, 5 countries, and 4 years in my life as a basketball vagabond* (pp. v–vii). New York, NY: Villard-Random House.

15. **BOOK WITH A TITLE WITHIN THE TITLE**

Do not italicize or enclose in quotation marks a title within a book title.

> Klarman, M. J. (2007). *Brown v. Board of Education and the civil rights movement*. New York, NY: Oxford University Press.

Print periodicals

Begin with the author name(s). (See models 1–5.) Then include the publication date (year only for journals, and year, month, and day for other periodicals); the article title; the periodical title; the volume number and issue number, if any; and the page numbers. The source map on pp. 530–31 shows where to find this information in a sample periodical.

16. **ARTICLE IN A JOURNAL PAGINATED BY VOLUME**

> O'Connell, D. C., & Kowal, S. (2003). Psycholinguistics: A half century of monologism. *The American Journal of Psychology, 116,* 191–212.

17. **ARTICLE IN A JOURNAL PAGINATED BY ISSUE**

If each issue begins with page 1, include the issue number (in parentheses and not italicized) after the volume number (italicized).

> Hall, R. E. (2000). Marriage as vehicle of racism among women of color. *Psychology: A Journal of Human Behavior, 37*(2), 29–40.

18. **ARTICLE IN A MAGAZINE**

> Ricciardi, S. (2003, August 5). Enabling the mobile work force. *PC Magazine, 22,* 46.

19. **ARTICLE IN A NEWSPAPER**

> Reynolds Lewis, K. (2011, December 22). Why some business owners think now is the time to sell. *The New York Times,* p. B5.

20. **EDITORIAL OR LETTER TO THE EDITOR**

> Zelneck, B. (2003, July 18). Serving the public at public universities [Letter to the editor]. *The Chronicle Review,* p. B18.

21. **UNSIGNED ARTICLE**

> Annual meeting announcement. (2003, March). *Cognitive Psychology, 46,* 227.

22. **REVIEW**

> Ringel, S. (2003). [Review of the book *Multiculturalism and the therapeutic process*]. *Clinical Social Work Journal, 31,* 212–213.

23. **PUBLISHED INTERVIEW**

> Smith, H. (2002, October). [Interview with A. Thompson]. *The Sun,* pp. 4–7.

APA SOURCE MAP: Articles from Print Periodicals

1 **Author.** List all authors' last names first, and use only initials for first and middle names. For more about citing authors, see models 1–5.

2 **Publication date.** Enclose the date in parentheses. For journals, use only the year. For magazines and newspapers, use the year, a comma, the month (spelled out), and the day, if given.

3 **Article title.** Do not italicize or enclose article titles in quotation marks. Capitalize only the first word of the article title and subtitle and any proper nouns or proper adjectives.

4 **Periodical title.** Italicize the periodical title (and subtitle, if any), and capitalize all major words. Follow the periodical title with a comma.

5 **Volume and issue numbers.** Give the volume number (italicized) and, without a space in between, the issue number (if given) in parentheses. Follow with a comma.

6 **Page numbers.** Give the inclusive page numbers of the article. For newspapers only, include the abbreviation *p.* ("page") or *pp.* ("pages") before the page numbers. End the citation with a period.

A citation for the periodical article on p. 531 would look like this:

Etzioni, A. (2006). Leaving race behind: Our growing Hispanic population creates a golden opportunity. *The American Scholar, 75*(2), 20–30.

The A M E R I C A N
SCHOLAR

④ Periodical Title

Spring 2006 | Vol. 75, No. 2

⑤ Volume and Issue Numbers

② Publication Date

The A M E R I C A N
SCHOLAR

③ Article Title

RICHA

Leaving Race Behind

Our growing Hispanic population creates a golden opportunity

AMITAI ETZIONI ● ① Author

ANN BEA
EDWARD H
PHYLLIS R

AL
JOSEPH W. G
D

J

For a subscription to THE AMERICAN S
$48 two years, $69 three years; for in
international subscriptions, add $15.
Newstand Services. For more inform
advertising please contact: Linda Mill
THE AMERICAN SCHOLAR, a quarterly j
Phi Beta Kappa Society, 1606 New
scholar@pbk.org. Manuscripts may b
AMERICAN SCHOLAR assumes no respons
Periodical postage paid at Washingto
P.O. Box 354, Mt. Morris, IL 61054-0
additional revenues, the Phi Beta Kap
deleted should send their name and

Some years ago the United States government asked me what my race was. I was reluctant to respond because my 50 years of practicing sociology—and some powerful personal experiences—have underscored for me what we all know to one degree or another, that racial divisions bedevil America, just as they do many other societies across the world. Not wanting to encourage these divisions, I refused to check off one of the specific racial options on the U.S. Census form and instead marked a box labeled "Other." I later found out that the federal government did not accept such an attempt to de-emphasize race, by me or by some 6.75 million other Americans who tried it. Instead the government assigned me to a racial category, one it chose for me. Learning this made me conjure up what I admit is a far-fetched association. I was in this place once before. When I was a Jewish child in Nazi Germany in the early 1930s, many Jews who saw themselves as good Germans wanted to "pass" as Aryans. But the Nazi regime would have none of it. Never mind, they told these Jews, *we determine* who is Jewish and who is not. A similar practice prevailed in the Old South, where if you had one drop of African blood you were a Negro, disregarding all other facts and considerations, including how you saw yourself.

You might suppose that in the years since my little Census-form protest

⌣ Amitai Etzioni is University Professor at George Washington University and the author of *The Monochrome Society*.

Digital written-word sources

Updated guidelines for citing electronic resources are maintained at the APA's Web site (www.apa.org).

24. ARTICLE FROM AN ONLINE PERIODICAL

Give the author, date, title, and publication information as you would for a print document. Include both the volume and issue numbers for all journal articles. If the article has a digital object identifier (DOI), include it. If there is no DOI, include the URL for the periodical's home page or for the article (if the article is difficult to find from the home page). For newspaper articles accessible from a searchable Web site, give the site URL only.

> Barringer, F. (2008, February 7). In many communities, it's not easy going green. *The New York Times.* Retrieved from http://www.nytimes.com
>
> Cleary, J. M., & Crafti, N. (2007). Basic need satisfaction, emotional eating, and dietary restraint as risk factors for recurrent overeating in a community sample. *E-Journal of Applied Psychology, 2*(3), 27–39. Retrieved from http://ojs.lib.swin.edu.au/index.php/ejap/article/view/90/116

25. ARTICLE FROM A DATABASE

Give the author, date, title, and publication information as you would for a print document. Include both the volume and issue numbers for all journal articles. If the article has a DOI, include it. If there is no DOI, write *Retrieved from* and the URL of the journal's home page (not the URL of the database). The source map on pp. 534–35 shows where to find this information for a typical article from a database.

> Hazleden, R. (2003, December). Love yourself: The relationship of the self with itself in popular self-help texts. *Journal of Sociology, 39*(4), 413–428. Retrieved from http://jos.sagepub.com
>
> Morley, N. J., Ball, L. J., & Ormerod, T. C. (2006). How the detection of insurance fraud succeeds and fails. *Psychology, Crime, & Law, 12*(2), 163–180. doi:10.1080/10683160512331316325

26. ABSTRACT FOR AN ONLINE ARTICLE

> Gudjonsson, G. H., & Young, S. (2010). Does confabulation in memory predict suggestibility beyond IQ and memory? [Abstract]. *Personality & Individual Differences, 49*(1), 65–67. doi: 10.1016/j.paid.2010.03.014

AT A GLANCE

Citing Digital Sources

When citing sources accessed online or from an electronic database, include as many of the following elements as you can find:

- *Author.* Give the author's name, if available.

- *Publication date.* Include the date of electronic publication or of the latest update, if available. When no publication date is available, use *n.d.* ("no date").

- *Title.* If the source is not part of a larger whole, italicize the title.

- *Print publication information.* For articles from online journals, magazines, or reference databases, give the publication title and other publishing information as you would for a print periodical (see models 16–23).

- *Retrieval information.* For a work from a database, do the following: if the article has a DOI (digital object identifier), include that number after the publication information; do not include the name of the database. If there is no DOI, write *Retrieved from* followed by the URL for the journal's home page (not the database URL). For a work found on a Web site, write *Retrieved from* and include the URL. If the work seems likely to be updated, include the retrieval date. If the URL is longer than one line, break it only before a punctuation mark; do not break *http://*.

---

27. DOCUMENT FROM A WEB SITE

Include all of the following information that you can find: the author's name; the publication date (or *n.d.* if no date is available); the title of the document; the title of the site or larger work, if any; volume and issue numbers (if any); page numbers (if any); *Retrieved from* and the URL. Provide your date of access only if an update seems likely. The source map on pp. 536–37 shows where to find this information for an article from a Web site.

Behnke, P. C. (2006, February 22). *The homeless are everyone's problem.* Retrieved from http://www.authorsden.com/visit/viewArticle.asp?id=21017

Hacker, J. S. (2006). The privatization of risk and the growing economic insecurity of Americans. *Items and Issues, 5*(4), 16–23. Retrieved from http://publications.ssrc.org/items/items5.4/Hacker.pdf

What parents should know about treatment of behavioral and emotional disorders in preschool children. (2006). *APA Online.* Retrieved from http://www.apa.org/releases/kidsmed.html

1 Author. Include the author's name as you would for a print source. List all authors' last names first, and use initials for first and middle names. For more about citing authors, see models 1–5.

2 Publication date. Enclose the date in parentheses. For journals, use only the year. For magazines and newspapers, use the year, a comma, the month, and the day if given.

3 Article title. Capitalize only the first word of the article title and the subtitle and any proper nouns or proper adjectives.

4 Periodical title. Italicize the periodical title.

5 Volume and issue number. For journals and magazines, give the volume number (italicized) and the issue number (in parentheses).

6 Page numbers. For journals only, give inclusive page numbers.

7 Retrieval information. If the article has a DOI (digital object identifier), include that number after the publication information; do not include the name of the database. If there is no DOI, write *Retrieved from* followed by the URL of the journal's home page (not the database URL).

A citation for the article on p. 535 would look like this:

Chory-Assad, R. M., & Tamborini, R. (2004). Television sitcom exposure and aggressive communication: A priming perspective. *North American Journal of Psychology, 6*(3), 415–422. Retrieved from http://www.najp.8m.com

❸ Article Title

Television Sitcom Exposure and Aggressive Communication: A Priming Perspective.

❺ Volume and Issue Number

Vol. 6 Issue 3

❻ Page Numbers

p415-422, 8p

❶ Authors

Chory-Assad, Rebecca M.

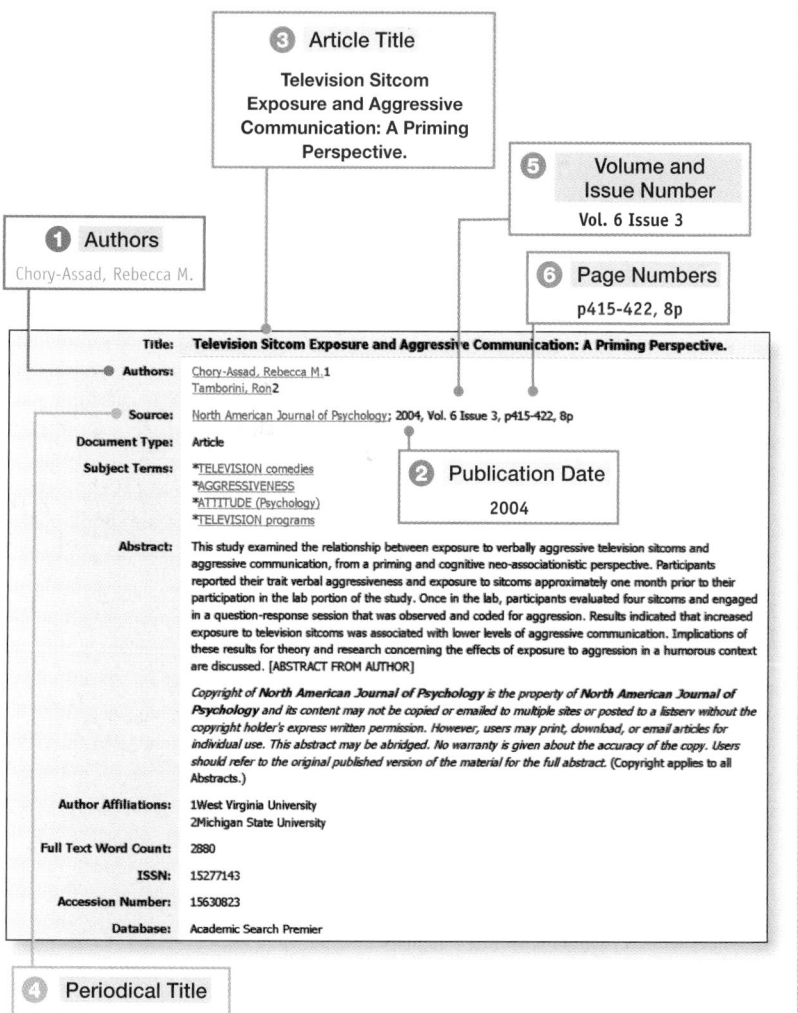

Title:	**Television Sitcom Exposure and Aggressive Communication: A Priming Perspective.**
Authors:	Chory-Assad, Rebecca M.1 Tamborini, Ron2
Source:	North American Journal of Psychology; 2004, Vol. 6 Issue 3, p415-422, 8p
Document Type:	Article
Subject Terms:	*TELEVISION comedies *AGGRESSIVENESS *ATTITUDE (Psychology) *TELEVISION programs
Abstract:	This study examined the relationship between exposure to verbally aggressive television sitcoms and aggressive communication, from a priming and cognitive neo-associationistic perspective. Participants reported their trait verbal aggressiveness and exposure to sitcoms approximately one month prior to their participation in the lab portion of the study. Once in the lab, participants evaluated four sitcoms and engaged in a question-response session that was observed and coded for aggression. Results indicated that increased exposure to television sitcoms was associated with lower levels of aggressive communication. Implications of these results for theory and research concerning the effects of exposure to aggression in a humorous context are discussed. [ABSTRACT FROM AUTHOR]
	*Copyright of **North American Journal of Psychology** is the property of **North American Journal of Psychology** and its content may not be copied or emailed to multiple sites or posted to a listserv without the copyright holder's express written permission. However, users may print, download, or email articles for individual use. This abstract may be abridged. No warranty is given about the accuracy of the copy. Users should refer to the original published version of the material for the full abstract. (Copyright applies to all Abstracts.)*
Author Affiliations:	1West Virginia University 2Michigan State University
Full Text Word Count:	2880
ISSN:	15277143
Accession Number:	15630823
Database:	Academic Search Premier

❷ Publication Date

2004

❹ Periodical Title

North American Journal of Psychology

535

APA SOURCE MAP: Works from Web Sites

1 Author. If one is given, include the author's name (see models 1–5). List last names first, and use only initials for first names. The site's sponsor may be the author. If no author is identified, begin the citation with the title of the document.

2 Publication date. Enclose the date of publication or latest update in parentheses. Use *n.d.* ("no date") when no publication date is available.

3 Title of work. Capitalize only the first word of the title and subtitle and any proper nouns or proper adjectives.

4 Title of Web site. Italicize the title. Capitalize all major words.

5 Retrieval information. Write *Retrieved from* and include the URL. If the work seems likely to be updated, include the retrieval date.

A citation for the Web document on p. 537 would look like this:

Alexander, M. (2001, August 22). Thirty years later, Stanford Prison Experiment lives on. *Stanford Report*. Retrieved from http://news-service.stanford
.edu/news/2001/august22/prison2-822.html

Retrieval Information

Publication Date

August 22, 2001

Title of Work

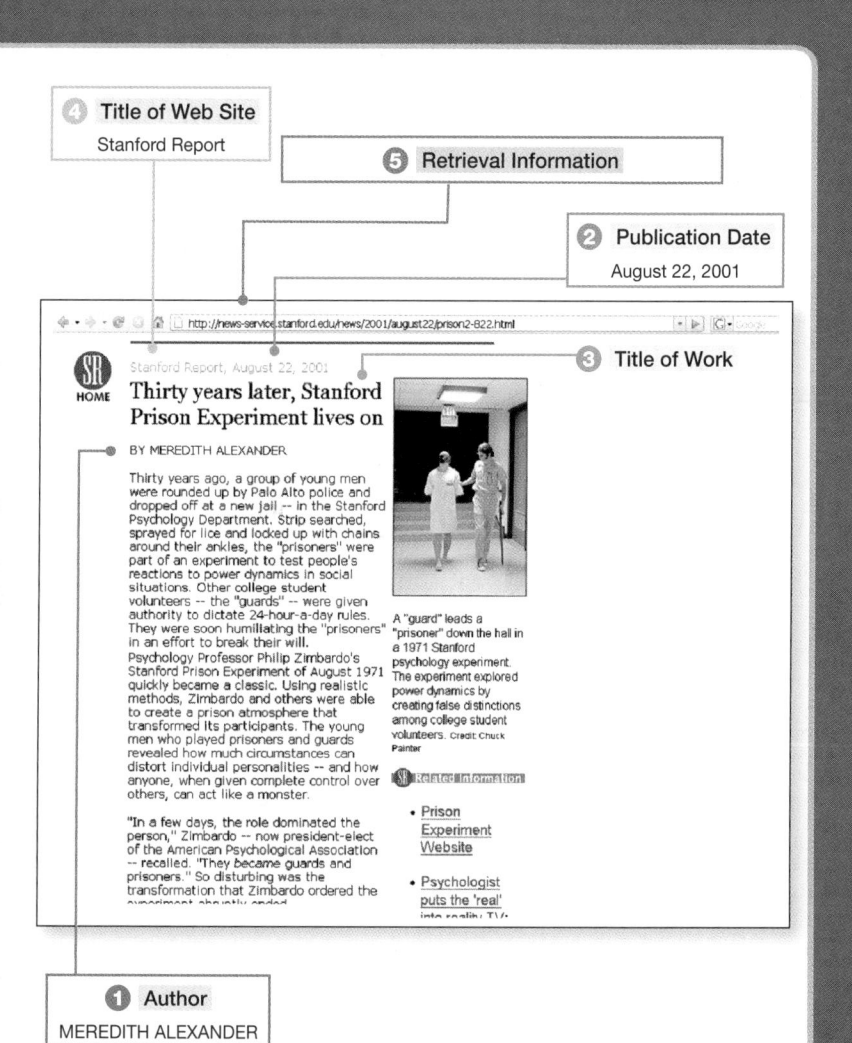

SR HOME

Thirty years later, Stanford Prison Experiment lives on

BY MEREDITH ALEXANDER

Thirty years ago, a group of young men were rounded up by Palo Alto police and dropped off at a new jail -- in the Stanford Psychology Department. Strip searched, sprayed for lice and locked up with chains around their ankles, the "prisoners" were part of an experiment to test people's reactions to power dynamics in social situations. Other college student volunteers -- the "guards" -- were given authority to dictate 24-hour-a-day rules. They were soon humiliating the "prisoners" in an effort to break their will. Psychology Professor Philip Zimbardo's Stanford Prison Experiment of August 1971 quickly became a classic. Using realistic methods, Zimbardo and others were able to create a prison atmosphere that transformed its participants. The young men who played prisoners and guards revealed how much circumstances can distort individual personalities -- and how anyone, when given complete control over others, can act like a monster.

"In a few days, the role dominated the person," Zimbardo -- now president-elect of the American Psychological Association -- recalled. "They became guards and prisoners." So disturbing was the transformation that Zimbardo ordered the experiment abruptly ended.

A "guard" leads a "prisoner" down the hall in a 1971 Stanford psychology experiment. The experiment explored power dynamics by creating false distinctions among college student volunteers. Credit Chuck Painter

SR Related Information

- Prison Experiment Website

- Psychologist puts the 'real' into reality TV:

Author

MEREDITH ALEXANDER

537

28. CHAPTER OR SECTION OF A WEB DOCUMENT

Follow model 27. After the chapter or section title, type *In* and give the document title, with identifying information, if any, in parentheses. End with the date of access (if needed) and the URL.

Salamon, Andrew. (n.d.). War in Europe. In *Childhood in times of war* (chap. 2). Retrieved April 11, 2008, from http://remember.org/jean

29. EMAIL MESSAGE OR REAL-TIME COMMUNICATION

Because the APA stresses that any sources cited in your list of references be retrievable by your readers, you should not include entries for email messages, real-time communications (such as IMs), or any other postings that are not archived. Instead, cite these sources in your text as forms of personal communication (see p. 520).

30. ONLINE POSTING

List an online posting in the references list only if you are able to retrieve the message from an archive. Provide the author's name, the date of posting, and the subject line. Include other identifying information in square brackets. End with the retrieval statement and the URL of the archived message.

Troike, R. C. (2001, June 21). Buttercups and primroses [Electronic mailing list message]. Retrieved from http://listserv.linguistlist.org/archives/ads-l.html

Wittenberg, E. (2001, July 11). Gender and the Internet [Newsgroup message]. Retrieved from news://comp.edu.composition

31. BLOG (WEB LOG) POST

Spaulding, P. (2010, April 27). Who believes in a real America? [Web log post]. Retrieved from http://pandagon.net/index.php/site/2010/04

32. WIKI ENTRY

Use the date of posting, if there is one, or *n.d.* for "no date" if there is none. Include the retrieval date because wiki content can change frequently.

Happiness. (2007, June 14). Retrieved March 24, 2008, from PsychWiki:

http://www.psychwiki.com/wiki/Happiness

Other sources (including online versions)

33. COMPUTER SOFTWARE

PsychMate [Computer software]. (2003). Available from Psychology Software

Tools: http://pstnet.com/products/psychmate

34. GOVERNMENT PUBLICATION

Office of the Federal Register. (2003). *The United States government manual*

2003/2004. Washington, DC: U.S. Government Printing Office.

Cite an online government document as you would a printed government work, adding the URL. If there is no date, use *n.d.*

U.S. Public Health Service. (1999). *The surgeon general's call to action to prevent*

suicide. Retrieved from http://www.mentalhealth.org/suicideprevention

/calltoaction.asp

35. DATA SET

U.S. Department of Education, Institute of Education Sciences. (2009).

NAEP state comparisons [Data set]. Retrieved from http://nces.ed.gov

/nationsreportcard/statecomparisons/

36. DISSERTATION

If you retrieved the dissertation from a database, give the database name and the accession number, if one is assigned.

Lengel, L. L. (1968). *The righteous cause: Some religious aspects of Kansas*

populism. Retrieved from ProQuest Digital Dissertations. (6900033)

If you retrieve a dissertation from a Web site, give the type of dissertation, the institution, and year after the title, and provide a retrieval statement.

Meeks, M. G. (2006). *Between abolition and reform: First-year writing programs,*

e-literacies, and institutional change (Doctoral dissertation, University of

North Carolina). Retrieved from http://dc.lib.unc.edu/etd/

37. TECHNICAL OR RESEARCH REPORT

Give the report number, if available, in parentheses after the title.

McCool, R., Fikes, R., & McGuinness, D. (2003). *Semantic Web tools for enhanced authoring* (Report No. KSL-03-07). Retrieved from www.ksl.stanford.edu /KSL_Abstracts/KSL-03-07.html

38. CONFERENCE PROCEEDINGS

Robertson, S. P., Vatrapu, R. K., & Medina, R. (2009). YouTube and Facebook: Online video "friends" social networking. In *Conference proceedings: YouTube and the 2008 election cycle* (pp. 159–76). Amherst, MA: University of Massachusetts. Retrieved from http://scholarworks.umass.edu/jitpc2009

39. PAPER PRESENTED AT A MEETING OR SYMPOSIUM, UNPUBLISHED

Cite the month of the meeting if it is available.

Jones, J. G. (1999, February). *Mental health intervention in mass casualty disasters.* Paper presented at the Rocky Mountain Region Disaster Mental Health Conference, Laramie, WY.

40. POSTER SESSION

Barnes Young, L. L. (2003, August). *Cognition, aging, and dementia.* Poster session presented at the 2003 Division 40 APA Convention, Toronto, Ontario, Canada.

41. FILM, VIDEO, OR DVD

Nolan, C. (Director). (2010). *Inception* [Motion picture]. United States: Warner Bros.

42. ONLINE AUDIO OR VIDEO FILE

Klusman, P. (2008, February 13). An engineer's guide to cats [Video file]. Retrieved from http://www.youtube.com/watch?v=mHXBL6bzAR4

O'Brien, K. (2008, January 31). Developing countries [Audio file]. *KUSP's life in the fast lane.* Retrieved from http://kusp.org/shows/fast.html

43. TELEVISION PROGRAM, SINGLE EPISODE

Imperioli, M. (Writer), & Buscemi, S. (Director). (2002). Everybody hurts [Television series episode]. In D. Chase (Executive Producer), *The Sopranos.* New York, NY: Home Box Office.

44. TELEVISION SERIES

> Abrams, J. J., Lieber, J., & Lindelof, D. (2004). *Lost.* [Television series]. New York, NY: WABC.

45. AUDIO PODCAST (DOWNLOADED AUDIO FILE)

> Noguchi, Yugi. (2010, 24 May). BP hard to pin down on oil spill claims. [Audio podcast]. *NPR morning edition.* Retrieved from http://www.npr.org

46. RECORDING

> The Avalanches. (2001). Frontier psychiatrist. On *Since I left you* [CD]. Los Angeles, CA: Elektra/Asylum Records.

53d A student research essay, APA style

On the following pages is a paper by Tawnya Redding that conforms to the APA guidelines described in this chapter. Note that this essay has been reproduced in a narrow format to allow for annotation.

Student Writer

Tawnya Redding

Student Writing
APA

Running Head: MOOD MUSIC   1

Running head (fifty characters or fewer) appears flush left on first line of title page

Page number appears flush right on first line of every page

Mood Music: Music Preference and the Risk for Depression

and Suicide in Adolescents

Tawnya Redding

Psychology 480

Professor Ede

February 23, 2009

Title, name, and affiliation centered and double-spaced

Annotations indicate effective choices or APA-style formatting.

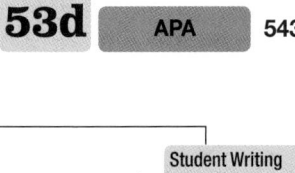

**Student Writing
APA**

Abstract

There has long been concern for the effects that certain genres of music (such as heavy metal and country) have on youth. While a correlational link between these genres and increased risk for depression and suicide in adolescents has been established, researchers have been unable to pinpoint what is responsible for this link, and a causal relationship has not been determined. This paper will begin by discussing correlational literature concerning music preference and increased risk for depression and suicide, as well as the possible reasons for this link. Finally, studies concerning the effects of music on mood will be discussed. This examination of the literature on music and increased risk for depression and suicide points out the limitations of previous research and suggests the need for new research establishing a causal relationship for this link as well as research into the specific factors that may contribute to an increased risk for depression and suicide in adolescents.

Heading
centered

No indentation

Use of
passive voice
appropriate for
social sciences

Clear,
straightforward
description
of literature
under review

Conclusions
indicated

Double-spaced
text

MOOD MUSIC   3

Mood Music: Music Preference and the Risk for Depression and

Suicide in Adolescents

Music is a significant part of American culture. Since the

explosion of rock and roll in the 1950s, there has been a concern

for the effects that music may have on listeners, and especially

on young people. The genres most likely to come under suspicion

in recent decades have included heavy metal, country, and blues.

These genres have been suspected of having adverse effects on

the mood and behavior of young listeners. But can music really

alter the disposition and create self-destructive behaviors in

listeners? And if so, which genres and aspects of those genres are

responsible? The following review of the literature will establish

the correlation between potentially problematic genres of music

such as heavy metal and country and depression and suicide risk.

First, correlational studies concerning music preference and suicide

risk will be discussed, followed by a discussion of the literature

concerning the possible reasons for this link. Finally, studies

concerning the effects of music on mood will be discussed. Despite

the link between genres such as heavy metal and country and

suicide risk, previous research has been unable to establish the

causal nature of this link.

The Correlation Between Music and Depression and Suicide Risk

Studies over the past two decades have set out to answer

this question by examining the correlation between youth music

preference and risk for depression and suicide. A large portion

of these studies have focused on heavy metal and country music

as the main genre culprits associated with youth suicidality

and depression (Lacourse, Claes, & Villeneuve, 2001; Scheel &

Westefeld, 1999; Stack & Gundlach, 1992). Stack and Gundlach

(1992) examined the radio airtime devoted to country music in 49

metropolitan areas and found that the higher the percentages of

Margin annotations:

Full title centered

Paragraphs indented

Background information about review supplied

Questions focus reader's attention

Boldface headings help organize review

Parenthetical references follow APA style

country music airtime, the higher the incidence of suicides among whites. The researchers hypothesized that themes in country music (such as alcohol abuse) promoted audience identification and reinforced a preexisting suicidal mood, and that the themes associated with country music were responsible for elevated suicide rates. Similarly, Scheel and Westefeld (1999) found a correlation between heavy metal music listeners and an increased risk for suicide, as did Lacourse et al. (2001).

Reasons for the Link: Characteristics of Those Who Listen to Problematic Music

Unfortunately, previous studies concerning music preference and suicide risk have been unable to determine a causal relationship and have focused mainly on establishing a correlation between suicide risk and music preference. This leaves the question open as to whether an individual at risk for depression and suicide is attracted to certain genres of music or whether the music helps induce the mood—or both. Some studies have suggested that music preference may simply be a reflection of other underlying problems associated with increased risk for suicide (Lacourse et al., 2001; Scheel & Westefeld, 1999). For example, in research done by Scheel and Westefeld (1999), adolescents who listened to heavy metal were found to have lower scores on the Reason for Living Inventory, a self-report measure designed to assess potential reasons for not committing suicide. These adolescents were also found to have lower scores on several subscales of the Reason for Living Inventory, including responsibility to family along with survival and coping beliefs. Other risk factors associated with suicide and suicidal behaviors include poor family relationships, depression, alienation, anomie, and drug and alcohol abuse (Lacourse et al., 2001). Lacourse et al. (2001) examined 275 adolescents in the Montreal region with a preference for heavy metal and found that this preference was not significantly related to suicide risk when other

Discussion of correlation vs. causation points out limitations of previous studies

Alternative explanations considered

MOOD MUSIC   5

risk factors were controlled for. This was also the conclusion of Scheel and Westefeld (1999), in which music preference for heavy metal was thought to be a red flag for suicide vulnerability, suggesting that the source of the problem may lie more in personal and familial characteristics.

George, Stickle, Rachid, and Wopnford (2007) further explored the correlation between suicide risk and music preference by attempting to identify the personality characteristics of those with a preference for different genres of music. A sample of 358 individuals was assessed for preference of 30 different styles of music along with a number of personality characteristics, including self-esteem, intelligence, spirituality, social skills, locus of control, openness, conscientiousness, extraversion, agreeableness, emotional stability, hostility, and depression (George et al., 2007). The 30 styles of music were then categorized into 8 factors: rebellious (for example, punk and heavy metal), classical, rhythmic and intense (including hip-hop, rap, and pop), easy listening, fringe (for example, techno), contemporary Christian, jazz and blues, and traditional Christian. The results revealed an almost comprehensively negative personality profile for those who preferred to listen to the rebellious and rhythmic and intense categories, while those who preferred classical music tended to have a comprehensively positive profile. Like Scheel and Westefeld (1999) and Lacourse et al. (2001), this study also supports the theory that youth are drawn to certain genres of music based on already existing factors, whether they be related to personality or situational variables.

Reasons for the Link: Characteristics of Problematic Music

Transition links
paragraphs
                Another possible explanation is that the lyrics and themes of the music have an effect on listeners. In this scenario, music is thought to exacerbate an already depressed mood and hence

contribute to an increased risk for suicide. This was the proposed reasoning behind higher suicide rates in whites in Stack and Gundlach's (1992) study linking country music to suicide risk. In this case, the themes associated with country music were thought to promote audience identification and reinforce preexisting self-destructive behaviors (such as excessive alcohol consumption). Stack (2000) also studied individuals with a musical preference for blues to determine whether the genre's themes could increase the level of suicide acceptability. The results demonstrated that blues fans were no more accepting of suicide than nonfans, but that blues listeners were found to have low religiosity levels, an important factor for suicide acceptability (Stack, 2000). Despite this link between possible suicidal behavior and a preference for blues music, the actual suicide behavior of blues fans has not been explored, and thus no concrete associations can be made.

Need for more research indicated

The Effect of Music on Mood

While studies examining the relationship between music genres such as heavy metal, country, and blues have been able to establish a correlation between music preference and suicide risk, it is still unclear from these studies what effect music has on the mood of the listener. Previous research has suggested that some forms of music can both improve and depress mood (Lai, 1999; Siedliecki & Good, 2006; Smith & Noon, 1998). Lai (1999) found that changes in mood were more likely to be found in an experimental group of depressed women versus a control group. It was also found that both the experimental and control groups showed significant increases in the tranquil mood state, but the amount of change was not significant between the groups (Lai, 1999). This study suggests that music can have a positive effect on depressed individuals when they are allowed to choose the music they are listening to. In a similar study, Siedliecki and

Discussion of previous research

MOOD MUSIC   7

Good (2006) found that music can increase a listener's sense of power and decrease depression, pain, and disability. Researchers randomly assigned 60 African American and Caucasian participants with chronic nonmalignant pain to a standard music group (offering them a choice of instrumental music types—piano, jazz, orchestra, harp, and synthesizer), a patterning music group (asking them to choose music to ease muscle tension, to facilitate sleep, or to decrease anxiety), or a control group. There were no statistically significant differences between the two music groups. However, the music groups had significantly less pain, depression, and disability than the control group (Siedliecki & Good, 2006). On the other hand, Martin, Clark, and Pearce (1993) identified a subgroup of heavy metal fans who reported feeling worse after listening to their music of choice. Although this subgroup did exist, there was also evidence that listening to heavy metal results in more positive affect, and it was hypothesized that those who experience negative effects after listening to their preferred genre of heavy metal may be most at risk for suicidal behaviors (Martin et al., 1993).

    Smith and Noon (1998) also determined that music can have a negative effect on mood. Six songs were selected for the particular theme they embodied: (1) vigorous, (2) fatigued, (3) angry, (4) depressed, (5) tense, and (6) all moods. The results indicated that selections 3–6 had significant effects on the mood of participants, with selection 6 (all moods) resulting in the greatest positive change in the mood and selection 5 (tense) resulting in the greatest negative change in mood. Selection 4 (depressed) was found to sap the vigor and increase anger/hostility in participants, while selection 5 (tense) significantly depressed participants and made them more anxious. Although this study did not specifically comment on the effects

MOOD MUSIC   8

of different genres on mood, the results do indicate that certain themes can indeed depress mood. The participants for this study were undergraduate students who were not depressed, and thus it seems that certain types of music can have a negative effect on the mood of healthy individuals.

Is There Evidence for a Causal Relationship?

Despite the correlation between certain music genres (especially heavy metal) and increased risk for depression and suicidal behaviors in adolescents, it remains unclear whether these types of music can alter the mood of at-risk youth in a negative way. This view of the correlation between music and suicide risk is supported by a meta-analysis done by Baker and Bor (2008), in which the authors assert that most studies reject the notion that music is a causal factor and suggest that music preference is more indicative of emotional vulnerability. However, it is still unknown whether these genres can negatively alter mood at all, and if they can, whether the themes and lyrics associated with the music are responsible. Clearly, more research is needed to further examine this correlation, as a causal link between these genres of music and adolescent suicide risk has yet to be shown. However, even if the theory put forth by Baker and Bon and other researchers is true, it is still important to investigate the effects that music can have on those who may be at risk for suicide and depression. Even if music genres are not the ultimate cause of suicidal behavior, they may act as a catalyst that further pushes adolescents into a state of depression and increased risk for suicidal behavior.

Conclusion indicates need for further research

MOOD MUSIC   9

References
begin on new
page

Journal
article from a
database, no
DOI

Print journal
article

Journal
article from a
database with
DOI

References

Baker, F., & Bor, W. (2008). Can music preference indicate mental
health status in young people? *Australasian Psychiatry, 16*(4),
284–288. Retrieved from http://www3.interscience.wiley.com
/journal/118565538/home

George, D., Stickle, K., Rachid, F., & Wopnford, A. (2007). The association
between types of music enjoyed and cognitive, behavioral, and
personality factors of those who listen. *Psychomusicology, 19*(2),
32–56.

Lacourse, E., Claes, M., & Villeneuve, M. (2001). Heavy metal music
and adolescent suicidal risk. *Journal of Youth and Adolescence,
30*(3), 321–332.

Lai, Y. (1999). Effects of music listening on depressed women in
Taiwan. *Issues in Mental Health Nursing, 20,* 229–246. doi:
10.1080/016128499248637

Martin, G., Clark, M., & Pearce, C. (1993). Adolescent suicide: Music
preference as an indicator of vulnerability. *Journal of the American
Academy of Child and Adolescent Psychiatry, 32,* 530–535.

Scheel, K., & Westefeld, J. (1999). Heavy metal music and adolescent
suicidality: An empirical investigation. *Adolescence, 34*(134),
253–273.

Siedliecki, S., & Good, M. (2006). Effect of music on power, pain,
depression and disability. *Journal of Advanced Nursing, 54*(5),
553–562. doi: 10.1111/j.1365-2648.2006.03860.x

Smith, J. L., & Noon, J. (1998). Objective measurement of mood
change induced by contemporary music. *Journal of Psychiatric
& Mental Health Nursing, 5,* 403–408.

Stack, S. (2000). Blues fans and suicide acceptability. *Death
Studies, 24,* 223–231.

Stack, S., & Gundlach, J. (1992). The effect of country music on
suicide. *Social Forces, 71*(1), 211–218. Retrieved from http://
socialforces.unc.edu/

Chicago Style **54**

The style guide of the University of Chicago Press has long been used in history as well as in other areas of the arts and humanities. The Sixteenth Edition of *The Chicago Manual of Style* (2010) provides a complete guide to *Chicago* style, including two systems for citing sources. This chapter presents the notes and bibliography system. For easy reference, examples of notes and bibliographic entries are shown together in 54b.

 bedfordstmartins.com/everydaywriter
Documenting Sources

54a The basics of *Chicago* style

Why does academic work call for very careful citation practices when writing for the general public may not? The answer is that readers of academic work expect to get certain information from source citations:

- Source citations demonstrate that you've done your homework on your topic or issue and that you are a part of the conversation surrounding it.
- Source citations show that you understand the need to give credit where credit is due when you make use of someone else's intellectual property. (See Chapter 18 for more details.)
- Source citations give explicit directions to guide readers who want to look for themselves at the works you're using.

Guidelines from *The Chicago Manual of Style* will tell you exactly what information you need to include in your citation and how you should format that information.

TYPES OF SOURCES

You will need to be careful to tell your readers whether you read a print version or a digital version of a source that consists mainly of written words. Digital magazine and newspaper articles may include updates or corrections that the print version lacks; digital books may not number pages or screens the same way the print book does. If you are citing a source that has important media elements—such as a film, song, or artwork—consult the "Other Sources" section of the directory (p. 554). And if you can't find a model exactly like the source you've selected, see the box on p. 559.

ARTICLES FROM WEB AND DATABASE SOURCES

You need a subscription to look through most databases, so individual researchers almost always gain access to articles in databases through the computer system of a school or community library that pays to subscribe. The easiest way to tell whether a source comes from a database, then, is that its information is *not* generally available free to anyone with an Internet connection. Many databases are digital collections of articles that originally appeared in edited print periodicals, ensuring that an authority has vouched for the accuracy of the information. Such sources often have more credibility than much of what you find free on the Web.

Connecting parts of citations

Citations in *Chicago* style appear in three places in your text — a note number in the text marks the material from the source, a footnote or an endnote includes information to identify the source (or information about supplemental material), and the bibliography provides the full citation.

Use superscript numbers (1) to mark citations in the text. Place the superscript for each note after the relevant quotation, sentence, clause, or phrase. Type the number after any punctuation mark except the dash, and do not leave space before the superscript. Number citations sequentially throughout the text. When you use signal phrases to introduce quotations or other source material, note that *Chicago* style requires you to use the present tense (*citing Bebout's studies, Meier points out*).

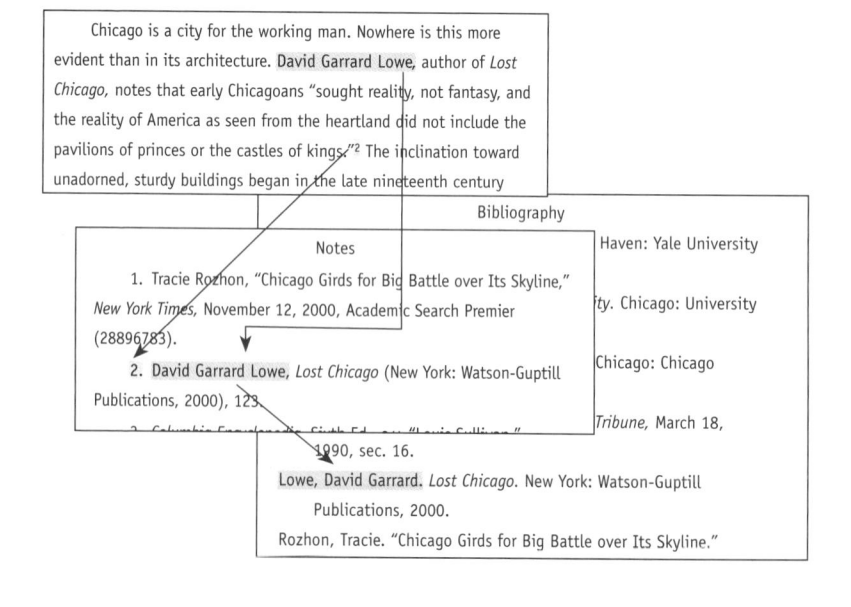

Type footnotes at the bottom of the page on which the superscript appears; type endnotes on a separate page at the end under the heading *Notes*. (Check which your instructor prefers.) The first line of each note is indented one-half inch and begins with a number, a period, a space, and the name of the source's author. All remaining lines of the entry are flush with the left margin. Footnotes and endnotes should be single-spaced, with a double space between notes, unless your instructor prefers double-spaced notes.

IN THE TEXT

Sweig argues that Castro and Che Guevara were not the only key players in the Cuban Revolution of the late 1950s.[19]

IN THE FIRST NOTE REFERRING TO THE SOURCE

19. Julia Sweig, *Inside the Cuban Revolution* (Cambridge, MA: Harvard University Press, 2002), 9.

After giving complete information the first time you cite a work, shorten additional references to that work: list only the author's last name, a comma, a short version of the title, a comma, and the page number. If you refer to the same source cited in the previous note, you can use the Latin abbreviation *Ibid.* ("in the same place") instead of the name and title.

IN FIRST AND SUBSEQUENT NOTES

19. Julia Sweig, *Inside the Cuban Revolution* (Cambridge, MA: Harvard University Press, 2002), 9.

20. Ibid., 13.

21. Ferguson, "Comfort of Being Sad," 63.

22. Sweig, *Cuban Revolution*, 21.

The alphabetical list of the sources in your text is usually titled *Bibliography* in *Chicago* style. You may instead use the title *Sources Consulted, Works Cited,* or *Selected Bibliography* if it better describes your list.

In the bibliographic entry, include the same information as in the first note for that source, but omit the page reference. Give the *first* author's last name first, followed by a comma and the first name; separate the main elements of the entry with periods rather than commas; and do not enclose the publication information for books in parentheses.

IN THE BIBLIOGRAPHY

Sweig, Julia. *Inside the Cuban Revolution*. Cambridge, MA: Harvard University Press, 2002.

Start the bibliography on a separate page after the main text and any notes. Continue the consecutive numbering of pages. Center the title *Bibliography*

DIRECTORY TO *CHICAGO* STYLE

Chicago style for notes and bibliographic entries

Print and online books
1. One author, *555*
   SOURCE MAP, *556–57*
2. Multiple authors, *555*
3. Organization as author, *555*
4. Unknown author, *555*
5. Online book, *558*
6. Electronic book (e-book), *558*
7. Edited book with no author, *558*
8. Edited book with author, *558*
9. Selection in an anthology or chapter in a book, with an editor, *558*
10. Introduction, preface, foreword, or afterword, *558*
11. Translation, *559*
12. Edition other than the first, *559*
13. Multivolume work, *559*
14. Reference work, *559*
15. Work with a title within the title, *560*
16. Sacred text, *560*
17. Source quoted in another source, *560*

Print and online periodicals
18. Article in a print journal, *560*
19. Article in an online journal, *561*
20. Journal article from a database, *561*

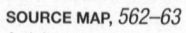

SOURCE MAP, *562–63*
21. Article in a print magazine, *561*
22. Article in an online magazine, *561*
23. Magazine article from a database, *561*
24. Article in a newspaper, *564*
25. Article in an online newspaper, *564*
26. Newspaper article from a database, *564*
27. Book review, *564*

Online sources
28. Web site, *565*
29. Work from a Web site, *565*
   SOURCE MAP, *566–67*
30. Blog (Web log) post, *565*
31. Email and other personal communications, *565*
32. Podcast, *565*
33. Online audio or video, *568*

Other sources
34. Published or broadcast interview, *568*
35. Video or DVD, *568*
36. Sound recording, *568*
37. Work of art, *569*
38. Pamphlet, report, or brochure, *569*
39. Government document, *569*

(without italics or quotation marks). *The Chicago Manual of Style* recommends single-spacing entries and double-spacing between entries.

54b *Chicago* style for notes and bibliographic entries

The following examples demonstrate how to format both notes and bibliographic entries according to *Chicago* style. The note, which is numbered, appears first; the bibliographic entry, which is not numbered, appears below the note.

Print and online books

For the basic format for citing a print book, see the source map on pp. 556–57. The note for a book typically includes six elements: author's name, title and subtitle, city of publication, publisher, year, and page number(s) or electronic locator information for the information in the note. The bibliographic entry usually includes all but the page number (and does include a URL or other locator if the book is electronically published), but it is styled differently: commas separate major elements of a note, but a bibliographic entry uses periods.

1. **ONE AUTHOR**

 1. Nell Irvin Painter, *The History of White People* (New York: W. W. Norton, 2010), 119.

 Painter, Nell Irvin. *The History of White People.* New York: W. W. Norton, 2010.

2. **MULTIPLE AUTHORS**

 2. Margaret Macmillan and Richard Holbrooke, *Paris 1919: Six Months That Changed the World* (New York: Random House, 2003), 384.

 Macmillan, Margaret, and Richard Holbrooke. *Paris 1919: Six Months That Changed the World.* New York: Random House, 2003.

 With more than three authors, you may give the first-listed author followed by *et al.* in the note. In the bibliography, list all the authors' names.

 2. Stephen J. Blank et al., *Conflict, Culture, and History: Regional Dimensions* (Miami: University Press of the Pacific, 2002), 276.

 Blank, Stephen J., Lawrence E. Grinter, Karl P. Magyar, Lewis B. Ware, and Bynum E. Weathers. *Conflict, Culture, and History: Regional Dimensions.* Miami: University Press of the Pacific, 2002.

3. **ORGANIZATION AS AUTHOR**

 3. World Intellectual Property Organization, *Intellectual Property Profile of the Least Developed Countries* (Geneva: World Intellectual Property Organization, 2002), 43.

 World Intellectual Property Organization. *Intellectual Property Profile of the Least Developed Countries.* Geneva: World Intellectual Property Organization, 2002.

4. **UNKNOWN AUTHOR**

 4. *Broad Stripes and Bright Stars* (Kansas City, MO: Andrews McMeel, 2002), 10.

 Broad Stripes and Bright Stars. Kansas City, MO: Andrews McMeel, 2002.

CHICAGO SOURCE MAP: Books

Take information from the book's title page and copyright page (on the reverse side of the title page), not from the book's cover or a library catalog. Look carefully at the differences in punctuation between the note and the bibliographic entry.

1 **Author.** In a note, list the author(s) first name first. In a bibliographic entry, list the first author last name first. List other authors first name first.

2 **Title.** Italicize the title and subtitle and capitalize all major words.

3 **City of publication.** List the city (and country or state abbreviation for an unfamiliar city) followed by a colon. In a note only, city, publisher, and year appear in parentheses.

4 **Publisher.** Drop *Inc.*, *Co.*, *Publishing*, or *Publishers*. Follow with a comma.

5 **Publication year.** In a bibliographic entry only, end with a period.

6 Page number. In a note only, end with the page number and a period.

Citations for the book on p. 557 would look like this:

ENDNOTE

    1. Alex von Tunzelmann, *Red Heat: Conspiracy, Murder, and the Cold War in the Caribbean* (New York: Picador, 2011), 178.

BIBLIOGRAPHIC ENTRY

Von Tunzelmann, Alex. *Red Heat: Conspiracy, Murder, and the Cold War in the Caribbean.* New York: Picador, 2011.

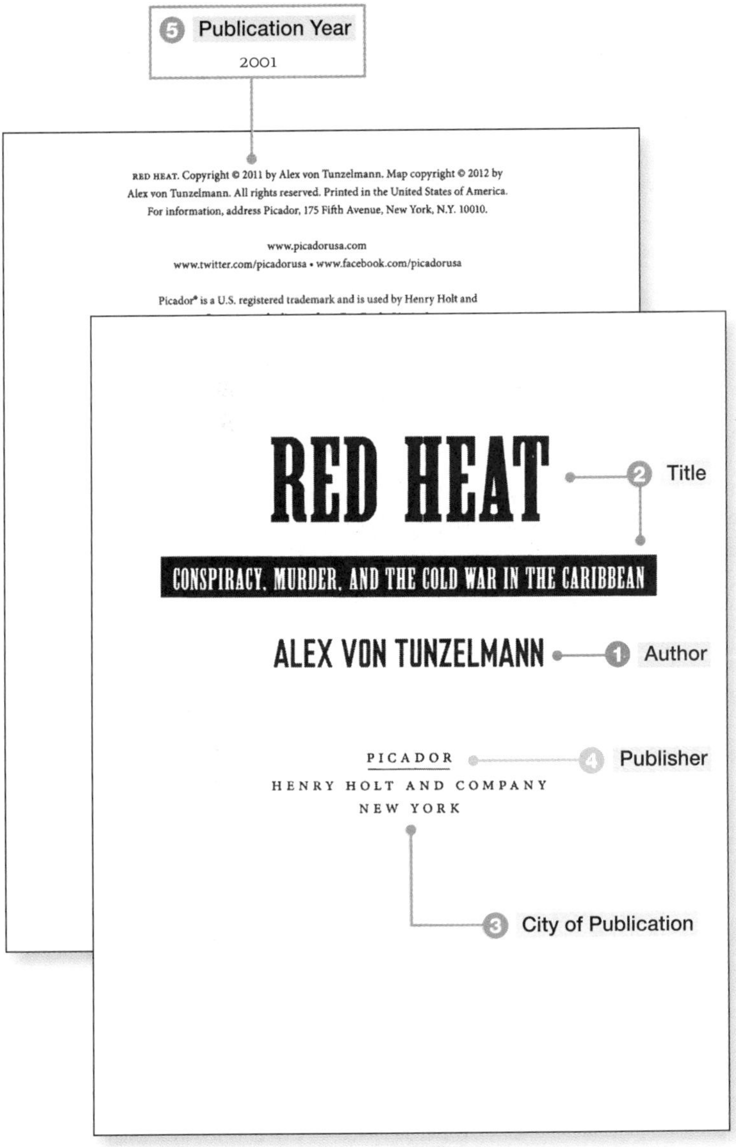

5 Publication Year
2001
RED HEAT. Copyright © 2011 by Alex von Tunzelmann. Map copyright © 2012 by
Alex von Tunzelmann. All rights reserved. Printed in the United States of America.
For information, address Picador, 175 Fifth Avenue, New York, N.Y. 10010.
www.picadorusa.com
www.twitter.com/picadorusa • www.facebook.com/picadorusa
Picador® is a U.S. registered trademark and is used by Henry Holt and
RED HEAT
2 Title
CONSPIRACY, MURDER, AND THE COLD WAR IN THE CARIBBEAN
ALEX VON TUNZELMANN
1 Author
PICADOR
4 Publisher
HENRY HOLT AND COMPANY
NEW YORK
3 City of Publication

5. ONLINE BOOK

5. Dorothy Richardson, *Long Day: The Story of a New York Working Girl, as Told by Herself* (1906; UMDL Texts, 2010),159, http://quod.lib.umich.edu/cgi/t/text/text-idx?c=moa;idno=AFS7156.0001.001.

Richardson, Dorothy. *Long Day: The Story of a New York Working Girl, as Told by Herself.* 1906. UMDL Texts, 2010. http://quod.lib.umich.edu/t/text/text-idx?c=moa;idno=AFS7156.0001.001.

6. ELECTRONIC BOOK (E-BOOK)

6. Manal M. Omar, *Barefoot in Baghdad* (Naperville, IL: Sourcebooks, 2010), Kindle edition, ch. 4.

Omar, Manal M. *Barefoot in Baghdad.* Naperville, IL: Sourcebooks, 2010. Kindle edition.

7. EDITED BOOK WITH NO AUTHOR

7. James H. Fetzer, ed., *The Great Zapruder Film Hoax: Deceit and Deception in the Death of JFK* (Chicago: Open Court, 2003), 56.

Fetzer, James H., ed. *The Great Zapruder Film Hoax: Deceit and Deception in the Death of JFK.* Chicago: Open Court, 2003.

8. EDITED BOOK WITH AUTHOR

8. Leopold von Ranke, *The Theory and Practice of History,* ed. Georg G. Iggers (New York: Routledge, 2010), 135.

von Ranke, Leopold. *The Theory and Practice of History.* Edited by Georg G. Iggers. New York: Routledge, 2010.

9. SELECTION IN AN ANTHOLOGY OR CHAPTER IN A BOOK, WITH AN EDITOR

9. Denise Little, "Born in Blood," in *Alternate Gettysburgs,* ed. Brian Thomsen and Martin H. Greenberg (New York: Berkley Publishing Group, 2002), 245.

Give the inclusive page numbers of the selection or chapter in the bibliographic entry.

Little, Denise. "Born in Blood." In *Alternate Gettysburgs.* Edited by Brian Thomsen and Martin H. Greenberg, 242–55. New York: Berkley Publishing Group, 2002.

10. INTRODUCTION, PREFACE, FOREWORD, OR AFTERWORD

10. Robert B. Reich, introduction to *Making Work Pay: America after Welfare,* ed. Robert Kuttner (New York: New Press, 2002), xvi.

Reich, Robert B. Introduction to *Making Work Pay: America after Welfare,* vii–xvii. Edited by Robert Kuttner. New York: New Press, 2002.

11. TRANSLATION

11. Suetonius, *The Twelve Caesars,* trans. Robert Graves (London: Penguin Classics, 1989), 202.

Suetonius. *The Twelve Caesars.* Translated by Robert Graves. London: Penguin Classics, 1989.

12. EDITION OTHER THAN THE FIRST

12. Dee Brown, *Bury My Heart at Wounded Knee: An Indian History of the American West,* 4th ed. (New York: Owl Books, 2007), 12.

Brown, Dee. *Bury My Heart at Wounded Knee: An Indian History of the American West,* 4th ed. New York: Owl Books, 2007.

13. MULTIVOLUME WORK

13. John Watson, *Annals of Philadelphia and Pennsylvania in the Olden Time,* vol. 2 (Washington, DC: Ross & Perry, 2003), 514.

Watson, John. *Annals of Philadelphia and Pennsylvania in the Olden Time.* Vol. 2. Washington, DC: Ross & Perry, 2003.

14. REFERENCE WORK

In a note, use *s.v.,* the abbreviation for the Latin *sub verbo* ("under the word") to help your reader find the entry.

14. *Encyclopedia Britannica,* s.v. "carpetbagger."

Do not list reference works such as encyclopedias or dictionaries in your bibliography.

AT A GLANCE

Citing Sources without Models in *Chicago* Style

To cite a source for which you cannot find a model, collect as much information as you can find — about the creator, title, date of creation or update, and location of the source — with the goal of helping your readers find the source for themselves, if possible. Then look at the models in this section to see which one most closely matches the type of source you are using.

In an academic writing project, before citing an electronic source for which you have no model, also be sure to ask your instructor's advice.

15. WORK WITH A TITLE WITHIN THE TITLE

Use quotation marks around any title within a book title.

> 15. John A. Alford, *A Companion to "Piers Plowman"* (Berkeley: University of California Press, 1988), 195.

> Alford, John A. *A Companion to "Piers Plowman."* Berkeley: University of California Press, 1988.

16. SACRED TEXT

> 16. Luke 18:24–25 (New International Version)

> 16. Qur'an 7:40–41

Do not include a sacred text in the bibliography.

17. SOURCE QUOTED IN ANOTHER SOURCE

Identify both the original and the secondary source.

> 17. Frank D. Millet, "The Filipino Leaders," *Harper's Weekly,* March 11, 1899, quoted in Richard Slotkin, *Gunfighter Nation: The Myth of the Frontier in Twentieth-Century America* (New York: HarperCollins, 1992), 110.

> Millet, Frank D. "The Filipino Leaders." *Harper's Weekly,* March 11, 1899. Quoted in Richard Slotkin, *Gunfighter Nation: The Myth of the Frontier in Twentieth-Century America* (New York: HarperCollins, 1992), 110.

Print and online periodicals

The note for an article in a periodical typically includes the author's name, the article title, and the periodical title. The format for other information, including the volume and issue numbers (if any), the date of publication, and the page number(s) to which the note refers, varies according to the type of periodical and whether you consulted it in print, on the Web, or in a database. In a bibliographic entry for a journal or magazine article from a database or a print periodical, also give the inclusive page numbers.

18. ARTICLE IN A PRINT JOURNAL

> 18. Karin Lützen, "The Female World: Viewed from Denmark," *Journal of Women's History* 12, no. 3 (2000): 36.

> Lützen, Karin. "The Female World: Viewed from Denmark." *Journal of Women's History* 12, no. 3 (2000): 34–38.

19. ARTICLE IN AN ONLINE JOURNAL

Give the DOI if there is one. If not, include the article URL. If page numbers are provided, include them as well.

19. Jeffrey J. Schott, "America, Europe, and the New Trade Order," *Business and Politics* 11, no. 3 (2009), doi:10.2202/1469-3569.1263.

Schott, Jeffrey J. "America, Europe, and the New Trade Order." *Business and Politics* 11, no. 3 (2009). doi:10.2202/1469-3569.1263.

20. JOURNAL ARTICLE FROM A DATABASE

For basic information on citing a periodical article from a database in *Chicago* style, see the source map on pp. 562–63.

20. W. Trent Foley and Nicholas J. Higham, "Bede on the Britons," *Early Medieval Europe* 17, no. 2 (2009), 157, doi:10.1111/j.1468-0254.2009.00258.x.

Foley, W. Trent, and Nicholas J. Higham. "Bede on the Britons." *Early Medieval Europe* 17, no. 2 (2009). 154–85. doi:10.1111/j.1468-0254.2009.00258.x.

21. ARTICLE IN A PRINT MAGAZINE

21. Terry McDermott, "The Mastermind: Khalid Sheikh Mohammed and the Making of 9/11," *New Yorker,* September 13, 2010, 42.

McDermott, Terry. "The Mastermind: Khalid Sheikh Mohammed and the Making of 9/11." *New Yorker,* September 13, 2010, 38–51.

22. ARTICLE IN AN ONLINE MAGAZINE

22. Tracy Clark-Flory, "Educating Women Saves Kids' Lives," *Salon,* September 17, 2010, http://www.salon.com/life/broadsheet/2010/09/17/education_women/index.html.

Clark-Flory, Tracy. "Educating Women Saves Kids' Lives." *Salon,* September 17, 2010. http://www.salon.com/life/broadsheet/2010/09/17/education_women/index.html.

23. MAGAZINE ARTICLE FROM A DATABASE

23. Sami Yousafzai and Ron Moreau, "Twisting Arms in Afghanistan," *Newsweek,* November 9, 2009, 8, Academic Search Premier (44962900).

Yousafzai, Sami, and Ron Moreau. "Twisting Arms in Afghanistan." *Newsweek,* November 9, 2009. 8. Academic Search Premier (44962900).

CHICAGO SOURCE MAP: Articles from Databases

1 **Author.** In a note, list the author(s) first name first. In the bibliographic entry, list the first author last name first, comma, first name; list other authors first name first.

2 **Article title.** Enclose the title and subtitle (if any) in quotation marks, and capitalize major words. In the notes section, put a comma before and after the title. In the bibliography, put a period before and after.

3 **Periodical title.** Italicize the title and subtitle, and capitalize all major words. For a magazine or newspaper, follow with a comma.

4 **Journal volume and issue numbers.** For journals, follow the title with the volume number, a comma, the abbreviation *no.*, and the issue number.

5 **Publication date.** For journals, enclose the publication year in parentheses and follow with a comma (in a note) or with a period (in a bibliography). For other periodicals, give the month and year or month, day, and year, followed by a comma.

6 **Page numbers.** In a note, give the page where the information is found. In the bibliographic entry, give the page range.

7 **Retrieval information.** Provide the article's DOI, if one is given, the name of the database and an accession number, or a "stable or persistent" URL for the article in the database. Because you provide stable retrieval information, you do not need to identify the electronic format of the work (i.e., PDF, as in the example shown here). End with a period.

Citations for the journal article on p. 563 would look like this:

ENDNOTE

> 1. Howard Schuman, Barry Schwartz, and Hannah D'Arcy, "Elite Revisionists and Popular Beliefs: Christopher Columbus, Hero or Villain?" *Public Opinion Quarterly* 69, no. 1 (2005), 13, doi:10.1093/poq/nfi001.

BIBLIOGRAPHIC ENTRY

> Schuman, Howard, Barry Schwartz, and Hannah D'Arcy. "Elite Revisionists and Popular Beliefs: Christopher Columbus, Hero or Villain?" *Public Opinion Quarterly* 69, no. 1 (2005). 2–29. doi:10.1093/poq/nfi001.

④ Journal Volume and Issue Numbers
Vol 69, No. 1

③ Periodical Title
Public Opinion Quarterly

⑥ Page Numbers
pp. 2–29

Public Opinion Quarterly, Vol. 69, No. 1, Spring 2005, pp. 2–29

⑤ Publication Date
Spring, 2005

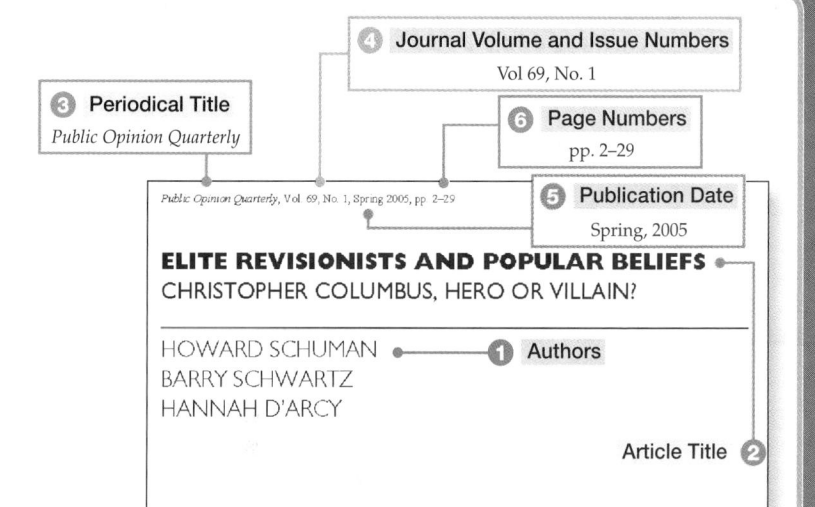

ELITE REVISIONISTS AND POPULAR BELIEFS
CHRISTOPHER COLUMBUS, HERO OR VILLAIN?

HOWARD SCHUMAN ● ——— **① Authors**
BARRY SCHWARTZ
HANNAH D'ARCY

Article Title ②

Abstract According to revisionist historians and American Indian activists, Christopher Columbus deserves condemnation for having brought slavery, disease, and death to America's indigenous peoples. We ask whether the general public's beliefs about Columbus show signs of reflecting these critical accounts, which increased markedly as the 1992 Quincentenary approached. Our national surveys, using several different question wordings, indicate that most Americans continue to admire Columbus because, as tradition puts it, "he discovered America," though only a small number of mainly older respondents speak of him in the heroic terms common in earlier years. At the same time, the percentage of Americans who reject traditional beliefs about Columbus is also small and is divided between those who simply acknowledge the priority of Indians as the "First Americans" and those who go further to view Columbus as a villain. The latter group of respondents, we find, show a critical stance toward modal American beliefs much more broadly.

We also analyze American history school textbooks for evidence of influence from revisionist writings, and we consider representations of Columbus in the mass media as well. Revisionist history can be seen as one consequence of the "minority rights revolution" that began after World War II and has achieved considerable success, but the endurance of Columbus's reputation—to a considerable extent even among the

HOWARD SCHUMAN is a research scientist and professor emeritus at the University of Michigan. BARRY SCHWARTZ is a professor emeritus at the University of Georgia. HANNAH D'ARCY is an independent statistical consultant who previously worked for the University of Michigan's Center for Statistical Consultation and Research. We thank Lawrence Bobo and Stanley Presser for stimulating us to do multiple validations, and we are grateful to the editor of *Public Opinion Quarterly* for recommendations that substantially improved our final presentation. In addition, we are much indebted for help during the course of the research to Virginia Hopcroft, Government Documents Librarian at Bowdoin College; Maria Krysan, University of Illinois at Chicago; Alyssa Miller, Evanston, Illinois; and Irina Poznansky, Departmental Librarian, Teachers College, Gottesman Libraries, Columbia University. Support for the research was drawn in part from a National Science Foundation grant (SES-0001844). Address correspondence to Howard Schuman; e-mail: hschuman@umich.edu.

doi:10.1093/poq/nfi001

⑦ Retrieval Information
doi:10.1093/poq/nfi001

24. **ARTICLE IN A NEWSPAPER**

Do not include page numbers for a newspaper article, but you may include the section, if any.

> 24. Caroline E. Mayer, "Wireless Industry to Adopt Voluntary Standards," *Washington Post,* September 9, 2003, sec. E.

> Mayer, Caroline E. "Wireless Industry to Adopt Voluntary Standards." *Washington Post,* September 9, 2003, sec. E.

If you provide complete documentation of a newspaper article in a note, you may not need to include it in the bibliography. Check your instructor's preference.

25. **ARTICLE IN AN ONLINE NEWSPAPER**

If the URL for the article is very long, use the URL for the newspaper's home page.

> 25. Andrew C. Revkin, "Arctic Melt Unnerves the Experts," *New York Times,* October 2, 2007, http://www.nytimes.com.

> Revkin, Andrew C. "Arctic Melt Unnerves the Experts." *New York Times,* October 2, 2007. http://www.nytimes.com.

26. **NEWSPAPER ARTICLE FROM A DATABASE**

> 26. Demetria Irwin, "A Hatchet, Not a Scalpel, for NYC Budget Cuts," *New York Amsterdam News,* November 13, 2008, Academic Search Premier (35778153).

> Irwin, Demetria. "A Hatchet, Not a Scalpel, for NYC Budget Cuts." *New York Amsterdam News,* November 13, 2008. Academic Search Premier (35778153).

27. **BOOK REVIEW**

After the information about the book under review, give publication information for the appropriate kind of source (see models 18–26).

> 27. Arnold Relman, "Health Care: The Disquieting Truth," review of *Tracking Medicine: A Researcher's Quest to Understand Health Care,* by John E. Wennberg, *New York Review of Books* 57, no. 14 (2010), 45.

> Relman, Arnold. "Health Care: The Disquieting Truth." Review of *Tracking Medicine: A Researcher's Quest to Understand Health Care,* by John E. Wennberg. *New York Review of Books* 57, no. 14 (2010), 45–48.

Online sources

In general, include the author (if given); the title of a work from a Web site (in quotation marks); the name of the site (in italics, if the site is an online publication, but otherwise neither italicized nor in quotation marks); the sponsor of the site, if different from the name of the site or name of the author; the date of publication or most recent update; and a URL. If the online source does not indicate when it was published or last modified, or if your instructor requests an access date, place it before the URL.

For basic information on citing works from Web sites in *Chicago* style, see the source map on pp. 566–67.

28. WEB SITE

28. Rutgers School of Arts and Sciences, *The Rutgers Oral History Archive,* 2010, http://oralhistory.rutgers.edu/.

Rutgers School of Arts and Sciences. *The Rutgers Oral History Archive.* 2010. http://oralhistory.rutgers.edu/.

29. WORK FROM A WEB SITE

29. Rose Cohen, "My First Job," *The Triangle Factory Fire,* Cornell University School of Industrial and Labor Relations, 2005, http://www.ilr.cornell.edu /trianglefire/texts/.

Cohen, Rose. "My First Job." *The Triangle Factory Fire.* Cornell University School of Industrial and Labor Relations. 2005. http://www.ilr.cornell.edu /trianglefire/texts/.

30. BLOG (WEB LOG) POST

Treat a blog post as a short work from a Web site (see model 29).

30. Jai Arjun Singh, "On the Road in the USSR," *Jabberwock* (blog), November 29, 2007, http://jaiarjun.blogspot.com/2007/11/on-road-in-ussr.html.

Chicago recommends that blog posts appear in the notes section only, not in the bibliography, unless the blog is cited frequently. Check your instructor's preference. A bibliography reference to an entire blog would look like this:

Singh, Jai Arjun. *Jabberwock* (blog). http://jaiarjun.blogspot.com/.

31. EMAIL AND OTHER PERSONAL COMMUNICATIONS

Cite email messages and other personal communications, such as letters and telephone calls, in the text or in a note only, not in the bibliography. (*Chicago* style recommends hyphenating *e-mail.*)

31. Kareem Adas, e-mail message to author, February 11, 2010.

32. PODCAST

Treat a podcast as a short work from a Web site (see model 29) and give as much of the following information as you can find: the author or speaker, the title or a description of the podcast, the title of the site,

CHICAGO SOURCE MAP: Works from Web Sites

1 **Author.** In a note, list the author(s) first name first. In a bibliographic entry, list the first author last name first, comma, first name; list additional authors first name first. Note that the host may serve as the author.

2 **Document title.** Enclose the title in quotation marks, and capitalize all major words. In a note, put a comma before and after the title. In the bibliography, put a period before and after.

3 **Title of Web site.** Capitalize all major words. If the site's title is analogous to a book or periodical title, italicize it. In the notes section, put a comma after the title. In the bibliography, put a period after the title.

4 **Sponsor of site.** If the sponsor is the same as the author or site title, you may omit it. End with a comma (in the note) or a period (in the bibliographic entry).

5 **Date of publication or last modification.** If no date is available, or if your instructor requests it, include your date of access (with the word *accessed*).

6 **Retrieval information.** Give the URL for the Web site. If you are required to include a date of access, put the word *accessed* and the date in parentheses after the URL. End with a period.

Citations for the Web site on p. 567 would look like this:

ENDNOTE

1. Rebecca Edwards, "The Populist Party," *1896: The Presidential Campaign: Cartoons & Commentary,* Vassar College, 2000, http://projects .vassar.edu/1896/populists.html.

BIBLIOGRAPHIC ENTRY

Edwards, Rebecca. "The Populist Party." *1896: The Presidential Campaign: Cartoons & Commentary. Vassar College.* 2000. http://projects.vassar .edu/1896/populists.html.

projects.**vassar.edu**/1896/populists.html

2 Document Title

The Populist Party

The Rise of Populism

The People's Party (or Populist Party, as it was widely known) was much younger than the Democratic and Republican Parties, which had been founded before the <u>Civil War</u>. Agricultural areas in the West and South had been hit by <u>economic depression</u> years before industrial areas. In the 1880s, as drought hit the wheat-growing areas of the Great Plains and prices for Southern cotton sunk to new lows, many tenant farmers fell into deep debt. This exacerbated long-held grievances against railroads, lenders, grain-elevator owners, and others with whom farmers did business. By the early 1890s, as the depression worsened, some industrial workers shared these farm families' views on <u>labor</u> and <u>the trusts</u>.

In 1890 Populists won control of the Kansas state legislature, and Kansan **William Peffer** became the party's first U.S. Senator. Peffer, with his long white beard, was a humorous figure to many Eastern journalists and politicians, who saw little evidence of Populism in their states and often treated the party as a joke. Nonetheless, Western and Southern Populists gained support rapidly. In 1892 the national party was officially founded through a merger of the Farmers' Alliance and the Knights of Labor. In that year the Populist presidential candidate, James B. Weaver, won over one million votes. Between 1892 and 1896, however, the party failed to make further gains, in part because of fraud, intimidation, and violence by Southern Democrats.

By 1896 the Populist organization was in even more turmoil than that of <u>Democrats</u>. Two main factions had appe...
orga...
"fus...

3 Title of Web Site

<u>Homepage</u>

© 2000, Rebecca Edwards, Vassar College

5 Date of Publication

4 Sponsor of Site

1 Author

the site sponsor (if different from the author or site name), the type of podcast or file format, the date of posting or access, and the URL.

> 32. Barack Obama, "Weekly Address: A Solar Recovery," *The White House,* podcast video, July 3, 2010, http://www.whitehouse.gov/photos-and-video/video /weekly-address-a-solar-recovery.

> Obama, Barack. "Weekly Address: A Solar Recovery." *The White House.* Podcast video. July 3, 2010. http://www.whitehouse.gov/photos-and-video/video /weekly-address-a-solar-recovery.

33. ONLINE AUDIO OR VIDEO

Treat an online audio or video source as a short work from a Web site (see model 29). If the source is downloadable, give the medium or file format before the URL (see model 32).

> 33. Alyssa Katz, "Did the Mortgage Crisis Kill the American Dream?" YouTube video, 4:32, posted by NYCRadio, June 24, 2009, http://www.youtube.com /watch?v=uivtwjwd_Qw.

> Katz, Alyssa. "Did the Mortgage Crisis Kill the American Dream?" YouTube video, 4:32. Posted by NYCRadio. June 24, 2009. http://www.youtube.com /watch?v=uivtwjwd_Qw.

Other sources

34. PUBLISHED OR BROADCAST INTERVIEW

> 34. Nina Totenberg, interview by Charlie Rose, *The Charlie Rose Show,* PBS, June 29, 2010.

> Totenberg, Nina. Interview by Charlie Rose. *The Charlie Rose Show.* PBS, June 29, 2010.

Interviews you conduct are considered personal communications (see model 31).

35. VIDEO OR DVD

> 35. Edward Norton and Edward Furlong, *American History X,* directed by Tony Kaye (1998; Los Angeles: New Line Studios, 2002), DVD.

> Norton, Edward, and Edward Furlong. *American History X.* Directed by Tony Kaye, 1998. Los Angeles: New Line Studios, 2002. DVD.

36. SOUND RECORDING

> 36. Paul Robeson, *The Collector's Paul Robeson,* recorded 1959, Monitor MCD-61580, 1989, compact disc.

> Robeson, Paul. *The Collector's Paul Robeson.* Recorded 1959. Monitor MCD-61580, 1989, compact disc.

37. WORK OF ART

Begin with the artist's name and the title of the work. If you viewed the work in person, give the medium, the date, and the name of the place where you saw it.

37. Mary Cassatt, *The Child's Bath,* oil on canvas, 1893, The Art Institute of Chicago, Chicago, IL.

Cassatt, Mary. *The Child's Bath.* Oil on canvas, 1893. The Art Institute of Chicago, Chicago, IL.

If you refer to a reproduction, give the publication information.

37. Mary Cassatt, *The Child's Bath,* oil on canvas, 1893, on *Art Access,* The Art Institute of Chicago, last modified August 2004, http://www.artic.edu /artaccess/AA_Impressionist/pages/IMP_6.shtml#.

Cassatt, Mary. *The Child's Bath.* Oil on canvas, 1893. On *Art Access,* The Art Institute of Chicago. Last modified August 2004. http://www.artic.edu /artaccess/AA_Impressionist/pages/IMP_6.shtml#.

38. PAMPHLET, REPORT, OR BROCHURE

Information about the author or publisher may not be readily available, but give enough information to identify your source.

38. Jamie McCarthy, *Who Is David Irving?* (San Antonio, TX: Holocaust History Project, 1998).

McCarthy, Jamie. *Who Is David Irving?* San Antonio, TX: Holocaust History Project, 1998.

39. GOVERNMENT DOCUMENT

39. U.S. House Committee on Ways and Means, *Report on Trade Mission to Sub-Saharan Africa,* 108th Cong., 1st sess. (Washington, DC: Government Printing Office, 2003), 28.

U.S. House Committee on Ways and Means. *Report on Trade Mission to Sub-Saharan Africa.* 108th Cong., 1st sess. Washington, DC: Government Printing Office, 2003.

54c An excerpt from a student research essay, *Chicago* style

Student Writer

Amanda Rinder

On the following pages is an essay by Amanda Rinder that conforms to the *Chicago* guidelines described in this chapter. Note that this essay has been reproduced in a narrow format to allow for annotation.

 **bedfordstmartins.com/everydaywriter**
Student Writing

Student Writing
Chicago

Title announces topic clearly and succinctly

Sweet Home Chicago: Preserving the Past,
Protecting the Future of the Windy City

Title and writer's name centered

Amanda Rinder

Course title, instructor's name, and date centered at bottom of title page

Twentieth-Century U.S. History
Professor Goldberg
November 27, 2006

Annotations indicate effective choices or *Chicago*-style formatting.

Rinder 2

Only one city has the "Big Shoulders" described by Carl Sandburg: Chicago (fig. 1). So renowned are its skyscrapers and celebrated building style that an entire school of architecture is named for Chicago. Presently, however, the place that Frank Sinatra called "my kind of town" is beginning to lose sight of exactly what kind of town it is. Many of the buildings that give Chicago its distinctive character are being torn down in order to make room for new growth. Both preserving the classics and encouraging new creation are important; the combination of these elements gives Chicago architecture its unique flavor. Witold Rybczynski, a professor of urbanism, told Tracie Rozhon of the *New York Times*, "Of all the cities we can think of . . . we associate Chicago with new things, with building new. Combining that with preservation is a difficult task, a tricky thing. It's hard to find the middle ground in Chicago."[1] Yet finding a middle ground is essential if the city is to retain the original character that sets it apart from the rest. In order to

Fig. 1. Chicago skyline, circa 1940s. (Postcard courtesy of Minnie Dangburg.)

First page of body text is p. 2

Paper refers to each figure by number

Thesis introduced

Double-spaced text

Source cited using superscript numeral

Figure caption includes number, short title, and source

Opening
paragraph
concludes
with thesis
statement

maintain Chicago's distinctive identity and its delicate balance
between the old and the new, the city government must provide a
comprehensive urban plan that not only directs growth, but calls
for the preservation of landmarks and historic districts as well.

Chicago is a city for the working man. Nowhere is this more
evident than in its architecture. David Garrard Lowe, author of *Lost
Chicago,* notes that early Chicagoans "sought reality, not fantasy, and
the reality of America as seen from the heartland did not include the
pavilions of princes or the castles of kings."[2] The inclination toward
unadorned, sturdy buildings began in the late nineteenth century
with the aptly named Chicago School, a movement led by Louis
Sullivan, John Wellborn Root, and Daniel Burnham and based on

Second
paragraph
provides
background

Sullivan's adage, "Form follows function."[3] The early skyscraper, the
very symbol of the Chicago style, represents the triumph of function
and utility over sentiment, America over Europe, and perhaps, as
Daniel Bluestone argues, even the frontier over the civilization of
the East Coast.[4] These ideals of the original Chicago School were
expanded upon by architects of the Second Chicago School. Frank
Lloyd Wright's legendary organic style and the famed glass and steel
constructions of Mies van der Rohe are often the first images that
spring to mind when one thinks of Chicago.

Clear transition
from previous
paragraph

Yet the architecture that is the city's defining attribute is being
threatened by the increasing tendency toward development. The root
of Chicago's preservation problem lies in the enormous drive toward
economic expansion and the potential in Chicago for such growth. The
highly competitive market for land in the city means that properties
sell for the highest price if the buildings on them can be obliterated

Notes

1. Tracie Rozhon, "Chicago Girds for Big Battle over Its Skyline," *New York Times,* November 12, 2000, Academic Search Premier (28896783).

Newspaper article in database

2. David Garrard Lowe, *Lost Chicago* (New York: Watson-Guptill Publications, 2000), 123.

Book

3. *Columbia Encyclopedia,* Sixth Ed., s.v. "Louis Sullivan."

4. Daniel Bluestone, *Constructing Chicago* (New Haven: Yale University Press, 1991), 105.

5. Alan J. Shannon, "When Will It End?" *Chicago Tribune,* September 11, 1987, quoted in Karen J. Dilibert, *From Landmark to Landfill* (Chicago: Chicago Architectural Foundation, 2000), 11.

Indirect source

6. Steve Kerch, "Landmark Decisions," *Chicago Tribune,* March 18, 1990, sec. 16.

7. John W. Stamper, *Chicago's North Michigan Avenue* (Chicago: University of Chicago Press, 1991), 215.

8. Alf Siewers, "Success Spoiling the Magnificent Mile?" *Chicago Sun-Times,* April 9, 1995, http://www.sun-times.com/.

Newspaper article online

9. Paul Gapp, "McCarthy Building Puts Landmark Law on a Collision Course with Developers," *Chicago Tribune,* April 20, 1986, quoted in Karen J. Dilibert, *From Landmark to Landfill* (Chicago: Chicago Architectural Foundation, 2000), 4.

10. Ibid.

Reference to previous source

11. Rozhon, "Chicago Girds for Big Battle."

Second reference to source

12. Kerch, "Landmark Decisions."

13. Robert Bruegmann, *The Architects and the City* (Chicago: University of Chicago Press, 1997), 443.

Bibliography
starts on new
page

Bibliography

Bluestone, Daniel. *Constructing Chicago*. New Haven: Yale University
Press, 1991.

Book

Bruegmann, Robert. *The Architects and the City*. Chicago: University
of Chicago Press, 1997.

Pamphlet

Dilibert, Karen J. *From Landmark to Landfill*. Chicago: Chicago
Architectural Foundation, 2000.

Newspaper
article

Kerch, Steve. "Landmark Decisions." *Chicago Tribune,* March 18,
1990, sec. 16.

Lowe, David Garrard. *Lost Chicago*. New York: Watson-Guptill
Publications, 2000.

Article from
database

Rozhon, Tracie. "Chicago Girds for Big Battle over Its Skyline."
New York Times, November 12, 2000. Academic Search Premier
(28896783).

Bibliography
entries use
hanging indent
and are not
numbered

Siewers, Alf. "Success Spoiling the Magnificent Mile?" *Chicago
Sun-Times,* April 9, 1995. http://www.sun-times.com/.

Stamper, John W. *Chicago's North Michigan Avenue*. Chicago:
University of Chicago Press, 1991.

CSE Style **55**

W riters in the physical sciences, the life sciences, and mathematics use the documentation and format style of the Council of Science Editors (CSE). Guidelines for citing print and electronic sources can be found in *Scientific Style and Format: The CSE Manual for Authors, Editors, and Publishers,* Seventh Edition (2006).

> ➔ **bedfordstmartins.com/everydaywriter**
> **Documenting Sources**

55a CSE style for in-text citations

In CSE style, citations within an essay follow one of three formats.

- The *citation-sequence format* calls for a superscript number or a number in parentheses after any mention of a source. The sources are numbered in the order they appear. Each number refers to the same source every time it is used. The first source mentioned in the paper is numbered *1,* the second source is numbered *2,* and so on.

- The *citation-name format* also calls for a superscript number or a number in parentheses after any mention of a source. The numbers are added after the list of references is completed and alphabetized, so that the source numbered *1* is alphabetically first in the list of references, *2* is alphabetically second, and so on.

- The *name-year format* calls for the last name of the author and the year of publication in parentheses after any mention of a source. If the last name appears in a signal phrase, the name-year format allows for giving only the year of publication in parentheses.

Before deciding which system to use, check a current journal in the field or ask an instructor about the preferred style in a particular course or discipline.

1. IN-TEXT CITATION USING CITATION-SEQUENCE OR CITATION-NAME FORMAT

VonBergen[12] provides the most complete discussion of this phenomenon.

For the citation-sequence and citation-name formats, you would use the same superscript ([12]) for each subsequent citation of this work by VonBergen.

2. IN-TEXT CITATION USING NAME-YEAR FORMAT

VonBergen (2003) provides the most complete discussion of this phenomenon.

Hussar's two earlier studies of juvenile obesity (1995, 1999) examined only children with diabetes.

The classic examples of such investigations (Morrow 1968; Bridger et al. 1971; Franklin and Wayson 1972) still shape the assumptions of current studies.

55b CSE style for a list of references

The citations in the text of an essay correspond to items on a list titled *References,* which starts on a new page at the end of the essay. Continue to number the pages consecutively, center the title *References* one inch from the top of the page, and double-space before beginning the first entry.

The order of the entries depends on which format you follow:

- *Citation-sequence format:* number and list the references in the order the references are first cited in the text.
- *Citation-name format:* list and number the references in alphabetical order.
- *Name-year format:* list the references, unnumbered, in alphabetical order.

In the following examples, you will see that the citation-sequence and citation-name formats call for listing the date after the publisher's name in references for books and after the periodical name in references for articles. The name-year format calls for listing the date immediately after the author's name in any kind of reference.

CSE style also specifies the treatment and placement of the following basic elements in the list of references:

- *Author.* List all authors last name first, and use only initials for first and middle names. Do not place a comma after the author's last name, and do not place periods after or spaces between the initials. Use a period after the last initial of the last author listed.
- *Title.* Do not italicize titles and subtitles of books and titles of periodicals. Do not enclose titles of articles in quotation marks. For books and articles, capitalize only the first word of the title and any proper nouns or proper adjectives. Abbreviate and capitalize all major words in a periodical title.

As you refer to these examples, pay attention to how publication information (publishers for books, details about periodicals for articles) and other specific elements are styled and punctuated.

DIRECTORY TO CSE STYLE

CSE style for references

Books
1. One author, *577*
   SOURCE MAP, *578–79*
2. Two or more authors, *577*
3. Organization as author, *580*
4. Book prepared by editor(s), *580*
5. Section of a book with an editor, *580*
6. Chapter of a book, *580*
7. Paper or abstract in conference proceedings, *581*

Periodicals
8. Article in a journal, *581*

9. Article in a weekly journal, *581*
10. Article in a magazine, *582*
11. Article in a newspaper, *582*

Digital sources
12. Material from an online database, *583*
    SOURCE MAP, *584–85*
13. Article in an online journal, *583*
14. Article in an online newspaper, *583*
15. Online book, *586*
16. Web site, *586*
17. Government Web site, *586*

Books

For the basic format for citing a book, see the source map on pp. 578–79.

1. ONE AUTHOR

CITATION-SEQUENCE AND CITATION-NAME

1. Buchanan M. Nexus: small worlds and the groundbreaking theory of networks. New York: Norton; 2003.

NAME-YEAR

Buchanan M. 2003. Nexus: small worlds and the groundbreaking theory of networks. New York: Norton.

2. TWO OR MORE AUTHORS

CITATION-SEQUENCE AND CITATION-NAME

2. Wojciechowski BW, Rice NM. Experimental methods in kinetic studies. 2nd ed. St. Louis (MO): Elsevier Science; 2003.

Note that, depending on whether you are using the citation-sequence or citation-name format or the name-year format, the date placement will vary.

① **Author.** List author(s) last name first, and use initials for first and middle names, with no periods or spaces. Use a period only after the last initial of the last author.

②, ⑥ **Publication year.** In name-year format, put the year of publication immediately after the author name(s). In citation-sequence or citation-name format, put the year of publication after the publisher's name.

③ **Title.** Do not italicize or put quotation marks around titles and subtitles of books. Capitalize only the first word of the title and any proper nouns or proper adjectives.

④ **City of publication.** List the city of publication (and the country or state abbreviation for unfamiliar cities) followed by a colon.

⑤ **Publisher.** Give the publisher's name. In citation-sequence or citation-name format, follow with a semicolon. In name-year format, follow with a period.

A citation for the book on p. 579 would look like this:

CITATION-SEQUENCE OR CITATION-NAME FORMAT

1. Wilson EO. The diversity of life. Cambridge: Belknap Press of Harvard University Press; 1992.

NAME-YEAR FORMAT

Wilson EO. 1992. The diversity of life. Cambridge: Belknap Press of Harvard University Press.

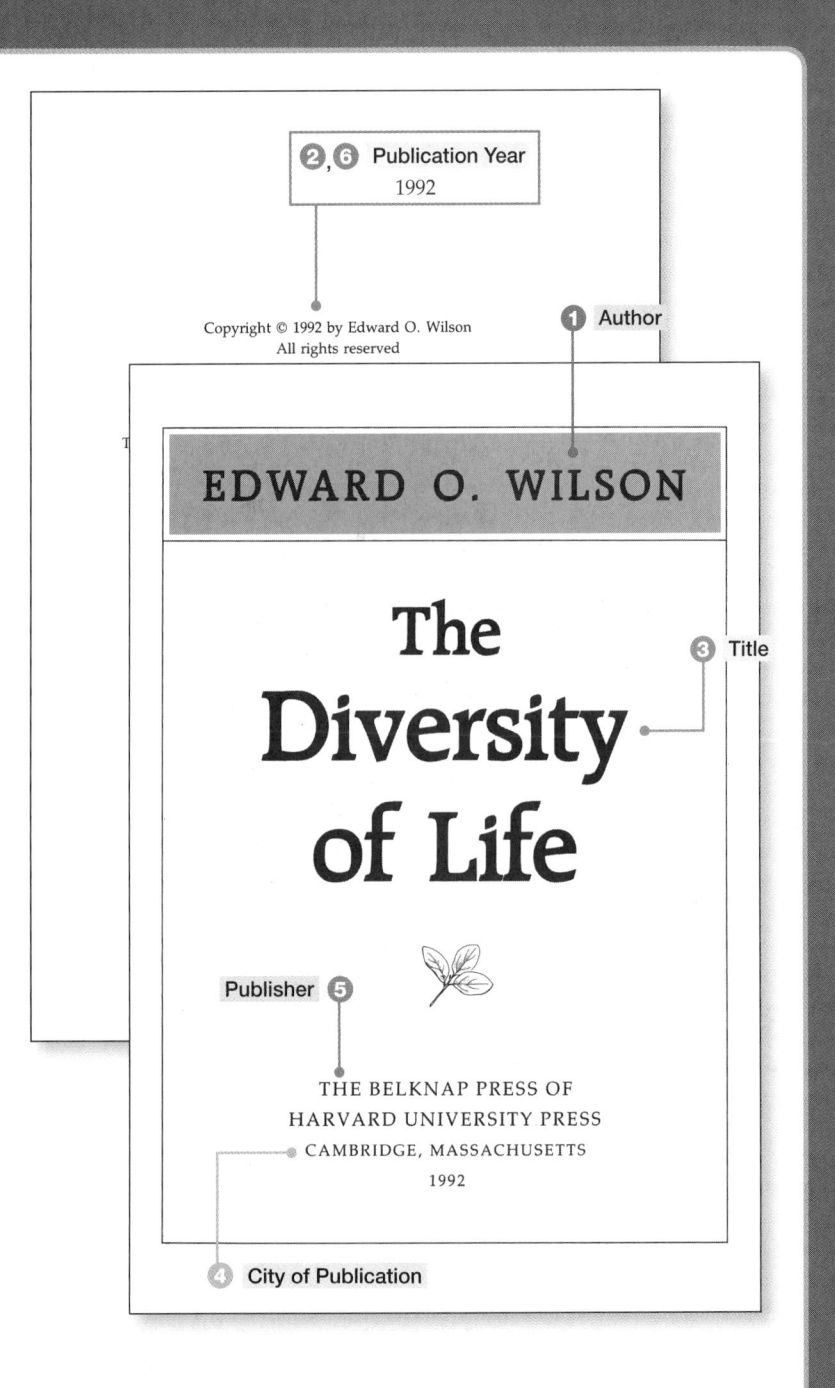

2,6 Publication Year
1992

Copyright © 1992 by Edward O. Wilson
All rights reserved

1 Author

EDWARD O. WILSON

The
Diversity
of Life

3 Title

Publisher **5**

THE BELKNAP PRESS OF
HARVARD UNIVERSITY PRESS
CAMBRIDGE, MASSACHUSETTS
1992

4 City of Publication

579

NAME-YEAR

Wojciechowski BW, Rice NM. 2003. Experimental methods in kinetic studies. 2nd ed. St. Louis (MO): Elsevier Science.

3. **ORGANIZATION AS AUTHOR**

CITATION-SEQUENCE AND CITATION-NAME

3. World Health Organization. The world health report 2002: reducing risks, promoting healthy life. Geneva (Switzerland): The Organization; 2002.

Place the organization's abbreviation at the beginning of the name-year entry, and use the abbreviation in the corresponding in-text citation. Alphabetize the entry by the first word of the full name, not by the abbreviation.

NAME-YEAR

[WHO] World Health Organization. 2002. The world health report 2002: reducing risks, promoting healthy life. Geneva (Switzerland): The Organization.

4. **BOOK PREPARED BY EDITOR(S)**

CITATION-SEQUENCE AND CITATION-NAME

4. Torrence ME, Isaacson RE, editors. Microbial food safety in animal agriculture: current topics. Ames: Iowa State University Press; 2003.

NAME-YEAR

Torrence ME, Isaacson RE, editors. 2003. Microbial safety in animal agriculture: current topics. Ames: Iowa State University Press.

5. **SECTION OF A BOOK WITH AN EDITOR**

CITATION-SEQUENCE AND CITATION-NAME

5. Kawamura A. Plankton. In: Perrin MF, Wursig B, Thewissen JGM, editors. Encyclopedia of marine mammals. San Diego: Academic Press; 2002. p. 939–942.

NAME-YEAR

Kawamura A. 2002. Plankton. In: Perrin MF, Wursig B, Thewissen JGM, editors. Encyclopedia of marine mammals. San Diego: Academic Press. p. 939–942.

6. **CHAPTER OF A BOOK**

CITATION-SEQUENCE AND CITATION-NAME

6. Honigsbaum M. The fever trail: in search of the cure for malaria. New York: Picador; 2003. Chapter 2, The cure; p. 19–38.

NAME-YEAR

Honigsbaum M. 2003. The fever trail: in search of the cure for malaria. New York: Picador. Chapter 2, The cure; p. 19–38.

7. **PAPER OR ABSTRACT IN CONFERENCE PROCEEDINGS**

CITATION-SEQUENCE AND CITATION-NAME

7. Gutierrez AP. Integrating biological and environmental factors in crop system models [abstract]. In: Integrated Biological Systems Conference; 2003 Apr 14–16; San Antonio, TX. Beaumont (TX): Agroeconomics Research Group; 2003. p. 14–15.

NAME-YEAR

Gutierrez AP. 2003. Integrating biological and environmental factors in crop system models [abstract]. In: Integrated Biological Systems Conference; 2003 Apr 14–16; San Antonio, TX. Beaumont (TX): Agroeconomics Research Group. p. 14–15.

Periodicals

Provide volume and issue numbers for journals. For newspaper and magazine articles, include the section designation and column number, if any, and the date. For all periodicals, give inclusive page numbers. For rules on abbreviating journal titles, consult the CSE manual, or ask an instructor to suggest other examples.

8. **ARTICLE IN A JOURNAL**

CITATION-SEQUENCE AND CITATION-NAME

8. Mahmud K, Vance ML. Human growth hormone and aging. New Engl J Med. 2003;348(2):2256–2257.

NAME-YEAR

Mahmud K, Vance ML. 2003. Human growth hormone and aging. New Engl J Med. 348(2):2256–2257.

9. **ARTICLE IN A WEEKLY JOURNAL**

CITATION-SEQUENCE AND CITATION-NAME

9. Holden C. Future brightening for depression treatments. Science. 2003 Oct 31:810–813.

NAME-YEAR

Holden C. 2003. Future brightening for depression treatments. Science. Oct 31:810–813.

10. ARTICLE IN A MAGAZINE

CITATION-SEQUENCE AND CITATION-NAME

10. Livio M. Moving right along: the accelerating universe holds secrets to dark energy, the Big Bang, and the ultimate beauty of nature. Astronomy. 2002 Jul:34–39.

NAME-YEAR

Livio M. 2002 Jul. Moving right along: the accelerating universe holds secrets to dark energy, the Big Bang, and the ultimate beauty of nature. Astronomy. 34–39.

11. ARTICLE IN A NEWSPAPER

CITATION-SEQUENCE AND CITATION-NAME

11. Kolata G. Bone diagnosis gives new data but no answers. New York Times (National Ed.). 2003 Sep 28;Sect. 1:1 (col. 1).

NAME-YEAR

Kolata G. 2003 Sep 28. Bone diagnosis gives new data but no answers. New York Times (National Ed.). Sect. 1:1 (col. 1).

Digital sources

These examples use the citation-sequence or citation-name system. To adapt them to the name-year system, delete the note number and place the update date immediately after the author's name.

The basic entry for most sources accessed through the Internet should include the following elements:

- *Author.* Give the author's name, if available, last name first, followed by the initial(s) and a period.
- *Title.* For book, journal, and article titles, follow the style for print materials. For all other types of electronic material, reproduce the title that appears on the screen.
- *Medium.* Indicate, in brackets, that the source is not in print format by using designations such as *[Internet]*.
- *Place of publication.* The city usually should be followed by the two-letter abbreviation for the state. No state abbreviation is necessary for well-known cities such as New York, Chicago, Boston, and London or for a publisher whose location is part of its name (for example, University of Oklahoma Press). If the city is implied, put

the city and state in brackets. If the city cannot be inferred, use the words *place unknown* in brackets.

- **Publisher.** For material other than journal articles from Web sites and online databases, include the individual or organization that produces or sponsors the site. If no publisher can be determined, use the words *publisher unknown* in brackets.

- **Dates.** Cite three important dates if possible: the date the publication was placed on the Internet or the copyright date; the latest date of any update or revision; and the date the publication was accessed by you.

- **Page, document, volume, and issue numbers.** When citing a portion of a larger work or site, list the inclusive page numbers or document numbers of the specific item being cited. For journals or journal articles, include volume and issue numbers. If exact page numbers are not available, include in brackets the approximate length in computer screens, paragraphs, or bytes: [2 screens], [10 paragraphs], [332K bytes].

- **Address.** Include the URL or other electronic address; use the phrase *Available from:* to introduce the address. Only URLs that end with a slash are followed by a period.

12. MATERIAL FROM AN ONLINE DATABASE

For the basic format for citing an article from a database, see the source map on pp. 584–85. (Because CSE does not provide guidelines for citing an article from an online database, this model has been adapted from CSE guidelines for citing an online journal article.)

12. Shilts E. Water wanderers. Can Geographic [Internet]. 2002 [cited 2010 Jan 27];122(3):72–77. Academic Search Premier. Ipswich (MA):EBSCO. Available from: http://www.ebscohost.com/ Document No.: 6626534.

13. ARTICLE IN AN ONLINE JOURNAL

13. Perez P, Calonge TM. Yeast protein kinase C. J Biochem [Internet]. 2002 Oct [cited 2008 Nov 3];132(4):513–517. Available from: http://edpex104.bcasj.or .jp/jb-pdf/132-4/jb132-4-513.pdf

14. ARTICLE IN AN ONLINE NEWSPAPER

14. Brody JE. Reasons, and remedies, for morning sickness. New York Times Online [Internet]. 2004 Apr 27 [cited 2009 Apr 30]. Available from: http://www .nytimes.com/2009/04/27/health/27BROD.html

CSE SOURCE MAP: Articles from Databases

Note that date placement will vary depending on whether you are using the citation-sequence or citation-name format or the name-year format.

1 **Author.** List author(s) last name first, and use only initials for first and middle names.

2, 5 **Publication date.** For name-year format, put publication date after author name(s). In citation-sequence or citation-name format, put it after periodical title. Use year only (for journals) or year month day (for other periodicals).

3 **Article title.** Capitalize first word and proper nouns/adjectives.

4 **Periodical title.** Capitalize major words. Abbreviate journal titles. Follow with *[Internet]* and a period.

6 **Date of access.** In brackets, write *cited* and year, month, and day. End with a semicolon.

7 **Publication information for article.** Give volume number, issue number (in parentheses), a colon, and page numbers. End with a period.

8 **Name of database.** End with a period.

9 **Publication information for database.** Include the city, the state abbreviation in parentheses, a colon, the publisher's name, and a period.

10 **Web address.** Write *Available from* and the brief URL.

11 **Document number.** Write *Document no.* and identifying number.

A citation for the article on p. 585 would look like this:

CITATION-SEQUENCE OR CITATION-NAME FORMAT

1. Miller AL. Epidemiology, etiology, and natural treatment of seasonal affective disorder. Altern Med Rev [Internet]. 2005 [cited 2010 25 May]; 10(1):5–13. Academic Search Premier. Ipswich (MA): EBSCO. Available from http://www.ebscohost.com Document No.: 16514813.

NAME-YEAR FORMAT

Miller AL. 2005. Epidemiology, etiology, and natural treatment of seasonal affective disorder. Altern Med Rev [Internet]. [cited 2010 25 May]; 10(1):5–13. Academic Search Premier. Ipswich (MA): EBSCO. Available from http://www.ebscohost.com Document No.: 16514813.

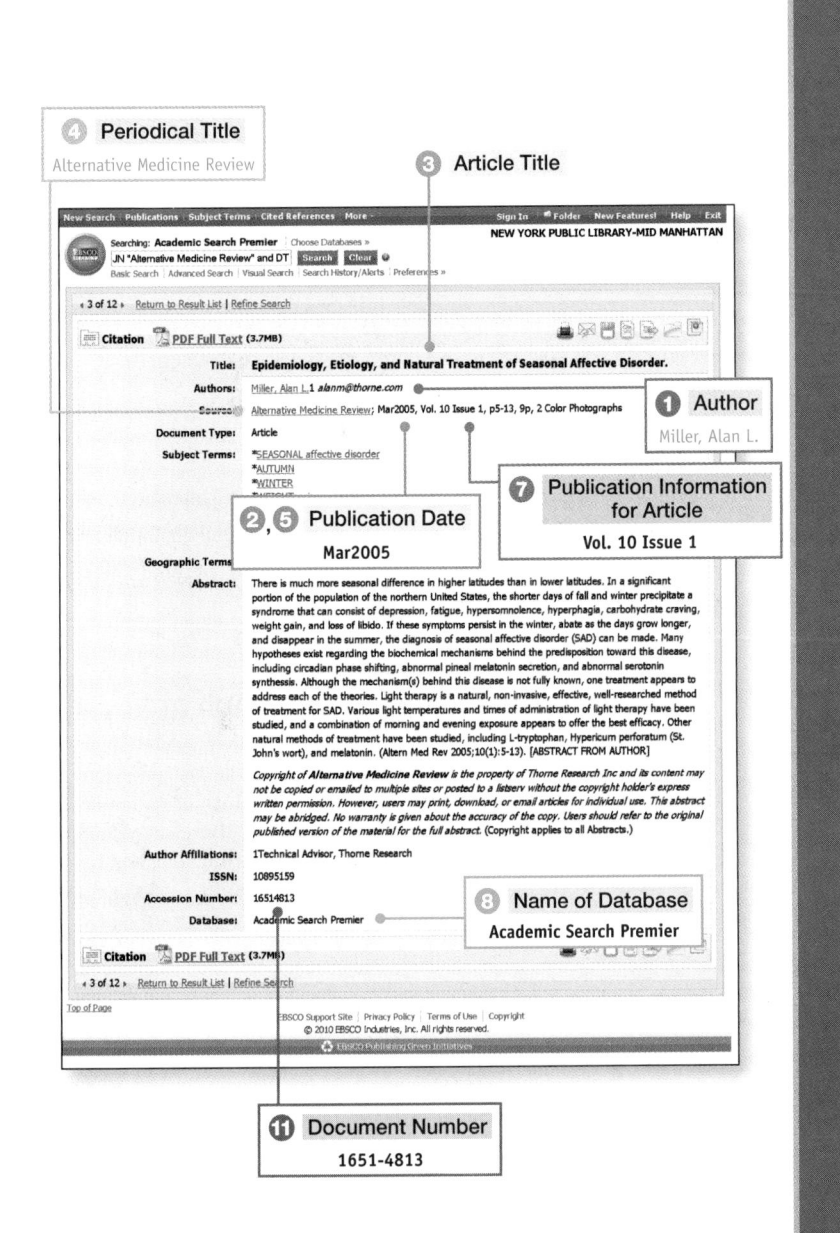

4 Periodical Title
Alternative Medicine Review

3 Article Title

Searching: **Academic Search Premier** | Choose Databases »
JN "Alternative Medicine Review" and DT | Search | Clear |
Basic Search | Advanced Search | Visual Search | Search History/Alerts | Preferences »

‹ 3 of 12 › Return to Result List | Refine Search

Citation | PDF Full Text (3.7MB)

Title:	Epidemiology, Etiology, and Natural Treatment of Seasonal Affective Disorder.
Authors:	Miller, Alan L.1 *alanm@thorne.com*
Source:	Alternative Medicine Review; Mar2005, Vol. 10 Issue 1, p5-13, 9p, 2 Color Photographs
Document Type:	Article
Subject Terms:	*SEASONAL affective disorder *AUTUMN *WINTER

1 Author
Miller, Alan L.

2, 5 Publication Date
Mar2005

7 Publication Information for Article
Vol. 10 Issue 1

Geographic Terms:

Abstract:
There is much more seasonal difference in higher latitudes than in lower latitudes. In a significant portion of the population of the northern United States, the shorter days of fall and winter precipitate a syndrome that can consist of depression, fatigue, hypersomnolence, hyperphagia, carbohydrate craving, weight gain, and loss of libido. If these symptoms persist in the winter, abate as the days grow longer, and disappear in the summer, the diagnosis of seasonal affective disorder (SAD) can be made. Many hypotheses exist regarding the biochemical mechanisms behind the predisposition toward this disease, including circadian phase shifting, abnormal pineal melatonin secretion, and abnormal serotonin synthesis. Although the mechanism(s) behind this disease is not fully known, one treatment appears to address each of the theories. Light therapy is a natural, non-invasive, effective, well-researched method of treatment for SAD. Various light temperatures and times of administration of light therapy have been studied, and a combination of morning and evening exposure appears to offer the best efficacy. Other natural methods of treatment have been studied, including L-tryptophan, Hypericum perforatum (St. John's wort), and melatonin. (Altern Med Rev 2005;10(1):5-13). [ABSTRACT FROM AUTHOR]

Author Affiliations:	1Technical Advisor, Thorne Research
ISSN:	10895159
Accession Number:	16514813
Database:	Academic Search Premier

8 Name of Database
Academic Search Premier

Citation | PDF Full Text (3.7MB)

‹ 3 of 12 › Return to Result List | Refine Search

Top of Page

11 Document Number
1651-4813

15. ONLINE BOOK

> 15. Patrick TS, Allison JR, Krakow GA. Protected plants of Georgia [Internet]. Social Circle (GA): Georgia Department of Natural Resources; c1995 [cited 2010 Dec 3]. Available from: http://www.georgiawildlife.com/content/displaycontent .asp?txtDocument=89&txtPage=9

To cite a portion of an online book, give the name of the part after the publication information: *Chapter 6, Encouraging germination.* See model 6.

16. WEB SITE

> 16. Geology and public policy [Internet]. Boulder (CO): Geological Society of America; c2010 [updated 2010 Jun 3; cited 2010 Sep 19]. Available from: http://www.geosociety.org/geopolicy.htm

17. GOVERNMENT WEB SITE

> 17. Health disparities: reducing health disparities in cancer [Internet]. Atlanta (GA): Centers for Disease Control and Prevention (US); 2010 [updated 2010 Apr 5; cited 2010 May 1]. Available from: http://www.cdc.gov/cancer/ healthdisparities/basic_info/disparities.htm

55c An excerpt from a student research proposal, CSE style

The following excerpt from a research proposal by Tara Gupta conforms to the citation-sequence format in the CSE guidelines described in this chapter. Note that these pages have been reproduced in a narrow format to allow for annotation.

Student Writer

Tara Gupta

bedfordstmartins.com/everydaywriter
Student Writing

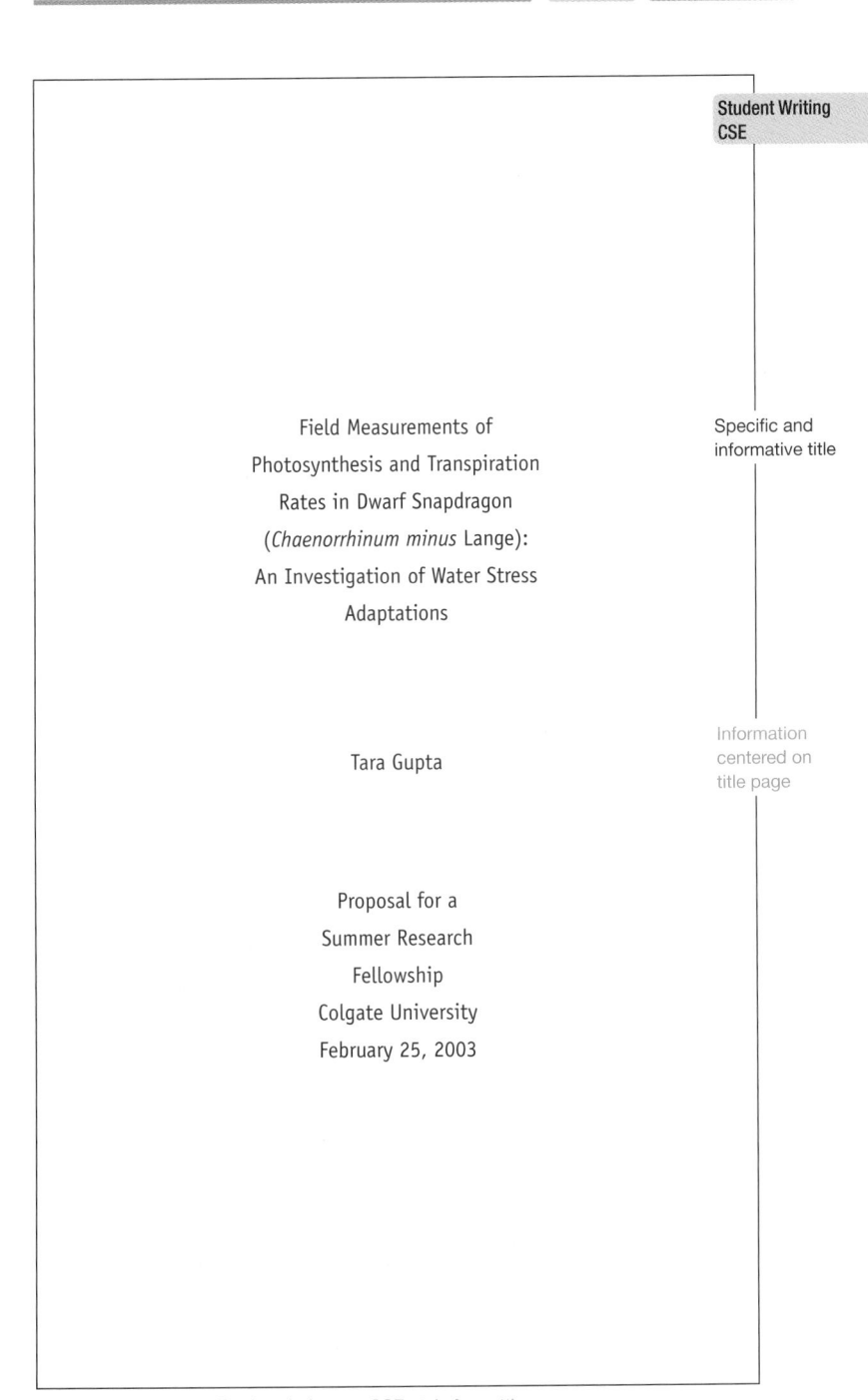

Field Measurements of
Photosynthesis and Transpiration
Rates in Dwarf Snapdragon
(*Chaenorrhinum minus* Lange):
An Investigation of Water Stress
Adaptations

Specific and
informative title

Tara Gupta

Information
centered on
title page

Proposal for a
Summer Research
Fellowship
Colgate University
February 25, 2003

Annotations indicate effective choices or CSE-style formatting.

Water Stress Adaptations 2

Headings
throughout
help organize
the proposal

Introduction
states
scientific
issue, gives
background
information

Documentation
follows CSE
citation-
sequence
format

Personal
communica-
tion cited in
parentheses
within text but
not included in
references

Introduction

Dwarf snapdragon (*Chaenorrhinum minus*) is a weedy pioneer plant found growing in central New York during spring and summer. Interestingly, the distribution of this species has been limited almost exclusively to the cinder ballast of railroad tracks[1] and to sterile strips of land along highways[2]. In these harsh environments, characterized by intense sunlight and poor soil water retention, one would expect *C. minus* to exhibit anatomical features similar to those of xeromorphic plants (species adapted to arid habitats).

However, this is not the case. T. Gupta and R. Arnold (unpublished) have found that the leaves and stems of *C. minus* are not covered by a thick, waxy cuticle but rather with a thin cuticle that is less effective in inhibiting water loss through diffusion. The root system is not long and thick, capable of reaching deeper, moister soils; instead, it is thin and diffuse, permeating only the topmost (and driest) soil horizon. Moreover, in contrast to many xeromorphic plants, the stomata (pores regulating gas exchange) are not found in sunken crypts or cavities in the epidermis that retard water loss from transpiration.

Despite a lack of these morphological adaptations to water stress, *C. minus* continues to grow and reproduce when morning dew has been its only source of water for up to 5 weeks (2002 letter from R. Arnold to me). Such growth involves fixation of carbon by photosynthesis and requires that the stomata be open to admit sufficient carbon dioxide. Given the dry, sunny environment, the time required for adequate carbon fixation must also mean a significant loss of water through transpiration as open stomata exchange carbon dioxide with water. How does *C. minus* balance the need for carbon with the need to conserve water?

Student Writing
CSE

Water Stress Adaptations 5

References

1. Widrlechner MP. Historical and phenological observations of the spread of *Chaenorrhinum minus* across North America. Can J Bot. 1983;61(1):179–187.

2. Dwarf Snapdragon [Internet]. Olympia (WA): Washington State Noxious Weed Control Board; 2001 [updated 2001 Jul 7; cited 2003 Jan 25]. Available from: http://www.wa.gov/agr/weedboard/weed _info/dwarfsnapdragon.html

3. Boyer JS. Plant productivity and environment. Science. 1982 Nov 6:443–448.

4. Manhas JG, Sukumaran NP. Diurnal changes in net photosynthetic rate in potato in two environments. Potato Res. 1988;31:375–378.

5. Doley DG, Unwin GL, Yates DJ. Spatial and temporal distribution of photosynthesis and transpiration by single leaves in a rainforest tree, *Argyrodendron peralatum*. Aust J Plant Physiol. 1988;15(3):317–326.

6. Kallarackal J, Milburn JA, Baker DA. Water relations of the banana. III. Effects of controlled water stress on water potential, transpiration, photosynthesis and leaf growth. Aust J Plant Physiol. 1990;17(1):79–90.

7. Idso SB, Allen SG, Kimball BA, Choudhury BJ. Problems with porometry: measuring net photosynthesis by leaf chamber techniques. Agron J. 1989;81(4):475–479.

Article from government Web site

Article in weekly journal

Article in journal

Includes all published works cited; numbers correspond to order in which sources are first mentioned

For Multilingual Writers

The whole idea of America . . . is imported; we're all imported.

— DEREK WALCOTT

For Multilingual Writers

56 Writing in U.S. Academic Genres *593*
a Meet expectations for U.S. academic writing *593*
b Understand genre conventions *594*
c Adapt structures and phrases from a genre *595*
d Check usage with search engines *595*

57 Clauses and Sentences *596*
a Include explicit subjects and objects *597*
b Follow English word order *597*
c Use noun clauses appropriately *598*
d Choose between infinitives and gerunds *598*
e Use adjective clauses appropriately *600*
f Use conditional sentences appropriately *601*

58 Nouns and Noun Phrases *602*
a Use count and noncount nouns appropriately *602*
b Identify proper nouns *603*
c Use determiners appropriately *603*
d Use articles conventionally *605*
e Arrange modifiers appropriately *607*

59 Verbs and Verb Phrases *609*
a Form verb phrases appropriately *609*
b Use modal auxiliaries (helping verbs) appropriately *612*
c Indicate present and past tenses *613*
d Form perfect and progressive verb phrases *614*
e Use participial adjectives correctly *616*

60 Prepositions and Prepositional Phrases *617*
a Use prepositions idiomatically *617*
b Use two-word verbs idiomatically *619*

For Multilingual Writers
591–620

For visual analysis Look carefully at the illustration on the front of this tab. What do you think this image suggests about what it means to write in more than one language?

Writing in U.S. Academic Genres **56**

Xiaoming Li, now a college English teacher, says that before she came to the United States as a graduate student, she had been a "good writer" in China—in both English and Chinese. Once in the United States, however, she struggled to grasp what her teachers expected of her college writing. While she could easily use grammar books and dictionaries, her instructors' unstated expectations seemed to call for her to write in a way that was new to her.

Of course, writing for college presents many challenges; such writing differs in many ways from high school writing as well as from personal writing like text messaging or postings to social networking sites. If you grew up speaking and writing in other languages, however, the transition to producing effective college writing can be even more complicated. Not only will you have to learn new information and new ways of thinking and arguing, but you also have to do it in a language that may not come naturally to you—especially in unfamiliar rhetorical situations.

56a Meet expectations for U.S. academic writing.

The expectations for college writing are often taken for granted by instructors. To complicate the matter further, there is no single "correct" style of communication in any country, including the United States. Effective oral styles differ from effective written styles, and what is considered good writing in one field of study is not necessarily appropriate in another. Even the variety of English often referred to as "standard" covers a wide range of styles (see Chapter 22). In spite of this wide variation, several features are often associated with U.S. academic English:

- conventional grammar, spelling, punctuation, and mechanics
- organization that links ideas explicitly
- readable type, conventional margins, and double spacing
- explicitly stated claims supported by evidence (Chapter 14)

- careful documentation of all sources (Chapters 49–55)
- consistent use of an appropriate level of formality (23a)
- conventional use of idioms (Chapter 60)
- conventional academic formats, such as literature reviews, research essays, lab reports, and research proposals

This brief list suggests features of the genre often described as U.S. academic writing. Yet these characteristics can lead to even more questions: What does *conventional* mean? How can a writer determine what is appropriate in any given rhetorical situation?

Most students can benefit from some instruction in how new contexts require the use of different sets of conventions, strategies, and resources. This is especially the case for multilingual writers.

56b Understand genre conventions.

Those who read your college writing—your teachers and peers—will hold some expectations about the features of the texts you produce. Many writers learn these expectations through practice. But if you

---

AT A GLANCE

Features of Genres

Study the features of the kind of text you need to write.

- What does the genre look like? How is the text laid out on the page? How are any visual features incorporated into the main text?
- How long is the whole text, each section, and each paragraph?
- How does the text introduce the topic? Is the main point stated explicitly or implicitly?
- What are the major divisions of the text? Are they marked with transitions or headings?
- How does each section contribute to the main point? How is the main point of each section supported?
- How are the key terms defined? What kind of background information is provided?
- What is the level of formality? Does the text use technical terms or contractions (such as *I'm* and *isn't* instead of *I am* and *is not*)?
- Does the text take a personal stance (*I*, *we*), address the audience directly (*you*), or talk about the subject without explicitly referring to the writer or the reader?
- How many sources are used in the text? How are they introduced?

have had limited exposure to various types, or *genres*, of academic writing in English, it may be helpful to think about these conventions explicitly.

Genres of texts

At some point in your writing process, you should consider the genre or kind of text the instructor expects you to write. In many cases, the assignment will not be explicit about what the text should look like or accomplish. If you are not sure what kind of text you are supposed to write, ask your instructor for clarification. (Examples may also be available at your school's writing center.) You may want to find multiple examples so that you can develop a sense of how different writers approach the same writing task.

56c Adapt structures and phrases from a genre.

If English is not your strongest language, you may find it useful to borrow and adapt transitional devices and pieces of sentence structure from other people's writing in the genre you are working in. You should not copy the whole sentence or sentence structure, however, or your borrowed sentences may seem plagiarized (Chapter 18). Find sample sentence structures from similar genres but on different topics so that you borrow a typical structure (which does not belong to anyone) rather than the idea or the particular phrasing. Write your own sentences first, and look at other people's sentences only to guide your revision.

The example on p. 596 illustrates effective borrowing. The student writer borrows phrases that are commonly used in academic writing in the social sciences to perform particular functions. Notice how the student also modifies these phrases to suit the needs of the writing situation.

56d Check usage with search engines.

To multilingual writers, search engines such as Google can provide a useful way of checking sentence structure and word usage. For example, if you are not sure whether you should use an infinitive form (*to* + verb) or a gerund (*-ing*) for the verb *confirm* after the main verb *expect* (57d), you can search for both *"expected confirming"* and *"expected to confirm"* in quotation marks to see which search term yields more results. A Google search for *"expected confirming"* yields many entries with a

Original Abstract from a Social Science Paper	Effective Borrowing of Structures from a Genre
Using the interpersonal communications research of J. K. Brilhart and G. J. Galanes, and W. Wilmot and J. Hocker, along with T. Hartman's personality assessment, I observed and analyzed the leadership roles and group dynamics of my project collaborators in a communications course. Based on results of the Hartman personality assessment, I predicted that a single leader would emerge. However, complementary individual strengths and gender differences encouraged a distributed leadership style, in which the group experienced little confrontation and conflict. Conflict, because it was handled positively, was crucial to the group's progress.	Drawing on the research of Deborah Tannen on men's and women's conversational styles, I analyzed the conversational styles of six first-year students at DePaul University. Based on Tannen's research, I expected that the three men I observed would use features typical of male conversational style and the three women would use features typical of female conversational style. In general, these predictions were accurate; however, some exceptions were also apparent.

comma between the two words, indicating that one phrase ends with *expected* and another begins with *confirming*.

On the other hand, a search for *"expected to confirm"* yields many more hits than a search for *"expected confirming."* These results indicate that *expected to confirm* is the more commonly used expression. Be sure to click through a few pages of the search engine's results to make sure that most results come from ordinary sentences rather than from headlines or phrases that may be constructed differently from standard English.

57 Clauses and Sentences

Short phrases, or sound bites, are everywhere—from the Dairy Council's "Got Milk?" to Volkswagen's "Drivers Wanted." These short, simple slogans may be memorable, but they don't say very much. In writing, you usually need more complex sentences to convey meaning. The requirements for forming sentences can differ across languages, and English has its own sets of rules.

57a Include explicit subjects and objects.

English sentences consist of a subject and a predicate. While many languages can omit a sentence subject, English very rarely allows this. Though you might write *Responsible for analyzing data* on a résumé, in most varieties of spoken and written English, you must explicitly state the subject. In fact, with only a few exceptions, all clauses in English must have an explicit subject.

▶ They took the Acela Express to Boston because ^*it*^ was fast.

English even requires a kind of "dummy" subject to fill the subject position in certain kinds of sentences.

▶ **It** is raining.
▶ **There** is a strong wind.

Transitive verbs (31k) typically require that objects—and sometimes other information—also be explicitly stated. For example, it is not enough to tell someone *Give!* even if it is clear what is to be given to whom. You must say *Give it to me* or *Give her the passport* or some other such sentence. Similarly, saying *Put!* or *Put it!* is not enough when you mean *Put it on the table* or *Put it down!*

Many dictionaries identify whether a verb is transitive (requiring an object) or intransitive (not followed by an object).

57b Follow English word order.

In general, subjects, verbs, and objects (31k) must be placed in specific positions within a sentence.

SUBJECT VERB OBJECT ADVERB
▶ **Mario left Venice reluctantly.**

The only word in this sentence that can be moved to different locations is the adverb *reluctantly* (*Mario reluctantly left Venice* or *Reluctantly, Mario left Venice*). The three key elements of subject, verb, and object are moved out of their normal order only to create special effects.

57c   Use noun clauses appropriately.

Examine the following sentence:

> In my last year in high school, my adviser urged that I apply to several colleges.

This complex sentence is built out of two sentences, one of them (B) embedded in the other (A):

A. In my last year in high school, my adviser urged B.
B. I (should) apply to several colleges.

When these are combined as in the original sentence, sentence B becomes a noun clause introduced by *that* and becomes the object of the verb *urged* in sentence A. Now look at the following sentence:

> It made a big difference that she wrote a strong letter of recommendation.

Here the two component sentences are C and D:

C. D made a big difference.
D. She wrote a strong letter of recommendation.

In this case, the noun clause formed from sentence D functions as the subject of sentence C so that the combination reads as follows:

> That she wrote a strong letter of recommendation made a big difference.

This sentence is gramatically acceptable but not typical. When a long noun clause is the subject, it is usually moved to the end of the sentence. The result is *It made a big difference that she wrote a strong letter of recommendation*, which inserts the dummy subject *It* as the subject.

57d   Choose between infinitives and gerunds.

Infinitives are verbs in the *to* + verb form (*to write, to read, to go*); gerunds are verbs that end in *-ing* and act as subjects or objects within a sentence. In general, infinitives tend to indicate intentions, desires, or expectations, and gerunds tend to state facts. Knowing whether to use a *to* form or an *-ing* form in a particular sentence can be a challenge. Though no simple explanation will make it an easy task, some hints might be helpful (see 56d for another strategy).

▶ My adviser urged me to apply to several colleges.
▶ Applying took a great deal of time.

In the first sentence, *to apply* conveys the message that the act of applying was something wanted, not yet a fact. In the second sentence, *applying* calls attention to the fact that the application process was actually carried out.

Using infinitives (to forms) to state intentions

▶ **Kumar expected to get a good job after graduation.**

▶ **Last year, Fatima decided to become a math major.**

▶ **The strikers have agreed to go back to work.**

At the moment indicated by the verbs *expect*, *decide*, and *agree* in these sentences, those actions or events were merely intentions. These three verbs, as well as many others that specify intentions (or negative intentions, such as *refuse*), must always be followed by an infinitive, never by a gerund. Many learner dictionaries provide information about verbs that must be followed by an infinitive instead of a gerund.

Using gerunds (-ing forms) to state facts

▶ **Jerzy enjoys going to the theater.**

▶ **We resumed working after our coffee break.**

▶ **Kim appreciated getting candy from Sean.**

In all of these cases, the gerund indicates that the action or event that it expresses has actually occurred. Verbs like *enjoy*, *resume*, and *appreciate* can be followed only by gerunds, not by infinitives. In fact, even when these verbs do not convey clear facts, the verb form that follows must still be a gerund. Again, many dictionaries provide this information.

▶ **Kim would appreciate *getting* candy from Sean, but he hardly knows her.**

Understanding other rules and guidelines

A few verbs can be followed by either an infinitive or a gerund. With some, such as *begin* and *continue*, the choice makes little difference in meaning. With others, however, the difference in meaning is striking.

▶ **Carlos was working as a medical technician, but he stopped to study English.**

The infinitive *to study* indicates that Carlos intended to study English when he left his job. We don't know whether he actually did study English.

▶ **Carlos stopped studying English when he left the United States.**

The gerund *studying* indicates that Carlos actually did study English but then stopped when he left.

The distinction between fact and intention is not a rule but only a tendency, and it can be outweighed by other rules. For example, use a gerund—never an infinitive—right after a preposition.

eating.
▶ **This fruit is safe for to eat.**
^

▶ **This fruit is safe for to eat.**

us
▶ **This fruit is safe for to eat.**
^

For a full list of verbs that can be followed by an infinitive and verbs that can be followed by a gerund, see *Grammar Troublespots*, Third Edition, by Ann Raimes (Cambridge UP, 2004), or *Cambridge International Dictionary of English* (Cambridge UP, 1999).

57e Use adjective clauses appropriately.

An adjective clause provides more information about a preceding noun.

▶ **The company *Yossi's uncle had invested in* went bankrupt.**

The subject is a noun phrase in which the noun *company* is modified by the article *the* and the adjective clause *Yossi's uncle invested in*. The sentence as a whole says that a certain company went bankrupt, and the adjective clause identifies the company more specifically by saying that Yossi's uncle had invested in it.

One way of seeing how the adjective clause fits into the sentence is to rewrite it like this: *The company (Yossi's uncle had invested in it) went bankrupt*. This is not a normal English sentence, but it helps demonstrate a process that leads to the sentence we started with. Note the following steps:

1. Change the personal pronoun *it* to the relative pronoun *which*: *The company (Yossi's uncle had invested in which) went bankrupt*.
2. Either move the whole prepositional phrase *in which* to the beginning of the adjective clause, or move just the relative pronoun: *The company in which Yossi's uncle had invested went bankrupt* or *The company which Yossi's uncle had invested in went bankrupt*. While both of these are correct English sentences, the first version is somewhat more formal than the second.
3. If no preposition precedes the relative pronoun, substitute *that* for *which*, or omit the relative pronoun entirely: *The company that Yossi's uncle had invested in went bankrupt* or *The company Yossi's uncle had invested in went bankrupt*. Both of these are correct English sentences. While they are less formal than the forms in step 2, they are still acceptable in much formal writing.

57f Use conditional sentences appropriately.

English distinguishes among many different types of conditional sentences—that is, sentences that focus on questions of truth and that are introduced by *if* or its equivalent. The following examples illustrate a range of different conditional sentences. Each of these sentences makes different assumptions about the likelihood that what is stated in the *if* clause is true.

▶ **If you *practice* (or *have practiced*) writing frequently, you *know* (or *have learned*) what your chief problems are.**

This sentence assumes that what is stated in the *if* clause may be true; as the alternatives in parentheses indicate, any tense that is appropriate in a simple sentence may be used in both the *if* clause and the main clause.

▶ **If you *practice* writing for the rest of this term, you *will* (or *may*) *understand* the process better.**

This sentence makes a prediction about the future and again assumes that what is stated may very well be true. Only the main clause uses the future tense (*will understand*) or some other modal (59a) that can indicate future time (*may understand*). The *if* clause must use the present tense.

▶ **If you *practiced* (or *were to practice*) writing every single day, it *would* eventually *seem* much easier to you.**

This sentence shows doubt that what is stated will happen. In the *if* clause, the verb is either past tense—actually, past subjunctive (32h)—or *were to* + the base form, even though it refers to future time. The main clause contains *would* + the base form of the main verb.

▶ **If you *practiced* writing on Mars, you *would find* no one to read your work.**

This sentence imagines an impossible situation. As with the preceding sentence, the past subjunctive is used in the *if* clause, although past time is not being referred to, and *would* + the base form is used in the main clause.

▶ **If you *had practiced* writing in ancient Egypt, you *would have used* hieroglyphics.**

This sentence shifts the impossibility back to the past; obviously, you aren't going to find yourself in ancient Egypt. But a past impossibility demands a form that is "more past": the past perfect in the *if* clause and *would* + the perfect form of the main verb in the main clause.

EXERCISE 57.1

Revise the following sentences as necessary. Not all sentences contain an error.

1. In the 1870s, a group of New York City dog owners formed officially the West-minster Kennel Club.

2. Members of the club enjoyed to tell stories about their dogs' talents.

3. Soon the group began hosting an annual dog show which dogs were judged and awarded prizes in it.

4. Was this show that eventually became the Westminster Dog Show, a popular event still held every January.

5. The Westminster Kennel Club contributes to charities that help many dogs and pet owners.

6. If you want to know more about purebred dogs, you have enjoyed watching the Westminster Dog Show.

bedfordstmartins.com/everydaywriter
Exercise Central > For Multilingual Writers

58 Nouns and Noun Phrases

Although all languages have nouns, English nouns differ from those in some other languages in various ways, such as their division into count and noncount nouns and the use of plural forms, articles, and other modifiers.

58a Use count and noncount nouns appropriately.

Look at the following sentences:

▶ **Research shows that this chemical can be dangerous.**

▶ **Studies show that this chemical can be dangerous.**

Studies is a count noun, and *research* is a noncount noun. Count nouns (also called countable nouns) refer to separate individuals or things that you can count: *a study, a doctor, a book, a tree; studies, doctors,* three *books,* ten *trees.* Noncount nouns (also called mass nouns or uncountable nouns) refer to masses or collections without distinctly separate parts: *research, milk, ice, blood, grass.* You cannot count noncount nouns unless you use a quantifier: *one blade of grass, two glasses of milk, three pints of blood.*

Count and noncount nouns also differ in their use of plural forms. Count nouns generally have singular and plural forms: *study, studies.* Noncount nouns generally have only a singular form: *research.*

COUNT	NONCOUNT
facts	information
suggestions	advice
people (plural of *person*)	humanity
tables, chairs, beds	furniture
letters	mail
pebbles	gravel
beans	rice

Some nouns can be either count or noncount, depending on the meaning.

COUNT Before there were video games, children played with marbles.

NONCOUNT The floor of the palace was made of marble.

When you learn a noun in English, it is useful to know whether it is count, noncount, or both. Many dictionaries provide this information.

58b Identify proper nouns.

In addition to count and noncount nouns, English has proper nouns. These nouns include names of people, places, objects, and institutions—for example, *California, Yolanda, IBM,* and *First National Bank.* Proper nouns are always capitalized and generally cannot vary in number, so they are either singular (*John,* the New York Times) or plural (*the Netherlands, the Rocky Mountains*).

58c Use determiners appropriately.

Determiners are words that identify or quantify a noun, such as *this study, all people, his suggestions.*

COMMON DETERMINERS

- the articles *a/an, the*
- *this, these, that, those*
- *my, our, your, his, her, its, their*
- possessive nouns and noun phrases (*Sheila's* paper, *my friend's* book)

- *whose, which, what*
- *all, both, each, every, some, any, either, no, neither, many, much, (a) few, (a) little, several, enough*
- the numerals *one, two,* etc.

Some determiners, such as *a, an, this, that, one,* and *each,* can only be used with singular nouns; others, such as *these, those, all, both, many, several,* and *two,* can only be used with plural nouns. Still other determiners—*my, the,* and *which,* for example—can be used with singular or plural nouns. See the chart below for additional examples.

Determiners with singular count nouns

Every singular count noun must be preceded by a determiner. Place any adjectives between the determiner and the noun.

▶ *my*
  sister
  ^

▶ *the*
  growing population
  ^

▶ *that*
  old neighborhood
  ^

These determiners . . .	. . . can precede these noun types	Examples
a, an, every, each	singular count nouns some proper nouns	*a* book, *an* American *each* word *every* Buddhist
this, that	singular count nouns noncount nouns	*this* book *that* milk
(a) little, much	noncount nouns	*a little* milk *much* affection
some, enough	noncount nouns plural count nouns	*some* milk, *enough* trouble *some* books *enough* problems
the	singular count nouns plural count nouns noncount nouns	*the* doctor *the* doctors *the* information
these, those, (a) few, many, both, several	plural count nouns	*these* books, *those* plans *a few* ideas *many* students *both* hands, *several* trees

Determiners with plural count nouns or with noncount nouns

Noncount and plural count nouns sometimes have determiners and sometimes do not. For example, *This research is important* and *Research is important* are both acceptable but have different meanings.

Remembering which determiners go with which types of noun

The chart on p. 604 describes which determiners can be used with which types of nouns.

58d Use articles conventionally.

Articles (*a*, *an*, and *the*) are a type of determiner. In English, choosing which article to use—or whether to use an article at all—can be challenging. Although there are exceptions, the following general guidelines can help.

Using a or an

Use *a* and *an*, indefinite articles, with singular count nouns. Use *a* before a consonant sound (*a car*) and *an* before a vowel sound (*an uncle*). Consider sound rather than spelling: *a house, an hour*. Do not use indefinite articles with plural count nouns or with noncount nouns.

A or *an* tells readers they do not have enough information to identify specifically what the noun refers to (in other words, it's an unspecified, or indefinite, noun). The writer may or may not have a particular thing in mind but in either case will use *a* or *an* if the reader lacks the information necessary for identification. Compare these sentences:

▶ I need *a* new coat for the winter.
▶ I saw *a coat* that I liked at Dayton's, but it wasn't heavy enough.

The coat in the first sentence is hypothetical rather than actual. Since it is indefinite to the writer and the reader, it is used with *a*, not *the*. The second sentence refers to a particular coat, but since the writer cannot expect the reader to know which one, it is used with *a* rather than *the*.

If you want to speak of an indefinite quantity rather than just one indefinite thing, use *some* or *any* with a noncount noun or a plural count noun. Note that *any* is used in negative sentences.

▶ This stew needs *some* more *salt*.
▶ I saw *some plates* that I liked at Gump's.
▶ This stew doesn't need *any* more salt.
▶ I didn't see *any* plates that I liked at Gump's.

Using the

The definite article *the* is used with both count and noncount nouns whose identity is already known or is about to be made known to readers. The necessary information for identification can come from the noun phrase itself, from elsewhere in the text, from context, from general knowledge, or from a superlative.

▶ Let's meet at *the* fountain in front of Dwinelle Hall.

The phrase *in front of Dwinelle Hall* identifies the specific fountain. We know from the use of *the* that there is only one fountain in front of Dwinelle Hall.

▶ Last Saturday, a fire that started in a restaurant spread to a

nearby clothing store. *The* Store was saved, although it suffered

water damage.

The word *store* is preceded by *the*, which directs our attention to the information in the previous sentence, where the store is first identified.

▶ She asked him to shut *the* door when he left her office.

She expects him to understand that she is referring to the door in her office.

▶ *The* Pope is expected to visit Africa in October.

There is only one living pope, and *the* before *pope* signals that this sentence refers to him. Similar examples include *the president (of the United States)*, *the earth*, and *the moon*.

▶ Bill is now *the* best singer in the choir.

The superlative *best* identifies the noun *singer*.

Using the zero article

If a noun appears without *the*, *a* or *an*, or any other determiner (even if it is preceded by other adjectives), it is said to have a zero article. The zero article can be used with plural count nouns (*plans, assignments*), noncount nouns (*homework, information*), and proper nouns (*Carmen, New York*). With plural count nouns and noncount nouns, the zero article is used to make generalizations.

▶ In this world nothing is certain but death and taxes.

— BENJAMIN FRANKLIN

Modifier Type	Arrangement	Example
determiners	at the beginning of the noun phrase	*these old-fashioned tiles*
all or *both*	before any other determiners	*all these tiles*
numbers	after any other determiners	*these six tiles*
noun modifiers	directly before the noun	*these kitchen tiles*
adjectives	between determiners and noun modifiers	*these old-fashioned kitchen tiles*
phrases or clauses	after the noun	*the tiles on the wall* *the tiles that we bought*

> The zero article indicates that Franklin refers not to a particular death or specific taxes but to death and taxes in general.

Here English differs from many other languages that would use the definite article to make generalizations. In English, a sentence like *The snakes are dangerous* can refer only to particular, identifiable snakes, not to snakes in general.

It is sometimes possible to make general statements with *the* or *a/an* and singular count nouns.

▶ *First-year college students* **are confronted with many new experiences.**

▶ *A first-year student* **is confronted with many new experiences.**

▶ *The first-year student* **is confronted with many new experiences.**

These sentences all make the same general statement, but the emphasis of each sentence is different. The first sentence refers to first-year college students as a group, the second focuses on a hypothetical student taken at random, and the third sentence, which is characteristic of formal written style, projects the image of a typical student as representative of the whole class.

58e Arrange modifiers appropriately.

Modifiers are words that give more information about a noun; that is, they *modify* the meaning of the noun in some way. Some modifiers precede the noun, and others follow it, as indicated in the chart above.

If there are two or more adjectives, their order is variable, but English has strong preferences, described below.

- Subjective adjectives (those that show the writer's opinion) go before objective adjectives (those that merely describe): *these beautiful old-fashioned kitchen tiles.*
- Adjectives of size generally come early: *these beautiful large old-fashioned kitchen tiles.*
- Adjectives of color generally come late: *these beautiful large old-fashioned blue kitchen tiles.*
- Adjectives derived from proper nouns or from nouns that refer to materials generally come after color terms and right before noun modifiers: *these beautiful large old-fashioned blue Portuguese ceramic kitchen tiles.*
- All other objective adjectives go in the middle, and adjectives for which no order is preferred are separated by commas: *these beautiful large decorative, heat-resistant, old-fashioned blue Portuguese ceramic kitchen tiles.*

Of course, the very long noun phrases presented above would be out of place in most kinds of writing. Academic and professional writing tend to avoid long strings of adjectives.

EXERCISE 58.1

Each of the following sentences contains an error. Rewrite each sentence correctly.

1. Before a middle of the nineteenth century, surgery was usually a terrifying, painful ordeal.
2. Because anesthesia did not exist yet, only painkiller available for surgical patients was whiskey.
3. The pain of surgical procedures could be so severe that much people were willing to die rather than have surgery.
4. In 1846, one of the hospital in Boston gave ether to a patient before he had surgery.
5. The patient, who had a large on his neck tumor, slept peacefully as doctors removed it.

EXERCISE 58.2

Insert articles as necessary in the following passage from *The Silent Language*, by Edward T. Hall. Some blanks may not need an article.

Hollywood is famous for hiring _____ various experts to teach _____ people technically what most of us learn informally. _____ case in point is _____ story about _____ children of one movie couple who noticed _____ new child in _____ neighborhood climbing _____ tree. _____ children immediately wanted to be given _____ name of his instructor in _____ tree climbing.

 bedfordstmartins.com/everydaywriter
Exercise Central > For Multilingual Writers

Verbs and Verb Phrases **59**

V erbs can be called the heartbeat of every language, but in English the metaphor is especially meaningful. With a few stylistic exceptions, all written English sentences must include a verb. Some of the distinctive features of English verbs include modals, perfect tenses, and progressive forms.

59a Form verb phrases appropriately.

Verb phrases can be built up out of a main verb and one or more helping (auxiliary) verbs (32b).

▶ **Immigration figures rise every year.**
▶ **Immigration figures are rising every year.**
▶ **Immigration figures have risen every year.**
▶ **Immigration figures have been rising every year.**

Verb phrases have strict rules of order. If you try to rearrange the words in any of these sentences, you will find that most alternatives are impossible. You cannot say *Immigration figures rising are every year* or *Immigration figures been have rising every year*. The only permissible change to word order is to form a question, moving the first helping verb to the beginning of the sentence: *Have immigration figures been rising every year?*

Putting helping verbs in order

In the sentence *Immigration figures may have been rising*, the main verb *rising* follows three helping verbs: *may*, *have*, and *been*. Together these helping and main verbs make up a verb phrase.

- *May* is a modal (59b) that indicates possibility; it is followed by the base form of a verb.
- *Have* is an auxiliary verb (32b) that in this case indicates the perfect tense (32e); it must be followed by a past participle (*been*).
- Any form of *be*, when it is followed by a present participle ending in *-ing* (such as *rising*), indicates the progressive tense (32e).
- *Be* followed by a past participle, as in *New immigration policies have been passed in recent years*, indicates the passive voice (32g).

As shown in the chart below, when two or more auxiliaries appear in a verb phrase, they must follow a particular order based on the type of auxiliary: (1) modal, (2) a form of *have* used to indicate a perfect tense, (3) a form of *be* used to indicate a progressive tense, and (4) a form of *be* used to indicate the passive voice. (Very few sentences include all four kinds of auxiliaries.)

Only one modal is permitted in a verb phrase.

> ▶ She will <u>can</u> speak Czech much better soon.

be able to

Forming helping verbs

Whenever you use a helping verb, check the form of the word that follows. The guidelines that follow describe the appropriate forms.

	Modal	Perfect *Have*	Progressive *Be*	Passive *Be*	Main Verb	
Sonia	—	has	—	been	invited	to visit a family in Prague.
She	should	—	—	be	finished	with school soon.
The invitation	must	have	—	been	sent	in the spring.
She	—	has	been	—	studying	Czech.
She	may	—	be	—	feeling	nervous.
She	might	have	been	—	expecting	to travel elsewhere.
The trip	will	have	been	being	planned	for a month by the time she leaves.

MODAL + BASE FORM

Use the base form of a verb after *can, could, will, would, shall, should, may, might,* and *must.*

▶ Alice **can read** Latin.

▶ Sanjay **should have** studied for the test.

▶ They **must be** going to a fine school.

In many other languages, modals such as *can* and *must* are followed by an infinitive (*to* + base form). In English, only the base form follows a modal.

▶ Alice can ~~to~~ read Latin.

Notice that a modal auxiliary can express tense (for example, *can* or *could*), but it never changes form to agree with the subject.

PERFECT *HAVE* + PAST PARTICIPLE

To form the perfect tenses, use *have, has,* or *had* with a past participle.

▶ Everyone **has gone** home.

▶ They **have been** working all day.

PROGRESSIVE *BE* + PRESENT PARTICIPLE

A progressive form of a verb is signaled by two elements, a form of the helping verb *be* (*am, is, are, was, were, be,* or *been*) and the *-ing* form of the next word: *The children* **are** studying.

▶ The children _∧ studying in school.   *are*

▶ The children are ~~study~~ in school.   *studying*

Some verbs are rarely used in progressive forms. These verbs express unchanging conditions or mental states rather than deliberate actions: *believe, belong, hate, know, like, love, need, own, resemble, understand.*

PASSIVE *BE* + PAST PARTICIPLE

Use *am, is, are, was, were, being, be,* or *been* with a past participle to form the passive voice.

▶ Tagalog **is spoken** in the Philippines.

Notice that with the progressive *be* the following word (the present participle) ends in *-ing,* but with the passive *be* the following word (the past participle) never ends in *-ing.*

▶ Takeo **is studying** music.

▶ Natasha **was taught** by a famous violinist.

If the first helping verb in a verb phrase is *be* or *have*, it must show either present or past tense, and it must agree with the subject: *Meredith has played in an orchestra* or *Meredith had played in an orchestra before she joined the band.*

59b Use modal auxiliaries (helping verbs) appropriately.

The nine basic modal auxiliaries (helping verbs) are *can, could, will, would, shall, should, may, might,* and *must.* There are a few others as well, in particular *ought to,* which is close in meaning to *should.* Occasionally *need* can be a modal rather than a main verb.

The nine basic modals fall into the pairs *can/could, will/would, shall/ should, may/might,* and the loner *must.* In earlier English, the second member of each pair was the past tense of the first. The second form still functions occasionally as a past tense, especially in the case of *could.*

▶ Ingrid **can** ski.
▶ Ingrid **could** ski when she was five.

But, for the most part, in present-day English, all nine modals typically refer to present or future time. When you want to use a modal to refer to the past, you follow the modal with a perfect form of a helping verb.

▶ If you have a fever, you **should see** a doctor.
▶ If you had a fever, you **should have seen** a doctor.

In the case of *must,* refer to the past by using *had to.*

▶ You **must** renew your visa by the end of this week.
▶ You **had to** renew your visa by the end of last week.

Using modals to make requests or to give instructions

Modals are often used in requests and instructions. Imagine making the following request of a flight attendant:

▶ **Will** you bring me a pillow?

This request may appear demanding or rude. Using a modal makes the request more polite by acknowledging that fulfilling the request may not be possible.

▶ **Can** you bring me a pillow?

Another way of softening the request is to use the past form of *will*, and the most discreet choice is the past form of *can*.

▶ **Would you bring me a pillow?**
▶ **Could you bring me a pillow?**

Using the past tense of modals seems more polite than using their present forms because it makes any statement or question less assertive.
Consider the meanings of each of the following instructions:

1. You *can* submit your report electronically.
2. You *may* submit your report electronically.
3. You *should* submit your report electronically.
4. You *must* submit your report electronically.
5. You *will* submit your report electronically.

Instructions 1 and 2 give permission to submit the report electronically but do not require it; 2 is more formal. Instruction 3 makes a strong recommendation; 4 allows no alternative; and 5 implies, "Don't even think of doing otherwise."

Using modals to indicate doubt or certainty

Modals can also indicate how confident the writer is about his or her claims. Look at the following set of examples, which starts with a tentative suggestion and ends with an indication of complete confidence:

▶ **The study might help explain the findings of previous research.**
▶ **The study may help explain the findings of previous research.**
▶ **The study will help explain the findings of previous research.**

59c Indicate present and past tenses.

Every sentence in standard written English must have at least one verb or verb phrase that is not an infinitive (*to write*), a gerund (*writing*), or a participle (*written*) without any auxiliaries. Furthermore, every such verb or verb phrase must have a tense (32e).

In some languages, such as Chinese and Vietnamese, the verb form never changes regardless of when the action takes place. In standard written English, the time of the action must be clearly indicated by the tense form of every verb, even if the time is obvious or it is indicated elsewhere in the sentence.

▶ During the Cultural Revolution, millions of young people ~~cannot~~ go
could not

to school and ~~are~~ sent to the countryside.
were

▶ Last night I ~~call~~ my aunt who ~~live~~ in Santo Domingo.
called ... *lives*

Direct and indirect quotations

Changing direct quotations to indirect quotations can sometimes lead to tense shifts.

DIRECT	She said, "My work *is* now complete."
INDIRECT	She *told* me that her work *was* now complete.
INDIRECT	She *tells* me that her work *is* now complete.

In general, the verb introducing the indirect quotation (sometimes called the reporting verb) will agree in tense with the verb in the indirect quotation; there are, however, some exceptions. For example, if the reporting verb is in the past tense but the information that follows holds true in the present, shifting to a present-tense verb is acceptable.

▶ She *told* me that her work *is* as exciting as ever.

In academic writing, reporting verbs are used regularly to refer to ideas from other texts or authors. Depending on the documentation style you use, you will probably use the present tense, the present perfect tense, or the simple past for these verbs.

Lee *claims* that . . .
Lee *writes* . . .
Lee *has argued* that . . .
Lee *found* that . . .

59d Form perfect and progressive verb phrases.

The perfect and progressive auxiliaries combine with the present or past tense, or with modals, to form complex verb phrases with special meanings (32f).

Distinguishing the simple present and the present perfect

▶ My sister **drives** a bus.

The simple present (*drives*) tells us about the sister's current job. But if you were to add the phrase *for three years*, it would be incorrect to say *My sister drives a bus for three years*. Instead, you need a time frame that goes from the past up to the present. The present perfect or present perfect progressive expresses this time frame.

▶ **My sister has driven a bus for three years.**

▶ **My sister has been driving a bus for three years.**

Distinguishing the simple past and the present perfect

▶ **Since she started working, she has bought a new car and a DVD player.**

The clause introduced by *since* sets up a time frame that runs from past to present and requires the present perfect (*has bought*) in the subsequent clause. Furthermore, the sentence does not say exactly when she bought the car or the DVD player, and that indefiniteness also calls for the perfect. It would be less correct to say *Since she started working, she bought a new car and a DVD player*. But if you say when she bought the car, you should use the simple past tense.

▶ **She bought the car two years ago.**

It would be incorrect to say *She has bought the car two years ago* because the perfect cannot be used with definite expressions of time. In this case, use the simple past (*bought*).

Distinguishing the simple present and the present progressive

Use the present progressive tense when an action is in progress right now. In contrast, use the simple present for actions that frequently occur during a period of time that might include the present moment (though the simple present does not necessarily indicate that the action is taking place now).

▶ **My sister drives a bus, but she is taking a vacation now.**

▶ **My sister drives a bus, but she takes a vacation every year.**

Many languages use the simple present (*drives, takes*) for both types of sentences. In English, however, the first sentence would be incorrect if it said *but she takes a vacation now*.

Distinguishing the simple past and the past progressive

▶ **Sally spent the summer in Ecuador.**

The simple past tense is used in this case because the action occurred in the past and is now finished.

The past progressive tense is used relatively infrequently in English. It is used to focus on duration or continuousness and especially to call attention to past action that went on at the same time as something else.

▶ Sally **was spending** the summer in Ecuador when she *met* her future husband.

59e Use participial adjectives correctly.

Many verbs refer to feelings—for example, *bore, confuse, excite, fascinate, frighten, interest*. The present and past participles of such verbs can be used as ordinary adjectives (see 31l). Use the past participle (which usually ends with *-ed*) to describe a person having the feeling.

▶ The **frightened** boy started to cry.

Use the present participle (which usually ends with *-ing*) to describe the thing (or person) causing the feeling.

▶ The **frightening** dinosaur display gave him nightmares.

Be careful not to confuse the two types of adjectives.

> *interested*
▶ I am **interesting** in African literature.

> *interesting.*
▶ African literature seems **interested.**

EXERCISE 59.1

Each of the following sentences contains an error. Rewrite each sentence correctly.

1. Over the past forty years, average temperatures in the Arctic increase by several degrees.
2. A few years ago, a robin was observe in Inuit territory in northern Canada.
3. Inuit people in previous generations will never have seen a robin near their homes.
4. The Inuit language, which called *Inuktitut*, has no word for *robin*.
5. Many Inuits are concerning that warmer temperatures may change their way of life.

EXERCISE 59.2

Rewrite the following passage, adapted from "Cold Comfort" by Atul Gawande (*New Yorker*, March 11, 2002), adding appropriate auxiliaries and verb endings where necessary. The total number of words required in each case is indicated in parentheses.

The notion that a chill _____ (put — 1) you at risk of catching a cold is nearly universal. Yet science _____ (find — 2) no evidence for it. One of the first studies on the matter _____ (lead — 2) by Sir Christopher Andrewes. He _____ (take — 1) a group of volunteers and _____ (inoculate — 1) them with a cold virus; previously, half of the group _____ (keep — 3) warm, and the other half _____ (make — 3) to take a bath and then to stand for half an hour without a towel while the wind _____ (blow — 2) on them. The chilled group _____ (get — 1) no more colds than the warm group.

⊙ **bedfordstmartins.com/everydaywriter**
Exercise Central > For Multilingual Writers

Prepositions and Prepositional Phrases **60**

Words such as *to, from, over,* and *under* show the relations between other words; these words are prepositions, and they are one of the more challenging elements of English writing. You will need to decide which preposition to use for your intended meaning and understand how to use verbs that include prepositions, such as *take off, pick up,* and *put up with.*

60a Use prepositions idiomatically.

Even if you know where to use a preposition, it can be difficult to determine which preposition to use. Each of the most common prepositions has a wide range of applications, and this range never coincides exactly from one language to another. See, for example, how *in* and *on* are used in English.

▶ The peaches are *in* the refrigerator.
▶ The peaches are *on* the table.
▶ Is that a diamond ring *on* your finger?

The Spanish translations of these sentences all use the same preposition (*en*), a fact that might lead you astray in English.

on
▶ Is that a ruby ring in your finger?

There is no easy solution to the challenge of using English prepositions idiomatically, but the strategies in the box on p. 618 can help.

AT A GLANCE

Using Prepositions Idiomatically

1. Keep in mind typical examples of each preposition.

IN The peaches are *in* the refrigerator.
   There are still some pickles *in* the jar.
   The book you are looking for is *in* the bookcase.

Here the object of the preposition *in* is a container that encloses something.

ON The peaches are *on* the table.
   There are still some pickles *on* the plate.
   The book you are looking for is *on* the top shelf.

Here the object of the preposition *on* is a horizontal surface with which something is in direct contact.

2. Learn other examples that show some similarities and some differences in meaning.

IN You shouldn't drive *in* a snowstorm.

Here there is no container, but like a container, the falling snow surrounds the driver. The preposition *in* is used for other weather-related expressions as well: *in a tornado, in the sun, in the rain.*

ON Is that a diamond ring *on* your finger?

The preposition *on* is used to describe things we wear: *the hat on his head, the shoes on her feet, the tattoo on his back.*

3. Use your imagination to create mental images that can help you remember figurative uses of prepositions.

IN Michael is *in* love.

The preposition *in* is often used to describe a state of being: *in love, in pain, in a panic.* As a way to remember this, you might imagine the person immersed *in* this state of being.

4. Try to learn prepositions not in isolation but as part of a system. For example, in identifying the location of a place or an event, you can use the three prepositions *at, in,* and *on.*

At specifies the exact point in space or time.

AT There will be a meeting tomorrow *at* 9:30 AM *at* 160 Main Street.

Expanses of space or time within which a place is located or an event takes place might be seen as containers and so require *in.*

IN I arrived *in* the United States *in* January.

On must be used in two cases: with the names of streets (but not the exact address) and with days of the week or month.

ON The airline's office is *on* Fifth Avenue.
   I'll be moving to my new apartment *on* September 30.

EXERCISE 60.1

Insert prepositions as necessary in the following paragraph.

The children's soccer game happened _____ 10:00 _____ Saturday morning. The families sat _____ blankets to watch the game. Everyone was _____ a good mood. When the game ended, both teams stood _____ a circle to cheer.

60b Use two-word verbs idiomatically.

Some words that look like prepositions do not always function as prepositions. Consider the following two sentences:

▶ **The balloon rose *off* the ground.**
▶ **The plane took *off* without difficulty.**

In the first sentence, *off* is a preposition that introduces the prepositional phrase *off the ground*. In the second sentence, *off* does not function as a preposition. Instead, it combines with *took* to form a two-word verb with its own meaning. Such a verb is called a phrasal verb, and the word *off*, when used in this way, is called an adverbial particle. Many prepositions can function as particles to form phrasal verbs.

The verb + particle combination that makes up a phrasal verb is a single entity that usually cannot be torn apart.

> *off*
▶ **The plane took without difficulty. off.**
>   ^   ^

The exceptions are the many phrasal verbs that are transitive, meaning that they take a direct object (31k). Some transitive phrasal verbs have particles that may be separated from the verb by the object.

▶ **I *picked up my baggage* at the terminal.**
▶ **I *picked my baggage up* at the terminal.**

If a personal pronoun (such as *it, her,* or *him*) is used as the direct object, it must separate the verb from its particle.

▶ **I *picked it up* at the terminal.**

Some idiomatic two-word verbs, however, are not phrasal verbs.

▶ **We *ran into* our neighbor on the train.**

In such verbs, the second word is a preposition, which cannot be separated from the verb. For example, a native speaker would not say *We ran our neighbor into on the train.* Verbs like *run into* are called prepositional verbs, which are another kind of two-word verb.

In the preceding sample sentence, *ran into* consists of the verb *ran* followed by the preposition *into*, which introduces the prepositional phrase *into our neighbor.* Yet *to run into our neighbor* is different from a normal verb + prepositional phrase, such as *to run into the room.* If you know the typical meanings of *run* and *into*, you can interpret *to run into the room.* Not so with *to run into our neighbor*; the combination *run + into* has a special meaning ("find by chance") that could not be determined from the typical meanings of *run* and *into.*

Prepositional verbs include such idiomatic two-word verbs as *take after*, meaning "resemble" (usually a parent or other older relative); *get over*, meaning "recover from"; and *count on*, meaning "trust." They also include verb + preposition combinations in which the meaning is predictable, but the specific preposition that is required is less predictable and must be learned together with the verb (for example, *depend on, look at, listen to, approve of*). There are also phrasal-prepositional verbs, which are verb + adverbial particle + preposition sequences (for example, *put up with, look forward to, give up on, get away with*).

EXERCISE 60.2

Each of the following sentences contains a two-word verb. In some sentences, the verb is used correctly; in others, it is used incorrectly. Identify each two-word verb, indicate whether it is a phrasal or prepositional verb, and rewrite any incorrect sentences correctly.

1. Soon after I was hired for my last job, I learned that the company might lay off me.

2. I was counting on the job to pay my way through school, so I was upset.

3. I decided to pick up a newspaper and see what other jobs were available.

4. As I looked the newspaper at, I was surprised to see that I was qualified for a job that paid much better than mine.

5. I gave my old job up and took the new one, which made attending school much easier.

bedfordstmartins.com/everydaywriter
Exercise Central > For Multilingual Writers

Writing in the Disciplines

Don't underestimate your readers'
intelligence, but don't overestimate their
knowledge of a particular field.

— JULIE ANN MILLER

Writing in the Disciplines

61 Academic Work in Any Discipline *623*
- **a** Reading and writing for every discipline *623*
- **b** Academic assignments and expectations *624*
- **c** Specialized vocabulary *625*
- **d** Disciplinary style *626*
- **e** Use of evidence *627*
- **f** Conventional patterns and formats *628*
- **g** Ethical issues *628*
- **h** Collaboration and communication *629*

62 Writing for the Humanities *630*
- **a** Reading texts in the humanities *630*
- **b** Writing texts in the humanities *632*
- **c** A STUDENT'S CLOSE READING OF POETRY *633*

63 Writing for the Social Sciences *639*
- **a** Reading texts in the social sciences *639*
- **b** Writing texts in the social sciences *640*
- **c** AN EXCERPT FROM A STUDENT RESEARCH ESSAY IN THE SOCIAL SCIENCES *642*

64 Writing for the Natural and Applied Sciences *647*
- **a** Reading texts in the natural and applied sciences *647*
- **b** Writing texts in the natural and applied sciences *648*
- **c** AN EXCERPT FROM A STUDENT CHEMISTRY LAB REPORT *650*

65 Writing for Business *655*
- **a** Reading texts for business *655*
- **b** Writing texts for business *655*
- MEMO *657*
- LETTER OF APPLICATION *659*
- RÉSUMÉ *662*
- SCANNABLE RÉSUMÉ *663*

For visual analysis Look carefully at the illustration on the front of this tab. What do you think this image suggests about what it means to write in more than one discipline?

Academic Work in Any Discipline **61**

A recent survey confirmed that good writing plays an important role in almost every profession. One MBA wrote, "Those who advance quickly in my company are those who write and speak well — it's as simple as that." But while writing is always a valuable skill, writing well means different things in different disciplines. As you prepare written assignments for various courses, then, you will need to become familiar with the expectations, vocabularies, styles, methods of proof, and conventional formats used in each field.

61a Reading and writing for every discipline

Writing is central to learning regardless of the discipline. So whether you are explaining the results of a telephone survey you conducted for a psychology class, preparing a lab report for chemistry, conducting a case study for anthropology, or working on a proposal for material sciences and engineering, writing helps you get the job done.

One good way to learn to write well in a discipline is to read the texts others write. So read a lot, and pay attention to the texts you are reading. To get started, choose an article in an important journal in the field you plan to major in and then answer the following questions:

- How does a journal article in this discipline begin?
- How is the article organized? Does it have specific sections with subheads?
- What sources are cited, and how are they used — as backup support, as counter-examples, or as an argument to refute?
- How does the article conclude?
- What audience does the text seem to address? Is it a narrow technical or disciplinary audience, or is it aimed at a broader reading public? Is it addressed to readers of a specific journal? Is it published in print or online?

Finally, make sure you know whether the articles you are reading are from juried or nonjuried journals (16a). Juried journals use panels of expert readers to analyze proposed articles, so articles in juried journals have been recommended for publication by experts in the field. Nonjuried journals can also offer valuable information, but they may bear the stamp of the editor's biases more strongly than a juried journal would. To find out whether a journal is juried or nonjuried, check the submissions guidelines for information about whether submitted articles are sent to reviewers before publication.

For additional guidelines on reading critically, see Chapter 12.

61b Academic assignments and expectations

When you receive an assignment, your first job is to be sure you understand what that assignment is asking you to do. Some assignments may be as vague as "Write a five-page essay on one aspect of the Civil War" or "Write an analysis of the group dynamics at play in your

---

AT A GLANCE

Analyzing an Assignment

- **What is the purpose of the assignment?** Are you expected to join a discussion, demonstrate your mastery of the topic in writing, or something else?

- **Who is the audience?** The instructor will be one audience, but are there others? If so, who are they?

- **What does the assignment ask of you?** Look for key terms such as *summarize, explain, evaluate, interpret, illustrate,* and *define.*

- **Do you need clarification of any terms?** If so, ask your instructor.

- **What do you need to know or find out to complete the assignment?** You may need to do background reading, develop a procedure for analyzing or categorizing information, or carry out some other kind of preparation.

- **What does the instructor expect in a written response?** How will you use sources? What kinds of sources should you use? How should you organize and develop the assignment? What is the expected format and length?

- **Can you find a model of an effective response to a similar assignment?**

- **What do other students think the assignment requires?** Talking over an assignment with classmates is one good way to test your understanding.

recent collaborative project for this course" (see 63c for one student's response to the latter assignment). Others may be fairly specific: "Collect, summarize, and interpret data drawn from a sample of letters to the editor published in two newspapers, one in a small rural community and one in an urban community, over a period of three months." Whatever the assignment, use the questions in the box on p. 624 (and the information in Chapter 5) to analyze it.

EXERCISE 61.1

Analyze the following assignment from a communications course using the questions in the At a Glance box on p. 624.

Assignment: Distribute a questionnaire to twenty people (ten male, ten female) asking these four questions: (1) What do you expect to say and do when you meet a stranger? (2) What don't you expect to say and do when you meet a stranger? (3) What do you expect to say and do when you meet a very close friend? (4) What don't you expect to say and do when you meet a very close friend?

When you have collected your twenty questionnaires, read them over and answer the following questions:

- What, if any, descriptions were common to all respondents' answers?
- How do male and female responses compare?
- What similarities and differences did you find between the responses to the stranger and to the very close friend?
- What factors (environment, time, status, gender, and so on) do you think had an impact on these responses?

Discuss your findings, using concepts and theories explained in your text.

61c Specialized vocabulary

Entering into an academic discipline or a profession is like going to a party where you don't know anyone. At first you feel like an outsider, and you may not understand much of what you hear or see. Before you enter the conversation, you have to listen and observe carefully. Eventually, however, you will be able to join in—and if you stay long enough, participating in the conversation becomes easy and natural.

To learn the routines, practices, and ways of knowing in a new field, you must also make an effort to enter into the conversation. A good way to get started is to study the vocabulary of the field you are most interested in.

Highlight the key terms in your reading or notes to learn how much specialized or technical vocabulary you will be expected to know. If you find only a small amount of specialized vocabulary, try to master the new terms quickly by reading your textbook carefully, looking up key words or phrases, and asking questions. If you find a great deal of specialized vocabulary, however, you may want to familiarize yourself with it methodically. Any of the following procedures may help:

- Keep a log of unfamiliar words used in context. Check definitions in your textbook's glossary or index, or consult a specialized dictionary.

- See if your textbook has a glossary of terms (see Chapter 24) or sets off definitions. Study pertinent sections to master the terms.

- Work with key concepts. Even if they are not yet entirely clear to you, using them will help you understand them. For example, in a statistics class, try to work out (in words) how to do an analysis of *covariance*, step by step, even if you are not sure of the precise definition of the term. Or try to plot the narrative progression in a story even if you are still not entirely sure of the definition of *narrative progression*.

- Take special note of the ways technical language or disciplinary vocabulary is used in online information related to a particular field.

61d Disciplinary style

Another important way to learn about a discipline is to identify its stylistic features. Study pieces of writing in the field with the following in mind:

- *Overall tone.* How would you describe it? (See 5f.)

- *Title.* Are titles generally descriptive ("Findings from a Double-Blind Study of the Effect of Antioxidants"), persuasive ("Antioxidants Proven Effective"), or something else? How does the title shape your expectations?

- *Stance.* To what extent do writers in the field strive for distance and objectivity? What strategies help them to achieve this stance? (See 5d.)

- *Sentence length.* Are sentences long and complex? Simple and direct?

- *Voice.* Are verbs generally active or passive? Why? (See 32g.)

- *Person.* Do writers use the first-person *I* or third-person terms such as *the investigator*? What is the effect of this choice? (See the box on p. 627.)

- *Visuals.* Do writers typically use elements such as graphs, tables, maps, or photographs? How are visuals integrated into the text?

TALKING THE TALK

The First Person

"Is it true that I should never use *I* in college writing?" In much writing in college, using the first-person *I* is perfectly acceptable to most instructors. As always, think about the context — if your own experience is relevant to the topic, you are better off saying *I* than trying too hard not to. But don't overdo it, especially if the writing isn't just autobiographical. And check with your instructor if you aren't sure: in certain academic disciplines, using *I* may be seen as inappropriate.

What role, if any, do headings and other formatting elements play in the writing? (See Chapter 9.)

- *Documentation style.* Do writers use MLA, APA, *Chicago*, or CSE style? (See Chapters 49–55.)

Of course, writings within a single discipline may have different purposes and different styles. A chemist may write a grant proposal, a lab notebook, a literature review, a research report, and a lab report, each with a different purpose and style.

61e Use of evidence

As you grow familiar with an area of study, you will develop a sense of what it takes to prove a point in that field. You can speed up this process, however, by investigating and questioning. The following questions will help you think about the use of evidence in materials you read:

- How do writers in the field use precedent and authority? What or who counts as an authority in this field? How are the credentials of an authority established? (See 14e.)

- What kinds of quantitative data (countable or measurable items) are used, and for what purposes? How are the data gathered and presented?

- How are qualitative data (systematically observed items) used?

- How are statistics used and presented? Are tables, charts, graphs, or other visuals important, and why?

- How is logical reasoning used? How are definition, cause and effect, analogy, and example used?

- How does the field use primary materials — the firsthand sources of information — and secondary sources that are reported by others? (See 16a.) How is each type of source presented?

- What kinds of textual evidence are cited?
- How are quotations and other references to sources used and integrated into the text? (See Chapter 18.)

Read a few journals associated with your prospective major or a discipline of particular interest to you, using the preceding questions to study the use of evidence in that discipline. If you are keeping a writing log, make an entry summarizing what you have learned.

61f Conventional patterns and formats

To produce effective writing in a discipline, you need to know the field's generally accepted formats for organizing and presenting evidence. Although these formats can vary widely from discipline to discipline and even from instructor to instructor, common patterns do emerge. A typical laboratory report, for instance, follows a fairly standard organizational framework and usually has a certain look (see 64c for an example). A case study in sociology or education or anthropology likewise follows a typical organizational plan. Ask your instructor to recommend good examples of the kind of writing you will do in the course; then analyze these examples in terms of format, design, and organization. You might also look at major scholarly journals in the field to see what types of formats seem most common and how each is organized.

61g Ethical issues

Writers in all disciplines face ethical questions. Those who plan and carry out research on living people, for example, must be careful to avoid harming their subjects. Researchers in all fields must be scrupulous in presenting data to make sure that others can replicate research and test claims. And although writers in any discipline should take into consideration their own interests, those of their collaborators, and those of their employers, they must also responsibly safeguard the interests of the general public.

Fortunately, a growing number of disciplines have adopted guidelines for ethics. The American Psychological Association has been a pioneer in this area, and many other professional organizations and companies have their own codes or standards of ethics. These guidelines can help you make decisions about day-to-day writing. Even so, you will no doubt encounter situations where the right or ethical decision is murky at best. In such situations, consult your own conscience first and then talk your choices over with colleagues you respect before coming to a decision on how to proceed.

61h Collaboration and communication

In contemporary academic and business environments, working with others is a highly valued skill. Such collaboration happens when classmates divide research and writing duties to create a multimedia presentation, when peer reviewers share advice on a draft, or when colleagues in an office offer their views on appropriate revisions for a company-wide document.

Because people all over the world now have the ability to research, study, write, and work together, you must be able to communicate effectively within and across cultures. Conventions for academic writing (or for forms of online communication) can vary from culture to culture, from discipline to discipline, and from one form of English to another. What is considered polite in one culture may seem rude in another, so those who communicate globally must take care to avoid giving offense—or taking it where none was intended. (For more information on writing across cultures, see Chapter 20.)

EXERCISE 61.3: THINKING CRITICALLY

Reading with an Eye for Disciplinary Discourse

The following abstract introduces an article titled "Development of the Appearance-Reality Distinction." This article appeared in *Cognitive Psychology*, a specialized academic journal for researchers in the subfield of psychology that focuses on human cognition. Read this abstract carefully to see what you can infer about the discourse of cognitive psychology — about its characteristic vocabulary, style, use of evidence, and so on.

> Young children can express conceptual difficulties with the appearance-reality distinction in two different ways: (1) by incorrectly reporting appearance when asked to report reality ("phenomenism"); (2) by incorrectly reporting reality when asked to report appearance ("intellectual realism"). Although both phenomenism errors and intellectual realism errors have been observed in previous studies of young children's cognition, the two have not been seen as conceptually related and only the former errors have been taken as a symptom of difficulties with the appearance-reality distinction. Three experiments investigated 3- to 5-year-old children's ability to distinguish between and correctly identify real versus apparent object properties (color, size, and shape), object identities, object presence-absence, and action identities. Even the 3-year-olds appeared to have some ability to make correct appearance-reality discriminations and this ability increased with age. Errors were frequent, however, and almost all children who erred made both kinds. Phenomenism errors predominated on tasks where

the appearance versus reality of the three object properties was in question; intellectual realism errors predominated on the other three types of tasks. Possible reasons for this curious error pattern were advanced. It was also suggested that young children's problems with the appearance-reality distinction may be partly due to a specific metacognitive limitation, namely, a difficulty in analyzing the nature and source of their own mental representations.

— JOHN H. FLAVELL, ELEANOR R. FLAVELL, AND FRANCES L. GREEN,
Cognitive Psychology

Thinking about Your Own Writing in a Discipline

Choose a piece of writing you have produced for a class in a particular discipline — a blog or other posting, a laboratory report, a review of the literature, or any other written assignment. Examine your writing closely for its use of that discipline's vocabulary, style, methods of proof, and conventional formats. How comfortable are you writing a piece of this kind? In what ways are you using the conventions of the discipline easily and well? What conventions give you difficulty, and why? You might talk to an instructor in this field about the conventions and requirements for writing in the discipline. Make notes about what you learn about being a better writer in the field.

Writing for the Humanities

Disciplines in the humanities are concerned with what it means to be human: historians reconstruct the past; literary critics analyze and interpret texts portraying the human condition; philosophers raise questions about truth, knowledge, beauty, and justice; scholars of languages learn to inhabit other cultures. In these and other ways, those in the humanities strive to explore, interpret, and reconstruct the human experience.

62a Reading texts in the humanities

The interpretation of texts is central to humanities disciplines. A reader in the humanities needs the tools to analyze a text — whether a primary or secondary source, ancient or modern, literary or historical, verbal or visual — and carefully consider the arguments it makes.

To read critically in the humanities (2c and Chapter 12), you will need to pose questions and construct hypotheses as you read. You may ask, for instance, why a writer makes some points or develops some examples but omits others. Rather than finding meaning only in the surface information that texts or artifacts convey, use your own questions

---

AT A GLANCE

Guidelines for Reading Texts in the Humanities

1. ***Be clear about the purpose of the text.*** The two most common purposes for works in the humanities are to provide information and to argue for a particular interpretation. Pay attention to whether the text presents opinions or facts, to what is included and omitted, and to how facts are presented to the audience. (17c)

2. ***Get an overall impression.*** What does the work make you think about — and why? What is most remarkable or memorable? What confuses you?

3. ***Annotate the text.*** Be prepared to "talk back," ask questions, note emerging patterns or themes, and point out anything out of place or ineffective. (See Chapter 12.)

4. ***Look at the context.*** Consider the time and place represented in the work as well as when and where the writer lived. You may also consider social, political, or personal forces that may have affected the writer.

5. ***Think about the audience.*** Who are the readers or viewers the writer seems to address? Do they include you?

6. ***Pay attention to genre.*** What category does the work fall into (graphic novel, diary, political cartoon, sermon, argumentative essay, Hollywood western)? What is noteworthy about the form? How does it conform to or subvert your expectations about the genre? (5f)

7. ***Note the point of view.*** Whose point of view is represented? How does it affect your response?

8. ***Notice the major themes.*** Are specific claims being advanced? How are these claims supported?

9. ***Understand the difference between primary and secondary sources.*** Primary sources provide firsthand knowledge, while secondary sources report on or analyze the research of others. (16a)

---

and hypotheses to create fuller meanings — to construct the significance of what you read.

To successfully engage texts, you must recognize that you are not a neutral observer, not an empty cup into which meaning is poured. If such were the case, writing would have exactly the same meanings for all of us, and reading would be a fairly boring affair. If you have ever gone to a movie with a friend and each come away with a completely different response, you already understand that a text never has just one meaning. Most humanities courses will expect you to exercise your interpretive powers; the following guidelines will help you build your strengths as a close reader of humanities texts.

62b Writing texts in the humanities

Strong writers in the humanities use the findings from their close examination of a text or artifact to develop an argument or to construct an analysis.

Assignments

Common assignments that make use of these skills of close reading, analysis, and argument include summaries, response pieces, position papers, critical analyses of primary and secondary sources, and research-based projects. A philosophy student, for example, might need to summarize an argument, critique a text's logic and effectiveness, or discuss a moral issue from a particular philosophical perspective. A literature assignment may ask a reader to look very closely at a particular text ("Examine the role of chocolate in Toni Morrison's *Tar Baby*") or to go well beyond a primary text ("Discuss the impact of agribusiness on modernist novels"). History students often write books or articles ("Write a critical review of Jane Addams's *Twenty Years at Hull-House,* paying special attention to the writer's purpose and goals and relating these to the larger settlement house movement in America") along with primary source analyses or research papers.

For papers in literature, modern languages, and philosophy, writers often use the documentation style of the Modern Language Association; see Chapters 49–52 for advice on using MLA style. For papers in history and other areas of the humanities, writers often use the documentation style of the University of Chicago Press; see Chapter 54 for advice on using *Chicago* style.

Analysis and critical stance

To analyze a text, you need to develop a critical stance—the approach you will take to the work—that can help you develop a thesis or major claim (see 5d and 7b). To evaluate the text and present a critical response to it, you should look closely at the text itself, including its style; at the context in which it was produced; and at the audience the text aims to reach, which may or may not include yourself.

A close look at the text itself includes considering its genre, form, point of view, and themes, and looking at the stylistic features, such as word choice, use of imagery, visuals, and design. Considering context means asking why the text was created—thinking about the original (and current) context and about how attitudes and ideas of its era may have influenced it. Considering audience means thinking about who the intended audience might be, and about how people outside this intended group might respond. Think about your personal response to the text as well. (See also Chapters 5, 12, and 13.)

Carrying out these steps should provide you with plenty of material to work with as you begin to shape a critical thesis and write your analysis. You can begin by grounding your analysis in one or more important questions you have about the work.

Writing a literary analysis

When you analyze or interpret a literary work, think of your thesis as answering a question about some aspect of the work. The guiding question you bring to the literary work will help you decide on a critical stance toward the work. For example, a student writing about Shakespeare's *Macbeth* might find her curiosity piqued by the many comic moments that appear in this tragedy. She could build on her curiosity by turning the question of why Shakespeare uses so much comedy in *Macbeth* into the following thesis statement, which proposes an answer to the question: "The many unexpected comic moments in *Macbeth* emphasize how disordered the world becomes for murderers like Macbeth and his wife."

 bedfordstmartins.com/everydaywriter
Writing about Literature

EXERCISE 62.1: THINKING CRITICALLY

Choose at least two projects or assignments you have written for different disciplines in the humanities — say, history and film. Reread these papers with an eye to their similarities. What features do they have in common? Do they use similar methods of analysis and value similar kinds of evidence, for instance? In what ways do they differ? Based on your analysis, what conclusions can you draw about these two disciplines?

62c A student's close reading of poetry

The following paper, a close reading of two poems by E. E. Cummings, was written by Bonnie Sillay, a student at the University of Georgia. This essay follows MLA style (see Chapters 49–52). Bonnie is creating her own interpretation, so the only works she cites are the poems she analyzes. Note that this essay has been reproduced in a narrow format to allow for annotation. (For sample research papers in MLA style, see 14k and Chapter 52.)

Student Writer

Bonnie Sillay

 bedfordstmartins.com/everydaywriter
Student Writing

¹/₂″

Sillay 1

1″

Bonnie Sillay

Name, instructor, course number, and date on left margin, double-spaced

Instructor Angela Mitchell

English 1102

December 4, 2011

Title centered

"Life's Not a Paragraph"

Present tense used to discuss poetry

Throughout his poetry, E. E. Cummings leads readers deep into a thicket of scrambled words, missing punctuation, and unconventional structure. Within Cummings's poetic bramble, ambiguity leads the reader through what seems at first a confusing and winding maze. However, this confusion actually transforms into a path that leads the reader to the center of the thicket where Cummings's message lies: readers should not allow their experience to be limited by reason and rationality. In order to communicate his belief that emotional experience should triumph over reason,

Foreshadows discussion of work to come

Cummings employs odd juxtapositions, outlandish metaphors, and inversions of traditional grammatical structures that reveal the illogic of reason. Indeed, by breaking down such formal

Introductory paragraph ends with thesis statement

boundaries, Cummings's poems "since feeling is first" and "as freedom is a breakfastfood" suggest that emotion, which provides the compositional fabric for our experience of life, should never be defined or controlled.

In "since feeling is first," Cummings urges his reader to reject attempts to control emotion, using English grammar as one example of the restrictive conventions present in society. Stating that "since feeling is first / who pays any attention / to the syntax

Quotation cited parenthetically

of things" (lines 1-3), Cummings suggests that emotion should not be forced to fit into some preconceived framework or mold. He carries this message throughout the poem by juxtaposing images of the abstract and the concrete—images of emotion and of English grammar. Cummings's word choice enhances his intentionally

Annotations indicate effective choices or MLA-style formatting.

strange juxtapositions, with the poet using grammatical terms that suggest regulation or confinement. For example, in the line "And death i think is no parenthesis" (16), Cummings uses the idea that parentheses confine the words they surround in order to warn the reader not to let death confine life or emotions.

The structure of the poem also rejects traditional conventions. Instead of the final stanzas making the main point, Cummings opens his poem with his primary message, that "feeling is first" (1). Again, Cummings shows that emotion rejects order and structure. How can emotion be bottled in sentences and interrupted by commas, colons, and spaces? To Cummings, emotion is a never-ending run-on sentence that should not be diagramed or dissected.

In the third stanza of "since feeling is first," Cummings states his point outright, noting "my blood approves, / and kisses are a better fate / than wisdom" (7-9). Here, Cummings argues for reveling in the feeling during a fleeting moment such as a kiss. He continues, "the best gesture of my brain is less than / your eyelids' flutter" (11-12). Cummings wants the reader to focus on a pure emotive response (the flutter of an eyelash)—on the emotional, not the logical—on the meanings of words instead of punctuation and grammar.

Cummings's use of words such as *kisses* and *blood* (8, 7) adds to the focus on the emotional. The ideas behind these words are difficult to confine or restrict to a single definition: kisses mean different things to different people, blood flows through the body freely and continually. The words are not expansive or free enough to encompass all that they suggest. Cummings ultimately paints language as more restrictive than the flowing, powerful force of emotion.

Paper header on each page includes last name and page number

Transition sentence connects the previous paragraph to this one

Quotation introduced effectively

Writer uses a metaphor that captures the spirit of Cummings's point

Quotation integrated into writer's sentence

Paragraph reiterates Cummings's claim and sums up his argument

Clear and explicit transition from discussion of first poem

The poet's use of two grammatical terms in the last lines, "for life's not a paragraph / And death i think is no parenthesis," warns against attempts to format lives and feelings into conventional and rule-bound segments (15-16). Attempts to control, rather than feel, are rejected throughout "since feeling is first." Emotion should be limitless, free from any restrictions or rules.

While "since feeling is first" argues that emotions should not be controlled, ordered, or analyzed, "as freedom is a breakfastfood" suggests the difficulty of defining emotion. In this poem, Cummings uses deliberately far-fetched metaphors such as "freedom is a breakfastfood" and "time is a tree" (1, 26). These metaphors seem arbitrary: Cummings is not attempting to make profound statements on time or freedom. Instead, he suggests that freedom and time are subjective, and attempts at narrow definition are ridiculous. Inversions of nature, such as "robins never welcome spring" and "water most encourage flame" (16, 7), underscore emotion's ability to defy reason. These inversions suggest the arbitrariness of what "since feeling is first" calls "the syntax of things" (3).

Although most of "as freedom is a breakfastfood" defies logic, Cummings shifts the tone at the end to deliver one last metaphor: "but love is the sky" (27). The word *but* separates this definition from the rest of the poem and subtly implies that, unlike the metaphors that have come before it, "love is the sky" is an accurate comparison. In order to reach this final conclusion, however, Cummings has taken his readers on a long and often ambiguous journey.

Nevertheless, the confusion has been deliberate. Cummings wants his readers to follow him through the winding path through the thicket because he believes the path of the straight and narrow limits the possibilities of experience. Through the unconventionality of his poetic structures, Cummings urges his readers to question order and tradition. He wants his readers to realize that reason and rationality are always secondary to emotion and that emotional experience is a free-flowing force that should not be constrained. Cummings's poetry suggests that in order to get at the true essence of something, one must look past the commonsensical definition and not be limited by "the syntax of things."

Writer returns to the image of the thicket from the introduction to create a closing that resonates with the opening

Works Cited

Cummings, E. E. "as freedom is a breakfastfood." *E. E. Cummings: Complete Poems 1904-1962*. Ed. George J. Firmage. New York: Liveright, 1991. 511. Print.

---. "since feeling is first." *E. E. Cummings: Complete Poems 1904-1962*. Ed. George J. Firmage. New York: Liveright, 1991. 291. Print.

Second work by same author uses three hyphens in place of name

Writing for the Social Sciences **63**

When do most workers begin to save toward retirement? What role do television ads play in a voter's decision-making process? How do children learn to read? The social sciences—psychology, anthropology, political science, speech, communication, sociology, economics, and education—try to answer such questions. The social sciences share with the humanities an interest in what it means to be human, and they share with the natural and applied sciences the goal of engaging in systematic, observable study. All the social sciences aim to identify, understand, and explain patterns of human behavior.

63a Reading texts in the social sciences

Strong readers in the social sciences—as in any subject—ask questions, analyze, and interpret as they read, whether they are reading an academic paper that sets forth a theoretical premise or overall theory and defends it, a case study that describes a particular case and draws out inferences and implications from it, or a research report that presents the results of an investigation into an important question in the field. Most of what students read in the social sciences is trying to prove a point, and readers need to evaluate whether that point is supported.

The social sciences, like other disciplines, often use specialized vocabulary as shorthand for complex ideas that otherwise would take paragraphs to explain.

Qualitative and quantitative studies

Different texts in the social and natural sciences may call for different methods and strategies. Texts that report the results of *quantitative* studies collect data represented with numerical measurements drawn from surveys, polls, experiments, and tests. For example, a study of voting patterns in southern states might rely on quantitative data such as statistics. Texts that report the results of *qualitative* studies rely on non-numerical methods such as interviews and observations to reveal social patterns. A study of the way children in one kindergarten class develop rules of play, for instance, would draw on qualitative data—observations of social interaction, interviews with students and teachers, and so on. Of course, some work in the social and behavioral sciences combines quantitative and qualitative data and methods:

an educational report might begin with statistical data related to a problem and then move to a qualitative case study to exemplify what the statistics reveal.

In the social sciences, both quantitative and qualitative researchers must determine what they are examining and measuring in order to get answers to research questions. A researcher who studies childhood aggression must first define and measure *aggression*. If the research is qualitative, a researcher may describe types of behavior that indicate aggression and then discuss observations of children and interviews with teachers and peers about those behaviors. A quantitative researcher, on the other hand, might design an experiment that notes how often children hit a punching bag or that asks children to rate their peers' aggression on a scale of one to ten.

It's important to recognize that both quantitative and qualitative studies have points of view, and that researchers' opinions influence everything from the hypothesis and the design of the research study to the interpretation of findings. Readers must consider whether the researchers' views are sensible and solidly supported by evidence, and they must pay close attention to the kind of data the writer is using and what those data can—and cannot—prove. For example, if researchers of childhood aggression define *aggression* in a way that readers find unpersuasive, or if they observe behaviors that readers consider playful rather than aggressive, then the readers will likely not accept their interpretation of the findings.

Conventional formats

Make use of conventional disciplinary formats to help guide your reading in the social sciences. Many such texts conform to the format and documentation style of the American Psychological Association (APA). In addition, articles often include standard features—an abstract that gives an overview of the findings, followed by the introduction, review of literature, methods, results, discussion, and references. Readers who become familiar with such a format can easily find the information they need. (For more on APA style, see Chapter 53.)

63b Writing texts in the social sciences

Perhaps because the social sciences share concerns with both the humanities and the sciences, the forms of writing within the social sciences are particularly varied, including summaries, abstracts, literature reviews, reaction pieces, position papers, radio scripts, briefing notes, book reviews, briefs, research proposals, research papers, quantitative research reports, case studies, ethnographic analyses, and meta-analyses. Such an array of writing assignments could seem overwhelming, but in fact these assignments can be organized under five main categories:

- *Writing that encourages student learning* — reaction pieces, position papers
- *Writing that demonstrates student learning* — summaries, abstracts, research papers
- *Writing that reflects common on-the-job communication tasks undertaken by members of a discipline* — radio scripts, briefing notes, informational reports
- *Writing that requires students to analyze and evaluate the writings of others* — literature reviews, book reviews, briefs
- *Writing that asks students to replicate the work of others or to engage in original research* — quantitative research reports, case studies, ethnographic analyses

Many forms of writing in the social sciences call either explicitly or implicitly for argument (see Chapter 13). If you write an essay reporting on the results of a survey you developed about attitudes toward physician-assisted suicide among students on your campus, you will make an explicit argument about the significance of your data. But even in other forms of writing, such as summaries and book reports, you will implicitly argue that your description and analysis provide a clear, thorough overview of the text(s) you have read.

The literature review

Students of the social sciences carry out literature reviews to find out the most current thinking about a topic, to learn what research has already been carried out on that topic, to evaluate the work that has been done, and to set any research they will do in context. The following guidelines are designed to help you explore and question sources, looking for flaws or gaps. Such a critical review could then lead to a discussion of how your own research will avoid such flaws and advance knowledge.

- What is your topic of interest? What is the dependent variable (the item or characteristic being studied)?
- What is already known about this topic? What characteristics does the topic or dependent variable have? How have other researchers measured the item or characteristic being studied? What other factors are involved, and how are they related to each other and to your topic or variable? What theories are used to explain the way things are now?

- How has research been done so far? Who or what has been studied? How have measurements been taken?
- Has there been change over time? What has caused any changes?
- What problems do you identify in the current research? What questions have not been answered yet? What conclusions have researchers drawn that might not be warranted?
- What gaps will your research fill? What new information or ideas does it contribute? What problems do you want to correct?

EXERCISE 63.1

Identify a literature review in a social-science field you are interested in (ask your instructor or a librarian for help in finding one), and read it carefully, noting how it addresses the questions on pp. 641–42. Bring your notes to class for discussion.

EXERCISE 63.2: THINKING CRITICALLY

Reading with an Eye for Writing in the Social Sciences

Choose two readings from a social-science discipline, and read them with an eye toward issues of style. Does the use of disciplinary terms and concepts seem appropriate? In what ways do the texts attempt to engage readers? If the texts are not clear and understandable, how might they be improved?

Thinking about Your Own Writing in the Social Sciences

Choose a text you like that you have written for a social-science discipline. Then examine your style in this paper to see how well you have engaged your readers. Note variation in sentence length and type (do you, for example, use any questions?), number of active and passive verbs, use of concrete examples and everyday language, and so on. How would you rate your writing as a social scientist?

63c An excerpt from a student research essay in the social sciences

An excerpt from an essay by Merlla McLaughlin appears on the following pages. It conforms to the APA guidelines described in Chapter 53. Note that this essay has been reproduced in a narrow format to allow for annotation.

Student Writer

Merlla McLaughlin

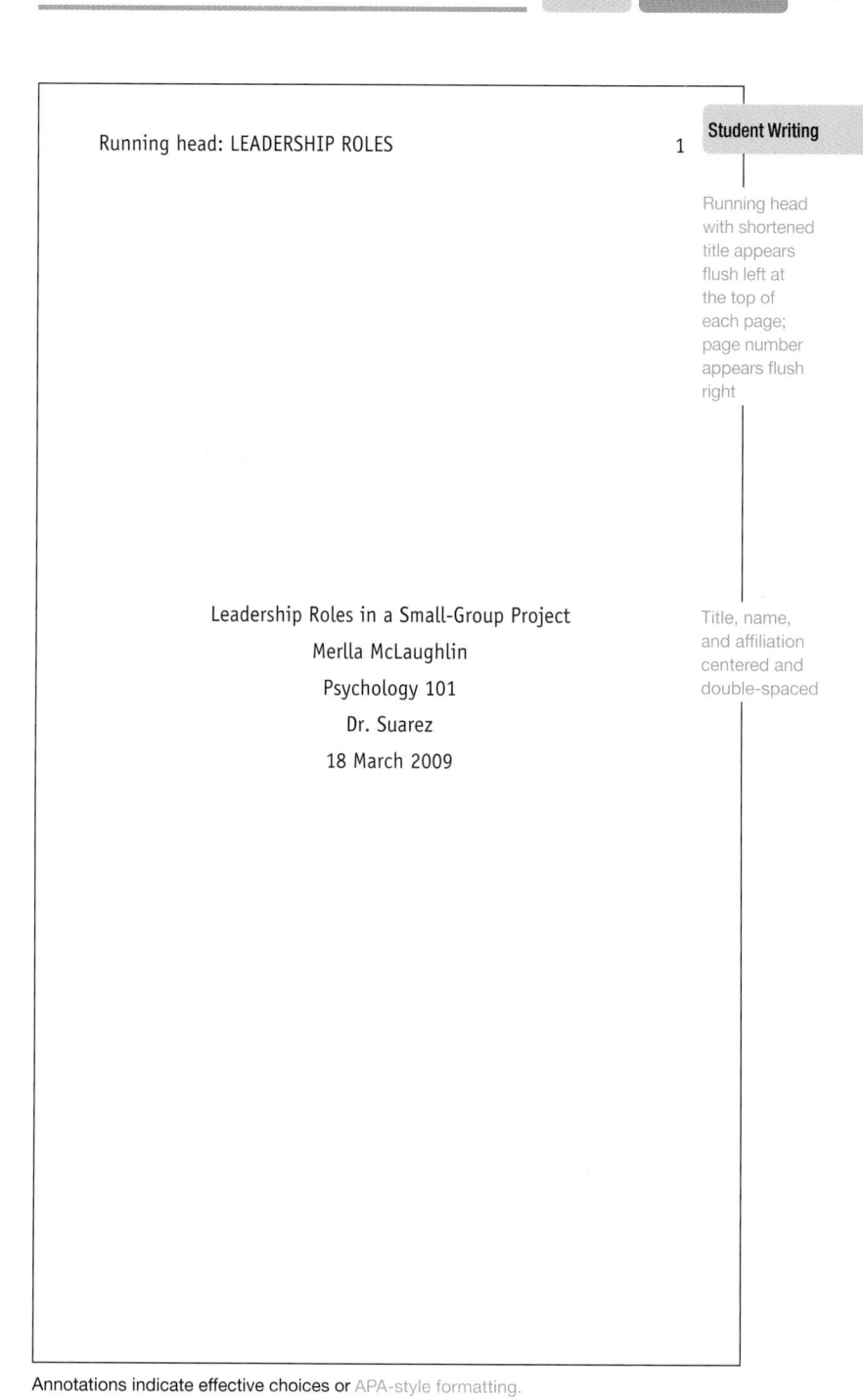

Student Writing

Running head with shortened title appears flush left at the top of each page; page number appears flush right

Leadership Roles in a Small-Group Project

Merlla McLaughlin

Psychology 101

Dr. Suarez

18 March 2009

Title, name, and affiliation centered and double-spaced

Annotations indicate effective choices or APA-style formatting.

LEADERSHIP ROLES   2

Heading
centered

No indentation

Study
described

Key points
of report
discussed

Double-spaced
text

                                    Abstract

Using the interpersonal communications research of J. K. Brilhart
and G. J. Galanes as well as that of W. Wilmot and J. Hocker, along
with T. Hartman's Personality Assessment, I observed and analyzed
the leadership roles and group dynamics of my project collaborators
in a communications course. Based on results of the Hartman
Personality Assessment, I predicted that a single leader would
emerge. However, complementary individual strengths and gender
differences encouraged a distributed leadership style, in which the
group experienced little confrontation. Conflict, because it was
handled positively, was crucial to the group's progress.

Leadership Roles in a Small-Group Project

Although classroom lectures provide students with volumes of information, many experiences can be understood only by living them. So it is with the workings of a small, task-focused group. What observations can I make after working with a group of peers on a class project? And what have I learned as a result?

Leadership Expectations and Emergence

The six members of this group were selected by the instructor; half were male and half were female. By performing the Hartman Personality Assessment (Hartman, 1998) in class, we learned that Hartman has associated key personality traits with the colors red, blue, white, and yellow (see Table 1). The assessment identified most of us as "Blues," concerned with intimacy and caring. Because of the bold qualities associated with "Reds," I expected that Nate, our only "Red" member, might become our leader. (Kaari, the only "White," seemed poised to become the peacekeeper.) However, after Nate missed the first two meetings, it seemed that Pat, who contributed often during our first three meetings, might emerge as leader. Pat has strong communications skills, a commanding presence, and displays sensitivity to others. I was surprised, then,

Table 1

Hartman's Key Personality Traits

Trait category	Color			
	Red	Blue	White	Yellow
Motive	Power	Intimacy	Peace	Fun
Strengths	Loyal to tasks	Loyal to people	Tolerant	Positive
Limitations	Arrogant	Self-righteous	Timid	Uncommitted

Note. Table is adapted from information found at The Hartman Personality Profile, by N. Hayden. Retrieved February 15, 2004, from http://students.cs.byu.edu/~nhayden/Code/index.php

(margin annotations) Full title, centered | Paragraphs indented | Questions indicate the focus of the essay | Headings help organize the report | APA-style parenthetical reference | Background information about team members' personality types | Chart displays information concisely | Chart referred to in preceding text | Source of table listed

LEADERSHIP ROLES   7

List starts on
new page

Book

Web site

Entries
alphabetized

First line of
entry flush left;
subsequent
lines indent

References

Brilhart, J. K., & Galanes, G. J. (1998). *Effective group discussion*
(9th ed.). Boston: McGraw-Hill.

Hartman, T. (1998). *The color code: A new way to see yourself, your
relationships, and your life*. New York: Scribner.

Hayden, N. (n.d.). *The Hartman Personality Profile*. Retrieved
February 15, 2009, from http://students.cs.byu.edu/
~nhayden/Code/index.php

Wilmot, W., & Hocker, J. (1998). *Interpersonal conflict* (5th ed.).
Boston: McGraw-Hill.

Writing for the Natural and Applied Sciences

64

Whether they are studying geological faults or developing a stronger support structure for suspension bridges, scientists and engineers in the natural and applied sciences want to understand how the physical and natural worlds work. Natural sciences such as biology, chemistry, and physics study the natural world and its phenomena; applied sciences such as nanotechnology and mechanical engineering apply knowledge from the natural sciences to practical problems. More than many other scholars, scientists and engineers are likely to leave the privacy of their office or lab to engage in fieldwork and experimentation. Whether done in the lab or the field, however, writing—from the first grant proposal to the final report or scientific paper—plays a key role in the natural and applied sciences.

64a Reading texts in the natural and applied sciences

Scientists and engineers work with evidence that can be observed, verified, and controlled. Though they cannot avoid interpretation, they strive for objectivity by using the scientific method—observing or studying phenomena, formulating a hypothesis about the phenomena, and testing that hypothesis through controlled experiments and observations. Scientists and engineers aim to generate precise, replicable data; they develop experiments to account for extraneous factors. In this careful, precise way, scientists and engineers identify, test, and write persuasively about theoretical and real-world problems.

Identifying argument

As you read in the sciences, try to become familiar with disciplinary terms, concepts, and formats as soon as possible, and practice reading—and listening—for detail. If you are reading a first-year biology textbook, you can draw upon general critical-reading strategies. In addition, charts, graphs, illustrations, models, and other visuals often play an important role in scientific writing, so your ability to read and comprehend these visual displays of knowledge is particularly important. (See Chapter 12.)

When you read a science or engineering textbook, you can assume that the information presented there is authoritative and as objective as possible. When you read specialized materials, however, recognize that although scholarly reports undergo significant peer review, they nevertheless represent arguments (see Chapter 13). The connection between facts and claims in the sciences, as in all subject areas, is created by the author rather than simply revealed by the data. So read both facts and claims with a questioning eye: Did the scientist choose the best method to test the hypothesis? Are there other reasonable interpretations of the experiment's results? Do other studies contradict the conclusions of this experiment? When you read specialized texts in the sciences with questions like these in mind, you are reading—and thinking—like a scientist. (For additional information on assessing a source's credibility, see 17c.)

Conventional formats

As you advance in your course work, you will need to develop reading strategies for increasingly specialized texts. Many scientific texts conform to the format and documentation style of the Council of Science Editors (CSE); for more on CSE style, see Chapter 55. (However, you should be prepared to follow an instructor's guidelines for citation and references if another style is used in your discipline or in a particular course.) In addition, articles often include standard features—an abstract that gives an overview of the findings, followed by an introduction, literature review, materials and methods, results, discussion, and references.

You might expect to read a journal article for a science or engineering course from start to finish, giving equal weight to each section. However, an experienced reader in sciences and engineering might skim an abstract to see if an article warrants further reading. If it does—and this judgment is based on the reader's own research interest—he or she might then read the introduction to understand the rationale for the experiment and then skip to the results. A reader with a specific interest in the methods will read that section with particular care.

EXERCISE 64.1

Choose a respected journal in a discipline in the natural or applied sciences that interests you. (Ask your instructor or a reference librarian if you need help identifying a journal.) Then read quickly through two articles, taking notes on the author's use of any headings and subheadings, specialized vocabulary, visuals, and evidence. Bring the results of your investigation to class for discussion.

64b Writing texts in the natural and applied sciences

Students in the sciences and engineering must be able to respond to a diverse range of writing and speaking tasks. Often, they must maintain lab or engineering notebooks that include careful records of experiments. They also write memos, papers, project proposals and reports, literature reviews, and progress reports; in addition, they may develop print and Web-based presentations for both technical and lay audiences (see 3c). Particularly common writing assignments in the sciences are the literature review, research proposal, and research report.

Scientists undertake *literature reviews* to keep up with and evaluate developments in their field. Literature reviews are an essential first step in any research effort, for they enable scientists to discover what research has already been completed and how they might build on earlier efforts. Successful literature reviews demonstrate a student's ability to identify relevant research on a topic and to summarize and in some instances evaluate that research.

For a student literature review, see 53d.

Most scientists spend a great deal of time writing research or *grant proposals* aimed at securing funds to support their research. Undergraduate writers often have an opportunity to make similar proposals—to an office of undergraduate research or to a science-based firm that supports student research, for instance. Funding agencies often have guidelines for preparing a proposal. Proposals for research funding generally include the following sections: title page, introduction, purpose(s) and significance of the study, methods, timeline, budget, and references. You may also need to submit an abstract.

For a student research proposal, see 55c.

Research reports, another common writing form in the sciences, may include both literature reviews and discussions of primary research, most often experiments. Like journal articles, research reports generally follow this form: title, author(s), abstract, introduction, literature review, materials and methods, results, discussion, and references. Many instructors ask students to write lab reports (64c), which are briefer versions of research reports and may not include a literature review.

Today, a great deal of scientific writing is collaborative. As students move from introductory to advanced courses and then to the workplace, they increasingly find themselves working as part of teams or groups. Indeed, in such areas as engineering, collaborative projects (6g) are often the norm.

Style in the natural and applied sciences

In general, use the present tense for most writing you do in the natural and applied sciences. Use the past tense, however, when you are describing research already carried out (by you or others) or published in the past (32e).

Writers in the sciences need to produce complex figures, tables, images, and models and use software designed to analyze data or run computer simulations. In addition, they need to present data carefully. If you create a graph, you should provide headings for columns, label axes with numbers or units, and identify data points. Caption figures and tables with a number and descriptive title. And avoid orphan data—data that you present in a figure or table but don't comment on in your text.

Finally, make sure that any writing you do is as clear, concise, and grammatically correct as possible to ensure that readers see you as capable and credible.

EXERCISE 64.2: THINKING CRITICALLY

Reading with an Eye for Writing in the Sciences

Identify one or more features of scientific texts, and consider their usefulness. Why, for instance, does an abstract precede the actual article? How do scientific nomenclatures, classification systems, and other features of scientific writing aid the work of scientists? Try to identify the functions that textual elements such as these play in the ongoing work of science. Finally, research the scientific method to see how it is served by the features of scientific writing discussed in this chapter.

Thinking about Your Own Writing in the Sciences

Choose a piece of writing you did for a natural or applied science class — a lab report, a research report, a proposal — and read it carefully. Note the format and headings you used, how you presented visual data, what kinds of evidence you used, and what citation system you used. Compare your piece of writing with a similar piece of writing published in a journal in the field. How well does your writing compare? What differences are most noticeable between your writing and that of the published piece?

64c An excerpt from a student chemistry lab report

The following piece of student writing is excerpted from a lab report on a chemistry experiment by Allyson Goldberg, a student at Yale University. Note that these sample pages have been reproduced in a narrow format to allow for annotation.

Student Writer

Allyson Goldberg

bedfordstmartins.com/everydaywriter
Student Writing

Chemistry 119L Laboratory Report
Evaluation of the Value of the Gas Constant R

Title page
includes
relevant
information
about lab

Allyson Goldberg

Date of Experiment: Monday, September 27, 2010

Introduction explains purpose of lab and gives overview of results

Introduction

The purpose of this investigation was to experimentally determine the value of the universal gas constant, R. To accomplish this goal, a measured sample of magnesium (Mg) was allowed to react with an excess of hydrochloric acid (HCl) at room temperature and pressure so that the precise amount and volume of the product hydrogen gas (H_2) could be determined and the value of R could be calculated using the ideal gas equation, $PV=nRT$.

Materials and methods section explains lab setup and procedure

Materials & Methods

Two samples of room temperature water, one about 250mL and the other about 400mL, were measured into a smaller and larger beaker respectively. 15.0mL of HCl was then transferred into a side arm flask that was connected to the top of a buret (clamped to a ringstand) through a 5/16" diameter flexible tube. (This "gas buret" was connected to an adjacent "open buret," clamped to the other side of the ringstand and left open to the atmosphere of the laboratory at its wide end, by a 1/4" diameter flexible tube. These two burets were adjusted on the ringstand so that they were vertically parallel and close together.) The HCl sample was transferred to the flask such that none came in contact with the inner surface of the neck of the flask. The flask was then allowed to rest, in an almost horizontal position, in the smaller beaker.

The open buret was adjusted on the ringstand such that its

Passive voice throughout typical of writing in natural sciences

20mL mark was horizontally aligned with the 35mL mark on the gas buret. Room temperature water was added to the open buret until the water level of the gas buret was at about 34.00mL.

A piece of magnesium ribbon was obtained, weighed on an analytical balance, and placed in the neck of the horizontal side arm flask. Next, a screw cap was used to cap the flask and form an airtight seal. This setup was then allowed to sit for 5 minutes in order to reach thermal equilibrium.

After 5 minutes, the open buret was adjusted so that the menisci on both burets were level with each other; the side arm flask was then tilted vertically to let the magnesium ribbon react with the HCl. After the brisk reaction, the flask was placed into the larger beaker and allowed to sit for another 5 minutes.

Next, the flask was placed back into the smaller beaker, and the open buret was adjusted on the ringstand such that its meniscus was level with that of the gas buret. After the system sat for an additional 30 minutes, the open buret was again adjusted so that the menisci on both burets were level.

This procedure was repeated two more times, with the exception that HCl was not again added to the side arm flask, as it was already present in enough excess for all reactions from the first trial.

Results and Calculations

Trial #	Lab Temp. (°C)	Lab Pressure (mbar)	Mass of Mg Ribbon Used (g)	Initial Buret Reading (mL)	Final Buret Reading (mL)
1	24.4	1013	0.0147	32.66	19.60
2	24.3	1013	0.0155	33.59	N/A*
3	25.0	1013	0.0153	34.35	19.80

*See note in Discussion section.

Results and calculations show measurements and calculations of final value of R

Goldberg 8

References

Ganapathi N. Chemistry 119L laboratory manual. New Haven (CT): Yale University Press; 2004.

Oxtoby DW, Gillis HP, Nachtrieb NH. Principles of modern chemistry. 5th ed. Farmington Hills (MI): Thompson Learning; 2002.

Writing for Business **65**

Written communication is essential in identifying and solving the complex problems of today's companies. To succeed in business, you need to know how to manage many kinds of writing—from negotiating an ever-increasing number of email messages to communicating effectively with readers from Manhattan, Montgomery, Mexico City, and Mumbai.

65a Reading texts for business

Readers in business face a dizzying array of demands. A team of businesspeople today has almost unlimited access to information and to people, such as economists and scientists, whose expertise can be of use in the business world. Somehow, the members of this team need to negotiate a huge stream of information and to evaluate that information.

To meet these demands, you can draw on general strategies for effective reading (see Chapter 12). One such strategy—keeping a clear purpose in mind when you read—is particularly important when you are engaged in work-related reading. Are you reading to solve a problem? to gather and synthesize information? to make a recommendation? Knowing why you are reading will increase your productivity. Time constraints and deadline pressures will also affect your decisions about what and how to read; the ability to identify important information quickly is a skill you will cultivate as a business reader.

65b Writing texts for business

Writing assignments in business classes serve two related functions. While their immediate goal is to help you master the theory and practice of business, these assignments also prepare you for the kinds of writing you will face in the world of work. For this reason, students in *every* discipline need to know how to write effective business memos, emails, letters, résumés, and reports.

Memo

Memos are a common form of print or electronic correspondence sent within and between organizations. Memos tend to be brief, internal documents, often dealing with only one subject.

AT A GLANCE

Guidelines for Writing Effective Memos

- Write the name of the recipient, your name, the subject, and the date on separate lines at the top.
- Begin with the most important information: depending on the memo's purpose, you may have to provide background information, define the task or problem, or clarify the memo's goal.
- Use your opening paragraph to focus on how the information you convey affects your readers.
- Focus each subsequent paragraph on one idea pertaining to the subject.
- Present information concisely and from the readers' perspective.
- Emphasize exactly what you want readers to do and when.
- Use attachments for detailed supporting information.
- For print memos, initial your memo next to your name.
- Adjust your style and tone to fit your audience.
- Attempt to build goodwill in your conclusion.

Following is a memo, written by two student writers, Michelle Abbott and Carina Abernathy, that presents an analysis and recommendation to help an employer make a decision.

Student Writer

Michelle Abbott

Student Writer

Carina Abernathy

 bedfordstmartins.com/everydaywriter
Student Writing

MEMO

❖ *Jenco* ❖

INTEROFFICE MEMORANDUM

TO: ROSA DONAHUE, SALES MANAGER

FROM: MICHELLE ABBOTT & CARINA ABERNATHY

SUBJECT: TAYLOR NURSERY BID

DATE: 1/30/2012

CC:

As you know, Taylor Nursery has requested bids on a 25,000-pound order of private-label fertilizer. Taylor Nursery is one of the largest distributors of our Fertikil product. The following is our analysis of Jenco's costs to fill this special order and a recommendation for the bidding price.

The total cost for manufacturing 25,000 pounds of the private-label brand for Taylor Nursery is $44,075. This cost includes direct material, direct labor, and variable manufacturing overhead. Although our current equipment and facilities provide adequate capacity for processing this special order, the job will involve an excess in labor hours. The overtime labor rate has been factored into our costs.

The absolute minimum price that Jenco could bid for this product without losing money is $44,075 (our cost). Applying our standard markup of 40% results in a price of $61,705. Thus, you could reasonably establish a price anywhere within that range.

In making the final assessment, we advise you to consider factors relevant to this decision. Taylor Nursery has stated that this is a one-time order. Therefore, the effort to free this special order will not bring long-term benefits.

Finally, Taylor Nursery has requested bids from several competitors. One rival, Eclipse Fertilizers, is submitting a bid of $60,000 on this order. Therefore, our recommendation is to slightly underbid Eclipse with a price of $58,000, representing a markup of approximately 32%.

Please let us know if we can be of further assistance in your decision on the Taylor Nursery bid.

Paragraphs not indented

Opening paragraph provides background and states purpose

Most important information emphasized

Double-spaced between paragraphs

Options presented

Relevant factors explained

Final recommendation

Closing builds goodwill by offering further help

Email

Business email can be formatted much like a print memo but is easier to create and store and faster to distribute. Remember, however, that email is essentially public and that employers have easy access to email written by employees. As always, it's best to use discretion and caution in email, especially on the job.

Letter

Despite the popularity of email, letter-writing remains an important skill. When you send a business or professional letter, you are writing either as an individual or as a representative of an organization. In either case, and regardless of your purpose, a business letter should follow certain conventions.

The letter of application or cover letter (p. 659) often accompanies a résumé. The purpose of a letter of application is to demonstrate how the experiences and skills you outline in your résumé have prepared you for a particular job; it is important to focus on how you can benefit the company, not how the company can help you. If you are responding to a particular advertisement, mention it in the opening paragraph. Finally, be sure to indicate how you can be reached for an interview.

The following application letter for a summer internship was written by Nastassia Lopez, a student at Stanford University. Note that the letter has been reproduced in a narrow format to allow for annotation.

Student Writer

Nastassia Lopez

 bedfordstmartins.com/everydaywriter
Student Writing

LETTER OF APPLICATION

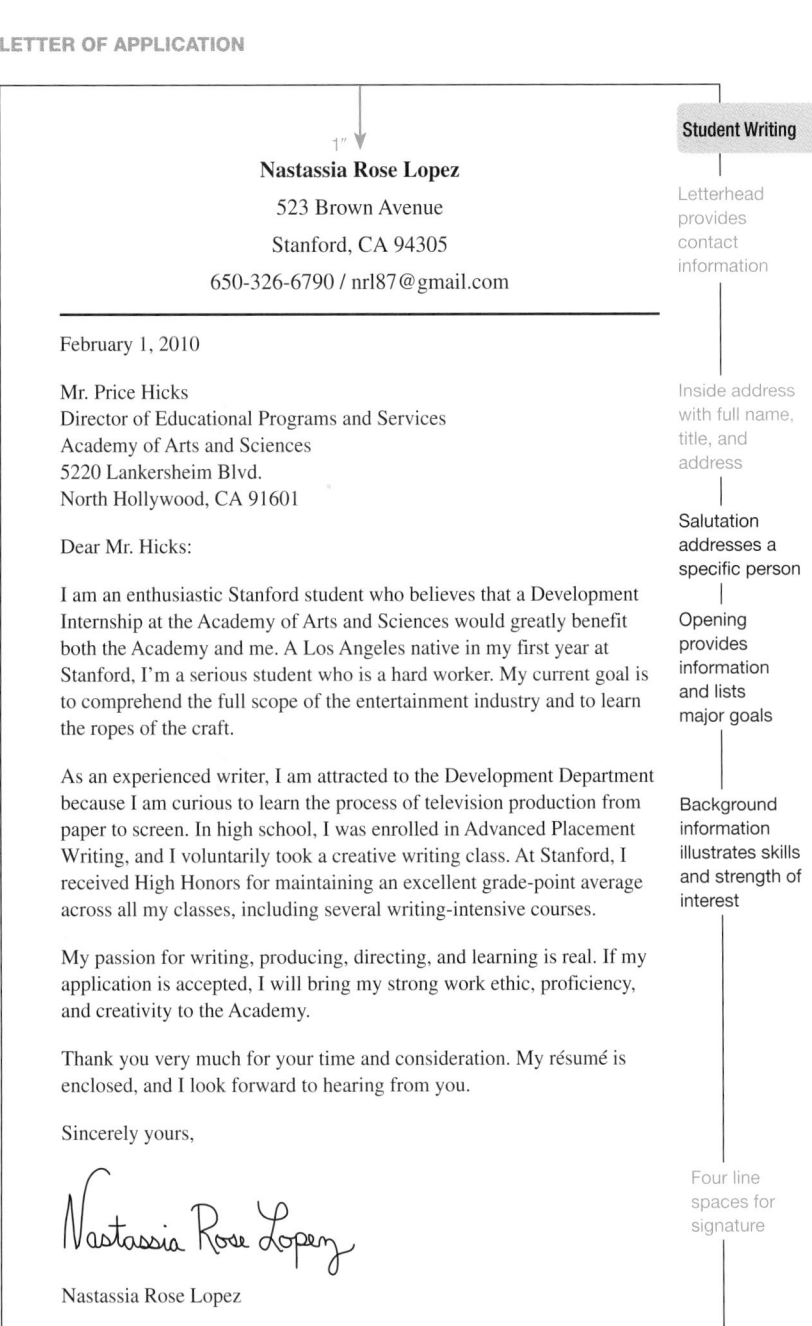

1"

Nastassia Rose Lopez

523 Brown Avenue

Stanford, CA 94305

650-326-6790 / nrl87@gmail.com

February 1, 2010

Mr. Price Hicks
Director of Educational Programs and Services
Academy of Arts and Sciences
5220 Lankersheim Blvd.
North Hollywood, CA 91601

Dear Mr. Hicks:

I am an enthusiastic Stanford student who believes that a Development Internship at the Academy of Arts and Sciences would greatly benefit both the Academy and me. A Los Angeles native in my first year at Stanford, I'm a serious student who is a hard worker. My current goal is to comprehend the full scope of the entertainment industry and to learn the ropes of the craft.

As an experienced writer, I am attracted to the Development Department because I am curious to learn the process of television production from paper to screen. In high school, I was enrolled in Advanced Placement Writing, and I voluntarily took a creative writing class. At Stanford, I received High Honors for maintaining an excellent grade-point average across all my classes, including several writing-intensive courses.

My passion for writing, producing, directing, and learning is real. If my application is accepted, I will bring my strong work ethic, proficiency, and creativity to the Academy.

Thank you very much for your time and consideration. My résumé is enclosed, and I look forward to hearing from you.

Sincerely yours,

Nastassia Rose Lopez

Nastassia Rose Lopez

Student Writing

Letterhead provides contact information

Inside address with full name, title, and address

Salutation addresses a specific person

Opening provides information and lists major goals

Background information illustrates skills and strength of interest

Four line spaces for signature

AT A GLANCE

Guidelines for Writing Effective Letters

- Use a conventional format. (See p. 659.)
- Whenever possible, write to a specific person (*Dear Tom Robinson* or *Dear Ms. Otuteye*) rather than to a general *Dear Sir or Madam*.
- Open cordially and be polite — even if you have a complaint.
- State the reason for your letter clearly. Include whatever details will help your reader see your point and respond.
- If appropriate, make clear what you hope your reader will do.
- Express appreciation for your reader's attention.
- Make it easy for your reader to respond by including contact information and, if appropriate, a self-addressed, stamped envelope.

Résumé

While a letter of application usually emphasizes specific parts of the résumé, telling how your background is suited to a particular job, a résumé summarizes your experience and qualifications and provides support for your letter. An effective résumé is brief, usually one or two pages.

Research shows that employers generally spend less than a minute reading a résumé. Remember that they are interested not in what they can do for you but what you can do for them. They expect a résumé to be formatted neatly, and your aim is to use clear headings and adequate spacing that will make it easy to read. Although you may be tempted to use colored paper or unusual type styles, avoid such temptations. A well-written résumé with a standard format and typeface is the best way to distinguish yourself.

Your résumé may be arranged chronologically (from most to least recent) or functionally (based on skills or expertise). Include the following information:

1. *Name, address, phone numbers, and email address.*
2. *Career objective(s).* List immediate or short-term goals and specific jobs for which you realistically qualify.
3. *Educational background.* Include degrees, diplomas, majors, and special programs or courses that pertain to your field of interest. List honors and scholarships and your grade-point average if it is high.
4. *Work experience.* Identify each job—whether a paying job, an internship, or military experience—with dates and names of organizations. Describe your duties by carefully selecting strong action verbs.
5. *Skills, personal interests, activities, awards, and honors.*

6. ***References.*** List two or three people who know your work well, first asking their permission. Give their titles, addresses, and phone or fax numbers. Or simply say that your references are available on request.

7. ***Keywords*** (for a scannable résumé). In general, nouns function as keywords for résumés that are scanned by search engines. Look for places where you can convert verbs (*performed laboratory tests*) to nouns (*laboratory technologist*). Place the most important keywords toward the beginning of the résumé.

Increasingly, job seekers are composing online résumés as hypertext screen documents, which make keywords more visible to search engines and thus tend to produce more hits. In addition, some businesses ask applicants to fill out résumé forms on company Web sites. In such cases, take special care to make sure that you have caught any error or typo before submitting the form.

The following pages show student Dennis Tyler's résumé in two formats, one in conventional print style, the other formatted for scanning.

Student Writer

Dennis Tyler Jr.

RÉSUMÉ

DENNIS TYLER JR.

CURRENT ADDRESS PERMANENT ADDRESS
P.O. Box 12345 506 Chanelle Court
Stanford, CA 94309 Baton Rouge, LA 70128
Phone: (650) 498-4731 Phone: (504) 246-9847
Email: dtyler@yahoo.com

CAREER OBJECTIVE Position on editorial staff of a major newspaper

EDUCATION

9/00–6/04 **Stanford University,** Stanford, CA
BA, ENGLISH AND AMERICAN STUDIES, June 2004
9/02–12/02 **Morehouse College,** Atlanta, GA
STANFORD STUDY EXCHANGE PROGRAM

EXPERIENCE

6/03–9/03 **Business Scholar Intern,** Finance, AOL Time Warner,
New York, NY
Responsible for analyzing data for strategic marketing
plans. Researched the mergers and acquisitions of
companies to which Time Inc. sells advertising space.

1/02–6/03 **Editor-in-Chief,** *Enigma* (a literary journal), Stanford
University, CA
Oversaw the entire process of *Enigma.* Edited numerous
creative works: short stories, poems, essays, and interviews.
Selected appropriate material for the journal. Responsible for
designing cover and for publicity to the greater community.

8/02–12/02 **Community Development Intern,** University Center
Development Corporation (UCDC), Atlanta, GA
Facilitated workshops and meetings on the importance of home
buying and neighborhood preservation. Created UCDC brochure
and assisted in the publication of the center's newsletter.

6/02–8/02 **News Editor,** *Stanford Daily,* Stanford University, CA
Responsible for editing stories and creating story ideas for
the newspaper. Assisted with the layout for the newspaper and
designs for the cover.

SKILLS AND HONORS

- Computer Skills: MS Word, Excel, PageMaker,
Microsoft Publisher; Internet research
- Language: Proficient in Spanish
- Trained in making presentations, conducting
research, acting, and singing
- Mellon Fellow, Gates Millennium Scholar, Public Service
Scholar, National Collegiate Scholar
- Black Community Service Arts Award, 2003–2004

REFERENCES Available upon request

SCANNABLE RÉSUMÉ

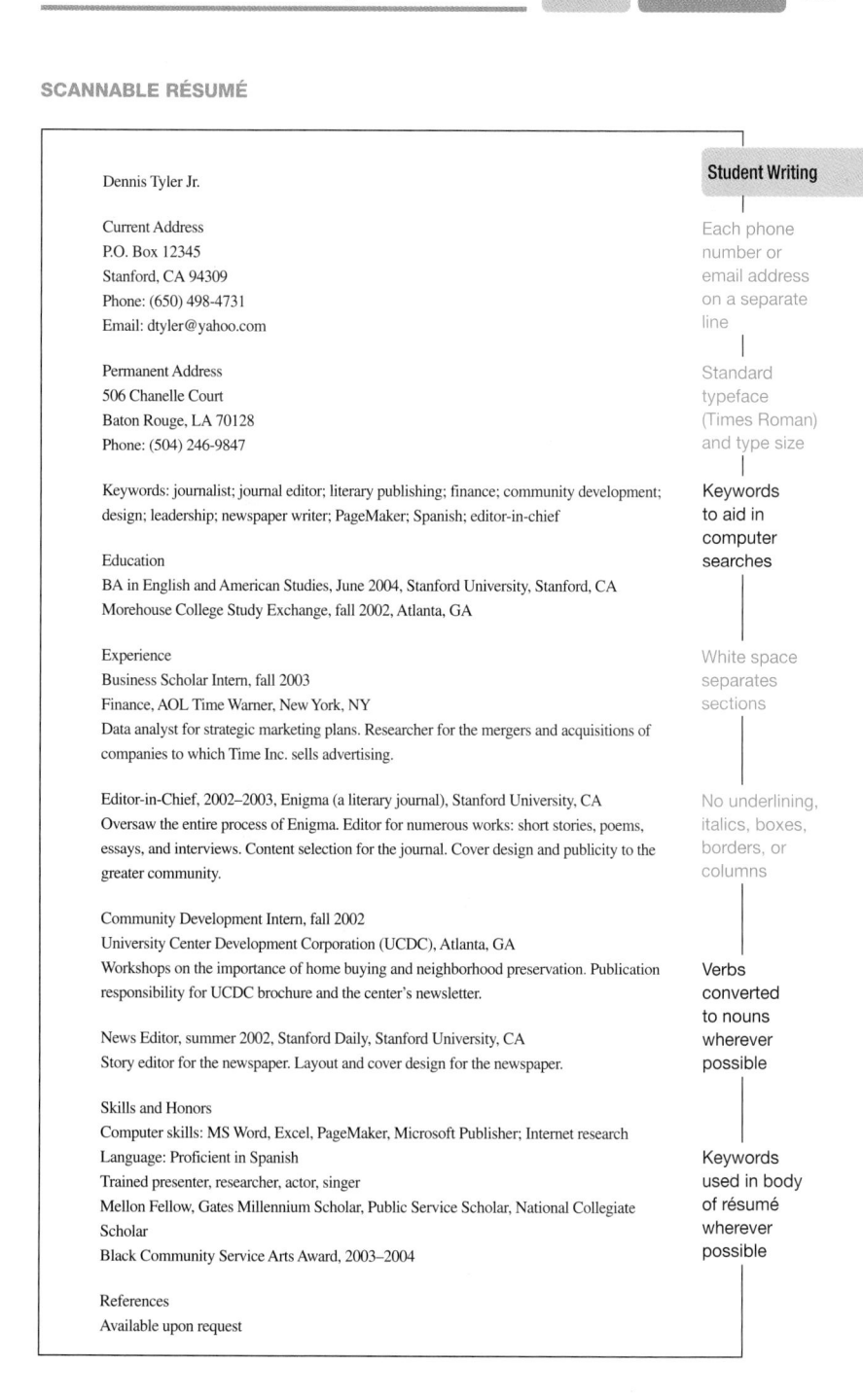

Dennis Tyler Jr.

Current Address
P.O. Box 12345
Stanford, CA 94309
Phone: (650) 498-4731
Email: dtyler@yahoo.com

Permanent Address
506 Chanelle Court
Baton Rouge, LA 70128
Phone: (504) 246-9847

Keywords: journalist; journal editor; literary publishing; finance; community development; design; leadership; newspaper writer; PageMaker; Spanish; editor-in-chief

Education
BA in English and American Studies, June 2004, Stanford University, Stanford, CA
Morehouse College Study Exchange, fall 2002, Atlanta, GA

Experience
Business Scholar Intern, fall 2003
Finance, AOL Time Warner, New York, NY
Data analyst for strategic marketing plans. Researcher for the mergers and acquisitions of companies to which Time Inc. sells advertising.

Editor-in-Chief, 2002–2003, Enigma (a literary journal), Stanford University, CA
Oversaw the entire process of Enigma. Editor for numerous works: short stories, poems, essays, and interviews. Content selection for the journal. Cover design and publicity to the greater community.

Community Development Intern, fall 2002
University Center Development Corporation (UCDC), Atlanta, GA
Workshops on the importance of home buying and neighborhood preservation. Publication responsibility for UCDC brochure and the center's newsletter.

News Editor, summer 2002, Stanford Daily, Stanford University, CA
Story editor for the newspaper. Layout and cover design for the newspaper.

Skills and Honors
Computer skills: MS Word, Excel, PageMaker, Microsoft Publisher; Internet research
Language: Proficient in Spanish
Trained presenter, researcher, actor, singer
Mellon Fellow, Gates Millennium Scholar, Public Service Scholar, National Collegiate Scholar
Black Community Service Arts Award, 2003–2004

References
Available upon request

Student Writing

Each phone number or email address on a separate line

Standard typeface (Times Roman) and type size

Keywords to aid in computer searches

White space separates sections

No underlining, italics, boxes, borders, or columns

Verbs converted to nouns wherever possible

Keywords used in body of résumé wherever possible

EXERCISE 65.1: THINKING CRITICALLY

Reading with an Eye for Writing in Business

Monitor your mail and email for a few days, saving everything that tries to sell a product, provide a service, or solicit information or money. Then go through these pieces of business writing and advertising, and choose the one you find most effective. What about the writing appeals to you or gets and holds your attention? What might lead you to buy the product, choose the service, or make a contribution? What might make the piece of writing even more effective? Bring the results of your investigation to class for discussion.

Thinking about Your Own Business Writing

Chances are, you have written a letter of application for a job, completed a résumé, or sent some business-related letters or email messages. Choose a piece of business-related writing that is important to you or that represents your best work, and then analyze it carefully. How clear is the writing? How well do you represent yourself in the writing? Do you follow the conventions for business letters, résumés, memos, and so on? Make notes on what you could do to improve this piece of writing.

Acknowledgments

Text credits: pp. 133–134, Cord Jefferson, "Is the Internet Warping Our Brains?" from *Good*, July 18, 2011, http://www.good.is/post/is-the-internet-warping-our-brains/. Copyright © 2011 by Good Worldwide, LLC. Reprinted by permission of Good World- wide, LLC; **pp. 155–157, Exercise 13.1,** "Protecting Freedom of Expression at Harvard" by Derek Bok. First published in the *Boston Globe*, March 25, 1991, p. 15. Reprinted with permission of the author; **pp. 160–161, Exercise 13.3,** James Hunter, "Outlaw Classics: The Albums That Kept Nashville Real in the Sixties and Seventies," p. 95 from *Rolling Stone,* March 9, 2006. Copyright © 2006 by Rolling Stone, LLC. All rights reserved. Reprinted by permission; **p. 269, Exercise 23.7,** Langston Hughes, "Harlem [2]" from *The Collected Poems of Langston Hughes* by Langston Hughes, edited by Arnold Rampersad with David Roessel, Associate Editor. Copyright © 1994 by The Estate of Langston Hughes. Used by permission of Alfred A. Knopf, a division of Random House, Inc., and Harold Ober Asso- ciates, Ltd.; **p. 302, Exercise 27.3 and p. 413,** Quotes from "The Ring of Time" from *Points of My Compass* by E. B. White. Copyright © 1956 by E. B. White. Originally appeared in *The New Yorker.* Reprinted by permission of Allene White and Martha White; **p. 424,** Excerpt from "The Road Not Taken" from *The Poetry of Robert Frost* edited by Edward Connery Lathem. Copyright 1916, 1969 by Henry Holt and Company. Copyright 1944 by Robert Frost. Reprinted by permission of Henry Holt and Company, LLC.

Art credits: p. 21, Mike Enright/www.menright.com; **p. 28,** Photograph by Shuqiao Song; **p. 41,** Courtesy of Joelle Hann; **p. 42,** Brian Swirsky; **p. 43,** © Seeds of Solidarity Education Center; **p. 70,** Mike Enright/www.menright.com; **p. 71,** Animal Locomotion/Bridgeman Art; **p. 72,** © 2010 Wolters Kluwer Health, Lippincott Williams and Wilkins; **p. 72,** Mike Enright/www.menright.com; **p. 81,** Mike Enright/www.menright.com; **p. 83,** Royalty Free/Getty Images; **p. 83,** Mike Enright/www.menright.com; **p. 85,** Bettmann/Corbis; **p. 86,** Mike Enright/www.menright.com; **p. 95,** Louis Mazatanta/National Geographic Stock; **p. 96,** Courtesy of www.airconditioning and refrigeration guide.com; **p. 102,** Doug Fowler; **p. 102,** Mike Enright/www.menright.com; **p. 103,** Mike Enright/www.menright .com; **p. 138,** Craig F. Walker/*The Denver Post*; **p. 142,** From *Fun Home: A Family Tragicomic* by Alison Bechdel. Reprinted by Permission of Houghton Mifflin Harcourt Publishing Company. All rights reserved; **p. 146,** Photograph by Wendy Annibell; **p. 147,** Spur Design; **p. 150,** Adbusters Media Foundation; **p. 154** (both images), David King Collection; **p. 167,** Sustainable Foods; **p. 168,** Jan Weber/As We Sow; **p. 172,** Emanuel Saez/University of California Berkeley; **p. 173,** Tom Tomorrow; **p. 174,** Getty Images; **p. 194** (upper left), *Michigan Quarterly Review;* (lower left) Courtesy of Ecology and Sociology; (upper right) *Scientific American;* (lower right) Salon.com; **p. 199,** University of North Carolina; **pp. 200–201,** EBSCOhost; **p. 213,** Harvard University/Nieman Reports; **p. 215,** Ungar, Mark. "Prisons and Politics in Contemporary Latin America," *Human Rights Quarterly* 25:4 (2003): 909–10. © 2003 The Johns Hopkins University Press. Reprinted with permission of The Johns Hopkins University Press; **p. 237,** courtesy of Shuqiao Song; **p. 258,** From "Today's Demon: Lost Worlds," *One! Hundred! Demons!* by Lynda Barry, Copyright © 2002 by Lynda Barry, published by Sasquatch Books; **p. 459,** EBSCOhost; **p. 460,** www.sutjhally.com; **p. 470,** *The Value of Nothing* by Raj Patel. Reprinted with permission of Picador Press; **p. 470,** courtesy of Alisa Quart, *Columbia Journalism Review;* **p. 471,** Nobelprize.org; **p. 471,** Mike Enright/www.menright.com; **p. 477,** *The Value of Nothing* by Raj Patel. Reprinted with permission of Picador Press; **p. 483,** courtesy of Alisa Quart, *Columbia Journalism Review;* **p. 487,** EBSCOhost; **p. 491,** Nobelprize.org; **p. 522,** Alexander, Meredith. "Thirty Years Later, Stanford Prison Experiment Lives On," Stanford Report (online), August 22, 2001, http://news.stanford.edu/news/2001 /august22/prison2-822.html. Photo: Chuck Painter/Stanford News Service; Palgrave Macmillan; Everett Collection; *The American Scholar;* **p. 527,** Palgrave Macmillan; **p. 531,** *The American Scholar;* **p. 535,** EBSCOhost; **p. 537,** Alexander, Meredith. "Thirty Years Later, Stanford Prison Experiment Lives On," Stanford Report (online), August 22, 2001, http:// news.stanford.edu/news/2001/august22/prison2-822.html. Photo: Chuck Painter/ Stanford News Service; **p. 554,** *Red Heat: Conspiracy, Murder, and the Cold War in the Carib- bean* by Alex Von Tunzelmann. Reprinted with permission of Picador Press; **p. 557,** *Red*

Heat: Conspiracy, Murder, and the Cold War in the Caribbean by Alex Von Tunzelmann. Reprinted with permission of Picador Press; **p. 563,** EBSCOhost; **p. 577** (upper), Reprinted by permission of the publisher from *The Diversity of Life* by Edward O. Wilson, Cambridge, Mass.: The Belknap Press of Harvard University Press, Copyright © 1992 by Edward O. Wilson; (lower) EBSCOhost; **p. 579,** Reprinted by permission of the publisher from *The Diversity of Life* by Edward O. Wilson, Cambridge, Mass.: The Belknap Press of Harvard University Press, Copyright © 1992 by Edward O. Wilson; **p. 585,** EBSCOhost.

Index

A

a, an (articles), 605
  deciding when to use, 324
  usage, 274
abbreviations, 442–47
  in different fields (Talking about
    Style), 445
  editing for (At a Glance), 442
  periods with, 416
  texting (Talking the Talk), 262
absolute concepts, 378
absolute phrases, 334
abstract and concrete words, 266–67
abstracts
  APA style, 543
  CSE style, 581
  dissertation, citing in MLA style,
    500
  for periodical articles, 200–201
  purpose of, 211
academic courses, citing Web sites
    (MLA style), 492
academic institutions, citing Web sites
    (MLA style), 492
academic reading. *See* critical reading
academic writing
  arguments, 143–61
  authority, establishing, 15
  for business courses, 655–63
  collaboration, 629
  compared to informal writing, 14
  cultural contexts. *See* multilingual
    writers
  directness, 15–16
  disciplinary language, 625–26
  disciplinary style, 626–27
  ethical guidelines, 628–29
  and evidence, 627–28
  first person in, 627
  formats, 628
  formatting. *See* designing texts
  genres, 594–95
  in humanities, 630–38
  instructor expectations, 12, 17, 593–94
  multimodal presentations, 20–36
  in natural and applied sciences,
    647–54
  purpose, understanding, 50–51
  research, planning, 17
  research project, 187–241
  in social sciences, 639–46
  stance, rhetorical, 50–52
  U.S. academic style, features of, 16,
    594
  visuals in. *See* visuals
accept, except, 274
active reading, strategies for, 16–17

active voice The form of a **verb** when
the **subject** performs the action: *Lata
sang the chorus.*

  advantages of, 120, 310, 352
  shifts between passive voice and, 303
addresses
  commas with, 408
  numbers in, 446
ad hominem fallacy, 151

adjective, 324, 374–80 A word that
modifies, quantifies, identifies, or
describes a **noun** or words acting as a
noun.

  adjective-adverb confusion, 376
  commas with, 406
  comparatives, superlatives, 324, 377
  editing (At a Glance), 375
  ending in *-ing* and *-ed*, 616
  and linking verbs, 374–75
  phrases, 334
adjective clauses, 336, 403–4
  for multilingual writers, 600

adverb, 324–25, 374–80 A word that
qualifies, modifies, limits, or defines a
verb, an **adjective**, another adverb, or a
clause, frequently answering the questions *where? when? how? why? to what
extent?* or *under what conditions?*

  adjective-adverb confusion, 376
  comparatives, superlatives,
    325, 377
  conjunctive adverbs, 325
  editing (At a Glance), 375
  phrases, 334
adverb clauses, 336–37, 403–4
advertisements, citing (MLA style), 499
advice, advise, 274
affect, effect, 274
afterwords, citing
  in *Chicago* style, 558
  in MLA style, 479

age, assumptions about, 254
aggravate, 274
agreement The correspondence
between a **pronoun** and its **antecedent**
in **person**, number, and gender (*Mr. Fox
and his sister*) or between a **verb** and its
subject in person and number *(She and
Moe are friends)*.
    pronoun-antecedent agreement, 10,
        369–73
    subject-verb agreement, 355–62
alignment, in design, 95
all ready, already, 274
all right, alright, 274
all together, altogether, 274
allude, elude, 274
allusion, illusion, 274
almanacs, 196
almost, 382
along with, 356
America, American, 254
American Psychological Association
    (APA). *See also* APA style
    ethical code, 628–29
    guide to electronic references,
        532–39
among, between, 275
amount, number, 275
ampersand (&), in in-text citations
    (APA style), 518–19
an, a (articles), 324, 605
analogy
    developing, paragraphs with, 86
    in emotional appeals, 173
analysis. *See also* academic writing;
        writing process
    literary analysis, 633–38
    rhetorical, student model, 157–60
AND, in electronic searches, 198
and/or, 275
annotated bibliography, 207–8
annotation
    for critical reading, 131–34
    of research sources, 223–24
antecedent, 322, 369–73 The **noun** or
noun **phrase** that a **pronoun** replaces.
anthologies, citing
    in *Chicago* style, 558
    in MLA style, 467, 474

anticlimax, and humor, 294
any body, anybody, 275
anybody, gender-neutral approach,
    371
any one, anyone, 275
anyplace, 275
anyway, anyways, 275
APA style, 515–50 The citation style
guidelines issued by the American
Psychological Association.
    content notes in, 516–17
    directory to in-text citation models,
        517
    directory to model references, 522
    formatting paraphrases and quota-
        tions in, 518
    formatting reference list in, 523
    in-text citations in, 517–21
    quotations, integrating in, 226
    references list, 521–41
        author listings, 523–25
        books, 525–28
        electronic sources, 532–39
        formatting (At a Glance), 523
        miscellaneous sources, 539–41
        print periodicals, 528–31
    student research essay in, 541–50
    verb tense guidelines, 348, 518
apostrophes, 419–22
    in contractions, 421
    editing for (At a Glance), 419
    errors (Top Twenty), 9
    in plurals, 421–22
    in possessive forms, 419–21
appeals, 145–48
    credibility, creating, 165–75
    emotional, 145–48, 172–74
    ethical, 146, 167
    logical, 146–47, 167–72
    in visual arguments, 147–48
applied sciences. *See* natural and
        applied sciences
appositive, 404–5 A **noun** or noun
phrase that adds identifying information
to a preceding noun or noun phrase:
Zimbardo, an innovative researcher,
designed the experiment.
appositive phrases, 335
apt, liable, likely, 275

Arab, usage, 254–55
arguable statements, 163
argument, 143–61 A text that makes and
supports a **claim**.
  analyzing, 143–61
  appeals, identifying, 145–48
  arguable statements, criteria for, 163
  audience analysis, 165
  claims in, 149, 163–64, 176
  classical structure, 175–76
  counterarguments, 166–67, 177
  credibility, creating, 165–75
  cultural contexts, 145
  designing, 177–78
  as exploration of ideas (Talking the
    Talk), 162
  fallacies, 151–55
  purposes of, 161–62
  reviewing (At a Glance), 162
  rhetorical analysis, student model,
    157–60
  sources, consulting, 175
  student model, 178–83
  Toulmin, 148–50, 176–77
  visual arguments, 140–41, 150
  working thesis for, 164
Aristotle, 145, 171
articles (*a, an, the*), 324, 605–6
articles in periodicals
  citing in APA style, 528–31
  citing in *Chicago* style, 560–64
  citing in CSE style, 581–82
  citing in MLA style, 480–84
  evaluating, 208–10, 214–15
  locating, 200–201
art works, citing
  in *Chicago* style, 569
  in MLA style, 497–98
as, 275
as if, like, 275
assignments. *See* common assignments;
  writing assignments
associational organization, 72
assumptions
  in arguments, 149, 164, 171,
    176
  unstated, avoiding, 251–56
assure, ensure, insure, 275
as to, 275

At a Glance boxes
  abbreviations and numbers, editing,
    442
  adjectives and adverbs, editing,
    375
  APA references list, formatting, 523
  apostrophes, editing for, 419
  appropriate language and spelling,
    editing for, 261
  arguments, analyzing, 144
  arguments, reviewing, 162
  assignments, analyzing, 624
  business letters, guidelines for
    writing, 660
  capitalization, editing for, 437
  commas, editing for, 401
  comma splices and fused sentences,
    editing, 386
  common ground, building with
    language, 250
  conciseness, editing for, 307
  consistency and completeness,
    editing for, 296
  coordination, subordination, and
    emphasis, editing for, 287–88
  cultures, communicating across,
    246
  electronic sources, citing, 533
  end punctuation, editing for, 415
  genres, features of, 594
  hyphens, editing for, 451
  interviews, conducting, 204
  italics, editing for, 448
  language variety, 257
  memo, guidelines for writing, 656
  misplaced or dangling modifiers,
    editing, 380
  MLA citation for visuals, 498
  MLA digital sources, citing, 484
  MLA list of works cited, formatting,
    472
  MLA print periodical entries, format-
    ting, 481
  models, combining parts of, 478, 524
  models, sources without, APA
    citation, 538
  note-taking guidelines, 220
  observations, conducting, 204
  online text, creating, 20
  oral presentations, preparing, 25

At a Glance boxes *(continued)*
parallelism, editing for, 299
paraphrasing guidelines, 222
plagiarism, avoiding, 233
potential sources, examining, 211
prepositions, idiomatic use, 618
pronouns, editing, 363
punctuation, effective use, editing
for, 429
quotation marks, editing for, 423
quoting, paraphrasing, summarizing, 225
semicolons, editing for, 412
sentence fragments, editing, 392
sentence patterns, basic, 329
sentence variety, editing for, 312
sexist pronouns, editing, 371
shifts, confusing, 304
sources without models, citing, 494,
559
subject-verb agreement, editing for,
356
summarizing guidelines, 223
survey questionnaire, designing, 205
Top Twenty (common errors), 4
U.S. academic style, 16
verbs, editing in own writing, 340
verb tense, editing, 350
visuals, attitude and point of view
in, 56
visuals, effective use, 104
writing inventory, taking, 11
writing to make something happen,
37
atlases, 196
audience, 53–54
for arguments, 165
formality of language and, 261–64
for online texts, 21–22
for oral presentations, 26
for public writing, 38
recognizing (Talking the Talk), 188
for research projects, 188
reviewing draft for, 105, 107
in rhetorical situation, 49, 52–54
sources, evaluating for, 208
and tone, 56
world audiences. *See* cultural
contexts

audio content
incorporating, 228–29
reviewing draft for, 106
revising, 116
tone of, 57
types of, 22
audio sources, citing
in APA style, 540–41
in *Chicago* style, 568
in MLA style, 495–97
authority
cultural contexts, 247
establishing your, 15
as evidence for argument, 169
authors
APA style, citing
in references list, 523–25
in text, 518–20
Chicago style, citing, 555–60
credibility of, evaluating, 208–10
CSE style, citing, 577–81
MLA style, citing
in text, 464–68
on works cited list, 470–74
a while, awhile, 275

B
bad, badly, 275, 376
bandwagon appeal fallacy, 151
bare, bear, 275
bar graphs, 101
base form, 340–45 The form of a **verb**
listed in dictionaries (*go*).
be, forms of
everyday use of (Talking about
Style), 341
as helping verbs, 320, 342, 610–11
nonstandard use, 341
progressive tenses, 611
and wordiness, 309
because of, due to, 275
begging the question fallacy, 152
being as, being that, 276
believing and doubting game,
144
beside, besides, 276
between, among, 275

bibliographies
    in APA style, 521
    in *Chicago* style, 553–54
    as library resources, 201
    working bibliographies, 206–7
biographical resources, 183
block quotations, 424
blogs (Web logs)
    citing in APA style, 538
    citing in *Chicago* style, 565
    citing in MLA style, 492
    features of, 22
    for research project, 191
bookmarking Web sites, 202–3
books
    citing in APA style, 525–28
    citing in *Chicago* style, 555–60
    citing in CSE style, 577–81
    citing in MLA style, 474–80, 488
    indexes, as research source, 199
    library search, 198–99
    titles of, italics for, 448
    in working bibliographies, 207
Boolean operators (AND, NOT, OR) for
    electronic searches, 198
brackets
    in direct quotations, 227
    usage, 430–31
brainstorming, 59–60
brake, break, 276
breath, breathe, 276
bring, take, 276
British, English, usage, 254
business writing, 655–63
    cultural contexts, 249
    email messages, 658
    letters, 658–60
    memos, 655–59
    résumés, 660–63
but, yet, 276
but that, but what, 276

C

can (modal auxiliary verb), 276,
    612–13
can, may, 276
can't hardly, 276
can't help but, 276

capitalization, 437–42
    editing for (At a Glance), 437
    headings, 100
    lines of poetry, 438
    proper adjectives and proper nouns,
        324, 438–39
    titles of persons, 439
    titles of works, 439–40
    in Top Twenty (common errors), 7
    unnecessary, 440–41
cartoons
    citing in MLA style, 468, 498–99
    as visuals, 102

case, 363–69 The form of a **noun** or
pronoun that reflects its grammatical
role: *He ate* (subjective). *His food was
cold* (possessive). *I saw him* (objective).

    in compound structures, 368
    in dependent clauses, 366–67
    in elliptical constructions, 368
    objective case, 364–65
    possessive case, 365
    subjective case, 364
    we and *us* before nouns, 368–69
    who, whom, whoever, whomever,
        366–67
catalogs, library, 195
cause and effect
    developing paragraphs with, 86
    supporting an argument with, 170
    transitions to signal, 91
CDs, citing
    in *Chicago* style, 568
    in MLA style, 495–96
censor, censure, 276
certainty, modals to indicate, 613
charts
    misleading, 154–55
    MLA style, citing, 468–69, 498
    symbols in, abbreviating, 444
    as visuals, 101

Chicago style, 551–74 Citation
guidelines based on the *Chicago Manual
of Style.*

    directory, 554
    formatting guidelines, 553–54
    in-text citations, 552–53

Chicago style *(continued)*
  notes and bibliographic entries,
    554–69
      books, 555–60
      electronic sources, 561–68
      miscellaneous sources, 568–69
      periodicals, 560–64
  quotations, integrating, 226
  student research essay, 569–74
chronological organization
  of information, 71
  of narratives, 82
  of process descriptions, 87
  résumés, 660
citation-name format (CSE style), 575–76
citation-sequence format (CSE style), 575
claim, 149, 163–64, 176 An arguable
statement.
class discussions, guidelines, 24
classical format for arguments, 175–76
classification, developing paragraphs
  with, 84–85
clause, 335–37 A group of words
containing a **subject** and a **predicate**.
An **independent clause** can stand
alone as a sentence, while a **dependent
clause** must be attached to an independent clause.
  and comma splices, 385–90
  conjunctive adverbs with, 325
  in fused (run-on) sentences, 385–90
clichés, 268
climactic order, position of ideas in
  sentences, 293–94
close reading. *See* literary analysis
clustering, 62–63
coherence, 89–92, 90 Also called "flow,"
the quality that makes a **text** seem
unified.
collaboration, 64–65, 629
collective nouns, 321
  pronoun-antecedent agreement with,
    369
  subject-verb agreement with, 10,
    358–59
college writing. *See* academic writing
colloquial language, 262
colons, 432–33
  with quotation marks, 426

color, in text design, 97
comics, citing (MLA style), 498–99
commands (imperative mood), 353
commas, 400–412
  with absolute phrases, 334
  with addresses, 408
  with appositives, 404–5
  for clarity, 410
  in compound sentences, 9, 338, 402
  with contrasting elements, 407
  with coordinating conjunctions, 7, 9,
    387, 402
  with dates, 408
  with direct address, 407
  editing for (At a Glance), 401
  with independent clauses, 335, 387
  with interjections, 407
  with introductory elements, 400
  with items in series, 405–6
  with nonrestrictive elements, 8, 403–5
  with numbers, 408–9
  with parentheses, 430
  with parenthetical expressions,
    406–7
  with quotation marks, 6–7, 409, 426
  with tag questions, 407
  with transitional expressions, 406–7
  unnecessary, 368, 402
comma splice, 385–90 An error in formal
writing resulting from joining two **independent clauses** with only a comma.
  in context (Talking about Style), 389
  editing (At a Glance), 386
  in literary writing, 389
  in Top Twenty, 9–10
commenting on a draft, 110–11
comments, instructor, 111–13
common assignments. *See also* writing
  assignments
  in business classes, 655–61
  in humanities, 632–33
  in natural and applied sciences, 648–49
  in social sciences, 641–42
common errors. *See* Top Twenty
common ground, language that builds,
    250–56
  establishing credibility with, 166
  using (At a Glance), 250
common knowledge, 231
communicator, in rhetorical situation, 49

company names
abbreviations in, 444
capitalizing, 439
comparative, 324–25 The *–er* or *more*
form of an **adjective** or **adverb** used
to compare two things (*happier, more
quickly*).
compare to, compare with, 276
comparison and contrast, developing
paragraphs with, 85
comparisons
complete, editing for, 298
as evidence in argument, 173
transitions to signal, 91
compass directions, capitalizing, 440
complement, compliment, 276
complete sentence. *See* sentence
complex sentences, 338
compose, comprise, 276
compound adjectives, hyphens with,
11, 451
compound antecedents, pronoun-
antecedent agreement, 369–70
compound-complex sentences, 338
compound constructions and commas,
411
compound nouns
hyphens in, 451
possessive forms of, 420
compound numbers, hyphens with,
451
compound predicates, 331
as sentence fragments, 394
compound sentences, 338
commas in, 9, 402
missing commas in (Top Twenty), 9
pronoun case in, 368
compound subjects, 330
subject-verb agreement, 357–58
compound words
and hyphens, 451–52
spell-checker errors, 269
comprise, compose, 276
concession, transitions to signal, 92
conciseness, 307–11 Using the
fewest possible words to make a point
effectively.
editing for (At a Glance), 307
in headings, 100

conclusions, 93, 238–39
of oral presentations, 26–27
revising, 115–16
of sentences, dash for emphasis, 431
of sentences, emphasis in, 293
in syllogisms, 170–71
transitions to signal, 92
concrete words, 266–67
conditional sentences, 601
conference proceedings, citing
in APA style, 540
in *Chicago* style, 581
in MLA style, 500
conjunction, 326–28 A word or words
joining **words, phrases,** or **clauses.**
and emphasis, 287
parallelism with, 300–301
conjunctive adverbs, 325, 328
commas with, 407
linking clauses with semicolons and,
413
connotation, 265
conscience, conscious, 276
consensus of opinion, 276
consequently, subsequently, 276
consistency, editing for (At a Glance), 296
context for writing, 49–50
continual, continuous, 277
contractions, 421
contrast
developing paragraphs with, 85
in visual design, 94
contrasting elements
commas with, 407
transitions to signal, 91
conventions (Talking the Talk), 14
coordinate adjectives, commas to
separate, 406
coordinating conjunctions, 327 The
words *and, but, for, nor, or, so,* and *yet,*
which give the same emphasis to both
the elements they join: *Restaurants are
expensive, *so* I cook.*
commas with, 7, 9, 387, 402
with compound predicates, 331
in compound sentences, 338
with compound subjects, 330
linking clauses with, 387, 413
parallelism with, 300–301

coordination, 288–89

corporate authors. *See* organizations as authors, citing

correlative conjunctions, 327 Paired conjunctions (*both . . . and, either . . . or, neither . . . nor, not only . . . but also*) used to connect equivalent elements.

with compound subjects, 330
parallelism with, 301

could, as modal, 320, 342, 612–13

could of, 277

Council of Science Editors (CSE) style. *See* CSE style

count and noncount nouns, 321, 602–3

counterarguments, 166–67, 217

cover letters, 658–60

credibility
in arguments, establishing, 165–75
in sources, evaluating, 208–10
of statistics, 155
and variety of English used, 259

criteria, criterion, 277

critical reading, 129–43
as active reading, 16–17
analyzing text, 136–39
annotating text, 131–34
business texts, 655
in humanities (At a Glance), 631
in natural and applied sciences, 647–48
previewing text, 129–31
in social sciences, 639
of sources, 210–15
student writing model, 140–43
summarizing text, 135–36

critical stance, 632–33

critical thinking
arguments, analyzing, 143–61
critical reading, 129–43

CSE style, 575–86 The citation style guidelines issued by the Council of Science Editors.

directory, 577
in-text citations, 575–76
citation-name format, 575
citation-sequence format, 575
name-year format, 576

references list, 576–81
author listings, 577–81
books, 577–81
electronic sources, 582–86
periodicals, 581–82
student research proposal, 586–89

cultural contexts, 247–50. *See also* multilingual writers
of arguments, 145
and authority of writer, 247
and business writing, 249
communicating across cultures (At a Glance), 246
evidence, nature of, 248
and formality, 249–50
meaning, clarifying, 246–47
norms and culture, 245–46
and organizing writing, 248–49
and writing style, 249–50

D

dangling modifiers, 384
editing (At a Glance), 380

dashes, 431–32
linking clauses with, 390
with quotation marks, 427

data, 277

data analysis, research data, 205

databases, 196–98
abstracts in, 200–201
in APA style, citing, 532–33
in *Chicago* style, citing, 561–64
in CSE style, citing, 583–85
and digital object identifier (DOI), 532–33
full-text, 200
in MLA style, citing, 467–68, 485–87
periodical indexes, 200–201
search options, 197–98
for social sciences. *See also* articles in periodicals

dates
commas with, 408
numbers in, 446

declarative sentences, 339

deductive reasoning, 170–71

definitions
  cultural contexts and, 246–47
  developing paragraphs with, 83–84
  quotation marks for, 425
demonstrative pronouns, 323
denotation, 265
dependent clause, 289–94, 338 Some-times called a "subordinate clause," a word group that contains a **subject** and a **predicate** but can't stand alone as a sentence because it begins with either a **subordinating conjunction** (*because, although*) or a **relative pronoun** (*that, which*).
  relative pronouns in, 323
  as sentence fragments, 394–95
  sentence variety, 313
  who, whom, whoever, whomever in, 366–67
depend on, 620
descriptions, development, 83
designing texts, 94–104
  for arguments, 177–78
  design principles, 94–95
  editing, 120
  for portfolio, 123–24
  print versus electronic delivery, 94
  research project, 236
  revising, 116
details
  concrete, 173
  in description, 83
  developing paragraphs with, 80
  and emotional appeals, 173
  and subordination, 289–90
  of visuals, 81
determiners, 324, 603–5
diagrams, 101
diction. *See* word choice
dictionary entry, citing (MLA), 467
different from, different than, 277
digital object identifier (DOI), 532–33
digital sources
  citing in APA style, 532–39
  citing in *Chicago* style, 561–68
  citing in CSE style, 582–86
  citing in MLA style, 484–93
  guidelines (At a Glance), 484 (MLA),
    533 (APA)
direct address, 408
direct discourse, shifts in, 304–5

directness, in writing, 15–16
direct objects
  explicit, 597
  infinitives as, 598–600
  noun clauses as, 336
  noun phrases as, 333
  pronoun case in, 365
direct quotations
  changing to indirect, 614
  and quotation marks, 423–24
disabilities, considering
  audience analysis, 55
  color perception, 97
  freespeaking, 60
  knowing your readers, 255
  oral presentation accessibility, 27
  references to, 255
  and spelling, 273
  Web texts accessibility, 23
disciplinary language, 625–26
disciplinary style, 626–27
discourse, shifts in, 304–5
discreet, discrete, 277
disinterested, uninterested, 277
disruptive modifiers, 383
dissertations, citing
  in APA style, 539
  in MLA style, 500
distinct, distinctive, 277
division, developing with, 84
do, forms of, as helping verbs, 342
documentation. *See also* APA style;
    Chicago style; CSE style; MLA style
  missing or incomplete (Top Twenty),
    5–6
  need for, 231
  of visuals, 102
document design. *See* designing texts
doesn't, don't, 277
DOI (digital object identifier), 532–33
dots. *See* ellipses
doublespeak, 264
doubt, modals to indicate, 613
doubting game, 144
drafting. *See also* writing process
  guidelines for planning and, 73–74
  research project, 238–41
  reviewing draft, 105–13
  working thesis, 67–69

due to, because of, 275
DVDs, citing
  in APA style, 540
  in *Chicago* style, 568
  in MLA style, 494

E

each
  pronoun-antecedent agreement with, 368
  subject-verb agreement with, 358
each other, one another, 277
e-books, citing (*Chicago*), 558
-ed, -d endings
  for adjectives, 616
  for past forms of regular verbs, 342
editing, 117–22. *See also* At a Glance
  adjectives, 375
  adverbs, 375
  colons, 433
  comma splices, 386–90
  for coordination and subordination, 292
  design, 120
  for emphasis, 287–88
  fused (run-on) sentences, 386–90
  misplaced or dangling modifiers, 380
  for misspelling, 120
  paragraphs, 78
  for parallelism, 299–302
  research project, 239
  sentence length, 117–18, 311–13
  for sentence variety, 311–13
  word choice, 119
editions of books, citing
  in APA style, 528
  in *Chicago* style, 559
  in MLA style, 479
editorials, citing
  in APA style, 529
  in MLA style, 481, 488
editors, citing
  APA style, 525
  Chicago style, 558
  CSE style, 580
  MLA style, 474–75
effect, affect, 274
either-or fallacy, 153
electronic communication, 17–19

electronic sources. *See* digital sources
elicit, illicit, 277
ellipses, for omitted words, 227, 434–35
elliptical structures, 297, 368
elude, allude, 274
email
  APA style, citing, 520, 538
  business use of, 658
  capital letters in, 441
  Chicago style, citing, 565
  MLA style, citing, 493
  writing, guidelines for, 18
emigrate from, immigrate to, 277
emotional appeals, 145–48, 172–74
emphasis, 287–88
  dashes for, 431–32
  italics for, 448
  order for, 293–94
encyclopedias, 196
endnotes, *Chicago* style, 554–69
end punctuation, editing for (At a Glance), 415
English, British, usage, 254
English, varieties of, 256–59
ensure, assure, insure, 275
enthused, enthusiastic, 277
enthymeme, 149
equal ideas, relating with coordination, 288–89
equally as good, 277
-er, -est. See comparative; superlative
errors, common. *See* Top Twenty
-es, -s endings
  plural nouns, 273, 321
  verbs, 341, 355
essays. *See* academic writing; writing assignments; writing process
ethical appeals, 146, 147–48, 165–66
ethical guidelines, 628–29
ethnic groups
  assumptions about, 253–54
  capitalizing name of, 438
  language varieties, 259
ethos, 145
euphemisms, 264
evaluating sources, 206–15
every day, everyday, 277
every one, everyone, 278
everyone, gender-neutral approach, 371

evidence, 148–49 Support for an argument's **claim**.

in cultural contexts, 248
evaluating, 211, 627–28
examples
colons with, 432
developing paragraphs with, 84
establishing credibility with, 167–69
transitions to signal, 91
except, accept, 274
exclamation points, 409, 417
with quotation marks, 427
exclamatory sentences, 339
experts, using as sources, 203–4
explanatory notes, MLA style, 462–63
expletive constructions, 310
explicit, implicit, 278
exploring ideas, 59–65
brainstorming, 59–60
clustering, 62–63
collaboration for, 64–65
freespeaking, 60
freewriting (looping), 60–61
imagery for, 61–62
narrowing topic, 66–67
questions for, 63–64
research project, 187–88
sources, using for, 64

F
Facebook
event invitation, 42
posting, citing (MLA), 493
fairness, and credibility, 166–67
fallacies, 151–55
ad hominem, 151
bandwagon appeal, 151
begging the question, 152
charts and graphs, misleading, 154–55
in-crowd appeal, 152
either-or, 153
false analogy, 152
false authority, 151
flattery, 151–52
guilt by association, 151
hasty generalization, 153
non sequitur, 152
oversimplification, 153
photographs, misleading, 153–54

post hoc, 152
straw man, 153
veiled threat, 152
false analogy, 152
false authority, 151
family relationship words, capitalizing, 7, 440
farther, further, 278
faulty predication, 296–97

faulty sentence structure, 296–97 A common writing problem in which a sentence begins with one grammatical pattern and switches to another (also called "mixed structure").

fewer, less, 278
field research, 203–5
figurative language, 173–74, 267–68
for topic selection, 61–62
figures, citing, 468, 498
films, citing
in APA style, 540
in MLA style, 494
finalize, 278
firstly, secondly, 278
first person (*I*) in academic writing, 627
flattery, 151–52
flaunt, flout, 278
flow. *See* coherence
flyer, student model, 40
fonts. *See* typefaces
footnote numbers with quotation marks, 426
footnotes, citing
in *Chicago* style, 554–69
in MLA style, 462–63
foreign languages, using words from, 54, 259–60, 449
forewords, citing
in *Chicago* style, 558
in MLA style, 479
formality, appropriate, 261–64
cultural contexts, 249–50
formal outlines, 74
formal rhetorical situations, 49
formal writing, 18–19, 49. *See also* academic writing
correctness or stuffiness (Talking the Talk), 366
formal audiences, 53–54

formatting. *See also* designing texts
APA references list (At a Glance), 523
APA style, 523
Chicago style, 553–54
MLA list of works cited (At a Glance), 472
online texts, 23
former, latter, 278
forums, online, guidelines for, 18–19
fractions
hyphens in, 451
numbers in, 446
slashes in, 434
subject-verb agreement with, 358

fragment, 12, 392–96 A group of words that is not a complete sentence but is punctuated as one. Usually a fragment lacks a **subject**, a **verb**, or both, or it is a **dependent clause**.

freespeaking, 60
freewriting (looping), 60–61
further, farther, 278

fused sentence, 9, 385–90 Sometimes called a "run-on," a sentence in which two **independent clauses** are run together without a **conjunction** or punctuation between them (*My dog barked he woke me up*).

future tenses, 349
future perfect, 349
future perfect progressive, 349
future progressive, 349
simple future, 349

G
games, computer, citing (MLA), 496
gender-neutral language, 251–53, 371
general and specific words, 265–66
general indexes, 199
generalizations
inductive, 170–71
with zero article, 606–7

genre, 55, 594–95 A form of communication used for a particular purpose and incorporating certain conventional features. Some common examples include lab reports, researched essays, brochures, invitations, etc.

for public writing, 38
reviewing draft for, 106
geographical area, assumptions about, 254–55
geographical names, capitalizing, 438

gerund, 334 A verbal form that ends in *-ing* and functions as a **noun**: *Sleeping is a bore.*

and possessive-case pronouns, 365
to state facts, 599
glossary of usage, 274–83
good, well, 278, 376
good and, 278
Google, 202, 595
Google Scholar, 203
government institutions
abbreviations in, 443
capitalizing names, 439
government sources, 202–3
citing in APA style, 539
citing in *Chicago* style, 569
citing in CSE style, 586
citing in MLA style, 467, 499–500
grammar, 318–96. *See also* parts of speech
grammatical terms (Talking the Talk), 319
graphic narratives, citing (MLA), 478
graphs
bar graphs, 101
citing, 468–69, 498
misleading data in, 154–55
symbols in, abbreviating, 444
group authors. *See* organizations as authors, citing
guilt by association fallacy, 151

H
hanged, hung, 278
hasty generalizations, 153
have, forms of
as helping verbs, 320, 342, 610–11
perfect tenses, 611
third-person singular, 356

having, present-perfect participle, 351
he, she (personal pronouns), 278
headings
   and document design, 94, 99–100
   in formal outlines, 74
   of notes, 218
   typefaces, 98
   wording of, 100
helping verb, 320, 342, 609–12 A **verb** such as a form of *be*, *do*, or *have* or a **modal** combined with a main verb.

her, his (possessive pronouns), 278, 322
here, opening sentences with, 330
herself, himself, myself, yourself (reflexive pronouns), 278, 322
hierarchical organization, 75
his, her (possessive pronouns), 278, 322
hisself, 278
historical sources, evaluating, 195
homonyms, errors with, 6, 269
hopefully, 278
however. See conjunctive adverbs
humanities, writing for, 630–38
   assignments, types of, 632–33
   critical reading (At a Glance), 631
   critical stance of writer, 632–33
   literary analysis, 633–38
humor, and anticlimax (Talking about Style), 294
hundred, 447
hung, hanged, 278
hyphens, 11, 450–53
   editing for (At a Glance), 451
   unnecessary, 452
   unnecessary or missing (Top Twenty), 11
hypothesis to working thesis, 192

I

ibid. (in the same place), 553
ideas
   equal, linking with coordination, 288–89
   paired, 300–301
   for writing, exploring, 59–65
idioms, learning, 268
i.e. (that is), 444
if, 353, 601

illusion, allusion, 274
illustrations, as visuals, 102
IM (instant messaging). *See* texting
imagery, 61–62
immigrate to, emigrate from, 277
impact, 279
imperative mood (commands), 303, 353
imperative sentences, 339
   you as implied subject of, 330
implicit, explicit, 278
implicit thesis statements, 67
imply, infer, 279
in-crowd appeal fallacy, 152
indefinite pronoun, 359 A word such as *each*, *everyone*, or *nobody* that does not refer to a specific person or thing.

   apostrophes, 419–20
   pronoun-antecedent agreement, 10, 369
   sexist pronouns, 371
independent clause, 335–37 A word group containing a **subject** and a **predicate** that can stand alone as a **sentence**.

indexes, for research, 199–201
indicative mood, 303, 353
indirect discourse, shifts in, 304–5
indirect objects, 332
   pronoun case with, 365
indirect questions, 416
indirect quotations, 409, 427, 614
indirect sources, citing
   in APA style, 520
   in MLA style, 466
inductive reasoning, 170–71
infer, imply, 279
infinitive, 334, 351 *To* plus the **base form** of a verb (*to go, to run, to hit*), which can serve as a noun, an adverb, or an adjective: *One option is to leave* (noun). *We stopped to rest* (adverb). *He needs time to adjust* (adjective).

   disruptive modifiers in, 383
   and gerunds (multilingual writers), 598–600
   subjects of, pronoun case in, 365
infinitive phrases, 334

informal rhetorical situations, 49
informal writing, 12–14, 19
    audiences for, 53–54
    compared to academic writing, 19
-ing words
    as adjectives, 334, 616
    as nouns (gerunds), 334, 598–99
    as present participles of verbs, 341
    in progressive tenses, 347–49, 616
inside of, outside of, 279
instant messaging (IM). *See* texting
instructions, modals to indicate,
    612–13
instructor comments, 111–13
instructor expectations, 12, 17, 593–94
insure, ensure, assure, 275
integrating sources, 224–29
intensive pronouns, 322
intentions, infinitives for, 599
interact, interface, 279

interjection, 328, 407 An exclamation of
surprise or other strong emotion: *Ouch!*

interlibrary loans, 202
Internet searches, 202
    to check usage, 595–96
Internet sources
    annotating, 223–24
    authoritative sources online, 203
    citing. *See* digital sources
    evaluating, 212–13
    wikis (Talking theTalk), 196
    in working bibliographies, 207
interrogative pronouns, 323
interrogative sentences, 339
interviews
    APA style, citing, 520, 529
    conducting (At a Glance), 204
    MLA style, citing, 495, 500
in-text citations
    APA style, 517–21
    CSE style, 575–76
    MLA style, 463–69
intransitive verbs, 332, 346, 597
introductions
    citing in *Chicago* style, 558
    citing in MLA style, 479
    developing, 92–93, 238
    oral presentations, 26–27
    research projects, 238

reviewing draft for, 107
    revising, 115–16
introductory elements, commas with,
    5, 400
irony, quotation marks with, 425
irregardless, regardless, 279
irregular forms
    comparatives and superlatives, 377
    plural nouns, 321, 360–61
    verbs, 342–45

irregular verb, 342–45 A **verb** that
does not form the past tense and past
participle by adding *-ed* or *-d* to the **base
form**.

issues, exploring, 162
is when, is where, 279, 296
it
    opening sentences with, 119, 310
    vague use of, 372
italics, 448–49
items in series
    colons with, 433
    commas with, 405–6, 411
    parallelism, 299–302
    semicolons with, 413–14
it is, avoiding, 310
its, it's, 279, 322, 421

J

jargon, 262–63
journal articles
    in APA style, 529–31
    in *Chicago* style, 560–64
    in CSE style, 581, 583
    in MLA style, 480, 485
journalistic questions, 64
journals, italics for names of, 448
just as, so, 327

K

key words
    in oral presentations, 27
    in paragraphs, 89–90
    and purpose for writing, 188
    in scannable résumés, 661, 663
keyword searches, 197
kind, sort, type, 279

kind of, sort of, 279
know, no, 279
knowledge, credibility established
      with, 165–66

L

lab reports, 650–54
language. *See also* word choice
      appropriate, editing for (At a
            Glance), 261
      assumptions, avoiding, 251–56
      bringing in another, 54, 259–60
      colloquial, 262
      and common ground, 250–56
      doublespeak and euphemisms, 264
      figurative, 267–68
      gender-neutral, 251–53
      glossary of usage, 274–83
      jargon, 262–63
      pompous, 263
      and rhetorical situation, 54
      slang, 262
      stereotypes, avoiding, 251
      use and cultural contexts,
            250–56
      varieties of (At a Glance), 257
      for world audience. *See* cultural
            contexts
language names, capitalizing, 438
language that builds common ground,
      250–56
language variety, 256–59
later, latter, 279
latter, former, 278
lay, lie, 279, 346
leave, let, 279
lectures and speeches, citing (MLA),
      496–97
legal sources, citing, 501
lend, loan, 279
less, fewer, 278
less, least, 324
let, leave, 279
letters (texts), 658–60
      APA style, citing, 520
      Chicago style, citing, 565
      guidelines for writing (At a Glance),
            660

letter of application, student sample,
      658–59
      MLA style, citing, 500
      reflective statements, 124
letters of the alphabet
      italics for, 449
      plurals, 422
letters to the editor
      APA style, citing, 529
      MLA style, citing, 481, 488
Library of Congress, online, 203
*Library of Congress Subject Headings
      (LCSH),* 197
library research, 195–202
      catalogs, 195, 198–99
      databases, 196–98
      indexes, 199–201
      reference librarians, 195
      search options, 197–98
lie, lay, 279, 346
like, as if, as, 275
"like" buttons, 23
limiting modifiers, 382
linear organization, 75
linking verb, 331 A verb that suggests a
state of being, not an action.
      and adjectives, 324, 374–75
      and subject-verb agreement, 360
links, in online texts, 23
listen to, 620
list of works cited. *See* MLA style
lists
      colon in, 433
      numbers in, 430
literally, 280
literary analysis, 633–38
literary works, citing (MLA), 466
literature review
      in natural and applied sciences,
            649
      in social sciences, 641–42
live performances, citing (MLA), 497
loan, lend, 279
logical appeals, 146–47, 167–72
logical organization, 71–72
logos, 145, 146–47
logs, research, 191
looping, 60–61
loose, lose, 280

lots, lots of, 280
-*ly* words (adverbs), 325, 375–76

M

magazine articles, citing. *See also*
    articles in periodicals
    APA style, 529
    Chicago style, 561
    CSE style, 582
    MLA style, 480
magazines
    online, 203
    as research source, 194
    titles, italics for, 425, 448
main clauses. *See* independent clause
main idea
    developing in paragraphs, 78–79
    distinguishing with subordination,
        289–91
    topics. *See* exploring ideas; topic
        selection
main verbs. *See* verb
major premise of syllogism, 170–71
man, mankind, 280
manuscripts, MLA style, 501
maps
    MLA style, citing, 468–69, 498
    as visuals, 101
margins, white space and, 96–97
may, as modal, 276, 610, 612–13
may be, maybe, 280
meaning
    clarifying for other cultures, 246–47
    reviewing draft for, 105
meanwhile, 328
media, 280
memos, 655–59
    guidelines for writing (At a Glance),
        656
messaging. *See* texting
metaphors, 267
    and emotional appeals, 173
might, as modal, 342, 612–13
mine, my, 322
minor premises, of syllogisms, 170–71
misplaced modifiers, 380–81
mixed metaphors, 267–68
mixed structures in sentences,
        296–97

MLA style, 457–511 The citation
style guidelines issued by the Modern
Language Association.
    block quotations, lines of prose or
        poetry, 424
    directory to in-text citations, 463–64
    directory to works-cited models,
        470–71
    explanatory and bibliographic notes,
        462–63
    in-text citations, 463–69
    list of works cited, 470–501
        author listings, 471–74
        books, 474–80
        digital sources, 484–93
        formatting guidelines (At a
            Glance), 472
        government publications,
            499–500
        multimedia sources, 494–99
        print periodicals, 480–84
    quotations, integrating, 226
    student research essay, 501–11
    visuals, 229, 468–69

modal, 342, 612–13 A kind of **helping
verb** that has only one form and shows
possibility, necessity, or obligation: *can,
could, may, might, must, shall, should,
will, would, ought to.*

modifier, 380–85 A word, phrase, or
clause that acts as an **adjective** or
an **adverb**, qualifying the meaning of
another word, phrase, or clause.
    adjectives and adverbs, 375–76
    order in sentences, 607–8
    placement, 380–85

mood, 303, 353–54 The form of a **verb**
that indicates the writer's attitude toward
the idea expressed. The indicative mood
states fact or opinion (*I am happy*); the
imperative gives commands (*Keep calm*);
and the subjunctive refers to a condition
that does not exist (*If I were rich . . .*).

moral, morale, 280
more, most, 324
multilingual writers, 593–620
    adjective clauses, 600
    adjective sequence, 377

adjectives with plural nouns, 375
American spellings, recognizing, 271
articles, 324, 605–6
British English, 258
capitalization, 440
class participation, 25
conditional sentences, 601
count and noncount nouns, 321, 602–3
determiners, 603–5
English, global varieties of, 258
explicit points, 79
fancy words, avoiding, 264
genres, understanding, 594–95
genre structures and phrases, adapting, 595
gerunds, 598–600
helping verbs, 609–12
hundred, use of term, 447
idioms, learning, 268
infinitives, 598–600
modal auxiliaries (helping verbs), 342, 609–12
modifiers, 607–8
noun clauses, 598
participial adjectives, 616
past tense, 613–14
peer review, 107
perfect and progressive tenses, 614–16
personal experience, 166
plagiarism as a cultural concept, 232
prepositions, idiomatic, 617–20
present tense, 613–14
proper nouns, 603
quotation marks, 427
quotations, tense shifts, 614
reading patterns, 98
reported speech, shifting tenses in, 306
reviewing drafts, 105
reviewing thesis, 235
sentence length, 388
sources, identifying, 223
subjects and objects of sentences, 597
subjunctive mood, 354
thesis, stating explicitly, 69
topic, choosing, 62

U.S. academic style, 593–94
usage, checking online, 595–96
verb phrases, 609–12
word order, 597
multimedia, library resources, 202
multimodal text, 20–36 A **text** that may include oral, visual, or audio elements in addition to (or instead of) words on a page.
multiple negatives, 379
multivolume works, citing, (MLA) 466, 479, (APA) 528, (*Chicago*) 559
musical works
    MLA style, citing, 496
    titles, italics for, 448
Muslim, Moslem, usage, 255
must, as modal, 320, 342, 612–13
my, mine, 322
myself, himself, herself, yourself (reflexive pronouns), 322

N
name-year format (CSE), 576
narratives
    developing paragraphs with, 82
    establishing credibility with, 168–69
narrowing topics, 66–67
natural and applied sciences, 647–54
    assignments, types of, 648–49
    critical reading for, 647–48
    formats for writing, 648
    lab report, student model, 650–54
    style in, 649–50
n.d. (no date), 520, 539
negatives, multiple (Talking about Style), 379
newsletters, 41–42
newspaper articles, citing
    APA style, 529
    Chicago style, 564
    CSE style, 582
    MLA style, 481, 485
no, know, 279
noncount nouns, 321, 602–3, 604–7
none, 322

nonrestrictive element, 8, 403–5 A word, **phrase**, or **clause** that provides more information about, but does not change, the essential meaning of a sentence. Nonrestrictive elements are set off from the rest of the sentence with commas: *My instructor, who is perceptive, liked my introduction.*

NOT, in electronic searches, 198
note cards, for oral presentations, 30
notes. *See also* endnotes; footnotes
    APA style, 516–17
    Chicago style, 552–53
    ibid. (in the same place), 553
    MLA style, 462–63
note-taking, 218–24
    guidelines (At a Glance), 220
    paraphrasing, 220–22
    quoting, 219–20
    summarizing, 222–23
noun, 321, 602–5 A word that names a person, place, thing, or idea.

noun clauses, 336, 598
noun phrases, 333
number, amount, 275
number, shifts in, 304
numbers, 446–47
    commas with, 408–9
    in different fields (Talking about Style), 445
    editing (At a Glance), 442
    hyphens with, 451
    plurals, 422
    used as terms, italics for, 449

O

object A **noun** or **pronoun** receiving the action of a **verb** (*We mixed paints*) or following a **preposition** (*on the road*). *See* direct objects; indirect objects.

object complements, 329, 332
objective case, 364–65
    in compound structures, 368
observations, 204
    conducting (At a Glance), 204
off, of, 280
OK, O.K., okay, 280

omissions, ellipses for, 434–35
on account of, 280
one another, each other, 277
online searches. *See* Internet searches
online sources, citing. *See* digital sources, citing
online texts, 20–24. *See also* informal writing
    accessible, 23
    creating (At a Glance), 20
    features of, 22–23
    structure, designing, 24
or (coordinating conjunction), 402
    in compound antecedent, 338
    subject-verb agreement and, 358
OR, in electronic searches, 198
oral presentations, 25–36
organization of writing, 70–73
    and cultural contexts, 248–49
    instructor comments on, 112
    for online texts, 24
    reviewing draft for, 105–6, 107
    revising, 115–16
    by subject, 236–37
    visuals, 73
organizations as authors, citing
    in APA style, 524
    in *Chicago* style, 555
    in CSE style, 580
    in MLA style, 465, 473
ought to, as modal auxiliary, 342
our, ours, 322
ourselves, 322
outlines, 74, 237
oversimplification fallacy, 153
owing to the fact that, 280

P

page numbers
    in APA in-text citations, 518
    in MLA in-text citations, 463–68
    pagination, formats for, 98
    sources without, 467–68 (MLA), 521 (APA)
pamphlets, citing, 569
paper, quality of, for print texts, 97–98

papers
  presented at conference, citing (CSE),
    581
  presented at symposium, citing
    (APA), 540
  writing. *See* academic writing; writ-
    ing assignments; writing process
paragraphs, 78–93
  coherence (flow), 89–92
  conclusions, 93
  details in, 80
  development of, 82–88
  introductions, 92–93
  length, 80, 88–89
  topic sentences, 79
parallelism, 299–302
  for paragraph coherence, 90
paraphrases, 220–22, 227–28
  in APA style, 518
  avoiding plagiarism in, 220–22
  guidelines for (At a Glance), 222
  as indirect discourse, 304
  present tense in, 348
  signal verbs with, 227
  sources of, acknowledging, 231
  when to use (At a Glance), 225
parentheses, 429–30
  with other punctuation, 430
  question marks in, 417
  searches using, 198
parenthetical expressions, commas to
    set off, 406–7
participial adjectives, 616
participial phrases, 334, 351
  restrictive and nonrestrictive,
    404
participle, 340–46, 611 A word formed
from the **base form** of a **verb**. The present
participle always ends in -*ing* (*going*). The
past participle ends in -*ed* (*ruined*) unless
the verb is **irregular**. A participle can
function as an **adjective** (*the singing frog, a
ruined shirt*) or form part of a **verb phrase**
(*You have ruined my shirt*).

parts of speech, 320–28 The eight
grammatical categories describing how
words function in a sentence (**adjectives,
adverbs, conjunctions, interjections,
nouns, prepositions, pronouns,
verbs**).

passed, past, 280

passive voice, 303–4, 352 The form of a
verb when the **subject** is being acted on,
not acting: *The batter was hit by a pitch.*
  constructing, 611–12
past, passed, 280
past participles, 341
  -*ed, -d* endings, 342
  of irregular verbs, 342–45
past perfect progressive tense, 349
past perfect tense, 349
past progressive tense, 349, 615–16
past subjunctive, 353
past tense forms, 341, 349
  of *be*, 341
  -*ed, -d* endings, 342
  of irregular verbs, 342–45
  for multilingual writers, 613–14
pathos, 145
PDF files, citing
  in APA style, 521
  in MLA style, 468
peer review, 107–11
per, 280
percent, percentage, 280

perfect progressive tense, 347–49 The
tense of a **verb** showing an ongoing
action completed at some point in the
past, present, or future: *The workers
had been striking for a month before the
settlement. He has been complaining for
days. The construction will have been
continuing for a year in May.*

perfect tense, 347–49 The **tense** of a
verb showing a completed action in the
past, present, or future: *They had hoped
to see the parade but got stuck in traffic.
I have never understood this equation. By
then, the governor will have vetoed the bill.*
  for multilingual writers, 614–16
periodicals. *See also* articles in
    periodicals
  APA style, citing, 528–31
  articles in, locating, 200–201
  Chicago style, citing, 560–64
  CSE style, citing, 581–82

periodicals *(continued)*
    evaluating articles in, 208–10, 214–15
    indexes, 200–201
    MLA style, citing, 480–84
    scholarly and popular sources, 194
    in working bibliographies, 207
periods, 416
    with parentheses, 430
    with quotation marks, 426
person, 304 The point of view of a
subject. The first person refers to itself
(*I*); the second person addresses *you*; the
third person refers to someone else *(they)*.

    in academic writing, 627
    and verb forms, 320
personal communication, citing
    in *Chicago* style, 565
    in MLA style, 520
personal pronouns, 322
persuasive writing. *See* argument; writ-
    ing assignments; writing process
photographs, 102
    citing in MLA style, 468–69, 497–98
    misleading, 153–54
phrasal verbs, 320, 619–20
phrase, 333–35 A group of words that
lacks a **subject**, a **verb**, or both.

    restrictive and nonrestrictive, 404
    verb, 320, 333, 609–12
phrase fragments, 393
pie charts, 101
place, transitions to signal, 91
plagiarism, avoiding, 220–22, 232–34
plenty, 281
plurals
    count and noncount nouns, 321, 602–3
    first, second, and third person, 341
    irregular forms, 321
    possessive nouns, 321, 420
    spelling rules, adding *-s* or *-es*, 273,
        321
    subject-verb agreement and, 355–62
plus, 281
podcasts
    citing in APA style, 541
    citing in *Chicago* style, 565, 568
    citing in MLA style, 497
    features of, 22

poetry
    capitalization, 438
    literary analysis, student model,
        633–38
    MLA style
        block quotations, 424
        in-text citations, 424, 448, 466
        slashes between lines, 434
        titles, 425, 449
pompous language, 263
popular sources, 194
portfolios, preparing, tips for,
    123–24
possessive form, 9, 321, 419–20 The
form of a **noun** or **pronoun** that shows
possession. Personal pronouns in the
possessive case don't use apostrophes
(*ours, hers*), but possessive nouns
and indefinite pronouns do (*Harold's,
everyone's*).

possessive pronouns, 322, 365
    as antecedents, 373
posters
    in oral presentations, 30
    student model, 39
post hoc fallacy, 152
PowerPoint. *See* presentations
precede, proceed, 281
precedents, 168
predicate, 318–19, 331–32 The **verb** and
related words in a **clause** or sentence. The
predicate expresses what the subject does,
experiences, or is. The simple predicate is
the verb or **verb phrase**: *We have been
living in the Atlanta area.* The complete
predicate includes the simple predicate and
its **modifiers**, **objects**, and complements:
We have been living in the Atlanta area.

prefaces, citing
    in *Chicago* style, 558
    in MLA style, 479
prefixes, hyphens with, 452
premises, in syllogisms, 170–71
preposition, 325–26, 617–20 A word or
word group that indicates the relationship
of a **noun** or **pronoun** to another part of
the sentence: *From the top of the ladder
we looked over the rooftops.*

prepositional phrases, 333
  commas with, 404
presentations, 25–26
  audience analysis, 26
  guidelines for, 35–36
  introductions and conclusions, 26–27
  notes, speaking from, 30
  organization, 27
  preparing for (At a Glance), 25
  purposes for speaking, 26
  scripts, 28–30
  signpost language in, 27, 30
  student model script and slides, 29
  transitions in, 27
  visuals, integrating, 30–35
present participles, 341, 611
present perfect participles, 351
present perfect progressive tense, 348
present perfect tense, 348, 614–16
present progressive tense, 348,
    614–16
present subjunctive, 353
present tense, 347–48, 614–16
  be, forms of, 341
pretty, 281
Prezi. *See* presentations

primary source, 193 A research source
that offers firsthand knowledge of its
subject.

principal, principle, 281
problem and solution, developing
    paragraphs with, 87
proceed, precede, 281
process, developing paragraphs with, 87

progressive tense, 347–49, 614–16 The
tense of a **verb** showing a continuing
action in the past, present, or future:
*He was snoring during the lecture. The
economy is improving. Business schools
will be competing for this student.*

pronoun, 321–23, 363–74 A word used
in place of a **noun**.

  gender-neutral, 252, 371
  as subject complements, 331
pronoun-antecedent agreement, 10,
    369–73
pronoun reference, vague (Top
    Twenty), 6

proofreading, 120, 241
  for spelling, 270
proper adjectives
  capitalization, 7, 324, 438
  order in sentences, 608
proper nouns, 321
  capitalization, 7, 438, 603
  for multilingual writers, 603, 606
  spell-checker errors, 269
  zero article with, 606–7
proximity, in document design, 95
public speaking. *See* presentations
public writing, 36–44
  writing to make something happen
    (At a Glance), 37
publisher's imprint, citing (MLA), 480
punctuation, 400–436
  apostrophes, 419–22
  brackets, 430–31
  colons, 432–33
  commas, 400–412
  dashes, 431–32
  effective use, editing for (At a
    Glance), 429
  ellipses, 434–35
  exclamation points, 417
  hyphens, 450–53
  parentheses, 429–30
  periods, 416
  question marks, 416–17
  quotation marks, 422–27
  semicolons, 412–15
  slashes, 434
purposes
  arguments, 161–62
  and choosing visuals, 56
  key words for, 188
  for online texts, 21
  for oral and multimedia presenta-
    tions, 26
  for public writing, 37
  reviewing draft for, 105, 107
  understanding assignments, 50–51

Q
qualifiers in arguments, 149–50
qualitative studies, 639–40
quantitative studies, 639–40

question marks, 416–17
  with quotation marks, 409, 417, 427
questionnaires, designing, 205
questions
  to explore a topic, 63–64
  in indicative mood, 353
  indirect, 416
  interrogative pronouns, 323, 365–67
  interrogative sentences, 339
  for questionnaires, 205
  research, 190, 210
  subject of sentence in, 330
  tag, 407
quotation, quote, 281
quotation marks, 422–27
  commas with, 6, 409
  for definitions, 425
  editing for (At a Glance), 423
  in electronic searches, 198
  with end punctuation, 366, 417,
    426–27
  for irony and invented terms, 425
  with lines of poetry, 424
  misused, 427
  single, 423–24
  for titles of works, 425
quotations
  in APA style, 226
  block quotations, 424
  brackets for changed words, 227
  brief versus long, incorporating, 226
  colons with, 433
  as direct discourse, 304
  direct quotations, 423–24
  ellipses for deleted words in, 227
  indirect quotations, 409, 427
  integrating into writing, 226–27
  mechanical errors with (Top
    Twenty), 6–7
  in MLA style, 226
  note-taking guidelines (At a Glance),
    220
  note-taking with, 219–20
  poorly integrated (Top Twenty), 10
  within quotations, 423–24
  signal words for, 227
  sources of, acknowledging, 231
  tenses with, 348
  when to use (At a Glance), 225

R

race, assumptions about, 253–54
raise, rise, 281, 346
rarely ever, 281
ratios, colons in, 433
reading, 123–26. *See also* critical reading
real, really, 281
real-time communications, citing
  (APA), 538
reasoning, critical, 170–71
  Toulmin's system, 171
reason . . . is because constructions, 296
reasons, in arguments, 149, 171
reason why, 281
reciprocal pronouns, 323
reference librarians, 195
references list
  in APA style, 521–41
  in CSE style, 576–81
  formatting for APA (At a Glance),
    523
reference works, citing
  in APA style, 528
  in *Chicago* style, 559
  in MLA style, 479, 489
reflecting on writing, 122–25
  for portfolios, 124
  questions to ask, 123
reflective writing, student sample, 124–25
reflexive pronouns, 322
regardless, irregardless, 279
regional varieties of language, 256–59
regular verb, 342 A **verb** that forms
the **past tense** and **past participle** by
adding *-d* or *-ed* to the **base form** (*care,
cared, cared; look, looked, looked*).

reiteration, developing paragraphs
  with, 87–88
relative pronouns, 290, 323, 336
  and subject-verb agreement, 360
religion, assumptions about, 255
repetition
  in document design, 95
  transitions, to signal, 92
reports. *See also* academic writing;
  writing assignments
  APA style, citing, 540
  Chicago style, citing, 569

lab, student model, 650–54
MLA style, citing, 499
online, sample, 43
psychology, student research essay,
    642–46
requests, modals to signal, 612–13
research (research project), 187–241
    audience analysis, 188
    conclusions, 238–39
    design, 236
    drafting, 238–41
    field research, 203–5
    hypotheses in, 190
    introductory paragraphs, 238
    for natural and applied sciences, 649
    with open mind (Talking the Talk),
        208
    organizing, 236–37
    planning, 17, 190–91
    prewriting choices, refining, 234–35
    research logs, 191
    research question, 190, 210
    reviewing drafts, 239
    revising, 113–16
    revising and editing, 239–40
    rhetorical stance, 188
    for social sciences, 639–46
    sources, 193–234
    supporting information for, 70
    thesis statements, 190, 235–36
    titles, 238
    topics, exploring, 187–88
    working thesis, 67–69, 192
research questions
    evaluating, 210
    formulating, 190
respectively, respectfully, 281
restrictive element, 403–5 A word,
phrase, or **clause** that changes the
essential meaning of a sentence. A
restrictive element is not set off from the
rest of the sentence with commas or other
punctuation: *The tree that I hit was an oak.*
    commas, unnecessary, 7, 403, 410
résumés, 660–63
review indexes, 199
reviewing drafts, 105–13
    of arguments, 162
    elements to review, 105–6
by instructors, 111–13
    peer review, 107–11
    of research project, 239
reviews, citing
    in *Chicago* style, 564
    in MLA style, 481, 488
revision, 113–16
    of research project, 239–40
    scope of (Talking the Talk), 115
    student sample, 121–22
rhetorical analysis. *See also* argument
    student sample, 157–60
rhetorical situation, 48–59 The whole
context for a piece of writing, including
the person communicating, the topic and
the person's attitude toward it, and the
intended audience.
    audience analysis, 53–54
    context in, 55–57
    formal and informal, 49
    of online texts, 21–22
    purpose, 50–51
    stance, 52
    student sample situation, 57–58
    time/length factors, 55
    visuals, choosing, 56
rhetorical stance, 50–51
    for research project, 188
    reviewing draft for, 105, 107
    of sources, evaluating, 209–10
    synthesis from sources, 216–17
rise, raise, 281, 346
run-on sentence. *See* fused sentence

S

-s, -es endings
    plural nouns, 273, 321
    verbs, 341, 355
sans serif fonts, 98
scholarly sources, 194
    online, locating, 203
sciences, forms of writing in, 641
science terms, abbreviations in,
    443
scores, numbers in, 446
scripts for oral presentations, 28–30
search engines, usage, for multilingual
    writers, 595–96

searching
  keyword. *See* keyword searches
  library sources, 197–98
secondary source, 193–94 A research
source that reports information from
research done by others.
secondly, firstly, 278
second person, 303–4, 341
semicolons, 412–15
  clauses, linking with, 328, 387–88,
    402, 412–13
  in compound sentences, 338
  editing for (At a Glance), 412
  equal ideas, relating with, 288–89
  misused, 414
  with quotation marks, 427
sentence, 318–19, 329–33, 337–39 A
group of words containing a **subject** and
a **predicate** and expressing a complete
thought.
  length of, 117–18, 311–12, 388
  for multilingual writers, 597–98
  patterns, basic (At a Glance), 329
sentence fragment, 12, 392–96 A group
of words that is not a grammatically
complete sentence but is punctuated as
one. Usually a fragment lacks a **subject**,
a **verb**, or both, or it is a **dependent
clause**.
sentence variety, 311–13
  editing for (At a Glance), 312
sequence, transitions to signal, 91
series. *See* items in series
serif fonts, 98
set, sit, 281, 346
sexist language, 251–52, 371
  pronouns, editing (At a Glance), 371
sexual orientation, assumptions about,
    255–56
shall, as modal, 320, 342, 612–13
she, he, 278
shifts, 303–7
  confusing (At a Glance), 304
  between direct and indirect
    discourse, 304–5
  in mood, 303
  in person/number, 304
  in tone, 305–6

  in verb tense, 8, 303
  in voice, 303–4
  in word choice, 305–6
should, as modal, 320, 342, 612–13
sic (so), 431
signal phrases, 227
signal words
  for APA in-text citations, 518–19
  for MLA in-text citations, 463–64
  for quotations, 227
signpost language, in oral presenta-
    tions, 27, 30
similes, 267
  and emotional appeals, 173
simple predicates, 331
simple sentences, 338
simple subjects, 329–30
simple tenses, 347–49, 614–16 Past (*It
happened*), present (*Things fall apart*), or
future (*You will succeed*) forms of verbs.
since, 281
sit, set, 281, 346
situations for writing. *See* rhetorical
    situation
slang, 262
slashes, 434
slides, PowerPoint, 30–35
so (coordinating conjunction), 281, 402
social bookmarking sites, 202–3
social classes, assumptions about,
    254
social media. *See also* Facebook;
    informal writing
  and informal writing, 12–14
  sites, MLA style, citing, 493
social sciences, writing for, 639–46
  critical reading, 639
  student model, 642–46
someplace, 282
some time, sometime, sometimes, 282
song titles, quotation marks for, 425
sort, kind, type, 279
sort of, kind of, 279
sound recordings. *See* audio sources,
    citing
sources, 193–234
  for arguments, 175
  articles, evaluating, 210–15
  citations, abbreviations in, 392

data interpretation, 205
digital. *See* digital sources, citing
documenting. *See* documentation
evaluating credibility, 208–10
excessive use, avoiding, 229–30
historical, 195
importance of, 206
integration in writing, 224–29,
    241
interviews, 203–4
library. *See* library research
list of, preparing, 241
note-taking, 218–24
observations, 204
online texts, giving credit, 23
plagiarism, avoiding, 232–34
popular sources, 194
potential, examining (At a Glance),
    211
primary sources, 193
for research project, 190–91
scholarly sources, 194
secondary sources, 193–94
surveys, 204–5
synthesizing, 216–18
working bibliography, 206–7
spatial organization, 70–71
specialized indexes, 200–201
spell checkers, 269–70
    limitations of, 120
    and spelling errors (Top Twenty), 6
    and wrong-word errors (Talking the
        Talk), 270
    and wrong-word errors (Top
        Twenty), 5
spelling, 272–73
    editing for (At a Glance), 261
    errors, in Top Twenty, 6
    homonym errors, 6, 271
spoke-and-hub organization, 76
squinting modifiers, 382
stance, rhetorical, 52
standard English, 256–57
states abbreviations, 445
stationary, stationery, 282
statistics, 154–55
    numbers in, 446
stereotypes, avoiding, 251

storyboards, to organize information,
    75–76
straw man fallacy, 153
streaming media, 22
styles, disciplinary, 626–27
subheadings, purpose of, 211
subject, 318–19, 329–30 The **noun** or
pronoun and related words that indicate
who or what a sentence is about. The
simple subject is the noun or pronoun:
The timid gray mouse ran away. The
complete subject is the simple subject
and its modifiers: *The timid gray mouse
ran away.*
    explicit, 597
subject complements
    as adjectives, 329
    hyphens, unnecessary, 452
    and linking verbs, 331, 374–75
    noun clauses as, 336
    pronoun case, 364
subjective case, 364
    in compound structures, 368
subject-verb agreement, 355–62
    and ambiguous antecedents, 372
    editing for (At a Glance), 356
    and possessive antecedents, 373
    and third-person singular subjects,
        355–56
subject word searching, 197
subjunctive mood, 303, 353–54 The
form of a **verb** used to express a wish, a
suggestion, a request or requirement, or
a condition that does not exist: *If I were
president, I would change things.*
subordinate clause. *See* dependent
    clause
subordinating conjunction, 287–88,
290, 327, 335 A word or **phrase** such as
although, because, or *even though* that
introduces a **dependent clause**: *Think
carefully before you answer.*
subordination, 289–94
    editing for (At a Glance), 287–88
    excessive, avoiding, 292
    main ideas, distinguishing with,
        289–91
    power of (Talking about Style), 291

suffixes
  hyphens with, 452
  and spelling rules, 272
summary A brief retelling of the main points of a **text**.
  guidelines for (At a Glance), 223
  incorporating in writing, 227–28
  for notes, 222–23
  sources, acknowledging, 231
  when to use (At a Glance), 225
superlative The *–est* or *most* form of an **adjective** or **adverb** used to compare three or more items (*happiest, most quickly*).
superscript numbers
  APA style, content notes, 516–17
  Chicago style citations, 552–53
  CSE style citations, 575
  MLA style, explanatory/biblio-graphic notes, 463
supporting evidence. *See also* sources
  reviewing draft for, 107
  revising, 115
  and working thesis, 70
supposed to, used to, 282
sure, surely, 282
surface errors, 3
surveys, 204–5
syllogisms, elements of, 170–71
syntax The arrangement of words in a sentence.
synthesis, 205, 216–18 Grouping ideas and information together in such a way that the relationship among them is clear.

T
tables
  in MLA style, 468–69
  as visuals, 101
tag questions, commas with, 407
take, bring, 276
Talking about Style boxes
  abbreviations and numbers in differ-ent fields, 445
  anticlimax and humor, 294
  be, everyday use of, 341
  comma splices in context, 389
  multiple negation, 379

subordination, 291
technical and scientific writing, voice for, 352
technical writing, 312
Talking the Talk boxes
  arguments, 162
  assignments, 52
  audience, recognizing, 188
  conventions, 14
  first person (*I*) in academic writing, 627
  formality, correctness, or stuffiness, 366
  grammatical terms, 319
  research with an open mind, 208
  revision, 115
  spell checkers and wrong-word errors, 270
  texting abbreviations, 262
  visual texts, 137
  writing something new, 230
technical writing
  disciplinary style, 626–27
  disciplinary vocabulary, 625–26
  passive voice, use of, 352
  sentence length (Talking about Style), 312
television shows, citing
  in APA style, 540–41
  in MLA style, 494–95
tense, 347–51 The form of a **verb** that indicates the time when an action takes place — past, present, or future. Each tense has **simple** (*I enjoy*), **perfect** (*I have enjoyed*), **progressive** (*I am enjoy-ing*), and **perfect progressive** (*I have been enjoying*) forms.
testimony, as evidence, 169
text Traditionally, words on paper, but now anything that conveys a message.
  online, 20–24
  in rhetorical situation, 49
  visual (Talking the Talk), 137
texting, 19, 262
than, then, 282
that
  introducing quotation with, 409
  as relative pronoun, 323
  vague use of, 372
that, which, 282
the (article), 324, 606

their, theirs, 322
theirselves, 282
themselves, 322
then, 328
there, opening sentences with, 119, 309, 330
therefore, 325, 328
there is, there are, 310
there was, there were, 361
thesis statements, 67–69, 235–36
   research project, 190
   revising, 114–15
they, indefinite use of, 372–73
thinking, critical. *See* critical thinking
third person, 304
   singular and plural, 341, 355–56
this, vague use of, 372
thorough, threw, through, 282
time
   numbers in, 446
   subordinating conjunctions, 327
   transitions to signal, 91
time management, 24, 189
titles
   capitalizing, 440
   colons in, 433
   italics for, 425, 448–49
   quotation marks for, 425
   for research projects, 238
   reviewing draft for, 107
   revising, 115–16
   and subject-verb agreement, 361
   within titles, citing, 480, 528, 560
   of visuals, 102
titles of persons
   abbreviating, 442–43
   capitalizing, 439
   commas with, 408
to, too, two, 282
to forms (infinitives), 334, 351, 598–99.
   See also infinitive
tone
   considering for assignment, 56–57
   shifts in, 305–6
   of source, evaluating, 210
tone of voice, oral presentations, 35
topic selection, 49–50. *See also* exploring ideas
topic sentences, 79
Top Twenty (common errors), 4–12
   apostrophe, unnecessary or missing, 9
   capitalization, unnecessary or missing, 7
   commas, missing after introductory element, 5
   commas, missing in compound sentences, 9
   commas, missing with nonrestrictive element, 8
   commas, unnecessary, 7
   comma splice, 9–10
   documentation, incomplete or missing, 5–6
   fused (run-on) sentences, 9
   hyphens, unnecessary or missing, 11
   listing of (At a Glance), 4
   pronoun-antecedent agreement errors, 10
   pronoun reference, vague, 6
   quotations, mechanical errors, 6–7
   quotations, poorly integrated, 10
   sentence fragments, 12
   sentence structure, faulty, 8
   spelling errors, 6
   verb tense shifts, 8
   words, missing, 7–8, 298
   wrong-word errors, 3–5
Toulmin arguments, 148–50
   organization of, 176–77
   reasoning system of, 171
transition, 90–92 A word or **phrase** that signals a progression from one sentence or part of a sentence to another.
   sentence variety with, 313
   signpost language, 27
transitive verb, 331–32, 597 A **verb** that acts on an **object**: *I posted my review online.*
translations, citing
   in APA style, 525
   in *Chicago* style, 559
   in MLA style, 475, 478
Twitter, 13, 307. *See also* informal writing
two, too, to, 282
type, sort, kind, 279
typefaces, 98–99
typos, 269

U

uninterested, disinterested, 277
unique, 282
units of measurement, 444
unknown authors, citing
 in APA style, 524
 in *Chicago* style, 555
 in MLA style, 465, 473, 478
unpublished works, citing, 501
unsigned articles, citing, 529
URLs, slashes in, 434
U.S. academic style
 features of (At a Glance), 16
 and multilingual writers, 593–94
used to, supposed to, 282
U.S. Government Printing Office (GPO Access), 202
us or *we* before nouns, 368–69

V

veiled threat fallacy, 152
verb, 320, 331–32, 340–55 A word or **phrase**, essential to a sentence, that expresses the action of a sentence or **clause**. Verbs change form to show **tense**, number, **voice**, and **mood**.
 base forms, 340–45
 be, forms of, 330
 editing (At a Glance), 340
 to forms (infinitives), 334
 helping, 320, 342
 intransitive, 331–32
 irregular forms, 342–45
 linking, 331
 mood, 303, 353–54
 for multilingual writers, 619–20
 predicates, 331–32
 regular forms, 342
 revising, 120
 strong, 309
 tense, 347–51
 transitive, 331–32
 voice, 352
verbals, 334
verb phrase, 320, 609–12 A **main verb** and one or more **helping verbs**, acting as a single verb.
verb tense. *See* tense

very, 282
video content
 reviewing draft for, 106
 revising, 116
 types of, 22
videos, citing
 in APA style, 540
 in *Chicago* style, 568
 in MLA style, 494
visual argument, 147–48, 167, 174
visual rhetoric, 94
visuals, 100–104
 attitude and point of view in, 56
 documentation of, 103
 effective use of (At a Glance), 104
 incorporating, 228–29
 misleading, 154–55
 MLA style
  in-text citations, 228–29, 468–69
  in list of works cited, 497–99
 numbers and titles for, 102
 online texts, formatting, 23
 for oral presentations, 30–35
 organizing, 73
 point of view in, 56
 to provide details, 81
 reviewing draft for, 106
 tone of, 57
 visual texts (Talking the Talk), 137
visual structure, in design, 94–95
voice, 320, 352 The form of a **verb** that indicates whether the subject is acting or being acted on. In the active voice, the subject performs the action: *Parker played* the saxophone. In the **passive voice**, the subject receives the action: *The saxophone was played* by *Parker.*

W

warrant, 149 An assumption, sometimes unstated, that connects an argument's **claim** to the reasons for making the claim.
way, ways, 283

Webcasts. *See* podcasts
Web logs. *See* blogs (Web logs)
Web sites
    citing in APA style, 533–38
    citing in *Chicago* style, 565–67
    citing in CSE style, 586
    citing in MLA style, 489–92
    features of, 22
well, good, 278, 376
we or *us* before nouns, 368–69
where, 283
which
    adjective clause with, 403–4
    as determiner, 604
    as interrogative pronoun, 323
    subject-verb agreement, 360
    vague use of, 372
which, that, 283
whichever, 323
white space, and design, 96–97
who
    as interrogative pronoun,
        323
    subject-verb agreement, 360
who, whom, 283
    in dependent clauses, 366–67
    in questions, 366
whoever, 323
whoever, whomever, in dependent
        clauses, 367
whose, as determiner, 604
who's/whose, 283
wikis
    citing in APA style, 539
    citing in MLA style, 492–93
    features of, 22
    as research source (Talking the Talk),
        196
wildcards, in searches, 198
will, as modal, 320, 342, 612–13
winning, and arguments, 161
word choice, 261–69
    disciplinary language, 625–26
    editing, 119
    instructor comments on, 112
    oral presentations, 27–28
    shifts in, 305–6
    unnecessary, redundant, and empty
        words, 308–9
word errors (Top Twenty)

missing word, 7–8, 298
    wrong word, 3–5, 270
words as words, subject-verb agree-
        ment in, 361
working bibliography, 206–7
working thesis, 67–69
    of arguments, 164
    for research project, 192
    supporting information for, 70
    testing, 236
works cited. *See* MLA style
world audiences. *See* cultural contexts
would, as modal, 320, 342, 601,
        612–13
writing assignments. *See also* academic
        writing
    analyzing (At a Glance), 624
    argument, 143–61
    business writing, 655–63
    changes in (Talking the Talk), 52
    in humanities, 632–33
    narratives, 82
    in natural and applied sciences,
        648–49
    reflective statement, 124
    in social sciences, 641–42
writing inventory, taking (At a Glance),
        11
writing process, 45–125
    designing texts, 94–104
    drafting, 76–77
    editing, 117–22
    ideas for writing, exploring,
        59–65
    narrowing topic, 66–67
    paragraph development,
        78–93
    reflecting on writing, 122–25
    reviewing drafts, 105–13
    revising, 113–16
    thesis, working, 67–69
    writing situations, 48–59
writing situation. *See* rhetorical
        situation
writing to make something happen in
        the world, 36–44
wrong word (Top Twenty),
        3–5
    and spell checkers, 270

Y

yet, but, 276
you (second person)
   as implied subject, 330
   indefinite use of, 372
your, you're, 283
your, yours, 322
yourself, myself, himself, herself (reflexive
   pronouns), 278, 322

yourselves, 322
YouTube, 23
   podcasts, citing (MLA), 497

Z

zero article, 606–7

Directories

Directory of Storyboard Art

Rhetorical Situations: Choose Your Topic   *50*
Rhetorical Situations: Consider Your Purpose and Stance   *51*
Rhetorical Situations: Imagine Your Audience   *53*
Working Thesis: Plan Your Approach   *66*
Working Thesis: Refine Your Topic   *67*
Working Thesis: Craft Your Message   *68*
Peer Review: Work with a Writer   *108*
Peer Review: Work with Reviewers   *110*
Revision: Read All Comments Carefully   *113*
Revision: Plan Your Next Draft   *114*
Editing: Polish Your Draft   *117*
Critical Reading: Preview   *130*
Critical Reading: Read Carefully   *132*
Critical Reading: Summarize   *135*
Critical Reading: Analyze   *137*
Synthesis: Finding Patterns   *216*
Synthesis: Combining Ideas   *217*

Directory of Student Writing

In the Book

Twitter posts: Parker   *13*
Facebook post: Michalski   *13*
Oral presentation excerpts: Song,"Residents of a Dys*FUN*ctional
    HOME"   *26–35*
Poster: Rao   *39*
Flyer: Mumford   *40*
Event promotion: Swirsky   *42*
Final draft: Lesk, "Red, White, and Everywhere"   *58*
Portfolio cover letter: Kung   *124*
Critical reading: Song, "Residents of a Dys*FUN*ctional *HOME*"   *140*
Rhetorical analysis: Ateyea, "A Curse and a Blessing"   *157*
Argument essay: Pfeifer, "Devastating Beauty"   *178*
MLA-style research essay: Craig, "Texting and Messaging: The Language
    of Youth Literacy"   *501*
APA-style literature review: Redding, "Mood Music: Music Preference and
    the Risk for Depression and Suicide in Adolescents"   *541*
Chicago-style research essay: Rinder,"Sweet Home Chicago: Preserving the
    Past, Protecting the Future of the Windy City"   *569*

CSE-style research essay: Gupta, "Field Measurements of Photosynthesis and Transpiration Rates in Dwarf Snapdragon" *586*

Close reading of poetry: Sillay, "Life's Not a Paragraph" *633*

Psychology research essay: McLaughlin, "Leadership Roles in a Small-Group Project" *642*

Chemistry lab report: Goldberg *650*

Memo: Abbott and Abernathy *656*

Letter of application: Lopez *658*

Print résumé: Tyler *662*

Scannable résumé: Tyler *663*

On the Web Site

Go to **bedfordstmartins.com/everydaywriter** > **Student Writing** for model essays, drafts, research projects, annotated bibliographies, presentations, and work created for disciplines other than English.

For Multilingual Writers

CHAPTERS OF ADVICE

Chapter 56: Writing in U.S. Academic Genres *593*

Chapter 57: Clauses and Sentences *596*

Chapter 58: Nouns and Noun Phrases *602*

Chapter 59: Verbs and Verb Phrases *609*

Chapter 60: Prepositions and Prepositional Phrases *617*

BOXED TIPS

Speaking Up in Class *25*

Bringing In Other Languages *54*

Using Your Native Language to Explore Ideas *62*

Stating a Thesis Explicitly *69*

Being Explicit *79*

Reading Patterns *98*

Asking an Experienced Writer to Review Your Draft *105*

Understanding Peer Review *107*

Counting Your Own Experience *166*

Identifying Sources *223*

Plagiarism as a Cultural Concept *232*

Asking Experienced Writers to Review a Thesis *235*

Global Varieties of English *258*

Avoiding Fancy Language *264*

Learning Idioms *268*
Recognizing American Spellings *271*
Shifting Tenses in Reported Speech *306*
Using Count and Noncount Nouns *321*
Deciding When Articles Are Necessary *324*
Using Modal Auxiliaries *342*
Using the Subjunctive *354*
Using Adjectives with Plural Nouns *375*
Determining Adjective Sequence *377*
Judging Sentence Length *388*
Quoting in American English *427*
Learning English Capitalization *440*
Using the Term *Hundred* *447*

IF YOU SPEAK . . .

Arabic *254, 440*
British English *240, 271, 427*
Chinese *248, 440, 613*
Dutch *440*
French *427*
German *427, 440*
Hebrew *440*

Hindi *440*
Indian English *259, 271*
Japanese *247*
Russian *375*
Spanish *253, 259, 375, 617*
Tagalog *246*
Vietnamese *613*

Considering Disabilities

Accessible Web Texts *23*
Accessible Presentations *27*
Your Whole Audience *55*
Freespeaking *60*

Color for Contrast *97*
Knowing Your Readers *255*
Spelling *273*

Talking the Talk

Conventions *14*
Assignments *52*
Paragraph Length *80*
Revision *115*
Critical Thinking *131*
Visual Texts *137*
Arguments *162*
Reaching an Audience *188*
Wikis as Sources *196*

Research with an Open Mind *208*
Saying Something New *230*
Texting Abbreviations *262*
Spell Checkers and Wrong-Word
    Errors *270*
Grammatical Terms *319*
Correctness or Stuffiness? *366*
The First Person *627*

Revision Symbols

Some instructors use these symbols as a kind of shorthand to guide you in revision. The numbers refer to a chapter number or a section of a chapter.

abb	abbreviation **46a–g**		//	faulty parallelism **8e, 27**
ad	adjective/adverb **35**		*para*	paraphrase **17d, 18**
agr	agreement **33, 34f**		*pass*	inappropriate passive **28c, 32g**
awk	awkward			
cap	capitalization **45**		*ref*	unclear pronoun reference **34g**
case	case **34c–d**			
cliché	cliché **11a, 23d**		*run-on*	run-on (fused) sentence **37**
co	coordination **25a**		*sexist*	sexist language **21b, 34f**
coh	coherence **8e**		*shift*	shift **28**
com	incomplete comparison **26e**		*slang*	slang **23a**
			sp	spelling **23e–f**
concl	weak conclusion **8f, 19b**		*sub*	subordination **25b**
cs	comma splice **37**		*sum*	summarize **17d, 18, 62b**
d	diction (word choice) **23**		*t*	tone **10d, 17c, 23a, 23d**
def	define **8c**		*trans*	transition **8e, 30b**
dm	dangling modifier **36c**		*u*	unity **8a**
doc	documentation **49–55**		*vague*	vague statement
emph	emphasis unclear **25**		*verb*	verb form **32a–d**
ex	example needed **8b–c**		*vt*	verb tense **32e–h**
frag	sentence fragment **38**		*wv*	weak verb **32**
fs	fused sentence **37**		*wrdy*	wordy **29**
hyph	hyphen **48**		*ww*	wrong word **1, 11a, 23a–b**
inc	incomplete construction **26**		,	comma **39**
			;	semicolon **40**
intro	weak introduction **8f, 19b**		. ? !	period, question mark, exclamation point **41**
it	italics (or underlining) **47**			
jarg	jargon **23a**		'	apostrophe **42**
lc	lowercase letter **45**		" "	quotation marks **43**
lv	language variety **22**		( ) [ ] —	parentheses, brackets, dash **44a–c**
mix	mixed construction **26a**			
mm	misplaced modifier **36**		: / ...	colon, slash, ellipsis **44d–f**
ms	manuscript form		∧	insert
no ,	no comma **39j**		∿	transpose
num	number **46h–j**		⌒	close up
¶	paragraph **8**		X	obvious error

Contents

☑ = LearningCurve adaptive quizzing content online

How to Use This Book v
Preface xiii

Writing for College and Beyond

1 The Top Twenty 3
2 Expectations 12
3 Multimodal Assignments 20
 • STUDENT PRESENTATION
4 Writing to Make Something Happen 36
 • SAMPLE WRITING

The Writing Process

5 Rhetorical Situations 48
6 Exploring Ideas 59
7 Planning and Drafting 66
8 Developing Paragraphs 78
9 Making Design Decisions 94
10 Reviewing and Revising 104
11 Editing and Reflecting 117
 • REVISED STUDENT DRAFT
 • STUDENT STATEMENT

Critical Thinking and Argument

12 Critical Reading 129
 • STUDENT CRITICAL READING
13 Analyzing Arguments 143
 • STUDENT ANALYSIS
14 Constructing Arguments 161
 • STUDENT ESSAY

Research

15 Preparing for a Research Project 187
 a Analyze assignment
 b Formulate hypothesis
 c Plan research
 d Set up research log
 e Draft working thesis
16 Doing Research 193
 a Kinds of sources
 b Start with the library
 c Library resources
 d Internet
 e Field research

17 Evaluating Sources and Taking Notes 206
 a Purpose of sources
 b Working bibliography
 c Evaluate
 d Read and interpret
 e Synthesize
 f Take notes and annotate
18 Integrating Sources and Avoiding Plagiarism 224
 a Quote, paraphrase, or summarize
 b Integrate text
 c Integrate visuals
 d Excessive use of sources
 e Why to acknowledge sources
 f Which sources to acknowledge
 g Avoid plagiarism
19 Writing a Research Project 234
 a Refine plans
 b Organize and draft
 c Incorporate sources
 d Get responses
 e Revise and edit
 f Prepare source list
 g Create final copy

Language

20 Writing to the World 245
 a What is "normal"
 b Clarify meaning
 c Meet expectations
21 Language That Builds Common Ground 250
 a Unstated assumptions
 b About gender
 c About race and ethnicity
 d Other kinds of difference
22 Language Variety 256
 a Standard varieties
 b To evoke a place
 c To build credibility
 d Other languages
23 Word Choice and Spelling 260
 a Appropriate formality
 b Denotation and connotation
 c General and specific words
 d Figurative language
 e Spell checkers
 f Spelling rules
24 Glossary of Usage 274

Sentence Style

25 Coordination, Subordination, and Emphasis 287
 a Relate equal ideas
 b Distinguish main ideas
 c Opening, closing positions
26 Consistency and Completeness 295
 a Faulty sentence structure
 b Subjects and predicates
 c Elliptical structures
 d Missing words
 e Comparisons
27 Parallelism ☑ 299
 a With items in a series
 b With paired ideas
 c With necessary words
28 Shifts 303
 a In verb tense
 b In mood
 c In voice
 d In person and number
 e Direct, indirect discourse
 f In tone and word choice
29 Conciseness 307
 a Unnecessary words
 b Redundant words
 c Empty words
 d Wordy phrases
 e Sentence structure
30 Sentence Variety 311
 a Length
 b Openings

Sentence Grammar

31 Basic Grammar 318
 • PARTS OF SPEECH
 • PARTS OF SENTENCES
 • TYPES OF SENTENCES
32 Verbs 340
 a Verb forms
 b Helping verbs
 c Regular, irregular verbs
 d *Lie, lay; sit, set; rise, raise*
 e Tenses ☑
 f Sequence
 g Active, passive voice ☑
 h Mood
33 Subject-Verb Agreement ☑ 355
 a Third-person singular
 b Subjects separated from verbs
 c Compound subjects
 d Collective-noun subjects